Fourth Edition

Computer Education for Teachers

Integrating Technology into Classroom Teaching

Vicki F. Sharp

California State University,

Boston   Burr Ridge, IL   Dubuque, IA   Madison, WI   New York   San Francisco   St. Louis
Bangkok   Bogotá   Caracas   Kuala Lumpur   Lisbon   London   Madrid   Mexico City
Milan   Montreal   New Delhi   Santiago   Seoul   Singapore   Sydney   Taipei   Toronto

McGraw-Hill Higher Education

*A Division of The **McGraw-Hill** Companies*

COMPUTER EDUCATION FOR TEACHERS:
INTEGRATING TECHNOLOGY INTO CLASSROOM TEACHING
Published by McGraw-Hill, an imprint of The McGraw-Hill Companies, Inc. 1221 Avenue of the Americas, New York, NY, 10020. Copyright © 2002, 1999, 1996 by The McGraw-Hill Companies, Inc. All rights reserved. No part of this publication may be reproduced or distributed in any form or by any means, or stored in a database or retrieval system, without the prior written consent of The McGraw-Hill Companies, Inc., including, but not limited to, in any network or other electronic storage or transmission, or broadcast for distance learning. Some ancillaries, including electronic and print components, may not be available to customers outside the United States.

All Terrapin Logo art in Chapter 15 is used with permission of Terrapin Software, Inc., Portland, ME. Reprinted by permission of Terrapin Software.

This book is printed on acid-free paper.

1 2 3 4 5 6 7 8 9 0 FGR/FGR 0 9 8 7 6 5 4 3 2 1

ISBN 0-07-239772-1

Editorial director: *Jane Karpacz*
Sponsoring editor: *Beth Kaufman*
Editorial assistant: *Terri Wise*
Senior marketing manager: *Daniel M. Loch*
Project manager: *Diane M. Folliard*
Senior production supervisor: *Lori Koetters*
Media producer: *Lance Gerhart*
Freelance design coordinator: *Gino Cieslik*
Cover design: *Gino Cieslik*
Cover image: *R.S. Rogers*
Supplement coordinator: *Matthew Perry*
Printer: *Quebecor World Fairfield, Inc.*
Typeface: *10/12 Palatino*
Compositor: *Carlisle Communications, Ltd.*

Library of Congress Cataloging-in-Publication Data

Sharp, Vicki F.
    Computer education for teachers : integrating technology into classroom teaching / Vicki F. Sharp.—4th ed.
        p. cm.
    Includes bibliographical references and index.
    ISBN 0-07-239772-1 (alk. paper)
    1. Education—Data processing. 2. Computers—Study and teaching. 3. Computer-assisted instruction. I. Title.
    LB1028.43 .S55 2002
370'.285—dc21   2001030690

www.mhhe.com

This book is dedicated to my mother, Bobbie E. Friedman, who died December 3, 2000. She was a wonderful mother and I miss her!

About the Author

Vicki F. Sharp is currently a professor at California State University and is a former elementary school teacher. She received her Ph.D. in Quantitative Research from St. Louis University and a Bachelor of Arts degree from Washington University. She teaches math/science methods courses and computer courses, and she supervises student teachers. She has been the author or co-author of more than 25 books, including *Statistics for the Social Sciences* (Little, Brown), *HyperStudio in an Hour* and *PowerPoint in an Hour* (ISTE), *Make It with Office* and *Make It with Inspiration* (Visions Technology in Education). She serves as a computer consultant and trainer for software publishers and school districts in southern California. She speaks at computer conventions such as Computer User Educators (CUE) and the National Education Computer Conference (NECC). She is currently a member of the Educational Advisory Board for Knowledge Adventure, one of the top publishers of educational software. Her special interests include integrating the computer into the classroom, teacher education, and school improvement.

Preface

We have come a long way from the 1940s and 1950s when computers consisted of vacuum tubes, data were recorded on magnetic tapes and magnetic drums, and the machines were used primarily by scientists and engineers. In 1969, when I was working on my Ph.D., I typed cards on a keypunch machine, and the cards were then read by a computer that filled a large room. Then, in 1977, Steve Jobs and Steve Wozniak introduced a fully assembled version of their Apple computer, called the Apple II. I thought this compact desktop computer with its 4K of memory, priced at $1,298, was a marvel. In the early 1980s I wanted to bring computers to teachers, so I bought pocket computers and taught programming off campus. Using the Apple IIe as a demonstration machine, I showed software like *Lemonade Stand* and used a word processor program called *Bank Street Writer*. At that time, educational software was limited and inadequate, and the focus was teaching the programming language BASIC, followed shortly thereafter by Logo.

Since the mid-1990s, there have been many technological changes, and the computer has emerged as an important tool in society and in education in particular. With the production of quality software, the computer's role has changed from a device used for computer programming to an instrument that can be efficiently integrated into the curriculum. Teachers utilize computers for word processing, database management, graphics generation, desktop publishing, Internet access, and multimedia. Our machines are now smaller, contain gigabyte hard drives, and have gigabyte processing speeds. We use the Internet as a huge library resource, and electronic mail has proliferated. (In fact, we communicate by e-mail to such an extent that I am relieved when our server breaks down.) Today, computers are being used to help students with special needs realize their potential. In the next 10 years, the computer and the Internet will become even more pervasive influences on how we teach and what happens in the classroom. It will be an exciting time for teachers and students, and we can scarcely predict what the future will bring.

✖ Book Audience

Computer Education for Teachers: Integrating Technology into Classroom Teaching, fourth edition, assumes no prior experience with computers and is designed to meet the needs of the computer novice. It is written for undergraduate and graduate students who want an up-to-date, readable, practical, concise introduction to computers. Covering a large range of topics, this book should help students acquire the knowledge and skills necessary to effectively integrate computers into the classroom.

⚔ Contents of the Text

The content of the text is arranged in a logical teaching order. However, the chapters are not dependent on each other and can be taught in the order the instructor requires.

This edition offers the following salient features:

- **Internet chapters.** In this edition, I have devoted two chapters to the Internet, covering topics such as search engines, integrating the Internet into the classroom, and website evaluation. Each chapter presents a multitude of websites with varying curriculum, classroom activities, and projects.
- **A new chapter on special education.** Chapter 12 covers hardware, software, laws, lesson plans, issues, and ways to integrate the computer into the classroom to teach students with special needs using the latest technology.
- **A chapter on desktop publishing.** Desktop publishing is one of the primary applications for the computer. Chapter 5 teaches the student to create such products as newspapers, bulletins, and signs that can enrich the curriculum and enhance the classroom atmosphere.
- **A chapter on multimedia.** This chapter introduces the student to ways of using the computer to combine text, graphics, and sound into effective multimedia presentations.
- **Brand-new OLC.** The brand-new Online Learning Center for *Computer Education for Teachers* contains resources for professors and students including self-quizzes, links and lesson plans, study tools, Internet exercises, an online instructor's manual with *PowerPoint* slides, and much more.
- **New student CD-ROM.** The *Computer Education for Teachers Student CD-ROM* includes quizzes and Internet links, covers the evaluation of Web resources, offers ideas for integrating technology into the classroom with links to lesson plans, and more!
- **Lots of clear illustrations.** This edition features more than 300 illustrations to highlight pertinent points, facilitate understanding, and explain software.
- **Chapter objectives.** The objectives at the beginning of each chapter serve as a map of the chapter's contents, thus guiding the reader through the book.
- **Evaluation instruments.** Numerous evaluation instruments appear throughout chapters.
- **Internet sites.** At the end of each chapter, I have included a list of Internet sites that offer additional lesson plans, resources, tutorials, historical information, and utilities to use in the classroom.

- **Chapter mastery tests.** Questions selected according to sound learning principles appear at the end of each chapter to help readers ascertain how well they understand the material.
- **Recommended annotated software listing.** A complete, up-to-date annotated listing of software helps the reader make more informed purchasing decisions. This can be found in Appendix A.
- **A discussion of standards.** The book addresses the technology standards that are expected for K–12 students, preservice teachers, and education professionals.
- **Summaries of current computer research.** These summaries provide readers with an understanding of past and current research, effective and ineffective uses of the computer, and promising new directions for further research.
- **Exposure to state-of-the-art technology developments.** Explorations of advances in computer technology keep the student on the cutting edge of computer knowledge.
- **Extensive bibliographies.** The reader can use the selected bibliographies at the end of each chapter to investigate a wide spectrum of topics related to educational technology.
- **A revised teacher's manual.** This manual supplies the teacher with chapter summaries, lecture outlines, answers to mastery test questions, suggested activities and projects, transparency masters, additional test items, and sample software evaluations.

✄ New to the Fourth Edition

Computer Education for Teachers has been updated in a wide variety of ways to reflect the changes that are occurring in educational technology. Chapters have been reorganized, combined, and revised and new chapters have been written. The new edition offers the following features:

- Brand new Chapter 12, "Computers in Special Education."
- More than 150 new illustrations.
- Hundreds of tips for integrating the computer into the classroom.
- Brand-new student CD-ROM.
- Brand-new OLC.
- Basic terms defined.
- New annotated list of software (Appendix A), updated directory of software publishers and mail-order and online software sources (Appendixes B and C).
- Expanded and updated Internet chapters with lesson plans and other curriculum resources, including WebQuests.
- An expanded and updated multimedia chapter.
- Additional chapter questions and projects.
- Updated bibliographies and glossary.
- New instructor's manual.

✖ A Message to Readers

If you would like to see some topic in a future edition or have any comments or questions, please send your thoughts to me at one of the following addresses:

1. America Online address: VickiFS@aol.com

2. Internet address: vicki.sharp@csun.edu

3. University address: Dr. Vicki Sharp, California State University, Northridge, School of Education, 18111 Nordhoff, Northridge, CA 91330-8265

✖ Acknowledgments

This book could never have been completed without the help of a number of kind individuals.

First, I would like to thank my husband, Dick Sharp, for his invaluable contributions. He not only gave me emotional support, but he contributed to the writing of this book. He searched for the best websites, wrote descriptions, checked the software directory for errors, made phone calls, and was my severest critic. Furthermore, he was a loving husband and a wonderful father to our son, David.

Second, I would like to thank the terrific Special Education Department at California State University, Northridge. The chairman of the department, Dr. Claire Cavallaro, critiqued my special education chapter, offered great suggestions, and spent time discussing issues. Dr. June Downing, Dr. Tamarah Ashton, Joyce Linden, Dr. Sarah Hall, and Dr. Michael Spagna loaned me books and tapes and also gave up their valuable time. Furthermore, Tobey Shaw, principal and technology coordinator at Frostig Center and a student at CSUN, gave suggestions for this chapter.

Third, I want to express special appreciation to Terri Wise, developmental editor at McGraw-Hill, for her suggestions and support. Terri is a very conscientious individual who really cares about the product. She was always available with help. The project manager, Diane Folliard, a very special person, also gave me invaluable assistance and I am indebted to her. The McGraw-Hill team is a wonderful group of people to work with and I am proud to be a part of this team.

Fourth, a special thanks to Anthony Nguyen, network administrator at CSUN, and Dr. George Friedman, adjunct professor at USC, formerly research director at the Space Studies Institute, Princeton. Anthony, thank you for the interview along with the insights into wireless networks and distance learning. George, thank you for your insights into the future of the computer in education.

Fifth, the terrific individuals who critiqued this book and offered many wonderful suggestions that were incorporated into this new edition:

Patti S. Abraham, *Mississippi State University*

Carolyn Adler, *Nova Southeastern University*
Rosemary Buteau, *Chicago State University*
Laurie B. Dias, *Georgia State University*
Linda S. Eller, *Christian Brothers University*
Deborah Gartland, *Towson University*
Tim Green, *California State University–Fullerton*
Glenn Growe, *Grand Valley State University*
Bruno Hicks, *University of Maine–Fort Kent*
Doris G. Johnson, *Wright State University*
Russell Lee, *University of West Florida*
Jon Margerum-Leys, *Eastern Michigan State University*
David McCarthy, *The University of Minnesota–Duluth*
Roberta Lynne Ruben, *Western Illinois University*
Catherine C. Schifter, *Temple University*

Sixth, Judy Lombardi, California State University, Northridge, deserves special recognition for the time and effort she gave to the teacher's manual, an excellent resource for the instructor. She did an outstanding job and it is greatly appreciated.

Last but not least, the many software houses that contributed to the completion of this textbook:

Barnum Software: Christopher Wright
Corel: Chip Maxwell
Critical Thinking Books & Software: Linda L. Barbour, Ph.D.
Don Johnston: Christine A. Filler, Angie LeBoida
Edmark: Andrea Fullerton
Encore: Jill Griffin
Equilibrium: Dave Gardner
FileMaker Inc.: Stephen F. Ruddock
FTC Group: Mike Kessler, Marsha Kessler
Grolier Electronic Publishing: Veronica Scheer
Harmonic Visions: Joel Brazy
Ingenuity Works: Brigetta Baron
Inspiration: Robin Christensen, John Cromett
Jay Klein Productions: Jay A. Klein
Knowledge Adventure: Mary Ann Scovall
Lawrence Productions: Michelle Shelton
The Learning Company: Mark Clark
Logo Computer Systems Inc. (LCSI): Lea M. Laricci
Microsoft: Irving Kwong, Sally McDonald, Wendy Morris
Nova: Dorie Liang
Optimum Resources, Inc.: Christopher J. Gintz
Scholastic Software: Eileen Hilbrand, Veronica Scheer
SmartStuff: Maria Crawford
Sunburst Communications: Clair Kubasik
Tech4Learning: Melinda Kolk, David Wagner
Terrapin Logo: Bill Glass
T/Maker: Diane La Mountaine

Tom Snyder Productions: Kim Goodman

Ventura Educational Systems: Fred Ventura

Visions Technology in Education: John Crowdner, president; Arnie Uretsky, Nickola Frye, Michael Wise, Garth Upshaw, David Hoeger, and Richard Otto

A very special thanks to Mark Clark (The Learning Company), Dave Gardner (Equilibrium), Roger Wagner and Chris Saulpaugh, and Jeff Kelly (Roger Wagner/Knowledge Adventure), Mary Ann Scovall and Eileen Moskowitz (Knowledge Adventure), Claire Kubasik (Sunburst), John Crowder (Visions Technology in Education), Brigetta Baron (Ingenuity Works), and Andrea Fullerton (Edmark). These individuals selflessly gave of their time and provided expert advice.

Thanks to Equilibrium for use of *DeBabelizer* to batch-produce the screen shots and enhance the images.

Brief Contents

Contents

CHAPTER 13   *Teacher Tool Software, Graphics, Art, and Music 336*

CHAPTER 14   *Multimedia for the Classroom 363*

CHAPTER 1

History of Computers and Educational Technology

Computer Literacy

To become computer literate, you should be familiar with some of the major developments in computer technology. Did you realize that computers are derived from primitive humans' practice of counting with fingers, toes, and rocks? By reading this chapter, you will learn what led to the development of modern-day computers and how education fits into this big picture. We will discuss current technology, educational milestones, and lessons we have learned from our past. It is only by studying our past that we gain perspective and prepare for the future.

Objectives

Upon completing this chapter, you will be able to:

1. Identify and place in proper sequence five of the major inventions in the history of computing;
2. Discuss succinctly the contributions of each of the following individuals to the field of computing:
   a. Charles Babbage,
   b. Herman Hollerith,
   c. Howard Aiken,
   d. John Atanasoff,
   e. John Mauchly and J. Presper Eckert, and
   f. John Von Neumann;
3. Differentiate among the generations of computers according to their technological advances; and
4. Be able to list three ways the computer has changed education.

Historical Background

Early Times

Primitive humans found it necessary to count and the natural instruments to use were their fingers. With their fingers, they could show how many animals they had killed on a hunt or the number of people in a village. To indicate large numbers, they used all 10 fingers; since humans have 10 fingers, 10 became the basis of our number system.

As time passed, life became more complex, and people needed a way to keep track of their possessions. They began to use rocks as a way to store information, using one rock to represent each animal they owned, for example. Later, wanting a record of this information, they carved notches and symbols in stone or wood, an effective record-keeping method until the abacus was invented.

The Abacus

The **abacus** was different from any recording device that came before it because it allowed manipulation of data.

In 1854, at Senkereh near Babylon, archaeologists found a clay tablet resembling a primitive abacus. They believed it was nearly 4,000 years old (Pullan, 1968). This artifact, which now resides in the British Museum, indicates that some form of calculation existed in Babylon about 3000 B.C. Records show that ancient civilizations, such as India, China, Egypt, and Mesopotamia, were using calculating devices several thousand years ago. The abacus (Fig. 1.1) user manipulates beads in a wood frame to keep track of numbers and place values. Users can perform calculations almost as quickly as people who use calculators can. Of all the early aids to calculation, the abacus is the only one used today.

FIGURE 1.1
Abacus

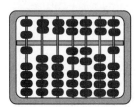

The Pioneers

There were many pioneers of computational devices. We next discuss individuals such as Napier, Pascal, Leibniz, and Jacquard and their inventions prior to the computer.

John Napier, a Scottish mathematician, invented **Napier's Rods** or **Bones** in 1617. This device let you multiply large numbers by manipulating rods. In 1642, **Blaise Pascal** built a calculating machine (Fig. 1.2) that could add and subtract. This was the standard until **Baron Gottfried Wilhelm Von Leibniz,** a German mathematician, designed an instrument called the **Stepped Reckoner,** which he completed in 1674. Leibniz's machine (Fig. 1.3)

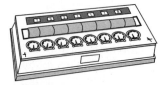

FIGURE 1.2 *The Pascaline*

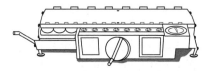

FIGURE 1.3 *Lebiniz's Stepped Reckoner*

was more versatile than Pascal's because it could multiply and divide as well as add and subtract; it used cylinders instead of gears to do its calculations. Leibniz's most important contribution to the computer's evolution was not his machine but his binary arithmetic, a system of counting that uses only two digits, 0 and 1. Leibniz never completed his work on binary arithmetic.[1] It wasn't until 1854, nearly two centuries later, that **George Boole** devised a system of logic based on the binary system called *Boolean algebra*. Finally, in the late 1930s inventors built a computer that used this binary system, the standard internal language of today's digital computers.

Though not a calculating device, **Jacquard's Loom** was the next invention of great significance in the development of the computer. In 1804, **Joseph Marie Jacquard** used punched cards to create patterns on fabric woven on a loom. The hole punches directed the threads up or down, thus producing the patterns. Jacquard's device was the forerunner of the keypunch machine (Fig. 1.4).

FIGURE 1.4
Jacquard's Loom

Each of these men brought us closer to the invention of the computer. (These pioneers are discussed on the Internet sites listed at the end of this chapter and the books listed in the suggested readings.)

A Brief History of Computers

All the mechanical gadgets discussed so far could do only arithmetic. The first individual to conceptualize a real computer was **Charles Babbage,** a Cambridge mathematics professor.

Charles Babbage

Aggravated by the errors in the mathematical tables that were being printed, Babbage resigned his position at Cambridge to work on a machine that would solve this problem. He called this machine the *Difference Engine* because it worked on solving differential equations. Using government funds and his own resources, he labored on the computer for 19 years but was unable

---

[1]Refer to Chapter 2 for a discussion of the binary code.

to complete it. Babbage constructed only a few components, and people referred to his engine as *Babbage's Folly.*

After the government withdrew its funding, Babbage proceeded to work on another, more sophisticated version of this machine, which he called the **Analytical Engine** (Fig. 1.5). A close friend of his, **Augusta Ada Byron, Countess**

FIGURE 1.5
Babbage's Analytical Engine

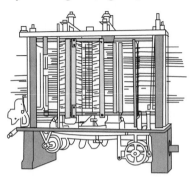

of Lovelace, the only legally recognized daughter of Lord Byron, tried to help him. She raised money for his invention and wrote a demonstration program for the Analytical Engine. Because of this program, she is considered the first computer programmer, and the programming language **Ada** was named after her.

In 1835, Babbage designed a system with provision for printed data, a control unit, and an information storage unit, but the Analytical Engine was never completed because construction of the machine required precision tools that did not exist at the time. Babbage did not publish many details of his work, although some notes were taken of a lecture he gave at the British Association. He did leave behind enough detailed drawings with a notebook and a portion of the machine so that, in 1906, his son Henry P. Babbage was able to complete part of the engine, get it to compute, and publish samples of its work.

The logic of Babbage's machine was important for other computer inventors. Babbage is responsible for the two classifications of the computer: the *store,* or memory, and the *mill,* a processing unit that carries out the arithmetic calculations for the machine. For this achievement he is called the "father of computers," and historians have even said that all modern computers were descended directly from Babbage's Analytical Engine, ironic given that in his day Babbage was considered a failure. He died in poverty; just 19 years later, the punched-card aspect of the Analytical Engine appeared in a working machine, a tabulator built by Herman Hollerith.

Herman Hollerith

No history would be complete without discussion of the American inventor **Herman Hollerith.** When Hollerith worked at the Census Bureau in the 1880s, he met Colonel John Shaw Billings, who was the director of the division of vital statistics. They became friends, and during an evening discourse, Billings discussed the possibility of a hypothetical machine that could do the mechanical work of tabulating the population. Billings envisioned the possibility of using cards with notches punched on the edges, with the notches representing each individual's description. Hollerith was so fascinated with the idea, he decided to leave his job at the Census Bureau and go to MIT to teach and work on this **Tabulating Machine.** Many years later, Hollerith applied for several patents on punched-card data processing, and he devised several experimental test systems (Fig. 1.6).

FIGURE 1.6
Hollerith's Tabulating Machine

When Hollerith took out a patent for the first punched-card calculator, Robert Porter offered him a job in the Census Bureau. He refused this offer because he was interested in winning the contract to do the 1890 census. In 1889, there was a contest held and Hollerith's system won by a landslide against two competing systems.

Hollerith's innovative Tabulating Machine relied heavily on Jacquard's punched-card idea. Hollerith designed his machine so that it pushed pins against cards that were the size of an old-fashioned dollar bill. The holes made by the pins represented characteristics of the population, such as sex, birthplace, and number of children. If a pin went through a hole, it made contact with a metal surface below and a circuit was completed. This census item was then counted and added to the total. If there was no hole, the census item was not counted and there was nothing added to the total. The census office bought 56 of Hollerith's machines and commissioned him to repair them as needed. Because of Hollerith's invention, the census was completed in just two years, compared to the seven years it took for the 1880 census.

Eventually, Herman Hollerith organized his own company called the Tabulating Machine Company. In the 1900s, he rented his more sophisticated tabulating machines for the census. His business prospered and merged with other companies. The company went through a series of name changes, and the last name change came in 1924 when it became known as *International Business Machines,* or *IBM.*

Let's conclude our discussion of these early pioneers with a summary of their achievements in Table 1.1.

In the 20th century, the Census Bureau bought a machine designed by James Powers to replace Hollerith's machines. Powers founded a company called Powers Accounting Machine Co., which merged with others to become known as Remington Rand and then Sperry Rand. Today, these companies are part of the conglomerate *Unisys.*

Hollerith's company and Powers's company produced machines that primarily served the business community. However, the scientific community still

TABLE 1.1
Computing Devices Before the 20th Century

Inventor	Invention	Year
Unknown	Abacus	3000 B.C.?
John Napier	Napier's Bones	1617
Blaise Pascal	Pascaline	1642
Gottfried Leibniz	Stepped Reckoner	1674
Joseph Marie Jacquard	Punched-Card Loom	1804
Charles Babbage	Analytical Engine	1835
Herman Hollerith	Tabulating Machine	1887

needed machines that could do more complex processing and therefore there was a demand for scientific data processing machines.

The Modern Computer

In 1944, the age of the modern computer began. World War II created a need for better data handling that spurred on advances in technology and the development of computers. While the war was going on, a brilliant team of scientists and engineers (among them Alan Turing, Max Newman, Ian Fleming, and Lewis Powell) gathered at Bletchley Park, north of London, to work on a machine that could solve the German secret code. They worked with electronic decoders to decipher the Germans' electromechanical teleprint, the Enigma. Much of this innovative work remains classified.

Howard Aiken

In 1937, **Howard Aiken** was working at Harvard to complete his research for his Ph.D. Faced with tedious calculations on nonlinear, differential equations, he decided that he needed an automatic calculating machine to make the chore less arduous. In a memo written in 1937, he proposed to create a computer. Initially, Aiken found little support at Harvard for his machine, so he turned to private industry. Fortunately, IBM was taken with Aiken's idea and agreed to back him in his effort.

Aiken headed a group of scientists whose task was to build a modern equivalent to Babbage's Analytical Engine. In 1943, the **Mark I,** also called the IBM Automatic Sequence Controlled Calculator, was completed at IBM Development Laboratories at Endicott, New York. It was 51 feet long, 8 feet high, and 2 feet thick; it had 750,000 parts and 500 miles of wire; and it weighed 5 tons. Noisy, but capable of three calculations per second, it accepted information by punched cards and then stored and processed this information. The results were printed on an electric typewriter.

The first electromechanical computer was responsible for making IBM a giant in computer technology. After the completion of the Mark I, IBM produced several machines that were similar to the Mark I, and Howard Aiken also built a series of machines (the Mark II, Mark III, and Mark IV).

Besides building computers, Howard Aiken had many publications in the *Annals of Harvard Computation Laboratory Series.* Perhaps his biggest contribution was the environment he helped to create at Harvard, enabling this institution to develop an illustrious program for computer scientists.

An interesting aside on Aiken pertains to the coining of the word **debug.** In 1945, the Mark II was housed in a building without air conditioning. Because the computer generated tremendous heat, the windows were left open. Suddenly this giant computer stopped working, and everyone tried frantically to discover the source of the problem. Grace Hopper, a brilliant scientist, and her coworkers found the culprit: a dead moth in a relay of the computer. They removed the moth with a tweezers and placed it in the Mark II logbook. When Aiken came back to see how things were going with his associates, they told him they had to debug the machine. Today the Mark II logbook is preserved in the Naval Museum in Dahlgren, Virginia.

There was a need now for computers that would operate faster and more efficiently. After the Mark II, the computers were much faster because electrical circuits replaced the moving parts.

John Atanasoff

In 1939 at Iowa State University, **John Atanasoff** designed and built the first electronic digital computer while working with **Clifford Berry,** a graduate student. Atanasoff and Berry then went to work on an operational model called the **ABC,** the Atanasoff-Berry Computer. This computer, completed in 1942, used binary logic circuitry and had regenerative memory. No one paid much attention to Atanasoff's computer except John Mauchly, a physicist and faculty member from the University of Pennsylvania. In 1941, he took a train to Ames, Iowa, to learn more about the ABC. Staying five days as Atanasoff's house guest, he had an opportunity to read Atanasoff's handbook explaining the electronic theories and construction plans of the ABC (Mollenhoff, 1990). Mauchly then returned home to the Moore School of Electrical Engineering at the University of Pennsylvania, where he became involved in a secret military project with J. Presper Eckert, an astronomer. (He never told Eckert of his visit with Atanasoff in Ames, Iowa.)

John Mauchly and J. Presper Eckert

With the emergence of World War II, the military wanted an extremely fast computer that would be capable of doing the thousands of computations necessary for compiling ballistic tables for new Naval guns and missiles. **John Mauchly** and **J. Presper Eckert** believed the only way to solve this problem was with an electronic digital machine, so they worked on this project together. In 1946, they completed an operational electronic digital computer called the **ENIAC** (Electronic Numerical Integrator and Calculator), derived from the ideas of Atanasoff's unpatented work.[2] It worked on a decimal system and had all the features of today's computers. The ENIAC, shown in Figure 1.7, was tremendous in size, filling up a very large

FIGURE 1.7
ENIAC

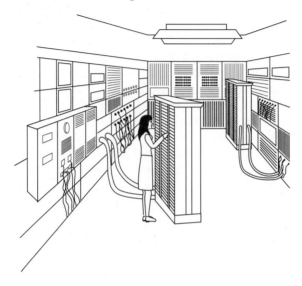

room and weighing 30 tons. It conducted electricity through 18,000 vacuum tubes, generating tremendous heat; it had to have special air conditioning to keep it cool.

This computer operated at a rate that was 500 times faster than any electromechanical computer of that day. A problem that took an electromechanical machine 30 to 32 hours to calculate, this machine solved in three minutes. The ENIAC's limitations were a small memory and a problem in shifting from one program to another. When the user wanted to shift to another program, the machine had to be rewired. These problems might have taken years to solve if it hadn't been for a meeting between Herman Goldstine, a mathematician and liaison officer for the ENIAC project, and **John Von Neumann,** a famous logician and mathematician. Because of that meeting, John Von Neumann joined the Moore team, which was about to embark on a new computer called the **EDVAC,** the Electronic Discrete Variable Automatic Computer.

John Von Neumann

After John Von Neumann arrived in Philadelphia, he helped the Moore group get the contract for the EDVAC. He also assisted the group with the logical

---

[2]Atanasoff's work was ignored for years; he was rejected by IBM, Remington Rand, and Iowa State. He was unheard of until 1973, when he received recognition as one of the fathers of computing. At this time, Sperry Rand brought a suit against Honeywell, and Federal District Judge Earl R. Larson invalidated the ENIAC patent. Judge Larson said that Eckert and Mauchly had derived some of their ideas from Atanasoff's unpatented work.

makeup of this machine. As a result of the Moore team's collaboration, a major breakthrough came in the form of the stored-program concept. Until this time, a computer stored its program externally, either on plugboards, punched tape, or cards. The ENIAC used 18,000 vacuum tubes and required a pair of these tubes joined in a particular manner to hold in memory a single bit of data.

Mauchly and Eckert discovered that one mercury delay line could replace dozens of these vacuum tubes. They figured that the delay lines would mean gigantic savings in cost of tubes and memory space. This advance contributed to the design of the EDVAC. The EDVAC stored information in memory in the same form as data. The machine then manipulated the stored information.

Although Von Neumann and his group were credited with using the stored-program concept, theirs was not the first machine. That honor goes to a group at Cambridge University who developed the **EDSAC,** Electronic Delay Storage Automatic Computer. The EDSAC and the EDVAC computers were the first to use binary notation.

Before 1951, the computer had not been manufactured on a large scale. In 1951, with the arrival of the UNIVAC, the era of **commercial computers** began. Only two years later, IBM started distributing its IBM 701, and other companies manufactured computers such as the Burroughs E101 and the Honeywell Datamatic 1000. The computers that were developed during the 1950s and 1960s were called *first-generation computers* because they had one common feature, the vacuum tube.

Generations of Computers

Since its inception, the computer has gone through several stages of development. Generally writers classify these technological advances in *generations,* a marketing term. Even though there is some overlap, it is convenient to view the computer's technological development in this manner.

The First Generation of Computers

The first generation of computers began in the 1940s and extended into the 1950s. During this period, computers used **vacuum tubes,** such as the one in Figure 1.8, to conduct electricity. The employment of vacuum tubes made the computers big, bulky, and expensive because the tubes were continually burning out and having to be replaced. At this time, computers were classified by the main memory storage device they used. The UNIVAC I used an ingenious device called the *mercury delay line,* which relied on ultrasonic pulses. Mercury delay line storage was a reliable device, but it was very slow compared to modern storage devices.

During the first generation, pioneering work was done in the area of magnetic storage. Data were recorded on magnetic tapes and magnetic drums, which were used for auxiliary memory. In magnetic tape storage, the data were recorded on tapes similar to the audiocassette tapes used today.

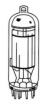

FIGURE 1.8
Vacuum Tube

Data were held on the tapes in serial manner, which meant the user could not access the information directly, resulting in slower access time. Similar to magnetic tapes were magnetic drums. These two means of storage were important until magnetic disks appeared in the third generation.

The Second Generation of Computers

FIGURE 1.9
Transistor

The second generation of computers began when the **transistor** (Fig. 1.9) replaced the vacuum tube in the late 1950s. In 1947, John Bardeen, Walter H. Brattain, and William Shockley, a team of physicists working at Bell Labs, invented the transistor. In 1956, they shared the Nobel Prize for this invention.

The transistor, an electrically operated switch similar to an old-fashioned relay, was a landmark in the development of the computer. The transistor is created by melting silicon, an element found in common sand. Transistors conduct electricity more efficiently, consume less energy, need less space, and generate less heat than vacuum tubes. In addition, they don't burn out as the tubes did. The computer with transistors became smaller, more reliable, faster, and less expensive than a computer with vacuum tubes. Small- and medium-size businesses now found it more economical to buy computers.

A new development that started in the early 1950s came to fruition during the second generation. Magnetic-core memory was responsible for data being retrieved and stored at a millionth of a second. *Core memory* became synonymous with the main memory of the computer.

The Third Generation of Computers

The third generation of computers began in 1964 with the introduction of the IBM 360, the computer that pioneered the use of **integrated circuits** on a chip. In that year, computer scientists developed tiny integrated circuits and installed hundreds of these transistors on a single silicon chip, which was as small as a fingertip. The computer became smaller, more reliable, and less expensive than ever before. The integrated circuit chips made it possible for minicomputers to find their way into classrooms, homes, and businesses. They were almost a thousand times faster than the first generation of computers, and manufacturers mass-produced them at a low price, making them accessible to small companies.

The integrated circuits were now used as main memory, and magnetic disks replaced magnetic tape as auxiliary memory. These disks allowed information to be retrieved nonsequentially, speeding up access time. Computer terminals flourished, and an increasing number of individuals used them to communicate with computers at other locations. In the beginning, the terminal was like a typewriter and produced a printed output. As time went on, the video display terminals replaced the punched cards for entering data and programs into the computer. Hollerith's cards became obsolete.

The 1970s began with the development of **large-scale integration (LSI),** a method that put hundreds of thousands of transistors on a single silicon chip. The chip was as minute as a speck of dust and so delicate that miniature scientific instruments were devised to create it. The development of the LSI led to the insertion of computers in cameras, television sets, and cars. Another result of LSI was the personal computer.

The Fourth Generation of Computers

The development of microprocessor technology resulted in the fourth generation. The **microprocessor chip** (Fig. 1.10) is a central processing unit, the brains of the computer, built on a single chip. It is hard to believe, but on this single chip the processing and computing take place.

Magnified Chip

Actual Chip Size

FIGURE 1.10
Microprocessor Chip

In 1971, a group of individuals working at Intel introduced the 4004 microprocessor. They intended that this chip be used in items such as the calculator because the chip lacked the power needed to run a microcomputer. Three years later, they introduced the 8080 version, which was capable of running the processing unit of a computer. *Radio Electronics,* in 1974, published an article on a home-built computer that used this technology. Subsequently, *Popular Electronics* ran a story on Altair, a computer that had the 8080 chip. In the article, the writers mentioned that Micro Instrumentation Technology Systems was selling kits for this computer. The response to this article was overwhelming, and it inspired other companies to develop new products.

Apple computers came into being in the 1970s. Steve Wozniak and Steve Jobs worked out of a garage where they began selling Apples for the price of $666.66. Figure 1.11 shows the Apple I. Wozniak and Jobs placed ads in hobbyist publications with the money that they raised by selling their personal possessions.

FIGURE 1.11
Apple I Computer

This duo provided software for their machines free of charge and they achieved a modicum of success. They hired professional help and support and in 1977 introduced, in what was a historic moment for computers, a new fully assembled version of their Apple machine called the Apple II. The Apple II was the first computer accepted by business users because of a spreadsheet simulation program called *VisiCalc*. It was a compact desktop computer with 4 kilobytes (4K) of memory, priced at $1,298, with a clock speed of 1.0.[3]

Four years later, IBM entered the personal computer market with the IBM PC. This computer was tremendously successful and became a bestseller. Because of IBM's successful entrance in the field, other computer makers chose to capitalize on its popularity by developing their own "clones." These personal computers had many of the same features as the IBM machines and could run the same programs. Widespread use of personal computers became a reality.

The Fifth Generation of Computers

Starting in the mid-1990s the fifth generation heralded incredibly fast computer chips capable of carrying out thousands of operations simultaneously. This generation of computers delivers gigahertz speeds and utilizes millions of transistors. Computers now use voice recognition, natural and foreign language translation, fiber optic networks, and optical discs. Computers are smaller with increased data storage and gigahertz memory. In a few years, computers will be ultrathin, weigh less than a pound, and operate on batteries that will last years. Many systems now have touch screens and handwriting recognition software that let the user employ a pencil-like stylus as the input device. Students and teachers are increasingly using electronic organizers such as the Palm. There are wearable computers where voice and data are transmitted by a built-in cellular radio. Holographic storage is still in the research laboratories, but could be another viable alternative. The data storage system will eventually come in the form of laser cards the size of a small plastic credit card that can hold terabytes of information.

This generation of computers is based on logical inference and the extensive use of **artificial intelligence (AI)**. AI is "a computer science field that tries to improve computers by endowing them with some of the characteristics associated with human intelligence, such as the capability to understand natural language and to reason under conditions of uncertainty" (Pfaffenberger, 2000). Such machines will shortly be able to reason to the point of making decisions, drawing conclusions, understanding everyday speech, and learning from experience. There are already some accomplishments today in this area: Medical programs aid in diagnosing various diseases, and mining programs help mining companies in their explorations. AI elements already exist in educational software programs such as *Mavis Beacon Teaches Typing!* (Learning Company) and *The Time Warp of Dr. Brain* (Knowledge Adventure). Artificial intelligence

---

[3]Clock speed is the speed of the internal clock of a microprocessor. It is measured in megahertz, and higher clock speed brings gains in microprocessor-intensive tasks (Pfaffenberger, 2000).

has been used on board games such as chess and backgammon. Some of the chess and backgammon programs have been known to defeat their creators. Alan Turing proposed a test in 1950 that could determine if a computer was reasoning as a human being. Some computers are getting close, and who knows?—in years to come people might prefer talking to a computer rather than to an actual person. Computers will communicate in English or Chinese rather than in a computer language. They will respond to a human voice, not to a keyboard or disk drive. In Stanley Kubrick's film *2001: A Space Odyssey*, the computer HAL understood every word it heard and all the subtleties of the person talking. This very thoughtful film predicted many things that are a reality today or will become a reality tomorrow. Today, the voice synthesizers that are used in computers sound more human than those used a few years ago. Up until very recently, only higher-end computers had voice recognition, but now the majority of these machines have this capability.

Presently, printers and computers are communicating through wireless networks and machines have parallel processing; that is, the computer performs two or more operations simultaneously. There are flat-panel displays that are larger, in color, and detachable. The **Internet**, a worldwide system for linking small computer networks, is having an increasingly pervasive influence on our everyday lives. Teachers and students will eventually have new ways to work from their homes and in schools. Through the use of wireless telecommunication services, they will be spending less time in the classroom and more time on the Internet via voice, data, and video conferencing. Teachers and students will use the Internet's research tools and communicate through online courses almost exclusively. Exciting new technologies will deliver huge increases in bandwidth capacity, making Internet access occur with lightning-fast speed. With these new developments come new forms of interactive content, realistic 3-D, virtual reality,[4] multiplayer games, and interactive educational video forums. Chapter 16 and the Epilogue will discuss the many new advances in computer technology and speculate on its future. Table 1.2 highlights the major technological advances in the development of computers.

TABLE 1.2
Generations of Computers

Generation of Computer	Years	Technological Advance
First	Early 1950s	Vacuum tube
Second	Mid-1950s	Transistor
Third	Early 1960s	Integrated circuits
Fourth	1970–mid-1990s	Microprocessor
Fifth	Mid-1990s–2000s	AI, Internet, parallel processing, virtual reality

---

[4]Virtual reality (VR) is a computer system that can immerse the user in the illusion of a computer-generated world and permit the user to navigate throughout this world at will. (Pfaffenberger, 1997). (See Chapter 14 for further discussion.)

Brief History of Computers in Education

By reading the preceding material, you should have an understanding of the historical origins of computers. At this point, you are probably wondering how computer technology developments have influenced educational technology. The following section will briefly discuss some of the major developments in computer technology that have had an impact on educational technology.

Before the Microcomputer

The oldest technique for learning with a computer was **programmed instruction**. This technology is the forerunner of the computer tutorial. In 1950, the Harvard psychologist B. F. Skinner first used the term "programmed instruction." For this type of instruction, material is broken down into small bites or segments of information. Students work through the programmed materials at their own rate, and after each step they are tested on their comprehension by answering questions. The students are immediately given the right answer or additional material to help them master the subject. Books, teaching machines, or computers can be used to present this material. Most teachers started to use computers when the microcomputer came into the classroom. However, computer culture was in existence roughly 21 years before the microcomputer era.

In 1950, the first documented instructional use of the computer occurred at MIT. Teachers used a computer flight simulator to train pilots. In 1959, the first documented instructional use of computers with elementary students occurred in New York City. An IBM computer was used to teach schoolchildren binary arithmetic. During this time frame there were federally funded projects that supported research with mainframe-based computer systems. Furthermore, there was a growing interest in **computer-assisted instruction (CAI)**. In this instance, computer-assisted instruction referred to the student being involved in some instructional activity on the computer.

During the 1970s and 1980s, companies such as the Computer Curriculum Corporation (CCC), Control Data Corporation, and IBM were major players in the educational computing field. Stanford University was the first university to use an IBM computer system dedicated to instruction with a programming language called **Coursewriter**. This system had the first multimedia learning station, which consisted of a cathode-ray tube screen, microphone, audiotape player, earphones, and slide projector. At this time universities, faculty, and students used mainframe systems to teach programming, develop programs, and share programs with other institutions.

Patrick Suppes, president of Computer Curriculum Corporation, worked extensively on research and development. He produced math drill and practice software on a mainframe computer, a large computer that was the size of a standard classroom. The computer screen displayed a problem, the student responded, and the computer provided immediate feedback. Don Bitzer, along with a team of specialists, developed an instructional system called Programmed Logic for Automatic Teaching Operations **(PLATO)**. This system had a terminal with a plasma screen, a specially designed keyboard, and an authoring system called Tutor. This authoring system developed tutorial lessons and complete courses. There were other products such as Time-Shared Interactive Computer-Controlled Information Television (TICCIT), Program for Learning in Accordance with Needs (PLAN), and Individually Prescribed Instruction (IPI) systems.

With the growth of computer applications such as spreadsheets, computer organizations strove to computerize their administrative activities. For example, they wanted to computerize report cards, attendance records, and student and staff records. Because these mainframe systems were expensive and complex, the district office controlled the hardware and software operation. There had been an interest in computer-assisted instruction, but this interest declined because there seemed to be more potential for using the computer for administrative tasks.

The Time of the Microcomputer

In 1977, computers were placed in schools, and the focus shifted from mainframes to desktop microcomputer systems. Teachers organized into computer interest groups. In 1979, academic groups decided to come together for the first meeting of the National Education Computing Conference (NECC), presently the largest computer conference in the United States. Classroom teachers began to use their own computers. Before microcomputers, software came from hardware manufacturers such as IBM. With the advent of the microcomputer, there emerged a new software market that was directed by teachers. The nonprofit Minnesota Educational Computing Consortium (MECC) developed a good portion of the mainframe software and transferred this software to microcomputers. The MECC became a major influence in the software field for education. Many other software companies began producing educational software. MicroSIFT project and the Educational Products Information Exchange (EPIE), as well as professional organizations, magazines, and journals, began to evaluate this software. Many software evaluation magazines went out of business because the schools formed committees to evaluate software. Teachers then wanted a voice in the design of the software, and they were highly vocal in their opinions.

Authoring Systems

Software developers responded by producing authoring systems such as PILOT and SuperPILOT. The authoring systems were the precursor of modern applications such as *HyperCard, Linkway,* and *HyperStudio.* (See Chapter 14 for a detailed discussion.) The interest in this type of software waned as teachers realized how much time and expertise were needed to develop good courseware. They felt their time could be used more productively by purchasing software.

Programming and Literacy

During the early 1980s there was a movement to teach programming, and languages such as BASIC and Logo were taught. Apple even built BASIC into the ROM of its computers. Because BASIC was free, the majority of teachers taught it to their students. In addition, software for students was almost non-existent, and what was available was expensive. Logo was developed and promoted as a programming language for young students by Seymour Papert. (See Chapter 15 for a more in-depth discussion.) Papert was an MIT mathematics professor who based his philosophy of computer use on the work of Jean Piaget. He expressed his contructivist approach to education in a popular book called *Mindstorms.* There was now an intense interest in Logo activities, Logo products, and Logo research. In the mid-1980s interest in teaching programming languages declined. Teachers wanted students to use the computer as a tutor—a way to help students who were academically behind (Molnar, 1978). There was an interest in **computer literacy,** which is the ability to understand and use computers. This resurgence of interest became so strong in the 1990s that many states required computer literacy courses for prospective teachers.

Networking and the Internet

Administrators and school districts began to see the value of **networking** computers: connecting a group of computers and peripherals to a communication system. Integrated learning systems similar to the drill and practice software developed by Suppes were introduced in school districts. School districts realized that computers networked to a central server could provide instruction more efficiently and at a lower cost than stand-alone machines. There was a movement away from the stand-alone machines used by individual teachers toward centralized control by schools and districts.

In the midst of this movement the Internet came into its own (see Chapter 8). The U.S. Department of Defense created the Internet for military research purposes. The department's major concerns were to ensure widespread communication of information while providing maximum security. University professors and scientists used the Internet for research and worldwide communication, but it was difficult for the novice to use. In 1993, this changed when Marc Andreessen developed *Mosaic* at the University of Illinois's National Center for Supercomputing Applications. *Mosaic,* a software breakthrough, was a navigator tool for interactive material. This software browser (Fig. 1.12) allowed users to view pictures and documents by simply clicking on a mouse. A simple interface let users travel through the online world of electronic information along any path they wished in order to discover the wonders contained on the Internet. Educators all over the world now became interested in technology and began to see the potential for this powerful tool. Distance learning—that is, people receiving educational training from a remote teaching site via a computer—increased rapidly. People now attended classes and conferences on the Internet in the privacy of their

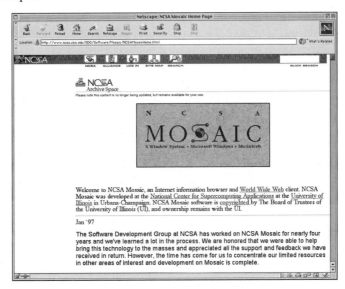

**FIGURE 1.12
Mosaic**

Mosaic™, NCSA Mosaic™, and the "spinning globe" logo are proprietary trademarks of the University of Illinois. These trademarks identify "Web" browser products developed and owned by the University of Illinois. Used by permission.

own home (see Chapter 8). Table 1.3 summarizes the major events in educational computing.

TABLE 1.3

Educational Technology

Major Event	Year
Computers used for instructional purposes	1950
Computers first used in the schools	1959
PLATO, an instructional system, is developed	1970
BASIC and Logo taught in the schools	1980s
MECC begins courseware development	1980s
Network systems increase	1990s
Use of Internet becomes widespread	1994

Summary

The origin of computers can be traced back to inventors who were interested in processing information and wanted devices to simplify tedious arithmetic calculations. In the 1800s, Jacquard used punched cards in his loom to produce beautiful patterns, an invention that inspired Charles Babbage; Babbage used the concept of the punched card in his Analytical Engine. Babbage's work was forgotten for nearly a century. Near the end of the 1800s, Herman Hollerith improved on Jacquard's idea and pioneered processing of statistical data in the 1890 census. Today, this is a major application for the computer. In the 1900s, inventors constructed the earliest electromechanical computer, quickly replaced by the faster electronic computer.

The machines that superseded the early experimental machines were classified in generations. In the first generation, computers used vacuum tubes to conduct electricity. In the second generation, transistors replaced tubes, followed in the 1970s by integrated circuits in the third generation. The fourth generation saw the advent of large-scale, integrated circuit chips. The fifth generation of computers offers the development of artificial intelligence, computers based on logical inference and parallel processing, and radical changes in the Internet, as we know it today. While the computer was evolving, there were major breakthroughs occurring in educational technology. There were developments ranging from PLATO, an instructional system, to the widespread use of the Internet. The development of the computer has become like a stone rolling down a hill, gathering other stones and creating an explosion in technology.

What follows is an annotated list of top-rated Internet sites. These sites contain historical information, timelines, historical treatment of educational technology, and photos of machines from the earliest to the present.

✍ COMPUTER HISTORY INTERNET SITES

History of Apple Computer
http://www.apple-history.com/
A brief history of Apple Computer is discussed from the launching of the Apple I to the company's recent financial trouble. The centerpiece is a graphical catalog (see gallery) of almost every Apple computer ever produced.

Calculating Machines
http://www.webcom.com/calc/
The history, classification, and pictures of mechanical calculating machines.

Computer Museum History Center
http://www.computerhistory.org/
This site provides a comprehensive collection of 2,000 computer-related artifacts which includes an 1890 Hollerith Census machine, a Cray-3 supercomputer, a World War II ENIGMA device, a see-through Palm Pilot; parts of MIT's Whirlwind computer, and a computer-generated *Mona Lisa*!

Triumph of the Nerds
http://www.pbs.org/nerds/
This companion website for the PBS television special gives a history of computers.
http://www.pbs.org/nerds/game.html
You can find a charming guessing game called "Guess the Computer" here.

Historic Computer Images
http://www.asap.unimelb.edu.au/hstm/data/199.htm
This is a photo collection of 200 computer images.

Past Notable Women of Computing
http://www.cs.yale.edu/~tap/past-women-cs.html
This site has information on the pioneering computing women from Ada Byron King, Countess of Lovelace, to Joan Margaret Winters. The site also includes a photo gallery of women and computers.

Yahoo List of Online Computer Museums
http://dir.yahoo.com/Computers_and_Internet/History/Museums/
Yahoo has a comprehensive list of computer museums.

Science: Click-N-Learn
http://www.kids-online.net/learn/c_n_l.html
This site gets at the heart of computers, giving detailed descriptions of the insides of a typical CPU. Simply drag your mouse over the exposed skeleton of the computer and click to get full descriptions of the hardware. There are three different knowledge levels for your students to explore; and teachers can benefit from knowing the ins and outs of computers as well.

Vintage Calculators
http://www.vintagecalculators.com/
This catalog of "old-school" calculators includes the 25-pound Comptometer, the Addiator, and a pinwheel contraption dubbed the Muldivo. All of these models feature actual working gears and levers that can be viewed

with the naked eye. When was the last time you fixed your Palm Pilot by replacing a worn washer? You're also invited to browse a timeline of calculator history (beginning with the abacus and ending in 1978) and peruse an array of early pocket calculators that appear roughly the size of toasters.

World War II Codes and Ciphers
http://www.codesandciphers.org.uk/
This homespun site was created by Tony Sale, a man instrumental in preserving and restoring the historical collection at Bletchley Park. Bletchley Park was headquarters of British code-breaking during World War II. There are detailed tutorials for the mathematically inclined and a Bletchley Park photo album.

ERIC Clearinghouse on Information and Technology
http://ericir.syr.edu/ithome/
ERIC Clearinghouse on Information and Technology is dedicated to the areas of library and information science and educational technology.

Dear Parents
http://www.dearparents.com/
Dear Parents is advice on learning and technology from Edmark.

AIL 601: Theories of Learning Applied to Technological Instruction
http://www.bamaed.ua.edu/ail601/INDEX. HTM
Theories of Learning Applied to Technological Instruction is written by George E. Marsh II. This site covers Dr. Marsh's course contents. There is extensive information on topics that include problem-based learning, a brief history of instructional technology, teaching and learning on the Internet, and distance learning.

Apple Museum
http://www.applemuseum.seastar.net/
This site features informative articles, timelines, galleries, and detail of Apple's greatest machines.

1946: ENIAC First Operated
http://www.library.upenn.edu/special/ gallery/mauchly/jwmintro.html
The world's first electronic digital computer, the Electronic Numerical Integrator and Calculator (ENIAC) was turned on for the first time in 1946. This 30-ton monster was about as powerful as the tiny computers inside today's "singing" greeting cards. The story of ENIAC, as seen by one of its creators, is told on this site.

Chapter Mastery Test

To the Instructor: Refer to the Instructor's Manual for the Answers to the Mastery Questions. This manual has additional questions and resource materials.

Let's check for chapter comprehension with a short mastery test. Basic Terms, Classroom Projects, and Suggested Readings and References and follow the test.

1. Discuss briefly the contributions made to the computer field by the following individuals:
   a. Howard Aiken;
   b. Charles Babbage;
   c. Herman Hollerith; and
   d. John Atanasoff.

2. Identify and place in correct order four of the major inventions in the field of computing.

3. Differentiate the generations of computers by their technological advances.

4. Explain the significance of punched cards and vacuum tubes in the development of early computers.

5. Explain the importance of transistors and microprocessors in the development of modern computers.

6. What was George Boole's lasting contribution to computer history?

7. What computer opportunities would a sixth grader have in 1953 as opposed to a sixth grader in 2002?

8. Why was Hollerith's tabulating machine for the 1890 census significant for the future of computing?
9. Explain the importance of the discovery that made personal computers possible.
10. Explain why Charles Babbage might be considered to have been born in the wrong time.
11. What were some of the problems of first-generation computers?
12. What are Steve Jobs's and Steve Wozniak's major achievements in the computer field?
13. Explain why Ada Lovelace deserves an important place in the history of computers.
14. What spearheaded the development of the electronic digital computer?
15. Why did the Internet suddenly become popular?
16. Name two major events that increased the use of the computer in education.
17. Who was B. F. Skinner and what was his contribution?
18. Why did programming suddenly fall out of favor?

Basic Terms

abacus (2)
Ada (4)
analytical engine (4)
artificial intelligence (AI) (12)
computer-assisted instruction (CAI) (14)
computer literacy (16)
Coursewriter (14)
debug (7)
integrated circuits (10)

Internet (13)
large-scale integration (LSI) (10)
microprocessor chip (11)
networking (16)
PLATO (15)
programmed instruction (14)
transistor (10)
vacuum tubes (9)

Classroom Projects

1. Prepare a paper on the 1973 court trial between Sperry Rand and Honeywell. In this case, Judge Larson ruled that "Eckert and Mauchly did not themselves invent the electronic digital computer, but instead derived the subject matter from one John V. Atanasoff."
2. Use three magazines to investigate developments in educational computing that occurred during the last five years. Write a brief summary of the findings.
3. Using a computer timeline program such as Tom Snyder's TimeLiner, list at least 10 significant computer events from 1863 to 2001.
4. Prepare an in-depth research report on the life of an important inventor and his or her contribution to the history of computers.
5. What are today's schools covering in terms of computer literacy? What are second and seventh graders learning about computer history?
6. Write three biographical sketches on important women in the computer field discussing their achievements.

Suggested Readings and References

Asimov, Isaac. *How Did We Find Out About Computers?* New York: Walker, 1984.

Aspray, William. "John Von Neumann's Contributions to Computing and Computer Science." *Annals of the History of Computing,* 11, no. 3 (1989): 165.

Austrian, G. *Herman Hollerith: Forgotten Giant of Information Processing.* New York: Columbia University Press, 1982.

Bernstein, J. *The Analytical Engine.* New York: Morrow, 1981.

Burks, A., and A. Burks. "The ENIAC: First General-Purpose Electronic Computer." *Annals of the History of Computing,* October 1981, pp. 310–400.

Dunn, Ashley. "UCLA, Hewlett-Packard Scientists' Finding Could Speed Up Computing." *Los Angeles Times,* January 3, 2000, p. B5.

Evans, Christopher. *The Making of the Micro: A History of the Computer.* New York: Van Nostrand Reinhold, 1981.

Evans, Christopher. *The Micro Millennium.* New York: Viking Press, 1979.

Feigenbaum, Edward A., and Pamela McCorduck. *The Fifth Generation.* Reading, Mass.: Addison-Wesley Publishing Company, 1983.

Freedman, A. *The Computer Desktop Encyclopedia.* New York: Amacom, 2000.

Freedman, A. *The Computer Glossary.* New York: Amacom, 1995.

Gardner, David, W. "Will the Inventor of the First Digital Computer Please Stand UP?" *Datamation* 20 (February 1974): 84–90.

Gates, Bill, Nathan Myhrvold, and Peter Rinearson. *The Road Ahead.* New York: Viking Penguin, 1996.

Goldstine, H. *The Computer from Pascal to Von Neumann.* Princeton, N.J.: Princeton University Press, 1972.

Holmes, Stanley. "Software Giant Hears Footsteps on Internet." *Los Angeles Times,* December 27, 1999, p. C7.

Levy, Steven. "The Computer." *Newsweek,* February 6, 1998, pp. 28–30.

Macintosh, Allan R. "Dr. Atanasoff's Computer." *Scientific American* 259, no. 2 (August 1, 1988): 90.

Magid, Lawrence J. "The Meanest, Fastest Machine on the Block Isn't for Everyone." *Los Angeles Times,* November 1, 1999, p. C7.

McDonald, Glenn, and Cameron Crotty. "The Digital Future." *PC World,* January 1, 2000, pp. 116–34.

Metropolis, N., J. Howlett, and G. C. Rota, eds. *A History of Computing in the Twentieth Century.* New York: Academic Press, 1980.

Mollenhoff, Clark R. "Forgotten Father of the Computer." *The World & I,* March 1990, pp. 319–32.

Molnar, Andrew R. "Computers in Education a Brief History." *T.H.E. Journal* 24, no. 11 (June 1997): 59–62.

Molnar, Andrew R. "The Next Great Crisis in American Education: Computer Literacy." *AEDS Journal* 12, no. 1 (1978): 11–20.

Moore, Johanna D. "Making Computer Tutors More Like Humans." *Journal of Artificial Intelligence in Education* 7, no. 2 (1996): 181–214.

Moreau, Rene. *The Computer Comes of Age: The People, the Hardware, and the Software.* Translated by J. Howlett. Cambridge, Mass.: MIT Press, 1984.

Morgenstern, David. "Exponential: No Fast Start for New Chips." *MacWeek* 11, no. 13 (March 31, 1997): 1.

Morrison, P., and E. Morrison, eds. *Charles Babbage and His Calculating Engines.* New York: Dover, 1961.

Naisbitt, John. *Megatrends: Ten New Directions Transforming Our Lives.* New York: Warner Books, 1982.

Naisbitt, John. *Megatrends 2000: Ten New Directions for the 1990s.* New York: Morrow, 1990.

Niemiec, Richard P., and Richard J. Walberg. "From Teaching Machines to Microcomputers: Some Milestones in the History of Computer-Based Instruction." *Journal of Research on Computing in Education* 21, no. 3 (Spring 1989): 263.

Norr, Henry. "MacHandwriter Puts Pen on Desktop." *MacWeek* 8, no. 5 (January 31, 1994): 1.

Pfaffenberger, Bryan. *Dictionary of Computer Terms.* 6th ed. Carmel, Ind.: Que, 1996.

Pfaffenberger, Bryan. *Webster's New World Dictionary of Computer Terms.* 6th ed. New York: Que, 1997.

Pullan, J. M. *A History of the Abacus.* New York: Praeger Publishers, 1968.

Quain, John R. "Going Mainstream." *PC Magazine* 13, no. 4 (February 22, 1994): 110.

Ralston, Anthon, and C. L. Meek, eds. *Encyclopedia of Computer Science.* New York: Petrocelli, 1976.

Resick, Rosalind. "Pressing Mosaic." *Internet,* October 1994, pp. 81–88.

Ritchie, David. *The Computer Pioneers: The Making of the Modern Computer.* New York: Simon and Schuster, 1986.

Roblyer, M. D., and Jack Edwards. *Integrating Educational Technology into Teaching.* 2nd ed. Upper Saddle River, N.J.: Prentice Hall, 2000.

Rochester, J., and J. Gantz. *The Naked Computer.* New York: Morrow, 1983.

Slater, Michael. "PowerPC Steps into Right with Pentium." *MacWEEK* 8, no. 11 (March 14, 1994): 1.

Smarte, Gene, and Andrew Reinhardt. "15 Years of Bits, Bytes and Other Great Moments: A Look at Key Events in Byte, the Computer Industry." *Byte* 15, no. 9 (September 1, 1990): 369–400.

Stone, David, M. "Even Faster and Smaller." *PC Magazine* 16, no. 6 (March 25, 1997): 186–89.

Takahashi, D. "A Dogged Inventor Makes the Computer Industry Say: Hello, Mr. Chip." *Los Angeles Times,* October 21, 1990, p. C1.

Zilber, Jon. "Why 2004 Won't Be Like 1994." *MacUser* 8, no. 1 (January 1, 1994): 92.

Zorpette, Glen. "Science and Medicine." *Los Angeles Times,* December 30, 1991, p. B5.

CHAPTER 2

Getting Started on the Computer

Integrating the Computer into the Classroom

Did you know that originally there were three classifications of computers: mainframes, minicomputers, and microcomputers? Did you know the advent of microcomputers brought the Apple II series of computers into the schools? Today, a typical computer system found in any classroom might have a monitor, keyboard, mouse, printer, internal disk drive, hard disk drive, CD-ROM drive or DVD drive, modem, and speakers. This chapter will discuss what a computer is and how it works. In addition, you will become familiar with Internet sites that contain online stores, educational resources, and operating systems as well as software downloads, searchable databases, tips and tricks, and news.

Objectives

Upon completing this chapter, you will be able to:

1. Discuss how the basic components of a computer system operate.
2. List three precautions for handling floppy disks and optical discs.
3. Give an explanation of the following:
   a. formatting or initializing a disk,
   b. making a backup copy of a disk, and
   c. copying or deleting a file.
4. List the differences and similarities between a mainframe, minicomputer, and microcomputer; and
5. Explore some useful Internet sites that include online stores, operating system sites, computer terms, and tips and tricks.

Computer Classification

Computers are frequently divided into categories: mainframes, minicomputers, and microcomputers. In the past, there was a technical distinction among these computers, but today the differences are in terms of cost and speed. These categories have become blurred because many new microcomputers have the same capabilities as the old mainframes. Many professors have added two more categories, the laptop and the Palm (see Chapter 3).

In the early 1960s, all computers were called **mainframes** in reference to the cabinet that held the central processing unit. As time progressed, very large computers began to be called mainframe computers. Mainframes cost thousands of dollars, had enormous memory and speed, and took up the space of a standard-size classroom. Because of the machine's memory, it could dispatch complex programs very quickly and it could execute these programs while many individuals utilized the computer simultaneously. Computer technicians usually managed the machine at a prepared site for the large corporations or financial institutions that used it. Mainframes were usually connected to terminals that resembled small computers without a central processing unit or computing component. These devices had a keyboard to input information and a videoscreen or printer to output information. The terminals relayed information to and from the mainframe housed in the same building or even in another city. If the terminals were in another city, they communicated with the mainframe via telephone.

The largest and fastest of the mainframe computers are called **supercomputers.** These state-of-the-art machines, produced by the United States and Japan at a cost of millions of dollars, have the most advanced processing abilities, with peak speeds exceeding 1 trillion calculations per second. In the 1960s, government laboratories developed these computers under top secrecy. For years the U.S. government was the only market for supercomputers; only a few scientists had access to these machines, and they did not develop the computers' capabilities aggressively because the government did not allow it. In the 1980s, access to the supercomputers increased, and today they are used worldwide.

Cray Computers, founded by Seymour Cray, was the only American company to manufacture supercomputers (Fig. 2.1) until the company di-

FIGURE 2.1 *Cray-1 Supercomputer 1976*
Freedman Desktop Encyclopedia, 2000.

vided into two corporations in May 1989 to become Cray Research Incorporated and Cray Computer Corporation. Because of the supercomputers' high cost, the aerospace industry, the military, the National Weather Service, and oil conglomerates at one time were the primary users. Now, as business and technical enterprises intermingle, companies such as Cray and Sun are producing lower-cost machines for commercial use.

In 1965, Digital Equipment Corporation (DEC) introduced the **minicomputer.** Universities and large companies needed a machine that did not require a staff of professionals or large storage space, and the minicomputer met this need. This machine was smaller and less costly than the mainframes and usually fit in a large cabinet in a corner of a room. Usually, its terminals were housed in the same building or room. The minicomputer did not have the diversified input/output devices of the mainframe or its memory capacity. However, like the mainframe, the minicomputer could handle more than one task at a time. The minicomputer was still too expensive and too sophisticated for most individuals, but it was used in small businesses and by school districts. Because it cost less than the mainframe, this computer was prevalent until the microcomputer came on the scene in the mid-1970s.

The **microcomputer** came into being because computer engineers were able to etch many circuits on a single chip. This advance in computer technology produced a computer that was less costly, more powerful, and smaller than the minicomputer. Today, the microcomputer is a powerful piece of equipment, small enough to sit on a desk or fit in a briefcase.

Microcomputers originally were differentiated as either *personal computers* or *business computers.* Most software developed for personal machines, such as the Apple II series, was educational or had applications in the home: home management, computer literacy, and word processing. Most software developed for business machines, IBM, PC compatibles, and the Macintosh consisted of complex spreadsheets, elaborate databases, professional word processing programs, statistical applications, scientific programs, and desktop publishing programs. Now, these distinctions among microcomputers are not clear-cut, and educational software and business software are developed for all machines.

To appreciate the beauty and sophistication of these machines, let's spend a little time exploring what a computer is and how it operates.

What Is a Computer?

A computer is a machine that can handle huge amounts of information at an incredible speed. Computers do not have brains, feelings, or the ability to solve their own problems; they can solve only those problems they have been programmed to solve. A typical computer system found in a normal classroom might have a monitor, keyboard, mouse, printer, internal disk drive, hard disk drive, CD-ROM drive, modem, and speakers. Figure 2.2 is an example of a computer and its components.

A computer performs four tasks:

1. receiving input such as figures, facts, or sets of instructions;
2. storing information by placing it in its memory;

FIGURE 2.2
*Computer and Its
Components*
Nova Development
Corporation 1997–2000.

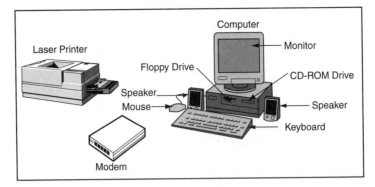

3. processing the data by acting on the information; and
4. outputting the information by generating the results of the processing.

Professor Friedman's research study serves as a hypothetical example of how the computer performs the preceding four tasks. She has collected her data carefully and now wants the computer to do some statistical analysis on the data. She installs her statistical program onto the hard drive of her computer. Next, using the keyboard, she enters her data into the spreadsheet of the statistical program and chooses "analysis of variance" from the statistical procedures. The computer stores the data she enters in memory and then processes this information by performing the necessary statistical calculations in its central processing unit of the computer, discussed later in this chapter. The professor sees the results of the analysis on the screen or as a printout from the printer.

This example sheds some light on how the computer works. Let's continue by examining the computer in more detail. A computer system consists of a central processing unit and the peripheral devices connected to it, along with the computer's operating system. The central processor, or CPU, is contained on one single chip called a **microprocessor.** The memory, RAM (random access memory) and ROM (read only memory), of the computer is also contained on computer chips. Before discussing these various chips, let's define the term **computer chip.**

The Computer Chip

A computer chip is a silicon wafer, approximately 1/16 inch wide and 1/30 inch thick, that holds from a few dozen to millions of electronic components. The term *chip* is synonymous with *integrated circuit*. Computer chips are encased in plastic to protect them, and metal pins enable these chips to be plugged into a computer circuit board. Figure 2.3 shows a chip encased in its plastic protection.

FIGURE 2.3
*Computer Chip
Encased in Plastic*

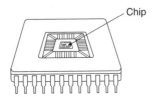

If you look carefully at this chip, you can see tiny circuits etched on the metal. The process of putting these circuits on one chip and connecting them together is called **large-scale integration (LSI)** or **very-large-scale integration (VLSI).** This complex procedure, which involves engineering, plotting, photography, baking, and magnetism, permits silicon chips to be produced in large quantities at a very low cost. Today, there are millions of transistors on a single chip, and with wafer scale integration, eventually these circuits will be built in overlapping layers and there will be billions of transistors.

In the microcomputer, the RAM chips, ROM chips, CPU chips, and other components are plugged into a flat board called a **printed circuit board** (Fig. 2.4). The other side of this board is printed with electrical conductive

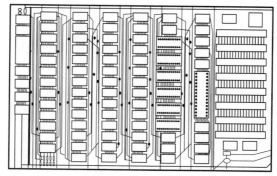

FIGURE 2.4   *Printed Circuit Board*

pathways between the components. A circuit board in 1960 connected discrete components together; in the 2000s the boards connect chips that each contain hundreds of thousands and millions of elementary components (Freedman, 2001).

Computer systems have different components on their boards, and there is no standard way of designing them. Nevertheless, the main component of any computer system is the central processing unit, the brain of the computer.

Central Processing Unit

The **central processing unit (CPU),** also called the **processor,** is the computing part of the computer. A personal computer's central processor is contained on one single chip called a microprocessor, which is smaller than a fingernail. This unit is essential because it controls the way the computer operates. Whenever programmer designs software that gives instructions to the computer, the processor executes these instructions. The central processor gets instructions from memory and either carries out the instructions or tells other components to follow the instructions. Then it goes back to get the next set of instructions. This procedure is repeated until the task is completed.

The central processing unit (Fig. 2.5) consists of three components: the control unit, the arithmetic unit, and the logic unit. In most microcomputers, the arithmetic unit and the logic unit are combined and are referred to as the **arithmetic logic unit (ALU).**

FIGURE 2.5
Central Processing Unit

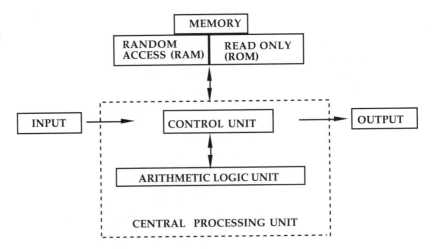

The **control unit** verifies that the computer carries out instructions, transfers instructions to the main memory for storage, and relays information back and forth between the main memory and the ALU. The arithmetic logic unit carries out all the arithmetic operations and logical decisions. Since the central processing unit can work only on small amounts of information at a time, it needs a way to store information while it is not being processed. It needs memory.

Memory

There are two types of chips that take care of the computer's internal memory: **read only memory (ROM)** chips and **random access memory (RAM)** chips.

ROM chips store information permanently in the computer's memory, and this memory supplies the computer with a list of operating instructions. These instructions are burned into the computer during the manufacturing process. ROM is called *nonvolatile memory* because it does not disappear when the computer is turned off. There is nothing an ordinary computer user can do to remove or replace the instructions of ROM because the computer can only read information burned onto these ROM chips. Most computers have a program in ROM that puts on the screen symbols, such as a cursor (usually in the form of a blinking square or line). BASIC was stored in the ROM of the Apple II line of computers, and today there are ROM chips in microwave ovens, watches, and calculators.

The information on RAM chips, however, can be modified; users can write, read, and erase this information. The problem with this type of memory is that it needs a constant power supply so that the data are not lost. RAM is referred to as *volatile memory* because of its temporary nature. Whenever an individual turns off the computer, he or she loses whatever information is in RAM. The basic unit for RAM storage is a **byte,** the space available to hold letters, numbers, and special characters.[1] Because a computer user normally manipulates thousands of characters at a time, the RAM size is usually measured in **kilobytes,** or thousands of bytes (the symbol for kilobytes is K). For example, a computer that has 512K is capable of holding approximately 512,000 numbers, symbols, and letters.[2]

The amount of RAM chips a computer has determines the amount of information that can be retained in memory, the size and number of programs that can be run simultaneously, and the number of data that will be processed immediately. Programs vary in their memory requirements; for example, *AppleWorks* 6.0 needs 24 MB (**megabytes**)[3] of RAM memory to run on a Macintosh with System 8.1 or later, while 16 MB of RAM is required for the Windows version of *DeBabelizer.* Fortunately, the RAM size of most computers can be expanded by adding RAM chips. In the early 1980s, computers usually had a memory size of 64K, then considered more than adequate for a personal computer. Today, the RAM size of a computer is usually described in terms of megabytes or **gigabytes.**[4] Tomorrow, the RAM size will be in trillions of bytes, or **terabytes.**

So now we know about the physical properties of memory, but how does the computer store this information since it cannot store it as a printed page? What does it use to translate information? The fundamental principle behind digital computers' storage is **binary notation.**

Binary Notation

All computer input is converted into binary numbers consisting of two digits, 0 and 1. An instruction that is read as a 1 tells the computer to turn on a circuit, and an instruction read as a 0 tells the computer to turn off the circuit. The digits 0 and 1 are called **bits,** short for **b**inary dig**its**. The computer can represent letters, numbers, and symbols by combining these individual bits into a binary code. Each character or letter typed is translated into a byte by turning circuits off and on. This whole procedure happens at lightning speed whenever a user hits a key on the computer keyboard. For example, when the user types the letter Z, the computer translates it into 01011010. When the user types the number 1, it is translated into 00110001. Every character on the keyboard has a different code combination.

Before leaving memory, let's look briefly at how the computer user stores data permanently.

---

[1] Byte is discussed in more detail in the Binary Notation section of this chapter.
[2] The accurate number is 524,288 (512 × 1,024) because the computer uses powers of 2, and 2^{10} is 1,024. A kilobyte then represents 1,024, or approximately 1,000, bytes.
[3] A megabyte is equivalent to 1,048,576 bytes.
[4] A gigabyte is equivalent to 1 billion bytes.

Disks

The most prevalent method of storage is still the disk. In the early 1990s, one of the most used methods of storage was the 5 1/4-inch disk, but it has disappeared like the dinosaur. The 3 1/2-inch floppy disk is going in the same direction as the 5 1/4. In 1998, Apple computer introduced the iMac, the first personal computer without a floppy disk drive. The four most frequently used storage devices today are pictured in Figure 2.6: the optical disc, infor-

FIGURE 2.6
Four Commonly Used Storage Methods

ClickArt Images © 1995 T/Maker Company.

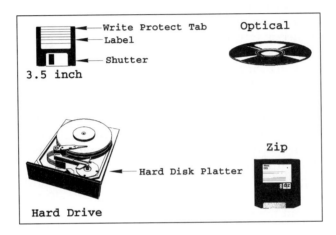

mation stored in the form of tiny pits and read by laser beam; the 3 1/2-inch disk and Zip disk, flexible tapelike material encased in a firm plastic cover; and the hard disk, positioned in a sealed unit. The 3 1/2-inch disk, the Zip disk, and the hard disk store data in the same way: The disk spins on a surface that can be magnetized or demagnetized.

    The number of tracks that are on a disk is a function of how accurately the disk is constructed, how fast the disk spins, how sensitive the disk is to magnetization, and so forth. It is for this reason that the Zip disk holds more information than the 3 1/2-inch disk, and the hard disk is capable of holding more information than either one.

Hard Disk

The **hard disk** is made of metal and covered with a magnetic recording surface. The read/write head, an electronic device that electromagnetically records and reads the information from the disk, travels across this surface via an air cushion, without touching the disk. This disk is fixed or removable and can hold anywhere from 20 gigabytes to 80 gigabytes of information. This is a much greater storage capacity than a 3 1/2-inch floppy disk, which holds anywhere from 800 kilobytes to 2 megabytes of information. Hard disk storage capacity is the amount of room on the hard disk and should not be confused with RAM, the amount of memory necessary to run a program. Presently, the 40-gigabyte hard disk is commonplace, and by the year 2003, you will see drives that are 10 times this amount.

Floppy Disk

Covered with a magnetic coating, such as iron oxide, a floppy disk (or diskette) looks like a small phonograph record divided into tracks invisible to the human eye. The information is sorted on the cylindrical tracks on the disk's surface. Whenever the computer records or reads from the disk, the disk revolves at a constant speed inside its disk drive and the slightest separation between the drive head(s) and the disk surface can lead to the loss of data. The storage capacity of this disk depends on whether data can be stored on both sides of the diskette and on the storage density on each side of the disk. A floppy disk is delicate, and a user should protect this disk from damage by adhering to the following eight suggestions:

1. Always hold a disk by its label and refrain from touching the shutter (refer to Fig. 2.5).
2. Never store 3 1/2-inch disks in plastic envelopes because of the static thus created.
3. When the red in-use light is on or the disk drive is working, do not remove or insert a disk.
4. Never bend the disk or use rubber bands or paper clips on it.
5. Keep the disk away from television, magnets, or severe heat.
6. Do not smoke, eat, or drink near a disk.
7. Do not write on the disk label with a ballpoint pen because it will leave impressions. Always use a felt-tip pen.
8. Stand the disks up in their storage container.

Optical Disc

An **optical disc** holds a huge capacity of information that is stored at high density in the form of small pits that are read by a laser beam. There are a variety of optical discs such as CD-ROM (compact disc read only memory), CD-rewritable or recordable, DVD-ROM discs (digital versatile disc or digital video disc), WORM (write once, read many). The CD-ROMs are an economical means for storing read only programs and data; they hold 650 MB of data, which is equivalent to 250,000 pages of text. CD-rewritable discs store the same amount of data but allow the user to write to the CD-ROMs. Many computers are equipped with CD-rewritable drives, and this will soon be the standard on PCs in the schools. The DVD-ROM discs are a step beyond the CD-ROM; they can hold up to 17 gigabytes (GB) of data and have a faster access time than the CD-ROM discs. (See chapter 3 for a more complete explanation on this topic.) Table 2.1 presents guidelines for handling optical discs.

TABLE 2.1

Optical Disc Care Guidelines

1. Do not expose discs to excessive heat or cold.
2. Do not touch the bottom of the disc.
3. Do not write on the disc.
4. Do not stack the discs on top of one another.

Zip Disk

With the advent of Iomega's Zip disk, the disk storage media changed forever. People had an alternative to the floppy disk that holds only 2 MB of data. The Zip presently stores 250 MB, is small, and is removable (refer to Fig. 2.6). In addition to the Zip, Iomega produces the Jaz drive, which holds 2 GB of storage.

Formatting or Initializing a Disk

If a disk is not formatted, it cannot save or store data. **Formatting a disk** prepares the disk to store information by instructing the computer to record some magnetic reference marks on the disk. These reference marks define the number and size of the sectors on a soft-sectored disk. The storage layout of the disk is determined by the computer operating system's access method. Disks must be initialized with the particular operating system of the computer; operating system A cannot use a disk from operating system B. Each disk is formatted only once unless the user wants to erase everything on the disk. Disks are presently sold unformatted or formatted; the formatted ones are slightly more expensive, but they save time and effort.

Operating Systems

In the early days of computing, a person controlled the operation of a computer by using an elaborate control panel. Later, computer programmers designed a program that would allow the computer to control its own operation. This control program is the **operating system** of the computer, and its major task is to handle the transfer of data and programs to and from the computer's disks. The operating system can display a directory showing the names of programs stored on the disk; it can copy a program from one disk to another; it can display and print the contents of any file on the screen. The operating system controls the computer components and allows them to communicate with each other. (The term DOS is an abbreviation for **d**isk **o**perating **s**ystem.) There are many other functions that an operating system performs; the computer's system manual enumerates them.

Different computers have different operating systems. The same computer, moreover, may have more than one operating system available to it. For example, the old Apple II computers used DOS 3.3, ProDOS, and OS/GS operating systems. Some other well-known operating systems are MS-DOS, Microsoft Windows 95, Microsoft Windows 2000, UNIX, OS/2, and Macintosh System 6 and System 8. Macintosh OS X is the most recent Apple OS (operating system), and Windows XP is the most recent Microsoft operating system. Lacking a single standard operating system, all computers are not compatible. However, many companies are seeking a solution to this incompatibility problem. *Virtual PC* (Connectix) is a software program that lets your

Macintosh computer run many PC-based operating systems. This economical software product requires plenty of memory and a fast computer to run effectively. The IBM 615-based system runs X86, Macintosh, UNIX, and OS/2 software. There are other manufacturers, such as Orange Micro and Daystar, that produce cards that can be placed inside computers to allow them to run more than one system. In the past, different models of computers varied in the way the operating system was supplied to the computer. Some computers had the entire operating system built into the ROM of the machine, while others had their operating systems placed on separate floppy disks. Presently, the majority of computers have hard disk drives, and their operating systems are installed from CD-ROM onto the hard disks.

When the operating system was stored on a disk, the computer, when turned on, would run a small program usually stored in the ROM of the computer. This program's purpose was to *load* the operating system into the main memory of the computer and then turn over its authority to the operating system. The procedure of starting the computer so that it could load its operating system became known as **booting the system,** a term that has interesting origins. In the past, when the computer first loaded the operating system into main memory, the small program that helped it do this was called a *bootstrap loader* because the initial loading was analogous to "lifting yourself by your own bootstraps." As time went on, computer experts began referring to the procedure of starting the computer system as "booting the system."

How does one physically boot a system? If the operating system was on a disk, the user simply put the disk in a disk drive, turned on the machine, and waited for it to boot. Some computers' operating systems requested that the user supply information, such as date or time of day, before the operating system would respond to the person's commands. Currently, the operating system is on the hard disk and the user simply turns on the computer.

Since its inception, the Macintosh's trademark has been its ease of use. It had the most workable operating system, a characteristic that distinguished it from other systems. Practically every Macintosh application program used the same user interface, so the user did not have to relearn commands each time he or she used a different application. The success of the Macintosh interface led Microsoft to introduce Windows for the IBM, which has an interface that is similar to the Macintosh. Both Apple Macintosh OS X (System 10), and Microsoft's Windows 2000 feature **graphical user interfaces (GUIs)** in which the user points to a picture or icon to select a program instead of typing commands.

Let's take a look at the opening screens of these particular versions of the Macintosh and Windows operating systems.

Macintosh Opening Screen

The new Macintosh operating system has translucent buttons and an aqua interface. At the bottom of the screen, Mac OS X has folders, applications, documents, storage, minimized windows, QuickTime movies, digital images, links to websites, and applications that you need for instant access (Fig. 2.7). The system's Finder gives you extremely fast access to finding files, running applications, and communicating with people. This system is built to easily access the Internet.

FIGURE 2.7
Macintosh Opening Screen

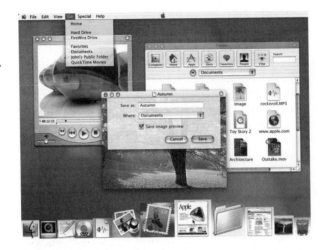

Windows 2000

The Windows 2000 operating system is a combination of *Office 2000* and *Windows 2000*. The system is built to take advantage of the Internet and provide support for mobile users. As you can see from Windows' opening screen (Fig. 2.8), the system eliminates menu clutter; it is less artistic and more analytical looking than the Macintosh.

FIGURE 2.8
Windows Opening Screen

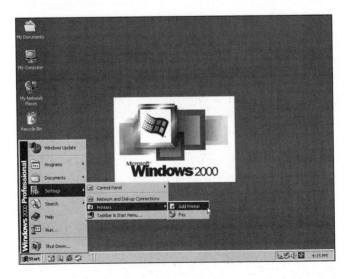

Basic System Utilities

During a normal session of computing, the utility functions usually requested are formatting, copying disks, copying files, and deleting files.

Formatting lets the user store data on a disk. Copying disks makes backup copies of data files or applications; this is imperative because original disks can become defective or accidentally erased. Copying files copies a few files instead of the whole disk. Finally, deleting files removes unwanted files from a disk.

Although the Macintosh and Windows systems are both graphical interfaces that rely heavily on icons or pictures, their respective systems handle their basic functions in unique ways.

For further discussion of the Macintosh and Microsoft Windows operating systems, consult your operating system's manual.

Getting Started on the Computer

Before you turn on the computer, familiarize yourself with the following accepted sequence for turning most computers on and off. This sequence provides a safeguard against electrical problems.

Computer Checklist

1. Turn on the printer.
2. Turn on the monitor.
3. Turn on any other peripherals.
4. Turn on the computer.
5. When finished working, remove the disk from the disk drive.
6. Turn off the computer.
7. Turn off the printer, monitor, and peripherals.[5]

Even though this sequence is very common, some computers require a different sequence. Check the manual or consult the Read Me First document before proceeding.

Summary

Even though advances in technology have blurred the distinctions, memory capacity, speed, capability, price range, and size classify computers. The three classifications are mainframe, minicomputer, and microcomputer. In education, the student uses the computer to perform three functions: logic comparisons, arithmetic operations, and storage and retrieval. The computer accomplishes these functions at high speed, storing huge amounts of data in a binary format. The central processing unit, the brain of the computer, consists of a control unit that controls what is happening; an arithmetic logic unit (ALU) that does the arithmetic and logic operations; and primary memory, ROM and RAM, that stores all data and instructions necessary for operation. ROM, read only memory, cannot be changed

---

[5]Use a power strip to safeguard your equipment from power surges.

and is hard-wired into the machine. RAM, random access memory, is temporary memory that stores data and programs that need processing. Because of its erasable characteristics, RAM allows a program to be executed as many times as the user needs. Since RAM is temporary, disks are very important permanent storage media. The floppy disk is delicate and requires special handling. The operating system, the control program that handles the transfer of data and programs to and from computer disks, makes it possible to enter and run programs.

What follows is a list of helpful Internet sites. These sites include online stores, operating system sites, computer terms, and tips and tricks.

ONLINE STORES AND OPERATING SYSTEM SITES

PC–Mac Connection
http://www.macconnection.com
http://www.pcconnection.com
Mac and PC Connection, Inc., is a mail order company that offers more than 100,000 brand-name products at competitive prices.

PC–Mac Warehouse
http://www.warehouse.com
Mac and PC Warehouse, Inc., is a mail order company that offers brand-name products at competitive prices.

Educational Resources
http://www.edresources.com
Educational Resources, in operation since 1985, has more than 5,000 software titles, supplemental software, and mixed-media curriculum courseware, as well as peripherals and accessories.

Learning Services
http://www.learnserv.com
Learning Services has been operation for more than 20 years and features over 5,000 software titles. It has supplemental software and mixed-media curriculum courseware, as well as peripherals and accessories.

Windows 95
http://www.gate.net/~jsharit/windows_95/win95tips_and_tweaks.html
Tips and Tweaks contains numerous Windows 95 references and resources, as well as helpful tip and tweaks.

Windows 95 and 98 Tips and Tricks
http://www.window95.com
This site is dedicated to helping you through the Windows 98 operating system. It contains Windows 98 tips and tricks.

WINDOWS 2000 Tips and Tricks
http://win2000tips.home.att.net/
This site is dedicated to helping you through the Windows 2000 operating system. It contains Windows 2000 tips and tricks.

CPM's TechWeb
http://winmag.com/win98
This site fulfills your Windows 98 information needs through its news, tips, related articles, free e-mail newsletter, downloads, and a forum.

Microsoft
http://microsoft.com
Microsoft's home page contains an assortment of items ranging from news to downloads to product information.

Apple Computer
http://apple.com
Apple's home page consists of a range of items—reviews, news, products, and downloads.

MacFixIt
http://macfixit.com/
Created in 1996 by author Ted Landau, this site brings together experts who discuss conflicts and fixes for things that go in or on or are connected to the Macintosh.

Foldoc Free Online Dictionary of Computing
http://wombat.doc.ic.ac.uk/foldoc/
The *Free Online Dictionary of Computing* (FOLDOC) is a searchable database, which has

more than 13,000 entries and is still growing. You can search it using a search engine or clicking on an alphabetical index.

Supercomputer sites
www.netlib.org/benchmark/top500.html
A list of the 500 most powerful computers and their installations is updated biyearly and posted on Web servers in the United States, Germany, and Japan.

Chapter Mastery Test

To the Instructor: Refer to the Instructor's Manual for the Answers to the Mastery Questions. This manual has additional questions and resource materials.

Let's check for chapter comprehension with a short mastery test. Some suggested readings and references follow the activities.

1. What are the major differences among these categories of computers: mainframe, minicomputer, and microcomputer?
2. Give some pointers on how to protect a floppy disk and an optical disc from harm.
3. Compare and contrast RAM and ROM.
4. Explain how the different components of a central processing unit work.
5. What is an operating system and what function does it perform?

6. Discuss the microprocessor, the CPU, and memory and explain how they function independently and as a complete unit.
7. Why is it important to have enough RAM for your computer?
8. Why is it necessary to initialize or format a disk?
9. Define and explain the following terms: bit, byte, kilobytes, and megabytes.
10. What does "to boot a computer" mean?
11. Explain the following terms: formatting or initializing, copying disks, copying files, and deleting files.
12. Explain what an optical disc is and what distinguishes it from a floppy disk.
13. Why are erasable optical discs the wave of the future?
14. What is the function of a Zip disk and why did it become so popular?

Basic Terms

arithmetic logic unit (ALU) (28)
binary notation (29)
bit (29)
booting the system (33)
byte (29)
central processing unit (27)
computer chip (26)
control unit (28)
formatting a disk (32)
gigabyte (29)
graphical user interface (GUI) (33)
hard disk (30)
kilobyte (29)
large-scale integration (LSI) (27)

mainframe (24)
megabyte (29)
microcomputer (25)
microprocessor (26)
minicomputer (25)
operating system (32)
optical disc (31)
printed circuit board (27)
random access memory (RAM) (28)
read only memory (ROM) (28)
supercomputer (24)
terabyte (29)
very-large-scale integration (VSLI) (27)

Classroom Projects

LAB ACTIVITIES

1. Start computer.
2. Initialize or format a disk.
3. Copy a file.
4. Delete a file.

CLASSROOM ACTIVITIES

1. Write a paper on the history of computer memory and in this paper explain the following:
   A. How data is stored in the computer,
   B. The speed and cost of memory, and
   C. The limitations and advantages of the system used.
2. At the library, find a recent article on microchips and discuss recent developments in this technology.
3. Compare and contrast two operating systems.

Suggested Readings and References

Alessi, S. M., and S. R. Trollip. *Computer-Based Instruction: Methods and Development.* Englewood Cliffs, N.J.: Prentice Hall, 1985.

American National Standards Institute. *American National Standard Code for Information Interchange.* New York: ANSI, 1986.

Baron, Cynthia L., and Robin Williams. *Windows for MacUsers: The Macintosh-to-Windows Guide.* Berkeley, Calif.: Peachpit Press, 1999.

Barr, Christopher. "First Sub-Mini Hard Disk." *PC Magazine* 11, no. 1 (January 14, 1992): 30.

Bott, Ed. "The Top Secret Windows: Memphis." *PC Computing,* August 1997, pp. 154–82.

Brown, Margaret. *Learning Windows 95.* New York: DDC Publishing, 1995.

DeMillion, John A. "Another View of PC vs. Mac." *School Business Affairs* 64, no. 2 (February 1998): 44–47.

Eoyang, Christopher. "The Second Generation of Japanese Computers." *SuperComputer Review.* San Diego, Calif.: Myrias Research Corporation, 1988, pp. 26–27.

Freedman, Alan. *The Computer Desktop Encyclopedia.* New York: Amacom, 2001.

Freedman, Alan. *The Computer Glossary.* 5th ed. New York: Amacom, 1995.

Goodman, A. *The Color-Coded Guide to Microcomputers.* New York: Barnes and Noble, 1983.

Langer, Maria. *MAC OS 8 Visual QuickStart Guide.* Berkeley, Calif.: Peachpit Press, 1997.

Laurie, Peter. *The Joy of Computers.* Boston: Little, Brown, 1983.

Maran, Ruth. *Windows 95 Visual Pocket Guide.* Foster City, Calif.: IDG Books , Worldwide, Inc., 1995.

Maran, Ruth. *Windows 98 Simplified.* Foster City, Calif.: IDG 3-D Visual Series, Worldwide, Inc., 1998.

Mello, Adrian. "Into the Next Decade." *Macworld,* February 1994, pp. 21–22.

Moore, John Frederick. "Making the Most of a Mobile OS." *Mobile Computing & Communications,* April 2000, pp. 28–30.

Neel, Dan, and Geneva Sapp. "Windows 2000 Launch: Moment of Truth Arrives." *InfoWorld* 22, no. 7 (February 14, 2000): 134.

Norr, Henry. "Rhapsody Tunes Up." *MacUser,* September 1997, pp. 76–77.

Patton, Peter. "Survey Forecasts Super Computer Market Growth at 35% to 40%." *SuperComputer Review.* San Diego, Calif.: Myrias Research Corporation, 1988, pp. 28–29.

Poultney, John. "Apple-IBM Subnotebook Due to Hit U.S. in Summer." *MacWeek* 11, no. 12 (March 24, 1997): 1.

Reed, Sandy. "Microsoft to Launch Its Windows 2000 to a More Skeptical Marketplace." *InfoWorld* 22, no. 6 (February 7, 2000): 77.

Richman, Ellen. *Spotlight on Computer Literacy.* Rev. ed. New York: Random House, 1982.

Rollwagen, John A. *Cray Research Inc. Annual Report.* Eagan, Minn.: Cray Research Inc., 1997.

Stone, David. "Future Mass Storage." *PC Magazine* 16, no. 6 (March 25, 1997): 182–84.

Trott, Bob, and Ed Scannell. "Win3000 Bandwagon Fills." *InfoWorld* 22, no. 7 (February 14, 2000): 34.

Zorpette, Glenn. "Science and Medicine." *Los Angeles Times,* December 30, 1991, p. B5.

CHAPTER 3

Computer Hardware for the Classroom

Integrating Computer Hardware in the Classroom

Did you know that you cannot integrate educational software in the classroom, you need to know about computer hardware. Did you know you need some understanding about how these hardware devices operate? This chapter will discuss the major input devices and output devices that are found in schools. In the process of reading the chapter, you will learn how to pick out hardware for the classroom by using specific criteria. You will see a checklist designed to help you select the right computer or monitor for your classroom. In addition, you will become familiar with Internet sites that contain information about hardware, hardware companies, lesson plans, news, and reviews.

Objectives

Upon completing this chapter, you will be able to:

1. Describe the major input devices and explain how each works;
2. Describe the major output devices and explain how each works;
3. List the salient features of different printers, monitors, and storage devices;
4. Choose appropriate hardware in terms of established criteria; and
5. Explore some useful Internet sites.

Background

The **hardware** of a computer system includes the electronic components, boards, wires, and peripherals. The **software** instructs the computer hardware to perform various tasks. If you have only hardware, you are powerless to accomplish anything with the computer, much as if you had a car without fuel. Buying hardware for your classroom is a complicated and time-consuming job that requires an examination of many factors. Before you begin the process of selecting hardware, you first choose the software that meets the needs of your class. When you select the software, you determine primary needs and then estimate future needs. For example, you might be satisfied initially with software such as *Ultimate Writing and Creativity Center* but might soon require a sophisticated desktop package such as *QuarkXpress*. If you want to use an advanced spreadsheet or statistical software, you will need computer hardware with ample memory. You have to spend time learning about available hardware, its capabilities, and its functions. Current magazines (such as *MacWorld* or *PC World*) alert you to the latest hardware developments. You can save time and money by being prepared to ask appropriate questions. In the course of this discussion you will look at some of the factors that most influence a teacher or student's decision and examine some of the basic hardware equipment available. The most popular input devices used in the classroom are the keyboard, mouse, trackball, and touchpad.

Input Devices

An input device gives information to the computer system so that it can perform its tasks. Years ago, the keypunch machine was the major means of input; today, it is the keyboard.

Keyboard

The computer **keyboard** is similar to that of a standard typewriter, but it includes extra keys such as the function keys and the numeric pad. Figure 3.1 shows a standard keyboard with a numeric pad on the right for quick data entry. Although the keyboard is the primary way of entering data, it is not as efficient for making screen selections. Furthermore, if you are an inexperienced typist, you are more likely to make mistakes when using the keyboard for screen selections. As a result, computer manufacturers created pointing devices that would lessen the need for a keyboard. Today, most computers use both a keyboard and supplemental pointing devices.

FIGURE 3.1
Computer
Keyboard
Courtesy of Nova
Development Corporation.

Pointing Devices

Mouse

Originally designed by Xerox, the **mouse** was popularized by the Apple Macintosh computer. The original mouse was a palm-size box with a button on it. It was connected to the computer by either a cable or a wire. Today, mouses come in different shapes and sizes, some are cordless, and they can have from one to three buttons. They have two different internal mechanisms: mechanical and optical. The mechanical mouse has a rubber-coated ball on the bottom of its case; when you move the mouse, the ball rotates. The optical mouse shows its position by detecting reflections from a light-emitting diode[1] that aims the beam downward. This mouse usually required a special pad to reflect the beam correctly. However, Apple's Pro mouse, based on high-precision tracking (Fig. 3.2), does not require a special pad.

FIGURE 3.2
Mouse
Courtesy of Apple Computer.

The movement of the mouse is represented by a cursor or blinking light on the screen. If you move the mouse to the right, the cursor moves to the right. If you push the mouse's button, the cursor is positioned at that particular location. Furthermore, the mouse can be used to select items from a pulldown menu, to delete and insert text, and to draw or paint when used with paint or draw software such as *Corel Draw 9*.

The mouse is easy to use and install; however, it is awkward for delicate drawing and it requires space. An alternative device that is stationary and requires less desk space is the trackball.

Trackball

The **trackball** (Fig. 3.3), which performs the same tasks as the mouse, operates with a rotating metal ball inset in a small, boxlike device and does not re-

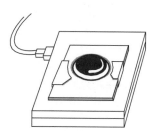

FIGURE 3.3
Trackball

quire a desktop. With your fingers, you roll the exposed part of the trackball, producing cursor movement on the screen. This device was very popular in portable computers until Apple introduced the touchpad.

---

[1]A diode, an electronic component that acts primarily as a one-way valve, is used as a temperature or light sensor (Freedman, 2000).

FIGURE 3.4
Touchpad
Photo courtesy MicroQue,
1994.

Touchpad

The **touchpad** is a pressure-sensitive pad that is smaller, more accurate, thinner, and less expensive to build than the trackball. You slide your finger over this pad with the same movements that you would use with a mouse. The faster your fingers travel on the pad, the greater the distance you will cover on the computer screen. You can also tap on the pad's surface instead of pushing the touchpad keys.

QuePoint (MicroQue) was one of the first external touchpads, sold for desktop and portable systems (Fig. 3.4). The QuePoint was based on the same technology that is used in today's modern portable computers.

Alternative Input Devices

In addition to pointing devices, many other input devices are used in the workplace. These devices include optical scanning devices that utilize laser capabilities. The laser searches for groups of dots that represent marks, characters, or lines. These input devices differ from each other in terms of the programs used and the way the computers massage the data.

Optical Mark Reader

The **optical mark reader** (**OMR**) was designed initially to read penciled or graphic information on exam answer sheets. Lamps furnish light that reflects from test paper. The amount of reflected light is measured by a photocell. When a mark is made on a sheet of paper, it blocks light from reflecting. The Scanmark's optical mark reader (Fig. 3.5) compares the pattern of marks on

FIGURE 3.5
Optical Mark Reader
Courtesy of Scanmark's ES 2010.

test papers with the correct pattern stored in the computer's memory. Many schools and school districts use the optical mark reader to grade standardized tests. With the proper software, the OMR will also keep library and attendance records and will report grades.

Scanners

The **scanner** is now being rediscovered in the schools because of its affordability and its usefulness for desktop publishing, faxing, and **optical character recognition (OCR).** OCR is machine recognition of typed or printed text. By using OCR software with a scanner, a student can scan a printed page and the characters can be converted into text. Figure 3.6 shows the results of using the scanner in conjunction with *TextBridge* (Xerox), a full-featured optical character recognition software, to input text. *TextBridge,* a relatively inexpensive

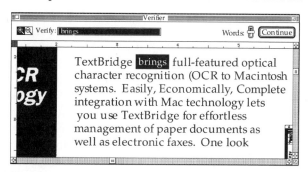

FIGURE 3.6
TextBridge
Used with permission of
Xerox Imaging Software.

product, eliminates the time, expense, and potential errors of typing the material to input it. Advanced OCR systems let students recognize hand printing.

The scanner transforms images into electronic images. Figure 3.7 is a photograph of my son that was scanned into the computer.

FIGURE 3.7
*Scanned
Photograph*
Courtesey of Vicki Sharp.

Scanners digitize photographs or line art and store the image as a file that can be transferred into a paint program or directly into a word processor. If you create a newsletter and want to insert a picture into the text, you scan the picture, copy it, and then "paste" it into the document. Scanners used for this purpose come in a variety of forms (Fig. 3.8): You could use a full-size flatbed scanner, a handheld scanner, an overhead scanner, a sheet-fed scanner, or a film scanner.

Flatbed   Overhead

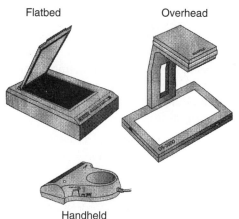

FIGURE 3.8
Scanners

Handheld

A flatbed scanner easily scans documents, books, or periodicals. You simply open the lid of the scanner and place the materials on the "bed." It is more versatile than a hand scanner, but it is more expensive.

A handheld scanner fits in the palm of your hand. You slide it across the image or document slowly, at the rate of about an inch every 10 seconds. It works well on four-inch columns, but it is not able to scan an entire line of text in a single pass. The only alternative is to stitch or paste the material together, which is time-consuming but does produce acceptable results.

The overhead scanner scans large documents as a flatbed does. It also scans three-dimensional objects. The sheet-fed scanner can only scan paper rather than three-dimensional objects or books. This scanner moves the paper across a stationary head. An example of this type of scanner is Visioneer's Strobe Pro Color Sheetfed scanners.

Finally, the film scanner is designed for scanning slides, negatives, or photographic prints. This scanner delivers resolutions that range from 1,000 to 4,096 dots per inch, and it can read 16.8 million colors.

Scanners differ in **resolution,** or degree of sharpness. The more dots a scanned image contains, the sharper it is. An inexpensive scanner produces images at about 600 dots per inch. The more expensive scanners produce images at a higher resolution. In the past, most scanners produced black-and-white and half-tone images, and the color scanner was too expensive for the ordinary person. Today, however, an inexpensive color scanner can be purchased for under $200. Let us conclude this discussion with an examination of digital cameras and the handheld computer.

Digital Cameras

Digital cameras record images in digital format. These cameras operate on the same fundamental principles as a basic camera, but they are better suited for desktop publishing. The primary difference between a basic camera and a digital one is that they employ different media for capturing images. The traditional camera uses film, while the digital camera uses a charge-coupled device (CCD) that is readable by the computer.[2]

One of the first digital cameras was FotoMan by Logitech. This camera delivered eight-bit, gray-scale photo images to a Macintosh computer without photo paper, scanner, chemicals, or film. Currently, interest in digital cameras is increasing in schools. A standard digital camera's resolution is up to $1,280 \times 960$; it uses flash memory card, floppy disks, or hard disk to store pictures. The images are transferred to the computer with a serial or Universal Serial Bus (USB) cable or via the storage medium itself if the computer has a corresponding reader.

---

[2]A charge-coupled device (CCD) is "electronic memory that can be charged by light. CCDs can hold a variable charge, which is why they are used in cameras and scanners to record variable shades of light" (Freedman, 2000).

The Sony Digital Maverick cameras (Fig. 3.9) use standard floppy disks to transfer photos into your PC. These cameras are very popular in the schools because of their convenient floppy disk storage, which lets the teacher easily transfer images to any computer or hand off images to a student. There are no

FIGURE 3.9
Sony Digital Maverick
Courtesy of Sony Corporation.

adapters and no extra hardware to buy, and many of the units let you save low-resolution video clips that you can post on the Web or attach to an e-mail. Most of the major camera companies such as Canon, Kodak, Olympus, and Fuji have low-cost digital cameras retailing for $125 to $300.

There are many important considerations when purchasing a digital camera for your school; we will touch on only a few here. The teacher should look at the camera's *image quality.* The more expensive cameras have the higher image quality. One factor that determines image quality is pixel density or pixel depth (see Video Output, page 58). Present digital cameras are capable of storing 3 million pixel images. Another factor that determines image quality is the quality of the lens system, which varies with the type of camera you buy. *Camera use* is a very important factor in determining what features you must have in a camera. Buying the most expensive camera could be overkill when all you want to do is put images on a Web page. Another issue is how the camera *stores images* and *transfers images* to the computer. Since teachers and students need a quick and easy way to transfer these images to their computer, a floppy disk or a USB cable might be the best solution.

Digital cameras make picture taking easy, their image editing program gives you control over your pictures, and you don't have to work in a darkroom or drop film off at the local drugstore. The only trouble with digital cameras is that they cost as much or more than the 35-mm single-lens reflex film camera, and many have simple optics and limited abilities. Nevertheless, the digital camera is a quick way to get photos into computer-readable form, which can be used for school reports, for quick security badges, or for shooting pictures for Web pages. Digital cameras are still evolving and every three or four months manufacturers increase resolution, lower price, and reduce size. Any school that is on a strict budget can use the small **videoconferencing cameras** as an alternative.

Videoconferencing Cameras

These inexpensive cameras may cost as little as $50. They usually have built-in microphones, and they have an easy way to capture still pictures and moving images for your presentations. Logitech (Fig. 3.10) has a series of these cameras that start at $50. Teachers and students can quickly build Web pages, make live video, and do simple e-mail videos and pictures to share with their classmates or other school districts or talk to students around the world.

FIGURE 3.10
Logitech Camera
Courtesy Logitech.

Handheld Electronic Organizers

Students and teachers are increasingly using electronic organizers. These handheld computers are small mobile computers that accept input through a penlike instrument called a *stylus* that you use to write on the computer's screen. These devices let you take notes, send and receive faxes, send e-mail, search the Internet, keep a calendar, and collect information from distant databases. The Palm, formerly known as the PalmPilot (Fig. 3.11), is the leading electronic organizer in the field (Freedman, 2001).

FIGURE 3.11
The Palm III XE
Courtesy of Palm Computing, Inc.

Digital Video Magazine (Fig. 3.12) envisions the handheld computers of the future as having picture capabilities so that users can see the person with whom they are communicating.

FIGURE 3.12
Next Generation of Computers
Courtesy of DV Magazine.

For the education market, Apple was the first to sell the eMate 300, an affordable mobile computer. Apple's eMate combined many of the features of a personal computer and the flexibility of a mobile computer with the ability to interact with a desktop computer and the Internet. This machine was an important breakthrough that was unfortunately discontinued. However, there are machines that provide computer access for every student in the classroom and are quite inexpensive. For example, the AlphaSmart 3000 (Alpha Smart, Inc.; Fig. 3.13) works with virtually any Macintosh or PC running

FIGURE 3.13
AlphaSmart 3000
Courtesy of AlphaSmart, Inc.

any application. The device prints directly to the printer and downloads files to the computer. The students can do most of their work wherever they happen to be—in a classroom, lab, on a field trip, or at home. Weighing 2 pounds, these rugged units have a word processor and spelling checker. Furthermore, there are features for special needs: sticky keys, which stay down when you press them; key repeat control; and four keyboard layouts. Brother also produces an inexpensive computerlike device called the GeoBook, which teaches keyboarding, screen navigation, file management, word processing, and spreadsheet skills; it also gives the user e-mail and Internet access.

Output Devices

Printers

One of the most notable output devices is the **printer,** which gives you a permanent record of your work by producing a printout, or hard copy. Let's look at three different types of printers that are currently found in the classroom, the dot-matrix, laser, and inkjet.

Dot-Matrix Printer

For years, the dot-matrix printer was the most widely used printer. With the price reduction of laser printers and the advances in inkjet technology, this situation has changed and the dot-matrix printer has disappeared from the majority of classrooms. The dot-matrix printer (Fig. 3.14) is an impact printer that

FIGURE 3.14
Dot-Matrix Printer
ClickArt Images © 1995 T/Maker Company.

produces characters and graphic images by striking an inked ribbon with tiny metal rods called pins. When the movable print head with its pins is pressed against ribbon and paper, it causes small dots to print on the paper (Fig. 3.15).

FIGURE 3.15
Letter A *on a Dot-Matrix Printer*

The print quality depends on the number of pins the printer has; that is, a 24-pin printer produces better-looking characters than a 9-pin printer.

Inkjet Printer

The **inkjet printer** uses a nozzle to spray a jet of ink onto paper. These small, spherical bodies of ink are released through a matrix of holes to form characters. Inkjet printers produce high-quality output, have few moving parts, and are quiet because they do not strike the paper with metal parts. Inkjet printers are still slower than good-quality laser printers, but they are faster than most low-cost laser printers. Even though the cost of the color inkjet has been steadily decreasing, there is a significant cost associated with the purchase of the ink cartridges. Because of improvements in technology, color inkjet printers have become very popular. These printers cost under $200, inexpensive compared to color laser printers, which cost $2,000 or more.

Laser Printer

Producing near-professional quality print, the **laser printer** (Fig. 3.16) operates like a copying machine—with one important difference. The

FIGURE 3.16
Laser Printer
ClickArt Images © 1995 T/Maker Company.

copying machine produces its image by focusing its lens on paper, while the laser printer traces an image by using a laser beam controlled by the computer.

Laser printers produce text and graphics with high resolution; however, the print quality is not as high as that obtained by a phototype machine used by commercial textbook publishers. Many inexpensive laser printers that print in black and white are on the market today. Brother's latest laser printer, HL-1240, costs under $300 and prints 12 pages per minute. The laser is a sought-after printer because of its beautiful print and graphics capabilities. In the next few years you will see color laser printers at drastically reduced prices.

Screen Displays

The computer could function without peripherals such as the digital camera or a set of speakers, but the monitor is an essential piece of equipment. The two most frequently used types of monitors are the **cathode ray tube (CRT)** monitor and the **liquid crystal display (LCD)** monitor.

CRT Monitors

Cathode ray tube (Fig. 3.17) refers to a vacuum tube that is used as a display screen in a video terminal or TV. Currently, the term refers to the entire monitor rather than the tube (Freedman, 2001).

FIGURE 3.17
Cathode Ray Tube (CRT)

The best of the CRT monitors is the **red, green, and blue (RGB) monitor.** Using three electronic guns, the red, green, and blue monitor generates three colors. This monitor, the most expensive, produces the sharpest images because of the separate video signals used for each of these guns. The RGB monitor (Fig. 3.18) generates a better image than the television, which merges the three colors together.

FIGURE 3.18
Red, Green, and Blue (RGB) Monitor
© Corel Draw 3.0.

LCD Monitors

The most common flat-screen displays are the liquid crystal displays (LCDs). The LCD is created by positioning a liquid crystal material between two sheets of polarizing material squeezed between two glass panels. This display depends on reflected light, so the viewing angle is important; the image can disappear with the wrong angles and with inadequate adjustment of the contrast controls. Used in calculators, watches, and laptops, LCD technology is also becoming popular for flat-panel desktop monitors. The LCD flat panels not only take up less space, but they resist glare, use less energy, and emit less radiation.

There are two types of LCDs: the *active matrix* and the *passive matrix*. In the active matrix display, each of the screen's tiny electrodes has its own transistor. The passive matrix display has only a single transistor that controls an entire column of the display's electrodes. The active matrix is superior in contrast and resolution, but it is much more expensive. LCD panels have always been available for laptops (Fig. 3.19). Teachers and students are constantly using these laptops for presentation, networking, and carrying their work with them.

FIGURE 3.19
iBook
Courtesy of Apple Computer.

In the next few years expect the CRT monitors to disappear and be replaced by the LCD monitors (see Chapter 17).

Demonstrating for the Class

The classroom teacher needs a way to use the computer to demonstrate a program or concept to the entire class. Currently, three methods are used: the LCD projection panel, the projector, and video scan converter.

LCD Projection Panel

The LCD projection panel is important because it enables the classroom teacher to use the computer for the entire class. The LCD panel is a projector that receives computer output and displays it on a liquid crystal screen placed on top of an overhead projector. The overhead becomes the projector, displaying the programs that the computer generates on a larger screen for the whole class to see. The size of the panel varies depending on the manufacturer. The LCD projection panel is certainly an alternative to the more expensive computer projectors.

Projectors

Teachers use the projector to project images from the computer to a screen or television. The LCD projector can connect directly to the school's PC, Mac, VCR, or video source and is an excellent way to view a software program or see an Internet site. These projectors range in price from $2,000 and up. The InFocus projectors are compact, are portable, and have a zoom lens. For teachers who need a lightweight traveling projector, the LP330 (Dragonfly; Fig. 3.20) weighs only 4.8 ounces and is high quality.

FIGURE 3.20
LP330 InFocus Projector
Courtesy of InFocus.

Scan Converters

For the teacher who is working on a budget and wants to use existing equipment, a video **scan converter** will accomplish the task. These converters can turn any standard television into a large-screen display. This is great for presentation, training educators, or viewing Internet sites. FOCUS Enhancements has a series of video scan converters that accomplish this simply and inexpensively, costing about $150 to $275. The TView Gold video scan converter (Fig. 3.21) connects almost any computer, is both Mac and PC compatible, and it has pan, zoom, and freeze capabilities. Up to this point, input or out-

FIGURE 3.21
TView Gold Scan Converter
Courtesy of FOCUS Enhancements.

put devices have been considered separate categories; now let's consider devices that perform a dual function.

Storage Devices

In the classroom, storage devices that are commonly available are the floppy drive, Zip drive, Jaz drive, hard disk drive, optical discs, CD-ROM drive, and DVD drive.

Floppy Disk

In the 1970s, IBM introduced the 8-inch floppy disk (diskette) for data storage. It consists of a circular piece of plastic, oxide-coated matter enclosed in a protective jacket, similar in appearance to an audiocassette tape. When the disk is placed in a disk drive, it rotates inside its jacket, thus allowing data to be stored on it and viewed later. This disk was replaced by the 5 1/4-inch disk, which was subsequently replaced by the 3 1/2-inch disk (Fig. 3.22). This 3 1/2, which is not adequate for multimedia, will shortly be replaced.

FIGURE 3.22
Floppy Disk
ClickArt Images © 1995
T/Maker Company.

Zip Drive

In 1995 Iomega Corporation introduced the Zip drive, a removable storage device (Freedman, 2001). These drives, which could be internal or external, were responsible for the decline of the floppy. Currently, the Zip drives (Fig. 3.23) provide 100 or 250 MB of storage inexpensively on disks that are just a little larger than a floppy disk (see Chapter 2). There are other companies such as Imation manufacturing disks that are similar in nature.

FIGURE 3.23
Zip Drive
Courtesey of Iomega.

Jaz Drive

The Jaz disk is a portable means of storage that provides 2 GB of disk space on each 3.5-inch cartridge. This device is invaluable for users who want to back up their hard drive or huge graphic files. The Jaz drive provides storage and has very quick access time, which makes moving files around a pleasure.

Hard Disk

The hard disk drive provides increased storage capabilities and faster access. Hard disks were developed by IBM in 1973. The early ones were extremely expensive; however, with mass production of the personal computer, a hard disk drive is now available for as little as $200, and it is incorporated into the computer system. A fixed, hard disk usually has one or more disk platters coated with a metal oxide substance that allows information to be magnetically stored on it. This storage system includes the disk, a read/write head assembly, and the connections between the drive and the computer (Fig. 3.24).

FIGURE 3.24
*Hard Disk and
Drive Components*
Copyright © Pearson
Computer Systems Pty., Ltd.

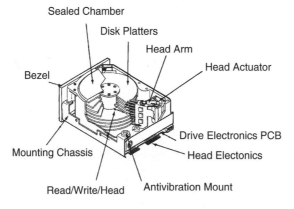

Sealed Chamber
Disk Platters
Head Arm
Head Actuator
Bezel
Drive Electronics PCB
Head Electonics
Mounting Chassis
Read/Write/Head
Antivibration Mount

At first, these disk drives used 14-inch disks, but now they use 5 1/4-inch, 3 1/2-inch, 2-inch, and 1 4/5-inch diameters. In contrast to the floppy disk drive, hard disk drives hold from 80 megabytes to gigabytes and terabytes of information. When purchasing a hard disk, consider *storage capacity* and *seek time*, a measure of a hard disk's access speed. The smaller the numbers, the faster the disk. In the past, 65 milliseconds was the standard access time, but today the standard is less than 7 milliseconds. The *Firwire* hard drives (VST) provide blazing-fast, high-density storage for your desktop and laptop system. They can hold 6 GB and more, are light and small, and they are perfect for multimedia transfer and storage. Because the hard drive can wear out in three to five years, the optical disc is its likely successor.

Optical Disc

An **optical disc,** a direct-access disk, has information recorded on it with a laser beam that burns pits into its surface. Another laser beam reads back information that it detects from these pits. Optical storage currently found in the schools is in the form of compact discs (CDs), compact disc read only memory discs (CD-ROMs), digital versatile discs (DVD-ROM), DVD-video, and laser discs.

These optical discs are recorded at the time of manufacture and cannot be erased. Introduced in 1982, the CD is a digital audio disk that is 4.75 inches in diameter and contains up to 74 minutes of hi-fi stereo sound. CD-ROM discs store text, graphics, and hi-fi stereo sound in a digital format.

CD-ROM Disc

The CD-ROM disc is similar to the music CD, but it uses a different tracking system. A CD-ROM disc handles at least 650 MB of data—the equivalent of 250,000 pages of text, four hundred 3 1/2-inch high-density floppy disks, or fifteen 40 MB hard disks. This medium is invaluable for storing large volumes of data such as the *Grolier Electronic Encyclopedia.*

DVD-ROM, DVD-Video, and Laser Discs

DVD discs are double-sided optical discs that are the same overall size as a CD-ROM but have significantly higher capacities. The DVD-ROM discs are double sided, whereas CD-ROMs are single sided, and they read CD-ROM media as well as their own discs. A DVD-ROM can hold as much as 17 GB of information using this double-sided technology. DVD-Video is DVD-ROM with a little different logical format. DVD-Video uses Multimedia Personal Computer-2 (MPEG-2) compression and provides roughly 133 minutes of video per side (Freedman, 2001).[3]

---

[3]Multimedia Personal Computer-2 is the minimum computer configuration needed to run multimedia applications (Pfaffenberger, 2000).

A laser disc is a read- only optical disc that stores and retrieves still and moving pictures, sound, or color. This disc looks like a large CD, holds from 30 minutes to 2 hours of video, and provides direct access to any location on its disc. Many laser disc systems were introduced in the 1970s. The laser disc has become increasingly scarce in the classroom with the introduction of CD-ROMs and DVD.

Erasable Optical Discs

Erasable optical discs are like floppy disks and can be recorded on repeatedly. Since the laser beam scans the disc without physical contact, the optical disc does not wear out like a magnetic disk. The disks are small, 3 1/2 inches in diameter, and lightweight; they are unaffected by cold, dust, or heat, and they hold huge amounts of data (Fig. 3.25). They come close to magnetic disk

FIGURE 3.25
Erasable Disc

speeds, are not subject to head crashes or corruption from stray magnetic fields, and have a 30-year life expectancy. Three examples of erasable optical discs are CD-RW, and DVD-RAM, DVD-RW.

CD-RW

CD-Rewritable, known as CD-RW, is more expensive then a CD-ROM drive, but these discs are recordable and excellent for archiving. The CD-RW has six layers, with an outer layer that is the same as a CD-ROM. The drives are slower and are designated by three numbers, for example, 8X4X32X. The first number refers to the writing speed of the CD-RW, the second number is the writing speed of the CD-RW, and the last number is the reading speed of the CD-ROM media. Eventually, these drives will be replaced by DVD when a DVD standard is adopted.

DVD-RAM, DVD-RW, and DVD+RW

Several rewritable DVD technologies are now in competition to set an industrial standard. They all accomplish the same purpose, but they use different technologies. DVD-RAM was the first one to produce a drive. DVD-RAM drives can read DVD-ROM media, but DVD-RAM media cannot be used with other DVD drives. Digital Video RAM discs are a CD-ROM format that is capable of playing a full-length movie; they have full read/write capabilities and store 17 GB of data. The DVD-RAM rewritable drive lets you record and erase. The companies that manufacture them claim 100,000 rewrites per disc. Accomplishing the same result, the DVD-RW uses technology like the CD-RW and promises backward compatibility, and the DVD+RW uses phase change technology and is supported by Sony, HP, and Philips. For more information, visit the Tech Encyclopedia at CPMnet's site at http://www.techweb.com/encyclopedia/.

Fax Machine

Another input/output device, the facsimile (fax) machine, lets you transmit text and images between distant locations. Chapter 8 features a detailed discussion of the fax machine.

Modem

The **modem** lets two computers communicate with each other. When you connect one computer to another, you use hardware and software. In the majority of cases, the hardware consists of equipment that sends the data over some type of communications line, such as a telephone line. The software controls the flow of the data. The necessary hardware consists of a modem, telephone lines, and computer.

There are two types of modems: internal and external. Internal modems reside in the computer and are plugged into an open slot. They do not require any special cabling, nor do they take up any extra desk space. External modems (Fig. 3.26) are separate units that sit outside the computer;

FIGURE 3.26
External Modem
© Corel Draw 3.0.

the modem is connected to the telephone jack with a telephone cable. External modems usually have diagnostic lights so users can monitor what is transpiring. This type of modem is portable and easily accessible for repair.

Modem is a contraction of **MO**dulator/**DEM**odulator. The modem *modulates* the computer output to an acceptable signal for transmission and then *demodulates* the signal back for computer input. The modem on the transmitting computer converts the digital signals to modulated, analog signal tones and transmits them over the telephone lines. The receiving computer's modem transforms the incoming analog signals back to their digital equivalents in order to understand them. Figure 3.27 illustrates this modem-to-modem transmission. The software that is required to operate a modem is usually included in the operating system. For example, in Windows, the Dial-up Networking "Make New Connection" wizard takes you through the steps of setting up your modem.

FIGURE 3.27
Modem-to-Modem
Transmission
© Corel Draw 3.0.

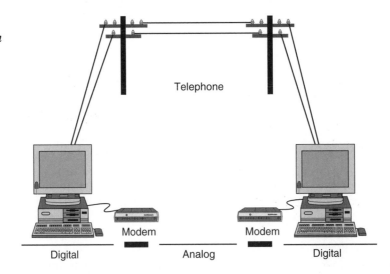

Overview of Hardware

Table 3.1 lists the devices discussed in this hardware chapter. After perusing this table, let's consider some criteria for selecting hardware.

TABLE 3.1

Hardware Summary

Input	Output	Input/Output
Keyboard	Printers	Disk drive
Mouse	Dot-matrix	Floppy
Trackball	Inkjet	Zip drive
Touchpad	Laser	Iomega Jaz
Optical mark reader	Screen display	Hard drive
Scanner	RGB monitor	Optical discs
Flatbed	LCD monitor	CD-ROM
Handheld	LCD projection panel	DVD-ROM
Overhead	Projectors	Erasable optical discs
Sheet-fed	Scan converters	CD-RW
Film		DVD-RAM, DVD-RW, and DVD+RW
Digital camera		Fax machine
Handheld computers		Modem

Hardware Selection Criteria

Type of Computer

Is the computer compatible with other computers in the school district? How easy is it to use the equipment? Is the documentation well written? Are the weight and size of the machine important considerations? How durable is the machine? Is it too delicate for classroom use? One of your main decisions is whether to buy a computer equipped with a Windows system or a Macintosh system. The Macintosh is still easier to use, set up, and expand than is a Windows computer. However, Windows computers have a wider selection of peripherals and software. If you are interested in ease of use and expansion, graphics, multimedia, and video, buy a Macintosh; if you need spreadsheets and databases and a wider assortment of peripherals, buy a Windows system.

Memory

A very important consideration during the hardware selection process is the computer's random access memory, the working memory. (See Chapter 2 for a complete discussion of RAM.) In the early 1980s, 64K of RAM was considered more than adequate for running educational software. Today, many applications need 16 MB or more of memory, and these memory requirements are continually increasing. For example, *Site Central* (Knowledge Adventure) requires 32 MB to effectively run its Windows version. Every time software publishers upgrade programs, they add more features requiring more memory. The amount of RAM a computer has affects the kind of software it is capable of running. Any new system you are purchasing should have a minimum of 128 MB of RAM. Buy as much RAM as you can afford because you can never have too much.

Expandability

Consider these questions when your computer system is not powerful enough for your needs. Can you upgrade the processor chip? Can the memory of the computer be increased? Can special equipment be added to the machine for the disabled student? Is the computer designed so that extra peripherals such as a scanner can be added easily? Does your computer have **expansion slots**? In other words, does your computer have a receptacle inside that will accept expansion boards or printed circuit boards? These boards or cards, as they are called, expand the computer's ability so that it can accept other peripheral devices such as sound cards.

Speed

The speed at which the microcomputer accesses the instructions is another important consideration. Speed depends on clock speed and word size.

Clock speed is the number of electronic pulses per second, measured in megahertz (MHz) up to gigahertz (GHz). The more pulses the computer has per second, the faster it executes the instructions. The clock speed on a microcomputer can vary from 1 MHz to greater than 1.6 GHz. For example, the old Apple II had a clock speed of 1 MHz, the Macintosh LC and the newer HP Pavilion has a clock speed of 1.5 GHz. Some programs, such as sophisticated spreadsheet programs, require more speed than others.

Keyboard

You should test out the keyboard feel by sitting at the computer and checking how comfortable it is to type on the keys. Keyboards today have many different ergonomic designs. One computer might have impressive specifications, but typing on the keyboard may be uncomfortable. See if an extended keyboard is available. Extended keyboards have additional keys that can be programmed to perform different functions and numeric pads that speed up number entry.

Hard Disk Space

Like everything else on computers, hard disk space has gotten larger and less expensive. Most new computers are being sold with a minimum of 40 GB (gigabytes). You need a gigantic hard disk if you plan to store digitized photographs or edit videos; the bigger the better!

Video Output

When it comes to the computer monitor, the CRT is the most economical for word processing, spreadsheets, and educational software. The higher the resolution of the screen, the clearer the screen display. Resolution is expressed as the number of linear dots, or pixels, that are displayed on the screen. The more pixels, the clearer the image or the better the resolution. The size of a monitor screen varies from 5 inches to 40 inches; usually, a screen displays 24 or 25 lines of text. The size of your monitor should not be smaller than 15 inches and for a few dollars more you can buy a 17-inch monitor. The dot pitch, which is the smallest dot your monitor displays, should be .28mm or less. The refresh rate, the "rate at which a monitor and video adapter pass the electron guns of a cathode ray tube (CRT) from the top of the display to the bottom" (Pfaffenberger, 1997), should be 85 Hz at the resolution you use. In a couple years, LCD monitors will be affordable for most schools.

Video RAM (VRAM)

Video RAM (VRAM), or graphic memory, is "a type of memory in a video display board that holds the image that appears on the video screen" (Freedman, 1995). Make sure you have at least 2 MB of graphic memory. If you play multimedia software and video games, 4 MB is preferred.

Sound

The quality of sound is very important for playing musical compositions or educational games. Ask about the number of voices the system has. You should get a minimum of 32 voices. If you want a realistic sound, purchase more voices. Find out the octave ranges of the voices. Most computers offer speech synthesizers capable of pronouncing words.

Peripherals

Study the peripherals that you need and know the features that are available. Read magazines to determine which peripherals are best to purchase. Find out which peripherals have the lowest rate of repair and the fastest access time.

Hardware Reliability and Dealer Support

There are some questions you should ask: Are the local dealers reputable? (Find a local store that can easily service the machine.) Does the store give free training on newly purchased machinery? Is there a service contract? Is the equipment warranted for a year, and is there quick turnaround on computer repair?

Ease of Operation

Ask these questions: Is the machine relatively easy to operate? Do you need hours to study its thick manuals? (For a young student or an easily frustrated adult, these considerations are important.) Is there quality documentation for the computer?

Cost

Prices that are quoted by manufacturers are discounted, so check the *Computer Shopper*, the local newspaper ads, and magazines to determine the price structure of a system. Is the machine too costly compared to similar machines? Does the manufacturer include free software? Is there a warranty on the product, on-site repair, or, at the very least, a place to ship the machine for quick repair?

The hardware checklist should serve as a handy guide in analyzing your hardware needs.

HARDWARE CHECKLIST

Directions: Examine the following items and determine which ones you feel are important for your particular class situation. Evaluate the hardware and place an X on each line where it meets your needs.

Computer Type _____   Model _____   Manufacturer _____

A. Features
___ 1. Screen size
___ 2. Text/graphics display
___   a. Number of lines
___   b. Characters per line
___   c. Resolution
___   d. Number of colors
___ 3. Sound
___   a. Number of voices
___   b. Number of octaves
___   c. Loudness
___ 4. Portability
___ 5. Keyboard design
___   a. Number of keys
___   b. Numeric keypad
___ 6. Ease of expansion
___ 7. Color capabilities
___ 8. Equipment compatibility
___ 9. Networking
___ 10. Memory (RAM)
___ 11. Hard disk capacity
___ 12. CD-ROM drive (8×, 16×, 24×, 32×, etc.)
___ 13. Zip drive
___ 14. DVD drive
___ 15. CD-RW or DVD-RW drive

B. Ease of Use
___ 1. Easy program loading
___ 2. Flexibility

___ 3. Easy equipment setup
___ 4. Tutorial manual

C. Consumer Value
___ 1. Cost of basic unit
___ 2. Cost of peripherals
___   a. Disk drive
___   b. Interfaces/cables
___   c. Memory expansion
___   d. Modem
___   e. Monitor
___   (1) Included in price
___   (2) Size
___   f. Printer
___   g. Other
___   h. Software included
___   i. Speech synthesizer
___ 3. Total investment

D. Support
___ 1. Service contract
___ 2. Nearby dealer support
___ 3. Readable manuals
___   a. Tutorial
___   b. Index
___ 4. Money-back guarantee
___ 5. Warranty period: carry in or on-site
___ 6. Teacher training

Rating Scale
Rate the hardware by placing a check in the appropriate box.

Excellent ___ Very Good ___ Good ___ Fair ___ Poor ___

Comments

Summary

This chapter has explored the functions of the major input, output, and input/output devices used in the classroom. We considered the following examples of input devices: (1) keyboards, (2) mouses, (3) trackballs, (4) touchpads, (5) optical readers, and (6) scanners. The two most important output devices considered were the printer, which produces a hard copy of the work, and the screen display, which shows the information on the screen. Examples of the display screens discussed are the liquid crystal display (LCD) and the cathode ray tube (CRT). The major printers discussed were (1) dot-matrix, (2) inkjet, and (3) laser. The dot-matrix printer has a print head with wires to create its characters; the inkjet printer sprays ink; and the laser printer uses a process similar to photocopying. We discussed and compared floppy disks, hard disks, and optical discs. Floppy disks and hard disks are still the most popular storage media, while optical discs are gaining in popularity. We also considered criteria for hardware selection.

What follows is an annotated list of top-rated Internet sites. These sites will contain information about hardware, hardware companies, lessons on computer hardware, news, and reviews.

HARDWARE SITES

PC Webopedia
http://www.pcwebopedia.com/
PC Webopedia is a resource for information about PCs. It contains definitions of 2,000 computer terms, with links to sites related to each term.

PC Webopedia's Hardware Companies
http://webopedia.internet.com/Hardware/
Hardware_Companies/
This site links to leading PC hardware companies.

Tip World
http://www.topica.com/
Tip World provides daily free e-mail tips for the Windows and the Mac OS operating systems and for keeping your hardware humming along.

Computer Lessons for Kids and Small Adults
http://www.kidsandcomputers.com/kids/
lessons/starter.htm
Computer Lessons for Kids and Small Adults offers easy-to-understand lessons on the parts and the operating systems of a personal computer.

What's in That Box?
http://members.aol.com/wbox/wbox.htm
This site is a presentation on what's in your computer and how it works.

Yahoo! Hardware
http://dir.yahoo.com/Computers_and_
Internet/Hardware/Systems/
Yahoo! Hardware offers an extensive list of links to hardware companies from the ill-fated Amiga to the highly successful iMAC computer.

Hardware Central
http://www.hardwarecentral.com/
Hardware Central features the latest in hardware news and reviews.

Yahoo! Peripherals
http://dir.yahoo.com/Computers_and_
Internet/ Hardware/Peripherals/
Yahoo! Peripherals is a list of links to peripheral companies from digital cameras to modems.

Ultimate Memory Guide
http://www.kingston.com/tools/umg/
Everything you ever wanted to know about computer memory. See table of contents on the left panel in blue.

Chapter Mastery Test

To the Instructor: Refer to the Instructor's Manual for the Answers to the Mastery Questions. This manual has additional questions and resource materials.

Let's check for chapter comprehension with a short mastery test, look at some basic terms, and see some classroom projects. Some suggested readings and references follow the classroom projects.

1. What is a digital camera and how would you use it in the classroom?
2. Explain the difference between a CD-ROM disc and a DVD-RAM disc.
3. Name two input and two output devices. Explain how each works.
4. Name four factors to consider when examining hardware.
5. Compare a laser printer with an inkjet printer.
6. What is a scan converter and how would you use it in the classroom?
7. Compare a floppy disk to a Zip disk.
8. How are hard disks similar to and different from floppy disks?
9. What are optical discs? Why are they considered the wave of the future?

Basic Terms

cathode ray tube (CRT) (p. 49)
clock speed (p. 58)
digital cameras (p. 44)
expansion slots (p. 57)
hardware (p. 39)
inkjet printer (p. 48)
keyboard (p. 40)
laser printer (p. 48)
liquid crystal display (LCD) (p. 49)
modem (p. 55)
mouse (p. 40)
optical character recognition (OCR) (p. 42)
optical disc (p. 53)

optical mark reader (OMR) (p. 42)
printer (p. 47)
red, green, and blue (RGB) monitor
   (p. 49)
resolution (p. 44)
scan converter (p. 51)
scanner (p. 42)
software (p. 39)
touchpad (p. 42)
trackball (p. 41)
videoconferencing cameras (p. 45)
video RAM (p. 59)

Classroom Projects

1. Visit a computer store and compare the output of laser and inkjet printers. Report on the differences.
2. Take a field trip to a school that uses digital cameras and report how they are incorporated in student writing projects.
3. Using a digital camera, illustrate a book report or a creative story.
4. Prepare and illustrate a report discussing the different storage technologies.

Suggested Readings and References

"The Best of What's New." *Popular Science,* December 1997, pp. 44–81.

Bruder, Isabelle. "Schools of Education: Four Exemplary Programs." *Electronic Learning* 10, no. 6 (March 1991): 21–24, 45.

Crawford, Walt. "Jargon that Computes: Today's PC Terminology." *Online* 21, no. 2 (March–April 1997): 36–41.

Darrow, Barbara. "IBM Develops Prototype of Color Touch Screen for Laptops." *InfoWorld* 13, no. 16 (April 22, 1991): 6.

Flanagan, Patrick. "The 10 Hottest Technologies in Telecom." *Telecommunications* 31, no. 5 (May 1997): 25–28, 30, 32.

Freedman, Alan. *Desktop Encyclopedia.* New York: American Management Association, 2001.

Fritz, Mark. "DVD Dream." *Presentations,* March 2000, pp. 38–45.

Grossman, Evan. "Tut Modem Boasts 2Mbps over Standard Phone Wire." *InfoWorld* 19, no. 40 (October 6, 1997): 74.

Morris, John. "1 Gig Gets Real." *PC Magazine,* April 18, 2000, pp. 30–32.

Pfaffenberger, Bryan. *Webster's New World Dictionary.* New York: Que, 2000.

Pownell, David, and Gerald D. Bailey. "The Next Small Thing." *Learning and Leading with Technology* 27, no. 8 (May 2000): 47–49.

Randall, Neil. "Setting Up a Webcam." *PC Magazine,* April 18, 2000, pp. 138–40.

Roberts, Nancy, George Blakeslee, Maureen Brown, and Cecilia Lenk. *Integrating Telecommunications into Education.* Englewood Cliffs, N.J.: Prentice Hall, 1990.

Robertson, S. "The Use and Effectiveness of Palmtop Computers in Education." *British Journal of Educational Technology* 28, no. 3 (July 1997): 177–89.

Takezaki, Noriko. "Mobile Computing and the Internet." *Computing Japan,* October 1997, pp. 31–33.

Trosko, Nancy. "Making Technology Work for Your Students." *Technology Connection* 4, no. 2 (April 1997): 20–22.

Turner, Sandra, and Michael Land. *Tools for Schools.* 2nd ed. Belmont, Calif.: Wadsworth, 1996.

Vizard, Frank, ed. "Web TV Gets More Muscle." *Popular Science,* December 1997, pp. 44–81.

Wong, William G. "Optical Drive Technologies." *Computer Buyer's Guide and Handbook Presents Essential Peripherals Buying Guide,* April 2000, pp. 38–45.

Woodcock, Joanne, Senior Contributor. *Computer Dictionary.* Redmond, Washington: Microsoft Press, 1991.

CHAPTER 4

Word Processing

Integrating Word Processing into the Classroom

Did you know that word processing is the most popular computer application? Did you know that students at all grade levels can use word processing software to create a variety of projects? Students can create book reports, lab sheets, letterhead stationery, and flyers. In the lower grades students can use large-size fonts when they create stories, alphabet books, and journals. Teachers can have students write letters to people in the class and across the country. This chapter will discuss how to select a word processor for the classroom and consider the general features of a word processor. You will see a checklist designed to help you choose the right word processor. Furthermore, you will be given exercises to help you integrate word processing into the classroom. You will become familiar with Internet sites that include creative writing tips, forums, writing clubs, and lesson plans.

Objectives

Upon completing this chapter, you will be able to:
1. Define the term *word processor;*
2. Describe the features and functions of a word processor;
3. Demonstrate how a word processing program operates;
4. Evaluate word processing software based on standard criteria;
5. Utilize and create a repertoire of word processing activities for the classroom;
6. Evaluate a word processing program utilizing the criteria given in this book; and
7. Explore Internet sites on word processing that range from creative writing tips to lesson plans.

In a 1991 study of teachers' perceptions, word processing was ranked as the primary need for students and teachers (Woodrow, 1991). Pfaffenberger (2000) noted that word processing programs are the most widely used computer application in the office, classroom, and home. Bearing this in mind, we examine how word processing evolved.

Historical Background

At the onset, there were simple typewriters, eventually followed by more so-phisticated ones. In 1961, IBM introduced the elite Selectric typewriter, a fast electric model with changeable print balls, typefaces, and type sizes. Ten years later, Wang Laboratories inaugurated its Wang 1200, a small-screen typing workstation capable of reading output and storing information on a cassette tape. System users could retrieve documents whenever needed and could edit text. Several years later, Wang expanded and improved the 1200 by develop-ing a disk storage system that could store approximately 4,200 pages.

Altair 8800, a microcomputer kit introduced in 1974, was the first com-mercially successful microcomputer. This computer could store a small amount of data in memory; however, it had neither a keyboard nor a moni-tor screen. The user entered data and programs by flipping small toggle switches. The microcomputer did not have disks as a workable storage medium until 1976, when Digital Research Corporation introduced the Com-puter Program Management (CP/M) operating system. Three years later, Seymour Rubenstein created *WordStar,* a word processor for the CP/M oper-ating system, and in 1980, Alan Ashton and Bruce Bastian produced *Word-Perfect,* another word processor for the Data General minicomputer. Dedi-cated word processors, machines designed solely for word processing, soon dominated the office market.

This situation changed in 1981, when IBM introduced its personal com-puter, the PC. Simultaneously, Unlimited Software announced the first piece of software to run on this new machine: a word processor program called *EasyWriter.* A few months before the announcement, Lifetree Software devel-oped a program called *Volkswriter.*[1] From 1981 to 1985, word processing pro-grams, such as *MacWrite* (Apple), *Microsoft Word* (Microsoft Corporation), *Bank Street Writer* (Scholastic), *PFS Write* (Software Inc.), and *AppleWorks* (Ap-ple), flourished. *AppleWorks,* introduced in 1983, was an integrated program combining word processor, database, and spreadsheet. In the 1980s, helpful features such as spell checker, mail merge, font capabilities, and electronic thesaurus were introduced. Because of the popularity of the **graphical user interface (GUI)** systems, such as Macintosh and personal computers that ran Windows, programs could now display different types of fonts and font size choices on the screen as well as handle simple desktop publishing functions such as newsletters.

The 1980s marked the beginning of a trend away from the stand-alone word processing programs toward products that sell several software tools in one package. In the education field these packages have become popular be-cause they are economical, with costs beating the cost of each tool purchased separately. Recently, manufacturers began selling two types of these pack-ages, the integrated program such as *AppleWorks 6.0* and *Microsoft Works 2000* and the suites such as *WordPerfect* and *Microsoft Office 2001.* An **integrated**

---

[1]Lifetree is now called Writing Tools Groups, a subsidiary of Wordstar International.

software package usually consists of a word processor, spreadsheet, database, graphic tools, and communication software; a **software suite** usually contains additional programs and comes in a variety of combinations tailored to meet the needs of the educator or businessperson. (Chapter 7 explains in more detail how integrated programs work.)

Now that we have some background on the evolution of word processing, we need to define the term *word processing* and see what it involves.

What Is a Word Processor?

A **word processor** is software program designed to make the computer a useful electronic writing tool that can edit, store, and print documents. Before the computer, the typewriter was the principal means of writing reports, and a typist took great pains to avoid making mistakes because correcting and revising were tedious tasks. Word processing changed all that because the user could make changes quickly and efficiently simply by pressing a few keys on the keyboard. He or she could easily save a document on a disk, make multiple copies, and put the disks away for safekeeping.

In the past, businesses used computers that were designed primarily for word processing (**dedicated word processors**). They had a special keyboard with keys programmed to perform such tasks as underline and change to italics. These machines were inexpensive and perfectly adequate for typing projects only. Now, the microcomputer, packaged with sophisticated word processing software, is found in the office. The majority of these computers are networked so that programs and correspondence can be handled electronically.

Today, when writers discuss word processing they usually are talking about personal computers with word processing software. Such software programs are for sale at local software stores usually on a CD-ROM disc. The buyer installs the program onto a computer. Then, after opening the program, he or she can create a document, edit text, underline, delete, and add and remove words.

Components of Word Processing

A word processor usually involves interaction among the components pictured in Figure 4.1. Through the software, the user enters the text using the

FIGURE 4.1
Word Processing
Components
ClickArt Images © 1995
T/Maker Company.

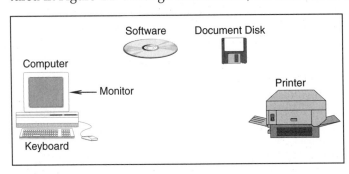

keyboard, views it on the monitor, changes it as necessary, saves the document on disk, and prints it on the printer.

Integrating a Word Processor into the Classroom

Teachers, as well as students, can use the word processing program in a variety of ways. The teacher can prepare lesson plans, worksheets, memos, lab sheets (Fig. 4.2) and book report forms, assignment sheets, course syllabi, and

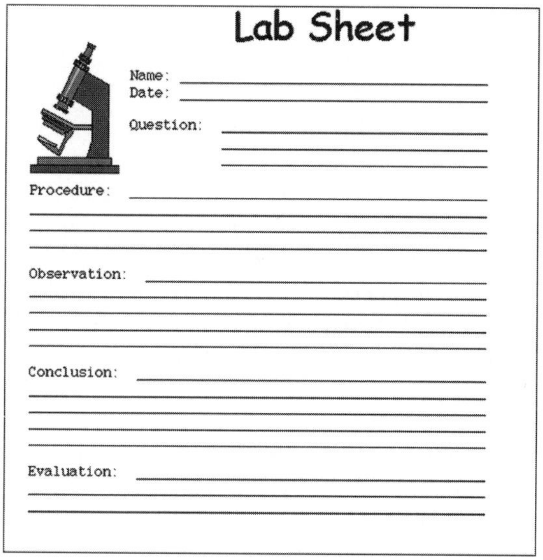
Lab Sheet

Name:
Date:
Question:
Procedure:
Observation:
Conclusion:
Evaluation:

FIGURE 4.2
Word Processing Document
ClickArt Images ©1995 T/Maker Company.

other instructional materials. They can create quizzes, tests, and different types of evaluation forms. Furthermore, they can write letters and create weekly newsletters for parents.

Students at all grade levels can use word processing software to create an assortment of projects. In the lower grades, they can use large-size fonts when they create stories, alphabet books, and journals. Students can create classroom reports, outlines, flyers, book reports, and lab reports using tables and graphs. Furthermore, students can create a class newspaper using clip art or create their own letterhead stationery. After their letterhead stationery has been designed, students can write letters to people in the class, across the country, or around the globe. Finally, they can use the word processor to edit papers with grammar and spelling errors, changing underlined words with a thesaurus.

Since word processing is a primary use for a personal computer, you should exercise care in choosing the right package. The next section explains the factors you should consider before purchasing word processing software. However, before continuing to the next section, experiment with a word processor package. After you're comfortable with the software, you'll be ready to learn how to select a word processor for the classroom.

How to Select a Word Processor for the Classroom

There are numerous word processing packages on the market today, complete with every imaginable feature. Among these programs are word processors well-suited for classroom use. Some word processing programs that fit into this category are *Write:OutLoud; Paint, Write & Play!; Kid Works Deluxe; Storybook Weaver Deluxe; AppleWorks;* and *Microsoft Works. WordPerfect* and *Microsoft Word* are for the advanced junior high, high school, and college student. Software reviewers recommend programs such as *Write:OutLoud; Paint, Write & Play!;* and *Storybook Weaver Deluxe* for elementary school students because they have fewer features and are easier to use. The features included in most programs are those that will help students the most, such as delete, which removes unwanted text, and insert, which inserts lines or passages. The word processors for the upper grades have become more complicated, offer multiple features, and occupy more disk space and memory. A case in point is *Microsoft Word*, which contains many desktop publishing features, charting tools, and custom toolbars.

Choosing software for the classroom is a five-step process: (1) determine the hardware compatibility; (2) study the program's general features; (3) examine its standard editing features; (4) review formatting functions; (5) consider instructional design, cost effectiveness, and technical support.

Hardware Compatibility

Check out the computers that are available at your school. For example, do you have old Apple IIes, Macintosh G4s, or IBM compatibles? How much memory do these machines have: 128K, 64 MB, or 224 MB of RAM? How much storage space does the hard disk drive contain? What other peripherals or external devices are available? For instance, does the school district have a CD-ROM, DVD-RAM player, or a scanner?

General Features

Most word processors have cursor control, word wrap, and page break. Since cursor control is an important feature, it warrants discussion first.

Cursor Control

A **cursor** (Fig. 4.3) is usually a blinking white block of light that shows the position of a character. It is a place marker that lets the computer user quickly find the place to correct or enter data. The equivalent on a typewriter is the place on the paper where the next keystroke will strike.

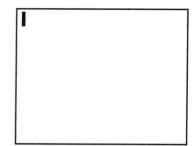

FIGURE 4.3
Cursor

You use the cursor to move within the text and handle editing functions faster than you could with keystrokes. As you type, the cursor moves ahead or under each character that is on the screen. The cursor can move one character at a time, line by line, or over a block of text. You can also move it with the mouse.

Word Wrap

Word wrap lets you type as much as you want without paying attention to the end of lines. When you reach the right-hand margin, the cursor automatically moves to the beginning of the next line; you do not have to hit the return key. If the word does not fit on a line, it automatically moves to the next line. You hit the return key only to show a new paragraph or to move down a line.

Page Breaks

Most word processors display some mark on the screen that tells where the pages in the document break. Before printing your document you can thus check to make sure there are no bad breaks.

Standard Editing Features of a Word Processor

Word processors vary in their editing capabilities because some are more powerful than others. However, they all usually have the same basic editing features: insert, delete, find and replace, and block operations.

Insert

The **insert** function allows you to insert lines of text, words, and paragraphs anywhere in the document, without retyping any information preceding or following the inserted material.

Delete

The **delete** function allows you to erase words, lines, or paragraphs of text. After you delete the material, the remaining text arranges itself so that the layout is proper.

Find and Replace

The **replace** function (Fig. 4.4) in *Microsoft Word* allows you to search a doc-

**FIGURE 4.4
Microsoft Word
2001** *Replace
Function*
Box shot reprinted with
permission from © Microsoft
Corporation.

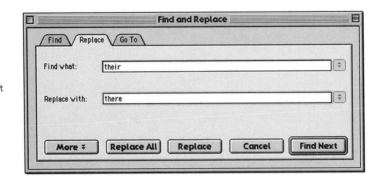

ument for a word or phrase and then to replace it. For example, if you mis-use the word *their,* you can later instruct the computer to find every inci-dent of *their* so you can replace it with *there.* This function also allows you to conduct a global search. So, in the example, you can tell the computer to automatically change all entries of *their* to *there.* This particular function is extremely useful for editing a manuscript, because it makes locating cor-rections a simple matter.

Block Operations

A **block** is a part of text found between two marked points. The advantage of working with blocks of text is that instead of deleting, inserting, or copying one word or line at a time, you perform these operations on many lines or paragraphs of text. To delete a block of text, select or highlight the text, then apply the cut function. In the past, if you wanted to change the order of para-graphs, you had to cut the original typewritten sheet of paper and paste the sections into the new sequence. Today, thanks to modern technology, you can use the **cut and paste** function by following these steps:

1. Highlight the block of text that will be moved.
2. Using the cut function, remove the specified portion of text.
3. Position the cursor where you want the material to be placed and then instruct the computer to paste or insert. The text will arrange itself automatically with the proper spacing.

Today, most word processors have **drag-and-drop** text editing. With the mouse, select a small block of text. Then, while pressing the mouse button, drag the text to a new location. This function is very handy for moving text short distances within a document.

The **copy** function works similarly. Choose some text or a picture by highlighting it. Use the copy function to copy it. Once you've copied it, you can paste or insert it in a new location in the document or even in another document.

Standard Formatting Functions

Besides editing features, word processors offer numerous formatting functions. We'll examine only a few of the more pertinent ones such as spacing, justification, and margins. Formatting is the process of making the text appear a certain way on the printed page. First, we'll consider the formatting functions concerned with space, and second, we'll consider those concerned with form.

Space Functions

The most common space functions are margins, tabs, justification, centering, headers and footers, and line spacing.

Margins   The **margin** is the spacing between the edge of the page and the main text area. A *margin* is set for the entire document, whereas an *indent* is set for individual paragraphs. Margins can be adjusted easily to meet your needs.

Tabs   **Tabs** are similar to the tabs on a typewriter, which position text precisely within a line in a document or within a column in a table. When you press the tab key, you move the cursor across the page quickly to a predetermined point. These points are adjustable.

Justification   **Justification** aligns the margins of text. Text can be aligned along the left side, it can be aligned along the right side, it can fill the type

FIGURE 4.5
Justification Types

A. Left-Justified Text

Suddenly this giant computer stopped working, and everyone was frantically attempting to discover the source of the problem.   Grace Hopper and her coworkers found the culprit was a dead moth in a relay of the computer. They removed the moth with a tweezer and placed it in the Mark II logbook.

B. Right-Justified Text

Suddenly this giant computer stopped working, and everyone was frantically attempting to discover the source of the problem.   Grace Hopper and her coworkers found the culprit was a dead moth in a relay of the computer. They removed the moth with a tweezer and placed it in the Mark II logbook.

C. Full-Justified Text

Suddenly this giant computer stopped working, and everyone was frantically attempting to discover the source of the problem.   Grace Hopper and her coworkers found the culprit was a dead moth in a relay of the computer. They removed the moth with a tweezer and placed it in the Mark II logbook.

D. Center-Justified Text

Suddenly this giant computer stopped working, and everyone was frantically attempting to discover the source of the problem.   Grace Hopper and her coworkers found the culprit was a dead moth in a relay of the computer. They removed the moth with a tweezer and placed it in the
Mark II logbook.

space to align both left and right, or it can be centered. In left-justified text (Fig. 4.5A), the left margin is aligned and the right margin is uneven. This is the most common type of justification, and word processing programs usually have this as their default. In right-justified text (Fig. 4.5B), the right margin is aligned and the left margin is uneven. Full-justified text (Fig. 4.5C) is aligned along both margins. The computer achieves this alignment by adding space between words in a line of text to extend it. In center-justified text (Figure 4.5D), all the lines of text are aligned in the center of the page. This type of justification is often used to make headings more attractive on a page.

The *WordPerfect* processing program uses buttons identical to those shown in Figure 4.6 for the different types of justification. For example, for left-justified text, select the top button.

FIGURE 4.6 *Justification Buttons*

WordPerfect 9 Copyright © 1999 Corel Corporation and Corel Corporation Unlimited. All rights reserved.

Headers and Footers   A **header** is text that appears at the top margin of each page of manuscript, while a **footer** is text that prints in the bottom margin of a page of manuscript. Headers and footers usually include descriptive text, such as page numbers, titles, and dates.

Line Spacing   Line spacing is the amount of space between lines of text. You can single-, one and one-half-, or double-space text in the document with the line spacing function. For *AppleWorks 6.0,* you just click on the left or right icon ▣ 1 li ▣ depending how much space you need between the lines.

Formatting Functions

The formatting functions include boldface, underlining, superscripts, subscripts, fonts, and numbering.

Boldface   Boldfacing darkens words or sentences and slightly enlarges the text in a document. **This sentence is an example of boldfaced text.** Some programs show actual boldfacing on the screen, while others indicate with special characters what words are to be boldfaced. When a program shows boldfacing with special characters, the selected words are not seen as boldface until printed.

Underlining   Underlining is simply putting a <u>line</u> under a word or sentence. Some software programs will show the word underlined; other programs will indicate the underlining with special characters.

Superscripts and Subscripts   Superscripts and subscripts are used in mathematical formulas and with footnote markers. The 8 in 2^8 is a superscript while the 1 in A_1 is a subscript.

Font   **Font** refers to the physical characteristics of a typed character. These characteristics include typeface, spacing, pitch, point size, and style. **Typeface** refers to the design of the characters, such as *Flora* text; **pitch** represents characters per inch; *point size* is the height of characters; *style* includes italicizing and boldfacing. Programs vary in the number of fonts that can be used. Figure 4.7 shows examples of different fonts, sizes, and styles that

Font Styles And Sizes

Flora Medium 9 Point Plain

New York 10 Point Bold

Courier 14 Point Shadow

Palatino 18 Point Bold

Helvetica 24 Point Italic

FIGURE 4.7   *Font Styles and Sizes*

can be generated on a Macintosh computer. Fonts can be printed as bit map, in a pattern of dots, or as outlines defined by a mathematical formula.

Numbering   Many word processors offer automatic numbering functions. These number the pages in a document.

After examining formatting functions, look carefully at the instructional design and features of your program. The next few pages should give you an idea of what to scrutinize.

Instructional Design and Features

For the lowest grade levels, a word processor should offer at least the following functions: insert, delete, center, underline, double space, save text, and print. A word processor program should be easy for the student to learn and not require hours of instruction.

Write:OutLoud is a talking word processor that provides auditory feedback for students with or without learning disabilities. Students hear the words, letters, or sentences as they are typed. There is a talking spelling checker and a toolbar. The word processor also has large font sizes to make the letters easier to read. *Write:OutLoud* has its functions displayed at the top of the screen (Fig. 4.8). This is ideal for beginners because it saves them from

FIGURE 4.8
Write:OutLoud
Used with permission of Don Johnston, Inc.

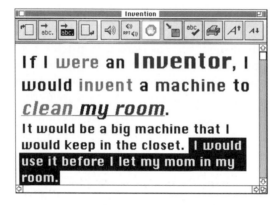

having to remember the functions. For example, to print a document, the user chooses the printer icon on the toolbar; to save the work, he or she chooses the floppy disk icon on the toolbar. This word processor is a perfect example of a picture- or icon-based application.

FIGURE 4.9
AppleWorks 6.0
Startup Screen
Copyright© of Apple Computer, Inc. All rights reserved.

AppleWorks 6.0 has an easy starting point (Fig. 4.9) and useful help function. The most recent version (Fig. 4.10) has a spelling checker, a thesaurus, hypermedia functions, and presentation and desktop capabilities. In this version of *AppleWorks 6.0,* the major functions appear at the top of the screen.

In your search for a word processor, examine only those that have easy-to-remember keys for functions. Find out how the word processor carries out simple functions such as underlining or boldfacing.

In the higher grade levels, students make considerable use of word processing, so they need a word processor like *WordPerfect* (Corel Corp.). This program has many advanced features but it still retains its simplicity. At this upper grade level, a word processor should have features such as those listed in Table 4.1 (page 76). An instructor must know what the students' requirements are and what word processing features are available.

Safety Features

Are there safety devices that prevent a student from making a mistake? These types of queries warn both the novice and advanced user that they may be making errors. Many word processing programs try to protect against data loss by automatically saving material intermittently. Other programs remind the user to save the document. *Microsoft Word* displays the screen in Figure 4.11

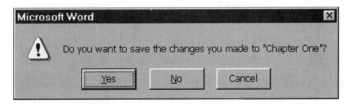

TABLE 4.1

Advanced Word Processing Features

Feature	Description
AutoCorrect	When you type words, the AutoCorrect feature automatically corrects common spelling, typing, and grammatical errors.
AutoFormat	The AutoFormat feature automatically applies formatting to the text. For example, it can convert a Web address to a hyperlink, or number a list.
Charts	Insert and create charts in document.
Columns	The majority of word processors let you create columns, but the advanced ones let you wrap words to the next line within the column.
Desktop capabilities	Graphic objects can be resized, rotated, and scaled. Borders can be created.
Equation editor	Builds complex equations using special math symbols. $$\frac{-b \pm \sqrt{b^2 - 4ac}}{2a}$$
Footnotes	Reserves space at the bottom of each page for footnote[1] text like the following: ——— [1]A footnote is a reference at the bottom of a page.
Glossary creation	Helps create a list of technical words and definitions for the end of the textbook such as **ABC** An abbreviation for the Atanasoff-Berry-Computer, the first electronic digital computer. **Access time** The time a computer needs from the instant it asks for information until it receives it.
Hyperlink creation	You can create hyperlinks that let you jump to a location in the current document or Web page. http://www.csun.edu/

Index	A list of key words in a document along with page numbers that the reader can use to find information. An example follows:
	
	QuickTime movie 179–186
	   Creating 183–186
	   Playing 179–181
	Quit HyperStudio 33, 46, 61, 72

Mail merge	Creates a personalized document by inserting information such as the person's name and address into a form letter.
Outlining	Creates headings for key ideas.

TABLE 4.1
Advanced Word Processing Features

Feature	Description
Picture insertion	Using the word processor, the user inserts images with different types of graphic format such as PICT, GIF, PCX, BMP, or EPS.
Speech recognition	You can speak into the computer and the words will be displayed on the screen.
Style sheets	Once a document is created, its format can be used repeatedly. Fonts, tabs, margins, etc., can be stored in a style sheet file and applied to a new document.
Table of contents	Using codes that are assigned to words in the document, the word processor generates a list of major headings.
Tables	By simply typing in the number of rows and columns, you can use the word processor to create a table like this one for advanced features.
Templates	A template is formatted document for a specific document type. For example, a word processor might have a résumé template or a fax cover sheet template containing the proper spacing and positioning of elements.
Tracking changes	If many people have to edit a particular document, this feature lets you color-code changes made by different users. It also lets you add comments without changing the document.
Voice annotation	You can add sound comments to explain the text.
Web page creation	Many word processors let you create Web pages.
Windows	This feature lets the user have two or more documents showing at the same time. The user can then move text from one document to the other.

when the user is about to quit an application without saving the changes. The user then has three options: not to save, to cancel, or to save.

Most word processing programs have **undo** features that reverse the last action performed on the document. *Nisus, Word,* and *WordPerfect* advanced-level word processing programs have unlimited undos. It is important to have as many of these safeguards as possible, especially when you are about to save material.

Screen Display

When it comes to screen displays, there are two primary concerns: What You See Is What You Get (WYSIWYG) and zooming. **WYSIWYG** is a feature that is commonplace in most word processors. It means text and graphics appear on screen the same as they will appear when printed. To have WYSIWYG text, a matching screen font must be installed for each printer font. It is a rare occurrence to get 100 percent exact representation because printer resolution and screen resolution rarely match. **Zooming** is also commonplace: You can zoom in to get a closer view or zoom out to see more of the page at a smaller size.

Consumer Value

Software is expensive, and for teachers, cost is often a consideration. Any **public domain software** package that can be purchased for a minimal price and duplicated as often as needed would be very advantageous for the teacher if the package is good. There is one catch: The program cannot be sold to anyone. **Shareware** is inexpensive software that is copyrighted, but it can be tried before you buy it. Usually, commercial software is more expensive, but there are exceptions.

Ease of Use

A major consideration when buying a word processor is how easy is it to learn the program. The program's features are immaterial if it is difficult to learn. Ask the following questions: Can a person in a reasonable amount of time learn to use this program? *Paint, Write & Play!* for grades K–2 (Learning Co., Fig. 4.12) is exceptionally easy to use. Most instructions appear on the

**FIGURE 4.12
Paint, Write &
Play!**

right side of the screen, so teachers do not have to read a large manual. There are icons every step of the way to remind you what each function does. For example, choose the printer picture to print the document, and the crocodile to dispose of the unwanted document. Are there help screens that tell the student what to do each step of the way? Is there a tutorial disk or manual that takes the user through the program? Can you set up the printer easily and is it ready to print immediately? Is there a spelling checker, grammar checker, or thesaurus? Even the more advanced word processors such as *Microsoft*

Word or *WordPerfect* have these icons at the top of the screen, so you can just click on them. Is there good online help—that is, resources that are available on the computer? The majority of software programs include online help, which you access by clicking help on the menu bar. Can you access help from a website?

Support

Support refers to personal as well as written help from the software company. Can you call a technician at the software company to get immediate help or must you sift through a series of messages and wait an unbearable amount of time? Is the technical support toll-free or is it a pay call? Are you charged for the amount of time you're on the telephone with the technician? Is there a yearly fee for unlimited support and is it reasonable? Is the manual readable, with activities and lesson plans and an index? The new and revised advanced programs are packaged with all three. Is there also a website on the Internet that provides support?

Spelling Checkers

The **spelling checker** is built into the majority of word processors. The spelling checker looks for spelling and typing errors by checking the spelling of the words in your document against a dictionary that is stored on the hard disk drive. If a word in the document does not appear in the dictionary, the spelling checker will display the word in question and give you the opportunity to override the query or select an alternative. In *AppleWorks 6.0* (Fig. 4.13), the word *looks* is misspelled; the spelling checker suggests

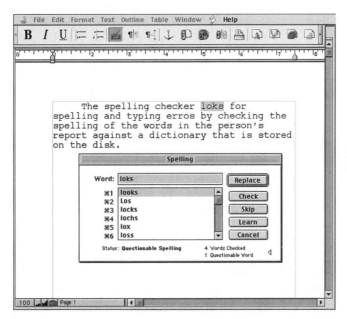

FIGURE 4.13
AppleWorks 6.0
Spell Checker
Copyright© Apple Computer, Inc. All rights reserved.

many alternatives and highlights the most likely. You can add any words you wish to the spelling checker's dictionary. Once you've added a word, the spelling checker will no longer question that particular spelling. The good spelling checker lets you see the misspelled word in context.

Grammar Checkers

Grammar checkers help with grammar, style, punctuation, and even spelling errors. The grammar checker identifies problems such as inconsistencies, awkward phrases, clichés, and wordiness. After it identifies the problem, it suggests corrections and provides an online tutorial explaining the grammar rule that applies. Usually, you make the correction with a click of the mouse. You also have the option of rewriting the incorrect sentence or leaving it just as it is.

The screen from *Grammarian 2* (Casady & Greene), a stand-alone grammar checker, in Figure 4.14 shows a dialog box that offers a correction or sug-

**FIGURE 4.14
Grammarian 2,
*Grammar Checker***

Reprinted with permission of Casady & Greene, Inc.

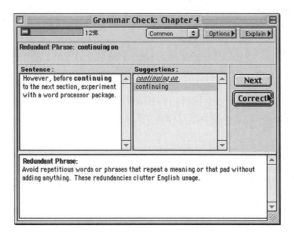

gestion to the writer in the top right pane, the pertinent part of the writer's document in the top left pane, and an explanation at the bottom of the dialog box. In this case, the user takes the suggestion by selecting *continuing* and clicking **Correct.** If the person did not like the suggestion, he or she could have typed in corrections directly in the top left pane. The **Next** button lets the writer skip the sentence entirely.

Early grammar checkers were limited because of their emphasis on mechanical and stylistic errors, but the new programs like the *Grammarian 2* are more versatile. The grammar checkers do not restrict the writer to one writing style but offer a choice, depending on the writer's purpose. For example, *Grammarian 2* gives the choice of eight different writing styles, from academic to technical. This program also compares the readability of the writing, sentence by sentence, to the educational level of the audience. If a particular sentence is too difficult for the selected audience to understand, the checker tells the writer immediately.

Grammar checkers that are integrated into word processors are as common as spelling checkers. For example, *Microsoft Word* and *WordPerfect 9* (Corel Corp.) have grammar checkers built into their programs. There are only a few grammar checkers sold today as stand-alone packages. Even though there have been advances in recent years, the grammar checkers are still in the process of evolving.

Thesaurus

The **thesaurus** has the capacity to generate synonyms for any word that it has in its dictionary. For example, if you want a different word for *peculiar*, *WordPerfect 9's Thesaurus* lists such words as *odd, curious, strange, unusual,* and *funny.* Figure 4.15 shows the *Word Perfect Thesaurus* screen. Select the word that you want to use—in this case *curious*—and click **Replace.** The program automatically substitutes the new word.

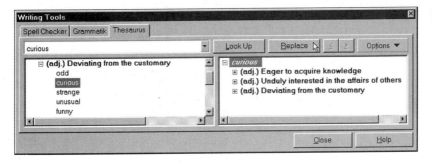

**FIGURE 4.15
WordPerfect 9
Thesaurus**

WordPerfect 9 Copyright © 1999 Corel Corporation and Corel Corporation Unlimited. All rights reserved.

The previous description of available features shows that word processing has come a long way from the Wang 1200. A teacher looking for a classroom word processing program now must weigh many factors. **Be sure to review the annotated list of award-winning word processing programs in Appendix A.** Next, examine any one of these programs by using the following checklist and evaluation rating instrument.

WORD PROCESSOR CHECKLIST

Directions: Examine the following items and determine which ones you feel are important for your class situation. Evaluate your word processor and place an X on each line where the software meets your needs.

Product Name _____   **Manufacturer** _____   **Grade Level** _____

A. Hardware
___ 1. CD-ROM or DVD
___ 2. Computer compatibility
___ 3. Hard disk space required
___ 4. Memory needed
___ 5. Printer compatibility

B. Standard Editing Features
___ 1. Block operations
___   a. Delete block
___   b. Copy block
___   c. Drag and drop
___ 2. Cursor control
___ 3. Find/replace
___ 4. Insert and delete
___ 5. Page breaks

C. Standard Formatting Functions
___ 1. Automatic numbering
___ 2. Boldfacing
___ 3. Centering
___ 4. Headers and footers
___ 5. Justification
___ 6. Line spacing
___ 7. Margins
___ 8. Superscripts and subscripts
___ 9. Tabs
___ 10. Underlining

D. Advanced Features
___ 1. AutoCorrect
___ 2. AutoFormating
___ 3. Automatic indexing
___ 4. Charting
___ 5. Columns
___ 6. Footnoting
___ 7. Glossary
___ 8. Hyperlink creation
___ 9. Importing different graphic file formats
___ 10. Mail merge

___ 11. Outlining
___ 12. Style sheets
___ 13. Table of contents
___ 14. Tables
___ 15. Tracking changes
___ 16. Voice annotation
___ 17. Web creation
___ 18. Templates
___ 19. Equation editor
___ 20. Windows

E. Safety Features
___ 1. Undo last move(s)
___ 2. Warning questions
___ 3. Automatic save

F. Screen Display
___ 1. WYSIWYG
___ 2. Zooming capabilities

G. Ease of Use
___ 1. Help screens
___ 2. Online tutorial
___ 3. Printer setup
___ 4. Talking processor

H. Support Features
___ 1. Technical support
___ 2. Tutorial material
___ 3. Readable manual
___   a. Activities and lesson plans
___   b. Tutorial
___   c. Index
___ 4. Spelling checker
___ 5. Grammar checker
___ 6. Thesaurus

I. Consumer Value
___ 1. Cost
___ 2. Free technical support
___ 3. Guarantees

Rating Scale
Rate the Word Processor by placing a check on the appropriate line.
Excellent ___ Very Good ___ Good ___ Fair ___ Poor ___

Comments

Practice Lessons for the Classroom

The following exercises are meant to be used in conjunction with any word processor. If a computer lab is not available, just follow this section to get a feel for what is involved in using a word processor.

Begin by installing a word processing program on your computer and formatting a disk to store files.

Looking at your screen and keyboard, notice the following. The cursor shows where the next letter or number will appear. The *delete* key will move the cursor to the left and delete letters. The *return* or *enter* key operates like the carriage return on a typewriter. After working through the following preliminary exercises, you will be ready to handle the six subsequent classroom activities.

Type the following jumbled sentence[2] as it appears:

> "LIS NOT THERE PRIZES HARD DIFFICULT WORK."

Do not press the *return* or *enter* key because it will move the cursor down a line.

1. Use the delete key in this instance to delete (a) the *L* in *LIS,* (b) the *T* in *NOT,* and (c) the word *DIFFICULT.* The *delete* key deletes characters, words, or paragraphs, depending on the writer's purpose.
2. Now insert the word *FOR* between *PRIZES* and *HARD.*
3. Next, learn to use the cut and paste function by positioning the word *THERE* at the beginning of the sentence.
4. Use the find/replace function to replace the word *PRIZES* with *SUBSTITUTE.* If you completed the word processing task correctly, the following quotation should appear:

> "THERE IS NO SUBSTITUTE FOR HARD WORK."

Before continuing with the next exercise, learn how to save the material you just typed and how to erase the screen.

To practice some basic word processing functions, let's unscramble a famous poem. First, type the following poem exactly as it appears:

Bananas

Stories are made by fools like me,

But only God can make a flea.

A flea whose hungry mouth is prest;

Against the earth's sweet flowing breaset;

---

[2]This quotation by Alva Edison appeared in *Life.*

A flea that looks at God all day,

And lifts his strong arms to pray;

A flea wear

A nest of robins in his hair;

Upon whose boosom snow has lain;

Who intimately lives with rain.

My love he is the one for me;

He is bound to me for eternity.

I think that I shall neever see

A poem lovely as a flea.

1. Use the find/replace option to exchange the word *Bananas* with the word *Trees.* Now exchange the word *strong* with the word *leafy,* and the word *Stories* with the word *Poems.* Use this option to exchange every instance of the word *flea* with the word *tree* and the word *his* with the word *her.*
2. Center the word *Trees* as the title of the poem.
3. Use the cut and paste option to exchange lines 1 and 2 of the poem with lines 13 and 14. Proceed by cutting lines 1 and 2 and moving them to the very end of the poem. Cut and move lines 13 and 14 to the top of the poem. These lines will fill the empty spaces left.
4. Use the delete option to delete lines 11 and 12. Now there are two blank lines, so hit the delete key twice to get rid of them. Next insert four words in the poem by putting the cursor on line 7, after the word *tree* and before the word *wear,* and then typing the following words:

that may in Summer

Use the spacebar to create a space where one is needed.

5. Use the spelling checker to find any spelling errors in the poem. The first word the spelling checker finds is *neever.* Change it to *never.* The second word the checker finds is *prest;* this word exists, so don't change it but do add the word to the dictionary. The next word is *breaset;* correct it by typing *breast.* The last word the checker finds is *boosom.* Correct it by typing *bosom.*
6. Now save the poem on the formatted disk.
7. As a final activity print the poem. The printout is the poem "Trees," by Sergeant Joyce Kilmer:[3]

---

[3]Reprinted from *Trees and Other Poems* by Sergeant Joyce Kilmer. George H. Doran Company, 1914.

Trees

I think that I shall never see

A poem lovely as a tree.

A tree whose hungry mouth is prest

Against the earth's sweet flowing breast;

A tree that looks at God all day,

And lifts her leafy arms to pray;

A tree that may in Summer wear

A nest of robins in her hair;

Upon whose bosom snow has lain;

Who intimately lives with rain.

Poems are made by fools like me,

But only God can make a tree.

8. To finish this exercise, learn how to retrieve a saved file and then reboot the computer and retrieve the poem that was just saved. Finally, learn how to boldface and underline the poem.

The following seven ready-to-use lesson plans test your students' ability to use successfully the different features of the word processor.

Classroom Lesson Plans

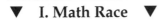

▼   I. Math Race   ▼

Objective

Students will improve their math skills and, in the process, practice editing on the word processor.

Procedure

1. Create a list of math problems from the work that the class is currently doing.

2. Develop a race sheet similar to the following:

Math Race

Starting---Position

$8 * ? = 64$ $4 * 5 = ?$

$54/9 = ?$

$25/5 = ?$ $? * 8 = 40$

$8 * 8 = ?$

$72/9 = ?$ $6 * 7 = ?$

$?/8 = 3$ $12 * 9 = ?$

Finish---Line

3. On this race sheet, vary the horizontal distance and the vertical spaces between the problems and diversify the missing parts of the problems.
4. Save the race sheet on the disk under the name *Math Race.*
5. Next, have the students load this program into their computers.
6. When you give the signal, the students race to solve the problems. They must use their arrow keys to reach each problem, delete the question mark, replace it with the correct response, and then cross the finish line. The student who has the fastest time and most correct answers wins the race.
7. Record a time after each student's name and check each problem, taking 10 percent off for each problem not solved correctly.

Variation

You can make this a group activity by dividing the class in half and creating two competing teams, Team A and Team B. Follow the same procedures as before and record the time score for each student. Next, compute Team A's score by adding together all the individual scores for Team A and deducting 10 percent for each problem not solved correctly. Then compute Team B's score in the same manner. The winning team is the one with the lowest combined time with the most correct answers.

▼   II. Unscramble the Story   ▼

Objective

Students will improve reading comprehension and learn how to use the word processor's move/block function.

Procedure

1. Choose a story that the students are currently reading.
2. Type the story or part of the story into the computer. For example, type "The Hare and the Tortoise,"[4] one of Aesop's Fables.

   The Hare and the Tortoise
   A hare was once boasting about how fast he could run when a tortoise, overhearing him, said, "I'll run you a race." "Done," said the hare and laughed to himself, "but let's get the fox for a judge." The fox consented and the two started. The hare quickly outran the tortoise, and knowing he was far ahead, lay down to take a nap. "I can soon pass the tortoise whenever I awaken." But, unfortunately, the hare overslept himself; therefore when he awoke, though he ran his best, he found the tortoise was already at the goal.
   Slow and steady wins the race.

3. Save this story under *Hare/Tortoise.*
4. Now scramble the story on the computer screen and use the cut and paste functions on the word processor to rearrange the story. The scrambled Tortoise and Hare story could look similar to this:

   The Scrambled Hare and the Tortoise
   The hare quickly outran the tortoise, and knowing he was far ahead, lay down to take a nap. "Done," said the hare and laughed to himself, "but let's get the fox for a judge." The fox consented and the two started. But, unfortunately, the hare overslept himself; therefore, when he awoke, though he ran his best, he found the tortoise was already at the goal. A hare was once boasting about how fast he could run when a tortoise, overhearing him, said, "I'll run you a race." "I can soon pass the tortoise whenever I awaken."

5. Save this scrambled fable under *AERH—Hare* scrambled.
6. Load *AERH* into each student's computer.
7. The students must use their word processors to rearrange the story correctly.
8. Record each student's score by writing down the time taken to complete the activity and the number of sentences arranged correctly.
9. The winner is the student who finishes first and arranges all the sentences correctly.

Variation

1. Divide the class into two teams, Team A and Team B.
2. Instruct Team A to scramble a story.

---

[4]From *The Children's Treasury,* Paula S. Goepfert, ed. New York: Gallery Books, 1987, p. 229.

3. Instruct Team B to rearrange the story.
4. Determine Team B's score by calculating the time it takes the team to rearrange the story and the number of sentences correct on completion.
5. Then have the teams swap roles.

▼   III. The Editor   ▼

Objective

Students will gain practice in basic word processing skills and in using the spelling checker.

Procedure

Enter into the computer two or three paragraphs from a story the students have been reading in class. Deliberately make four or five spelling errors. For purposes of illustration, let us use the following paragraphs:[5]

Programming the Calculator

Most people regard the calculator as an electrenic marvel, yet the principle on which it works is relativly simple. The heart of the calculator is an arithmetic and logical unit (which adds, subtracts, multiplies, divides, and compares numbers at highe speed by electronic means) and a memory unit, in which many thousands of numbers can be electornically stored

How Calculators Work

The value of the calculator over the human being lies in its ability to work without error and at immense speed; it can carry out hundreds of thousands of calculations every second, storing intermediate results in its memory and recalling them instantly when required. The various instrucitons for the stages in the program are stored in the computer memory in numerical form for instant access. The use of the calculator is based on the technique known as programming—the conversion of the problem the calculator is to solve, or the tasks it is to perform, into the simple steps the calculator can carry out. The computer is a very useful device.

Save these paragraphs under the name *Editor.* Now create five or six editing activities. An activity sheet sample follows:

1. Find and replace the word *calculator* with the word *computer.*
2. In paragraph 2 in the second line, insert the sentence "A programmer defines precisely what has to be done in each succeeding step."
3. Delete the last sentence in paragraph 2.

---

[5]James Mitchell, ed. "How Computers Work." *The Random House Encyclopedia.* New York: Random House, 1977, p. 1672.

4. In the last sentence of paragraph 1 after the word *stored,* insert "and recalled on command."
5. In paragraph 2, make the last sentence the first sentence.
6. Switch the titles of the paragraphs.
7. Use the spelling checker to correct the five spelling errors.

Have the students compete with each other and record the time it takes each of them to complete the editing activities. The numerical score is the time it takes each student to complete all six directions, plus a penalty for any incorrect items. The student with the fastest time and the most correct items wins.

Variation

The teacher can design this activity for two groups by dividing the class in half. Team A would design a paragraph and create a set of directions. Team B would take Team A's paragraph and follow the directions. Team A would time Team B. Then the teams would switch roles. The team with the fastest time and the most correct responses would win.

▼   IV. Punctuation Exercise   ▼

Objective

Students will improve punctuation skills and practice using the find/replace function.

Procedure

1. Design an activity sheet for the students. Type 6 to 10 sentences, eliminating all punctuation marks and putting in asterisks instead. A sample sheet follows:
   1. The sun is shining*
   2. I bought a computer* a monitor* a printer* and a modem at the computer store*
   3. Mom asked* *When will you clean your room*
   4. I have to teach a class at 1*30 this afternoon*
   5. "I am going to lunch*" said Dick
   6. The computer cost $3*700*
2. Save the punctuation exercise under *Punct* and load this file into each student's computer and save.
3. Have the students use their find/replace function to find each asterisk and replace each with the correct punctuation mark.
4. When the students finish, have them save their corrected work under their initials.
5. Correct the exercises and return the results.

▼   V. Insert the Adjectives   ▼

Objective

Students will improve their ability to recognize adjectives and practice using the find/replace function of the word processor.

Procedure

1. Design an activity sheet, eliminating adjectives. A sample sheet follows:
   1. The * mansion sat on top of the hill in a remote end of the forest.
   2. The * professor gave a very * lecture to the class.
   3. Jim flew the * plane into the sunset.
   4. The * horses raced to the end of the glen to see the * man.
   5. An * individual visited the classroom yesterday.
   6. She was a * * woman with * blue eyes.
2. Save this file under the name *Adj* and load it into each student's computer and save.
3. Have students search for the asterisk before each noun by using the find/replace function of the word processor and replace each asterisk with an adjective.
4. When the students finish, have them save the work under their initials.
5. Correct the exercises and return the results.

▼   VI. Replace the Sentences   ▼

Objective

Students will improve their writing skills and, in the process, use the cut/paste and find/replace functions.

Procedure

1. Have students independently create random sentences for a story file.
2. Instruct each student to write his or her sentence on a piece of paper. Ask the class to examine the sentences of two classmates, correcting grammar errors.
3. Next instruct the students to enter, one at a time, their sentences into the computer.
4. When the sentences are entered, separate them by a line and number them in the order they are entered.
5. The last student to enter his or her sentence should save the entire file of sentences under a name such as *Story 1.*

6. Go around the room asking students to call out random numbers no higher than the number of sentences that were recorded for *Story 1*.
7. Call up *Story 1* on the computer and record the random sequence of numbers the students gave at the top of the screen.
8. Have the students take turns using the find/replace function to locate the sentences in the random sequence and using the cut/paste function to move the sentences into the order of the random sequence.
9. Print out a copy of the ordered sentences for each student. During independent work time, ask the students to make stories out of their sentences, without changing the order of sentences, by adding sentences or words.
10. Ask students to share their finished stories.

An example follows:

Story 1

Use the find/replace and move/block functions to create a story from the sentences that follow. Arrange the sentences in the following sequence:

1 4 8 2 3 5 6 9 7

1. Do not judge food on calories alone.
2. The professor was frustrated with the paperwork he had to turn in next week.
3. The student was eagerly awaiting an exciting lecture on computers.
4. The wind blew a bee into the room.
5. "Don't forget to pick up the groceries at the store," said Paul.
6. "Did the emergency rations arrive?" asked Maria.
7. There were many children on the playground.
8. The centerfielder could not catch the ball.
9. The sound came from another room.

One student's story:

Do not judge food on calories alone. This is what the professor was saying as the wind blew a bee into the classroom. I was daydreaming as usual, watching the baseball team. The centerfielder could not catch the ball. The professor banged on the board. I looked up. He seemed crabby. I think he was frustrated with the paperwork he had to turn in next week. He called on Dewayne. The student was eagerly awaiting an exciting lecture on computers but instead he was invited up to the board to solve a complicated problem. I went back to daydreaming. There was something I was supposed to do after class. Suddenly I remembered. While I was brushing my teeth that morning, my roommate made a grocery list. "Don't forget to pick up the groceries at the store," said Paul as I ran out the door. Then at the bus stop, I ran into my friend Maria, who was heading up an earthquake disaster team. She was talking to someone else on the disaster team. "Did the emergency rations arrive?" asked Maria. As Dewayne tried to solve the problem, I decided I would donate some of my groceries to Maria's earthquake relief efforts. My daydreaming was interrupted by an explosion. The sound came from another room, the chemistry lab. Dewayne still wasn't finished. I looked back out the window. There were many children on the playground.

▼   VII. Fortune Cookie Word Processing   ▼

The idea for this activity came from a 1996 *Learning and Leading with Technology* article written by R. Reisman.

Objective

Students will improve their word processing skills by creating a booklet of sayings. In the process, they will learn about themselves and each other.

Procedure

1. Buy fortune cookies and have the class eat them and then discuss what the sayings mean.
2. Divide the class into small groups and have each group create some fortune cookie sayings on the computer.
3. After the class is through, have the students cut these sayings into strips and put them in a hat.
4. Randomly hand out the sayings to each student in the class.
5. Ask students to share their saying with the whole class and tell if they think the saying is true of them.
6. As a follow-up have the students use an art program to depict the meaning of their saying.
7. Finally, have the whole class use a desktop program to publish the class sayings in a class booklet.

Summary

This chapter traced the historical beginnings of word processing. We examined the merits of the word processor over the standard typewriter. We discovered how easy it is for users to change and edit documents by using word processors. We became familiar with the basic features of word processing and gained insight into what features to consider when selecting a word processor. The chapter presented a checklist and evaluation scale to facilitate this decision-making process, along with specific ideas on how to incorporate the word processor into the classroom. Seven word processing activities featured covered a range of curriculum areas. **Be sure to review the annotated list of award-winning word processing programs in Appendix A.**

What follows is an annotated list of top-rated Internet sites. These sites contain information about word processing software, lesson plans, activities, teaching suggestions for integrating writing into the curriculum, news, and reviews.

CLASSROOM ACTIVITIES AND LESSON PLAN SITES

AskERIC Computer Science Lesson Plans
http://askeric.org/cgi-bin/lessons.cgi/Computer_Science
This site offers a collection of technology lesson plans for grades K–12.

North Carolina Department of Instruction: Computer Skills Lesson Plans
http://www.dpi.state.nc.us/curriculum/Computer.skills/lssnplns/CompCurr.LP.html
Computer Skills Lesson Plans contains a table of keyboarding word processing, and other applications lesson plans.

Children's Literature Web Guide
http://www.acs.ucalgary.ca/~dkbrown/
David K. Brown, Doucette Library librarian at the University of Calgary, has collected extensive resources to facilitate and encourage the writing process. For example, the **More Links** section contains hundreds of sites to well-known children's authors and teacher resources.

Teachers @ Random
http://randomhouse.com/teachers/
This site offers instructional ideas for a wide range of novels indexed by grade, theme, and curriculum subject. It also includes author biographies.

Carol Hurst's Children's Literature Web Site
http://www.carolhurst.com/
This site is packed with hundreds of teaching suggestions for integrating writing into the curriculum using children's books.

Scholastic Lesson Plans and Reproducibles
http://teacher.scholastic.com/lessonrepro/
Scholastic provides a rich collection of lesson plans that range from pre-K to 8th grade.

OTHER INTERNET WORD PROCESSING RESOURCES

Sheldon Oberman's Writing and Storytelling
http://www.mbnet.mb.ca/~soberman/
Sheldon Oberman, a Canadian children's author, presents a wealth of writing tips from warm-up exercises to descriptive character sketches.

Aaron Shepard's RT Page
http://www.aaronshep.com/rt/
Aaron Shepard's *Reader's Theater Editions* provide scripts for getting the creative juices going.

The Young Writers Club
http://www.cs.bilkent.edu.tr/~david/derya/ywc.html
At this site, students can join a free online writers' club, send in their writing, read other kids' work, and take part in contests and activities.

Melisa C. Michaels
http://www.sff.net/people/Melisa/
The author of the Skyrider science fiction series offers writing tips, samples from her novels, short stories and poems, and story starters.

KidNews: Kids' Writing from Practically Everywhere
http://kidnews.com/
KidNews represents different forms of writing. Submissions from kids around the world include news, features, creative writing, pen pals, and book reviews.

NativeTech: Poems and Stories
http://www.nativetech.org/poetry/
The site, accompanied by illustrations, includes poetry shaped by Native American experiences. The poems feature imagery of nature, animals, and the seasons, and are divided into sections called "Beavers and Beyond" and "Medicine Dreams."

Interactive Poetry Pages
http://www.csd.net/cgibin/cgiwrap/cantelow/poem_view.pl/aha
This site is a link from a larger site that features many forums for poetry

http://www.faximum.com/aha!poetry

This site features poems in progress and encourages the viewer to add to, comment on, or finish the poem. You can also begin a new poem and have others add to it.

The Write Site
http://writesite.org/
It is an interactive language arts and journalism project for middle schools including information on how to conduct research and develop your own personal writing style.

Be sure to review the annotated list of award-winning word processing programs in Appendix A.

Chapter Mastery Test

To the Instructor: Refer to the Instructor's Manual for the Answers to the Mastery Questions. This manual has additional questions and resource materials.

Let's check for chapter comprehension with a short mastery test. What follows are basic terms, classroom projects, and suggested readings and references.

1. What is word processing and why is it important in education?
2. What distinguishes a typewriter from a word processor?
3. Identify and describe five features that are common to all word processors.
4. Discuss three different ways a word processor would be useful in the classroom.
5. Distinguish among a thesaurus, a spelling checker, and a grammar checker and explain which a 6th grader and a 10th grader would prefer.
6. Select two standard editing features and justify their use.
7. Explain the concept of line justification as it relates to the computer and give two examples.
8. Discuss the factors involved in selecting a word processor for a school district. Use Appendix A for an annotated list of word processing software.

9. Define the following terms:
    a. font,
    b. cut,
    c. block function,
    d. text insertion, and
    e. find and replace.
10. What safety features should be included in a word processor and why?
11. Evaluate a real or hypothetical word processing software program based on the criteria used in this chapter.
12. What is a dedicated word processor and how is it used?
13. Choose three advanced word processing features and explain how you would use them in a high school classroom.
14. If you were buying a word processing program for use in an elementary school, what three features would be essential and why?
15. Compare two word processors on the basis of their features; then review each one separately.
16. Americans generally use word processing software more than Europeans do. Explain why you think this situation will or will not change.
17. Explain why templates have become a highly popular word processing tool.

Basic Terms

block (p. 70)	grammar checkers (p. 80)
copy (p. 70)	graphical user interface (GUI) (p. 65)
cursor (p. 68)	header (p. 72)
cut and paste (p. 70)	insert (p. 69)
dedicated word processors (p. 66)	integrated software package (p. 66)
delete (p. 69)	justification (p. 71)
drag-and-drop (p. 70)	margin (p. 71)
font (p. 73)	pitch (p. 73)
footer (p. 72)	public domain software (p. 78)

replace (p. 70)
shareware (p. 78)
software suite (p. 66)
spelling checker (p. 79)
tabs (p. 71)
thesaurus (p. 81)

typeface (p. 73)
undo (p. 77)
word processor (p. 66)
word wrap (p. 69)
WYSIWYG (p. 77)
zooming (p. 78)

Classroom Projects

1. Create letterhead stationery.
2. Prepare a résumé.
3. Create a flyer.
4. Create a homework-to-do list.
5. Outline a chapter.
6. Prepare a table of contents.
7. Write a story.

Suggested Readings and References

Allen, Philip A. "Adult Age Difference in Letter-Level and Word-Level Processing." *Psychology and Aging* 6, no. 2 (June 1, 1991): 261.

Bahr, Christine M. "The Effects of Text-Based and Graphics-Based Software Tools on Planning and Organizing of Stories." *Journal of Learning Disabilities* 29, no. 4 (July 1996): 355–70.

Balajthy, E. "Keyboarding, Language Arts, and the Elementary School Child." *Computing Teacher,* February 1988, pp. 40–43.

Boone, R. *Teaching Process Writing with Computers.* Eugene, Ore.: ISTE, 1991.

Bowman, Marcus. "Children, Word Processors and Genre." *Scottish Educational Review* 31, no. 1 (May 1999): 66–83.

Campbell, George. "Get Their Attention with Voice Attachments." *PC World* 18, no. 3 (March 2000): 265.

Cerrito, Patricia. "Writing Technology and Experimentation to Explore the Concepts of Elementary Statistics." *Mathematics and Computer Education* 28, no. 2 (Spring 1994): 141.

Coats, Kaye, et al. "Ideas from Teachers! Writing Notebook." *Creative Word Processing in the Classroom* 7, no. 4 (April–May 1990): 40–41.

Cochran-Smith, Marilyn. "Writing Processing and Writing in Elementary Classrooms: A Critical Review of Related Literature." *Review of Educational Research* 61, no. 1 (Spring 1991): 107.

Daiute, C. *Writing and Computers.* Reading, Mass.: Addison-Wesley, 1985.

Drumm, John E., and Frank M. Groom. "Teaching Information Skills to Disadvantaged Children." *Computers in Libraries* 19, no. 4 (April 1999): 48–51.

Greenleaf, Cynthia. "Technological Indeterminacy: The Role of Classroom Writing Practices and Pedagogy in Shaping Student Use of the Computer." *Written Communication* 11, no. 11 (January 1, 1994): 85.

Howell, R., and P. Scott. *Microcomputer Applications for Teachers.* Scottsdale, Ariz.: Gorsuch, 1985.

Howie, S. H. *Reading, Writing, and Computers: Planning for Integration.* Needham Heights, Mass.: Allyn & Bacon, Longwood Division, 1989.

Jarchow, E. "Computers and Computing: The Pros and Cons." *Electronic Education,* June 1984, p. 38.

Joslin, E. "Welcome to Word Processing." *Computing Teacher,* March 1986, pp. 16–19.

Laframboise, Kathryn L. "The Facilitative Effects of Word Processing on Sentence-Combining Tasks with At-Risk Fourth Graders." *Journal of Research and Development in Education* 24, no. 2 (Winter 1991): 1.

Land, Michael, and Sandra Turner. *Tools for Schools.* 2nd ed. New York: Wadsworth Publishing Company, 1996.

Langone, John. "The Differential Effects of a Typing Tutor and Microcomputer-Based Word Processing on the Writing Samples of Elementary Students with Behavior Disorders." *Journal of Research on Computing in Education* 29, no. 2 (Winter 1996): 141–58.

Levy, Michael C., and S. Ransdell. "Computer-Aided Protocol Analysis of Writing Processes." *Behavior Research Methods, Instruments, & Computing* 26, no. 2 (May 1, 1994): 219.

MacArthur, Charles A. "Using Technology to Enhance the Writing Processes of Students with Learning Disabilities." *Journal of Learning Disabilities* 29, no. 4 (July 1996): 334–54.

MacArthur, Charles A. "Word Processing with Speech Synthesis and Word Prediction: Effects on the Dialogue Journal Writing of Students with Learning Disabilities." *Learning Disability Quarterly* 21, no. 2 (Spring 1998): 151–66.

Marcus, Stephen. "Word Processing: Transforming Students' Potential to Write." *Media and Methods* 27, no. 5 (May 1, 1991): 8.

Milone, Michael N. *Every Teacher's Guide to Word Processing: 101 Classroom Computer.* Englewood Cliffs, N.J.: Prentice Hall, 1985.

Montague, Marjorie, and Fionelle Fonseca. "Using Computers to Improve Story Writing." *Teaching Exceptional Children* 25, no. 4 (Summer 1993): 46–49.

Morton, L. L. "Lab-Based Word Processing for the Learning-Disabled." *Computers in the Schools* 8, no. 1/3 (1991): 225.

Nichols, Lois Mayer. "Pencil and Paper versus Word Processing: A Comparative Study of Creative Writing in the Elementary School." *Journal of Research on Computing in Education* 29, no. 2 (Winter 1996): 159–66.

Owen, Trevor. "Poems That Change the World: Canada's Wired Writers." *English Journal* 84, no. 6 (October 1995): 48–52.

Pfaffenberger, Bryan. *Webster's New World Dictionary of Computer Terms.* 8th ed. New York: IDG Worldwide, 2000.

Porter, Rebecca. "Word versus WordPerfect: Word-Processing Software on Trial." *Trial* 36, no. 3 (March 2000): 55.

Poulsen, Erik. "Writing Processes with Word Processing in Teaching English as a Foreign Language." *Computers & Education* 16, no. 1 (1991): 77.

Reissman, R. "Computerized Fortune Cookies: A Classroom Treat." *Learning and Leading with Technology* 23, no. 5 (1996): 25–26.

Robinette, Michelle. "Top 10 Uses for ClarisWorks in the One-Computer Classroom." *Learning and Leading with Technology* 24, no. 2 (October 1996): 37–40.

Roblyer, M. D. "The Effectiveness of Microcomputers in Education: A Review of the Research from 1980–1987." *T.H.E. Journal,* September 1988, pp. 85–89.

Schramm, Robert M. "The Effects of Using Word Processing Equipment in Writing Instruction." *Business Education Forum* 45, no. 5 (February 1, 1991): 7.

Sharp, Vicki. *Make It with Microsoft Office (Macintosh).* Eugene, Ore.: Visions Technology in Education, 1999.

Sharp, Vicki. *Make It with Microsoft Office (Windows).* Eugene, Ore.: Visions Technology in Education, 1999.

Solomon, Gil L. "Four Tips for More Efficient Word Processing." *Family Practice Management* 6, no. 8 (September 1999): 54.

Stone, M. David. "Choose Your Words." *PC Magazine* 19, no. 6 (March 21, 2000): 113.

Varblow, Judy. "Reading, Writing, and Word Processing: An Interdisciplinary Approach." *Balance Sheet* 72, no. 2 (Winter 1990): 22.

Woodrow, Janice F. J. "Teachers' Perceptions of Computer Needs." *Journal of Research on Computing in Education* 23, no. 4 (Summer 1991): 475–93.

Zorko, Leslie J. "Creative Writing: A Comparison Using the Computer vs. Handwriting." *National Association of Laboratory Schools Journal* 18, no. 2 (Winter 1993): 28.

CHAPTER 5

Desktop Publishing

Integrating Desktop Publishing into the Classroom

Did you know that desktop publishing is the second most popular computer application? Did you know that students can use desktop software to create a variety of projects? Students can create minibooks, book reports, yearbooks, newsletters, posters, and flyers. Teachers can use a desktop publishing program to create awards, worksheets, signs, flyers, and posters for classroom display. This chapter will discuss how to select a desktop publishing program for the classroom and the general features of a desktop publishing program. You will see a checklist designed to help you choose the right desktop publishing software. Furthermore, you will be given exercises that help you integrate desktop publishing into the classroom. You will become familiar with Internet sites that include tutorials, software tips, design basics, and classes for learning desktop publishing.

Objectives

Upon completing this chapter, you will be able to:

1. Explain what desktop publishing is;
2. Describe the features of desktop publishing;
3. Operate a desktop publishing program;
4. Evaluate different desktop publishing packages using standard criteria;
5. Create and apply a repertoire of desktop publishing activities for the classroom;
6. Discuss three guidelines for desktop publishing; and
7. Explore Internet sites that include desktop publishing articles, tips, tutorials, and lesson plans.

Historical Background

In Europe, before the 1400s, information was transmitted orally by troubadours who traveled from place to place. They would sing ballads or recite poems to broadcast the news or gossip of the day. Few people could read or write, and books were scarce because they had to be handwritten. Reading was mainly for religious instruction or entertainment.

Then around 1450, Johannes Gutenberg revolutionized communication with the invention of **movable type.** Modifying a winemaker's press to hold type, he poured hot metal into molds from which he created letters, numbers, and symbols. He placed his type and engravings on the bed of the press, inked the surface, and covered it with a sheet of paper. When he cranked the handle of the press, the pressure of the plate created an image on the paper (Fig. 5.1).

FIGURE 5.1
Early Printing Press
Dubl-Click Software, Inc.

Gutenberg's printing innovation gave more people the opportunity to read by making books more available. Even though Gutenberg's methods were refined over time, his basic concept remained unchanged for 400 years.

In the late 1880s, Ottmar Mergenthaler invented the **Linotype machine,** the first successful automated typecasting machine. This mechanical type-composing machine let the operator cast an entire line of type at once by using a keyboard. It was first used to typeset the *New York Tribune* in 1886. A year later, Tolbert Lanston invented the Monotype machine, which produced three characters of set type a second and was widely used for books.

The Linotype and Monotype, along with hand-set type, dominated typesetting until Intertype introduced the first phototypesetting machine in 1950. Phototypesetting replaced cast type because of its low cost, faster speed, and flexibility. Phototypesetting used film to reproduce type and images on metal plates that could then be inked for reproduction on paper.

The search for higher typesetting speeds resulted in the development of a method that would dispense with phototypesetting altogether by storing characters in electronic digital format. However, it wasn't until the mid-1960s that digital typesetting came into existence. Today, it coexists with photo-typesetting as the standards for setting type. Digital type uses computer type-setting equipment to describe letter forms as nearly invisible dots. This invention led the way for desktop publishing (DTP), a term coined by Paul Brainward of Aldus Software.

What Is Desktop Publishing?

Desktop publishing (DTP) is probably the second most popular use of computers in the school next to word processing (Kearsley, Hunter, and Furlong, 1992). Desktop publishing uses the personal computer (in conjunction with specialized software) to combine text and graphics to produce high-quality output on either a laser printer or a typesetting machine. This multistep process, which involves different types of software and equipment, is illustrated in Figure 5.2.

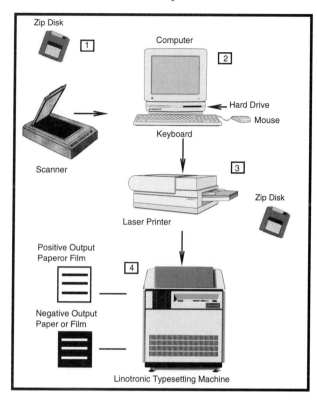

FIGURE 5.2
Desktop Publishing Process
Desktop Design by Laura Lamar, p.6 Crisp Publications Los Altos, CA 94022.

Your first step is to create and/or edit text using the word processor and to produce illustrations using a drawing, CAD, or painting program or to reproduce illustrations with a scanner. Desktop publishing programs are not generally used for original creation of a document. DTP's major purpose is to provide the ultimate in page-layout capabilities. For this reason, many programs lack a fully functioning word processor or graphics program. After text files and graphic files have been gathered, you turn to the DTP and

1. Input your material using the keyboard, a scanner, a zip disk, a Jaz disk, a CD-ROM, or a video digitizer. Also input illustrations from clip art, from a drawing or painting program, or from a program such as *SnagIt* (TechSmith Corporation), which captures images on the computer screen.
2. Lay out the text and graphics on the screen, revising and refining the material using the DTP's capabilities.
3. At this point, you have two choices: printing the finished document on a laser printer or, for better quality, printing it on a typesetting machine.
4. After obtaining proofs, make further changes and corrections and ready the final copy for printing or instruct the typesetter to do so.

Desktop publishing has become an all-encompassing term: It can refer to 14 Macintosh computers connected to a magazine's editorial and design departments; to an IBM user running *Print Shop II* (Learning Company) to produce a newsletter on an inkjet printer; or to an eight-year-old creating a sign to find a lost pet. DTP is no longer the exclusive property of the skilled technician or computer programmer. With a desktop publishing program, you can design a business newsletter, create a banner, or produce a school newspaper.

In the past each student working on the high school or college newspaper was assigned a different task. Typically, there was a designer, a writer, an illustrator, a typesetter, and a pasteup artist. Now DTP makes it possible for one person to perform all these functions. DTP permits the student to

1. create on-screen layouts,
2. use different typefaces or fonts,
3. right-justify text and lay out multiple columns,
4. insert and print art and text on the same page, and
5. print camera-ready copy.

The student can easily change the images, enlarge or shrink them, save them on a disk for later revision, and view the finished product early in the process.

There are many advantages to preparing student publications this way. DTP offers greater flexibility in designing graphics and headlines and gives more control over the final product than ever before. DTP is a more versatile, faster, and less expensive way to produce publications than the traditional methods because fewer people are involved and fewer revisions are necessary. It is a natural outgrowth of word processing programs such as the original *Bank Street Writer* (Scholastic) and *The Student Writing Center* (The Learning Company), which have limited desktop features.

As recently as 1985, there were few DTP programs, and the available ones were *PageMaker* (Adobe) and *Ready Set Go* (Manhattan Graphics),[1] programs designed only for the Macintosh computer. Today, there are more programs to choose from, and they exist for all computers. The software and hardware that the student needs for DTP range in price from inexpensive to very expensive. If you want to print an informal newsletter, you might use a program such as *Print Shop II* (The Learning Company) or *Microsoft Publisher 2000* and a simple color inkjet printer. If you are responsible for a business presentation, you might use expensive scanning equipment with programs such as *Adobe InDesign, Adobe PageMaker,* or *QuarkXPress* (Quark). Although the resolution from a laser printer would not be as high as that from professional typesetting equipment, the resulting copy would be exceptional.

Desktop programs differ in degree of complexity, cost, and features. Let's explore some of the basic characteristics of these programs.

Basic Desktop Publishing Features

Some of the features included in desktop publishing programs are a spelling checker, a thesaurus, a fully integrated word processor, text rotation, and var-

---

[1] This product is currently produced by Letraset USA.

ious graphics tools. Although desktop programs differ in their sophistication, all of them offer (1) page layout, (2) word processing, (3) style sheets and templates, (4) graphics, and (5) page view.

Page Layout

Page layout is the process of arranging the various elements on the page. During the process, you set the page margins, the number and width of the columns for regular text, and the position of the graphics and text. The most powerful programs, such as *Adobe PageMaker* and *QuarkXPress*, allow greatest control in page design; however, these programs are sophisticated and demand a steep learning curve. There are less powerful programs, such as *Print Shop II* and *Microsoft Publisher* (Windows version), that offer a wide variety of options but require less learning time. *Microsoft Publisher 2000* (Windows version) offers the choices shown in Figure 5.3.

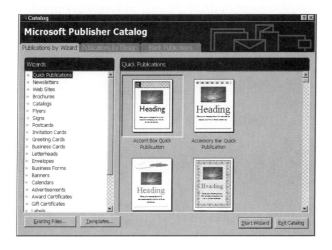

FIGURE 5.3 Microsoft Publisher 2000 *(Windows Version) Screen*
Screen shot reprinted with permission from Microsoft Corporation.

You select a calendar, a flyer, a newsletter, or some other publication format. Then you answer a series of questions; based on your answers, the program builds the publication. The program also lets you work from scratch. It is more complicated than *The Ultimate Writing & Creativity Center* or *Print Shop II*. Nevertheless, it does not have all the features of *PageMaker* or *QuarkXPress*.

In addition to these programs, there are word processing programs such as *The Student Writing Center* and *The Student Writing & Research Center* (The Learning Company) and *Print Shop II* that have sufficient desktop capabilities to fulfill the desktop publishing needs of students from age 10 and up. Finally, there are for the young user programs such as *Storybook Weaver Deluxe* (MECC/The Learning Company) and *The Ultimate Writing & Creativity Center* (The Learning Company). Using hundreds of graphics and sound effects, *Storybook Weaver Deluxe* lets students create a story with music and sound effects. The students can create and hear their story's text in either Spanish or English. *The Ultimate Writing & Creativity Center,* for users ages 6 to 10, creates reports, signs, journals, storybooks, and newsletters. Reports are limited to one-column pages, and newsletters have two or three fixed columns of text and a heading region that extends across the full width of the page. This program has the ability to have documents read aloud and can add animation.

In *PageMaker,* you determine the page size, set the margins, and choose the number of columns and the width of each column. This program has master pages, or templates, that allow you to design a template for the document with measuring rulers and guides to help with the placement of graphics and text on the page. The majority of DTP programs show an overview of the page to help you decide if the final design meets your approval. Many present programs can resize, reshape, and reposition text or graphics, and they all have automatic page numbering.

Most page-layout programs are based on **frames.** If you want to put text into a document, you either place it on the base page, an immovable frame that covers the entire page, or draw a frame and enter or import text or graphics into it. With the help of a screen ruler, you define the shape of a text block or the size of a graphic by drawing a box or frame on the page. Once the frame is defined, you can import the text or graphic to fill the space. The user can stack frames or create captions that overlay illustrations. The desktop publishing program should let you create as many frames as you want and put them anywhere on the page, stacking them and adjusting them as necessary. Using this type of frame-based page, you are able to more easily design a page visually to achieve a desired effect.

PageMaker, the program that set the standard for desktop publishing, originally was a variation on this frame-based model. The latest version now uses frames, similar to its rival *QuarkXPress.*

Word Processing

The power of the word processor varies with the desktop publishing program, but all DTPs can edit and format text to some degree.

Editing

The majority of these packages allow you to enter text, edit it, and import documents from other programs. The typical word processing functions are delete, insert, and copy. The majority of DTP programs have spelling checkers and thesauruses. For the high school student, it is important that there are move, search, and replace functions.

Formatting Text

The formatting features, such as type size, font, and typeface, determine how the page will look. The more control you have over the text, the more professional the document will appear. Many DTP programs let you center or align text, which makes uniform margins, and some programs let you define the space between letters,[2] words, and lines, which improves the readability and appearance of the document.

Style Sheets and Templates

A **style sheet** is a format that you can repeat throughout a paper. For example, you might design a style sheet with page numbers in the right corner, two inches from the top of the page. Once you've created the style sheet, all pages in your document will automatically have page numbers in the right corner. On your style sheet, you can set the margins, type style, line spacing, headers, footers, and quotations for your entire document.

Figure 5.4 shows the dialog box you would use to define a style. In this example, the style selected is *Body text,* and it is defined as Times at 12 points, with automatic leading, flush left justification, a 0.333 first indent,

FIGURE 5.4
PageMaker
Used with permission of Adobe Systems Incorporated. Adobe and Pagemaker are either registered trademarks or trademarks of Adobe Systems Incorporated in the United States and/or other countries.

and automatic hyphenation. To apply this style you would select the text and click on *Body text* in the Style dialog box. The style sheet then automatically would be applied to the selected text. It would look like this:

> "The longest running-computer crime. Double-entry inventory control at Saxon Industries. A Fortune 500 company that reported profits of $7.1 million and $5.3 million in 1979 and 1980, respectively, it went bankrupt in 1982. A bogus inventory record was maintained by computer by Saxon's Business Products Division. It was used to inflate the company's annual revenues. The double books were kept for thirteen years, and the crime might never have been revealed if the company had been profitable. Saxon was $53 million in the hole when it went under" (Rochester and Gantz, 1983, p. 117).

---

[2]*Kerning* is the adjustment of space between pairs of characters, so that the characters print in a visually pleasing manner.

Quite a few DTP programs contain their own style sheets and others let you import style sheets into their word processors. Many DTPs provide **templates**—guides already set up—and some companies let you create your own templates. The templates are time-savers because the user has a professionally designed document and does not have to worry about placement of text or pictures. The classroom template in Figure 5.5 is from *Print Shop II* (Windows). This program is packaged with a multitude of templates covering different topics.

**FIGURE 5.5
Print Shop II**

Screen shot courtesy of The Print Shop® Presswriter™ ©1998 Broderbund Software, Inc. All rights reserved. Used with permission.

The Print Shop Presswriter, and Broderbund are trademarks and/or registered trademarks of Broderbund Software, Inc.

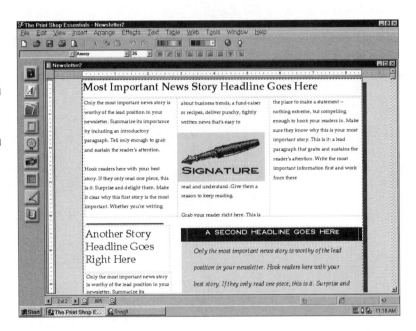

Graphics

Desktop publishing programs permit you to add different types of pictures or graphics to text either by drawing them or by importing them. Even though graphics can be created in the DTP program, these programs rarely have full-featured graphic capabilities. Typically the graphic is created in a draw or paint program and then imported into the publishing program.

A desktop program usually has a variety of tools similar to *QuarkXPress* (Fig. 5.6). Each tool serves a different function. Let us look at these tools. The Item tool ⊹ moves the boxes, items, or lines on the page, the Content tool ✋ manipulates the content within the box, the Rotation tool ↻ rotates the item, and the Zoom tool 🔍 lets you get a closer look at the item. The middle set of tools on the palette are called *creation tools* because they are used to create text boxes, picture boxes, and lines. The Text Box tool ▣ draws the text frames that are used to hold the text as illustrated by the following heading:
THE NEWS

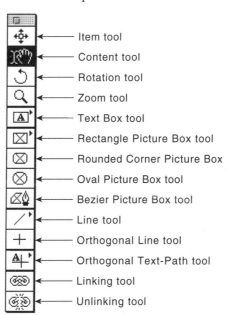

FIGURE 5.6
Tools from
QuarkXPress
Portions copyrighted Quark,
Inc. All rights reserved.

The Rectangle Picture Box tool ⊠ creates a rectangle box, whereas the Rounded-Corner Picture Box tool ⊠ creates a rounded-corner picture box. The Oval Picture Box tool ⊗ creates an oval box, and the Bézier Picture Box tool 🖉 creates a Bézier line or freehand Bézier line. The Line tool ╱ draws lines at any angle, while the Orthogonal Line tool ╋ draws vertical as well as horizontal lines. The Orthogonal Text-Path tool A⊥ creates a straight line that contains text and provides access to other text-path tools. The two bottom tools are used for linking and unlinking text. The Linking tool ⊕ connects text boxes, permitting the flow of text from one box to another. The Unlinking tool ⊕ breaks the connection between these text boxes.

Generally, DTPs offer features that customize artwork; reduce, enlarge, rotate, or flip a drawing; zoom in for detail; and edit, pixel by pixel.[3] Some programs can trace edges and change perspective, useful in producing halo effects around graphics, in outlining type, or even in converting silhouettes to simple outline form. With a DTP, you can crop or trim away part of an image and use it as a separate graphic. You can also repeat or duplicate an image. Figure 5.7 shows the same dolphin image duplicated in a regular border

FIGURE 5.7
Dolphin Border Pattern
ClickArt images ©1995
T/Maker Company.

---

[3]A *pixel* is a small element that in combination with other creates an image on the screen. It is the smallest manipulatable element in an image.

pattern. A student who can't draw to his or her own satisfaction can import artwork from other places, creating in the process artistic layouts or designs. Make sure you have a **text wrap** feature to take care of any graphic overlay problems caused by importing. If your program has this feature, it will wrap lines of text around the edge of the graphic.

Page View

After the page layout is completed, you invariably want to see how it looks before printing out the document. *The Student Writing & Research Center* shows what the layout will actually look like on the page, at least in a reduced size. High-end programs like *QuarkXPress* and *Pagemaker* give you a full range of **page view** magnifications.

Integrating Desktop Publishing into the Classroom

Teachers, as well as students, can use desktop publishing programs to produce a multitude of projects. Teachers can create worksheets, signs, flyers (Fig. 5.8), posters, or other graphical material to display in the class.

FIGURE 5.8
Clip Art
©Microsoft Corporation.
All rights reserved.

Wentworth Military Ball

Sunday, the seventeenth of April two-thousand and two at 8 o'clock in the Auditorium

They can write a class newsletter and send it home to parents. In addition, teachers can make brochures to advertise extracurricular activities at the school.

Students can use desktop publishing software to create minibooks, book reports, yearbooks, advertisements for a product, newsletters, posters, and flyers. Here are a few projects that can be created in your class.

Classroom Projects
1. Awards or certificates
2. Science experiment sheets

3. Résumés
4. Brochures
5. Letterheads
6. Booklets

Now that you have some idea of how to integrate desktop publishing into the classroom, let us look at some ways to select a good program that will meet your students' needs.

How to Choose a Good Desktop Publishing Program

Many desktop publishing packages are on the market today, and they come with every imaginable feature. Among these are DTP programs that lend themselves easily to classroom use, such as *Storybook Weaver Deluxe, Print Shop II* (Windows), *EasyBook Deluxe* (Sunburst), *The Ultimate Writing & Creativity Center, The Student Writing Center, Microsoft Publisher 2000* (Windows version), *Kid Works Deluxe* (Knowledge Adventure).

To choose a DTP program for the classroom, (1) examine the program hardware compatibility; (2) look at the program's general features; (3) study the program's instructional design; (4) find out how easy it is to use the package; (5) check out the program's cost effectiveness; and (6) check out the program's technical support.

Hardware Compatibility

Find out what computers are available at your school, Windows-based PCs or Macintoshes. Are these computers new, running the latest systems, or are they dinosaurs that are limited in the software they can run? How much memory does each machine have: 64 MB, 224 MB, or more? How large are their hard drives: 6 GB or 40 GB? What type of backup storage is available: a 250 MB Zip drive, a 2.2 GB ORB Removable Media Drive, or something else? What other equipment is available: video digitizers, printers, multipage monitors, modems, CD-Rewritable drives, or scanners?

General Features

How many columns can you create for a document? (*PageMaker* creates 20 columns, *The Student Writing Center* creates a maximum of 9 columns, and *The Ultimate Writing & Creativity Center* creates only 2 or 3 fixed columns.) Is the program a What You See Is What You Get (WYSIWYG) program? Can you enlarge or shrink the graphics you import? If you make a mistake, can you easily change it? When you load a program into the computer, what is displayed on the screen? Is there an untitled document with tools or an endless series of screens? How difficult is it to change the fonts and italicize or boldface the text? How many fonts are included, and can you mix type and font styles and sizes anywhere on the page? How easy is it to insert art in the document? What graphic formats does the program handle? What graphics tools are supplied to change the artwork that was imported or created? How extensive are the word processing features? Does the program have a find and replace feature; the ability to copy, cut, and paste text; and a spelling checker and thesaurus?

There are a myriad of features to consider, but the most important question to ask is, "Which features are necessary?" In choosing a computer for the elementary school child, the major concern should be a product that produces pleasant results. The high school student or novice should have a program that has more features and, thus, more versatility.

Instructional Design

A desktop publishing program design should be straightforward. Programs with a menu bar displayed at the top of the screen are ideal for beginners who do not then have to memorize the different functions. *The Ultimate Writing & Creativity Center* (Fig. 5.9) has such a menu bar. It clearly displays the choices that are available in this program.

FIGURE 5.9   The Ultimate Writing & Creativity Center™ *Menu Bar*

© The Learning Company. All rights reserved.

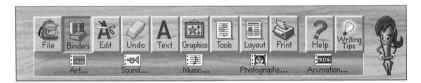

Any novice can change the font, add a picture, or use the printer by selecting the proper icon in the menu bar. The keys to programs such as *Print Shop II* and *Microsoft Publisher 2000* are the flexibility of their design and the many options available for the user. *Print Shop II* has an excellent manual and is easy to learn. *Microsoft Publisher* has a great on-screen tutorial that guides users step by step.

In looking at instructional design, you should ask the following questions: Is it a simple matter to make changes? Can you easily delete, add, or insert text? How fast is the general performance? (A program that is very slow can waste time—an annoyance if you are in a hurry to complete a job. For example, *Newsroom*, one of the first DTP programs for the elementary school, was a slow and cumbersome program.) How quickly can you change fonts, font style, characters, line spacing or leading, and paragraph justification? What flexibility does the program have in printing a newspaper? How easy is it to access the program functions? (Programs like *Microsoft Publisher 2000* have keyboard shortcuts for many of their functions, so it is not necessary to use their pull-down menus.)

Ease of Use

The program must be easy to learn and must use simple English commands. Ask the following questions: Can a student in approximately 60 minutes learn to use this program? Are there help screens that inform users what to do each step of the way, and are they easily accessible? Is there a menu bar across the screen so users do not have to memorize the different functions? Is there a tutorial disk or manual that takes students through the program? How difficult is it to figure out how to print a document? Can the printer be set up quickly? Is the program tedious to use because of too many help prompts and safety questions? Is there an automatic save feature?

Consumer Value

Cost has to be a major consideration in choosing a program for the classroom. *The Ultimate Writing & Creativity Center* can be purchased for around $48, whereas programs such as *PageMaker* and *QuarkXPress*, even with academic pricing, cost hundreds of dollars. Ask the following questions: Does the program include templates and graphic art? (*The Writing Center, Print Shop II,* and *Microsoft Publisher 2000* have templates and art included, which makes these programs better value for the money.) Are there on-site licenses, lab packs, or networked versions available? (Software companies, at a special price, offer on-site licenses so that you can freely copy the software for in-house use. Other manufacturers distribute lab packs that let you purchase software at a reduced price. Finally, many manufacturers offer networked versions of the software so that a set of software can be shared among many computers.)

Support

Is the documentation sent with the program helpful or bulky and unreadable? Can you call someone immediately to get help on the telephone, or must you wade through a series of messages and wait an unbearable amount of time? (Many software companies now tell you how many customers are in "line" before you and how long the wait is. When the wait is too long, some manufacturers have you leave your number and they call you back.) Do you have to pay a yearly fee or a fee per incident to get technical support? Is customer support available toll-free or do you pay long-distance rates? Is there a tutorial with the software package? Is the tutorial in the form of a manual, a disk, or both? (Many manufacturers provide both to simplify learning of their programs.) Is the manual readable, with activities, lesson plans, and an index? How easy is it to get a refund or a new disk if the disk is defective? Is it easy to get an update to buggy software?

Before selecting a desktop publishing program, look at the pupils' needs in the classroom. Determine what features meet these needs.

Refer now to Appendix A for an annotated bibliography of highly rated DTP programs for the classroom.

Next, examine one of these programs using the sample checklist and evaluation rating instrument on page 110.

After using this checklist a couple of times, you should be able to make a more informed decision when selecting software. Now let us explore how to use a desktop publishing program.

DESKTOP PUBLISHING CHECKLIST

Directions: Examine the following items and determine which ones you feel are important for your class situation. Evaluate your desktop publishing program and place an X on each line where the software meets your needs.

Product Name _____ **Manufacturer** _____ **Grade Level** _____

A. Hardware

_____ 1. Memory needed

_____ 2. Computer compatibility

_____ 3. Printer compatibility

_____ 4. Hard drive space

B. Features

_____ 1. Comprehensive undo

_____ 2. Page size selection

_____ 3. Adjustable column size

_____ 4. Page preview

_____ 5. Graphics

_____   a. Ruler guides

_____   b. Resize, position, crop

_____   c. Flip, rotate, invert

_____   d. Graphic importing

_____   e. File formats, EPS, Pict, GIF, JPEG, etc.

_____ 6. Wraparound graphics

_____ 7. Word processing

_____   a. Insert/delete

_____   b. Search/replace

_____   c. Copy/paste

_____   d. Spelling checker

_____   e. Thesaurus

_____   f. Tabs

_____   g. Automatic pagination

_____   h. Hyphenation

_____ 8. Typesetting

_____   a. Variety of type sizes

_____   b. Different type styles

_____   c. Variety of fonts

_____   d. Kerning (spacing between letters)

_____   e. Margin setting

_____ 9. Drawing/painting tools

C. Design

_____ 1. Speed of execution

_____ 2. Ease of graphics insertion

_____ 3. Simple saving function

_____ 4. Easy printing procedure

_____ 5. Number of columns possible

_____ 6. Type of page layout

_____ 7. Method of graphic importing

_____ 8. Formatting within program

D. Ease of Use

_____ 1. On-screen help

_____ 2. Tutorial disk

_____ 3. Easy printer setup

_____ 4. Minimal learning time

_____ 5. Automatic save

E. Consumer Value

_____ 1. Cost

_____ 2. Templates

_____ 3. Clip art included

_____ 4. Lab pack

_____ 5. Networked version

_____ 6. On-site license

F. Support Features

_____ 1. Technical

_____ 2. Tutorial material

_____ 3. Readable manual

_____   a. Activities

_____   b. Lesson plans

_____   c. Index

_____ 4. Money-back guarantee

Rating Scale

Rate the Desktop Publishing Program by placing a check on the appropriate line.

Excellent _____ Very Good _____ Good _____ Fair _____ Poor _____

Comments

Learning to Use a Desktop Publishing Program

This section gives an overview of how a desktop program operates. It should not serve as a substitute for the program's operational manual. For illustrative purposes, let's use *Microsoft Publisher,* a good middle-school desktop program. *Microsoft Publisher 2000* has many more advanced features than *The Ultimate Writing & Creativity Center,* a DTP program for grades 2–5. We'll consider how *Microsoft Publisher 2000* creates a layout, add text and graphics, and refines the product to produce a printout. When you open *Microsoft Publisher 2000,* you see an introductory screen that offers all sorts of options. You have the option of creating projects that include a letterhead, a newsletter, a banner, a flyer, an award certificate, and more. You can create from scratch or you can use a "Wizard" to speed the procedure. If you want to create newsletter, select **Newsletter** on the left and choose a newsletter template, for example, **School Newsletter** on the right of the screen then click on the **Start Wizard**

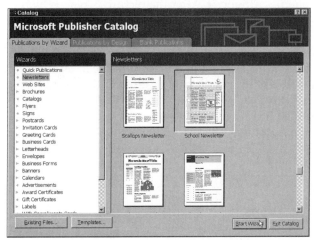

FIGURE 5.10
Microsoft Publisher 2000
Selecting Newsletter
Screen shot reprinted with permission from Microsoft Corporation.

(Fig. 5.10) to begin. The Wizard then asks a series of questions, which range from color scheme (Fig. 5.11) to number of columns.

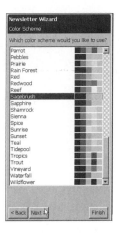

FIGURE 5.11
Microsoft Publisher 2000
Color Scheme
Box shot reprinted with permission from Microsoft Corporation.

Publisher has layout tool rulers, drawing tools, work areas, and storage areas. While creating your newsletter, you can change the margins, column size, borders, and page numbers. After determining these layout issues, you're ready to write or import text and pictures into the document. In many DTP programs, it is easier to edit text and graphics in your word processing program and import them into the DTP program only when they're nearly finished. In *Microsoft Publisher 2000,* the text is imported in the form of text frames that can be moved as a complete unit. *The Student Writing Center* imports text from word processing documents in a **text only format,** which means the imported text loses its formatting

Occasionally, you'll want to add graphics to illustrate a story; this usually means defining spaces or frames in which the graphics will fit. In *Microsoft Publisher 2000,* you insert the picture you want by selecting from the Clip Gallery, or from a separate file, using a scanner or digital camera, or linking to a picture outside of *Publisher.* The picture then appears with eight frame handles around it. After the picture is placed, you can resize it, move it, rotate it, or turn it sideways by using these frame handles. *Microsoft Publisher 2000*'s Clip Gallery has hundreds of pictures covering a range of subjects; you can also import pictures from clip art collections and pictures that you created with paint programs (unlike *The Student Writing Center,* this particular program has painting and graphics tools of its own).

As you experiment with layout and importing of art, you frequently need to view the entire page. Activate the page preview function to display the document in a reduced size that fits on-screen, as shown in Figure 5.12.

FIGURE 5.12
Microsoft
Publisher 2000
Page Preview
Function

Screen shot reprinted with permission from Microsoft Corporation.

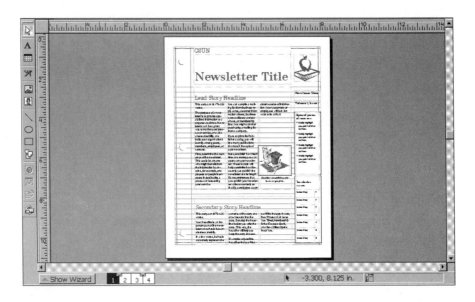

Many DTP programs have a zoom feature that lets you see a close-up of small sections of the document.

The last step is printing the document either on an inkjet or a laser printer. The laser printer produces a very professional quality copy, but this output does not approach the resolution of a professional typesetting machine.

As you can see, using a program like *Microsoft Publisher 2000* is not difficult. This program is appropriate for junior high and high school. *Microsoft Publisher 2000* is less expensive and does not have all the features of a professional program like *QuarkXPress,* which is more suitable for serious high school and college students. *QuarkXPress*'s introductory screen is simply a tool palette (Fig. 5.13). When you choose to create a new document, a dialog box

FIGURE 5.13
QuarkXPress *Tool Palette*
Portions copyrighted Quark, Inc. All rights reserved.

(Fig. 5.14) appears. At this point, you have to be knowledgeable enough to make choices about such items as number of columns, gutter width, and page

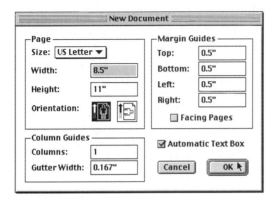

FIGURE 5.14
QuarkXPress *Dialog Box*
Portions copyrighted Quark, Inc. All rights reserved.

size. Working on a blank document, you then bring in text and graphics. After you are finished creating your document, you can view it in different ways such as a thumbnail sketch, 50 percent, or 200 percent or in a prearranged window (Fig. 5.15).

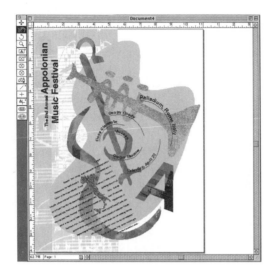

Although using a DTP program seems like a straightforward process, there always are compatibility problems between programs since different programs have different features and capabilities. Some are much easier to use and import graphics easily, while others offer more flexibility, include painting and drawing tools, but are more difficult to use.

Desktop Publishing Programs for the Classroom

Appendix A features an annotated list of highly rated desktop publishing programs. Let us quickly review a few of these programs in terms of age-level suitability. *Storybook Weaver Deluxe, The Ultimate Writing & Creativity Center, Kid Works Deluxe,* and *The Imagination Express Series* (Edmark) are early grade programs with desktop publishing features. *Storybook Weaver Deluxe* lets children design and publish their own illustrated books. The children can choose from hundreds of graphics to illustrate their books. *The Ultimate Writing & Creativity Center* lets children produce reports, newsletters, storybooks, and signs. The children can add animations to their stories, and the program has the ability to have documents read aloud. With *Kid Works Deluxe* the child creates stories combining text with graphics. *The Imagination Express Series* has rudimentary word processing features and bare-bones page-layout capabilities. Nevertheless, it lets the children create interactive stories by selecting background, scenery, and characters, by recording dialogue, and by adding text and sound effects. These programs have very limited word processing and picture handling features, but they are superior programs for the primary grades because of their low learning curve.

The Student Writing Center and *Print Shop II* are more advanced and suitable for the middle grades and because of their better picture handling and increased word processing capabilities. Although these programs offer improved features, they are by no means fully functioning desktop publishing programs. *The Student Writing Center* and *The Student Writing & Research Center* have basic word processing features with a spelling checker. These programs let students combine graphics and text to produce newsletters, book reports, research papers, journals, letters, résumés, and signs. *Print Shop II* (Windows) lets students choose from projects that include banners, certificates, greeting cards, newsletters, brochures, postcards, and more. Students can use headers and footers and edit their work using a spelling checker and thesaurus. When students graduate from this type of program, they might try programs such as *Microsoft Publisher 2000*, which fill a void by providing additional drawing tools and word processing and page-layout features that are useful for the junior high school and high school student.

Finally, at the advanced high school, college, and adult level, professional programs such as *Adobe PageMaker* and *QuarkXPress* are suitable because they possess a multitude of features, file-handling capabilities, and flexibility. They are very expensive, but academic versions exist for these products.

Guidelines for Desktop Publishing

1. Spend time planning ahead and collect the items that will be included in the proposed paper or newsletter. Make a sketch or a rough layout. Review what will be communicated. Who is the audience? What approach will be best for communicating the message? Be flexible and willing to experiment. Look for consistency on each page of the document and check for balance of design. Add interest when it is needed. Organize a page around a dominant visual.
2. Determine the format of the publication. Pay close attention to borders and margins. Provide a dramatic graphic for the front page. Use forceful headlines to organize the writing.
3. Add emphasis to the work. For example, use a large type size to emphasize important ideas when needed. When necessary, vary the type style by using boldface or italics. Use blank spaces to make the designs stand out. Highlight the ideas with artwork, but do not overdo it. Let the reader's eyes focus on a particular part of the page.
4. Be careful not to clutter the page with too many elements. At the same time, use a variety of items to avoid boring the audience.
5. Do not use too many typefaces because it detracts from the general feeling of the writing.
6. Select typefaces that are easy to read, like `Courier`; avoid typefaces like *Tekton*.
7. Type should be large enough so that any student can read it.
8. Use white space so that this focuses attention on areas that contain information.
9. Make the design fit the content of the document.

10. Make sure the information is easy to find and not buried. Have it flow from the upper left corner to the right following a logical sequence.
11. Balance related columns and facing pages. Make sure that the facing pages and columns are aligned within approximately one or two lines of each other.
12. Make the size of the components on the page consistent with the surrounding components.
13. Have the artwork face into the text.
14. Check the work thoroughly before printing out copies, and look at the printout again to apply finishing touches.
15. When possible, place titles below your illustrations and guide the reader with your headings.
16. Don't overuse pictures and elaborate graphics. Remember, they are to convey information and not distract the reader.
17. Avoid excessive underlining, lines composed of leftover single words, unequal spacing, and cramped logos.

There are many activities a teacher can use to motivate students to write with a DTP program. What follows are six such activities.

Classroom Lesson Plans

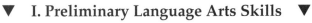

▼   I. Preliminary Language Arts Skills   ▼

Objectives

Students will learn some preliminary organizational skills and produce a simple picture with a few lines of text.

Procedure

1. Have the students bring in newsletters, newspapers, and magazines. Distribute these items around the class.
2. Divide the class into groups of five and have each group clip text and pictures from the newspapers and magazines.
3. Next, instruct each group to choose a picture and a line or two of text and put them together to communicate a message. Students might choose a headline from an article, a graphic from an advertisement, and a line of text from the front page, for example.
4. Now have each group use the desktop publishing program to translate its pasteup representation into print. Students will have to make some substitutions depending on the graphics available from their desktop publishing program.
5. End the process by having each group display its final design and discuss it with the entire class.

▼   II. Language Arts   ▼

Objective

Students will learn some preliminary DTP skills.

Procedure

1. Have each student in the class write a story.
2. Discuss each story with the student and as a class and make recommendations on how to improve it.
3. Have the students use their scissors to revise their stories.
4. Next, instruct each student to use the DTP program to enter his or her story.
5. Print out copies of each child's story for the entire class.
6. Divide the class in groups and have them read and discuss the stories.

▼   III. Math Stories   ▼

Objective

Students will learn how to write math word problems using their DTP program.

Procedure

1. Distribute a math story similar to the one shown in Figure 5.16.

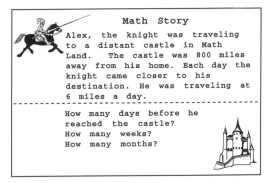

FIGURE 5.16
Math Story
© Dubl-Click Software Inc.
Used with permission.

2. Ask the students to read and solve the word problems found on this sheet.
3. Next, have the students write their own stories and related word problems.
4. After the students have finished writing their story problems, they should take turns entering these stories into the computer.
5. Have the students lay out and illustrate their stories with clip art, scanned images, or their own art created in a drawing program.
6. Use the printed stories as a math test for class.

▼   IV. Science Activity   ▼

Objective

Students will design their own science lab sheet and experiment.

Procedure

1. Help the students design individual experiments related to an overall classroom science topic.
2. Show students some sample lab sheets similar to the one in Figure 5.17.

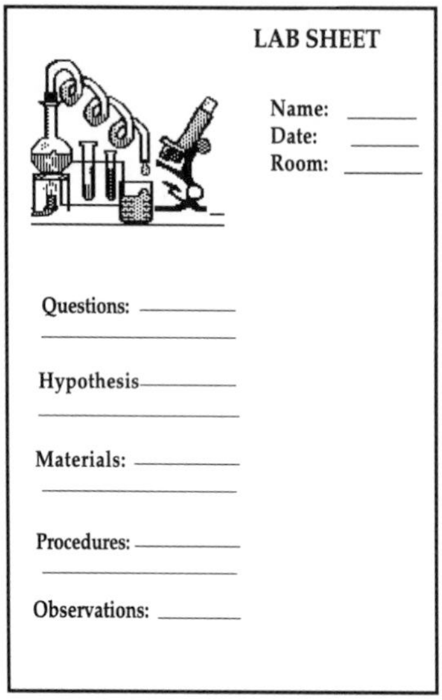

FIGURE 5.17
The Student
Writing Center
Lab Sheet

©1993, 1995–The Learning Company. Permission to use granted by The Learning Company. The Learning Company is a registered trademark of The Learning Company. Student Writing Center is a trademark of The Learning Company. All rights reserved.

LAB SHEET

Name: _____
Date: _____
Room: _____

Questions: _____

Hypothesis _____

Materials: _____

Procedures: _____

Observations: _____

3. Ask students to design with the DTP lab report forms for their experiments.
4. Have students conduct their experiments using their own lab reports. After the experiments, discuss how the students would modify their reports for the next experiment.

▼   V. History Activity   ▼

Objective

Students will create stationery that appears to be professionally produced. In the process, they will learn how to write a grammatically correct letter and at the same time learn something about a historical figure.

Procedure

1. Bring in sample letterhead stationery like that in Figure 5.18. If the desktop publishing program you are using has letterhead templates, show these templates to the class.

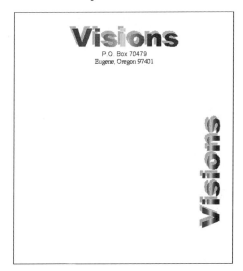

**FIGURE 5.18
WordArt
*Stationery***
Screen shot reprinted by permission of Microsoft Corporation.

2. Have each student design his or her own stationery.
3. Discuss the results in class.
4. Next, have each student write a letter as a historical figure such as Abraham Lincoln or Clara Barton. When the students write this letter, they must talk about some of the problems that are facing the individual in this particular time frame.
5. Next, have the students choose appropriate pictures to illustrate their letters. Talk about the importance of visual appeal and pictures that correlate with the time period.
6. The students should then check their work for grammar and spelling errors and historical accuracy.
7. Discuss the letters in class.

▼   VI. Newsletter Production   ▼

Objective
Students will be able to produce a newsletter for the class using word processing, page layout, and graphics programs.

Procedure
1. Bring in sample newspapers and newsletters and distribute them to everyone.
2. Divide the students into work groups and assign each group a different writing task. For example, one group might write a news article on dolphins while another group might write an editorial on a controversial issue and third group might be responsible for a gossip

column or movie reviews. Discuss with the students the process followed by journalists. Instruct them to determine who, what, why, where, and when in their reporting.

3. Have each work group write and revise its story.

4. Next, have the students write headlines and choose the pictures they want to use. Talk about the importance of visual appeal. Discuss how to be bold with headlines and how to place pictures effectively. The students should plan their placement of articles early in the process. Check their work for grammar and spelling errors. Use the sample from *PageMaker* in Figure 5.19 as a model.

FIGURE 5.19
Sample from
PageMaker

Used by permission of Adobe Systems Incorporated. Adobe and Pagemaker are either registered trademarks or trademarks of Adobe Systems Incorporated in the United States and/or other countries.

5. Ask students to use the DTP program to enter their articles for the paper. Make sure students view the entire document repeatedly to check its visual appeal.

6. After everyone is satisfied with the product, print out a copy. For later editions of the paper, rotate the tasks of the different groups in the class.

Students can write historical, autobiographical, art, sports, or science newsletters. Find out where your students' interest is and capitalize on that interest.

Additional Activities

The list of DTP activities is almost endless. Students can design awards, flyers, progress reports, questionnaires, and outlines for book reports. A sample award sheet created with *Print Artist* (Sierra) is shown in Figure 5.20.

FIGURE 5.20
Sample from **Print**
© **Artist** *(Sierra Home)*
© Sierra On-Line, Inc.

Summary

The computer has changed the steps involved in publishing a newsletter, magazine, or book. What was done mechanically is now handled electronically. Desktop publishing has altered the way school newspapers, business newsletters, and advertisements are produced.

This chapter traced the historical beginnings of desktop publishing. In the process, we considered the merits of desktop publishing. We discovered how easy it is for a user to produce a newsletter or lab report with one of these programs. We became familiar with the basic features of desktop publishing and gained insight into what features to consider when selecting a program. A checklist and evaluation scale presented in this chapter facilitate this decision-making process. The chapter also offered specific ideas on how to incorporate DTPs into the classroom. Six DTP activities that cover a range of curriculum areas were outlined. **Be sure to review the annotated list of award-winning desktop publishing programs in Appendix A.**

What follows is an annotated list of top-rated sites you can use in desktop publishing. These desktop publishing sites include articles, tips, tutorials, and lesson plans.

✎ INTERNET SITES: CLASSROOM ACTIVITIES AND LESSON PLANS

About.com's Desktop Publishing Page
http://desktoppub.about.com/
This site is an excellent starting place for articles about getting started in desktop publishing, design basics, software tips and tutorials, and classes for learning DTP.

About.com's Desktop Publishing Lesson Plans
http://desktoppub.about.com/compute/
desktoppub/library/weekly/aa082897.htm
DTP lesson plans for the K–12 classroom involving brochures, résumés, and business cards including step-by-step instructions.

Desktop Publishing.com
http://desktoppublishing.com/
http://www.desktoppublishing.com/
templates.html
The site is a premiere resource for clip art, desktop publishing, fonts, Web authoring, and placing your page on the Internet. Also offered are Free website templates allowing you to build

your home page in minutes using either Navigator or Explorer.

Desktop Movies in Education
http://www.apple.com/ca/education/k12/dv/
Desktop movies (digital video) allow you to develop stunning projects and activities with video (and audio)—right from your Macintosh. This capability can further the learning, the creating and the communicating environment for the K–12 classroom.

dtp-aus.com
http://www.dtp-aus.com/
The site offers free online publishing tutorials for learning HTML and DTP.

DTP.com
http://www.dtp.com/
DTP.com provides comprehensive lists of desktop publishing sites on the Web. The site brings you chat, discussions, clip art, fonts, and other relevant resources for desktop publishing online.

DTP Zone
http://www.powerup.com.au/~sevloid/ dtptips/dtpzone.htm
DTP Zone features a collection of tips and tricks for various DTP software including *PageMaker, Photoshop, Coreldraw,* and *Freehand.*

Microsoft Publisher
http://www.microsoft.com/office/publisher/
Microsoft Publisher 2000 helps you easily create, customize, and publish materials such as newsletters, brochures, flyers, catalogs, and Websites. You can publish easily on your desktop printer or directly to the Web.

Chapter Mastery Test

To the Instructor: Refer to the Instructor's Manual for the Answers to the Mastery Questions. This manual has additional questions and resource materials.

Let's continue with a short mastery test, basic terms, classroom projects, and suggested readings and references.

1. Explain the difference between a word processor and a desktop publishing program.
2. What is desktop publishing? Explain its importance in education.
3. Name and describe three features of a desktop publishing program.
4. Discuss a few general rules to follow when creating a newsletter or advertisement using desktop publishing software.
5. Which five DTP features are critical in producing a school publication? Explain your reasons.
6. Discuss three uses of DTP programs in the classroom.
7. Does DTP software make the traditional methods of producing newsletter and books obsolete? Justify your answer.
8. What is a layout? Briefly discuss why it is important to take considerable time when creating a layout.
9. Explain in general terms the way a newsletter might be produced with a DTP program.
10. Briefly trace the history of DTP from inception to the present.
11. What are some of the software, hardware, and design requirements of a typical DTP program?

Basic Terms

desktop publishing (DTP) (p. 98)   style sheet (p. 103)
frames (p. 102)   templates (p. 104)
Linotype machine (p. 98)   text only format (p. 112)
movable type (p. 97)   text wrap (p. 106)
page view (p. 106)

Classroom Projects

1. Develop a lesson plan using a DTP program.
2. Describe one DTP activity and show how a teacher can use it in a classroom situation.
3. Examine two DTP programs and compare their strengths and weaknesses.
4. Learn more about DTP by interviewing someone who uses a program. Have the individual demonstrate three or four features of the program. Identify any feature that is too complicated and then discuss some way of reducing the difficulty.
5. Read two articles about one DTP program and then use the program. Next, prepare a report that might persuade a school district to buy this program. In the presentation, discuss the benefits of using a DTP program.

Suggested Readings and References

Berman, Michael. "A New Desktop Publishing Contender." *Journal of Commerce* 423, no. 29671 (March 8, 2000): 6.

Braun, Ellen. "Word Processing, Desktop, Publishing Share Features." *Office* 117, no. 5 (May 1, 1993).

Breen, Christopher. "Desktop Publishing for the Home." *PC World* 17, no. 1 (January 1999): 77.

Clark, Sandra. "Desktop Publishing: Alive, Well & Growing." *Media and Methods* 27, no. 3 (January 1, 1991): 42.

Crawford, Walt. "Pages from the Desktop: Desktop Publishing Today." *Library Hi Tech* 12, no. 3 (1994): 101–19.

Ekhaml, Leticia. "Creating Better Newsletters." *School Library Media Activities Monthly* 12, no. 9 (May 1996): 36–38.

Ellis, Robert. "Creating a Studio Newsletter." *Clavier* 35, no. 3 (March 1, 1996): 27.

Franson, Paul "The Print Shop PressWriter." *PC Computing* 10, no. 8 (August 1997): 251.

Freedman, Alan. *The Computer Desktop Encyclopedia.* New York: Amacom, 2000.

Goldsborought, Reid. "Making Documents Look Good: Eight Tips." *Reading Today* 16, no. 4 (February/March 1999): 11.

Guthrie, Jim. "Designing Design into an Advanced Desktop Publishing Course (A Teaching Tip)." *Technical Communication: Journal of the Society for Technical Communication* 42, no. 2 (May 1995): 319–21.

Hane, Paula J. "Microsoft Debuts Vizact 2000, Releases Home Publishing Suite 2000." *Information Today* 16, no. 10 (November 1999): 45.

Hartley, James. "Thomas Jefferson, Page Design, and Desktop Publishing." *Educational Technology* 31, no. 1 (January 1, 1991): 54.

Johnson, Dave. "MICROSOFT Publisher." *PC Computing* 12, no. 6 (June 1999): 116.

Kearsley, G., B. Hunter, and M. Furlong. *We Teach with Technology.* Wilsonville, Ore.: Franklin, Beedle, and Associates, 1992.

Kramer, Robert, and Stephen A. Bernhardt. "Teaching Text Design." *Technical Communication Quarterly* 5, no. 1 (Winter 1996): 35–60.

Lamar, Laura. *Desktop Design*. Los Altos, Calif.: Crisp Publications, 1990.

Maxymuk, John. "Using Desktop Publishing to Create Newsletters, Handouts, and Web Pages: A How-To-Do-It Manual." *How-To-Do-It Manuals for Librarians* 74 (1997).

McCracken, Harry. "Publishing's Cheap with Print Shop and Canon." *PC World* 17, no. 11 (November 1999): 108.

Mendelson, Edward. "Microsoft Publisher 2000." *PC Magazine* 18, no. 1 (January 5, 1999): 36.

Mendelson, Edward. "Publishing the Easy Way." *PC Magazine* 16, no. 4 (February 18, 1997): 60.

Min, Zheng, and Roy Rada. "MUCH Electronic Publishing Environment: Principles and Practices." *Journal of the American Society for Information Science* 45, no. 5 (June 1994): 300–309.

Navarrete, Angela. "Complete Publisher '99." *PC World* 17, no. 4 (April 1999): 84.

Parker, R. *Aldus Guide to Basic Design*. Seattle, Wash.: Aldus Corporation, 1987.

Perreault, Heidi, and Lun Wasson. "Desktop Publishing: Considerations for Curriculum Design." *Business Education Forum* 45, no. 4 (January 1, 1991): 23.

Peterson, Nancy. "101 Expert Tips." *MacUser* 13, no. 8 (August 1997): 52.

Popyk, Marilyn K. "If Gutenberg Could See Us Now: Teaching Desktop Publishing." *Balance Sheet* 71, no. 3 (Spring 1990): 5.

Power, Brenda, "Newsletters; Web Sites; Teachers." *Instructor* 109, no. 3 (October 1999): 30.

Power, Brenda, "Strengthen Your Parent Connection." *Instructor* 109, no. 3 (October 1999): 30.

Roth, Evan. "Designs on Desktop." *Museum News* 70, no. 4 (July 1991): 59.

Sharp, Vicki. *Make It with Microsoft Office (Macintosh)*. Eugene, Ore.: Visions Technology in Education, 1999.

Sharp, Vicki. *Make It with Microsoft Office (Windows)*. Eugene, Ore.: Visions Technology in Education, 1999.

Simone, Luisa. "COREL Print Office 2000." *PC Magazine* 18, no. 1 (November 2, 1999): 66.

Sutton, Jayne O. "Stepping Up to Desktop Publishing." *Secretary* 57, no. 3 (March 1, 1997): 14.

Thompson, James A. "Producing an Institutional Fact Book: Layout and Design for a User-Friendly Product." *New Directions for Institutional Research* 91 (Fall 1996): 49–62.

Thompson, Patricia A. "Promises and Realities of Desktop Publishing." *Journalism Educator* 46, no. 1 (Spring 1991): 22.

Valle, Dwight, "Tools for Schools." *FamilyPC* 5, no. 8 (September 1998): 60.

Woody, Leonhard, Kyla K. Carlson, and Joel Enos. "Better Letters in Word." *PC Computing* 12, no. 6 (June 1999): 230.

CHAPTER 6

Databases

Integrating Databases into the Classroom

Did you know that teachers can use a database to prepare classroom materials and to do tasks that would otherwise be impossible? Did you know that teachers can use databases to locate instructional resources, motivate students, locate student records, and send personalized letters to parents? Students can use a database to engage in higher level thinking, to develop research skills, and to manage information. For example, students can use a keyword search to classify animals according to a characteristic. They can learn to locate entries that match a particular description. This chapter will discuss how to select a database program for the classroom along with the general features of a database program. You will see a checklist designed to help you choose the right database software. Furthermore, you will be given exercises that help you integrate the database into the classroom. You will become familiar with Internet sites that include tutorials, software tips, and discussion forums.

Objectives

Upon completing this chapter, you will be able to:

1. Explain what a database is and name its basic components;
2. Describe the basic features of a database;
3. Evaluate database software based on standard criteria;
4. Create and utilize a repertoire of database activities for the classroom;
5. Explain three methods of organizing data within a database;
6. Describe three different types of databases; and
7. Explore Internet sites that range from tutorials to searchable databases.

What Is a Database?

We are constantly bombarded by information in the workplace, at home, or at school. John Naisbitt, in his book *Megatrends,* writes, "We are drowning in information but starved for knowledge" (1982, p. 24). Since teachers cannot possibly retain all this information in memory, it is imperative that they develop skills in finding and interpreting data. Students also must master skills of organizing, retrieving, manipulating, and evaluating the information available.

Whenever there is a large amount of information to be managed, there is a need for **database management system** software that controls the storage and organization of data in a database. A **database** is a collection of information organized according to some structure or purpose. An all-encompassing term, *database* describes anything from an address book, recipe box, dictionary, or file cabinet to a set of computerized data files with sophisticated data relationships. To understand what a database is, you must be familiar with three terms: file, record, and field.

File. A file is a collection of information on some subject. For example, a class studying birds may place all its information on this topic in a file labeled *birds*.

Record. A record contains the information about one entry in the file. In our example on birds, a record would be information about a particular bird, say the *hummingbird*.

Field. Within a record there exist fields or spaces for specific information. The fields set aside for the hummingbird might include *beak type, scientific name, habitat,* and *migration patterns*.

The file cabinet, or database, in Figure 6.1 contains related files that store information in a systematic way. A principal using this file cabinet at

FIGURE 6.1
How a Database Works
ClickArt Images ©1995 T/Maker Company.

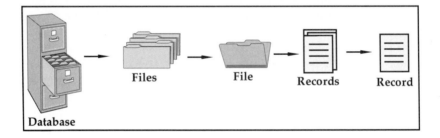

Database — Files — File — Records — Record

Clayton High School might take a stack of files out of the personal information drawer. She searches through the files for John Doe's file. This file contains a number of records, including a personal information record. She scans the information record for John Doe's address. The record is organized into five fields, or categories of information (Fig. 6.2): name, address, telephone

FIGURE 6.2
Fields

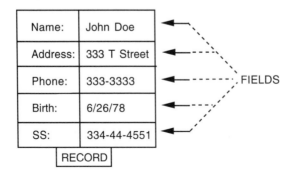

Name:	John Doe
Address:	333 T Street
Phone:	333-3333
Birth:	6/26/78
SS:	334-44-4551

FIELDS

RECORD

number, birth date, and social security number. When the principal wants John Doe's phone number, she gets it from the telephone field. In an electronic database, the information is stored on a disk. Figure 6.3 shows seven individual student records in *AppleWorks*.

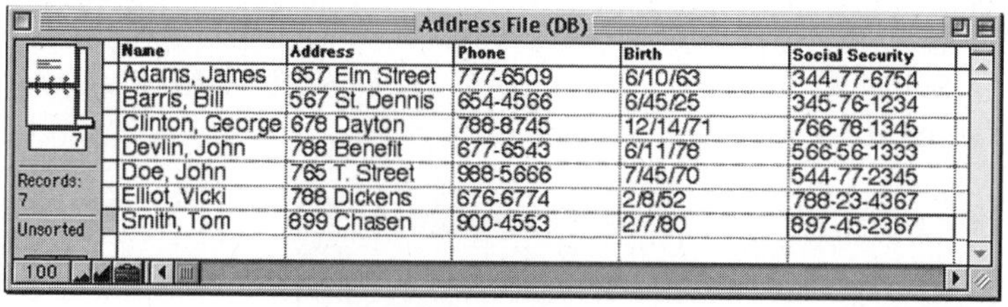

Address File (DB)				
Name	Address	Phone	Birth	Social Security
Adams, James	657 Elm Street	777-6509	6/10/63	344-77-6754
Barris, Bill	567 St. Dennis	654-4566	6/45/25	345-76-1234
Clinton, George	678 Dayton	788-8745	12/14/71	766-78-1345
Devlin, John	788 Benefit	677-6543	6/11/78	566-56-1333
Doe, John	765 T. Street	988-5666	7/45/70	544-77-2345
Elliot, Vicki	788 Dickens	676-6774	2/8/52	788-23-4367
Smith, Tom	899 Chasen	900-4553	2/7/80	897-45-2367

Records: 7
Unsorted
100

FIGURE 6.3
Sample Database

Advantages of an Electronic Database

The computerized database has many advantages over the file cabinet. Every database has a method of organization that lets a person retrieve information using some keyword. For example, Figure 6.3 has the address file arranged alphabetically. The problem with the nonelectronic listing of this information is it cannot be easily modified; after too many changes, the sheets of paper become unreadable and need retyping. This is not the case with an electronic database where the information is stored on disk. The computer database also minimizes data redundancy, that is, the same information being automatically available in different files. When a clerk searches through a file cabinet, he uses his fingers to locate key files, which can take a long time. The electronic database user can generate reports, retrieve files almost instantaneously, sort data in a variety of ways, edit, and print information with more flexibility and at faster speeds than the file clerk can. Furthermore, electronic files cannot easily be misplaced, and data can be shared easily among individuals. In addition, a user can execute a file search with incomplete information. With only the first half of a name and a brief description, for example, the police can search for a suspect. The only disadvantages to using a database are the time and effort expended in learning how to use it and the need to convert existing written files into the database format.

Computerized databases are used daily in government, occupational, and professional agencies. There are virtually thousands of repositories of information, such as Educational Resources Information Clearinghouse (ERIC), which students utilize for their research work. ERIC, the primary database for teachers, is the basic indexing and abstracting source for information about education. For example, a student searching for *problem solving* in *primary math* would input these keywords to locate abstracts on the recent research articles on this topic.

How a Database Operates

In this section, we'll use *FileMaker Pro* as an example of how an electronic database operates, but this discussion is not a substitute for *FileMaker Pro*'s documentation. Let's imagine that a teacher needs to keep track of the software she has accumulated haphazardly in a closet. The teacher wants to create a database to make order out of this chaos. This particular database has one file simply labeled *Software,* which represents the software collection. The teacher must first determine the number of fields for the record. She designs a record based on library referencing techniques that includes five fields: Title, Subject, Company, Copies, and Grade Level. In this example, the first field the teacher creates is *Title* (Fig. 6.4).

FIGURE 6.4
Selecting a Field
Courtesy of FileMaker, Inc.

After she designs the format, or template, the record is automatically saved. An example of her record is shown in Figure 6.5.

FIGURE 6.5
Sample Record
Courtesy of FileMaker, Inc.

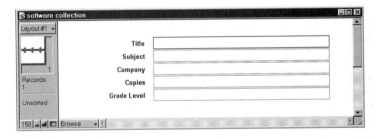

The next step is to enter the record data for each piece of software in the closet. A completed software file record is shown in Figure 6.6. The field *Title*

FIGURE 6.6
Software File Record
Courtesy of FileMaker, Inc.

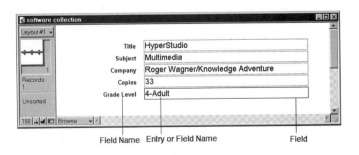

Field Name   Entry or Field Name   Field

has the entry *HyperStudio*, the field *Subject* has *Multimedia*, and the field *Company* has *Roger Wagner/Knowledge Adventure*. As the teacher enters the information, she has the option of adding or changing it. When one record is completed, she generates another. The teacher continues filling in records until she decides to stop or reaches the storage capacity of the particular database file program. When the task is finished, she has a database file that lists 10 records for the software file (Fig. 6.7).

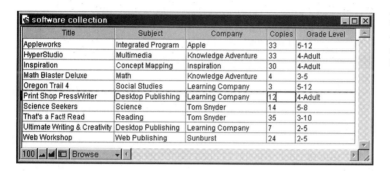

FIGURE 6.7
Records from Software File
Courtesy of FileMaker, Inc.

Functions of a Database

Now that the database is completed, the teacher can select or retrieve a file and sort the records.

Retrieving Information

One of the major tasks of any database is to retrieve information, which can be accomplished in a variety of ways:

1. Retrieve an entire file as shown by listing this file on the screen or printing it out.
2. Retrieve only a few field headings, such as *Title* and *Subject* (Fig. 6.8).

FIGURE 6.8 *Two Field Headings*
Courtesy of FileMaker, Inc.

university level; there are no shortcuts. This method can be inefficient and time-consuming when a user wants to access data from multiple groups and redefine part of the database. Second, the hierarchical database requires a complete restructuring each time the user adds a new field. On the positive side, once the data are set up, searching is fast and efficient because you don't have to search through all the records; you just search through specific groups.

The **network database** works the same as a hierarchical database except that a record can belong to more than one main group. This database is superior to the hierarchical database because it allows the user access to multiple data sets. Data can be accessed with speed and ease through different types of sources. However, networked databases still require every relationship to be predefined, and the addition of any new field requires a complete redefinition of the database.

Hierarchical and network databases enter data in a structured format. A **free-form,** or **encyclopedia, database** lets the user access data without specifying data type or data size. In this type of database, the user does not search for data in a field but instead uses a keyword or keywords. The software then searches all its text entries for matches. The advantage of an encyclopedia database is that a user who forgets the exact title of an article can find the article using a keyword search (Fig. 6.11).

**FIGURE 6.11
Grolier
Multimedia
Encyclopedia**

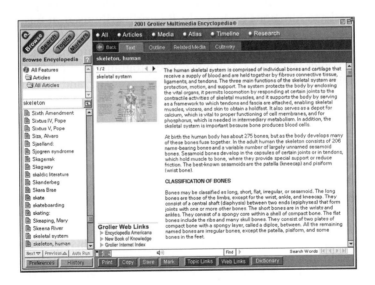

Many of the Internet search engines use keyword searches. The main application of the free-form database is the online encyclopedia. There is an example of this type of database in Chapter 8. The encyclopedia database maintains a large collection of information that is subject oriented. For example, an education database may group files according to different issues in education. You can then search by categories. Many times these databases are collections of data from other large free-form databases, giving you access to vast amounts of information. Typically these databases include such topics as news, microcomputer information, magazines articles, and medical information. *News* would let you access current news articles, newspapers, and information from news wire services. *Microcomputer information* would contain data from popular computing magazines. *Magazine articles* would let you access thousands of periodicals that focus on specialized areas such as medicine, education, and business. *Medical information* would give you access to medical journals.

Historically, *HyperCard,* a multimedia program, played an important role in changing the way databases are used in education. *HyperCard* was the first program to integrate data organization with graphics. Using *HyperCard,* the teacher and student can create individual cards or screens of data with both text and graphics. They can then link these cards to produce a stack, or group of cards. The *HyperCard* stack is equivalent to a database. In education, the ability to create cards, link these cards, and produce instructional data is a very potent tool. *HyperStudio* (Knowledge Adventure), along with other programs of this nature such as *mPower* (Tom Snyder Productions) and *Leonardo's Multimedia Toolbox* (NEC), are explored further in Chapter 14.

A **relational database** lets the user work with more than one file at a time and help with data redundancy. For example, a department chair might need several different files, such as test scores and transcript data on a particular student. If each of these files is a separate electronic file, he would have to duplicate information for each file to make it understandable. The relational database removes this problem by linking separate files or even entire databases through a common key field such as the student's social security number. The chair then can retrieve the data from any file by identifying the social security number of the student. In relational databases, changes made in one file are automatically reflected in the other files of the record. The product *dBase* (Borland International) is a classic example of this type of database. This database is very useful for the administration of elementary, high school, and college records. However, the majority of classroom teachers have little need for this type of data analysis.

Classroom teachers want a simple, straightforward way of entering their data, and the **flat-file database** fulfills this requirement. It works with only one data file at a time, and there is no linking to other data files. This database does not permit multiple access to data files or advanced questioning techniques. There is variation among flat-file databases, but generally they do not allow merging with other application programs.

In the past, the administrative office of a school district was the only place in the district that needed a database; the office is where student records, personnel files, and school resources were kept. Recently, however, classroom teachers are using computerized databases to keep track of students' progress and to store anecdotal comments on individual students. Furthermore, pupils are using prepared databases such as the *Compton's Interactive-World Atlas Classic* (The Learning Company), and the CD-ROM *New Millennium*

World Atlas Deluxe (Rand McNally) (Fig. 6.12). These databases provide users with a vast amount of geographic, historic, and demographic information. The *New Millennium World Atlas Deluxe* includes detailed three-dimensional maps and information on how geography has influenced important world events. A notebook feature organizes historic, scientific, cultural, and wildlife information into presentations and school reports. There is a powerful search tool, along with Internet links to thousands of sites and geographic articles covering most important events.

**FIGURE 6.12
New Millennium
World Atlas
Deluxe**

© Rand McNally. Printed with permission.

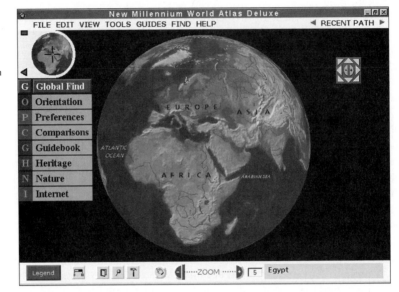

The database is the perfect tool for teaching higher level critical thinking skills, such as the ability to hypothesize, draw inferences, and use Boolean logic. Here's an example. Imagine that students in a class are instructed to search a hypothetical database for the names of students who took Dr. Gallio's computer class. After the students develop a strategy, they perform the search and find out who the students are. The teacher then asks them to hypothesize how many females received A's in the computer class. This time their strategy is more complex, as they are looking for names of people who meet two criteria: (1) students who are female and (2) students who received an A. Following this search, the students are asked to draw inferences about the results of the search and conduct further searches to see if there is any correlation among other items. Besides helping with higher level thinking, a database can help students learn content material in any of the curriculum areas. There are many databases on the Internet that cover specific academic areas. An excellent site from the federal government is *Digital Classroom* (http://www.nara.gov/education/classrm.html).

These databases have informational files on topics ranging from animals to countries. If students understand how to manipulate a database, they can gain deeper insight into any field of study; they can find patterns, draw relationships, or identify trends.

Today, students can use database files that they created themselves or files prepared by teachers or software houses. It is often more beneficial for students to enter their research into a design created by their teacher. The mastery of databases takes longer than the mastery of word processing because to learn databases, students need a good deal of hands-on experience and varied types of assignments.

The manuals supplied with databases include instructions on how to manipulate the data, student worksheets, and suggested activities. The database programs that exist for the middle grades should be used only on an elementary level, because schoolchildren cannot understand the logic behind database programs. They can, however, understand some essential concepts such as record, field, and search. It may be wise to save the complex searching for the junior high school students.

Integrating the Database into the Classroom

Teachers can use databases to help locate instructional material, to provide for students' needs, and to personalize letters. For example, a teacher may categorize books and resources in the classroom. The teacher then can easily search this database for instructional material to motivate the class. The teacher could create a database to store student information such as birthdays, reading levels, special medication, learning problems, students' favorite hobbies, who has authorization to pick up the student. Using the database, the teacher could retrieve information on birthdays to recognize a child's birthday with a special treat or banner. Furthermore, the teacher could use an address database to personalize letters to the parents.

Students can use databases for a multitude of classroom tasks. In language arts the students could use a database to write book reports. For data fields, the students could include title, author, type of book, setting, main character, and summary. After the books are catalogued, students could search for books that meet their interests. A synonyms database could help students write poetry. Other examples of language arts ideas are diaries, famous quotes, funny stories, legal terms, novelists, and parts of speech. Social studies is the perfect curriculum area to use databases. The students could create databases on countries, states, or famous people such as Albert Einstein, U.S. presidents, African American politicians, inventors and their inventions. There are all sorts of "Who am I?" games that can be executed in the classroom (see the lesson plan activities at the end of the chapter). In science there could be databases about animal groups, birds, insects, snakes, plant groups (flowers, vegetables, trees), and rocks and minerals. Furthermore, students could have databases about food groups, calories, nutrients, amphibians, animal behavior, chemical compounds, chemical elements, fish, gems, geological formations, planets, poisons, and antidotes. In the arts, students could have databases on artists, classical music, famous works of art, musical instruments, and popular music. Students could add pictures to any database to make it easier for the visual learner.

Classroom Projects Using a Database

1. Scheduling
2. Students' hobbies
3. Opinion survey
4. Planets, animal groups, rocks and minerals
5. Presidents of the United States
6. World events
7. Dictionary of spelling words

How to Choose a Database for the Classroom

There are many questions to ask when choosing a database program: How limited is the program in its ability to search? Can you easily add or change the data in the files? If there is a prepared database with the product, is the content proper for the students? Is the information accurate? What is the quality of the documentation? How easy is the program to use? Let us examine these factors more closely for the purpose of making a more informed decision.

The database packages on the market today have every imaginable feature, some more appropriate for classroom use than others. The more popular programs for the schools include *FileMaker Pro, Works 2000* (Windows only), *AppleWorks,* and *Microsoft Access.* Generally, these classroom-appropriate databases have fewer features and are easier to use than programs such as *dBase 2.* Choosing a database program for the classroom is a six-step process; consider the following: (1) hardware compatibility; (2) general features; (3) instructional design; (4) ease of use; (5) consumer value; and (6) support.

Hardware Compatibility

Check out the computer that your school is using. Is it an old Apple IIe, an IBM with a Pentium IV chip, or a Macintosh with a PowerPC chip? How much memory does it have: 64K, 128 MB, or more? (Some database programs need a huge amount of computer memory.) How large are their hard drives: 20 GB or 40 GB? What type of backup storage is available? What printers will work with this database program?

General Features

The most common functions provided by database programs are (1) sorting data; (2) changing or updating data; (3) searching for specific information; (4) deleting and adding information in the file; and (5) printing.

Sorting

In review, **sorting** is the ability to arrange the records in different ways. Programs should allow you to name the field type easily and to do the sort quickly. At the very least, the program should do the following: (1) an alphabetical sort from A to Z or Z to A, in any appropriate character field; (2) a numeric sort from lowest to highest and highest to lowest, in any numeric field. No matter what program you choose, you should be able to sort to the screen and the printer.

Changing and Updating

Every database can update and change a file. The questions that must be asked are the following: How difficult is it to accomplish this task? Is it easy to find the record and change it? How hard is it to add a record to the file, and is it a drawn-out procedure?

Searching or Retrieving

Database programs vary in the type of search criteria used to find forms in a file. For instance, there may be exact matches, partial matches, numeric matches, and numeric range matches. In an exact match, the program looks for the forms that exactly match the search criteria. An exact match for Florence Singer is Florence Singer or FLORENCE SINGER; however, Mrs. Florence Singer; Singer, Florence; and FlorenceSinger are not matches.

All database programs have exact matches, and many database programs have partial matches. You would use a partial match when you are unsure of how the information was entered into the database or when you are interested in locating different records with the same information. For instance, you might be able to find Florence Singer's file by just typing in Florence or Singer. You would use a partial match to find the records of students who have computer experience.

The more advanced the database, the more exotic the features. *Professional File* (Software Publishing Corporation), an advanced program for Windows, does quite a few numeric searches. This program lets you look for items less than, greater than, or equal to a given number. If you want to find the records for all children who were born later than 1982, you would enter Year: >1982. This program also has a numeric range match feature that allows you to search for numbers within a certain range. For instance, you might search for dates with the range of 1988 to 2002.

The database program should let you search using multiple criteria as well. For instance, you might want to search for the students eligible to take your advanced computer course. You would use two criteria: (1) students who are in 11th grade and (2) students who have computer experience. At the end of your search, the computer would generate the names of students who fit these qualifications.

Searching a file in some database programs can change the file if you're not careful. Because of this problem, it is desirable to choose a program in which the search feature is separate from the add feature. The ideal program has a way to lock files so they will not be accidentally erased.

Deleting and Adding

The database program should allow you to add information to or delete it from a record or field with minimum trouble. When you add a new field to one record, you want the new field to be added to all the records.

Printing

Your program should allow you to print a neat report. The instructions for this task should be easy to follow, and the printout should show the data fields that you want in the report.

Advanced Features

Some programs let you design the way the data will be displayed, and others perform mathematical calculations on the data. These programs do not perform the complex functions of a spreadsheet, but they let you total simple columns of numbers or compute student averages. Most database programs show the final list or report on the screen before it is printed. *FileMaker Pro, AppleWorks, Works 2000* (Windows only), *FoxPro* (Microsoft), and *Microsoft Access* let you select fields for different records and display them on the screen all at once. Some programs let you publish their database on the Web, and other programs let you store a picture with each record. The advanced student can merge data from a database document with a word processing document to produce a customized letter or report. With the **mail merge** function, you can send out form letters to parents or students, each letter with a different name, address, and grade. The mail merge function automatically places the name, address, and grade from the database into the word processing document's form letter. To produce a mail merge document, you start by writing a basic form letter, the general text you want to send each person on your mailing list. In this letter you do not include the names, address, or grades because these items will be inserted automatically from a mailing list. In their place you insert placeholders, or merge fields, that tell your word processor where to put the names, addresses, and grades. Next, you click on a mail merge tool. You select the list you want to merge and the word processor prints one personalized letter for each record received from your mailing list.

Instructional Design

A database program should require minimum learning time. The program that has a menu bar displayed at the top of the screen is ideal for beginners because users do not have to memorize the different functions. *AppleWork*'s database is very popular because of its design and its collection of templates (Fig. 6.13) that help you use the product quickly. The templates can be easily modified to suit your own needs. Just add or modify fields, layouts, or text when necessary.

The key to the success of database programs is their flexibility of design. How easy is it to make changes, and how easy is it to add a field or add information to a field in the database program? When you do, do you lose the information that already exists in the field? Does the database program make you start again when you want to make changes? What is the search speed of the program? What flexibility is there in printing a report? Can you be selective in printing certain columns or are you forced to print all the items as shown on the screen? What is the size limit of the database? *Professional File* theoretically can have 100 fields on a page and a file size of 8 MB. Is there a size limitation for the information in each field? *Professional File* allows 4,000 characters per page or field, while *AppleWorks* allows a total of 63 characters, including the field name. Database programs vary in the kinds of searches they are capable of accomplishing—what type of searches do you require? Can you conduct Boolean searches? Does the searching technique fit the skills you are emphasizing in the classroom?

Ease of Use

A major concern when buying a database program is how easy the program is to learn. Its features are immaterial if it is difficult to comprehend. Ask the following questions: Can you learn in a reasonable amount of time to use this program? Is there a tutorial disk that takes the user through the program? (*AppleWorks* uses simple English commands and has online help to teach you the program step by step.) Are there help screens that tell the user what to do each step of the way? Can you access these help screens whenever you need them? Are there menu bars across the screens so users do not have to memorize the different functions? Is the printer set up easily, and can you be ready to print immediately? Are there too many help prompts and safety questions?

Consumer Value

Because software is expensive, cost is a major consideration. Since public domain software costs very little, it is a natural alternative to commercial software. For example, there is free software available in California through the

California State Department of Education. Commercial software is more expensive, but there are many programs worth the cost. Many software companies let you use one disk to load the software on all your computers. Other companies offer an inexpensive on-site license that enables you to make as many copies as you need. Some companies have lab packs that let you purchase a large quantity of software at a reduced price.

Support

Ask these questions: Can you call someone on the telephone at the software company and get immediate help, or must you wade through a series of messages and wait an unbearable amount of time? (As mentioned previously, many houses will tell you how many customers are in line before you and how long you must wait.) Is the technical support available toll-free? (Many companies are charging a fee for technical support.) Does the software package have tutorial lessons to help the beginner learn the program? Is the manual readable and does it have an index? Does the program have templates or computer-based files? Do the software producers have data files for various content areas?

Before selecting the software, decide which features are important for your particular class. **Refer now to Appendix A for an annotated bibliography of highly rated database programs for the classroom.** Next, examine one of these programs using the sample checklist and evaluation rating instrument on page 141.

Teacher Practice Activities

The following exercises are meant to be used in conjunction with any database. If a computer lab is not available, just follow this section to get an idea of what kinds of activities can be used in the classroom. The first exercise is a step-by-step introduction to a database program.

Database 1

1. Open your database program.
2. From the main menu, select the option that creates a file and gives the file a name, such as Class.
3. Type in the following field names: Teacher, Students, Room, Grade, and Sex. Correct any mistakes made.
4. Using the add-a-record function, type the following information for each record:

TEACHER	STUDENTS	ROOM	GRADE	SEX
Smith	23	21	K	Male
Adams	16	14	4	Female
Gramacy	17	25	3	Female
Witham	33	29	1	Female
Youngblood	21	24	K	Male

DATABASE CHECKLIST

Directions: Examine the following items and determine which ones you feel are important for your class situation. Evaluate your database and place an X on each line where the software meets your needs.

Product Name _____ **Manufacturer** _____ **Appropriate Grade Level** _____

A. Hardware

___ 1. Memory needed
___ 2. Computer compatibility
___ 3. Printer compatibility
___ 4. Hard drive capacity

B. Features

___ 1. Selection of field types
___ 2. Sort
___   a. Alphabetic
___   b. Numeric
___   c. Chronological
___   d. Reverse order
___   e. To screen and printer
___ 3. Deleting and adding fields
___ 4. Search
___   a. Alphabetic
___   b. Numeric
___   c. And–or
___   d. Using multiple criteria
___ 5. Mathematical calculation of data
___ 6. Mail merge
___ 7. Display
___   a. Printout screen or printer
___   b. Can display selected fields
___ 8. Copy and paste
___ 9. Capacity to generate reports
___ 10. Publishing your database on the Web

C. Design

___ 1. Speed of search
___ 2. Ease of changing fields

___ 3. Ease of adding new fields
___ 4. Size requirements
___   a. Field size
___   b. Characters per field
___   c. Number of records in a file

D. Ease of Use

___ 1. Help screens
___ 2. Tutorial disk
___ 3. Easy printer setup
___ 4. Automatic save
___ 5. Warning questions

E. Consumer Value

___ 1. Cost
___ 2. Lab packs or on-site licensing

F. Support

___ 1. Technical
___ 2. Tutorial material
___ 3. Lab packs
___ 4. Templates
___ 5. Prepared software
___ 6. Readable manual
___   a. Activities
___   b. Lesson plans
___   c. Tutorial
___   d. Index

Rating Scale

Rate the database program by placing a check in the appropriate box.

Excellent _____ Very Good _____ Good _____ Fair _____ Poor _____

Comments

5. Add another record to the list: Teacher, Sharp; Students, 20; Room, 12; Grade, 3; and Sex, Female.
6. Change (a) the name Smith to Small and his room number 21 to 24 and (b) the name Adams to Allen and the number of students she has from 16 to 28.
7. Next, delete the Gramacy record.
8. Alphabetize the list of records A to Z in the teacher's name field. The list should now look like this:

TEACHER	STUDENTS	ROOM	GRADE	SEX
Allen	28	14	4	Female
Sharp	20	12	3	Female
Small	23	24	K	Male
Witham	33	29	1	Female
Youngblood	21	24	K	Male

9. Print out the results.
10. Next, numerically sort the field Grade from highest to lowest:

TEACHER	GRADE
Allen	4
Sharp	3
Witham	1
Small	K
Youngblood	K

11. Search for the following records:
    a. Youngblood (type the name Youngblood in the Teacher field);
    b. Allen; and
    c. the kindergarten records (type K in the field Grade).
       The program should find Small and Youngblood. The database shows the records that match the specifications you type. If there is no record, the program usually displays a 0. You also get a 0 if you spell the record name differently from the way it was spelled in the original entry in the database.
12. Search for records using two criteria: (a) teachers who are male, and (b) teachers who have exactly 21 students. Type 21 for the Students field and male for the Sex field. For this search, there is only one record: Youngblood.
13. Let's find the male kindergarten teachers' records. Type K for the grade and male for the sex. In this case, there are two teachers that fit these criteria: Small and Youngblood.

14. If the database program has a greater than (>) or less than (<) feature, find the following records:
    a. all the teachers who have a class size greater than 20;
    b. the male teachers who have 23 or more students; and
    c. the female teachers who have 18 or more students.

Database 2

For practice, create another database. Type in the following field names: Student, Sex, Hair Color, and Birth Date.

1. Using the add function, type the following information for each record:

Student Data Sheet

Pupil: Smith, Joan	Hair Color: Brown
Sex: Female	Birth Date: 1975
Pupil: Lorenzo, Max	Hair Color: Black
Sex: Male	Birth Date: 1977
Pupil: Chen, Mark	Hair Color: Black
Sex: Male	Birth Date: 1978
Pupil: Sharp, David	Hair Color: Brown
Sex: Male	Birth Date: 1977
Pupil: Schainker, Nancy	Hair Color: Red
Sex: Female	Birth Date: 1976
Pupil: Edwards, Bobbie	Hair Color: Blond
Sex: Female	Birth Date: 1979
Pupil: Lopez, Mary	Hair Color: Black
Sex: Female	Birth Date: 1980
Pupil: Jefferson, LeMar	Hair Color: Black
Sex: Male	Birth Date: 1979
Pupil: Jung, Nicky	Hair Color: Red
Sex: Female	Birth Date: 1979

2. Change the field name Pupil to Student.
3. Next, change David Sharp's birth date to 1950, Nicky Jung's description to a male with black hair, and Bobbie Edwards's hair color to red.
4. Add the following file: Student, Lee, Bessie; Hair Color, Brown; Sex, Female; Birth Date, 1980.
5. Alphabetize the list A to Z in the Student field and print out the list.
6. Find the following files:
    a. David Sharp;
    b. all students who are female;
    c. students who have red hair;
    d. students born after 1950;
    e. students born before 1977; and
    f. all students who are female and have red hair.

Classroom Lesson Plans

▼ I. General Database ▼

Materials

You will need the personal data sheet, a database program (*FileMaker Pro, AppleWorks, Works 2000*, etc.), and one computer or more.

Objective

Students will use the Boolean operators *and* and *or*.

Procedure

1. Discuss the use of *and* and *or* to connect two fields.
2. Have the students write personal data sheets about themselves using Figure 6.14 as a model.

FIGURE 6.14
Personal Data Sheet

```
PERSONAL DATA SHEET


1. YOUR LAST NAME

2. YOUR FIRST NAME

3. YOUR BIRTH MONTH

4. NUMBER OF BROTHERS

5. NUMBER OF SISTERS

6. FAVORITE SPORT

7. NUMBER OF PETS
```

3. Collect the data sheets from the students.
4. Enter the data into the computer database.
5. Have the students do the following tasks:
    a. Find every student whose first name starts with A or C.
    b. Sort the sheets by birth month.
    c. Print a list of students who have two pets and whose last names begin with S.
    d. Print out the names of students whose birth month is August and who have one brother.
    e. Find out which students have two brothers.
    f. Find out who has the most sisters.
    g. Find out how many students have one brother and one sister.
    h. Sort by the Last Name field.
    i. Find out how many people were born in April.
    j. Find out whose favorite sport is baseball.

▼ II. Science Database ▼

Materials

You will need the dinosaur database form, a database program (*FileMaker Pro, AppleWorks, Works 2000,* etc.), and one computer or more.

Objectives

Students will create a dinosaur database, learn about dinosaurs, sort alphabetically, practice using Boolean operators, and sort by number.

Procedure

1. Have each student read about a dinosaur.
2. After the reading assignment is completed, have each student fill out the dinosaur database form (Fig. 6.15).

DINOSAUR DATABASE FORM

NAME	HABITAT	FOOD	FEET	ARMORED

FIGURE 6.15
Dinosaur Database Form

3. Instruct each student to enter his or her information on the same data file disk.
4. Following are sample data for this database:

Dinosaur Database

NAME	HABITAT	FOOD	FEET	ARMORED
Ankylosaurus	Land	Plants	4	Yes
Tryannosaurus	Land	Meat	2	No
Brachiosaurus	Water-Swamp	Plants	4	No
Brontosaurus	Water-Swamp	Plants	4	No
Corythosaurs	Water-Swamp	Plants	2	No
Diplodocus	Water-Swamp	Plants	4	No
Iguanodon	Land	Plants	2	No
Proceratops	Land	Plants	4	Yes
Stegosaurus	Land	Plants	4	Yes
Coelophysis	Land	Meat	2	No

5. After this task has been completed, have the students do the following:
    a. Sort the file by the number of feet in the field, highest to lowest.
    b. Using the Boolean operator *and,* find out if there are any two-legged plant eaters and any four-legged meat eaters.
    c. Sort alphabetically by name and print out the list.

Additional Suggestions

Have students add fields such as weight, height, and nickname and sort the fields by (1) length (lowest to highest); (2) weight; and (3) characteristics.

▼   III. Language Arts Database   ▼

Materials

You will need a book report form, a database program (*FileMaker Pro, Apple-Works, Works 2000,* etc.), and one computer or more.

Objectives

Students will create a database book report file, learn to sort alphabetically, and read a book.

Procedure

1. Have each student read a book.
2. After the reading assignment is finished, have each student complete the book report form (Fig. 6.16).

FIGURE 6.16
Book Report Form

```
                BOOK REPORT FORM

STUDENT'S NAME_____
1. AUTHOR:
2. TITLE:
3. TYPE OF BOOK:
4. SETTING:
5. MAIN CHARACTER OF THE STORY:
6. SUMMARY OF THE STORY:


```

3. Instruct students to input their information under each field name on the same data file disk. This activity requires a database program that has a comment field. If the database program does not have this feature, eliminate this field name.

4. After this task has been completed, have the students do the following:
    a. Search for books they might like to read, using the search function.
    b. Print out a list of all the books in the database.
    c. Sort the database alphabetically by title and print out the list.
    d. Sort the database file alphabetically by author and print out the list.
    e. Find out how many students read baseball stories or biographies by using the find function of the database program.

▼ IV. Geographical Database ▼

Materials

You will need the state geographical sheet, a database program (*FileMaker Pro, AppleWorks, Works 2000,* etc.), and one computer or more.

Objectives

Students will create a geographical data file for each state, learn geographical information about each state, sort alphabetically, and search using the Boolean operators *and* and *or.*

Procedure

1. Have each student in the class choose a state to research.
2. Have the students use reference books to complete the state geographical sheet (Fig. 6.17).

STATE GEOGRAPHICAL SHEET	
FIELD NAME	DATA
1. LOCATION (Midwest, Northeast, etc.)	
2. SIZE (Square Miles)	
3. NATURAL RESOURCES	
4. CLIMATE	
5. TERRAIN (Desert, Mountains, etc.)	

FIGURE 6.17
State Geographical Sheet

3. Have the students enter the proper information under each field name on the data file disk.
4. After this task has been completed, have the student independently use the search function to answer *Who am I?* questions (Fig. 6.18).

WHO AM I?
1. I am a small state
2. I am known for my mountains.
3. I have red clover flowers.

FIGURE 6.18
Who Am I? Questions

▼   V. Math Database   ▼

Materials

You will need the state data sheet, a database program (*FileMaker Pro, Apple-Works, Works 2000,* etc.), and one computer or more.

Objectives

Students will create a state data file, learn statistical information about the United States, sort alphabetically, and search using the Boolean operators *and* and *or.*

Procedure

1. Have each student in the class choose a state to research.
2. Have the students use encyclopedias to complete the state data sheet (Fig. 6.19).

FIGURE 6.19
State Data Sheet

STATE DATA SHEET	
FIELD NAME	DATA
1. CAPITAL	
2. POPULATION	
3. NUMBER OF REPRESENTATIVES IN CONGRESS	
4. YEAR OF STATEHOOD	

3. Tell students to complete the proper information under each field name on the same data file disk.
4. After this task has been completed, have the students independently use the search function to carry out the following tasks:
   a. Search for the states that have populations over 2 million.
   b. Find the last state that was added to the United States.
   c. Sort the records according to population from lowest to highest.
   d. Sort the records alphabetically by the name of the state and print out a list.
   e. Sort the states by population and print out a list.
5. Next, divide the class into two teams and collect each team's state data sheets.
6. Read aloud one of the state data sheets without revealing the name of the state.
7. Ask Team One to try to figure out what state the data sheet describes.
8. Ask Team Two to check Team One's answer by using the computer. If Team One has answered correctly, it scores a point.
9. Read another data sheet.
10. Ask Team Two to try to identify the state and Team One to check Team Two's answer. The first team to reach 10 points wins.

▼ VI. Music ▼

Materials

You will need a database program (*FileMaker Pro, AppleWorks, Works 2000,* etc.) and one computer or more.

Objectives

Students will learn how to create a database by cataloging their own music CD collection or the school's CD collection. After they create their database, they will find information using certain criteria.

Procedure

1. Have the class decide which fields they are going to use to create their database. For example, they could use artist, title, description, style of music.
2. Have the students create their own database using their CD collection at home or school.
3. After the databases are created, have the students do the following:
   a. Find their favorite performer.
   b. Find the CDs that are rock and roll.
   c. Find female vocalist only.
   d. Find male vocalist only.
4. Next, have each student share his or her database with another member of the class.

Summary

The database is an effective manager of information and a powerful tool for learning in the classroom. With a database, students can look for relationships among data, test hypotheses, and draw conclusions. This chapter discussed the merits of an electronic database and its basic features. We examined a database checklist evaluation form and learned how to introduce the database to the class. Classroom activities presented covered a range of curriculum areas. **Be sure to review the annotated list of award-winning database software in Appendix A.**

What follows is an annotated list of top-rated Internet database sites. These sites include information about databases, tutorials, tips, and discussion forums.

 DATABASE SITES

What is?com
http://whatis.techtarget.com/
This site includes thousands of explanations of computer and software terms including relational and object-oriented databases.

About.com's Database for Beginners
http://databases.about.com/
Database for Beginners provides *Access* and *FileMaker Pro* tutorials and explains how the contents of organized data can easily be accessed, managed, and updated.

Access All Areas (A3)
http://athree.com/
Access All Areas provides help for Microsoft Access users. The site includes basic database information, reviews, and discussion forums.

FileMaker Today
http://www.filemakertoday.com/
This popular *FileMaker Pro* users site offers free *FileMaker Pro* training, templates, plug-ins, and the latest news from the FileMaker community. It also features the FileMaker Cafe, a *FileMaker Pro* question-and-answer forum.

Introducing AppleWorks 6
http://www.apple.com/appleworks/
This site offers information on the latest version of *AppleWorks*, which offers word processing, spreadsheet, database, presentation, and drawing and painting capabilities.

Tammy's Technology Tips for Teachers
http://www.essdack.org/tips/
This site shows how to use a database and other computer tools for making classroom management tasks easier.

Digital Classroom
http://www.nara.gov/education/classrm.html
The federal government's National Archives and Records Administration (NARA) offers a searchable database of historical documents useful for social studies teaching.

Filemaker Pro
http://www.claris.com/products/
http://www.claris.com/demos/fm_demo_1a.html
This site offers information about *Filemaker Pro 5*, which can used with *Microsoft Office* for Windows and Macintosh. It includes QuickTime videos showing how the program organizes your data.

Activity Search
http://www.eduplace.com/search/activity.html
The Education Place Activity Search, sponsored by Houghton Mifflin, is a searchable database of over 500 original K–8 classroom activities and lesson plans for teachers in all subject areas.

Chapter Mastery Test

To the Instructor: Refer to the Instructor's Manual for the Answers to the Mastery Questions. This manual has additional questions and resource materials.

Let's check for chapter comprehension with a short mastery test. Basic terms, classroom projects, and suggested readings and references follow.

1. What is a database and how can it be used in the classroom?
2. Define the following: file, record, and field.
3. Name and describe two ways of sorting data.
4. What differentiates a file cabinet from a database?
5. Discuss the advantages of using a computerized database.
6. Discuss the factors involved in selecting a database for a school district.
7. Name and describe three ways of searching for a file.
8. When should a student use a wildcard search?
9. Explain three methods of organizing data within a database.
10. What is a relational database?
11. Name two common functions of a database.
12. What is a free-form database?

Basic Terms

Boolean operators (p. 130)
database (p. 126)
database management system (p. 126)
data strings (p. 130)
encyclopedia database (p. 132)
field (p. 126)
file (p. 126)
flat-file database (p. 133)

free-form database (p. 132)
hierarchical database (p. 131)
mail merge (p. 138)
network database (p. 132)
record (p. 126)
relational database (p. 133)
sorting (p. 136)
wildcard search (p. 130)

Classroom Projects

1. Create a database file on famous composers.
2. Examine three database programs and compare their different features.
3. Choose a grade level and create a database activity for it.

Suggested Readings and References

Adams, Sharon, and Mary Burns. Connecting Student Learning & Technology. 1999.

Anders, Vicki, and Kathy M. Jackson. "Onliners. CD-ROM—The Impact of CD-ROM Databases upon a Large Online Searching Program." *Online* 12, no. 6 (November 1, 1988): 24.

Antonoff, Michael. "Using a Spreadsheet as a Database." *Personal Computing*, 1986, pp. 65–71.

Bachor, D. G. "Toward Improving Assessment of Students with Special Needs: Expanding the Database to Include Classroom Performance." *Alberta Journal of Educational Research* 36, no. 1 (March 1, 1990): 65.

Barbour, A. "A Cemetery Database Makes Math Come Alive." *Electronic Learning,* February 1988, pp. 12–13.

Bensu, Janet. "Use Your Database in New Ways." *HR Magazine* 35, no. 3 (March 1, 1990): 33.

Bernard, Deborah F., and Yolanda Hollingsworth. "Teaching Web-Based Full-Text Databases." *Reference & User Services Quarterly* 39, no. 1 (Fall 1999): 63.

Bock, Douglas B. "Solving Crime with Database Technology." *Journal of Systems Management* 39, no. 10 (October 1, 1988): 16.

Braun, Ellen. "Word Processing: Desktop Publishing Share Features." *The Office* 117, no. 5 (May 1, 1993): 9.

Braun, Joseph A., Jr. "Ten Ways to Integrate Technology into Middle School Social Studies." *Clearing House* 72, no. 6 (July 1999): 345–51.

Byers, John A. "Source. Database Program to Manage Slides and Images for Teaching and Presentations." *Educational Media International* 36, no. 1 (March 1999): 77–80.

Caughlin, Janet. *Claris Workshop for Students Secondary 7–12.* Eugene, Ore.: Visions, 1997.

Caughlin, Janet. *Claris Workshop for Teachers.* Eugene, Ore.: Visions, 1995.

Coe, Michael. "Keeping Up with Technology." *Computing Teacher* 18, no. 5 (February 1991): 14–15.

Coulson, C. J. "Creation of Inhouse Database." *Transactions* 17, no. 5 (October 1, 1989): 838.

Davey, Claire, and Adrian S. Jarvis. "Microcomputers for Microhistory: A Database Approach to the Reconstitution of Small English Populations." *History & Computing* 2, no. 3 (1990): 187.

Dunfey, J. "Using a Database in an English Classroom." *Computing Teacher* 12, no. 8 (1984): 26–27.

"Electronic Databases." *Media & Methods* 36, no. 4 (March/April 2000): 39.

Ennis, Demetria. "Interdisciplinary Database Activities for Fifth Graders at Tomas Rivera." *Journal of Computing in Childhood Education* 8, no. 1 (1997): 83–88.

Epler, D. M. *Online Searching Goes to School.* Phoenix, Ariz.: Oryx Press, 1989.

Fagan, Patsy J., and Ann D. Thompson. "Using a Database to Aid in Learning the Meanings and Purposes of Math Notations and Symbols." *Journal of Computers in Mathematics and Science* 8, no. 4 (Summer 1989): 26.

Ferraro, Joan M. "Teacher Education Reform: An ERIC Bibliography." *Journal of Teacher Education* 50, no. 4 (September/October 1999): 315.

Flynn, Marilyn L. "Using Computer-Assisted Instruction to Increase Organizational Effectiveness." *Administration in Social Work* 14, no. 1 (Winter 1990): 103.

Geoff, Duncan. "FileMaker Pro 5.0." *Macworld,* February 2000, p. 40.

Hannah, L. "The Database: Getting to Know You." *Computing Teacher,* June 1987, pp. 16–23.

Hodson, Yvonne D., and David Leibelshon. "Creating Databases with Students." *School Library Journal* 32 (May 1986): 12–15.

Hunter, Beverly. "Problem Solving with Databases." *Computing Teacher* 12 (1985): 20–27.

Kearsley, G., B. Hunter, and M. Furlong. *We Teach with Technology.* Wilsonville, Ore.: Franklin, Beedle, & Associates, 1992.

LaBare, Kelly M., and R. Lawrence Klotz. "Using Online Databases to Teach Ecological Concepts." *American Biology Teacher* 62, no. 2 (February 2000): 124–28.

Lathrop, Ann. "Online and CD-ROM Databases in School Libraries: Readings." *Libraries Unlimited,* Database Searching Series no. 2 (1989): 361–66.

Levetan, Janice. "Apples and Oranges and Lemons?" *Online Elementary Periodical Indices Library Talk* 12, no. 4 (September/October 1999): 38.

McIntyre, D. R., Hao-Che, Pu, and Francis G. Wolff. "Use of Software Tools in Teaching Relational Database Design." *Computers & Education* 24, no. 4 (1995): 279.

Mendelson, Edward. "The Complete Home Suite." *PC Magazine* 18, no. 21 (December 1, 1999): 66.

Mittlefehlt, Bill. "Social Studies: Problem Solving with Databases." *Computing Teacher* 18, no. 5 (February 1991): 54–55.

Mohan, C., and H. Pirahesh. "Parallelism in Relational Database Management Systems." *IBM Systems Journal* 33, no. 2 (1994): 2.

Naisbitt, J. *Megatrends.* New York: Warner, 1982.

O'Leary, Mick. "Online Comes of Age." *Online* 21, no. 1 (January–February 1997): 10–14, 16–20.

Peck, Jacqueline K., and Sharon V. Hughes. "So Much Success from a First-Grade Database Project!" *Computers in the Schools* 13, no. 1–2 (1997): 109–16.

Rae, John. "Getting to Grips with Database Design: A Step-by-Step Approach." *Computers & Education* 14, no. 6 (1990): 281.

Robinette, Michelle. "Top 10 Uses for ClarisWorks in the One-Computer Classroom." *Learning and Leading with Technology* 24, no. 2 (October 1996): 37–40.

Scharberg, Maureen A., and Oran E. Cox. "Creating and Using a Consumer Chemical Molecular Graphics Database: The 'Molecule of the Day.'" *Journal of Chemical Education* 74, no. 7 (July 1997): 869.

Sloane, Pam. "Presentation Software." *Technology & Learning* 20, no. 9 (April 2000): 54.

Smith, Nancy H. G. "Teaching Teachers to Search Electronically." *Book Report* 11, no. 3 (November/December 1992): 23.

Wakerfield, A. P. "Creating and Using a Database of Children's Literature." *Reading Teacher* 48, no. 4 (December/January 1994–95): 366–67.

Watson, J. *Teaching Thinking Skills with Databases.* Eugene, Ore.: International Society for Technology in Education, 1991.

Weib, J. H. "Teaching Mathematics with Technology: Data Base Programs in Mathematics Classroom." *Arithmetic Teacher* 37, no. 5 (January 1990): 38–40.

Yu, Clement, and Weiyi Meng. "Confronting Database Complexities." *IEEE Software* 11, no. 3 (May 1, 1994): 6.

CHAPTER 7

Spreadsheets

Integrating Spreadsheets into the Classroom

Did you know that an electronic spreadsheet is faster and more flexible than the traditional methods of numerical calculation and data prediction? The teacher can use a spreadsheet as a gradebook or for classroom budgets, attendance charts, surveys, and checklists. Students can use a spreadsheet to create timelines, gameboards, or graphs and to keep track of classroom experiments. This chapter will discuss how to select a spreadsheet program for the classroom and the general features of a spreadsheet program. You will see a checklist designed to help you choose the right spreadsheet software. Furthermore, you will be given exercises that help you integrate the spreadsheet into the classroom. Finally, you will become familiar with Internet sites that include tutorials, software tips, lesson plans, and discussion forums.

Objectives

Upon completing this chapter, you will be able to:
1. Define spreadsheet, integrated software, cell, windowing, macro, mail merge, and logical functions;
2. Describe the basic features and functions of spreadsheets and integrated programs;
3. Discuss ways of integrating the spreadsheet in the classroom;
4. Evaluate different spreadsheet software based on standard criteria;
5. Utilize and create a repertoire of spreadsheet activities for the classroom; and
6. Explore Internet sites that include spreadsheet information, tutorials, tips, and discussion forums.

Historical Overview

In this chapter, we examine the spreadsheet, one of the earliest applications of the microcomputer. We start with a short historical discussion and then explore what a spreadsheet is and how it operates. In the early 1970s, the microcomputer was used primarily by hackers and hobbyists. This all changed when Dan Bricklin, a Harvard student, and Robert Frankston, an MIT student, combined efforts to create the first spreadsheet, *VisiCalc*, introduced in 1979. *VisiCalc*, primarily designed for microcomputers, had a small grid size and limited features. Because the Apple Computer was the only computer that could run *VisiCalc*, it became the first computer to be accepted by business users. *VisiCalc* served as a prototype for many other programs, such as *Logic-Calc* and *Plannercalc,* designed for microcomputers. Within a decade, the spreadsheets improved vastly, offering more features (such as the ability to create graphic displays), faster execution speeds, and a larger grid size.

In 1982, *Lotus 1-2-3* (Lotus Development) initiated a new generation and became the leading spreadsheet. It was the first integrated spreadsheet, meaning that it combined several different programs so that information could be presented in different formats. Later versions of spreadsheets had extended capabilities: a communication component, expanded spreadsheet size, and word processing. The word processor feature let the user easily explain the figures presented in the spreadsheet, while the communication component let computers communicate with each other over telephone lines.

Spreadsheets

Every year people across the United States prepare their income tax forms. College students request government loans and families determine their budgets based on their income in order to predict their annual expenses. The businessperson keeps a record of transactions to determine profits and liabilities, while the scientist performs mathematical calculations on experimental data. A teacher enters pupils' test scores and assignments, performs calculations, and makes inferences about the numerical data. To accomplish their various tasks, these people use worksheets or electronic spreadsheets. A **spreadsheet** is "a graphical representation of an accountant's worksheet, replete with rows and columns for recording labels (headings and subheadings) and values" (Pfaffenberger, 2000).

Components of a Spreadsheet

Every electronic spreadsheet is organized in a similar manner with two axes: rows and columns. Figure 7.1 shows *Microsoft Excel's* blank spreadsheet

FIGURE 7.1
Spreadsheet from **Microsoft Excel 2000** *(Windows Version)*

Box shot reprinted with permission from Microsoft Corporation.

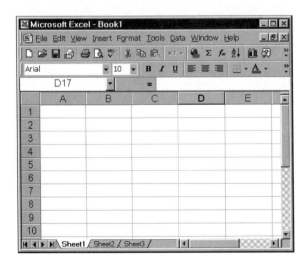

(Windows version). The letters across the top are used to identify the columns, and the numbers along the side identify the rows.[1] The intersection of each row and column forms a box, called a **cell.** A cell is identified by its column letter and row number. For example, in Figure 7.2, cell A1 is in the top left corner, and cell B1 is one cell to the right. To locate cell D4, you would count over to column D and then count down four cells to row 4. You would select cell D4 by clicking the cursor in its box. When selected, a cell shows a heavy border and its name appears in the indicator box above the A label.

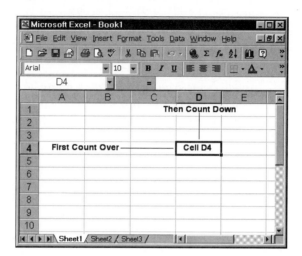

FIGURE 7.2
Spreadsheet Cells
Box shot reprinted with permission from Microsoft Corporation.

Three types of information can be entered into any single cell: number, text, or formula. The ability to enter formulas onto the spreadsheet makes it a powerful tool for business, science, and education.

How a Spreadsheet Operates

This section will explain how an electronic spreadsheet operates. For illustrative purposes, let's use *Microsoft Excel 2000* (Windows version) and a gradebook example, a popular educational use of the spreadsheet.

To use a *manual* spreadsheet for grade records, you would enter the students' names and their quiz scores. Let's say there are eight students and three quiz scores (Fig. 7.3). Next, using paper, pencil, and a calculator, you would add Richard Apple's scores, obtaining a total of 282. You would record the answer in the total column and then divide this total by 3 for an average of 94. You would continue this manual procedure for each subsequent student. If you made an error or changed a score, you would have to recalculate everything.

---

[1]Spreadsheets can differ in the system used to label rows and columns.

FIGURE 7.3
*Teacher's Grade
Roster*

Name	Quiz 1	Quiz 2	Quiz 3	Total	Average
1. Apple, Richard	99	97	86	282	94
2. Berger, Karen	85	82	76	243	81
3. Collins, Nancy	78	65	67	210	70
4. Diaz, Robert	88	85	79	252	84
5. Frank, Scott	98	88	81	267	89
6. O'Brien, Jeff	99	96	78	273	91
7. Sharp, David	99	94	95	288	96
8. Winters, Philip	88	87	83	258	86

An *electronic* spreadsheet offers many advantages over a manual one. Let's open *Microsoft Excel.* You see a blank spreadsheet (Fig. 7.1). You enter the same headings—Name, Quiz 1, Quiz 2, Quiz 3, and Average.[2] Then you type the eight pupils' names, last name first, and their respective quiz scores. While entering this information, you can easily make changes, corrections, deletions, or additions. You also can use the sort function to alphabetize the list of students by last name. When you're finished, your screen resembles the one in Figure 7.4.

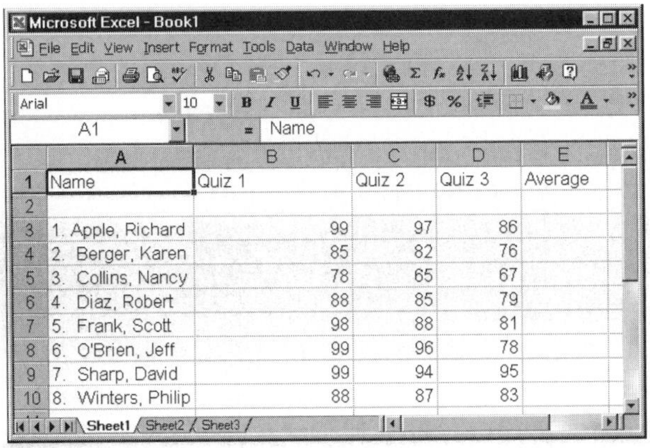

FIGURE 7.4
*Gradebook Roster
in* Microsoft Excel
2000

Box shot reprinted with
permission from Microsoft
Corporation.

The beauty of any spreadsheet is that each cell serves as an individual calculator that does computations quickly and accurately. For example, to determine each student's average score, select cell E3 and type in *Microsoft Excel's* formula tool bar: =(B3+C3+D3)/3. The spreadsheet calculates the mean for numbers 99, 97, and 86 and records the answer 94 instantaneously in cell E3. (The = sign that begins the formula (B3+C3+D3)/3 tells the computer to compute an average from cell B3 to D3; see Fig. 7.5.)

---

[2]It is unnecessary to have a total column in this electronic spreadsheet.

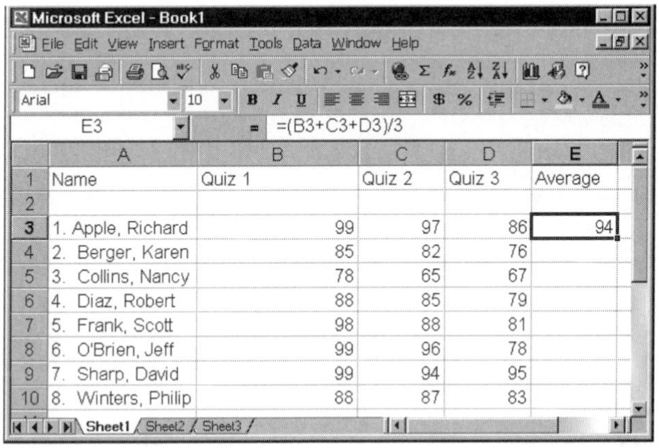

FIGURE 7.5
Gradebook Roster with Average
Box shot reprinted with permission from Microsoft Corporation.

To calculate the averages for the remaining pupils, you would not have to rewrite the formula, since every spreadsheet has a way of copying the original formula. In *Microsoft Excel*, you could use the Fill handle **Fill Handle** to select cells E3 through E10. The rest of the students' averages would be automatically displayed in the appropriate cells, as shown in the highlighted cells in column E of Figure 7.6.

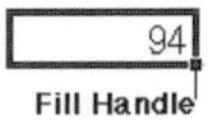

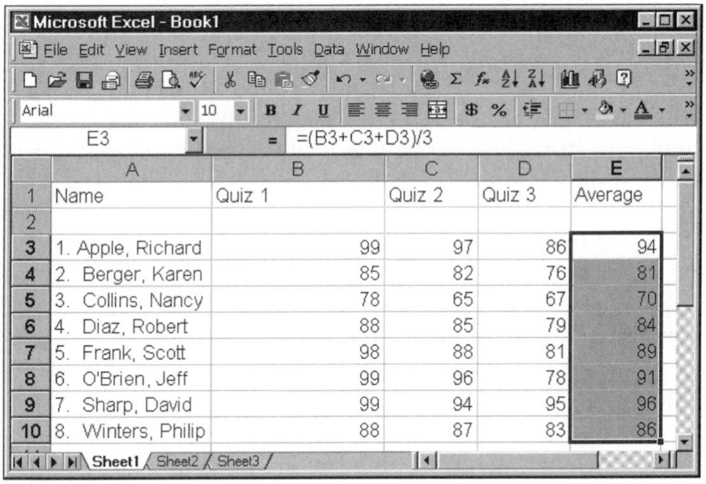

FIGURE 7.6
Microsoft Excel 2000 *Completed Roster*
Box shot reprinted with permission from Microsoft Corporation.

Furthermore, *Microsoft Excel* has more than 230 functions, or shortcuts, that save you from typing in formulas. A **function** is a built-in software routine that performs a task in the program. To apply the average function to the cell, click on **Edit formula (=)** in the formula toolbar and then select the average function from the pull-down menu that appears (Fig. 7.7).

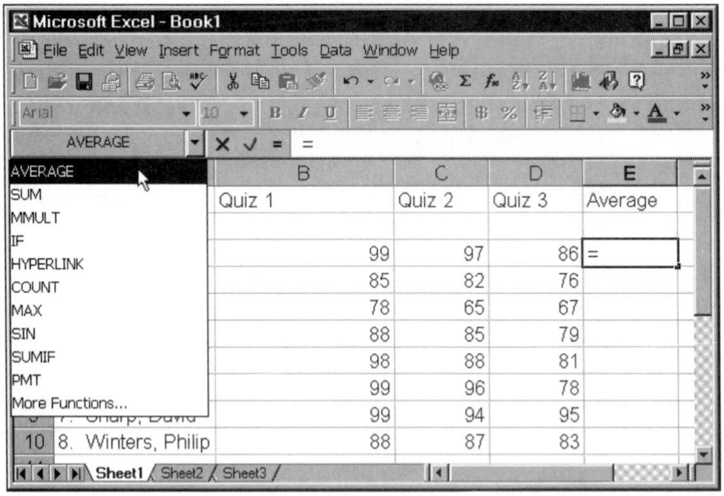

FIGURE 7.7
Average Function (Windows Version)

Box shot reprinted with permission from Microsoft Corporation.

Every spreadsheet has its own collection of built-in functions, ranging from *sum* to *average* to *sine*. These functions make the use and application of formulas quick and easy. You simply select the function and it is pasted into the spreadsheet. *AppleWorks* has more than 100 built-in functions, while *Cruncher 2* (Knowledge Adventure) has 23. Generally, the more built-in or predetermined functions, the more versatile the spreadsheet.

Why Use an Electronic Spreadsheet?

There are many reasons for a teacher to choose a computerized spreadsheet over a manual worksheet. The electronic spreadsheet is faster and more flexible than the traditional methods of numerical calculation and data prediction, permitting you to change the information on the screen as often as you want. A noncomputerized spreadsheet with a matrix of more than 25 rows and columns is cumbersome, whereas a computerized spreadsheet with a matrix of thousands of data entries performs instant calculations. Furthermore, on a computerized spreadsheet you can access any number instantaneously, simply by pressing a key or two. Another major feature of a spreadsheet is its ability to recalculate; that is, when you change the number in a cell, the spreadsheet automatically recalculates the other values. The recalculation feature of an electronic spreadsheet lets you employ **what-if analysis** strategies, used to answer questions such as "What would happen if Elena scored a 90 on this exam instead of a 60?" Another question commonly asked by students is, "What grade will I achieve in the course if I earn an 80 on the final exam?" Most homeowners ask, "If the interest rate drops from 8 to 7 percent, what will my mortgage payments be?" As a spreadsheet user, you would only have to enter the score or rate and see the effects or answers immediately.

There are still more advantages to the electronic spreadsheet. It lets you display and print the output in many visually appealing ways. Also, as long as you enter the formula correctly, your data will be accurate. Spreadsheets have the invaluable copy function, which lets you effortlessly repeat a formula once it's been defined. Clearly, the electronic spreadsheet has enormous advantage over a manual spreadsheet in terms of saving time and increasing productivity.

Integrating a Spreadsheet into the Classroom

The spreadsheet is not only a management tool; it's also a tool for learning in the classroom. The spreadsheet can be used as a gradebook (Fig. 7.8) or for classroom budgets, attendance charts, surveys, and checklists. Spreadsheets

Student's Math Grades

	A	B	C	D	E	F
1						
2			Math 101			
3	Name	Test 1	Test 2	Test 3	Student Average	Final Grade
4	Adams, Jayne	78	86	88	84	B
5	Bentley, David	88	98	88	91	A
6	Berger, Philip	95	88	85	89	A
7	Brown, Melissa	91	93	93	92	A
8	Friedman, Karen	77	67	77	74	C
9	Johnson, Alex	95	94	96	95	A
10	Kelly, Jim	83	84	83	83	B
11	Romero, Scott	87	78	96	87	B
12	Schainker, Holly	77	58	74	70	C
13						
14	Class Average	86	83	87		

FIGURE 7.8
Microsoft Excel 2000 *Gradebook*
Box shot reprinted with permission from Microsoft Corporation.

can be used to supplement instruction in a variety of curriculum areas. The teacher can use a spreadsheet as a study aid for history, for physics experiments, and for accounting problems. Teachers can improve learning by using spreadsheets to demonstrate numerical concepts like percentages, multiplication, electoral votes against popular votes. Using the spreadsheet, teachers can generate graphs to illustrate abstract concepts. Teachers can discuss stocks and have the class keep track of a stock portfolio's performance. The spreadsheet can aid teachers in preparing class materials or completing calculations.

Students can use the spreadsheet to do timelines, gameboards (Fig. 7.9), and graphs or to solve problems, keep track of classroom experiments, explore mathematical relationships, and delve into social studies or scientific investigation. Students can test various hypotheses and do what-if analyses. They can calculate averages and standard deviations for statistics problems and even keep track of their grades. They can also create their own what-if question to see what scores they need to raise their grades. They can use a spreadsheet to determine how much water and money are wasted by a dripping faucet. Furthermore, they can calculate the time to travel between cities by different means of transportation or they can explore relationships in the chemical periodic chart. They can convert Fahrenheit to Celsius temperatures, compare characteristics of the major groups of vertebrates or invertebrates, or

FIGURE 7.9
*Gameboard: Make
It With Microsoft
Office*
Screenshot reprinted with
permission from Microsoft
Corporation.

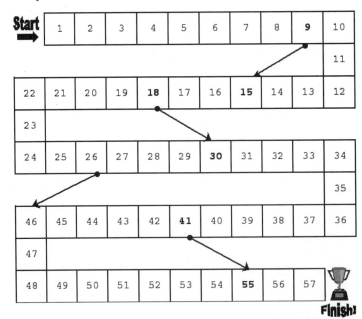

compare the climates of several countries. Students can learn about the weather and use the spreadsheet to store data about such items as temperature, precipitation, and barometer readings. Furthermore, they can use a spreadsheet in everyday life for comparison shopping, calculating the expense of keeping a pet, calorie counting, calculating income tax returns, figuring baseball statistics, and creating a budget. They can keep track of money from fund-raising activities such as magazine drives. In reality, you can use the spreadsheet to do activities that range from statistics to energy consumption to simple science experiments.

Projects with Spreadsheets

1. Developing a budget
2. Gradebook
3. Lesson plans
4. Seating charts
5. Gameboards
6. Plant growth calculation sheet

Now let's look at some of the basic features of the spreadsheet to see which ones would be most useful for the classroom teacher.

Basic Features of a Spreadsheet

Protected and Hidden Cells

Many spreadsheets have safeguards built into the program that protect a group of cells from being altered or erased. For example, you may have a formula that you want to keep safe from accidental erasure or deletion. Even when you remove this cell protection so that you can view the data, there may be a command you can give to prevent accidental erasure of data. In addition to this option, some spreadsheets allow you to take confidential information and hide it from view, even blocking it out in your printed reports. On a good spreadsheet, you should be able to retrieve easily the information from these hidden cells. Some spreadsheets require users to employ a secret password to access data.

Logical Functions

Powerful spreadsheets have **logical functions** that evaluate whether a statement is true or false. For example, let's say a teacher created a gradebook spreadsheet with four exam grades and an average score for each student. He now wants to invite into honors math only those students who received averages of 97 or above. Since the first average is in cell F4, he would enter a formula in G4 and repeat this formula for every student's score. With the spreadsheet program *Lotus 1-2-3*, this formula would read as follows: @If(F4>96,100,0).

The formula lets a 100 represent the honors class and a 0 represent the standard class. When the spreadsheet does its calculation, it checks to see whether the value entered (F4) is greater than 96, and if it is, the spreadsheet will print the first option (100) in cell G4. If the average in F4 is lower than 97, the spreadsheet will print the second option (0) in G4. All the students with 100s meet the requirements for honors class.

Predetermined Functions

The majority of spreadsheet programs have a range of built-in mathematical functions, including simple statistics, logarithmic functions, financial functions, and trigonometric functions. These **predetermined functions** are ready-made formulas that let you quickly solve problems.

Date and Time Function

The date and time function is another advanced feature. It automatically calculates how many days have elapsed between two dates in spreadsheet cells.

Macros

Macros are a group of routines or commands combined into one or two keystrokes. You can play these routines back at the touch of a key or two. This is how it works. First, you determine what keys you want to use, such as key F12. Then, you decide what the key will generate; for instance, F12 could generate a name, address, and telephone number. Finally, you program the macro so that when F12 is pressed, it automatically enters the name, address, and telephone number in the chosen cell. Some macros execute their commands to a certain point, wait for the input, and then continue with the command execution.

Graphing

Many spreadsheets generate bar or pie graphs based on the information contained in the spreadsheet. These graphs are great visual aids because as the data change, you can see the corresponding changes in the graphs.

Memory

When you enter data into a spreadsheet, you want to know how much memory remains so that you don't run out at a crucial point. A spreadsheet that has a running indicator of the memory available is better than one that simply flashes a message once the program is out of memory.

Cell Names

Some programs let you label the cells with words instead of the short cell address. For instance, if you record profit in Column C, Rows 3 through 15, you can tell the program to call these cells *Profit*. Then you can use the name *Profit* in any formula that refers to this range.

Windows

When you work on a large spreadsheet, you cannot see the whole spreadsheet on the screen but must use the cursor to scroll between sections. If you need to compare figures on different screens, it is helpful to be able to split the screen into two or three sections, each windowing a different part of the work, so that you can see your current location in the spreadsheet, see the effect your work has on cells in different locations, and easily compare figures from different sections. If the spreadsheet does not have a split-screen option, an alternative feature is a spreadsheet with the ability to set fixed titles. A fixed title option lets you keep designated rows and columns permanently on the screen, even as you scroll through sections.

Attached Notes

Some spreadsheets can attach notes, much as you would attach Post-it notes to your written work.

Editing and Sorting

When you make a mistake, the spreadsheet should offer a simple way of correcting the error. You should be able to insert and delete rows and columns. You should be able to quickly widen or narrow the spreadsheet's columns to meet your entry requirements. After the information is edited to your satisfaction, you should be able to sort it alphabetically and numerically.

Copying Command

The copying command on a spreadsheet copies the contents of a group of cells from one column to another, replicating formulas, values, and labels. The ability to copy and move from one location to another saves time on data entry. For instance, instead of retyping a formula, you quickly can copy it from one cell in the spreadsheet and then paste it into any other cells in which you need to use the same formula (Fig. 7.6).

Templates

It is very useful to have a spreadsheet that offers ready-to-use templates. A **template** is simply a spreadsheet that contains no data but has selected functions chosen for certain cells. You fill the appropriate cells of this spreadsheet with your own data. When you enter data in cells for which formulas are selected, the computer makes the calculations and the results are displayed in the appropriate cells. When you are finished, you save this altered spreadsheet under another name so that the template can be used for another spreadsheet. You can also create your own templates.

Online Help

Online help allows you to get help from the computer while using the program.

Formatting

Many spreadsheets have formatting capabilities that let you align numbers and text labels or apply different fonts and type styles. *Microsoft Excel* has an "AutoFormat" feature that lets you apply built-in table designs to give your spreadsheet a professional look. This AutoFormat feature uses distinctive formats for different elements of the table.

Advanced Features of a Spreadsheet

The more powerful spreadsheets can link other spreadsheets, have database capabilities, can chart or graph, and can print sideways. Linking spreadsheets allows you to get information from one spreadsheet and pull this information directly into your current sheet (this complicated feature is not meant for novices). *Lotus 1-2-3* has database capabilities, but these functions are not comparable to those of a database program; what they offer is a spreadsheet approach to dealing with database functions. Generally, printing is limited to 80 columns, or 136 if you use compressed type, but sometimes you need more room to fit all the columns on one sheet of paper. The best way to accomplish this is by using a utility program that allows you to print in the landscape mode. A few spreadsheet programs offer this convenience. The most advanced spreadsheets offer special fonts, multiple dimensions, sound, and add-on software. These spreadsheets have Internet capabilities that let you save your data to a website by converting the worksheet to HTML format. When you save the worksheet this way, you can see it in your Web browser (see Chapter 9). In addition, many spreadsheet programs let you add **hyperlinks** to your worksheet. This means that when you click on this text or graphic you go to a specific Web page, a file on your disk, or a file on a local network.

How to Select a Good Spreadsheet for the Classroom

Spreadsheets were originally designed for adults, but a handful of programs are suitable for the classroom. *Cruncher 2.0* is for grades 3 and up, while the high schools utilize *Microsoft Works 2000, AppleWorks, Microsoft Excel 2000* (Windows) or *Microsoft Excel 2001* (Macintosh), and *Quattro Pro 9* (Corel).

Choosing spreadsheet software for the classroom is a six-step process: (1) determine the hardware compatibility; (2) study the program's features; (3) test how easy it is to use the program; (4) examine the program's built-in functions; (5) investigate the program's consumer value; and (6) check out the technical support.

Hardware Compatibility

What computers are available in the school: old Apple IIGs, Windows-based machines, or Power Macintoshs? How much memory do these machines have? Is there enough memory to accommodate the spreadsheets the students are using?

General Features

Ask these questions: How is the labeling done on the spreadsheet? Can you easily center the labels or move them to the left or right? How does the spreadsheet handle decimal points and dollar signs? If you make a mistake, can you effortlessly modify the cell or cells? Can the width of the columns be easily adjusted? Can you protect the cells from being accidentally erased? Can you hide certain cells and not print them out? How does the spreadsheet show negative values? How many predetermined functions does the spreadsheet have? Does it have a date and time function? Can you easily calculate how many days have passed between two dates entered in the spreadsheet? Does the spreadsheet have macros? Can you generate bar or pie graphs? How does the spreadsheet indicate the amount of memory it has left? Does the spreadsheet have windows so that you can split the screen into two or three sections, each displaying a different part of the work? Can you link this spreadsheet with other spreadsheets or arrange the information in the spreadsheet alphabetically or numerically? Does the spreadsheet have enough columns and rows to meet the classroom needs?

Ease of Use

The spreadsheet is much more difficult to use than a database program because it involves working with numbers and formulas. Therefore, it is imperative that you choose a spreadsheet program that gives online help that can be accessed quickly. *Cruncher 2.0* fits these criteria with a step-by-step tutorial and online help. Figure 7.10 shows a screen from this tutorial.

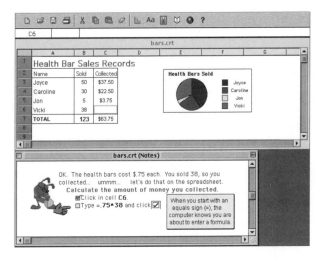

FIGURE 7.10
Cruncher 2.0
Reprinted with permission of Davidson and Associates.

AppleWorks, an integrated program, has a word processor, spreadsheet, database, drawing, painting, and presentation. The program lets the student quickly build graphs, slide shows, and pictures. It is packaged with clip art images, sounds, movies, and templates (Fig. 7.11) that duplicate what students are learning in school.

FIGURE 7.11
AppleWorks
Copyright Apple Computer, Inc. All rights reserved.

When considering ease of use, ask these questions: How fast can you edit the cells and enter the data? Can you smoothly delete and insert rows or columns? Is it hard to copy formulas from one row to another? How do you move the cursor from one cell to another?

Built-In Functions

What special functions do the students need to use in the class? For example, when students use the spreadsheet, is it to calculate sums, averages, or standard deviations?

Consumer Value

Software is expensive, so cost is an important consideration. *Cruncher 2.0* costs under $100, while *Microsoft Excel* sells for more than $250. Some software companies offer on-site licenses so that you can freely make copies of the software for in-house use. Other manufacturers distribute lab packs that let you purchase software at a reduced price. There are quite a few shareware spreadsheet programs; for examples, see *The Spreadsheet Page* at http://www.j-walk.com/ss/.

Support

A software company's willingness to support its product is an extremely important factor. Ask these questions: Can you call someone on the telephone at the company and get immediate help? Do you have to spend excessive time waiting on the phone? Is the technical support toll-free or are you charged by the minute? Do you have to pay a yearly fee to receive any type of assistance? Does the software package come with a tutorial? Is the manual readable— with an index? Does the program have templates? Use the following checklist when selecting a spreadsheet.

Teacher Practice

The following exercises are meant to be used in conjunction with any spreadsheet. If a computer lab is not available, simply read through this section to get an idea of how you would set up a spreadsheet. The first exercise introduces you step by step to a spreadsheet program.

1. Open the spreadsheet program.
2. Create a new file and give it the name *Gradebook*.
3. Begin by entering labels across the first row of the spreadsheet. Starting at cell B1, type the following labels: Exam 1, Exam 2, Exam 3, Exam 4, Exam 5. Place the label Exam 1 in cell B1, Exam 2 in C1, Exam 3 in D1, Exam 4 in E1, and Exam 5 in F1. Leaving cells A1 and A2

SPREADSHEET CHECKLIST

Directions: Examine the following items and determine which ones you feel are important for your class situation. Evaluate your Spreadsheet and place an X on each line where the software meets your needs.

Program Name _____   Manufacturer _____   Grade Level _____

A. Hardware

____ 1. Memory needed

____ 2. Computer compatibility

____ 3. Printer compatibility

____ 4. Hard disk space

____ 4. Windowing

____ 5. Macros

____ 6. Formulas

____ 7. Logical operators

____ 8. Fixed titles

____ 9. Transfer to word processing

____ 10. Link to other spreadsheets

____ 11. Integration with database

____ 12. Name ranges

____ 13. Graphing

____ 14. Flexibility of printing

____ 15. Manual recalculation

____ 16. Sound

____ 17. Internet capabilities

B. Features

____ 1. Protected cells

____ 2. Hidden cells

____ 3. Sorting

____   a. Alphabetical

____   b. Numerical

____ 3. Quick printer setup

____ 4. Easy editing of cells

____ 5. Simple command names

____ 6. Quick cell movement

____ 7. Warning questions

C. Editing

____ 1. Deleting and adding columns

____ 2. Changing column width

____ 3. Copying labels and formulas

____ 4. Formatting of cells

____ 5. Erasure

D. Ease of Use

____ 1. Help screens

____ 2. Tutorial disks

E. Consumer Value

____ 1. Cost

____ 2. On-site license

____ 3. Lab packs

____ 4. Network version

____ 5. Support

____   a. Technical

____   b. Tutorial material

____   c. Readable manual

____   d. Templates

Rating Scale

Rate the spreadsheet program by placing a check in the appropriate box

Excellent ____ Very Good ____ Good ____ Fair ____ Poor ____

Comments

empty, put the label Pupils in cell A3. These labels will describe the contents of the cells. The spreadsheet should look similar to the one in Figure 7.12, which is in *Microsoft Excel*.

FIGURE 7.12
Microsoft Excel
Spreadsheet

Screen shot reprinted with permission from Microsoft Corporation.

	A	B	C	D	E	F
1		EXAM 1	EXAM 2	EXAM 3	EXAM 4	EXAM 5
2						
3	PUPILS					
4						

4. Starting at A5, enter the pupils' last names: A5, Smith; A6, Sharp; A7, Garcia; A8, Raj; A9, Friedman; A10, Washington; A11, Reilly; A12, Hughes; A13, Sherrin; and A14, Jones.
5. Using the sort or arrange function, alphabetize the names and align each name on the left side of the cell.
6. Now enter the data in the gradebook. Enter Friedman's Exam 1 score as 89 in cell B5, his Exam 2 score as 46 in cell C5, Exam 3 as 69 in D5, Exam 4 as 74 in cell E5, and Exam 5 as 35 in cell F5. Now continue entering the exam scores for the remaining students; the spreadsheet should look like the one in Figure 7.13.

FIGURE 7.13
Microsoft Excel
Spreadsheet with
Grades

Screen shot reprinted with permission from Microsoft Corporation.

	A	B	C	D	E	F
1		EXAM 1	EXAM 2	EXAM 3	EXAM 4	EXAM 5
2						
3	PUPILS					
4						
5	FRIEDMAN	89	46	69	74	35
6	GARCIA	45	23	75	75	34
7	HUGHES	89	43	67	67	34
8	JONES	99	45	75	75	40
9	RAJ	98	50	73	73	39
10	REILLY	56	50	67	67	32
11	SHARP	98	45	72	71	39
12	SHERRIN	78	46	73	72	34
13	SMITH	99	45	74	74	40
14	WASHINGTON	87	45	72	72	34
15						

7. Next, type the label *AVERAGE* in cell G1. You want to enter a formula to calculate the average score for Friedman's five exams. Begin by putting the cursor on cell G5 and write the formula. There will be a variation in these formulas; for instance, if you are using *AppleWorks*, the formula is =AVERAGE(B5..F5). In *Microsoft Excel*, the formula is =AVERAGE(B5:F5). After you enter the formula, the average (62.6) should appear instantaneously in cell G5.
8. Next, use the copy or fill function to calculate the averages for the remaining students (Fig. 7.14).
9. Learn how to save the data on the formatted disk and print it out for inspection.

	A	G
1		AVERAGE
2		
3	PUPILS	
4		
5	FRIEDMAN	62.6
6	GARCIA	50.4
7	HUGHES	60
8	JONES	66.8
9	RAJ	66.6
10	REILLY	54.4
11	SHARP	65
12	SHERRIN	60.6
13	SMITH	66.4
14	WASHINGTON	62
15		

FIGURE 7.14
Calculating Averages in **Microsoft Excel**
Screen shot reprinted with permission from Microsoft Corporation.

Classroom Lesson Plans

What follows are five ready-to-use lesson plan activities that test the students' ability to use successfully the different features of the spreadsheet.

▼ I. Math/Science ▼

Objectives

Students will learn about speed and how to use a spreadsheet to do simple calculations.

Materials

You need a spreadsheet program like *AppleWorks, Excel 2000, Cruncher 2.0,* or *Quattro Pro 10.*

Procedure

1. Discuss how fast an automobile can travel and the relationship between distance, miles, and time.
2. Have the students create a spreadsheet similar to the one in Figure 7.15.

	A	B	C
1	RATE	TIME	DISTANCE
2	25	0.5	
3	30	1	
4	35	2	
5	40	2	
6	45	3	
7	50	3	
8	55	4	
9	60	5	
10	65	6	
11	70	7	

FIGURE 7.15
Speed Spreadsheet in **Microsoft Excel**
Screen shot reprinted with permission from Microsoft Corporation.

3. Next, pose the following question: What is the distance covered when traveling so many hours at a given speed?
4. Have the students type a formula in cell C2 that multiplies cell A2 by cell B2. Then copy this formula for cells C3 to C11.
5. After the students have accomplished this, have them examine the results and determine the answers to questions that you and they pose. If there are not enough computers, let the students use their calculators and a pencil and paper to complete this task.

Variations

You can generate other spreadsheets that would enable students to answer the following questions:

1. How much time does it take to travel a specified number of miles at a certain speed?
2. How much distance is covered when traveling so many hours at a given speed?

▼   II. Mathematics   ▼

Objective

Students will use a spreadsheet to keep track of expenses.

Materials

You need a spreadsheet program like *AppleWorks, Excel, Cruncher 2.0*, or *Quattro Pro 10*.

Procedure

1. Discuss the following problem with the students: The $10 Computer Club is having a fund-raiser to buy software for its club. The cost of the software is $700, and the club members expect to sell three raffle tickets apiece. They are selling these tickets for $3 each. Figure 7.16 shows how many tickets each student in the club sells.

FIGURE 7.16
Ticket Sales Spreadsheet

$10 CLUB	\	DAYS OF THE WEEK						AVERAGE
	1	2	3	4	5	6	7	
1. Adams	6	4	6	2	3	4	5	
2. Barrett	5	4	4	5	0	0	3	
3. Devlin	5	2	6	2	6	1	2	
4. Johnson	2	1	4	4	2	1	3	
5. Mason	3	0	0	0	10	0	2	
6. Garcia	1	2	3	4	3	2	1	
7. Youngblood	2	3	4	5	5	7	8	
8. Sands	1	3	2	5	0	4	3	

2. Have each student create the same spreadsheet and then finish this table by calculating the average for each student.

3. Tell the students to use the logical function to determine how many club members sold six or more tickets on a daily basis. Was the $10 Computer Club able to buy its software?

Variation

1. Change the totals in the spreadsheet for any two students not selling at least three raffle tickets daily to three raffle tickets and record the value the spreadsheet recalculates.

2. Have the students compute the averages again if the raffle ticket price were raised to $5.

▼   **III. Family and Consumer Education**   ▼

Objective

Students will use a spreadsheet to keep track of their expenditures for six months.

Materials

You need a spreadsheet program like *AppleWorks, Excel, Cruncher 2.0,* or *Quattro Pro 10.*

Procedure

1. Have each student record in a spreadsheet expenditures for the 10 items shown in Figure 7.17 during a six-month period.

EXPENSES	JAN.	FEB.	MARCH	APRIL	MAY	JUNE
Food						
Telephone						
Utilites						
Rent						
Automobile Loan						
Insurance						
Entertainment						
Clothes						
Medical Bills						
Savings						

FIGURE 7.17
Expenditures Spreadsheet

2. Have students use the sum formula to total each column.

3. Ask them to add an additional column to keep track of six-month totals.
4. Change values in the completed table so that the students can answer what-if questions such as "If I cut down on my entertainment, how much more can I save a year?"

Variation

From the savings row, create a spreadsheet that shows how much an initial deposit of $200 would grow at different interest rates and at different intervals of time.

▼   IV. The Pendulum   ▼

Objectives

Students will practice predicting, changing variables, and estimating and learn how to use a formula in a spreadsheet.

Materials

You will need string, thumbtacks, weights, and a spreadsheet program like *AppleWorks, Excel, Cruncher 2.0,* or *Quattro Pro 10.*

Procedure

Before beginning, students must understand how the pendulum works.

1. Have each student enter different weights, lengths, and amplitude values. The objective is to determine what affects the pendulum's period. A period is simply the time it takes the pendulum to swing from point A to point B and then back to point A again.
2. Ask each student to create a table like the one in Figure 7.18

FIGURE 7.18
Pendulum
Spreadsheet

Pendulum Investigations			
Length	Weight	Amplitude	Period

3. Have students use a formula to figure each period for the pendulum.

▼ V. Social Studies: The Election ▼

Objectives

Students will learn about elections and in the process how to use a spreadsheet to add and figure percentages.

Materials

The students will have to make voting booths and have access to a spreadsheet program like *Excel* or *Cruncher 2.0*. They will need ballots and tallies for each voting booth.

Procedure

Before beginning, students must understand the election process.

1. Have the students nominate candidates for president of the room or school.
2. Conduct an election with voting booths.
3. Create a table similar to Figure 7.19.

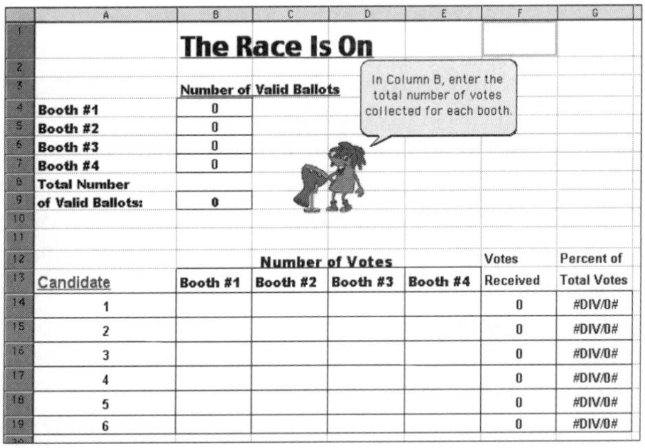

FIGURE 7.19
Cruncher 2.0 *Race Spreadsheet*
Used by permission of Knowledge Adventure/Havas Interactive.

4. Write the candidates' names and tally the votes.
5. Enter the number of valid ballots that were cast by the students.
6. Using the sum function, calculate the total number of valid ballots.
7. Using the percent function, calculate the percentage of the total vote that each candidate received.
8. Pose questions like the following: Was the election close? What percentage of the total votes did my candidate earn? How many votes were there all together?

This ends our discussion of spreadsheets; let's turn our attention to integrated programs and software suites.

Integrated Programs

Previously, we discussed three popular applications of the computer: the word processor, the database, and the spreadsheet. Each application was dedicated to a separate task: The word processor created and edited documents, the database organized information, and the spreadsheet worked with numerical data.

Once you are comfortable with these individual programs, you may require software that allows for the free interchange of data among programs. For example, you may need to take budget information stored in the spreadsheet and transfer it to a letter that you're writing on the word processor. Regardless of the software you have, you can accomplish this task by going through seven laborious steps: (1) write the report on the word processor, leaving space for the spreadsheet table; (2) print a hard copy of the report; (3) close the word processing application and open the spreadsheet; (4) enter data into the spreadsheet's cells and manipulate it; (5) generate a printout of this spreadsheet; (6) use actual scissors to cut the spreadsheet printout and paste the results onto the word processor hard copy; (7) photocopy the report. However, cutting and pasting among applications in this way is a time-consuming chore.

Stand-alone programs are generally not capable of communicating with other applications. There are many aspects of programming that limit the ability of these programs to address one another, and one important limitation is the differences among their command structures. For example, the *Cruncher 2.0* spreadsheet cannot electronically transfer information into the *AppleWorks* word processor because of their different commands.

The **integrated program,** on the other hand, includes in its most common configuration a word processor, a database, and a spreadsheet that can communicate with one another. *Lotus 1-2-3,* a pioneer in its field, was developed in the early 1980s as a spreadsheet. It was one of the first programs to offer as a part of its design a database with some graphics capabilities. After the success of *Lotus 1-2-3,* many programs followed its example. *SuperCalc 3* integrated database, spreadsheet, and graphics. *Microsoft Works* combined spreadsheet with file management and word processing. Integrated programs such as *Microsoft Works 2000* expanded to include more applications such as a calendar maker and an address book. *AppleWorks* (Fig. 7.20), another popular integrated program, offers word processor, spreadsheet, database manager, communications, painting, drawing, and presentation capabilities.

**FIGURE 7.20
AppleWorks**

The integrated program is a single program with applications that share a similar command structure. Because of similarity of command structure across the various applications, the program is easy to learn. Since each module is a component of one program, data are transferred seamlessly. You can effortlessly combine tables with text, for example. Finally, integrated programs cost much less than the several stand-alone programs that would offer similar applications. Nevertheless, this type of program does have two disadvantages: The integrated program typically needs more memory and has a weaker module than the stand-alone program. For example, the word processing application in an integrated program could have more limited functions than those in the stand-alone word processing package.

Alternatives to an Integrated Program

What are the alternatives to integrated programs?

1. You can use the stand-alone program as it is and cut and paste when necessary. If you are fortunate, your stand-alone program may have all the database or word processing capabilities that you require, even if they are limited.

2. You can retype your data into the separate applications. This sounds like a reasonable alternative, but it requires much typing and opens your data to errors since it is very easy to make a typo. Also, anytime you change a number in one application, you will have to retype it in the other applications.

3. You can file-share, which permits access to the files of the other programs. Because there is little standardization among the files of programs, these files cannot be directly read. If you want to read them, you need a special translator program like *MacLink Plus* (DataViz), which lets you input a file of one type, make it conform to the file structure of another type, and then output this transformed file. Unfortunately, these translator programs are not available for all software programs, and sometimes in the process of transforming the data it may lose its formatting.

In conclusion, if you do not need to transfer data among applications, a basic stand-alone application that fits your computer needs should suffice. However, if you are going to do work in which you need to transfer information from one application to another, you should buy an integrated software package or perhaps try another alternative a software suite.

Software Suites

In the 1990s the software companies started a new trend with the introduction of software suites. A **software suite** is a package of individual programs designed to work together to share data easily and quickly. The suite consists of stand-alone applications that are sold individually. Each application works together through special links that create a mock integration. Four popular examples of suites are *Corel WordPerfect Office 2000, Microsoft Office 2000, Microsoft Office 2001* (Macintosh version), and *Lotus SmartSuite*. A suite costs less than the individual pieces of software and offers more features. For example,

Corel WordPerfect Suite 2000 includes the following software: *WordPerfect, Quattro Pro, Corel Presentations, Trellix 2, Corel Print Office, Corel Central,* as well as hundreds of templates, hundreds of fonts, and thousands of clip art images. You can install the entire suite or only the programs that you want.

Similarities and Differences

There are many similarities between an integrated package and a suite. Both enable you to run many programs at once, and they are designed to work together. An integrated program and a suite feature a **clipboard,** a place to store text, graphic, audio, and video clips. You use this clipboard to move data among the suite or integrated programs applications. You copy the data to the clipboard and then paste it into the other applications. Both integrated programs and suites let you write more sophisticated reports and papers because you have access to a variety of programs.

The main difference between a software suite and an integrated program is that the suite's components are full-featured programs and not limited versions. These applications usually started as independent programs that were popular before being combined in a suite. In most cases, a suite is very economical, because software vendors use it to induce people to buy their products. It serves as a marketing strategy preventing the user from switching to a new product.

On the negative side, the various components in a suite do not work as smoothly as do those in an integrated program. There are very high hardware requirements to run a suite. The hard disk space, the memory, and the speed of the computer should all be taken into consideration. A suite like *Microsoft Office 2001* requires more than 160 MB of hard disk space to install its different components. It is preferable to have a more powerful computer to take full advantage of the programs' capabilities. Mastering a suite is definitely harder than mastering an integrated program. Expect to spend considerable time and effort if you want to learn more than just the basics.

Features

When you scrutinize an integrated program or suite you are concerned with the same features that you would be when considering separate applications. You should consider the same questions: How rapidly does the database sort? How much time is needed to load a file? How quickly does the spreadsheet calculate? How many columns and rows can you create using the spreadsheet document? Does the word processor have a thesaurus or grammar checker? You should find out how quickly and easily each module in the integrated package or software suite shares data and if the program has mail merge and windowing capabilities.

Mail Merge

Mail merge, as previously discussed in Chapter 6, gives you the ability to combine the database information with the word processing documents to produce a customized letter or report. In an integrated program, you may have a list of names and addresses in the database and a form letter in the word processor. The integrated program or suite merges the information from these applications to produce a customized letter.

Windowing

Windowing is the ability to display different parts of a worksheet on the screen so that you can work within each module window simultaneously. For example, one window might display a spreadsheet while another window might display a graph being generated from the spreadsheet. With windowing, you can change numbers in the spreadsheet and watch the effect on the graph as it is redrawn with the new values.

Summary

The electronic spreadsheet, which consists of a matrix of rows and columns intersecting at cells, was developed to handle complicated and tedious calculations. In this chapter, we became familiar with the basic features of a spreadsheet and discussed which features to consider when buying a spreadsheet program for the classroom. We also explored activities for introducing the spreadsheet to students.

In addition, we examined the integrated software package, a group of programs that freely exchange data with each other. In their most common configuration today, these integrated programs include a word processor, database, spreadsheet, telecommunication module, drawing module, and graphics module. Additionally, we discussed the software suite, a bundling of linked stand-alone programs. **Be sure to review the annotated list of award-winning spreadsheet and integrated programs in Appendix A.**

Spreadsheet Sites

What follows is an annotated list of top-rated spreadsheet sites. These sites include information about spreadsheets, tutorials, historical information, lesson plans, activities, and tips.

Microsoft Excel 2000
http://www.microsoft.com/office/excel/
http://www.microsoft.com/education/
tutorial/classroom/

The Microsoft site for *Excel 2000* provides information about the product as well as how-to articles and tips for using it. The Microsoft education site lists tutorials including *Excel 97*.

Excel 101
http://www.usd.edu/trio/tut/excel/
Excel 101 is a tutorial offering general information on using *Microsoft Excel* as well as specific instruction on formulas and formatting.

Dan Bricklin's Website
http://bricklin.com/
This site, maintained by Dan Bricklin, a co-creator *VisiCalc*, contains historical information about *VisiCalc*, the first computer spreadsheet program.

Using Spreadsheets to Keep Track of Students' Grades
http://www.math.berkeley.edu/~zach/
teaching/grades.html
This is a basic guide explaining the tasks for setting up a spreadsheet to keep a record of students' grades.

The Spreadsheet Page
http://www.j-walk.com/ss/
This extensive site provides information about spreadsheets of all types, including downloads, tips, and FAQs, with special emphasis on *Microsoft Excel*.

Mathematics and Spreadsheets
http://forum.swarthmore.edu/sum95/
math_and/index.html
http://forum.swarthmore.edu/workshops/
sum98/participants/sinclair/problem/
intro.html
http://forum.swarthmore.edu/alejandre/
spreadsheet.html
The forum site offers basic information for using spreadsheets in education, grades 8–12. See
also the lesson plan ideas in Margaret Sinclair's
Using Spreadsheets to Solve Algebraic Problems
and Suzanne Alejandre's *Graphs*.

Spreadsheet Lesson Plans
http://www.dpi.state.nc.us/Curriculum/
computer.skills/lssnplns/sstoc.html
The North Carolina Department of Education
offers spreadsheet lesson plans for middle
grades.

Robert 's Online Spreadsheet!
http://www.intrepid.com/~robertl/
spreadsheet1.html
Dr. Robert Lum offers a free Web-based spreadsheet program.

Productivity in the Classroom
http://microsoft.com/education/lesson/
productivity/
The site provides a variety of lessons and activities for integrating technology into the classroom using Microsoft software such as *Excel*.

Microsoft Office Template Gallery
http://officeupdate.microsoft.com/
templategallery/
Microsoft Office Template Gallery contains
hundreds of templates: résumés, cover letters,
legal documents, and much more. You can
browse by category, or search to find the template you need.

Chapter Mastery Test

*To the Instructor: Refer to the Instructor's Manual
for the Answers to the Mastery Questions. This
manual has additional questions and resource
materials.*

Let's check for chapter comprehension with a
short mastery test. What follows are basic
terms, classroom projects, and suggested
readings and references.

1. What is a spreadsheet?
2. Give an example of each of the following
   terms: (a) macro, (b) cell, (c) logical
   functions, (d) predefined functions,
   (e) windows.
3. What is the advantage of being able to
   copy a formula in a spreadsheet?
4. Explain how a spreadsheet can be useful
   in determining a classroom budget.
5. Describe five features of a spreadsheet
   and their functions.
6. Choose two important features of a
   spreadsheet and show how they can be
   utilized in the classroom.

7. Discuss the factors involved in selecting a
   spreadsheet for a school district.
8. Explain the advantage of a spreadsheet
   over a calculator.
9. Give an example of a situation in
   which an integrated software program
   has an advantage over a stand-alone
   program.
10. Explain two ways to integrate a
    spreadsheet into the classroom.
11. Define windowing and mail merge, and
    give an example of each.
12. Describe the advantage of using
    what-if analysis with a spreadsheet.
    Give some applications in which this
    type of comparison would be
    important.
13. Explain and suggest reasons for the
    popularity of software suites.
14. If you were buying an integrated
    program, what are some features you
    would look at before buying?

Basic Terms

cell (p. 155)	mail merge (p. 176)
clipboard (p. 176)	predetermined functions (p. 161)
function (p. 157)	software suite (p. 175)
hyperlinks (p. 164)	spreadsheet (p. 154)
integrated program (p. 174)	template (p. 163)
logical functions (p. 161)	what-if analysis (p. 158)
macros (p. 161)	windowing (p. 177)

Classroom Projects

1. Develop a spreadsheet activity for the classroom.
2. Create a spreadsheet similar to the gradebook example given in this chapter, but for this example have 12 students take three exams and a final. Calculate the final exam as 40 percent of the grade and the other three exams as 20 percent each.
3. Prepare a review comparing three spreadsheets.
4. Use a spreadsheet to compare the expenses with a devised budget.
5. Outline in a lesson plan format three different ways a spreadsheet would be useful in the classroom.
6. Prepare a report on integrated programs, comparing their strengths and weaknesses.
7. List the different ways an integrated program would be useful in the school district office.

Suggested Readings and References

Abramovich, Sergei, and Wanda Nabors. "Spreadsheets as Generators of New Meanings in Middle School Algebra." *Computers in the Schools* 13, no. 1–2 (1997): 13–25.

Anderson, Wynema. *Lotus 1-2-3 5.0 for Windows: Applications for Reinforcement.* Cincinnati, Ohio: South-Western Educational Publishing, 1997.

Arad, O. S. "The Spreadsheet Solving Word Problems." *Computing Teacher* 14, no. 4 (December/January 1986–1987): 13–15, 45.

Aranbright, Deane E. "Mathematical Applications of an Electronic Spreadsheet." *Computers in Mathematics Education.* Reston, Va.: NCTM 1984 Yearbook, 1984.

Berglas, Anthony, and Peter Hoare. "Spreadsheet Errors, Risks and Technique." *Management Accounting: Magazine for 77,* no. 7 (July/August 1999): 46.

Berit Fuglestad, Anne. "Spreadsheets as Support for Understanding Decimal Numbers." *Micromath* 13, no. 1 (1997): 6.

Birmingham, Stephen. "Spreadsheets at the Beach." *Wall Street Journal Eastern Edition,* June 25, 1999, p. W9.

Black, Thomas R. "Simulations on Spreadsheets for Complex Concepts: Teaching Statistics." *International Journal of Mathematical Education in Science & Technology* 30, no. 4 (July/August 1999): 473.

Bourgeois, Michelle. "The Cruncher 2.0." *T.H.E. Journal* 27, no. 1 (August 1999): 52.

Bowman, C. "Integrated Software Solves Scheduling Problems." *Electronic Learning,* April 1985, pp. 22–24.

Brooks, Lloyd D. *101 Spreadsheet Exercises for Lotus 1-2-3 and Other Spreadsheet Software.* 2nd ed. New York: Macmillan/McGraw-Hill, 1992.

Brown, J. M. "Spreadsheets in the Classroom." *Computing Teacher* 14, no. 3 (1987): 8–12.

Brown, J. M. "Spreadsheets in the Classroom Part II." *Computing Teacher* 14, no. 4 (February 1987): 9–12.

Carter, Ashley J. R. "Using Spreadsheets to Model Population Growth, Competition and Predation in Nature." *American Biology Teacher* 61, no. 4 (April 1999): 294.

Cooke, B. A. "Some Ideas for Using Spreadsheets in Physics." *Physics Education* 32, no. 2 (March 1997): 80–87.

"Got a Question? Ask Jeeves." *NEA Today* 18, no. 2 (October 1999): 32.

Gruet, Marie-Anne, Anne Philippe, and Christian P. Robert. "MCMC Control Spreadsheets for Exponential Mixture Estimation." *Journal of Computational and Graphical Statistics* 8, no. 2 (June 1999): 298.

Haugland, Ole Anton. "Spreadsheet Waves." *Physics Teacher* 37, no. 1 (January 1999): 14.

Holmes, Elizabeth. "The Spreadsheet—Absolutely Elementary!" *Learning and Leading with Technology* 24, no. 8 (May 1997): 6–12.

Hunt, William J. "Technology Tips: Spreadsheets—A Tool for the Mathematics Classroom." *Mathematics Teacher* 88, no. 9 (1995): 774–77.

Karlin, M. "Beyond Distance-Rate/Time." *Computing Teacher,* February 1988, pp. 20–23.

Koselka, Rita. "The Game of Life in Bits and Bytes—Spreadsheets Can't Solve All Problems. That's Why You Need Virtual People." *Forbes* 159, no. 7 (1997): 100.

Leonhard, Woody. "Excel Power Tips." *PC Computing* 12, no. 1 (January 1999): 264.

Lesser, Lawrence M. "Exploring the Birthday Problem with Spreadsheets." *Mathematics Teacher* 92, no. 5 (May 1999): 407.

Loeffler, Louis. "The Cruncher 2.0." *T.H.E. Journal* 27, no. 1 (August 1999): 54.

Luehrmann, Arthur. "Spreadsheets: More Than Just Finance." *Computing Teacher* 13 (1986): 24–28.

Manouchehri, Azita. "Exploring Number Structures with Spreadsheets." *Learning and Leading with Technology* 24, no. 8 (May 1997): 32–36.

Parker, J. "Using Spreadsheets to Encourage Critical Thinking." *Computing Teacher* 16, no. 6 (1989): 27–28.

Parker, O. J. *Spreadsheet Chemistry.* Englewood Cliffs, N.J.: Prentice Hall, 1991.

Pfaffenberger, Bryan. *Webster's New World Computer User's Dictionary.* 8th ed. New York: Macmillan, 2000.

Robinette, Michelle. "Top Ten Uses for ClarisWorks in the One-Computer Classroom." *Learning and Leading with Technology* 24, no. 2 (October 1996): 37–40.

Russell, J. C. "Probability Modeling with a Spreadsheet." *Computing Teacher* 14 (November 1987): 58–60.

Savel, Thomas G. "Organize Your Data with Microsoft Excel." *Family Practice Management* 6, no. 5 (May 1999): 51.

Sharp, Vicki. *Make It with Microsoft Office (Macintosh).* Eugene, Ore.: Visions Technology in Education, 1999.

Sharp, Vicki. *Make It with Microsoft Office (Windows).* Eugene, Ore.: Visions Technology in Education, 1999.

Smith-Gratto, Karen, and Marcy A. Blackburn. "The Computer as a Scientific Tool: Integrating Spreadsheets into the Elementary Science Curriculum." *Computers in the Schools* 13, no. 1–2 (1997): 125–31.

Stang, A., and M. Levinson. "Spreadsheets Come to School." *Media and Methods* (September 1984): 28–29.

"The Spreadsheet Tips." *PC World* 12, no. 3 (March 1, 1994): 180.

Walkenbach, John. "Display Multiple Charts on a Single Chart Sheet." *PC World* 18, no. 6 (June 2000): 271.

Walkenbach, John. "Surprise, Surprise! Excel Can Handle Fractions." *PC World* 18, no. 5 (May 2000): 254.

Weller, Erin J. "Selecting the Right Office Suite Can Be Easy . . . with a Little Guidance." *Book Report* 18, no. 5 (March/April 2000): 52.

CHAPTER 8

The Internet and the Web

Integrating the Internet into the Classroom

Did you know that the Internet comprises more than 65 million computers in more than 100 countries? Did you know that having access to the Internet means that you can tap into thousands of databases and talk electronically with experts all over the world on any subject? Students can explore this giant library with millions of sites and obtain information on any curriculum area, participate in online discussion groups, download lecture notes, and do research. They can create their own Web pages to showcase and share information. By reading this chapter you will learn about the Internet, distance learning, streaming video, and desktop videoconferencing. You will be given exercises that help you integrate the Internet into the classroom. Finally, you will become familiar with Internet sites that include articles on the Web's origins, online encyclopedias, online dictionaries, and distance education sites.

Objectives

Upon completing this chapter, you will be able to:
1. Describe networking and explain how it operates;
2. Discuss the Internet's historical background;
3. Explain the issues to consider when using the Internet;
4. Explain why the World Wide Web is an invaluable resource;
5. Identify and discuss three popular online services; and
6. Discuss distance learning and its implications for education.

Telecommunications and Networking

Telecommunications is the electronic transmission of information including data, television pictures, sound, and facsimiles. Usually involving a computer, a modem, software, and a printer, you can communicate with a friend in St. Louis, Missouri, or Paris, France, sending and receiving anything from a manuscript to a simple message over the telephone lines. Using the same method, a homebound child can interact with a teacher in the classroom, an office worker can work at home, and a doctor can access a remote computer for research data.

The reasons for using telecommunications are convincing:

1. It is expedient and efficient;
2. It decreases air pollution from auto emissions;
3. It saves time and money;
4. It allows the home to serve as an office; and
5. It promotes distance learning in which students can share information and computer research findings.

When you connect one computer to another, you use hardware and software. In the majority of cases, the hardware consists of equipment that sends the data over some type of communications line, such as a telephone line. This equipment includes a modem, telephone lines, and computer. The software controls the flow of data.

Networking is another way that computers communicate with each other. In a network, numerous computers are connected together. To have a computer network, you need to have the computers to connect, or network; these computers can be of any type. A network system generally includes a file server, which is a computer with a large data capacity that serves as a repository for information. The file server directs the flow of information to and from the computers in the network. You need a network card if the networking capabilities are not built or plugged into the computer; you also need cables, wires, hookups, and operating system software—available from companies such as Novell, Apple, and Microsoft—that gives access to the file server. Besides this special software and equipment, you need "networkable" software that runs on the network.

In addition, a network needs a variety of devices to connect parts of a network or handle traffic among the various components. For example, a hub is a central connecting devise that joins communication lines together on a network. **Routers and bridges** are devices used to organize the traffic among the people using the network. A network can have a permanent connection such as a cable or temporary connection made through the telephone or other communication device.

The computer's network cable connection can be either copper or fiber optic. The more expensive fiber optic cables, a transmission medium consisting of glass fibers, transmit digital signals in the form of pulses of light produced by a laser. Using this type of cabling, the network can handle more messages simultaneously than by using copper wiring or coaxial cable. "For example, two glass optical fibers can handle 6,000 telephone conversations at a time, a task that would take 250 copper wires" (Heinich, Molenda, Russell, and Smaldino, 1999).

A **wireless network** lets you transmit data between computers, servers, and other network devices without physically using cable or wire. The different means used to provide wireless transmission are infrared, cellular, microwave, and satellite. According to Chris Saulpaugh, a computer technical expert, "Infrared transmission has become very popular for small networks in one room or room to room. This type of transmission is very easy to install and all the user has to worry about is blocking or deflecting the signal to the computers." The current portable computers have infrared transceivers so they can send files to their printer, a desktop computer, or a handheld computer.

Apple's Airport Wireless is an example of a wireless technology that uses radio signals to communicate and does not require an unobstructed line of sight to make a connection. Airport delivers fast, affordable wireless technology to the home or classroom without cables or complicated networking hardware. Apple's Airport lets students go on the Internet wirelessly with their iBook, iMac, PowerBook, or Power Mac G4 at home, in the classroom, or in the dorm. Several students can be online simultaneously surfing on different websites, accessing e-mail, and exchanging files through one Internet service account. They can communicate up to 150 feet away, and it is fast at 11 megabits per second. To use Airport Wireless Internet access requires an Airport Card, Airport Base Station (Fig. 8.1), and Internet access. Some Internet service

iBook

Airport Base Station

FIGURE 8.1
Apple's Airport Wireless Technology
Copyright Apple Computer, Inc. All rights reserved.

providers (ISPs) are not currently compatible with Airport, and range may vary with the site conditions. Another example of a wireless network comes from Bluetooth Special Interest Groups (http://www.bluetooth.com). Bluetooth uses radio waves that can transmit through walls and nonmetal objects. Bluetooth is a technology that allows a variety of devices, such as laptops, PCs phones, personal data assistants (PDAs), and printers to communicate with each other without cables. A small group of users can also use this technology to create their own personal area network. Data can be sent from 750 kilobits to 1 megabit per second across distances of up to 100 meters.

The three most commonly known network arrangements are the ring, the star, and the shared-bus. The **ring network** is a communication network that connects devices such as computers in a closed loop or ring. This network does not rely on a file server or central computer, and if one computer goes down in the system, the others still operate (Fig. 8.2). This configuration

FIGURE 8.2
Ring Network
ClickArt Images ©1995 T/Maker Company.

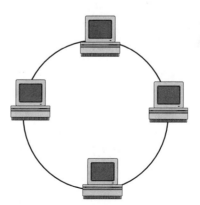

is found in university administrative offices in which each computer performs when needed and each computer has its own software.

In the second arrangement, the **star network** (Fig. 8.3), a file server is connected with several computers or terminals. The star network becomes inoperable if the file server fails because it has in its memory all the data that the other computers use for processing. A school computer center might use this type of network for its card catalog.

FIGURE 8.3
Star Network
ClickArt Images ©1995
T/Maker Company.

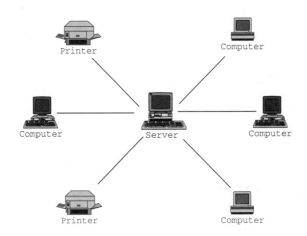

In the third arrangement, the **shared-bus network** (Fig. 8.4), a single bidirectional cable acts as a "bus line" to carry messages to and from devices. "Each node on the network has a unique address and failure at a single node will not disrupt the rest of the network" (Pfaffenberger, 2000). Information is stored in a central computer. To avoid the data collisions that occur when two or more nodes try to use the line at the same time, bus networks have collision detection to regulate traffic. Small local area networks use this configuration because it is an easy system to set up and use.

FIGURE 8.4
Shared-Bus Network
ClickArt Images ©1995
T/Maker Company.

Local area networks (LANs), wide area networks (WANs), and telephones are three types of networks. LANs provide communication within a local area, usually within 200 or 300 feet, such as in an office building. A school might have its card catalog stored on a file server's hard disk, accessible by other computers throughout the building through a LAN. WANs provide communication for a larger area that requires miles of communication linkage. A telephone network connects computers via telephone. The only difference between a WAN and a telephone network is the fact that the telephone's communication is intermittent, while the wide area network communicates all the time.

Networking computers offers many advantages:

1. It establishes communication among computers and is especially helpful when people work on different floors or in different buildings.
2. It improves the speed and accuracy of communication, preventing messages from being misplaced and automatically ensuring total distribution of key information.

3.   It saves money because users share software and equipment such as word processing programs and laser printers. Not only do users save on hardware; they save on software as well.
4.   A network allows users to share files with one another, which makes it suitable for class research.

However, this technology has some disadvantages:

1.   The costs of networking entail hardware, computer training, and maintenance, which can be high.
2.   Networking requires expertise that may not always be readily available, and school districts must consider the frustration level of teachers given the extra burden of learning a new system.
3.   It is difficult to find competent technicians to repair this equipment, and teachers who come to rely on their computers may be at a loss if the system crashes, a condition known as "computer dependency."
4.   The necessary networking software is not always available.
5.   The user must be mindful of system security; an unauthorized individual can access all information if the network is unprotected.

It was the Department of Defense's need for security that led to the creation of the Internet, the mother of all networks.

The Internet

The **Internet** is a large network that links smaller computer networks together. "The Internet is made up of more than 65 million computers in more than 100 countries covering commercial, academic and government endeavors" (Freedman, 2000). According to the National Center for Education Statistics, (http://nces.ed.gov/), 63 percent of U.S. public school classrooms were connected to the Internet in 1999. Having access to the Internet means that you can tap into thousands of databases and talk electronically with experts worldwide on any known subject. You can find jobs, communicate with teachers for educational planning, work out technical problems, sell products, conduct research, and find medical articles. Just how did this remarkable technology develop in such a relatively short time span?

Historical Background

In 1969, the Department of Defense created the Internet for military research purposes. The department's major concerns were to ensure mass communication of information while providing for maximum security. It wanted to connect the Pentagon with defense researchers in academia and business. The original network was called ARPAnet because the Advanced Research Projects Agency designed it. The goal was to build a decentralized network that would run even if nuclear war destroyed a portion of it. This network would continue to function during a disaster because it didn't rely on a single pathway for data transmission. The Department of Defense experimented with different ways of sending the data efficiently. Eventually, researchers devised a protocol that they called the Internet Protocol, or IP, to be used along with Transmission Control Protocol, or TCP.

In its first few years, this electronic highway provided a way of exchanging electronic mail service and linking online libraries to government agencies and universities. These agencies served as testers for the network's integrity. In the early 1980s, the original ARPAnet network divided into two networks, ARPAnet and Milnet. The connection between the networks was called the Defense Advanced Research Projects Agency, or DARPA Internet. In a short time, the name was shortened to the Internet.

In 1986, the National Science Foundation encouraged nondefense use of the Internet by creating a special network called NSFNet, which connected five new supercomputing centers across the country. Universities all over the country then started connecting into NSFNet. As the United States continued to develop its national and local networks during the 1980s, other countries did the same. This gave rise to connections among different national networks. As time passed, more countries joined the Internet to share its rich resources. By the late 1980s, students gained Internet access when they registered at their colleges. Since the Internet has become easier to use, more individuals and businesses have accessed it. In 1991, only 376,000 computers were registered on the Internet, but a year later this number had increased to 727,000. In the year 2001, the number of users on the Internet has ranged from 65 million to 108 million, depending on how researchers define Internet use. For instance, some researchers count Internet surfers at age 2, while other researchers count Internet surfing starting at age 18. Regardless, this figure could surge above 300 million by the end of 2003.

This growth is a far cry from the unenthusiastic reaction that U.S. Congressman Al Gore received in the 1980s when he called for the creation of a national network of "information highways" (Laquey and Ryer, 1992). In 1994, Apple, Microsoft, and IBM began including connectivity to online services as part of their operating systems (Farber, 1994), and software programs such as *ClarisWorks, Grolier Multimedia Encyclopedia,* and *HyperStudio* incorporated Internet components into their programs. Electronic services such as CompuServe and America Online offered **browsers,** software programs that allow subscribers to easily access the Internet, thus extending the Internet's influence even further.

Given the Internet's tremendous influence, we have to wonder, "Who pays the bill?" The answer is simple: University and research organizations pay to maintain their branches. Companies, organizations, and individuals who want direct access to the Internet also pay to connect. Finally, the government channels huge amounts of tax dollars through the National Science Foundation and various other governmental agencies such as NASA to help finance the Internet.

Recent Growth of the Internet

In the past, the Internet was difficult for the novice to use. However, Swiss researchers developed the **World Wide Web,** a system that lets the user move smoothly through the Internet, jumping from one document to another. Software tools were developed that made access to Internet resources uncomplicated. In 1993, Marc Andreessen developed *Mosaic* at the University of Illinois's National Center for Supercomputing Applications (NCSA). *Mosaic,* a software breakthrough, was a navigation tool for interactive material. This software browser allowed you to view pictures and documents by simply clicking on your mouse. A simple interface let you travel through the online world of electronic information along any path you wished in order to discover the wonders contained on the Internet. Figure 8.5 shows *Mosaic's* introductory screen.

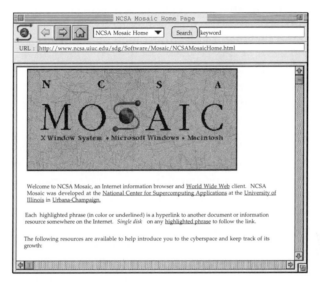

FIGURE 8.5
Mosaic

Mosaic™, NCSA Mosaic™, and the "spinning globe" logo are proprietary trademarks of the University of Illinois. These trademarks identify "Web" browser products developed and owned by the University of Illinois. Used with permission.

Some software houses purchased a nonexclusive license to sell and support *Mosaic.* At the time, Jim Clark, founder of Silicon Graphics Inc., decided not to license the source code but hired some of NCSA's programmers to reengineer a *Mosaic*-like browser. *Mosaic* author Marc Andreessen and Jim Clark formed a partnership they called Netscape Communications Corporation. They produced *Netscape Navigator,* which was a higher performance World Wide Web browser with multiple and simultaneous image loading. This browser was faster than *Mosaic* and much simpler to use. It also was more advanced than other browsers in the way it handled graphics (Morgenstern, 1995). In a short period of time, more browsers were developed, like Microsoft's *Internet Explorer;* these browsers made it unnecessary to learn the Unix commands that people had used on the Internet.

In the last half of the 1990s, two developments led to a surge in the Internet's growth. First, with the new graphics-based Web browsers, the World Wide Web exploded. Students and teachers found the Web easy to use, and it was no longer the private domain of scientists and hackers. Delphi was the first online service to offer access to the Web. Simultaneously, new Internet service providers offered access to individuals and companies. Internet service providers (ISPs) such as the award-winning Microsoft Software Network (MSN) provided Internet access and e-mail, and EarthLink Network, the world's largest independent ISP, provided network access and home pages. Many school districts gave students free ISP connection. There were also free commercial ISPs like Bluelight and Freelane. Liquid Slate gives a list of free Internet service providers (http://www.liquidslate.com/). Currently free services have begun to change and have restrictions. For example, Bluelight is limited to 12 hours per month.

The second development was the proliferation of e-mail. As online services such as America Online and CompuServe connected to the Internet, the Internet functioned as a central gateway: A member of one service could now send mail to a member of another. The Internet brought the world together for electronic mail (e-mail), and the Internet mail protocol is the world standard.

As a result of these developments, the Web provides a vast array of information and is the storehouse for drivers, updates, and demos that are downloaded by using the browser.

Problems with the Internet

There are quite a few security drawbacks on the Internet. People have been known to steal information, and some companies have had clients' correspondence violated. It is for this reason that Chrysler, Chevrolet, and Ford will not send designs over the Internet. Even though data are encrypted or encoded, it is difficult to verify a user's identity. Experts such as Taso Devetzis, a Bellcore lab researcher who does encryption work on the Internet, feel that the Internet is still not 100 percent secure. Because of security problems, many school districts are using a security system called **firewall** to protect their school's network against threats from hackers from other networks. A firewall is usually a combination of software and hardware that prevents computers in the school's network from communicating directly with computers outside the network, and vice versa. Another controversial issue is advertising over the network. Many people do not want to see advertising on the Internet, and yet it is there. Despite these problems, the Internet continues to grow rapidly because of the vast array of information and activities possible.

Using the Internet

Once you log onto the Internet, you can begin to use the tools that are available. You can look at a picture file of the Dead Sea Scrolls located in the Library of Congress. You can read an electronic copy of *Little Women*, obtain a weather satellite photograph, or chat with people around the world regarding a problem in physics. You can conduct legal research, consult job listings and career information, download public domain software or software updates for your computer. Most of the computers that connect to the Internet have resources such as electronic mail, searchable databases, and file transfer capabilities.

Internet Resources
Electronic Mail

Electronic mail, or **e-mail,** can be used to send messages to individuals at local or distant locations in a matter of seconds. What makes this system unique is the fact that the message recipient does not have to be present to receive a message. A host computer stores in memory any messages received; when the recipient logs on to the system, the screen displays a message informing him or her about the mail. There are many additional advantages to e-mail. You can quickly address an issue via e-mail without time-consuming social interaction. E-mail also conquers the problems of long-distance communication. People all over the world can easily communicate with each other instantly. E-mail can generate answers quickly and inexpensively.

A typical e-mail address has two parts: (1) the user's identification followed by the *at* symbol, @, and (2) the domain information consisting of the site name and type of organization. For example, the author's e-mail address is

vicki.sharp@csun.edu

The user's name identified in this example is *vicki.sharp.* The site name or domain name is *csun* (California State University, Northridge), and the domain type is *edu* (education). Examples of some domain types are government organization (*gov*), educational institution (*edu*), nonprofit organization (*org*), commercial organization (*com*). In the year 2000 the exponential growth of the Internet required the addition of new domain types such as *name, museum,* and *biz.*

It now seems hard to believe that electronic mail did not develop as rapidly as its innovators thought it would. There were two impediments to quick development. First, people were accustomed to fax machines (Fig. 8.6), which

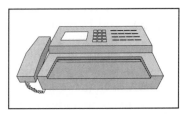

FIGURE 8.6
Fax Machine
ClickArt Images ©1995 T/Maker Company.

scan a piece of paper and convert its image into coded form for transmission over the telephone system; at the other end, a fax machine reconverts the transmitted code and prints out a facsimile of the original sheet of paper. This device does not require a computer or special knowledge in order for people to exchange information quickly. The second impediment was the existence of many incompatible, inadequately connected electronic mail systems. Although it seems likely that the competition among e-mail, fax, and the postal service will always exist, the Internet has solved the incompatibility problems of electronic mail systems. The Internet, a worldwide system of computer linkage, became the world forum for electronic mail and communications. This development resulted in a remarkable explosion of electronic mail. Figure 8.7 shows an electronic mail message sent via America Online, a commercial service provider.

FIGURE 8.7
America Online
AOL screenshots copyright 2001 America Online, Inc. Used with permission.

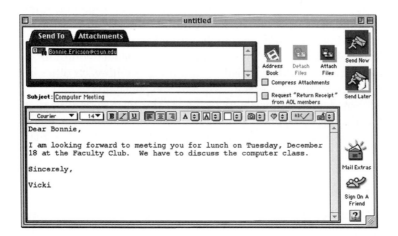

A browser, like Netscape, has e-mail applications integrated into its program.[1] Furthermore, there are stand-alone commercial programs like *Eudora Pro* (Qualcomm) that are loaded with features. Students who need fewer bells and whistles can download a freeware program like *Eudora Light* or *Pegasus* (David Harris, publisher) and use this program without restrictions. Both programs have basic components like sending and receiving messages, forwarding, replying, and setting up an address book.

Furthermore, there are free Web-based mail services such as *Yahoo! Mail, Email.com,* and *Hotmail. Yahoo! Mail* lets the user navigate by pointing and clicking. In addition, it has nice features like a signature file and mail filters. *Email.com,* owned by Snap.com, not only has all the standard features, but it lets the user have a simple e-mail address like vicki@email.com. Finally, *Hotmail,* one of the newest members to the Microsoft Network, besides being easy to use includes an antivirus scanner provided by McAfee. The *Free Email Address* reviews some of these e-mail services (http://www.free-email-address.com/).

The following resources are related to electronic mail:

---

[1] Netscape is now part of America Online, which is one of the most popular Internet service providers in the world. The Netscape browser does not come on many IBM-compatibles. To use it you have to download it from the Netscape website.

Netiquette When using e-mail, the writer must follow the proper etiquette. Getting along in the electronic environment (newsgroups and e-mail) is called **netiquette**, and here are a few suggestions for online usage:

1. Keep your messages to the point and brief.
2. Do not use ALL UPPERCASE LETTERS; this is considered shouting.
3. Never criticize a person's writing or spelling.
4. Don't overreact to items you see online.
5. Don't send excessive messages to multiple groups (cross-posting), in disregard of the members' interests.
6. Don't post items that are offensive.
7. Use discretion by not getting too personal with anyone.

You can find further suggestions on netiquette at the following sites: *Netiquette Home Page* (http://www.albion.com/netiquette/) and *Netiquette Life on the Internet* (http://www.cochran.com/start/guide/Netiquette.html).

Internet Relay Chat (IRC) **Internet Relay Chat (IRC)** allows you to do computer conferencing on the Internet. There are IRC channels on a wide range of topics that take place on IRC servers around the world. After you join a channel, your messages are broadcast to everyone listening on that channel.

Chat Rooms The **chat room** is a discussion by keyboard on a specific topic. These conversations address varied subjects. You can also choose an individual with whom to have a private conversation. Chat rooms are available from services such as America Online, many websites, and the Internet relay chat system.

Instant Messenger (or Instant Messaging) There are quite a few **instant messenger** programs such as AOL Instant Messenger which let you receive instant alerts, send instant messages, share photos and sound, and enjoy conversations online (Fig. 8.8). In addition, you can chat with friends and keep abreast of the news and stocks.

FIGURE 8.8
*America Online
Instant Messenger*
AOL screenshots copyright
2001 America Online, Inc.
Used with permission.

Searchable Databases and File Transfer Protocols

In addition to electronic mail, the Internet offers the following useful resources.

Wide-Area Information Service (WAIS)   **The Wide-Area Information Service (WAIS)** accesses many databases that are distributed around the Internet. For example, you can use it to access ERIC (Education Resources Information Clearinghouse). By specifying a list of keywords to use in a search, you are telling WAIS what databases to search. WAIS then searches every article in all the databases that you select. You can then view or print out the list of articles found in the search.

Telnet   **Telnet** is a software utility that lets you log on to a remote computer.

File Transfer Protocol (FTP)   Internet users may copy files that are spread around the Internet in large and small archives. These files contain text, pictures, sounds, and computer programs. The standard tool for copying these files is called **file transfer protocol (FTP)**. Using this tool, you can copy a file from the archive of a host computer to your own computer. If you do not have an account on the host computer, the host computer may recognize the special account name *anonymous*.

Archie Server   The **Archie server** helps you find a file stored at an anonymous FTP site. It is easy to download the file using FTP once you know the name of the site.

Gopher.   **Gopher** displays a simple series of menus through which you can access any type of textual information on the Internet. Gopher systems are locally administered and no longer as popular as they were before the Web existed.

Finger Service   **Finger service** lets you find out information about another Internet user, including the name of the person behind the user identification name (userid).

Usenet   The User's Network (**Usenet**) is not really a network, but it is a place for discussion groups. Through this network, individual articles can be distributed throughout the world. The estimate of users today is 7.9 million (Weise, 2000). Since the rise of the Web, Usenet is fading into obscurity.

Multiple User Dimension (MUD)   **The Multiple User Dimension (MUD)**, a program that involves rudimentary virtual reality, is similar to Dungeons and Dragons. You participate by taking on a role and exploring it in interactions with others.

Bulletin Board Systems (BBSs)   A **bulletin board system (BBS)** is a central computer that stores messages from other individuals. It is often set up in a person's home, and the individual who is in charge is called a **system operator**, or **sysop**. The bulletin board has three individual parts: (1) a message board where the user reads or posts messages; (2) a library of files where an individual can access programs ranging from graphics to public domain software; and (3) electronic mail (e-mail) for private communication with friends or colleagues.

Though they have declined in popularity, there are still bulletin boards across the world. The Internet has bulletin board systems at which messages and files devoted to certain topics are stored. An excellent bulletin board is BMUG, the Berkeley Macintosh Users Group. BMUG distributes information, gives help on Macintosh computer problems, and provides software for its members. In the 1990s, bulletin boards came under attack for harboring adult-only material that is easily seen by minors. Opponents of these types of bulletin boards encouraged the U.S. Congress to pass legislation criminalizing the distribution, creation, and availability of obscene material or communication that is indecent for minors. However, the U.S. Supreme Court upheld First Amendment protection for free speech and declared that this Communications Decency Act of 1996 was unconstitutional. Today, the bulletin boards are used where there is less direct Internet access, and many serve as e-mail channels to the Internet. Some software companies continue to maintain their bulletin boards as an alternative to their website for downloading software. The popularity of bulletin boards declined because browsers like Microsoft's *Internet Explorer* and *Netscape Communicator* make it easier to navigate the Internet and download files.

Newsgroups   Different from e-mail, **newsgroups** are like public bulletin boards in which you can read messages that others have written and write your own thoughts. An example of a website with a wide variety of bulletin boards is egroups at http://www.egroups.com. People discuss a range of topics from news to entertainment to grade-appropriate lesson plans.

World Wide Web   The Web is defined as "a global hypertext system that uses the Internet as its transport mechanism" (Pfaffenberger, 2000). The Web is a collection of computers containing documents accessed with special software that allows one to view text, graphics, video, and photos and to easily link to another document on the Web. (The World Wide Web will be discussed in this chapter and Chapter 9.)

This section has presented a small sample of the tools and resources that are available on the Internet.

Internet Access

The power of your modem compared to your personal computer is antiquated. Using a modern modem with today's Power G4 Macintosh machines or Pentium IV is like trying to power a race car with a lawnmower engine. Modems are certainly faster than they used to be. Each improvement in speed seems fast at first, but eventually, due to larger downloading and more complexity, the modem seems slow again. The villain responsible is the **bandwidth,** or the amount of data that can be transmitted through the computer network in a certain time period. An analogy would be the amount of water than can flow through different size pipes. New technologies promise to change this situation and increase bandwidth capacity. Presently your choices are limited to the following: 56-Kbps modems, cable modems, digital subscriber lines (DSLs), ISDN, and satellite data services.

The percentage of homes in the United States with **broadband** or high-speed-transmission Internet access will increase from 5 percent in 2000 to 66 percent in 2008, according to a study by the investment bank Goldman Sachs. Broadband growth will be driven by an increase in consumer adoption of cable modem and digital subscriber line (DSL) technology (Deveaux, 2000). Recently, companies providing DSL have been in competition with cable companies to provide faster service.

Modems

The **modem** is a device that adapts a computer to an analog telephone line by converting digital pulses to audio frequencies and the reverse (see Chapter 3). Currently 56 Kbps modems are standard equipment with computers and achieve their speed using the regular phone line. These modems are probably the last of their kind. They are half as fast as the ISDN modem, but lower monthly charges for using the 56 Kbps service make them attractive. A drawback is that you need a good-quality phone line in your house or you have to be within a mile or two of a phone company's switch, which means that rural areas do not have access to 56 Kbps services. Furthermore, you need an Internet service provider (ISP) that has hardware support for this kind of modem. Of the technologies briefly described here, we can't be sure which will dominate in the years to come. However, we can be sure that the connection speed will run faster and more individuals will be using high-speed digital lines.

A **cable modem** lets you connect to the Internet with the same cable that attaches to a standard television set. The cable modems, offered by many cable companies, provide shared point-to-point transmission. Cable modems offer a greater bandwidth (the amount of data transmitted in a fixed time period) than DSL. Even though this is the case, a cable modem is limited by the amount of use of the line, because the cable line is shared among many users. The speeds for cable vary, and heavy downloads are faster when few people are online. In the near future faster cable modems will be appearing.

Digital Connections

Digital subscriber lines (DSLs) and cable modems are different technologies, but both provide dedicated multimegabit connections to a service and they are always on, unlike a dial-up modem. DSL is a digital technology that offers high-speed transmission over standard copper telephone wiring. DSL is point-to-point technology providing downloading at speeds up to 8 megabits per second (Mbps). DSL can carry both voice and data signals at the same time, in both directions. There are many versions of DSL with varying transmission speeds. A benefit of DSL is that you can use the phone at the same time you use the Web, so you do not need a separate telephone line. However, DSL speeds are tied to the distance between the user and the central office. Also, DSL may not be available in your area.

The **Integrated Services Digital Network (ISDN)** was designed in the early 1980s as a replacement for analog telephone service. This service uses high-speed digital phone lines offered by the phone companies in most urban areas. The connection can range from 64 to 128 Kbps. When ISDN burst on the scene, it was difficult to order and particularly difficult to install the hardware. Moreover, ISDN is not universally available in the United States, and the combination of per-call connect charges and per-minute billing on data calls makes it expensive. Therefore, interest in this technology has diminished.

Satellite Data Service

Satellite data service uses a satellite dish to connect to your computer. A satellite data service can give you 400 kilobits per second (Kbps) for downloading. However, you connect to this service via an analog modem, and the installation charges are high.

The Internet and the World Wide Web

Even though the terms *Internet* and *Web* are used interchangeably, they are actually two different things. The Internet is the group of computers that carry data and make the exchange of information possible; the World Wide Web, a subset of the Internet, is a collection of interlinked documents that work together using a specific protocol called **Hypertext Transfer Protocol (HTTP).** The Internet exists independently of the Web, whereas the reverse is not true.

The World Wide Web is an invaluable resource for people interested in knowledge. You are only a mouse click away from a vast reservoir of information. The Web offers teachers a giant library with millions of sites that are increasing at a phenomenal rate each week. More than 10 million children are online, and it is predicted there will be 45 million online by 2002. The Software Publishers Association[2] conducted a survey and found that the two leading uses of the Internet were education and research/reference (Dyril, 1998). The Web is the multimedia part of the Internet—that huge worldwide network of connected computer networks with no single master control center or authority. The Web consists of a collection of electronic documents, called **home pages** or **websites,** full of text, pictures, sounds, and even video. **Hypertext markup language (HTML)** is the language used to design these home pages. (This simple language is discussed in Chapter 9.)

There are thousands of websites that take advantage of the Web's multimedia capabilities. Web users can do such things as get information on any curriculum area, talk to an expert, explore the human brain, participate in online discussion groups, and download chapters from books or lecture notes.

Websites, or home pages, have their own unique addresses called **uniform resource locators (URLs).** These individual addresses make websites easy to find. URLs start with *http://.* As an example, the URL for the website AskERIC is

http://www.askeric.org/

---

[2]The Software Publishers Association's new name is the Software Information Industry Association.

This site provides educational information to teachers, librarians, counselors, administrators, parents, and others throughout the United States and the world.

Once connected to a site, a reader will see that certain items on the Web pages are underlined. These underlined items, called *links,* are like threads in a spider's web and give the World Wide Web its name. Just by clicking on these links, the reader can jump from one page on the Web to another, be it a page on the same computer or a page on the other side of the world. One document is linked to another, which is linked to another, and so forth.

Connecting to an Online Service

To access the Web, you need a connection to the Internet. To start, you need a computer running Windows with at least a Pentium processor and 64 MB of RAM or a Macintosh computer running System 7 or higher with at least 64 MB of memory. Because of the memory requirements for most browsers, you will be happier with at least 96 MB of RAM. You will also need a modem with a transfer speed of 56 Kbps. Now you can get an Internet connection through a commercial online service such as America Online or CompuServe. In addition to providing access to information, many of these online services offer electronic mail and news and information about the weather, entertainment, sports, and finance. Furthermore, with such services you can download thousands of free programs, make contact with fellow computer users, obtain free help from experts, connect to the Internet, participate in conferences on a variety of topics, and obtain hardware and software support. When you join one of these services, you receive a starter kit with a subscriber identification number, a temporary password, and a manual explaining how to use the service. Most of the services initially give free online time, but after this initiation period, monthly charges vary widely and may include an extra fee for special services. Most of these commercial networks also have bulletin boards. What follows are brief summaries of the three most popular commercial services.

America Online

America Online (AOL) is the world's largest online information service (Freedman, 2000). This service (Fig. 8.9) features e-mail, AOL Instant Messenger, and chat, as well as customized news information; financial information and stock quotes; movie information; maps and driving directions; and local entertainment information. In addition, you can play games, access the encyclopedia, and more. AOL lets you point and click to find your way around the service. AOL has a quick-search function that can access the entire collection of files. It allows you to search all the databases with keywords. To download a file, simply select the file and click **Download.** When the file is finished, a voice says, "file done."

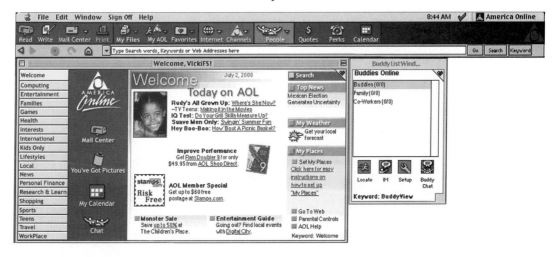

FIGURE 8.9   *America Online Introductory Screen*
AOL screenshots coyright 2001 America Online, Inc. Used with permission.

Prodigy

Prodigy has many of the same options that America Online offers. It was the first service with a built-in Web browser. One of its more popular services is home banking, which lets subscribers pay their bills electronically, transfer funds, and check their balances, all from the comfort of their own homes. Prodigy's family-oriented computer service now offers a simpler interface.

CompuServe

CompuServe is one of the oldest services and in the beginning was used mostly by businesspeople. At first, this service was very difficult to navigate, but it has changed its interface to resemble that of America Online. CompuServe provides services similar to the other commercial providers: Users can track stocks, play games, access encyclopedias, and obtain news and weather information.

Other Internet Service Providers

You can also get an Internet connection through an Internet service provider (ISP) like *Microsoft Software Network (MSN)* (http://essentials.msn.com/access/) or like *Earthlink* (http://www.earthlink.net/). Several places can help you find an ISP to fit your needs. If you already have access to the Internet through a commercial online service, you can check out a list of providers at http://www.thelist.com/. *The List* lets you search for providers by country, state, or area code.

Another place to find information about ISPs is in the local Yellow Pages or from a local computer user group.

Getting Started with a Browser

To take advantage of the Web, you need a software program called a browser. When you first launch your browser, in this case *Netscape Communicator* (Macintosh version) (Fig. 8.10), you see a toolbar at the top of its window. The toolbar has commands such as Print, Back, and Forward.

FIGURE 8.10   Netscape Communicator *Opening Screen*
Reprinted by permission of Netscape Communications.

From the **File** menu, choose **Open** then **Location in Navigator** (Note: You can also type the URL in the *Location* or *Netsite* line and press the Return or Enter key.)

Next, you type the following URL in the dialog box and then click **Open** (Fig. 8.11):

http://www.askeric.org/

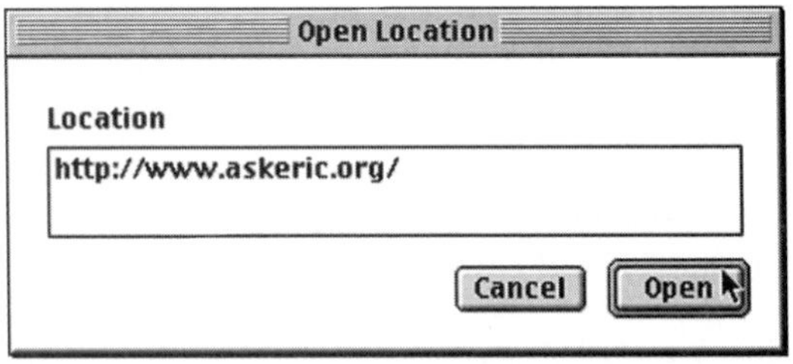

FIGURE 8.11   Netscape Communicator *Open Location*
Reprinted by permission of Netscape Communications.

After a few seconds, the home page corresponding to the URL will appear. Wait until the page is fully loaded on your screen. You are now ready to explore links, or connections, to other Web pages. Links are words that are underlined or displayed in a different color, or pictures that have a colored border around them (Fig. 8.12). *Note:* When you click on a live link, the pointer (or arrow) becomes a hand.

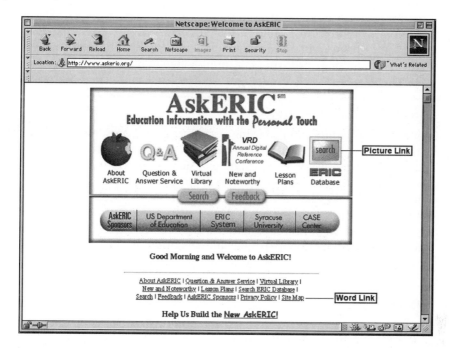

FIGURE 8.12
AskERIC's Home Page
Used by permission of ERIC.

Visual Communication Via the Internet

In the past, people used text only to communicate on the Internet. This situation changed with the explosion of the World Wide Web and the movement toward individuals and organizations creating websites. Visual communication became the cry as would-be authors demanded graphics, animations, and sounds. Students and teachers used visual images to communicate in distance learning, placing clip art, animations, photos, and scans on their Web pages. Furthermore, students shot movies with their camcorders and downloaded these movies to the Internet. Unfortunately, they had to wait a long time for the movies to download. Being impatient, they wanted to watch these videoclips as they downloaded them. Out of this need grew streaming video and streaming audio.

Streaming Video
Streaming videos are compressed movies that are sent in real time via the Internet. **Real time** is that time in which the event actually occurs. The receiving users can play these streaming movies with a streaming video player such as *RealVideo* or *QuickTime*. With streaming video the movies begin playing as

soon as you start to download. The quality of the movie depends on the speed of the computer connection. Videomaker's site on streaming video, found at http://www.streamingvideos.com, gives a more complete explanation of frequently asked questions about streaming video.

Streaming Audio

Streaming audio is audio transmission over the data network. The term means one-way transmission to the listener in which the listener and server cooperate to have uninterrupted sound. *RealPlayer* is a multimedia player that plays streaming audio and streaming video in real time.

Distance Education

As the number of individuals using the Internet increases, more people will be engaging in distance learning. **Distance learning** is "obtaining education and training from a remote teaching site via TV or computer" (Freedman, 2000). In distance learning, the learners are physically separated from one another during class and instructors use audio and videoconferencing and computer communication to teach. This type of communication can remove the barrier of distance and time because students can take classes from anywhere in the world, often with a flexible schedule.

FIGURE 8.13
Distance Learning
Used by permission of
ArtToday.com, Inc.

Distance learning is being used in medicine, law, education, and business. For years, doctors, lawyers, and engineers have used it to continue their educational studies. Many of these professionals are too busy in their work to participate in classroom study and they find home study their only option. Distance learning also reaches students who are in remote rural locations. Sometimes schools may not be able to spend money on a teacher to teach an advanced physics or chemistry course, and distance learning addresses this problem. Additionally, learners who are homebound due to serious illness or physical disability may not be able to travel to the educational institution. Furthermore, through distance learning the teacher can bring experts or special individuals into a classroom. Distance learning can link two classrooms so that students can communicate with each other.

Throughout the United States, professors are engaging in electronic instruction. Higher education institutions have used distance education to reach a diverse audience that would not be accessible through traditional classroom instruction. Many universities are offering virtual degrees via the Internet. Duke University and the University of Maryland are offering master's degree programs entirely through the Internet (Molnar, 1997). In 1999, Georgia Institute of Technology began offering courses over the Internet that could be applied toward a Master of Science degree in Mechanical Engineering. The University of Illinois at Champaign–Urbana (UICU) offers any student in the state the chance to take engineering courses without having to attend classes on campus. Presently, UICU students take exams, receive class assignments, are graded on their work, and engage in discussions with their teachers and classmates electronically, accomplished with conferencing software. In 1996, one of the first pre–college-level virtual schools, called the The Virtual High School, was started by the Hudson, Massachusetts, Public School System and the Concord Consortium. There are currently 43 high schools and 13 states registered. TEAMS Distance Learning, a service of the Los Angeles County Office of Education (LACOE), brings learning opportunities to K–8 students, teachers, and parents across the United States through nationally televised satellite broadcasts and the Internet.

Distance Learning Technologies

The first attempt at distance education was by correspondence. The student used self-study instructional material. This is still used today, but it is limited by the lack of interaction between the student and instructor. For correspondence the audiocassette and the videocassette can be used to supplement the printed text. As distance education developed, different technologies were used, such as television, radio, and the telephone. Let's discuss some of these technologies.

Radio
Radio reaches a large geographical area at a low cost. It can provide a uniform message to a diverse audience, and it is useful in curriculum areas such as music or language arts. Unfortunately, radio broadcasts have a fixed schedule and the communication is one way from the teacher to the student.

Telephone
Audio teleconferencing uses the telephone to permit interaction between individuals or groups at two or more locations. The individual(s) can use a speakerphone or additional equipment such as a microphone, amplifier, and speakers. The audience can have live two-way interaction between two physically separated locations. The person can be heard by an audience and can hear their reaction. When time and cost are factors, the audio teleconferencing method is an effective way to conduct a meeting, give simple instructions, or interview a person. A language arts teacher may interview an author this way, or a social studies teacher may interview a politician. The only negative aspect of this type of technology is that it uses only audio.

Video

Video can be delivered over distances using cable, television, satellite, microwave transmission, and closed circuit. There are different levels of video, for instance, one-way video and audio, one-way video with two-way audio, and two-way video and audio.

Television usually involves one-way transmission of information. There have been many experiments over the years on using television for educational purposes. Today schools use programs developed by the Public Broadcasting System and CNN's Newsroom and their local stations. The advantage of this system is it reaches a mass audience; the disadvantages are its dependence on time and the lack of interaction between the instructor and learner. To solve the latter problem, the instructor might add a simple telephone connection or a speakerphone between the two locations. With a talk-back capability students can then call the instructor with questions. The closest thing to face-to-face instruction in a classroom is two-way interactive video. The sending and receiving parties have cameras, video monitors, and microphones. The transmission is by cable, fiber optic, microwave, or digital-grade telephone lines that link the sites together. There are many experiments in this type of instruction in K–12 schools. This technology is still young and the video compression which is needed to support two-way interactive video can still cause some problems with picture quality. This system can be difficult and expensive to operate.

Computers

The learner can use the CD-ROM and instructional software to take a correspondence course. For this course, the student can use still pictures and graphics along with audio teleconferencing as aids. Audio teleconferencing can be conducted over the Internet. With the proper equipment, students can also engage in telephone calls over the Internet. This method is less expensive than placing a normal telephone call. Unfortunately, this technology is still new and the audio quality is not good. Furthermore, the computer can be used as a presentation tool or a slide projector to present text and graphics.

Desktop Videoconferencing

If you have the proper hardware and software, you can engage in **desktop videoconferencing.** (See Chapter 16 for a discussion.) For hardware, you need a network or modem connection, speakers, microphone, video camera, and computer. You can use software like White Pine's *CUSeeMe* or Microsoft's *NetMeeting*. The drawbacks to this software are it requires a lot of bandwidth and transmission is slow and jumpy. You need special high-speed connections for this to work more effectively. "The demand for videoconferencing is increasing and as soon as bandwidth issues and protocol issues are resolved this market will explode" (Merritt, 2000). Even with these drawbacks it is becoming quite popular in the classroom. It is not uncommon to find a microphone, a video camera, and speakers at a computer station. This equipment lets the teacher see and hear the students. Using the telephone lines and modem, the teacher and students can communicate with each other. The teacher can use a liquid crystal display (LCD) projection panel connected to the computer to enlarge the group of people that can see the screen video. Using compatible systems, the students can communicate with experts, students, or teachers in another state or country.

The teacher can supplement these computer devices for distance learning to include e-mail, computer conferencing, and the Web. E-mail allows the students to contact the teachers personally. Computer conferencing lets two or more individuals talk to each other. They talk one at time, as they would on a short-wave radio. The student can post from any location. The computer conference is an ongoing conversation among individuals who can leave when they want and not miss anything. When you want interaction to occur at the same time, the students use a chat function. Individuals interact by typing text back and forth. Chat rooms are very popular on the Internet for socialization. In the classroom, the students can use chat rooms to interact with students at another school or talk to experts in the field on other topics (Fig. 8.14).

FIGURE 8.14
Students Working on a Distance Learning Project
Used by permission of ArtToday.com, Inc.

Thanks to the computer, students can more easily communicate with instructors, and instructors can be more accessible and responsive to students' questions. More and more schools and universities are developing two-way audio and video capabilities; hence, distance learning is expanding. Teachers and students at distant locations are easily communicating with each other. Students are interacting more with other students in different countries. Instructors are communicating more by e-mail, chat rooms, and videoconferencing.

Drawbacks of Distance Learning

Distance learning offers many benefits; however, it is expensive and difficult to implement. For example, even though a simpler technology such as audio teleconferencing may cost only the charge of a long-distance call, this could be a problem in some schools. Two-way interactive can be very costly because the equipment needed is expensive and the cost of connecting two sites can be quite high. The cost of transmitting over telephone lines is high because of the huge bandwidth that the signal requires. Distance education is technically difficult to set up; videoconferencing requires an expert to coordinate personnel, vendors, technicians, and the telephone company. Extensive planning—scheduling of equipment and rooms—is needed. The rooms have to be planned in advance, and the equipment must be checked. Teachers need to redesign their lessons and activities to take advantage of distance learning technology, but first they need to be trained to effectively use this technology. This could involve on-site assistants, telephone help, e-mail. In other words, a lot of work is involved in distance learning, and only those who are able to expend the extra time, effort, and resources should undertake it. As this trend continues, the way we view the traditional school may change forever. At the very least, technology will change the way students learn and the time they spend in the school building (see Chapter 16).

Integrating the Internet into the Classroom

The Internet is becoming a pervasive influence on our lives. In 1994, only 35 percent of public schools had access to the Internet, whereas in 1996 some 65 percent of the schools had access to the Internet (Advanced Telecommunication in U.S. Public Elementary and Secondary Schools, Fall 1996, U.S. Department of Education, National Center for Education Statistics, 1997). In 1999, the ratio of students per instructional computer in public school was approximately six to one and 95 percent of public schools had access to the Internet (National Center for Education Statistics, 2000).

The Internet offers some exciting possibilities for the classroom. Because teachers and students have access to this huge library of information, teachers need to develop skill for determining the most relevant and best quality information. Here are a few suggestions on how to enhance the student's learning experiences.

Classroom Projects

1. Students can conduct online research using databases and online resources. For example, they can find information on topics such as whales, pandas, laws, distance learning, and the Civil War. Additionally, the students can obtain pictures and sounds.
2. The class can track current events through online magazines and newspapers. The students are no longer limited to hometown newspapers and magazines. Access to the Internet lets the students get critical stories from a variety of places. The students can compare local newspapers with what is being written by national and world news organizations.
3. New and experienced teachers can access databases of lesson plans, teaching methods, and instructional approaches. Students can find information on what to teach, hands-on experiments, drama techniques, and lesson plans.

4. Students can even access information on job possibilities, people to contact, and how to prepare a résumé.
5. Students can create multimedia projects or reports on the Web.

Some invaluable telecommunications tutorials accompany products such as *Microsoft Works* and *AppleWorks.* In addition to studying tutorials, students can engage in many activities that incorporate telecommunications into the classroom. What follows are five such lessons.

Classroom Lesson Plans

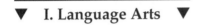

▼   I. Language Arts   ▼

Materials

You will need a computer, a word processing program, and a modem.

Objective

Students will e-mail a letter to another student.

Procedure

1. Introduce the students to telecommunications.
2. Demonstrate how the computer, software, modem, and printer work.
3. Discuss terms such as bulletin boards and electronic mail.
4. Show examples of completed pen pal letters.
5. Have students type and transmit letters to another school, using the modem.

▼   II. Science   ▼

Materials

You will need a computer with access to the Internet.

Objective

Students will identify and explain causes of chemical and physical weathering.

Procedure

1. Teach a unit on current environmental issues.
2. Have students measure local rainfall and its acidity level.

3. Access the Internet and have students use it to discover patterns of acidity in the rainwater across the continent.
4. Ask students to post their results online for other schools to use.
5. Have students download information from other students and draw maps and charts.

▼   III. General   ▼

Materials

You will need a computer, a communications package, a color monitor, a printer, a modem, a telephone line, and access to the Internet.

Objective

Using the Internet, college students will find online activities or lessons.

Procedure

1. Have the students search the Internet for useful sites.
2. Choose a lesson plan for a specific topic in a subject area with an online interactive activity.
3. Print the lesson plan and discuss it with your class.

▼   IV. Social Studies   ▼

Materials

You will need a computer and access to the Internet.

Objective

Students will learn about the American presidency by searching a site like "The American Presidency," found at the following URL:

http://gi.grolier.com/presidents/

Procedure

1. Discuss in class how to search the site.
2. Divide the students into small groups, for example, five groups.
3. Next, have the students use the "American Presidency" site or one like it to make up questions on the presidency.
4. Have the groups exchange questions and tell them to find the answers in a 15-minute time period. (Vary the time period according to the number and complexity of questions.)

5. The first group that answers the question correctly earns 5 points, the second group to finish earns 4, and so on. If you had divided the class into six groups, the first group to finish would receive 6 points.
6. Have the groups exchange questions again and continue the activity until every group has seen all the questions.
7. The winner is the group with the most points.

▼ V. Art ▼

Materials

You will need a computer and access to the Internet.

Objective

Students will use a site such as "Treasures of the Louvre," located at

http://www.paris.org/Musees/Louvre/Treasures/

to learn about the different art treasures found in the Louvre.

Procedure

1. Discuss some of the art treasures that people see in the Louvre.
2. Divide the students into small groups.
3. Using a site on the Louvre, have each group research a treasure that is located there and write a description of this art object.
4. In class, have each group discuss the art treasure they researched.
5. Now, each week the teacher can e-mail a set of clues to each group and have them find the particular art treasure.
6. The first group to come up with the answer gets a point.

Summary

In this chapter, we discussed the Internet, the mother of networks, in detail, including its history and the many available Internet resources. We discussed why the World Wide Web is invaluable and how it works. Briefly, we examined popular online services. Next we learned about distance learning and how it is being used in the classroom, its attributes, and its drawbacks. We also defined netiquette and listed some important rules. Finally, five classroom lessons or activities were shown.

 INTERNET SITES

What follows is an annotated list of Internet sites. These sites include information about search engines, tutorials, distance learning, lesson plans, activities, and tips.

Distance Learning on the Net
http://www.hoyle.com/distance.htm
Distance Learning on the Net, created by Glenn Hoyle, includes descriptions of distance education websites, along with links to lead you to further distance learning and education resources on the Internet.

Britannica.Com
http://www.britannica.com/
The Britannica.com site brings the best web-sites, leading magazines, related book, and the complete encyclopedia.

Internet Dictionary
http://www.oh-no.com/define.html
Internet Dictionary is a collection of terms common to the Internet.

Internet Society
http://www.isoc.org/internet-history/
The Internet Society articles range from those who made history to the World Wide Web past, present, and future.

University of South Dakota
http://www.usd.edu/trio/
University of South Dakota has a series of excellent basic tutorials on the Internet. Click on Tutorials and you have Internet Basics 101, which explains, tests, and illustrates basic Internet concepts.

Desktop Video Conferencing
http://www.coe.missouri.edu/~cjw/video/
Desktop Video Conferencing is a research project from the College of Education at the University of Missouri–Columbia. This site includes frequently asked questions, hardware and sofware, how to set up a two-way conference, and links to Web resources.

Barry's Clip Art Server
http://www.barrysclipart.com/
Barry's Clip Art Server contains thousands of images, all free for download.

The List
http://thelist.internet.com/
This ISP buyer's guide lets you search for providers by country, state, or area code.

Distant Learning Resource Network
http://www.dlrn.org/
The Distance Learning Resource Network (DLRN) is the dissemination project for the U.S. Department of Education Star Schools Program. This site contains information about distance learning, about other distance learning programs, Web-based instruction, news and publications, literature reviews and reports, and other resources.

Chapter Mastery Test

To the Instructor: Refer to the Instructor's Manual for the Answers to the Mastery Questions. This manual has additional questions and resource materials.

Let's check for chapter comprehension with a short mastery test. What follows are basic terms, classroom projects, and suggested readings and references.

1. How did the Internet begin and what led to its growth?
2. Define *networking*.
3. Discuss the advantages and disadvantages of using networking in the classroom.
4. Identify and briefly describe one of the more popular online services, elaborating on some of its resources.
5. Describe the Internet and discuss three of its resources.
6. What is the difference between e-mail and an electronic bulletin board?
7. What is *Mosaic* and why was it a technological breakthrough?
8. What distinguishes distance education from traditional classroom instruction?
9. Define the following terms: home page, URL, ISP, and HTML.
10. What is the World Wide Web and why is it an invaluable resource?
11. Give an example of a browser and explain why you need to use one.
12. Distinguish between 56-Kbps modems and cable modems.

Basic Terms

Archie server (p. 192)	modem (p. 194)
bandwidth (p. 193)	Multiple User Dimension (MUD) (p. 192)
broadband (p. 194)	netiquette (p. 191)
browsers (p. 186)	networking (p. 182)
bulletin board system (BBS) (p. 192)	newsgroups (p. 193)
cable modem (p. 194)	real time (p. 199)
chat room (p. 191)	ring network (p. 183)
desktop videoconferencing (p. 202)	routers and bridges (p. 182)
digital subscriber lines (DSLs) (p. 194)	satellite data service (p. 195)
distance learning (p. 200)	shared-bus network (p. 184)
e-mail (p. 189)	star network (p. 184)
file transfer protocol (FTP) (p. 192)	streaming audio (p. 200)
finger service (p. 192)	streaming videos (p. 199)
firewall (p. 188)	system operator (sysop) (p. 192)
gopher (p. 192)	telecommunications (p. 181)
home pages (p. 195)	Telnet (p. 192)
Hypertext Markup Language (HTML) (p. 195)	uniform resource locators (URLs) (p. 195)
Hypertext Transfer Protocol (HTTP) (p. 195)	Usenet (p. 192)
instant messenger (p. 191)	websites (p. 195)
Integrated Services Digital Network (ISDN) (p. 194)	Wide-Area Information Service (WAIS) (p. 192)
Internet (p. 185)	wide area networks (WANs) (p. 184)
Internet Relay Chat (IRC) (p. 191)	wireless network (p. 182)
local area networks (LANs) (p. 184)	World Wide Web (the Web) (p. 186)

Classroom Projects

1. E-mail someone in your class or at another school.
2. Take a field trip to a school that uses networking. Find out what type of network and what software are being utilized and how students are using networking in the classroom. Evaluate this school's program, listing its strengths and weaknesses.
3. Examine the different online services and compare their costs and benefits.

Suggested Readings and References

Altschuler, Glenn C., and Ralph Janis. "Promise and Pitfalls in Distance Education for Alumni." *Chronicle of Higher Education* 46, no. 41 (June 16, 2000): B8.

Biehle, James T. "Four Keys to Putting Tomorrow's Technology in Yesterday's Buildings." *School Planning and Management* 36, no. 2 (February 1997): 27–28.

Bork, Alfred. "The Future of Computers and Learning." *T.H.E. Journal* 24, no. 11 (June 1997): 69–77.

Braun, Joseph A., Jr. "Past, Possibilities, and Potholes on the Information Superhighway." *Social Education* 61, no. 3 (March 1997): 149–53.

Brown, Eric. "The Wireless Web." *Entrepreneur* 28, no. 7 (July 2000): 36.

Brownstein, Mark. "Butter Up for Broadband." *Byte,* October 1997, pp. 71–73.

Bull, Glen, Gina Bull, and Tim Sigmon. "Interactive Web Pages." *Learning and Leading with Technology* 24, no. 6 (March 1997): 22–27.

Burniske, R. W. "Netiquette." *Teacher Magazine* 9, no. 5 (February 1998): 44.

Carr, Stephen. "Putting It All Together." *Education Week* 17, no. 11 (November 10, 1997): 16–18.

Craig, Dorothy, and Jaci Stewart. "Mission to Mars." *Learning and Leading with Technology* 25, no. 2 (October 1997): 22–27.

Crawford, Walt. "Jargon That Computes: Today's PC Terminology." *Online* 21, no. 2 (March–April 1997): 36–41.

Darrow, Barbara. "IBM Develops Prototype of Color Touch Screen for Laptops." *InfoWorld* 13, no. 16 (April 22, 1991): 6.

Davis, Bob. "Internet in Schools: A National Crusade Backed by Scant Data." *Wall Street Journal Eastern Edition,* June 19, 2000, p. A1.

Davitt, John. "Need a Lesson Plan? Just Browse the Web." *Times Educational Supplement,* March 14, 1997, Computers Update, p. 10.

Dede, Chris. "The Evolution of Distance Education: Emerging Technologies and Distributed Learning." *American Journal of Distance Education* 10, no. 2 (1996): 4–36.

Desposito, Joseph. *Que's Computer Buyer's Guide.* Carmel, Ind.: Que Corporation, 2000.

Deveaux, Sarah, "Cable vs. DSL Is No Battle," *InfoWorld,* July 11, 2000 (http://www.infoworld.com).

Duffy, Bob. "Buttoning Down the Content Explosion." *Electronic Library* 15, no. 3 (June 1997): 227–29.

Dyril, Odvard, E. "Stats Making News." *Technology and Learning* 18, no. 7 (March 1998): 64.

Eklund, John, and Peter Eklund. "Collaboration and Networked Technology: A Case Study in Teaching Educational Computing." *Journal of Computing in Teachers Education* 13, no. 3 (April 1997): 14–19.

Farber, Dan. "Are You Experienced with What Internet Participation Takes?" *PC Week* 11, no. 31 (August 8, 1994): 3.

Flanagan, Patrick. "The 10 Hottest Technologies in Telcom." *Telecommunications* 31, no. 5 (May 1997): 25–28, 30, 32.

Fraser, Bruce. "Digital Cameras Coming into Focus." *MacWeek* 11, no. 31 (August 8, 1997): 11.

Freedman, Alan. *The Computer Glossary.* New York: Amacom, 2000.

Friedlander, Emily. "Access Denied." *FamilyPC* 7, no. 7 (July 2000): 28.

Gomes, Lee. "Internet Relay Chat Is Suspected Launch Pad of Web Hackers." *Wall Street Journal Eastern Edition,* February 14, 2000, p. B6.

Glossbrenner, Alfred, and Emily Glossbrenner. *Search Engines for the World Wide Web.* Berkeley, Calif.: Peachpit Press, 1998.

Grossman, Evan. "Tut Modem Boasts 2Mbps over Standard Phone Wire." *InfoWorld* 19, no. 40 (October 6, 1997): 74.

Hakes, Barbara, and others. *Compressed Video: Operations and Applications.* Washington, D.C.: Publisher Association Educational Communication and Technology, 1993.

Hahn, Harley. *Harley Hahn's Internet & Web Yellow Pages 2001.* New York: Osborne/McGraw-Hill, 2001.

Harris, Judy. "Ridiculous Questions! The Issue of Scale in Netiquette." *Learning and Leading with Technology* 25, no. 2 (October 1997): 13–16.

Heinich, Robert, Michael Molenda, James D. Russell, and Sharon Smaldino. *Instructional Media and the New Technologies Instruction.* 6th ed. New York: Merrill/Prentice Hall, 1999, p. 289.

Kirk, Rea. "A Study of the Use of a Private Chat Room to Increase Reflective Thinking in Pre-Service Teachers." *College Student Journal* 34 (March 2000): 115.

Kurland, Daniel, Richard Sharp, and Vicki Sharp. *Introduction to the Internet for Education.* Belmont, Calif.: Wadsworth, 1997.

Laquey, Tracy, and Jeanne Ryer (foreword by Al Gore). *Internet Companion.* Boston, Mass.: Addison-Wesley, 1992.

Leon, Ramon V., and William C. Parr. "Use of Course Home Pages in Teaching Statistics." *American Statistician* 54, no. 1 (February 2000): 44.

Lindroth, Linda. "Internet Connections." *Teaching Pre K–8* 27, no. 4 (January 1997): 62–63.

McCracken, Harry. "Search Engines with a Soul." *PC World* 18, no. 6 (July 2000): 43.

Mikat, Richard P. "Desktop Video Conferencing." *Journal of Physical Education, Recreation and Dance* 70, no. 7 (September 1999): 9.

Minkel, Walter. "The Chat's Out of the Bag." *School Library Journal* 46, no. 2 (February 2000): 33.

Merritt, Mark. "Videoconferencing." *Presentation,* June 2000, pp. 72–74.

Molnar, Andrew R. "Computers in Education: A Brief History." *T.H.E. Journal* 24, no. 11 (June 1997): 59–62.

Morgenstern, David. "Netscape to Add Tables." *MacWeek* 9, no. 10 (March 6, 1995): 1.

Morse, David. *Cyber Dictionary.* Boston: Knowledge Exchange, 1997.

Odvard, Dyrli. "The Internet Grows Up." *Technology and Learning* 17, no. 6 (March 1997): 42–47.

O'Leary, Mick. "Online Comes of Age." *Online* 21, no. 1 (January–February 1997): 10–14, 16–20.

Panepinton, Joe. "Family Parents' Guide to the Web." *Family PC,* February 1997, pp. 42–60.

Peha, Jon M. "Debates via Computer Networks: Improving Writing and Bridging Classrooms." *T.H.E. Journal* 24, no. 9 (April 1997): 65–68.

Pfaffenberger, Bryan. *Webster's New World Computer User's Dictionary.* 8th ed. New York: Macmillan, 2000.

Ralston, Anthon, and C. L. Meeks, eds. *Encyclopedia of Computer Science.* New York: Petrocelli, 1976.

Resick, Rosalind. "Pressing Mosaic." *Internet,* October 1994, pp. 81–88.

Roberts, Nancy, George Blakeslee, Maureen Brown, and Cecilia Lenk. *Integrating Telecommunications into Education.* Englewood Cliffs, N.J.: Prentice Hall, 1990.

Salpeter, Judy. "Industrial Snapshot: Where Are We Headed." *Technology and Learning* 17 no. 6 (March 1997): 22–32.

Selway, Mark. "Netiquette for Beginners." *Accountancy: International Edition,* April 1999, p. 47.

Sharp, Richard, Vicki Sharp, and Martin Levine. *Best Math and Science Web Sites for Teachers.* Eugene, Ore.: ISTE, 1997.

Sharp, Vicki. *Netscape Navigator 3.0 in an Hour.* Eugene, Ore.: ISTE, 1996.

Sharp, Vicki F. "Prospecting for Science Sites on the Internet." *CSTA Journal,* Fall 1996, pp. 26–34.

Sharp, Vicki, Richard Sharp, and Martin Levine. *Best Web Sites for Teachers.* 4th ed. Eugene, Ore.: ISTE, 2000.

Simkin, Mark G., and Robert H. Dependahl. *Microcomputer Principles and Applications.* Dubuque, Iowa: Wm. C. Brown Publishers, 1987.

Sisneros, Roger. "Telecomputing Takes the Mystery out of On-Line Communication." *Telecomputing,* Spring 1990, pp. 15–22.

Solom, G. "Students Can Compute by Just Touching the Screen." *Electronic Learning* 7, no. 7 (April 1988): 50–51.

Taaffee, Joanne, and Elinor Mills. "Users Still Like Java Despite the Sun–Microsoft Dispute." *InfoWorld* 19, no. 48 (December 1, 1997): 77.

Turner, Sandra, and Michael Land. *Tools for Schools.* 2nd ed. Belmont, Calif.: Wadsworth, 1997.

Tweney, Dylan. "Distance Learning Is No Substitute for Real-World Education." *InfoWorld Magazine,* May 17, 1999.

Van Horn, Royal. "The Electronic Classroom and Video Conferencing." *Phi Delta Kappan* 80, no. 5 (January 1999): 411.

Van Horn, Royal. "Technology." *Phi Delta Kappan* 81, no. 10 (June 2000): 795.

Weise, Elizabeth. "Successful Net Search Starts with Need." *USA Today,* January 24, 2000, p. 3D.

Wiggins, Richard W. "Examining Mosaic." *Internet,* October 1994, pp. 48–51.

Wilkerson, George J. "Teaching Composition via Computer and Modem." *Teaching English in the Two-Year College* 22, no. 3 (October 1995): 202–10.

Withrow, Frank B. "Technology in Education and the Next Twenty-Five Years." *T.H.E. Journal* 24, no. 11 (June 1997): 59–62.

Wu, Kamyin, and Amy B. M. Tsui. "Teachers' Grammar on the Electronic Highway: Design Criteria for 'Telegram.' " *System* 25, no. 2 (June 1997): 169–83.

CHAPTER 9

Integrating the World Wide Web (WWW) into the Classroom

Integrating the Web into the Classroom

Did you know that there are many ways to integrate the World Wide Web into the classroom? One way is to build a Web page using HTML. In creating this Web page students can learn about any academic subject and simultaneously express themselves through the Web page. Students can learn to use a search engine to find lesson plans and learn about any subject. Teachers can have students team with each other and do WebQuests on a variety of topics. For example, "What would Abraham Lincoln think about how teenagers live today?" In this chapter you will learn about the criteria for selecting websites. In addition, you will read about some useful Web utility programs, and you will be shown an excellent collection of Web lesson plans. Finally, you will become familiar with Internet sites that include information about search engines, tutorials, lesson plans, and activities and tips.

Objectives

Upon completing this chapter, you will be able to:
1. Differentiate between HTML, Java, and Java scripting;
2. Name two search engines and know their strengths;
3. Develop some strategies for searching;
4. Identify four criteria for selecting websites;
5. Follow guidelines for Web page design; and
6. Explain what a WebQuest is and why it is useful in the classroom.

Web Page Creation

With the growth of the Internet, computer-literate people everywhere want to express themselves by creating Web pages. Building Web pages has increased exponentially, and pages range from the informative to the ridiculous. Because of the popularity of Web pages, many programs were designed to create them. Among these programs are *Web Workshop* and *Web Workshop Pro* (Sunburst), *Site Central* (Knowledge Adventure), *PageMill* (Adobe), *Claris Home Page* (Filemaker, Inc.), and *Microsoft FrontPage*. These programs, which work similarly to a word processor, generally have a menu bar and toolbar that let users create the page as if they were viewing it through a Web browser. Tags[1] are inserted automatically, so knowledge of HTML (Hypertext Markup Language) is not necessary.

Web Workshop (Fig. 9.1) is perfect for the beginning student, grades 2 to 8. It contains clip art, familiar paint tools, and a simple interface that makes it

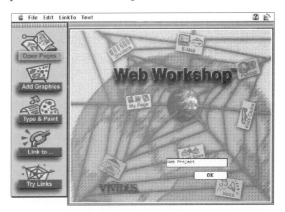

FIGURE 9.1
Web Workshop

Used by permission of Sunburst Communications (800) 321-7511.

easy for the student to create a Web page. All the student does is select backgrounds, add text, and place pictures with a click of the mouse. To create a link, students select an item and type in a World Wide Web address. This software is a perfect choice for the first-time Internet user. *Web Workshop Pro* is for the older students, from grades 6 to 12. This website design software provides tools and templates that prompt students to think about the content and function, purpose and navigability of their site. There is free one-step publishing on Sunburst's website.

SiteCentral (Fig. 9.2) is a Web page authoring tool for grade 4 and up. It can be used by junior high and high school students. There are ready-made

FIGURE 9.2
SiteCentral

Used by permission of Knowledge Adventure/Havas Interactive.

---

[1]Tags are pieces of code surrounded by the symbols < and > (Schart, 1998).

templates that help students make the website. This program is very easy to use because of its drag-and-drop interface. For example, when the students want a background they drag and drop it on the page. *SiteCentral* includes an extensive animation library and clip art, along with special art effects.

In the same manner, *Adobe PageMill, Claris Home Page,* and *Microsoft FrontPage* let you create full-featured Web pages without having to know anything about HTML or URLs. The software is simple and you can quickly add frames and tables to your Web page. There are more advanced programs like *Dreamweaver* and *GoLive Studio* (Adobe), but they are for the professional.

HTML editors are less intuitive but are available as shareware programs that can be purchased for a fraction of the cost of the others. Programs of this kind are *HTML Editor* (Rick Giles), *Hot Dog* (Sausage Software), and *Page-Spinner* (Jerry Aman, Optima System). In addition to these Web page creators, word processing programs like *WordPerfect* and *Microsoft Word* and Web browsers like *Netscape* and *Microsoft Explorer* have HTML features built into their programs. Furthermore, there are sites like Yahoo's *GeoCities* (http://geocities.yahoo.com/) that let you build your own Web pages. You can use page wizards to create a Web page in a matter of minutes. You simply answer a few questions and the wizard builds the page according to your answers (Fig. 9.3). The wizard creates a professional-looking page. In addi-

**FIGURE 9.3
Quick Start Web
Page Wizard**

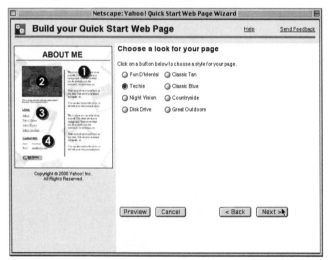

tion, there is a page builder on this site that lets you create pages from scratch. This page builder lets you drag and drop items and has many of the features of a high-end program. If you are a purist and want to work close to the code, you will have to learn **Hypertext Markup Language (HTML),** a formatting language for publishing documents on the Web.

Hypertext Markup Language (HTML)

HTML is the formatting language behind the documents that you see on the World Wide Web. (A browser, such as Netscape, has an option that lets you view the HTML source code for any existing Web page.) You use HTML tags to mark up text so that it can be read by your browser locally or over a network. This language lets authors insert tables, create forms that are used to get information from the user, style text, embed graphics, and create hyperlinks, which when clicked display another author's page. *NSCA Beginner's Guide to HTML* should further help you understand Web page creation. Here is its address:

http://www.ncsa.uiuc.edu/general/internet/www/htmlprimer.html

The following brief guide will give you some of the basics for creating an HTML document. For our discussion, we will use *HTML Editor* by Rick Giles, an inexpensive shareware product. This example is not meant to teach you HTML but to give you an overview of how it operates and help you format the most basic Web pages.

HTML Explanation

An HTML document consists of two parts: the *head* and the *body*. All orders are enclosed in brackets, for example, <TITLE>. These brackets, or tags, can be used by themselves, for example, <P>, or together in pairs, for example, <H1> and </H1>. Notice that the closing tag is the same as the opening one except that it is preceded by a slash. Tags that create forms and link files require different parts or arguments to work. In addition, graphic tags require additional information, like the file name and alignment information. Now refer to Figure 9.4 to follow the explanation.

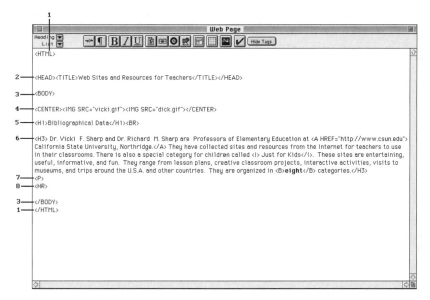

FIGURE 9.4
Example in **HTML Editor**
Courtesy of Richard Giles.

Key to Figure 9.4

1. Each document must begin with the <HTML> tag and end with an </HTML> tag.
2. The <HEAD> tag should be at the beginning of the document. Next comes the <TITLE> tag, the title "Web Sites and Resources for Teachers," and two ending tags: </TITLE> and </HEAD>.

3. Next type the document between two body tags: <BODY> and </BODY>.
4. To center a graphic, place the graphic between two center tags: <CENTER> and </CENTER>. In this example we have two graphics, so place the graphics by doing the following:
   a. Use a <CENTER> tag in front of the first graphic.
   b. To place a graphic on the page, type <IMG SRC= in front of the file name, which in this example is **vicki.gif.**
   c. Place the file name in quotes, "vicki.gif", and end with a bracket >:

<IMG SRC="vicki.gif">

   d. Do the same for the other graphic:

<IMG SRC="dick.gif">

   e. End with a closing center tag: </CENTER>.
   f. The result is:

<CENTER><IMG SRC="vicki.gif"><IMG SRC="dick.gif"></CENTER>

5. H1 creates a header in large type. The type is largest when surrounded by H1 tags; it is smaller when surrounded by H2 tags, and even smaller when surrounded by H3 tags.
   a. The beginning and ending tags <H1> and </H1> make the text "Biographical Data" appear very large.
   b. The <BR> ends a line and inserts a space:

<H1>Biographical Data</H1>

6. The next part of the document is made smaller and has a hypertext link as well as italicized and boldfaced words.
   a. The <H3> and </H3> tags make the print smaller.
   b. To create a hypertext link, start with the opening tag, <A HREF= which is placed in front of the URL, http://www.csun.edu/.
   c. The URL is enclosed in quotation marks and a bracket:

<A HREF="http://www.csun.edu/">

   d. A description for the URL is written as "California State University, Northridge." The end of the URL is a closing tag, </A>. The hypertext link should look like the following:

<A HREF="http://www.csun.edu/">California State University, Northridge </A>

   e. A beginning <I> tag and an ending </I> tag will format italic type, as in the following:

<I>Just for Kids</I>

f. A beginning <B> tag and the ending </B> tag will boldface whatever is between them; for example:

<B>eight</B>

7. The <P> tag indicates the end of a paragraph and adds a blank line.
8. The <HR> tag places a horizontal line on the page.

On the Web, this document would look like Figure 9.5.

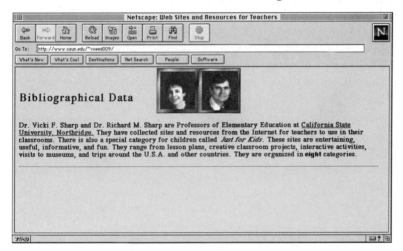

**FIGURE 9.5
Web Page
Example.**
Courtesy of Vicki Sharp.

Before creating your own Web page, read through the following guidelines.

Guidelines for Creating a Web Page

A good presentation, like a good Web page, has excellent overall design and well-chosen graphics. The following suggestions should help you generate an attractive Web page.

1. Plan ahead; that is, decide what type of information you want to put on the Web, then outline your ideas, write your text, and revise it. You need to present the information in a logical order and make every word count. Be sure to run your spelling checker and carefully proofread.
2. Organize your information; that is, on a fresh sheet of paper, organize your Web page. Create a sketch so you can visually see where you will place your text and graphics. In other words, storyboard your ideas. You can use a concept mapping program like *Inspiration* (Inspiration Software Inc.) for this purpose.
3. Decide where your navigational buttons[2] will be placed by creating a map to show these buttons. Rather than spending time scrolling, your reader should be able to jump easily from one location to another.

---

[2]A location on the computer screen, usually inside a hypermedia program, that causes an action when a person uses his or her mouse to click on its "hot spot."

4. Read your home page carefully: Does it communicate well, set a good tone, and catch people's attention? Good first impressions count in Web pages as well as in life.
5. Use graphics wisely to enhance content. Don't overload your page with pictures; no user enjoys long waits for graphics to load. Use an **interlaced GIF,** which displays graphics with one set of alternative lines at a time. (GIF stands for graphic interchange format.)
6. Be sure your site contains appropriate, relevant, timely, and engaging material.
7. Check the information on your site for reliability.
8. Be careful not to clutter the page with too many elements. Use of too many typefaces detracts from the general feeling of the writing.
9. Break up your text so it is more readable.
10. Keep the content interesting by using a variety of items so as not to bore the audience.

An example of a good website is *Cells Alive* (http://www.cellsalive. com/; Fig. 9.6). This site is a primer on cellular biology featuring a fascinating collection of pictures and animations with clear explanations. You can actually see how penicillin destroys bacteria and can view microscopic parasites.

FIGURE 9.6
Cells alive!

Cells alive! at www.cellsalive.com

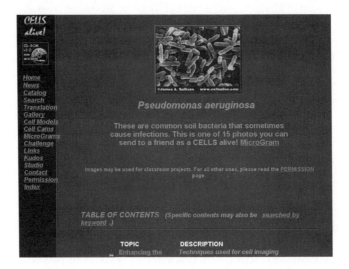

Along with HTML, Java and JavaScript are being used to create Web pages.

Java

Whereas HTML is a document display format that is constantly being changed to make it accomplish more, **Java** is a full-blown programming language. Java was developed in the early 1990s by a team at Sun Microsystems.

They were looking for a way to write programs for consumer electronic gadgets, ranging from televisions to pagers. Java was modeled after C++ and is a cross-platform programming language. This uncomplicated language eliminates features that programmers find time-consuming and tedious. Using Java, a person can write a program that will work on any computer that can run a Java interpreter, which is built into the majority of browsers today. The first browsers to run Java were *Netscape 2.0* and Sun's *HotJava* (Freedman, 2001). You find Java programs embedded in HTML documents on the World Wide Web. Java is typically used for creating games that run in a browser window, creating interactive Web graphics, and writing stand-alone applications. In 1996, Sun started selling stand-alone software applications written in Java.

Using Java you can create **applets,** or small computer programs, that provide a specific function such as displaying a scrolling, or ticker tape, message, a clock, or a calculator. These applets can be embedded in your Web page or in stand-alone applications. An example of a ticker tape applet follows:

Program

```
<APPLET CODE="TickerTape.class" HEIGHT=40 WIDTH=350>
<PARAM NAME="TEXT" VALUE="This is a Java program.">
<PARAM NAME="FONT" VALUE="Courier">
<PARAM NAME="FONTSIZE" VALUE=30>
<PARAM NAME="STYLE" VALUE="BOLD">
<PARAM NAME="FGCOLOR" VALUE="RED">
<PARAM NAME="BGCOLOR" VALUE="BLACK">
<PARAM NAME="DELAY" VALUE=50>
<PARAM NAME="CLICKURL"
VALUE="http://patriot.net/~gillette/applets/coffee.htm">
<PARAM NAME="SHADOWCOLOR" VALUE="BLUE">
<PARAM NAME="DEBUG" VALUE="">

</applet>
```

This Java applet has the text scroll in a message box across the screen. The scrolling text's message is "This is a Java program." The font used is Courier, its style is bold, the font color red, and the background of the message box black. Each letter is shadowed in blue and there is a 50-second delay.

Java is important because it is a promising new software technology that could power a new generation of devices that might make today's desktop personal computers obsolete (Hiltzik, 1997).

JavaScript

JavaScript is a scripting language developed by Netscape Communications for publishing on the World Wide Web. Most people confuse Java with JavaScript, even though their level of difficulty and use are quite different. Java is a full-blown programming language, while JavaScript is only a scripting language. According to Gesing and Schneider (1997), "scripting languages combine tools from programming languages to make them more concise and usable." JavaScript language has fewer features than Java, which makes this language less versatile. Nevertheless, it is easier for the novice or nonprogrammer to master. JavaScript's purpose is to expand the functionality of Web pages, and it is written as part of an HTML document. Both languages share syntax and structure. JavaScript is able to control and share information with Java applets. By using JavaScript, you are able to customize a Web page, depending on your browser; check for mistakes in a form before it's submitted; get visual feedback on your actions; create animations; and have interactive features on your Web pages.

Since Web page creation has become such a popular phenomenon, a cottage industry has developed around it. Some of the utilities that have become indispensable are bookmark managers, off-line browsers, seekers, printers, and security filters.

Web Utilities

URL Manager Pro (Kagi Shareware), authored by Alco Blom, is a professional **bookmark manager** for the Macintosh for use with *Netscape, Microsoft Internet Explorer,* and *iCab. URL Manager Pro* lets you organize and collect URLs in a hierarchical manner, organize bookmarks between folders with drag and drop, and access URLs on the Web. On the Windows platform there is a shareware bookmark program that is called *URL Manager* by Vince Sorensonby.

Web Wacker (Blue Squirrel) lets you save Internet sites that include text, graphics, and HTML links to your computer hard drive. This utility is ideal for presentations and working with students off-line. You can use this **off-line browsing tool** to preselect websites of interest and have the students explore the sites later.

Webzinger (ImageOn) is a fully automated **research engine.** Students type what they need and this Web research assistant locates websites by topic, visits and analyzes the sites, and downloads graphics and text.

WebPrinter (Blue Squirrel) can turn your printer into a printing press. *WebPrinter* takes Web pages (windows) that are going to be printed and automatically reduces, rotates, and realigns the pages to print as booklets on any printer.

Filtering and monitoring software helps ensure a safer online experience by not allowing access to inappropriate sites. There are many examples of filtering programs like *Cyber Patrol* (SurfControl Inc.), *Net Nanny* (Net Nanny Software International), and *CyberSnoop* (Pearl Software). *Cyber Patrol* lets the teacher customize lists of sites for individual students. *Cyber Patrol* also has an extensive array of fully researched websites that are updated on a daily basis. *Net Nanny* keeps a list of multiple users. It is a very user-friendly product and maintains a list of approved and blocked websites. Furthermore, users can view full website lists. Finally, *Cyber-*

Snoop (Fig. 9.7), developed for *Windows 95, 98, 2000,* and *NT,* easily lets users block unwanted content while focusing students on desirable sites. This program's features include time controls, unlimited user profiles, and report generation.

In addition to the software programs there are search engines such as *Searchopolis.com* (http://searchopolis.com) and *Yahooligans.com* (http://www.yahooligans.com), which are specially designed for students. These databases contain no sex or pornography sites.

These programs are only a few of the useful utilities that are available for Internet exploration.

Opening Web Pages

All Web pages displayed in this chapter were opened using *Netscape.* Other browsers work in a similar way, although the display of the home page on your monitor may look different. If you cannot open a site with a given URL, you can sometimes physically modify your URL to get the page you desire. For example, when you try to dial up the *Medical Matrix* home page at http://www.medmatrix.org/SPages/Patient_Education_and_Support.stm, you get an error message. Try deleting the final segment "Patient_Education_and_Support.stm" and press Return or Enter. Continue removing segments from the URL up to the forward slashes until it works. For this example, the URL is http://www.medmatrix.org/ (to access this particular site you must register). If this method of trying to find the URL doesn't work, try using a search engine to find the site.

Search Engines

Because the Web has millions of searchable pages, finding information is a difficult task. **Search engines** are software programs that help you locate information in a database on the Internet (Morse, 1997). Search engines have been around for years, but they have only come to the forefront since the explosion of the World Wide Web. Search engines locate Web pages on a subject or locate a specific page when you are lacking its URL. To use a search engine, type a word or phrase that is called a *keyword* or *search term* in the search engine's text box. For example, you might type "Fort Sumter" as your searching term. The search engine then returns results in the form of links to the relevant sites. Well-known search engines are *Excite, Google, HotBot, Yahoo, Lycos, Magellan,* and *AltaVista.* The kind of search site you use depends on the information you need. *Yahoo,* launched in 1994, was the first major online Web-based subject directory and search engine to gain attention.

Many of the search engine sites automatically send **spider programs** out on the Web to collect the text of the Web pages. These spiders are automated electronic software programs that follow the links on a page and put all the text into one huge database. You then search this database when you use the site. Some of the websites are a combination directory and search engine. Sites called **metasearch engines** do nothing but search other sites. For example, an excellent metasearch engine is *MetaCrawler.* These sites simultaneously bring you the results from many search engines. Many sites have become **portals,** sites that do not link to other sites but contain the information. For a list of all major search engines, how they work, and their significant features, visit http://www.searchenginewatch.com. Table 9.1 lists some popular sites that let you search for any topic.

All-In-One Search Page features a compilation of the various search tools that you can use to help you find things on the Internet. The URL is http://www.allonesearch.com/.

TABLE 9.1
Popular Search Engines

Search Engine	URL	Description
About.com	http://about.com/	Expert guidance is offered by real people searching for the best the Internet has to offer. They search in a wide range of subject areas.
AltaVista	http://www.altavista.com	*AltaVista* is an immense database of Internet resources including Word Wide Web pages and some Usenet newsgroups.
Ask Jeeves	http://www.askjeeves.com/	*Ask Jeeves* lets you type in an actual question. The software will identify a variety of possible answers to your question. There is a kid's version called *Ask Jeeves for Kids* at http://www.ajkids.com/.
Excite	http://www.excite.com	*Excite* attempts to collect the "most popular," frequently accessed Internet sites. It is unique because it searches by concept.
Google	http://www.google.com	*Google* searches for sites based on popularity, and these sites are ranked by how many sites have links to them.

Continued

Google Web Directory	http://directory.google.com	*Google Web Directory* is a database of sites organized by subject categories. This directory has over 1.3 billion pages and is considered the largest database.
Dogpile	http://www.dogpile.com	*Dogpile* searches 26 databases simultaneously and supports Boolean searches.
HotBot	http://www.hotbot.lycos.com	Lycos Network's *HotBot* provides a number of search options and ranks search results by relevancy.
Goto.com	http://goto.com	*Goto.com* is a fast, powerful, and easy-to-use search engine that ranks search results by relevancy and supports Boolean searches.
ix quick	http://ixquick.com	*ixquick* brings forth the best engines on the Internet and merges the results. It removes redundancies and puts the results into a grouping.
LookSmart	http://www.looksmart.com/	*LookSmart* is searchable, category-based Web directory.
Lycos	http://www.lycos.com	*Lycos* is a cross between *Yahoo* and *AltaVista*. It also lets you search for images.
MetaCrawler	http://www.metacrawler.com	*MetaCrawler* searches many search engines fast and at the same time. It also offers the winning *MiniCrawler*, which performs searches in a window on the desktop.
NBC Internet	http://home.nbci.com/	*NBCi*, replacing *Snap*, includes a Search & Find feature offering a directory of thousands of sites.
Northern Light	http://www.northernlight.com/	This is a powerful search engine that searches sites, including special collections of magazines, journals, and newspapers.
Open Directory Project	http://dmoz.org	*Open Directory Project* is one of the most comprehensive search engines, with millions of sites.
Raging	http://ragingsearch.altavista.com	This is a search engine that is provided by AltaVista and is very fast and organized.
Yahoo	http://www.yahoo.com	*Yahoo* is a popular hierarchical directory. There is a kid's version call *Yahooligans* at http://www.yahooligans.com.
Web Crawler	http://www.webcrawler.com	*Web Crawler* searches content areas and is also a Web directory.

How to Search

When you search, there are links to help you and search engines that will try to track down the information. However, to be a good searcher, you must have the mind of a detective and think creatively. After all, the Internet is a big database with thousands of links that vary in quality. What search tool you decide on is determined by what you are trying to find. If you just want to browse, directories like *Yahoo* and *Web Crawler* are good places to begin. If you are a beginner and want to ask a simple question, *Ask Jeeves* might be very useful. If you need a special type of database, try *All-in-One Search Page* (http://www.allonesearch.com/). Finally, if you are doing advanced searches, begin with *AltaVista*.

Here are a few general rules to follow when you search:

1. You can narrow your search and avoid thousands of unnecessary results or hits. For example, when using *Yahoo,* click the **advance search** link and try using an **exact phrase match.** After you get your results, in *Yahoo,* you can scroll to the bottom of the page and click on other search engines that are listed.

2. When searching, avoid generic or commonly used words. For instance, a search for the "Civil War" might be too general and will deliver a tremendous number of matches. For example, in *AltaVista,* using "Civil War" would deliver 897,315 pages as of March 18, 2001. If you the want to limit the search further, type the following: "Civil War U.S." This returns only 4,096 pages. Using quotation marks causes some search engines to use all the words listed.

3. Most search engines let you link your search terms with words such as "and," "or," or "minus" (-), as well as search for phrases by placing the words in quotation marks. For example, you might search for "Harry Truman and Pearl Harbor," which would give you information on both topics. If you replace "and" with "or," the search would be directed to identify one topic or the other. If you replace the "and" with the minus sign (no spaces), the engine will find the pages that contain references to Harry Truman but not Pearl Harbor. The connnectors vary with the search engines. Check your search engine's help page for more tips and tricks.

4. Use wildcards if the search engine allows it (surg* for surgery, surgeries, surgical).

5. Enter singular terms. Many search engines will find the substring and return mountains for mountain.

The following three sites give you tips and tricks for searching: University of California at Berkeley recommends search tools and search strategies, including advance searching techniques (http://www.lib.berkeley.edu/teaching Lib/Guides/Tools Tables.html/). The University of South Carolina's BareBones 101 (http://www.sc.edu/beaufort/library/bones.html) offers a basic Web search tutorial, including definitions, search strategies, and specific information about top directories and search engines. *Awesome Library* (http://www.awesomelibrary.org/help.html) shows simple as well as advanced searching techniques.

There are many ways a teacher can incorporate searching into the classroom. What follows is a lesson that can be used to teach students and motivate them to search.

▼ Scavenger Hunt Lesson Plan ▼

Materials

You will need a computer, a communications package, a modem, and access to the Internet.

Objective

Students will find factual information about topics ranging from history to current events.

Procedure

1. Discuss different searching techniques with the students.
2. Have the students form small groups.
3. Using the Scavenger Hunt form, have the students find the answer to each question by searching the specific site.

SCAVENGER HUNT

1. What is Michigan's state tree?

http://www.sos.state.mi.us/history/history.html

2. What animal made Jane Goodall famous?

http://www.wic.org/bio/idex_bio.htm

3. Why do leaves change color in the fall?

http://www.sciencemadesimple.com/

4. Who was the first American woman astronaut to orbit the earth?

http://quest.arc.nasa.gov/women/

5. Which president served the shortest term in the White House?

http://www.whitehouse.gov/WH/kids/html/home.html

6. What was the name of the Supreme Court decision that overturned legalized segregation?

http://www.infoplease.com/history.html

7. What is the currency in Zambia?

http://www.xe.com/ucc/

8. In what year was the last star sewn on our present-day flag?

http://www.ushistory.org/betsy/index.html

9. How many immigrants were processed at Ellis Island from 1892 to 1924?

http://www.ellisisland.org/history.html

10. Starting from the foot of the pedestal, how many steps must you climb to reach the torch of the Statue of Liberty?

http://www.libertystatepark.com/statueof.htm

---

4. When the students are finished, have them compare answers.

Searching the Internet without a Computer

A less expensive alternative to using the computer to search the Internet is to use the television set or use an Internet appliance. WebTV Networks Inc. was the first Internet service to distribute its boxes. WebTV uses an analog modem and telephone and lets the user access the Web on a television set. WebTV Plus has a 56 Kbps modem and a 1.08 GB hard drive. Furthermore, it has the ability to send video, still images, and audio via e-mail. You can also print out Internet material by connecting a printer to the back of the machine.

Internet appliances are low-cost devices that handle e-mail and Web browsing and do this job faster than the ordinary modem connection. These devices will not replace personal computers, but they serve as another alternative. An example of one such machine is NetPliance's i-opener (Fig. 9.8), which consists of a flat-panel color display and a keyboard. You plug the i-opener into a power outlet and phone jack, and it connects to the Internet, configuring itself for e-mail and Web browsing.

FIGURE 9.8
i-opener
Reprinted courtesy of Netpliance™.

Website Evaluation

Looking at sites on the Internet is a complex process; therefore, it is important to be able to distinguish a good website from one that is mediocre. Users must be cautious, because anyone can place information on a Web page, information that can be true, false, or just someone's own creation. Use the following criteria to aid you in evaluating websites.

Download Time

Does the home page download fast enough to use during full-class instruction? Does this page download efficiently enough to keep the students focused during small-group and independent study? Does the page download too slowly because the site is graphic-intensive?

Navigation Ease

Are your students able to easily move from page to page? Is the page designed in such a way that the students do not get confused or lost in cyberspace? Are the links and descriptions clearly labeled so the students have no trouble keeping at a task? Do the majority of the links work, with few dead links?

Appearance

Is the home page's design attractive and appropriate for students? Is the students' first impression positive, and will they be motivated to return repeatedly? Is the design clear so that the students can explore the page effectively? Are the screens easy to read?

Graphics, Videos, and Sounds

Do the graphics, videos, and sounds have a clear purpose, and are they appropriate for the intended students? Do the graphics, videos, and sounds help the students reach their objectives? Do the graphics enhance the content?

Content

Does the site offer information that covers the objective? Is this information clearly labeled and accurate? How is the site organized? Is the information at an appropriate grade level, and can it easily be understood by the student? Are the related links worthwhile and appropriate? Is the content free of bias and stereotype? Does the site provide interactivity that increases its instructional value?

Currency

Is the site updated on a regular basis?

Credibility

Is the site a trustworthy source of information? Does it provide author and source citations as well as a contact person to answer students' questions?

Now you have an idea of what is important when examining a website on the Internet. You might want to reproduce the following evaluation form and use these criteria to rate a site to see if it meets your curriculum objectives.

WEBSITE RATING SCALE

Site Title: _____

Subject: _____

URL (address): _____

Grade Level and Class: _____

Objective: _____

URLs for individual site pages (addresses):

Evaluate the website according to the following criteria. Circle the number that you feel the site deserves, 5 being outstanding and 1 being the worst.

1.	**Download Speed**					
	Quickly loads text	5	4	3	2	1
	Quickly loads graphics	5	4	3	2	1
2.	**Navigation Ease**					
	Easy movement link to link	5	4	3	2	1
	Links clearly labeled	5	4	3	2	1
	Links to other sites operate effectively	5	4	3	2	1
	Links for backward and forward movement	5	4	3	2	1
	Adequate number of links	5	4	3	2	1
	Links are apropos and helpful	5	4	3	2	1
3.	**Appearance**					
	Visual appeal	5	4	3	2	1
	Clarity	5	4	3	2	1
4.	**Content**					
	Information that meets objectives	5	4	3	2	1
	Clearly organized and labeled	5	4	3	2	1
	Linked to worthwhile sites	5	4	3	2	1
	Accurate and useful	5	4	3	2	1
	Provides interactivity	5	4	3	2	1
	Free of bias and stereotype	5	4	3	2	1
	Site author clearly identified	5	4	3	2	1
	Sufficient worthwhile information	5	4	3	2	1
	Authoritative source	5	4	3	2	1
	Readable by student at grade level	5	4	3	2	1
	Students collaborate with other sites	5	4	3	2	1
	Teachers share with others	5	4	3	2	1
5.	**Graphics, Videos, and Sounds**					
	Use clearly identified	5	4	3	2	1
	Clear purpose and appropriate	5	4	3	2	1
	Aids students to achieve objectives	5	4	3	2	1
	Relevant for the site	5	4	3	2	1
	Graphics enhance content	5	4	3	2	1
6.	**Currency (Frequency of Updating)**	5	4	3	2	1
7.	**Credible Source of Information**					
	Author and source citation	5	4	3	2	1
	Contact person	5	4	3	2	1

Add the total number of points that the site earns to determine the overall rating.

Overall rating: ____

Rating Scale

____ Website 5 (150–133 points) This site is of sound content, and I can let the students freely explore.

____ Website 5 (132–110 points) This site contains good instructional material, but the students will need very specific instructions to explore the site.

____ Website 5 (110–94 points) This site contains some worthwhile information, but students will need more specific links and a list of bookmarks along with frequent discussions to progress.

____ Website 5 (93–63) Although some useful information exists at this site, the best way to effectively use this site is through whole-class instruction and guiding the students.

____ Website 5 (62–52) This site contains some useful information, but other sites would be more appropriate, and I must supervise the students.

WebQuest

In 1995, at San Diego State University, Professor of Educational Technology Bernie Dodge developed and coined the concept **WebQuest** while teaching preservice teachers. He gave the students a format for online lessons that would foster high-order thinking. Shortly thereafter, Tom March, working as a fellow for Pacific Bell, developed the first WebQuest. Dr. Dodge's format for Web-based lessons was later published in *The Distance Educator Journal* (http://edweb.sdsu.edu/courses/edtec596/about_webquests.html). This paper, "Some Thoughts about WebQuests," defined a WebQuest as "an inquiry-oriented activity where most or all of the information that the students use comes from the Web." The WebQuest can take a single class session or be a month-long unit. The questions usually involve a group of students who divide their labor. The lessons consist of materials selected by the teachers and used by the students. Teachers do not spend their time and effort finding resources. WebQuests can be done on a variety of topics that are not well-defined and require creativity and problem-solving skills. Some examples are: What was it like to live during the American Revolution? What would Benjamin Franklin think about how teenagers live today? WebQuests are not meant for simple recall but are based on inquiry and logical constructivism incorporating collaborative learning.

What you need to create a WebQuest is the ability to design a Web page with links. Of course, if you are not talented this way, there are plenty of templates available on the Web. A server is not necessary, because you can copy the WebQuest on the hard drive. If you see a WebQuest that you want to use, you can use a program like *Web Wacker* to put it on the hard drive. (Naturally, you need to get the author's permission to "wack" the page.)

In a WebQuest there are six important components: (1) introduction, (2) task, (3) process, (4) resources, (5) evaluation, and (6) conclusions. The **introduction** gives students background information and assigns roles for them to play. For example, you are a member of a research team or you are an astronaut. The teacher gives an overview of the learning objectives to the students. The **task** tells the students what they will accomplish by the end of the WebQuest. For example, using *Planetary Web Quest* (Fig. 9.9; http://teacher. esuhsd.org/webquests/webquests/planetary.html), Jason Hovey has the

FIGURE 9.9
Planetary Web Quest
© Bernie Dodge.

team analyze the different planets and decide on which planet to colonize. At the end of the assignment, each team has to identify the planets, give general physical characteristics, and evaluate their sources. The **process** is the steps the students go through to accomplish the task that is set. There should be links for every step. The **resources** section should consist of a list of resources, either printed or bookmarked websites that the students need to complete the task. The resources are either listed separately or embedded in the **process** section. The students can also use other resources such as videos, audiocassettes, or maps. Each WebQuest must have some method for **evaluation.** The method should be fair and consistent for the tasks set. Finally, the **conclusion** component lets students discuss what they discovered and lets the teacher summarize what has transpired.

Since its beginning, teachers, curriculum specialists, and teacher educators at the university used Bernie Dodge's *WebQuest Page* (http://edweb.sdsu.edu/webquest/webquest.html) as a source of material and ideas. As time went on, the *WebQuest Page* grew and developed links to WebQuests all over the world. There are thousands of teachers who have created WebQuest lessons on the Web. You simply search with any search engine by typing in the search term "WebQuest." You can find WebQuest lessons such as *Mathart* (Fig. 9.10), which connects geometry with art

**FIGURE 9.10
MATHART**
© Bernie Dodge.

(http://u2.lvcm.com/esullivan/webquest.html), or the *EcoQuest: Desert Edition* site (http://members.aol.com/QuestSite/1/). *EcoQuest*, an interactive WebQuest designed for teachers in search of middle school science curricula, is structured to introduce students to Internet research and multimedia design. In addition, there is an excellent index of lessons developed by Bernie Dodge called *WebQuest* (http://www.macomb.k12.mi.us/wq/webqindx.htm). These WebQuests were created during a three-day in-service course in the summer of 1997. Lessons range from Clouds to Johnny Tremain: The Revolutionary. There are more WebQuest lessons at MISD, Macomb Intermediate School District Lessons, "WebQuest," and Projects (http://www.macomb.k12.mi.us/wq/). These lessons have a variety of topics from the U.S. Civil War to the nine planets of our solar system.

As is evident, the WebQuest is invaluable for integrating the Web into the classroom. Besides using a WebQuest, a teacher can use websites, projects, and activities to correlate to the state standards. What follows is a series of examples of websites and how to integrate them into the curriculum.

Integrating the Web into the Classroom

In this section, you will find websites that are particularly useful for teachers and students. They cover all curriculum areas and include an excellent collection of lesson plans. The sites were chosen for their currency, ease of use, comprehensiveness, and organization. They met the criteria listed on the Website Rating Scale. The sites are updated frequently and have the latest information. Many of the sites are award winners and have been cited for being valuable for their authoritative and reliable information. Many of these sites can be found in *Best Web Sites for Teachers* (Sharp, Sharp, and Levine, 2000).

Websites

Multisubject

Scholastic's Teacher Section

http://teacher.scholastic.com/

Scholastic provides standards-based lesson plans and reproducible materials for grades preK–8. Scroll also to online activities for Web-based, ready-to-use curriculum materials. The science lesson plan seen in Figure 9.11 is an example of what you find at this site.

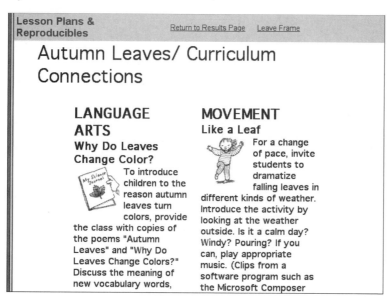

FIGURE 9.11 Scholastic Lesson Plans & Reproducibles.
SCHOLASTIC.COM. Copyright © Scholastic, Inc. Reprinted with permission of Scholastic, Inc.

CanTeach

http://www.track0.com/canteach/

CanTeach offers hundreds of lesson plans, thousands of links, and tons of other resources for elementary school teachers. For this example, the physical science lesson plan "Making a Pinhole Camera #2" (Fig. 9.12) was chosen.

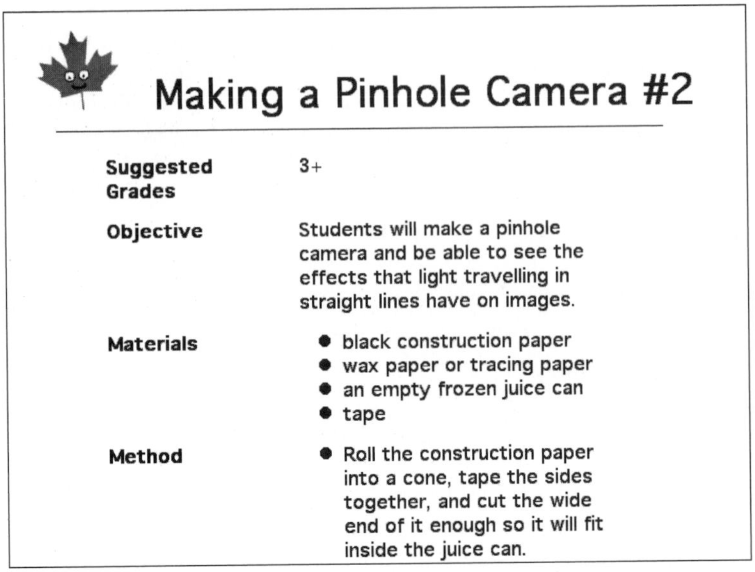

FIGURE 9.12
CanTeach.

Used by permission of CanTeach. Visit us at http://www.track0.com/canteach/elementary/physical14.html or http://www.track0.com/canteach/.

Making a Pinhole Camera #2

Suggested Grades	3+
Objective	Students will make a pinhole camera and be able to see the effects that light travelling in straight lines have on images.
Materials	● black construction paper ● wax paper or tracing paper ● an empty frozen juice can ● tape
Method	● Roll the construction paper into a cone, tape the sides together, and cut the wide end of it enough so it will fit inside the juice can.

Language Arts

Pals Activities

http://curry.edschool.virginia.edu/curry/centers/pals/pals-activities.html

This site offers an assortment of activities for reinforcing readiness reading skills. Activities covered are letter sounds, alphabet recognition, word concepts, word recognition, rhymes, beginning sounds, and blending. For beginning sounds, one of the game activities is the "Follow-the-Path Game" (Fig. 9.13).

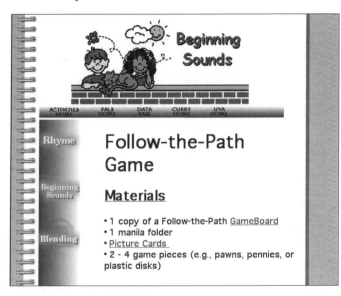

FIGURE 9.13
PALS website.

Reprinted with permission from the University of Virginia's Curry School of Education and the Virginia Department of Education.

Lesson Plans from the Teacher's Desk

http://www.knownet.net/users/Ackley/lessons.html

The Teacher's Desk contains a collection of over 250 language arts lesson ideas including a vocabulary activity of "Translating Fairy Tales" (Fig. 9.14).

http://www.knownet.net/users/Ackley/vocabtale.html

FIGURE 9.14
The Teacher's Desk.

Reprinted by permission. Visit us at http://www.knownet.net/~ackley/vocabtale.htm.

Translating Fairy Tales

Translating Fairy Tales is an activity designed to give students practice with synonyms and recalling familiar fairy tales. Given a newspaper headline for a familiar fairy tale that has been reworded with synonyms, students will determine the title of the fairy tale.

Directions:

1. Prepare a set of cards, one per headline.
2. With a marker, write one headline on the front of the card (see the table below). I prefer to use a word processing program to print the headlines on colorful paper. I then cut out the headlines and glue them to the cards.
3. With a marker, write the correct fairy tale title on the back (see the table below).
4. Laminate the cards for durability.

HEADLINE	TITLE
Rodent Terrified by Time Piece	Hickory, Dickory Dock
Arachnid Climbs Downspout	Little Miss Muffet
Fleece-Bearing Mammals Lost	Little Bo Peep
Dormant Shepherd Called for Musical Performance	Little Boy Blue, Come Blow Your Horn
Yule Pastry Contains Smooth-Skinned Fruit	Little Jack Horner
Swine Thief Brought to Justice	Tom, Tom, the Piper's Son
Feline Frightens Rodent in Royal Palace	Pussycat, Pussycat, Where Have You Been?
Man's Request for Baked Goods Denied	Simple Simon Met the Pie Man

CyberGuides: Teacher Guides and Student Activities

http://www.sdcoe.k12.ca.us/score/cyberguide.html

CyberGuides are supplementary, standards-based, Web-delivered units of instruction centered on core works of literature. Each *CyberGuide* contains a student and teacher edition, standards, a task, and a method for completion, teacher-selected websites, and a rubric. A sample lesson plan for the book *The Door in the Wall* is seen in Figure 9.15.

FIGURE 9.15
The Door in the Wall.

Used by permission of the San Diego County Office of Education.

Description of Materials, Activities, and Websites

- Class set of *The Door in the Wall* by Marguerite de Angeli
- At least one computer with Internet access and a printer
- Drawing paper and colored pencils (Castle and Armor Activity 1)
- Student created Medieval props (Skit or Puppet Show Activity 3)
- Parchment-like drawing paper (11x14") and crayons, paints or colored pencils, calligraphy pens (Illuminated Manuscripts Activity 4)

<u>Student Activity 1</u>: Illustrate/label parts of a castle and a knight in armor

Students will demonstrate a working knowledge of Medieval word meanings by drawing and labeling various parts of a castle and a knight's armor [Reading Vocabulary Standard 1.3]. Using the Internet, students will access a Medieval glossary, pictures of castles, and armored knights to learn specific vocabulary. Click on <u>Vocabulary</u> to view and print a copy of the words. Let students know that the best drawings from each class will be sent to Ian's Castle Site to be posted. Scan and send the drawings as e-mail attachments to nxd10@psu.edu.

<u>Medieval Glossary</u>:
http://netserf.cua.edu/glossary/home.htm
Comments: A readable guide for middle school students with quick access to terms. Extremely comprehensive database and user friendly site. Students will use this site to define castle terms.
<u>Medieval Castles</u>
http://vrlab.fa.pitt.edu/medart/menuengl/maineng.html
Comments: This site contains a map of England with clickable castle names. In addition to photographs, diagrams of the castles can be explored. Use this site for ideas when drawing the castle.
<u>British Castles</u>
http://www.radix.net/~mfeinberg/castles/individual.html#london
Comments: This site features six castles with a brief description of each and links to clarify some of the terms. The large font and middle school level readability are added benefits. Click on the forward arrow at the bottom of each page to learn about siege warfare and visit other castle sites. Use this site for ideas when drawing the castle.
<u>Arms and Armory Glossary</u>
http://www.chronique.com/Library/Glossaries/glossary-AA/armsindx.htm
Comments: Consists of a comprehensive glossary of terms with good readability. Use this site to define armor terms.

(http://wwwsdcoe.k12.ca.us/score/door/doortg.html)

The story takes place in the Middle Ages. Life during this time period is revealed through the experiences of Robin, a 10-year-old boy who hopes to become a knight. After becoming ill and losing the use of his legs, he struggles to overcome his handicap and proves himself a hero.

Math

SCORE Mathematics Lessons

http://www.kings.k12.ca.us/math/lessons/

SCORE mathematics lessons reflect California's and the National Council of Teachers of Mathematics' standards. Excellent sample lesson plans are "What's My Number?" (http://www.kings.k12.ca.us/math/lessons/100board.html). Students seek information on the Internet to find facts needed to arrive at a number on the 100 board, a number known only to the author. Students will use the information to work math problems using the 100 board. The other lesson is "Shopping for Toys" (Fig. 9.16; http://www.kings.k12.ca.us/math/lessons/

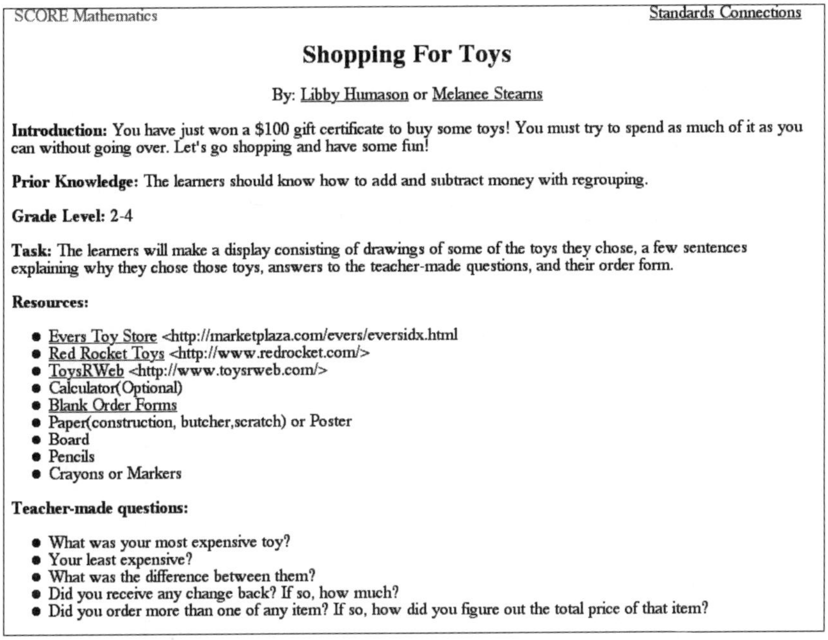

SCORE Mathematics   Standards Connections

Shopping For Toys

By: Libby Humason or Melanee Stearns

Introduction: You have just won a $100 gift certificate to buy some toys! You must try to spend as much of it as you can without going over. Let's go shopping and have some fun!

Prior Knowledge: The learners should know how to add and subtract money with regrouping.

Grade Level: 2-4

Task: The learners will make a display consisting of drawings of some of the toys they chose, a few sentences explaining why they chose those toys, answers to the teacher-made questions, and their order form.

Resources:

- Evers Toy Store <http://marketplaza.com/evers/eversidx.html
- Red Rocket Toys <http://www.redrocket.com/>
- ToysRWeb <http://www.toysrweb.com/>
- Calculator(Optional)
- Blank Order Forms
- Paper(construction, butcher,scratch) or Poster
- Board
- Pencils
- Crayons or Markers

Teacher-made questions:

- What was your most expensive toy?
- Your least expensive?
- What was the difference between them?
- Did you receive any change back? If so, how much?
- Did you order more than one of any item? If so, how did you figure out the total price of that item?

FIGURE 9.16 SCORE Mathematics
Used by permission of Kings County Office of Education. Visit us at http://www.score.kings.k12.ca.us/lessons/shop4toy.htm

shop4toy.htm). Students have won a $100 gift certificate and can spend up to that amount to buy some toys. They then make a display consisting of drawings of some of the toys they chose and a few sentences explaining why they chose those toys, answer teacher-made questions, and fill in their order forms.

MathStories

http://www.mathstories.com/

This website has more than 4,000 word problems classified according to grade level and topics. The worksheets can complement any math lesson, and teachers are allowed to make copies free of charge. Figure 9.17 reproduces Planets/Scientific Notation, a word problem sheet for grade 7 or 8.

**FIGURE 9.17
MathStories.
com™.**

Used by permission.

MathStories.com™

Copyright © 1999 *Math Stories . com* , Inc, 2416 Ramke Place , Santa Clara , California 95050 . All Rights Reserved.

Sheet # 43/Planets/Scientific Notation

Name: _____ Date_____

Fill the following table.

Planet	Average Distance From the Sun (in km)	Express in Scientific Notation
Mercury	58,000,000 .	
Venus	108,000,000 .	
Earth	150,000,000 .	
Mars	228,000,000 .	
Jupiter	778,000,000 .	
Saturn	1,429,000,000 .	
Uranus	2,875,000,000 .	

Math Forum Internet Mathematics Library

http://forum.swarthmore.edu/library/resource_types/lesson_plans/

This immense collection offers hundreds of topics from many sources, including Suzanne Alejandre's *Understanding Algebraic Factoring* (Fig. 9.18; http://mathforum.com/alejandre/algfac.html).

**FIGURE 9.18
Understanding
Algebraic
Factoring.**

Reprinted by permission of The Math Forum, Swarthmore College.

While working through algebraic factoring it is helpful to remember that all you are doing is working with breaking up and putting back together squares and rectangles!

■ **Objective:**

To show the geometric basis of algebraic factoring.

■ **Materials:**

One set of algebra tiles which includes:
- 15 - 1 unit by 1 unit squares
- 10 - 1 unit by "x" unit rectangles
- 3 - "x" unit by "x" unit squares

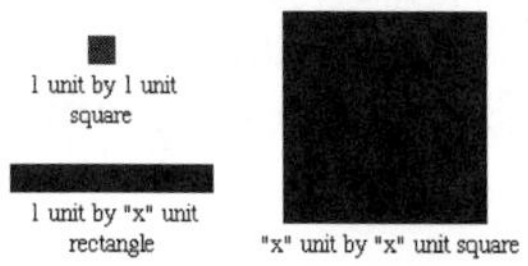

1 unit by 1 unit square

1 unit by "x" unit rectangle   "x" unit by "x" unit square

■ **Procedure:**

Introduce (or review) the notations used for multiplication.

3 X 3
3 . 3
(3)(3)

and show these ideas using an array of the 1X1 unit squares.

Social Studies

Archiving Early America

http://earlyamerica.com/

This site links to many primary sources of historical documents and portraits from 18th-century America. It includes portraits of famous 18th-century figures, original historical documents with abstracts, and chapters from books such as *The Autobiography of Benjamin Franklin.* It also has a script that scrolls to what happened on this day in history. For this example, the Declaration of Independence is seen in Figure 9.19.

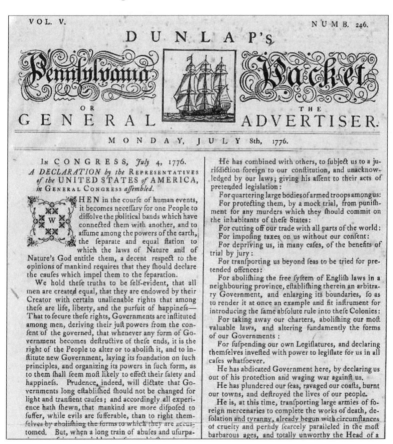

**FIGURE 9.19
Archiving Early America.**

The American Civil War

http://genealogy.org/%7Eajmorris/cw/cw.htm

This site offers short biographies written by descendents of Civil War soldiers. The biographies contain interesting quotes from diaries and letters (Fig. 9.20).

**FIGURE 9.20
Biographies.**

Reprinted by permission of
Andrew J. Morris. Visit
http://www.ajmorris.com/
roots/cw/cw.ht.

⊷*Letter from Granville Haller:* ⊷

March 17, 1897 Seattle, Washington

Dear Church:

Your letter requesting private information (confidentially) attending
General Grant's resignation from the 4th U.S. Infantry came to hand this
a.m. As you propose to write a *Life of Grant* , it is only proper that you
should have a fair knowledge of your subject, and therefore I write more
fully and plainly than I would under other circumstances.

Your letter might be construed to the effect that General Buchanan
heard that Grant had been under *"the influence of liquor"* as if this was
an accidental occurrence. Unfortunately such occurrence was *not once
only*. Grant had the habit of drinking in a peculiar way: he held the little
finger just even with the upper edge of the heavy glass bottom of the
tumbler, then lying his three fingers above the little one, filled in whiskey
to the top of his first finger, and drank it off, without mixing water in it.
This he would do, more or less frequently, each day, according to mingling
with more or less boon companions. The habit had become confirmed with
him.

I never was stationed at Fort Humboldt, but when on a visit here of Lewis
C. Hunt of the 4th Infantry when he was stationed at Fort Humboldt,
when Grant quit the service, we naturally spoke of Grant's case. I do not
remember if he mentioned the "military duty" Grant was performing at
the time for which drunkenness was alleged, or being arrested. However,

WPI Military Science

http://www.wpi.edu/Academics/Depts/MilSci/BTSI

This site features detailed descriptions of historic battles of Lexington and
Concord and Breed's Hill/Bunker Hill and the events that led to our Revolutionary War (Fig. 9.21).

WPI WORCESTER POLYTECHNIC INSTITUTE

MILITARY SCIENCE

Revolutionary War Battles - Battle of Lexington and Concord

Background

A Brief History:

On the 15 of April 1775, when General Thomas Gage, British Military Governor of Massachusetts, was ordered to destroy the rebel's military stores at Concord. To accomplish this he assembled the "Flanking units", including Light Infantry and Grenadiers, from his Boston Garrison. In charge he put Lieutenant Colonel Francis Smith and Marine Major John Pitcairn. He also composed a relief column under the command of Lord Hugh Percy to leave 6 hours after the main column. In an attempt at secrecy he did not tell his officers his plan until the last minute. The problem with his security measures were that Boston had become a glass fishbowl. All rebel eyes were watching to see the British' next action, and when the garrison committed to an action, the Americans knew their every move.

Minute Man Monument at Lexington Green

"By The Rude Bridge That Arched The Flood,
Their Flag to April's Breeze Unfurled,
Here Once The Embattled Farmers Stood,
And Fired The Shot Heard Round The World."

At midnight on the 19th of April the British column, consisting of 650-900 troops left Boston, crossed the Charles River, followed closely by the alarm rider Paul Revere. As the British marched towards Concord, the entire countryside had been alerted to their presence, and rebel militia was deployed to meet them.

Until this time there was no armed resistance to the British that had resulted in loss of British life. Several Months earlier, Gage had attempted to destroy miliary arms at Salem and met with resistance but no shots were fired, and the British retreated without completing their objective. Lexington Militia Captain John Parker had heard of the events at Salem, and collected his men on Lexington Green to face the British column.

FIGURE 9.21
Worcester Polytechnic Institute, Military Science.
Reprinted with permission.

Science

CEEE GirlTECH Lesson Plans

http://www.crpc.rice.edu/CRPC/Women/GirlTECH/Lessons/

GirlTECH has offered Internet science and math lesson plans for grades 7–12 since 1995. An excellent chemistry lesson activity, "It's ELEMENTary!" investigates the properties and characteristics of elements and promotes the understanding of the periodic table (Fig. 9.22; http://users.eul.net/~vklawinski/ptinternetact.htm). It includes an interactive quiz, links to other resources, a description of the project, project requirements, and Internet links that will enable the student to access the information to complete the project.

FIGURE 9.22
It's ELEMENTary!

Used by permission of Radica USA; for more information contact Lori Dawn Howl at ldhowl@radicausa.com

SCORE Science

http://scorescience.humboldt.k12.ca.us/

Click on **Lessons Search** to find a collection of lesson plans and activities organized by grade level and subject for grades K–12. An excellent example is "Newton's Laws," which explains clearly everything you've ever wanted to know about Isaac Newton and Newton's Laws (Fig. 9.23;

FIGURE 9.23
Newton's Laws

Used by permission of Humboldt County Office of Education.

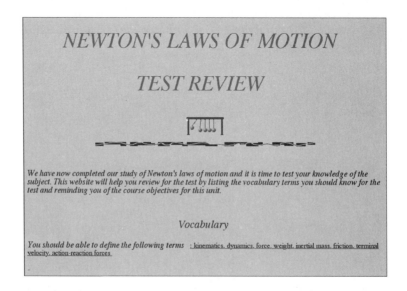

http://www.ced.appstate.edu/whs/goals2000/projects/97/michael/michael.htm).

I Can Do That!

http://www.eurekascience.com/ICanDoThat/

I Can Do That! is an amusing site that helps you learn about DNA, RNA, cells, protein, cloning, and other biotechnology topics (Fig. 9.24).

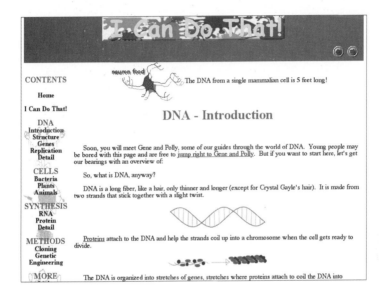

FIGURE 9.24
I Can Do That!

Reprinted by permission of Eureka! Science Corp.

Rock Hound

http://www.fi.edu/fellows/payton/rocks/index2.html

Learn about different types of rocks and rock collecting, and take a safety quiz from Rocky the Rock Hound (Fig. 9.25). To find other science lesson plans, visit the parent site, *The Franklin Institute Online Fellows Wired@School* (http://www.fi.edu/fellows/).

**FIGURE 9.25
Rocky the Rock
Hound.**

Used by permission of The
Franklin Institute Science
Museum. Please visit us at
http://www.fi.edu/educators.
html

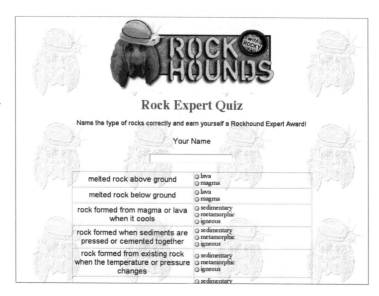

Newton's Apple

http://www.pbs.org/ktca/newtons/

This site contains a complete collection of teacher's guides, season 9 through 15, from the TV show *Newton's Apple*. All the guides are organized by topic and show number. Try this sample lesson plan on the human eye and some fun experiments (Fig. 9.26; http://www.pbs.org/ktca/newtons/14/humaeye01. html).

For a complete collection of Science Try-Its, visit http://www.pbs.org/ktca/newtons/tryits/14/sciencetryits.html.

**FIGURE 9.26
Science Try-Its™.**

Reprinted courtesy of Twin
Cities Public Television, Inc.

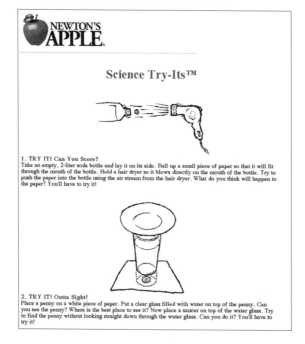

Other Ideas for Internet Projects

What follows are five classroom lessons that you can use with students on the Internet.

Combining Geography with Art

Students will learn how to use a map site such as *MapQuest* (http://www.mapquest.com) and a drawing or painting program such as *Corel Draw* or *AppleWorks*. They will find a map at *MapQuest* that covers an area they would like to visit. Next, they will copy and paste this map into their paint or draw program. Finally, they will add text, arrows, and pictures to illustrate their map.

Science

Students will use an Internet weather site such as *Weather.Com* (http://www.weather.com) to track the weather conditions around the world. They can create charts and graphs using a program like *Excel*. Finally, they will discuss the results with their classmates.

Language Arts

Students will make up a list of words to be used at an *Education Place's Wacky Web Tales* site (http://www.eduplace.com/m/mummy.html/). This site will generate wacky stories, "mad libs." Students can then share their funny stories with their classmates.

Social Studies

Students will use the a puzzle site such as *PuzzleMaker* (http://www.puzzlemaker.com) and create a crossword puzzle for their history vocabulary words. They will then exchange puzzles and see if their classmates can solve them. They can also use one of many crossword puzzles from the existing database.

Scavenger Hunts

Students will form groups and make up a scavenger hunt in science, social studies, music, art, or science. Their objective can be to find a picture of a hawk, or find out who the first American woman astronaut was. Next, students can exchange their scavenger hunts and search online for the required answers.

All Curriculum Areas

Students can make their own home page using an existing Web page builder such as *GeoCities*. The URL is http://www.geocities.yahoo.com.

Variation   In addition, students can use a scavenger hunt online and see who can solve it the fastest. For example, if they are studying black history month they might use *Dr. Martin Luther King, Jr., Scavenger Hunt* (http://users.massed.net/~tstrong/Martin.htm).

Summary

We discussed the World Wide Web with an emphasis on Web page creation, Hypertext Markup Language (HTML), and guidelines for creating a website. In the process, we discussed some useful Web utilities such as *Web Wacker* and *URL Manager Pro*. Dr. Bernie Dodge's WebQuest was explained and examples were given. Furthermore, we looked at the various search engines and gave a few pointers on how to search. We identified criteria for selecting websites and provided a Website Evaluation Scale. Finally, we showed ways to integrate the Web into the classroom.

INTERNET SITES

What follows is an annotated list of sites. These sites include information about search engines, tutorials on building a home page, lesson plans, activities, and tips and tricks.

Want to Make Your Own Home Page?
http://w3.trib.com/~dwood/createpage.html
This site is designed for the absolute beginner. It tells you everything you need to know to start creating your own home page.

The WebQuest Page
http://edweb.sdsu.edu/webquest/webquest.html
The creator of WebQuest, Dr. Bernie Dodge, has designed the site to serve as an extensive resource for individuals who are using the WebQuest model to teach. This site provides excellent examples and collected materials.

Concept to Classroom
http://www.wnet.org/wnetschool/concept2class/
At the *Concept to Classroom* site, you can learn how to use WebQuests to teach your students to think critically about information on the Internet. They can also learn how to design their own WebQuests here.

Creating a Web Page
http://www.marshall~es.marshall.k12.tn.us/jobe/webpage.html
Marshall Elementary School provides HTML tutorials, guideline, resources, free home pages, editors, graphics, and much more.

HTML Writers Guild Website
http://www.hwg.org/
The *HTML Writers Guild* provides resources, support, representation, and education for Web authors at all skill levels.

Practical Guide to HTML Publishing and Resources
http://members.aol.com/Rick1515/
This site contains HTML books, basics, editors, resources, and graphics.

How to Search the World Wide Web: A Tutorial for Beginners and Nonexperts
http://204.17.98.73/midlib/tutor.htm
David P. Habib and Robert L. Balliot created a guide to help the novice search the Internet.

How to Search the Web: A Guide to Search Tools
http://daphne.palomar.edu/TGSEARCH/
The site, created by Terry A. Gray, discusses search engines like *AltaVista*, *Excite*, *Web Crawler*, *Lycos*, and *Yahoo*. It has searching tips, useful articles, and a summary chart.

Evaluating Websites: Criteria and Tools
http://www.library.cornell.edu/okuref/research/webeval.html
The site discusses factors to consider when you evaluate a website. Furthermore, the qsite contains Web links, Web reviews, and rankings.

The Good, The Bad & The Ugly
http://lib.nmsu.edu/instruction/eval.html
Susan Beck's comprehensive site on evaluation criteria with samples, suggestions, and bibliography.

Kathy Schrock's Guide for Educators—Critical Evaluation Surveys
http://school.discovery.com/schrockguide/eval.html
Kathy Schrock has designed a series of evaluation surveys, one each at the elementary, middle, and secondary school level.

How to Create Web Pages
http://www.infopeople.org/Howto/htmlnote.html

Britannica
http://www.britannica.com/bcom/search/tips/
The best tutorial on how to search.

Open Directory
http://dmoz.org/
The *Open Directory* is a comprehensive Web directory, relying on a vast army of volunteer editors.

Yahoo WebQuests
http://dir.yahoo.com/Education/Instructional_Technology/Online_Teaching_and_Learning/WebQuests/
Yahoo's directory has hundreds of examples of WebQuests that can be used in K–12 classrooms.

Yahoo!Groups (formerly egroups)
http://groups.yahoo.com/
Yahoo!Groups lets anyone create a special interest group on the Internet with its own e-mail address and website. This free service allows you to discuss issues on a specific topic of interest to the group, stay in touch with your classmates, and share information.

Blackboard
http://blackboard.com/
The CourseSites channel, a free service, enables instructors to add an online component to their classes, or even host an entire course on the Web. Without knowing any HTML, instructors can quickly create their own learning materials, class discussions, and tests online.

Chapter Mastery Test

To the Instructor: Refer to the Instructor's Manual for the Answers to the Mastery Questions. This manual has additional questions and resource materials.

Let's check for chaper comprehension with a short mastery test. What follows are basic terms, classroom projects, and suggested readings and references.

1. Identify four criteria for selecting websites.
2. Offer a few generalized suggestions for searching the Web.
3. Explain what a search engine is and give an example.
4. Give three general rules to follow when creating a Web page.
5. What is the World Wide Web and why is it an invaluable resource?
6. Give an example of a browser and explain why you need to use one.
7. Name two ways you can use websites in the classroom.
8. What is HTML? Give an example of three tags and what they do.
9. What is a WebQuest and why is it valuable for students?
10. What is JavaScript and how does it different from Java?

Basic Terms

applets (p. 219)
bookmark manager (p. 220)
filtering and monitoring software (p. 220)
Hypertext Markup Language (HTML) (p. 214)
interlaced GIF (p. 218)
Internet appliances (p. 226)
Java (p. 218)
JavaScript (p. 219)

metasearch engines (p. 222)
offline browsing tool (p. 220)
portals (p. 222)
research engine (p. 220)
search engines (p. 221)
spider programs (p. 222)
WebQuest (p. 229)

Classroom Projects

1. Use the Website Rating Scale to rate five websites.
2. Investigate five different search engines and explain the advantages and disadvantages of each one.

3. Create simple Web page that
   a. displays a graphic,
   b. has a link, and
   c. has text.

Suggested Readings and References

Bakken, Jeffrey P., and Gregory F. Aloia. "Evaluating the World Wide Web." *Teaching Exceptional Children* 30, no. 5 (May/June 1998): 48.

Bond, Jill D., ed. *Internet Yellow Pages.* 6th ed. Indianapolis, Ind.: New Riders Publishing, 1997.

Cafolla, Ray, and Richard Knee. "Creating World Wide Web Sites." *Learning and Leading with Technology* 24, part I (November 1996): 3–9.

Carr, Stephen. "Putting It All Together." *Education Week* 17, no. 11 (November 10, 1997): 16–18.

Craig, Dorothy, and Jaci Stewart. "Mission to Mars." *Learning and Leading with Technology* 25, no. 2 (October 1997): 22–27.

Dyril, Odvard E. "Stats Making News." *Technology and Learning* 18, no. 7 (March 1998): 64.

Freedman, Alan. *Computer Desktop Encyclopedia.* Point Pleasant, PA.: Computer Language Company, 2001.

Frye, Nickola, and Michael Wise. Integrated Classroom Curriculum series. Visions Technology in Education, 1999–2000. (This series covers teaching units in math, science, social studies, and other areas. There is a CD-ROM included that gives activities, games, and quizzes.)

Gants, David L. "Peer Review for Cyberspace: Evaluating Scholarly Web Sites." *Chronicle of Higher Education* 45, no. 3 (October 9, 1999): B8.

Gesiny, Ted and Schneider, Jeremy. *Java Script for the World Wide Web.* Berkeley, Calif.: Peachpit Press, 1997, p. 3.

Hahn, Harley, and Rick Sout. *The Internet Complete Reference.* New York: Osborne McGraw-Hill, 1994.

Harris, Judy. "Ridiculous Questions! The Is   sue of Scale in Netiquette." *Learning and Leading with Technology.* 25 no. 2 (October 1997): 13–16.

Hiltzik, Michael Al. "Microsoft: Internet Explorer." *Los Angeles Times* (December 12, 1997): 1.

Junion-Metz, Gail. "Surf For." *School Library Journal* 46, no. 2 (February 2000): 35.

Kelly, Rebecca. "Working with WebQuests." *Teaching Exceptional Children* 32, no. 6 (July/August 2000): 4.

Kobler, Ron, ed. *PC Novice Guide to the Web*. Lincoln, Nebr.: PC Novice, 1997.

Kurland, Daniel, Richard Sharp, and Vicki Sharp. *Introduction to the Internet for Education*. Belmont, Calif.: Wadsworth, 1997.

Laquey, Tracy, and Jeanne Ryer (foreword by Al Gore). *Internet Companion*. Boston: Addison-Wesley, 1992.

Leebow, Ken, Randy Glasbergen (ill.), and Paul Joffe (ed.). *300 Incredible Things to Do on the Internet*. 3rd ed. Mass Market Paperback, 1999.

Levine, Martin G. "Social Studies Web Sites for Teachers and Students." *Social Studies Review* 36, no. 2 (Spring–Summer 1997): 95–98.

Lynch, Patrick J., and Sarah Horton. *Web Style Guide : Basic Design Principles for Creating Web Sites*. New Haven, Conn.: Yale University Press, 1999.

McCollum, Kelly. "Bookmark." *Chronicle of Higher Education* 46, no. 31 (April 7, 2000): A47.

Metcalfe, Bob. "Cable TV Modems Are Finally Delivering the Net to Homes and Small Offices." *InfoWorld* 20, no. 5 (February 2, 1998): 107.

Morse, David. *Cyber Dictionary*. Boston, Mass.: Knowledge Exchange, 1997.

Panepinto, Joe. "Family Parents' Guide to the Web." *FamilyPC*, February 1997, pp. 42–60.

Pfaffenberger, Bryan. *Webster's New World Dictionary*. New York: Que, 2000.

Randall, Neil. "Design Web Pages with Office 2000." *PC Magazine* 19, no. 5 (March 7, 2000): 122.

Ryder, James Randall, and Tom Hughes. *Internet for Educators*. Columbus, Ohio: Merrill, 1997.

Salpeter, Judy. "Industrial Snapshot: Where Are We Headed." *Technology and Learning* 17, no. 6 (March 1997): 22–32.

Santo, Christine. "Ultimate Guide to the Web." *FamilyPC*, October 1997, pp. 64–80.

Sharp, Vicki. *Netscape Navigator 3.0 in an Hour*. Eugene, Ore.: ISTE, 1996.

Sharp, Vicki, Richard Sharp, and Martin Levine. *Best Math and Science Web Sites for Teachers*. Eugene, Ore.: ISTE, 1997.

Sharp, Vicki, Richard Sharp, and Martin Levine. *Best Web Sites for Teachers*. 4th ed. Eugene, Ore.: ISTE, 2000.

Schart, Dean. HTML Visual Quick Reference, Indianapolis, Ind.: Que Corporation, 1998.

Sheppard, Nathaniel, Jr. "Building Your Place on the Web." *Emerge* 10, no. 8 (June 1999): 32.

Slater, James, and Brian Beaudrie. "Doing the Real Science on the Web." *Learning and Leading with Technology* 25, no. 4 (December/January 1997–1998): 28–31.

Sosinsky, Barrie, and Elisabeth Parker. *The Web Page Recipe Book*. Upper Saddle River, N.J.: Prentice Hall, 1996.

Stilborne, Linda, and Ann Heide. *The Teacher's Complete and Easy Guide to the Internet*. Ontario, Canada: Trifolium Books, 1996.

Taaffee, Joanne, and Elinor Mills. "Users Still Like Java Despite the Sun–Microsoft Dispute." *InfoWorld* 19, no. 48 (December 1, 1997): 77.

Turner, Marcia Layton, and Audrey Seybold. *Que's Official Internet Yellow Pages: Milennium Edition*. Carmel, Ind.: Que Education and Training, 2000.

Turner, Sandra, and Michael Land. *Tools for Schools*. Belmont, Calif.: Wadsworth, 1997.

Weinstein, Peter. "Tools for Becoming a Power Browser." *Technology and Learning* 20, no. 8 (March 2000): 49.

Williams, Robin, and Dave Mark. *Home Sweet Home Page*. Berkeley, Calif.: Peachpit Press, 1996.

Withrow, Frank B. "Technology in Education and the Next Twenty-Five Years." *T.H.E. Journal* 24, no. 11 (June 1997): 59–62.

Yahoo Editors. "Anatomy of a Web Site." *Yahoo Internet Life* 4, no. 2 (February 1998): 75–76.

CHAPTER 10

Software Evaluation

Integrating Software into the Classroom

Did you know that the computer can be used as an instructional tool? By using the computer this way, the student can be aided in subject areas such as math, language arts, science, social studies, and music. By reading this chapter you will learn about computer-assisted instruction and computer-managed instruction. You will be given criteria for selecting software for the classroom and learn how to distinguish between the constructivist learning model and the teacher-directed learning model. You will learn different ways of using educational software in the school. Finally, you will become familiar with Internet sites that include news, software reviews, shareware, educational resources, and links to software publishers and reviews.

Objectives

Upon completing this chapter, you will be able to:

1. Differentiate between computer-assisted instruction and computer-managed instruction;
2. Define these software terms: public domain, shareware, drill and practice, problem solving, simulation, and games;
3. Name and discuss the criteria for selecting quality software;
4. Evaluate a piece of software based on standard criteria;
5. Create a plan for organizing a software library; and
6. Distinguish between the constructivist learning model and the teacher-directed learning model.

Historical Background

In previous chapters, we considered the computer as a productivity tool in the classroom—its uses as a word processor, database, spreadsheet, and desktop publisher. This chapter will focus on the computer as an instructional tool, or tutor.

The computer has many purposes in the classroom, and it can be utilized to help a student in all areas of the curriculum. **Computer-assisted instruction (CAI)** refers to the use of the computer as a tool to facilitate and improve instruction. CAI programs use tutorials, drill and practice, simulation, and problem-solving approaches to present topics, and they test the student's understanding. These programs let students progress at their own pace, assisting them in learning the material. The subject matter taught through CAI can range from basic math facts to more complex concepts in math, history, science, social studies, and language arts.

In 1950, MIT scientists designed a flight simulator program for combat pilots, the first example of CAI. Nine years later, IBM developed its CAI technology for elementary schools and Florida State University offered CAI courses in statistics and physics. About the same time, John Kemeny and Thomas Kurtz created **Beginner's All-purpose Symbolic Instruction Code (BASIC),** at Dartmouth College, which provided a programming language for devising CAI programs.

In the early 1960s, CAI programs ran on large mainframe computers and were primarily used in reading and mathematics instruction. Computer programmers also produced simulation programs, modeled after real-life situations. Unfortunately, most of this early software was tedious, long on theory and short on imagination, lacking motivation, sound, and graphics.

The invention of the microcomputer led to the development of improved instructional software and, indirectly, to the resurgence of interest in classroom computer use because of public demand and the competition among companies. Today, software companies employ teams of educators to enhance their products, and textbook publishers are involved in producing software.

Computer-Assisted Instruction

Computer-assisted instruction facilitates student learning through various methods. CAI can provide the student with practice in problem solving in math; it can also serve as a tutorial in history and provide further drill and practice in English. Let us look at the different types of CAI: (1) tutorial, (2) simulation, (3) drill and practice, (4) problem solving, and (5) games.

Tutorial Programs

A **tutorial**'s job is to tutor by interactive means—in other words, by having a dialogue with the student. The tutorial presents information, asks questions, and makes decisions based on the student's responses. Like a good teacher, the computer decides whether to move on to new material, review past information, or provide remediation. The computer can serve as the teacher's assistant by helping the learner with special needs or the student who has missed a few days of school. The computer tutorial is very efficient, because it gives individual attention to the student who needs it. In addition, the student can progress at his or her own pace. A good tutorial is interesting and easy to follow; it enhances learning with sound and graphics. It has sound educational objectives, is able to regulate the instructional pace, and provides tests to measure the student's progress.

CAI tutorials are based on the principles of programmed learning: The student responds to each bit of information presented by answering questions about the material and then gets immediate feedback on each response. Each tutorial lesson has a series of frames. Each frame poses a question to the student. If the student answers correctly, the next frame appears on the screen. Educators disagree about the arrangement of these frames: Some educators are proponents of the linear tutorial, while others prefer the branching tutorial.

The **linear tutorial** presents the student with a series of frames, each of which supplies new information or reinforces the information learned in previous frames. The student has to respond to every frame in the exact order presented, and there is no deviation from this presentation, but the student does have the freedom to work through the material at his or her own speed.

The **branching tutorial** allows more flexibility in the way the material is covered. The computer decides what material to present to each student. The pupil's responses to the questions determine whether the computer will review the previous material or skip to more advanced work.

There are many tutorial programs, spanning the gamut of software. Encore Software produces *Math Advantage 2001* (Fig. 10.1). The program covers

FIGURE 10.1 Math Advantage 2001

eight core math subjects: pre-algebra, algebra I, algebra II, geometry, trigonometry, precalculus, calculus, and statistics. There are animated examples, narrated text, quizzes, games, and more than 3,000 problems. The in-depth tutorials have a hint system, with step-by-step problem solutions, and real-life examples of math applications. Encore also has *High School Advantage 2001*, which is a comprehensive core curriculum educational suite that helps students in eight subject areas that range from math to world history. *Typing Tutor 10*, produced by Knowledge Adventure, is an excellent typing tutorial that improves students' typing speed and accuracy.

Simulation Programs

In **simulation** programs, students take risks as if they were confronted with real-life situations without having to suffer the consequences of failure. Students can experiment with dangerous chemicals on the computer screen, for example, and not be in danger from the actual chemicals. With laboratory simulations, there is no expensive lab equipment to buy and students can observe the results without waiting a long time for the effects of experimental conditions. Moreover, students can repeat experiments easily as often as they wish. Simulations save time and money, reduce risks, and work well in decision-making situations. Many educators feel that a well-designed simulation software affords students the opportunity to apply classroom knowledge in more realistic situations than can otherwise be set up in a classroom, which enhances students' learning.

A classic example of a simulation program is *The Oregon Trail* (The Learning Company). In the fourth edition (Fig. 10.2), students try to survive various conditions and hardships as they travel across the Oregon Trail. They make significant decisions about resting, hunting, crossing rivers, and avoiding starvation, exposure, and death. In the process, the class gains an understanding of what it was like to be a settler of European descent during the pre–Gold Rush years between 1840 and 1848.

**FIGURE 10.2
The Oregon Trail
4th Edition:
Pioneer
Adventures**
The Learning Company, Inc.
All rights reserved.

Edmark has two interesting science simulations for grades 6 to 12. They are *Virtual Labs: Light* and *Virtual Labs: Electricity*. *Virtual Labs: Light* lets students safely run virtual laser experiments that would be dangerous and impractical to run in the real world. The students use virtual lasers and other optical tools to learn about the nature of light, mirrors, reflection, and more.

In the same vein, *Virtual Labs: Electricity* (Fig. 10.3) is a simulation program where students do experiments in a lab or create their own electricity

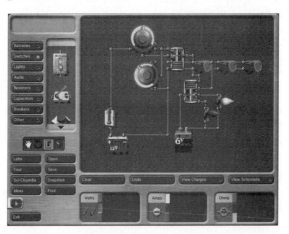

**FIGURE 10.3
Virtual Labs:
Electricity**
© Riverdeep Interactive
Learning Limited.

experiments without the hazards inherent in playing with electricity. This is a great program for hands-on learning in science. The students experiment, develop problem-solving skills, and improve their prediction skills.

The *Decisions, Decisions* series (Tom Snyder Productions) offers well-executed simulation social studies software programs. The series includes titles such as *Constitution, Revolutionary Wars, Immigrants,* and *Drinking and Driving.* There is an online version of the *Decisions, Decisions* series, with a different controversial topic to debate each month. For example, in *Gun Control*, students play the role of a senator and debate an upcoming bill. (http://ddonline.tomsnyder.com/; the price is free for a set time.)

Drill and Practice Programs

In 1963, Patrick Suppes and Richard Atkinson produced **drill and practice software** on a mainframe computer. The computer screen displayed a problem, the student responded, and the computer provided immediate feedback. The learner stayed with the problems until reaching a certain level of proficiency and then moved on to a more difficult level. With the arrival of the microcomputer in the 1970s, this drill and practice software began to be widely produced in all subject areas. It was so popular that 75 percent of the educational software developed at this time was drill and practice. In the 1980s, many educators argued that drill and practice software was being overused. They believed that the computer should be used to encourage higher-level thinking and not as an electronic workbook. Today's drill and practice programs are more sophisticated, offer greater capabilities, and are accepted in the schools. Most educators see the value of a good individualized drill and practice program; this software frees the students and the teacher to do more creative work in the classroom. Many of these programs serve as diagnostic tools, giving the teacher relevant data on how well the students are doing and what they need to work on. The programs also provide immediate feedback for students, allowing them to progress at their own speed and motivating them to continue.

Drill and practice software differs from tutorial software in a key way: It helps students remember and utilize skills they have previously been taught, whereas a tutorial teaches new material. Students must be familiar with certain concepts prior to working drill and practice programs in order to understand the contents.

The typical drill and practice program design includes four steps: (1) the computer screen presents the student with questions to respond to or problems to solve; (2) the student responds; (3) the computer informs the student whether the answer is correct; and (4) if the student is right, he or she is given another problem to solve, but if the student responds with a wrong answer, he or she is corrected by the computer. Figure 10.4 illustrates the four steps.

The computer program can handle incorrect responses in several different ways. The computer display might tell students to try the problem

FIGURE 10.4
Drill and Practice Program Steps

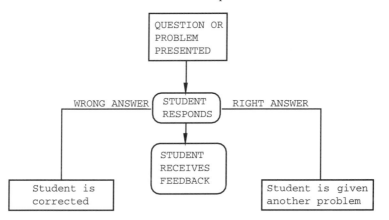

again. If they keep giving the wrong answer, the computer gives the right answer and then proceeds to the next problem. The computer might ignore all keys pressed except the right one or even beep when students try to type another response. It might display the answer that should have been typed. It might give students a hint when they respond incorrectly and a better hint if they miss the answer again. After three or four hints, it shows the right answer. Finally, it might give students additional information to help them respond to a question. This type of program is similar to a tutorial program.

Many drill and practice programs motivate students with their ingenious use of graphics and sound. Some programs are games in which players are rewarded points for the correct answers. *Math Blaster: Ages 6–9* (Knowledge Adventure) has the student play math and logic games to collect printable animal trading cards. The program has six activities, which include *Gnat Zapper* (Fig. 10.5).

FIGURE 10.5
Math Blaster: Ages 6–9
Used by permission of Knowledge Adventure/Havas Interactive.

Using an arcadelike game, the students try to improve their speed and accuracy in solving basic math facts. The object of the activity is to zap enough correct answers to math problems to win the race. The students use the arrow keys on the keyboard to move the Zapper and press the spacebar to zap the gnats. Another program of the same ilk is *Reading Blaster* (Knowledge Adventure). This multimedia program has a Word Zapper component that lets the student grab the letter group that completes a word.

Problem-Solving Programs

Problem-solving skills are necessary in a complex world, and a good way to develop these skills is to practice solving problems. The critical thinking needed for problem solving can be practiced in any content area. Problem-solving programs emphasize cooperation and are suitable for small groups or individual students.

A variety of computer programs focus on higher level thinking. The Learning Company produces *ClueFinders Reading Adventures Ages 9–12, ClueFinders 4th Grade Adventures with A.d.a.p.t, Where in the World Is Carmen Sandiego? Deluxe Edition,* and *Carmen Sandiego's ThinkQuick Challenge. Carmen Sandiego's ThinkQuick Challenge* is a multisubject quiz game where your objective is to stop Carmen Sandiego and recover the stolen knowledge.

Intellectum Plus produces a series of interactive problem-solving programs centering on elementary physics concepts such as force, motion, and friction. These programs are appropriate for junior high school to adult. The software is based on advanced problem-solving methodologies incorporating artificial intelligence features. In the *Friction Edition 2000* program (Fig. 10.6) you can see the problem that is defined and illustrated and the various multimedia features that are available to help solve the problem.

**FIGURE 10.6
Friction Edition
2000**
Reprinted by permission of
Intellectum Plus Inc.

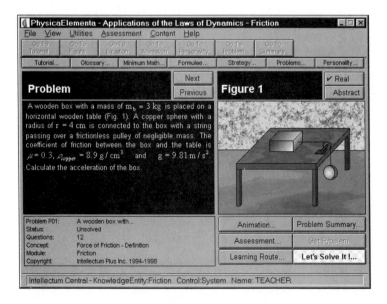

Kids Mensa (Grolier Interactive) offers 100 number puzzles with 10 levels of difficulty, while Sunburst's *Building Perspective Deluxe* promotes geometric and three-dimensional thinking skills while developing problem-solving abilities. Sunburst's *Math Arena* is a unique program that lets students practice the essential math skills, including money, probability, and geometry. The students play in training or a competition mode, by themselves or with two or three other people. There are 20 puzzles that range from Venn diagram sorting puzzles to probability exercises. In Figure 10.7 the student must choose the right change by hitting the Q buzz key.

**FIGURE 10.7
Math Arena**

Reprinted by permission of Sunburst Technology.

There is now a keen interest in problem-solving software, as evidenced by the number of entries in the commercial software catalogs. Teachers like this type of software because it helps students with testing hypotheses and taking notes. Similar to simulation, problem-solving programs easily can be used with only one computer and as many as 30 students. The whole class can be involved in critical thinking and making inferences. This type of software gives students more freedom to explore than drill and practice software does.

Game Programs

Game programs for the computer usually involve fantasy situations with some sort of competition. Game programs are classified as either entertainment or educational software. The educational programs have specific learning objectives, with the game serving as a motivational device, whereas the major goal of the entertainment programs is playing the game. Educational software offers a range of learning outcomes; entertainment software has little academic value except in learning game strategy.

Most CAI programs use a game format that ranges from drill and practice to logic programs. For example, *Reader Rabbit's Complete Learn to Read System—School Version* (The Learning Company) is an early reading, letter recognition, story reading and phonics, and sight word vocabulary program. In

"The Costume Creator" the student finds the correct sight words in order to dress the three chipmunks. Successful students are rewarded (Fig. 10.8). The

**FIGURE 10.8
Rabbit's
Complete Learn
to Read System—
School Version**

program *VisiFrog* (Ventura Educational Systems) helps students master the anatomy of a frog. This program accomplishes this purpose with interactive games. The program uses detailed graphics to represent the skeletal system, nervous system, cardiovascular system, reproductive system, and musculature. In the "Identification Game," the student types in the proper part to earn points. For this example (Fig. 10.9) the student is in the process of typing *small intestine*.

**FIGURE 10.9
VisiFrog**

Used by permission of Ventura Educational Systems, Grover Beach, CA 93483-0425. www.venturaes.com

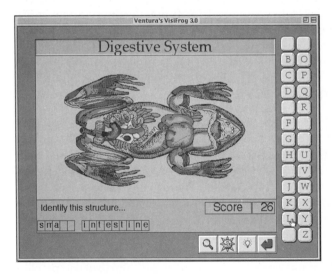

Because computer games are very popular, many educators think that CAI programs should be designed as games. A good educational game involves the active physical and mental participation of the players. Graphics, fast motion, and sound effects are used to enhance the program, not to detract from its educational value.

Most CAI programs incorporate more than one type of software in their design. For example, a program that is a tutorial may have a drill and practice element, while a simulation may have a game as an integral part of its program. The main element of *The Oregon Trail* is simulation; its game component is a hunting game.

Applications for Students with Special Needs

Much of the software that has been reviewed can be used with students who have special needs. The computer is patient, always waits for a response, and repeatedly gives the same explanation; thus it is an ideal tool for individualization and remediation. Furthermore, the teacher can add special hardware devices to the computer to overcome the physical limitations of the child with learning disabilities. For example, the instructor can install a special communication board that will respond to a student's spoken command. Students who have to stay at home can enjoy all the benefits of CAI with a terminal or modem connected to the school computer. (Refer to Chapter 12, which is dedicated to special education.)

Computer-Managed Instruction

We just explored CAI and how it focuses on the learner. In this section we examine **computer-managed instruction (CMI)**. CMI differs from CAI in that it focuses on the needs of the teacher, helping him or her manage the learning of students.

The computer in CMI manages instruction; keeps track of student test scores, attendance records, and schedules; and offers diagnostic-perspective instruction in all curricular areas. CMI makes the teaching environment more organized and productive, allowing the teacher to individualize instruction. It directs students so that they can proceed at their own pace, and it supervises instruction by telling the students to read certain books and listen to particular tapes. When the students finish their work, the computer tests them and gives further assignments. The computer grades the tests and records scores so that the teacher can see and evaluate the students' progress.

CMI is based on the underlying concept that all children can learn if they proceed at their own pace and are given the proper instructions and materials. CMI can be a comprehensive program for one or more areas of the curriculum. Many computer-managed instruction programs are based on pretest, diagnosis, prescription, instruction, and posttest. The results of the testing are then used by the instructor to determine the materials that are best for the individual student.

At the beginning of most CMI programs, the student takes a pretest on the computer. If the computer survey indicates an area of need, the student is given the appropriate test to pinpoint the area of weakness. If questions are missed on this exam, a prescription is given. If the student fails again, he or she must see the teacher. The teacher can customize the program, omitting tests for individuals in the class. The teacher also selects remediation assignments and decides when the testing ends. The instructor can call up records, class lists, tests, status reports on individuals, class reports, group reports, and graph reports.

An example of a computer management system is *ClassWorks Gold* (Knowledge Adventure), which is designed for pupils in grades K–8. *ClassWorks Gold* helps the teacher test, evaluate student progress (Fig. 10.10), and

**FIGURE 10.10
ClassWorks Gold**

Used by permission of Knowledge Adventure/Havas Interactive.

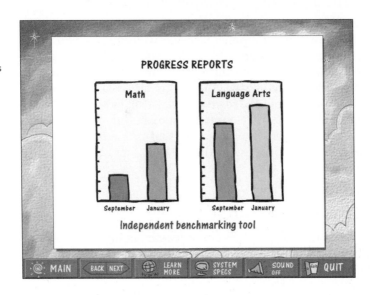

prescribe work. The teacher views a record of students' progress and is able to customize lessons with placement, assessment, and instruction tailored to students' needs. In addition, the teacher can effortlessly change lesson plans and learning levels. *ClassWorks Gold* can integrate thousands of subjects via the Internet and incorporate cross-curricular strands into subjects such as social studies, science, and English as a second language (ESL).

Many CMI packages are stand-alone packages like *ClassWorks Gold,* but some elements of CMI are being incorporated into drill and practice software, as well as tutorial software. For example, Sunburst's *Math Arena* has a teacher management tool that lets the teacher customize the students' experience and track their performance and progress. *Kaplan SAT & PSAT 2001 Edition* (Encore) tutorial program offers test-taking tips, tests, and an analysis of test-taking skills.

In theory CMI is sound, but in practice it poses some real problems. A common complaint is the difficulty of setting up the management module for students. It takes time to enter each student's name and define tasks, a job that normally would occur over a span of months but that with CMI has to be accomplished immediately. The CMI systems have moved toward more user-friendly software, but many programs are still difficult to use. Some researchers feel that use of CMI results in a decrease in the interaction between the student and teacher (Coburn et al., 1982, p. 48). Another frequent teacher complaint is the quality of the software. CMI tests basic skills only, using such instruments as multiple-choice and true/false questions. Another complaint is the cost, which can be exorbitant for the integrated learning systems; in addition, such systems may require considerable access to computers. Finally, there is some question about the capability of the computer to correctly assess the students' performance and provide the appropriate prescription for learning. Unfortunately, CMI has not been adequately researched and its results are inconclusive (Clements, 1989; Cuban and Kirkpatrick, 1998). Despite the effectiveness of CMI in college teaching (Sy, 1999), there is little use of this material in mainstream college teaching (Baker, 1997).

Public Domain Software and Shareware

Most software programs discussed in this book are commercial. The commercial programs can be expensive, especially in multiple copies. Fortunately, there is an alternative to commercial software: public domain software. **Public domain software** can be legally copied and shared with other users with no restrictions on use. Public domain is not copyrighted, and its authors choose not to seek formal rights or royalties. Users pay a one-time postage and handling fee. The software is distributed by electronic bulletin board services (BBSs) and software vendors, downloaded through a commercial service such as America Online (AOL) or from the Internet. User groups pass around public domain software to their members. The quality of this software varies considerably. There are very useful public domain programs, but you have to choose carefully and wisely; professional programmers and teachers write these programs in their free time.

Shareware is software that is distributed using the honor system. It is inexpensive and it may not be copyrighted. Its authors send their products directly to users. Usually, authors do not have to worry about marketing or promotion costs. The software is distributed on a trial basis through websites, BBSs, online services, mail-order vendors, and user groups. Users examine the program to see if it fits their needs. They also may give the software to friends for examination purposes. If, after looking over the software, the parties involved wish to use the product, they must register with the owner of the product and pay a fee. (If the buyer decides to use this program, he or she is obligated to pay for it.) A shareware fee to an author may be as low as $5 and as high as $50. The author's name and address are always on the disk. In return for the fee, the user usually gets documentation, technical support, and free updates. If the shareware is sold through the software vendors, the software price is usually higher, to cover the cost of distribution. There are tens of thousands of shareware programs; some are terrific, others mediocre. Two excellent sites for shareware software are *Tucows* at http://www.tucows.com and *CNET Shareware.com* at http://shareware.cnet.com.

Software Selection: A General Guide

In prior chapters, we examined different application software such as word processing and desktop publishing and learned how to evaluate these programs by using appropriate criteria. Now let's look at some general principles that apply to evaluating any software program.

Choosing good software is an eight-step process: (1) specify the software needs of your population; (2) locate the software; (3) research hardware compatibility; (4) examine the program's contents; (5) look at instructional design; (6) check out how easy the program is to learn; (7) evaluate the program in terms of consumer value; and (8) investigate the technical support and cost.

Specific Software Needs of Your Population

To make a wise decision, it is essential to know the learning/curriculum objectives that you wish to accomplish. After you have determined what these objectives are, you can better determine the software needs of your population. Ask the following questions: What type of program will best meet these objectives? Does the class need a math drill and practice program to reinforce some math skill? Does the group need a word processor or a remediation program to help the students learn something already taught? What are the grade level and ability level of the software program? How sophisticated should this software be? For example, should the program be a simple word processor for letter writing or a heavy-duty word processor for book writing? After making these decisions, list the features the classroom requires. If you are teaching first grade, you might want a word processor that produces a nice assortment of interesting large letter fonts. If you are working with high schoolers, you might want a word processor that has an outliner.

Locating Software

The major sources of software information are journals, indexes, educational organizations, magazines, software house catalogs, and the Internet.

A fast way to locate software is through catalogs such as Learning Services, Educational Resources, Educational Software Institute, Software Express, and CCV Software. These catalogs include program descriptions and often tell you the names of the company's best-selling programs. The companies operate via mail order and have discounted prices. **See Appendix C for a listing of recommended mail-order software sources.** There are numerous published reviews from professional journals and periodicals in the field. For example, the *Arithmetic Teacher* publishes reviews on math software and the *Journal of Learning Disabilities* prints occasional reviews for students with learning disabilities. Additional magazines like *T.H.E. Journal, Electronic Learning, Learning, Leading with Technology,* and *Journal of Special Education* all review software. Furthermore, there are many specialized resources such as *Only the Best Educational Software and Multimedia,* published by the Association for Supervising and Curriculum Development, the *Complete Teacher's SourceBook on Children's Software,* (Active Learning and Associates, Inc.) and the *Educational Software Preview Guide,* published by the International Society for Technology in Education. On the Internet there are sites that focus on reviewing software such as *Children's Software Revue, School House Software Reviews,* and *Techlearning.com.* At the end of this chapter are Internet sites that rate software.

Regardless of the source you use, you should read several reviews of the software to get different perspectives. Often there is disagreement among reviewers on what constitutes "good" software because every reviewer has a priority. For example, Reviewer A may feel that ease of use is the most important factor, while Reviewer B might be concerned with features. Also, look at advertisements for new products. You can see what new products are available just by scanning the magazine ads or asking the manufacturers to send a more detailed list. You might want to call the manufacturer of the product directly to find out about some features. Software developers such as Sunburst send preview copies if you guarantee their safe return. Many software publishers let you download from the Internet or order by phone demonstration versions of their software programs. There are other sources for previewing software: university software libraries, state departments of education, and software clearinghouses. And always keep in mind any computer enthusiast acquaintance or friend who may have used the product. *Microsoft Word* may be a hot-selling program, but by talking to a friend who is actually using it, you might learn it's not right for your particular situation. Computer user groups recommend good software, demonstrate it at their meetings, and answer questions. At the very least, these groups put you in touch with people who have the software, and they generally keep abreast of new developments in the field.

After you have properly researched different types of software, you'll be ready to enter the computer store or go online and examine the software package. Make sure the store is reputable and reliable, and ask about its policy on defective disks and returns. When examining a program, check the version number to be sure it's not an old version that has been lying around the store. Also, inspect the package to see if it is a teacher's version or a consumer version. The consumer edition may be less expensive, but it usually does not have a backup disk or an activity book.

Hardware Compatibility

Ask the following questions: Do the computers at the school have enough memory to run most programs? The more memory the better. How many gigabytes is the hard drive? What type of backup storage do the machines have? Do they have Zip drives or high-speed FireWire hard drives? How fast is the CD-ROM or DVD-ROM drive? Is it a CD-Rewritable drive? Most software programs today are in the CD-ROM format, but this will change as more machines are packaged with DVD drives. Does the software program you want to buy need more RAM to run faster and more efficiently? Is it a networkable program? What are the video-RAM requirements? What equipment is necessary? Does the program require a digital camera or a microphone? What type of printers does the program support?

Program Content

First, ask these questions: What are the objectives of this program? Do these objectives match my curriculum objectives? Are these objectives clearly stated? Does the program meet these objectives? (Many programs are not logically organized and lack a theoretical base. The objectives do not have to be seen on the computer screen. However, they should be found in the documentation that accompanies this software package.)

Next ask these questions: How appropriate is the program for the students? What knowledge or skills must a student possess to utilize this software program? Are the graphics and skills required reasonable for this grade level? (Be careful not to buy a program that is too easy or hard for the class.) Is the vocabulary appropriate for the grade level? (Many publishers supply readability scores that can serve as a benchmark.) How accurate is the material presented in the program? Is the program free of unnecessary computer jargon, and are the spelling and grammar correct? If it is a historical program, are the data accurate? How much time is needed to run the program? What about the program's transmitted values? Is the program free from prejudices or stereotypes? Is the program violent in nature?

Instructional Design

Many important factors relate to program design. These include learner control, reinforcement, sequencing, flexibility, and appearance.

Learner Control

Who controls the software program, the student or the computer? Can the student move back and forth in the lesson easily? Can the student quickly return to the previous frame? Can the student escape to the menu whenever he or she wants? Can the student control the speed of the program? Does the program move the academically bright students forward to more difficult problems, or does the level of difficulty remain the same? (It is important to be able to use the program at more than one ability level.) How easy is it for the student to exit the program or to restart an activity?

Reinforcement

How are the students reinforced? (The reinforcement should be delivered in a positive way. The software should be encouraging and not degrading. There should be little reinforcement for inappropriate responses. Some programs have reinforcement for wrong answers that is more rewarding than the reinforcement for right answers.) Does the program vary the reinforcement? Is the feedback active, passive, or interactive? (A student receives passive feedback when the program simply states that the answer is wrong or right. The student receives active feedback when animation appears on the screen such as a rabbit doing a jig.)

Sequencing

Is the instructional sequence appropriate? Does it start from the simple idea and move to the complex?

Flexibility

You should be able to adapt the program to small and large groups. You also should be able to modify the program to meet the individual needs of the students in the classroom. For example, *Fraction Operations* (Sunburst) enables you to change fractions that appear in each multimedia activity. Does the program provide a record of the student's progress?

Program Appearance

Does the program have colorful graphics, animation, and sound? Does the sound motivate the students or does it interfere with their learning? Are the graphics distracting or helpful? How is the screen laid out? Is it crowded or well organized? Is the full power of the computer being used? Are there too many instructions on the screen?

Ease of Use

Is the program easy to learn? Can the student immediately load the program and use it? Does the program use simple English commands? Can the student access a help screen whenever it is needed? Does a tutorial disk or manual take the user through the program? Is the printer easy to set? Can the student answer a few questions and then be ready to print immediately? Are there help prompts and safety questions? Is there an automatic save feature? What happens when the student hits a wrong key? Must the student reload the program or does the software crash? Does the program have error messages so that the student can correct problems? Are the directions clear and concise? Can the student follow the directions on the screen without going to the documentation that accompanies the software? Are the instructions brief and to the point?

Consumer Value

Cost is a concern because some software can run into the thousands of dollars. You have to decide whether that $395 word processor is really better than the $50 one. Are all the features found in that $395 package worth the cost? (Find out if a discount house or mail-order firm carries the software at a considerable savings; see Appendix C for a list of recommended mail-order sources.) Is the software protected? Do you have to type in a serial number or find a code word in the manual or use the original disk to install? For a reduction in software price per computer, you can order lab packs, a networkable version of the software, or a site license. **Lab packs** are multiple copies of a program with one set of documentation. **Networkable software** can run over a network without a reduction in performance. You simply install the program on a single file server at one school site with a varying number of computers connected. If you buy a **site license**, the teacher at a site can make a number of copies of the software from the original.

Support

How is the technical support? Can you call someone immediately to get help, or must you wait forever on the telephone? Do you have to make five or six menu choices and then get a recorded message that sends you online? Is the telephone call toll-free or is it a long-distance call? Does the company charge by the minute for technical help? Is there a tutorial with the software package? Is the tutorial on a disk or in book form? (Many manufacturers provide both to simplify learning their program.) Is the manual readable, with activities and lesson plans? (The documentation should be written for the target audience.) Is this publisher reputable? Will the company still be in business when you're having trouble with the software product? If you happen to get a defective disk, will the publisher replace it?

Shopping for software is an involved process. Using the software checklist on the next page should simplify this task.

Even if software purchased meets high standards, it can have its intent subverted when used. Purchasing software is not the only consideration; teachers must be given instruction and help in incorporating it into the classroom.

Software and Hardware Quality

Hardware manufacturers frequently rush out their new products while the products are still unfinished and bug-ridden. For example, a few years ago computers with Intel's Pentium chip had a flaw that resulted in inaccurate calculations. The original Power Macintosh would at first not support many peripheral devices. Software quality varies as well. In the past, a lack of sophistication in software development frequently led to errors in programs. Today, the most common reasons for poor quality software are greed, technical incompetence, and lack of instructional design.

SOFTWARE EVALUATION CHECKLIST

Directions: Examine the following items and determine which ones you feel are important for your class situation. Evaluate your program and place an X on each line where the software meets your needs.

Product Name _____   Manufacturer _____   Grade Level _____

Subject Area _____   Skill Level _____   Time _____

A. Program Type
_____   1. Drill and practice
_____   2. Tutorial
_____   3. Simulation
_____   4. Educational game
_____   5. Problem solving
_____   6. Teacher management
_____   7. Other _____

B. Hardware
_____   1. Memory needed
_____   2. Computer compatibility
_____   3. Printer compatibility
_____   4. Hard disk space
_____   5. CD-ROM drive speed
_____   6. DVD drive
_____   7. Peripherals

C. Program Content
_____   1. Objectives met
_____   2. Vocabulary appropriate
_____   3. Material accurate
_____   4. Free of bias or stereotype
_____   5. Motivational
_____   6. Grade-appropriate skills

D. Instructional Design
_____   1. Learner control
_____   a. Speed control
_____   b. Program movement
_____   2. Proper reinforcement
_____   3. Self-directed program
_____   4. Appropriate sequencing
_____   5. Student record keeping
_____   6. Disk crash safeguards

_____   7. Appropriate learning theory
_____   8. Wide range of abilities

E. Program Appearance
_____   1. No distracting sound/visuals
_____   2. Animation/sound/graphics
_____   3. Uncluttered screen
_____   4. Material clearly presented
_____   5. Product reliability

F. Ease of Use
_____   1. Easy program installation
_____   2. Simple screen directions
_____   3. On-screen help
_____   4. Tutorial manual—hard copy
_____   5. Easy printer setup
_____   6. Students can use without help
_____   7. Students can review directions on demand

G. Consumer Value
_____   1. Cost
_____   2. Extra programs
_____   3. Lab packs
_____   4. Network version
_____   5. Site license

H. Support
_____   1. Free technical help
_____   2. Toll-free number
_____   3. Readable manual
_____   a. Activities
_____   b. Lesson plans
_____   c. Tutorial
_____   d. Index
_____   4. Money-back guarantee
_____   5. Defective disk policy

Rating Scale

Rate the program by placing a check in the appropriate box.

Excellent _____ Very Good _____ Good _____ Fair _____ Poor _____

Comments

Greed

Some computer developers deliberately turn out products prematurely to keep up with the competition or beat it into the marketplace. They rely on clever advertising, catchy titles, and deceptive marketing to get the public to buy their products, which are so faulty that they need many revisions to run properly. The public buys these bug-ridden programs and unknowingly becomes a beta tester for the final product.

Technical Incompetence

Because hardware manufacturers are constantly turning out new machines, software manufacturers expend a great amount of effort just keeping up. Many of the new machines are not compatible with the current software. (The manufacturer usually makes some minor modification that prevents the existing software from working on the machine.) The software developer is then faced with angry customers who cannot understand why their programs are not working. The developer has to make modifications and send out revised versions to all customers, an expensive proposition. To save money, many manufacturers are posting updates to their products on the Internet.

Lack of Instructional Design

Many programs have good graphics and sound and are attractive. However, despite their slick appearance, these programs often have little value because they are not based on sound educational theory. It is therefore important that educators become involved in the process of software development. Incorporating learning theory is a crucial part of the instructional design of any first-rate classroom software package. Many educational programs are no different from what might be found in a workbook. Why spend thousands of dollars producing a software program when all a teacher has to do is buy a workbook? The software program should offer much more than a standard textbook or workbook.

Once you have the software, the most important job still remains ahead. Every teacher needs guidelines on how to organize a software collection. What follows is one approach to software organization.

Guidelines for Setting up a Software Library

1. Consult your school librarian for knowledge on cataloging and advice on time-saving techniques.
2. Choose the location for the collection wisely. It could be a classroom, library, or media center. The more central the location, the easier the access.

3. Use a database software program to keep a record of the software. Alphabetize the software by title, subject, type, age, and so on, and simultaneously make an annotated listing of the software.
4. Catalog the software. There is no standardized procedure, but one of the simplest and most effective ways is to color-code the software and documentation by subject area. For example, math software would be labeled with blue stickers or kept in blue folders. If you have a large software collection, use the Dewey Decimal System and the Sears List of Subject Headings.
5. Decide how the software is to be stored. Will you use hanging file folders, file cabinets, stands, or plastic containers?
6. Protect the collection. Make security arrangements and store disks, CD-ROMs, or DVD-ROMs vertically in containers. Protect these disks from dust, dirt, and strong magnetic fields.
7. Separate the computer disks from the documentation and serial numbers for security reasons.
8. Devise a set of rules for software use. For example, forbid food or drinks in any of the computer labs. Place software in its designated container.
9. Create a policy and procedures manual that handles the following issues:
   a. Who is responsible for this collection?
   b. What procedures will be used to evaluate, select, and catalog this software?
   c. How will the software be checked out?
   d. How does a teacher verify that the software is workable?
   e. How will the teacher report technical problems?

Organizing and maintaining a software library is a monumental task that requires someone to be in charge of it on a full-time basis. After this library is established, schools can benefit by devising a review procedure so that a continually growing library of software reviews can be developed and made available to all teachers.

Learning Theories and Technology Integration

Before 1980, educators debated whether to use the computer as a tool, as a teaching aid or tutor, or as a programming device. There was an absence of software and technology was limited. As different types of technologies have become available, choices have increased. To take advantage of these advances in technology, educators agree there has to be a change in education to help individuals achieve optimal learning.

Learning theories attempt to explain how an individual acquires knowledge and what factors contribute to this learning. The teaching that takes place in the classroom is often based on one or more learning theories. Using teaching strategies that have a solid theoretical base makes the computer a more effective tool. When evaluating software, it is important that the software includes elements of one or more learning theories. Jonassen (1988) discusses learning theories and their application to microcomputer courseware.

Behaviorism, cognitive theory, constructivism, situated cognition, and other theories, have been used to investigate the effect of the computer on teaching and learning. Learning theorists have disagreed on what strategies would be most useful in achieving educational goals. From this disagreement has evolved a recent interest in two different approaches, teacher-directed and constructivist (Roblyer, Edwards, and Havriluk, 2000). The **teacher-directed approach** is based on the behaviorism learning theory, while the **constructivist approach** comes from other branches of cognitive learning theory. (Since this textbook is not an instructional theory textbook, we will not cover this topic in depth.)

The Teacher-Directed Approach

The teacher-directed approach is derived from the behavioral theories of B. F. Skinner, Edward Thorndike, Richard Atkinson, David Ausubel, Robert Gagné, and Lee Cronbach. The teacher is seen as the manipulator of the classroom environment and the student as the receptacle. Famous for his work in behavior modification, B. F. Skinner favored programmed instruction. The lessons and drills are planned in small incremental steps to lessen the chance of incorrect responses on the part of the student. The idea is that the student can learn by tightly structuring the environment. The teacher focuses on teaching skills that begin at a lower level and build to higher skills, a systematic approach. There are clearly stated objectives, with test items that coincide. This approach stresses individual work and emphasizes the traditional teaching and assessment methods, such as lectures and worksheets.

During the 1970s and 1980s, when computers first appeared in the classroom, the behavioral theories were very popular. The software then was based on programmed instruction. Today thousands of educational software programs—such as *High School Advantage 2001* (Encore), *Quarter Mile* (Barnum Software), *Math Blaster: Ages 6–9* (Knowledge Adventure), *Type to Learn Junior* (Sunburst), *Kaplan SAT & PSAT ACT 2001 Edition* (Encore)—are based on the behavioral models of instruction. The programs are associated with drill and practice and tutorial software applications. They diagnose student skills, monitor student performance, and make changes in instruction when necessary. The software program usually generates student and class performance information for teacher use. The advocates of this approach praise the software for its individual pacing, self-instructional sequences, and remediation when the teacher's time is limited. The software generally makes learning faster, especially for instruction that is necessary for higher level skills. This software performs time-consuming tasks and frees the teacher for more complex student needs.

Opponents of this type of software criticize its lack of flexibility because it comes with predefined curricula. They say it uses only one type of educational technology, whereas other approaches use problem solving, multimedia, telecommunication, and cooperative problem solving.

Constructivism

The constructivist models have evolved from the work of developmental theorists such as Jerome Bruner, Jean Piaget, Lev Vygotosk, and Seymour Papert (see Chapter 15). The constructivist feels that learning occurs when the learner controls his or her own knowledge. These models focus on posing problems and searching for answers. Constructivism emphasizes exploration or discovery learning. Constructivism uses assessment by student portfolios, performance checklists, and tests with open-ended questions and narratives. It differs from the teacher-directed model because of its emphasis on group work as opposed to individual work. Students play an active rather than passive role, and they work to solve problems through cooperative learning activities. Even though the constructivist instructional theories and simulations have been around for years, the strategies used, such as annotated movies and hypertext, are recent innovations.

The application of simulations can be traced to 17th-century war games used to simulate the battles between opposite sides. In the mid-1950s simulations were introduced in business training, and in the 1970s the popular simulation program *Lemonade Stand* by Minnesota Educational Computing Corporation (MECC) was introduced and run on the Apple II computer. Today programs such as *Roller Coaster* (Microprose), the *Sim* series—*SimCity 3000, The Sims* (Electronic Arts)—and others are created to teach the concepts of supply and demand. Players make decisions about cost, production, price structure, and advertising. A further innovation in this field is virtual reality, in which the student feels a part of the environment, and programs like the classic *Myst Masterpiece Edition* (RedOrb) have come into their own. The advocates of constructivism say that it makes skills more relevant to students' experiences and that tasks are anchored in real-life visual situations. The students address problems through interactive situations and play active rather than passive roles. They work together in groups to solve problems through cooperative learning activities. This software emphasizes motivational activities that require high-level as well as low-level skills at the same time.

Both approaches attempt to identify what Gagné (1985) calls the "conditions of learning," or the circumstances that influence learning. Both approaches are based on work done by respected psychologists and learning theorists and the approaches differ only in the way they describe the environment in which learning occurs.

Table 10.1 compares the characteristics of the teacher-directed model with the constructivist model.

TABLE 10.1
Teacher-Directed versus Constructivist Instructional Models

Teacher-Directed	Constructivist
Worksheet and textbook based	Manipulatives, primary sources
Curriculum fixed	Curriculum flexible
Teacher transmits knowledge	Concept development
Didactic instruction	Student explores and discovers knowledge
Results in one correct answer	Large concepts
Assessment by testing	Interactive activities
Stresses individualized work	Concern with the process of learning
	Assessment by student products and student observation
	Stresses cooperative group work

Summary

The computer has many invaluable uses in all areas of the curriculum. Computer-assisted instruction (CAI) software uses the computer as a tool to improve instruction, provide the student with practice in problem solving, serve as a tutor, and supply drill and practice. CAI directly involves the learner, whereas computer-managed instruction (CMI) assists the teacher in managing learning. We considered eight criteria to apply when choosing software. We examined a software evaluation form (checklist) to aid in software selection. Following this discussion was a brief discourse on software quality, followed by guidelines for setting up a software library. The chapter concluded with a discussion of teacher-directed and constructivist approaches to learning. **Be sure to review the annotated list of award-winning special education programs listed in Appendix A.**

🌐 INTERNET SITES

The following Internet sites include, news, software reviews, shareware, and educational resources, and links to software publishers and reviews.

Children's Software Revue
http://www.childrenssoftware.com/

Children's Software Revue was started by former teachers in 1993. They publish a well-known magazine called *Children's Software Revue,* which contains authoritative reviews and ratings as well as helpful articles, tips, and spotlights on each school subject. You can browse their site for news, sample articles, and recommended software by age group and category. There are in-depth reviews to over 4,000 titles of the latest children's educational software.

SuperKids Educational Software Review
http://www.superkids.com/

SuperKids contains educational software for Mac and PC, a buyers' guide, and discounts for online orders. There are software reviews by parents, teachers, and students.

About.com's Shareware/Freeware-Educational Software
http://shareware.about.com/compute/software/shareware/msub_education_index.htm

This site provides links to software publishers, a multimedia tutorial, and an archive of previous features.

Techlearning.com
http://www.techlearning.com/review.html

Techlearning.com features a searchable database of reviews of educational software, taken from the print journal for K–12 educators.

School House Software Reviews
http://www.worldvillage.com/wv/school/html/scholrev.htm

The site contains professional reviews of the latest educational software for children and adults. *School House Software Reviews* is updated several times a week.

CNET DOWNLOAD.COM's Home and Education
http://download.cnet.com/downloads/0-10154.html

The Computer Network (CNET) is an index of Macintosh- and PC-compatible educational software (freeware, shareware, demos) available for download. The site includes program descriptions, reviews, and links to FTP sites. Users may search by keyword, browse by subject area, or display the newest, most popular, or highest rated titles. Categories are kids, language, literature, mathematics, miscellaneous, science, and teaching tools.

Kids Domain
http://www.kidsdomain.com/

Kids Domain is an educational site for children aged 2–12, parents, and teachers. This site includes sections with games and activities, stories, jokes and riddles, contests, and downloads. In addition, the site features software reviews and craft and activity ideas.

Game's Zone KidZone
http://www.GZKidZone.com/

The *GZKidZone's* mascot helps you find everything that is fun and informative about children's software. The main goal is to educate students and parents about the wide array of software on the market.

SafeKids.Com
http://www.safekids.com/

SafeKids.Com contains tips, advice and suggestions to make the online experience fun and productive.

Yahoo Directory of Children Software
http://dir.yahoo.com/Business_and_Economy/Shopping_and_Services/Children/Software/

Yahoo's directory contains an array of safe sites for children.

Education World: Technology in the Classroom
http://www.educationworld.com/a_tech/

The site offers a number of articles and tips for purchasing and using software and the Internet in the K–12 classroom. They range from "Online Encyclopedias" to "Software Bargains for Teachers!"

Simply the Best
http://www.simplythebest.net/

Simply the Best is a collection of the best shareware, music, metasearch, and so on.

Tucows
http://www.tucows.com/

The *Tucows* site offers more than 30,000 software titles in libraries located around the world.

CNET Shareware.com
http://shareware.cnet.com/

The Computer Network offers a searchable shareware database of software files for Windows and Macintosh platforms.

Chapter Mastery Test

To the Instructor: Refer to the Instructor's Manual for the Answers to the Mastery Questions. This manual has additional questions and resource materials.

Let's check for chapter comprehension with a short mastery test. What follows are basic terms, classroom projects, and suggested readings and references.

1. What is the most critical step in the evaluation of software? Explain its importance.
2. Discuss three criteria that a teacher should consider when choosing software for the classroom.
3. What is the main difference between shareware and public domain software?

4. Why is feedback a crucial element to consider when evaluating software?
5. Should the student or the computer control the direction of the program? Explain.
6. What is the major difference between a drill and practice program and a tutorial program?
7. Define simulation program and give an example.
8. Can a problem-solving program also be a simulation program? Explain in detail.
9. Give the paradigm for the typical drill and practice program design.
10. What is the major difference between computer-managed instruction and computer-assisted instruction?
11. Discuss two reasons for poor-quality software.
12. What are important considerations for setting up a software library?
13. As a student, are you more comfortable with teacher-directed or constructivist strategies? Explain your answer.
14. Name three characteristics associated with the constructivist learning model and three characteristics associated with the teacher-directed model.

Basic Terms

Beginner's All-purpose Symbolic Instruction Code (BASIC) (p. 249)
branching tutorial (p. 250)
computer-assisted instruction (CAI) (p. 248)
computer-managed instruction (CMI) (p. 257)
constructivist approach (p. 268)
drill and practice software (p. 252)
lab packs (p. 264)

linear tutorial (p. 250)
networkable software (p. 264)
public domain software (p. 259)
shareware (p. 259)
simulation (p. 250)
site license (p. 264)
teacher-directed approach (p. 268)
tutorial (p. 249)

Classroom Projects

1. Review a piece of software using the guidelines that were given in this chapter.
2. The software evaluation form that was used in this chapter was of a general nature. Develop a software checklist for a drill and practice software program in the area of math or science.
3. Go to the library and find three or four software review forms. Write a paper comparing these forms, discussing their similarities and differences.
4. Visit a high school or elementary school software library, and write a paper discussing its cataloging system.
5. Visit the library or use the Web to research a public domain software program. Write a review. What are the advantages and disadvantages of using this type of software program?
6. Using Appendix A or a software directory locate several math software packages for an eighth-grade class. Make a list.
7. Find a published review on a piece of software in the school's collection. Test out the product to determine the validity of the review. Write your own review.
8. Form small groups in the class; in each group develop a common evaluation form no more than three pages long. Make sure there is a consensus on all items and discuss the areas in which the group did not reach a consensus.

Suggested Readings and References

Baker, Warrant. "Technology in the Classroom: From Theory to Practice." *Educom Review* 32, no. 5 (September–October 1997): 42, 44, 46–50.

Berlin, D., and A. Wite. "Computer Simulations and the Transition from Concrete Manipulation of Objects to Abstract Thinking in Elementary School Mathematics." *School Science and Mathematics* 86, no. 6 (1986): 468–79.

"Best Products of 2000." *PC World* 18, no. 7 (July 2000): 98.

"Best Reading Software." *Children's Software Revue* 8, no. 2 (2000): 14–15.

Branzburg, Jeffrey, and Susan McLester. "Advice for Picking Out Great Software." *Technology and Learning* 20, no. 3 (October 1999): 44.

Buckleitner, Warren, ed. "The Elementary Teacher's Sourcebook on Children's Software." *Children's Software Revue* (Spring 2000).

Clements, F. H. *Computers in Elementary Mathematics*. Englewood Cliffs, N.J.: Prentice Hall, 1989.

Coburn, Peter et al. "How to Set Up a Computer Environment." *Classroom Computer News* 2, no. 3 (January–February 1982): 29–31.

Cohen, Steve, Richard Chechile, and George Smith. "A Method for Evaluating the Effectiveness of Educational Software. "*Behavior Research Methods, Instruments, and Computing* 26, no. 2 (May 1, 1994): 236.

Collopy, D. "Software Documentation: Reading a Package by Its Cover." *Personal Computing,* February 1983, pp. 134–44.

Cuban, Larry, and Heather Kirkpatrick. "Computers Make Kids Smarter—Right?" *Technos* 7, no. 2 (Summer 1998): 26–31.

Dede, C. "A Review and Synthesis of Recent Research in Intelligent Computer-Assisted Instruction." *International Journal of Man-Machine Studies* 24, no. 4 (1986): 329–53.

Edward, C. "Project MICRO." *Computing Teacher* 16, no. 5 (1989): 11–13.

Fruhauf, Karol, and Rob Gogher. "Comprehensive Guide to Software Quality Assurance Misses the Mark." *IEEE Software* 16, no. 5 (September/October 1999): 131.

Gagné, R. *The Conditions of Learning*. New York: Holt, Rinehart and Winston, 1985.

Goyne, June S., Sharon K. McDonough, and Dara D. Padgett. "Practical Guidelines for Evaluating Educational Software." *Clearing House* 73, no. 6 (July/August 2000): 345.

"Information Technology and Libraries." *Children's Software Revue* 16, no. 1 (1997): 45.

Jonassen, D. H. *Instructional Designs for Microcomputer Courseware.* Hillsdale, N.J.: Lawrence Erlbaum Associates, 1988.

Lindroth, Linda. "Blue Ribbon Software." *Teaching PreK–8* 30, no. 4 (January 2000): 16.

McLester, Susan. "Technology and Learning Software Awards of Excellence." *Technology and Learning* 20, no. 4 (November 1999): 13.

Only the Best Educational News Service. Association for Supervising and Curriculum Development 31250 North Pitt Street, Alexandria VA 22314-1453.

Pollack, Rachel H. "The Road to Software-Buying Success." *Currents* 23, no. 5 (May 1997): 36–40.

Pooley, Pam, and Eric Pooley. "Smart CD-ROMS. Best Products of 2000." *Family Life* 18, no. 7 (April 2000): 66.

Roblyer, M. D. "When Is It Good Courseware? Problems in Developing Standards for Microcomputer Courseware." *Educational Technology*, October 1981, pp. 47–54.

Roblyer, M. D., Jack Edwards, and Mary Anne Havriluk. *Integrating Educational Technology into Teaching*. Upper Saddle River, N.J.: Prentice Hall, 2000.

"Six Strategies for Raising a Scientist." *Software Revue* 8, no. 4 (2000): 12–16.

Sy, Leith. "Practice Tests as Formative Assessment Improve Student Performance on Computer-Managed Learning."*Assessment and Evaluation in Higher Education* 24, no. 3 (September 1999): 339.

TechTrends Media Reviews. *Association for Educational Communications and Technology,* 1 (202) 347–7834. Columns that have in-depth evaluations of educational multimedia.

Titus, Richard. "Finding Good Educational Software: Where to Begin." *Learning,* October 1985, p. 15.

Vargus, Julie S. "Instructional Design Found in Computer Assisted Instruction." *Phi Delta Kappan,* June 1986, pp. 738–44.

Voas, Jeffrey A. "New Generation of Software Quality Conferences." *IEEE Software* 17, no. 1, (January/February 2000): 22.

White, James A., and Stephanie S. VanDeventer. "A Successful Model for Software Evaluation." *Computers in the Schools* 8, no. 1/3 (1991): 323.

Zakrzewski, Stan, and Joanna Bull. "The Mass Implementation and Evaluation of Computer-Based Assessments." *Assessment and Evaluation in Higher Education* 23, no. 2 (June 1998): 141.

CHAPTER 11

Using the Computer in Major Curriculum Areas

Integrating the Computer into the Classroom
Did you know that there are strategies for using one computer with 30 or more students in the classroom? Did you know that there are ways of using language arts, math, social studies, and science computer software in conjunction with other resources in the classroom? In the process of reading this chapter, teachers will see examples of different types of software that make it easier for students to function successfully in the classroom setting. Furthermore, the chapter will give examples of lesson plans that can be used in a variety of situations and select Internet sites containing a rich assortment of lesson plan content.

Objectives

Upon completing this chapter, you will be able to:

1. List strategies for using one computer with 30 or more children in the math, science, social studies, and language arts areas;

2. Describe examples of the major software in four curricular areas;

3. Discuss ways of integrating the computer into the classroom; and

4. Examine useful lesson plans and Internet sites.

One Computer in the Classroom

The typical classroom used to have one computer for 30 or more children, but a recent survey shows that the typical U.S. school now has one computer for every 6 students (National Center for Education Statistics, 1999). Most of the time, however, these computers reside in a lab and the teacher has access to only one computer in the classroom. Some teachers store the computer encased in plastic wrap with strict rules to govern its use, and others, afraid to use the computer at all, let it gather dust in a remote corner of the room. In either situation, the computer is not being used to its potential. Here are seven suggestions that will help you better capitalize on the computer's capabilities in the classroom: (1) select the software according to students' needs; (2) collect the appropriate equipment; (3) organize the classroom; (4) use the team approach; (5) know the software's time factor; (6) encourage group participation; and (7) integrate computer use into the curriculum.

Selection of Software

In any good instruction, you adapt the material to students' needs. This principle holds for software as well. Students have varied abilities, interests, and preferences that warrant different teaching considerations and strategies. For example, if a student does not know how to type, he or she will have to search for the keys on the keyboard, thus becoming easily frustrated with the computer. At a third-grade level, a teacher's first strategy may be to instruct students in keyboarding skills, starting with the return, escape, and arrow keys.[1] Try this strategy for introducing the keyboard. Create a large keyboard and place it at the front of the room. Next, arrange students in pairs to practice the letter and number locations on a seat copy of the large-size keyboard. After students have had the experience of helping each other explore the keyboard, direct the whole class in finding designated keys. Eventually, have the children close their eyes while continuing this activity.

Typing programs such as *Kid Keys 2.0* (Knowledge Adventure) and *Type to Learn Junior* (Sunburst) provide excellent introductions to the keyboard. *Kid Keys 2.0* has five activities that are designed to introduce young children to the keyboard. This program has on-screen helping hands that show correct finger position, multiple levels that let students advance at their own pace, and closed captioning for youngsters who are hearing impaired. *Type to Learn Junior* features a learning tutorial and three interactive games to motivate early learners. One of the activities, called "Cassie's Empty Nest," emphasizes right-hand and left-hand placement. In Figure 11.1, a breeze is responsible for blowing different items out of Cassie's nest. The students type targets or letter combinations, in this case mmm, to help Cassie fill her nest again.

**FIGURE 11.1
Type to Learn
Junior**

Reprinted by permission of
Sunburst Technology.

---

[1]One research scientist at SRI International recommends delaying the formal introduction of keyboarding until third grade (Buckleitner, 2000).

Once the children are skilled in locating keys, they are ready to work with a typing program like *Mavis Beacon Teaches Typing 10* (The Learning Company), *All the Right Type* (Ingenuity Works), or *Typing Tutor 10* (Knowledge Adventure).

Mavis Bacon Teaches Typing 10 teaches typing for age 8 to adult through personalized typing lessons that focus on the student's strengths and weaknesses. The content is age-appropriate and so are the interesting activities. Teachers can personalize this program, adding custom content such as a vocabulary lesson, spelling words, or literature excerpts. There are eight different games, which focus on accuracy, speed, and rhythm.

All the Right Type 3.0 (age 9 and above) is an easy-to-use typing program that links the keyboarding program with a word processor. It includes a record-keeping feature, and the lessons are customized for the student's use in a classroom setting. The newest version is visually exciting with the addition of numeric keypad practice and a spaceship pacer game.

Finally, *Typing Tutor 10* provides you with easy-to-use navigation and customized lessons based on students' needs. This program is well designed and effective in improving older students' (grade 5 and above) typing. Just click the Lessons, Practice, Progress, or Games button (Fig. 11.2). Further-

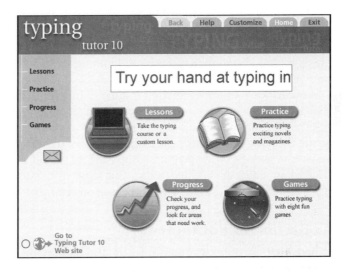

FIGURE 11.2
Typing Tutor 10
Used by permission of Knowledge Adventure/Havas Interactive.

more, there are eight action-packed games to motivate the learner. Once the students have achieved keyboard mastery, they can spend more time working with programs instead of working on the mechanics of finding keys.

If the students in the class need to improve their problem-solving abilities, a large range of programs is available. For example, **problem-solving software** such as *Where in the World Is Carmen Sandiego?* (The Learning Company) could work effectively for middle-grade students in the social studies area, while *Science Seekers—Hidden in Rocks* (Tom Snyder Productions) could work well for the same students in the science area. Using these programs, students can collectively improve their critical thinking skills by taking notes, manipulating variables, analyzing the results, drawing conclusions, and offering solutions to problems (Fig. 11.3).

**FIGURE 11.3
Science Seeker—
Hidden in Rocks**

Used by permission of Tom Snyder Productions.

If the class needs to study and research information about the United States, you can use a database software program such as *AppleWorks*. The students create information sheets, compose questionnaires, and collect appropriate data for computer entry. Each student might research two states and input information about each state's population, capital, number of representatives, and main crop. After information is entered into the database, students might search for a state in which the main crop is corn. When the state appears on the screen, the student at the computer calls out its name and the other students shade the state on a blank seat map. After the students find all the applicable states and shade them, you could study the maps and discuss where the corn-producing states are located. From this class discussion, the students could learn about the corn belt and why this region produces the most corn.

Collection of Equipment

When there is only one computer in the classroom, you need additional equipment to make the computer screen visible to the whole class. Projectors like the InFocus LP435z display enlarged images from a personal computer onto a wall screen. Another alternative is a portable **liquid crystal display (LCD) projection panel** and an overhead projector that uses the personal computer to display enlarged images on a screen. If the district cannot afford a projector or projection panel, there are less expensive alternatives. The T or Y adapter splits the signal coming from the class computer in order to display it on a larger television or monitor. Besides this device, a teacher can use a **video scan converter** like TView Gold to change the personal computer or laptop output for display on a television or NTSC (National Television System Committee) monitor. (For a full explanation of these products see Chapter 3.)

Many Macintosh computers have video out ports; you simply plug into that particular port for large-screen television reception capability. In most cases, these computers are ready for use with an additional monitor.

When you are cramped for space, you can improve the situation by elevating a large television or monitor to increase visibility. You also can tape a transparency on the TV screen and use a grease pencil to write on the screen to illustrate a point. Furthermore, you can create practice sheets that duplicate a screen from a computer program so that students can work along with the presentation.

Classroom Organization

Ask yourself questions to determine the best seating arrangement for viewing the computer. Are the students going to be in their seats or on the floor? Will the class be divided into small groups for discussion purposes? Will students be traveling to different learning stations in the room as they use manipulatives? Are they using an instrument such as a thermistor[2] to collect temperature data in different sections of the room?

Team Approach

Many students have been using computers since they were very young. If you have enough pupils who are familiar with the computer, organize them into a team. Under your tutelage, the team can practice giving directions, solving problems, and introducing new software. After the team is experienced, give the members identification badges and have them walk around the room answering questions on the current program. In addition to reducing the number of questions you'll receive, this team method reaches a larger number of pupils and gets them involved in helping each other.

Software Time Factor

For the computer program to be a success, in addition to selecting the appropriate program for the situation, you also must know the program's time constraints. For instance, when the time frame is short, don't choose open-ended software, because the students will be unhappy when they have to stop prematurely. *The Oregon Trail IV* (The Learning Company) takes at least 35 minutes to complete, and the students will object to quitting even though the program has a save function. *The Quarter Mile* (Barnum), on the other hand, ends quicker and therefore is easier to stop and start with a class. Additionally, in selecting a program, check whether it saves the game or activity instantaneously or at the end of a level. Software programs that require 15 or 20 minutes to finish a level might be inappropriate for a particular classroom situation.

---

[2]A thermistor is a sensoring device that converts temperature into electrical impulses.

Group Involvement

Your interactions with a class are very important and will determine how free your students feel to participate in class lessons involving computers. At the introduction of a lesson, explain that there are many acceptable answers and often there is no one solution to a problem. Try to reduce the students' anxiety about evaluation. At first, involve the whole class in discussion; later, break the class up into smaller groups. Ask probing questions and ask students for their next move. Search for the reasons behind their answers and give them time to think. You should be a facilitator, letting the students do most of the talking and never imposing ideas on the class discussion. Try not to be judgmental in responding to the students; they will pick up on your nonverbal body language. Encourage the students to cooperate in order to promote learning and social skills. Advance the students' thinking by making comments such as "That seems like a good idea, but expand on it."

Let the students practice problem solving by having them solve the same problem again, checking out their hypotheses and recording their collective answers. Give the students objects to manipulate at their desks to help them answer the questions that the software is posing. For example, *Puzzle Tanks* (Sunburst), a classic program, poses problems that involve filling tanks with Wonder Juice, Odd Oil, or Gummy Glue and moving this liquid over to a storage tank. At the simplest level, the program might ask the students to move 14 grams of Gummy Glue to a storage tank. For this problem, students are shown on the screen a tank that can hold seven grams and another tank that can hold one gram. You can involve the whole class in this activity by distributing measuring cups and beans at the students' desks. A favorite ploy is to divide the class into small groups that challenge each other to see which group answers the most problems correctly. At the end of the day, have the students work on the computer in pairs, one partner using the computer and the other coaching and recording. This pairing encourages students to develop strategies for handling the problems inherent in the software. Organize the time the students spend at the computer with a schedule similar to the one in Figure 11.4. The students should work on a program for a designated

FIGURE 11.4 Computer-Use Chart

PROGRAM: WHERE IN THE WORLD IS CARMEN SANDIEGO			
TIME	TEAMS		FINISHED
8:30-8:50	David	Scott	✔
8:50-9:10	Bobbie	Florence	✔
9:10-9:30	Jill	Judy	

time interval. When their time is up, the next pair of pupils listed in the chart takes a turn. If a team is absent or busy, the next available partnership fills the void. This way the computer can be used by everyone in the class.

Integrating the Computer into the Classroom

How do you make the computer an integral part of the core curriculum? The software should not substitute for the standard curriculum but rather should complement it on a regular basis. Let's look at four different software programs and how these programs can be included in classroom instruction.

If you want to improve students' writing skills, you might use a program such as *Hollywood High* (Grolier Interactive), which encourages creative writing and provides an opportunity for students to listen to their own written work and make revisions. When students use *Hollywood High* (Fig. 11.5),

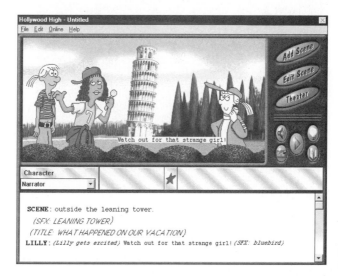

**FIGURE 11.5
Hollywood High**
© Theatrix. Used with permission.

they choose characters, expressions, and scenery for a play. They write scripts, add actions, edit these scripts, and then listen to and watch the characters perform. You can make suggestions for scripts that include recent events, historical occurrences, stories read, or class science experiments. Each student can work at his or her own desk to develop ideas for scripts, and the class can collectively brainstorm these ideas. Then, you and the class can discuss the characters, plot, purpose, and climax. The class then can form small groups to write their own scripts, and these scripts can be translated to the computer and viewed by the whole class.

In math, you can use a **simulation** program such as *Mighty Math Calculating Crew* (Edmark) to help students improve their math problem-solving skills. This program invites students into an animated world of math adventure. They are given practice in handling topics such as multiplication, division, number lines, money, and 3-D geometry. Many of the activities contain virtual manipulatives, which help students make connections between concrete and abstract math. Using this program, the students experiment with geometry by rotating a 3-D solid or by changing a 2-D net to see the effect on the corresponding solid. They build spatial orientation skills, which let them recognize the same object when viewed from different angles, and spatial visualization skills, which allow them to mentally rotate a 3-D solid or imagine it in different configurations.

For social studies, there is a truck-driving interactive simulation series entitled *Crosscountry* (Ingenuity Works), which includes such titles as *USA, Texas, Canada Platinum,* and *California* (Fig. 11.6). The *Crosscountry* programs

FIGURE 11.6 Crosscountry Canada Platinum
Used by permission of Ingenuity Works.

are effective for teaching map reading, geography, spatial relationships, and critical thinking skills. In *Crosscountry Canada Platinum,* students discover the geography of Canada by driving trucks to pick up commodities that the teacher or computer has selected from a list of 50 possibilities. These commodities are located in 79 Canadian cities. You could divide the class into two competing trucking companies and set them on their missions. (If one trucking company chooses to pick up only four commodities, its mission will require about 40 minutes.) You can customize the operation of the program so that both companies have to travel the same distance. Each team decides when to eat, sleep, and get gas; which cities to travel to; and how to get to the final destination. Obviously, each team's objective is to pick up and deliver its loads before the other team does. Members of the teams can record the trip routes, cities visited, population, locations, and other features. A winning team's strategy can be discussed, and each team can keep a journal of the journey.

The *Science Court* series (Tom Snyder Productions) teaches science concepts to elementary and middle school students. Some of the programs in the series cover sound, statistics, particles in motion, machines, the water cycle, fossils, and inertia. The program unfolds as a courtroom drama, and there are demonstrations and explanations as the lawyers battle over a case. In *Science Court—Fossils,* Jack Jenkins is accused of deliberately planting a fossil to halt construction of a café. During the trial, the students work in cooperative teams. They review the facts, engage in hands-on activities, and predict what will happen next. As the case progresses, the students attempt to answer questions correctly (Fig. 11.7). After the case is presented, the students predict how the jury will vote. The teacher can lead interesting discussions about the trial. At the same time, members of the class can be encouraged to take notes and then share their notes with the class. During the course of the trial, the

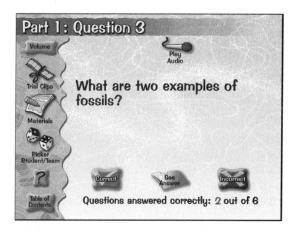

**FIGURE 11.7
Science Court—
Fossils**
Used by permission of Tom Snyder Productions.

students learn about the different types of fossils and conditions for fossilization. They engage in experiments such as creating imprints of hands, feet, and teeth, and then predict who made these imprints. Students also work as a team by listening and talking with others, sharing a goal, and becoming a member of a group. This series of programs is perfect for integrating the computer into the classroom.

In summation, you should select software that best satisfies the students' needs. You should also take time to collect the appropriate equipment, organize the room, and put the student experts to work. Learn the software, be aware of its time limitations, know how to integrate it into the classroom curriculum, and always encourage student participation by asking appropriate questions.

Subject Area Software

Now, let's examine some more educational software programs and see how they can be used in the classroom.

Mathematics Programs

Since most computer scientists have training in mathematics, the computer is usually associated with this field. The research literature offers no apparent agreement on how best to use computer software for improving math skills or for developing higher order thinking. In 2000, the National Council for Teachers of Mathematics (NCTM) published extensive standards for using technology. See the NCTM site for information on these standards at http://www.nctm.org/standards/. Even with these standards, teachers must decide how to use math software according to their own classroom needs. In the following section, math software is grouped as **drill and practice**, simulation, problem-solving, and **tutorial**.

Drill and Practice Programs

Drill and practice math programs help students become more proficient in their math skills and concepts. These programs give students the needed practice in a highly motivating format and assist the less academically adept child in mastering the concepts. Programs such as *MindTwisters* (Edmark) focus on math facts, rounding, measuring, telling time, counting money and much more. In this action-packed game show format, students race against the clock and other players to enter their answers. The teacher can set the program's challenge level to match individual students' skill levels. The *MindTwister Math* program can be used effectively in a one-computer or many-computer classroom. You can organize students into groups of two or three. For this particular example (Fig. 11.8), the player has to press the A key when he or she knows the answer, then press the correct answer, which is answer 1.

**FIGURE 11.8
MindTwister**
Challenge Screen
© Riverdeep Interactive
Learning Limited.

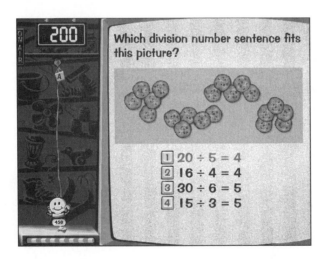

Another example of an addictive drill and practice program is *The Quarter Mile*. Barnum Software produces a series of these math programs that range from whole numbers to equations. *The Quarter Mile* is designed so that users are in a competitive drag race with themselves. (Students can opt to race "wild running horses" instead of cars.) When they answer a problem correctly, the car leaves the starting line at 55 miles per hour. Thereafter, the car accelerates by 5 mph with each correct answer, racing against an exact video replay of their own five best previous races. The car goes faster and faster as the racer accelerates to the accompanying sound effects, giving users the thrill of watching their improvement. The program features an excellent teacher management component. This program produces great results for the average or needier student (Fig. 11.9).

FIGURE 11.9
The Quarter Mile
Used with permission of Barnum Software.

Simulation Programs

In the past, mathematics was often taught as an abstract concept devoid of any real meaning, but today there are math simulation programs modeled after daily real-life situations.

Math for the Real World (Knowledge Adventure) teaches fractions, decimals, time, money, charts, and measurement. The program lets students use their math skills in a real-world context by joining a band and traveling to 10 cities across the United States. When traveling, they apply math concepts to earn points for a band contract. In this example, the student must move the correct number of pizza pieces to Rusty's plate (Fig. 11.10).

FIGURE 11.10
Math for the Real World
Used by permission of Knowledge Adventure/Havas Interactive.

Two other excellent simulation programs are *PrimeTime Math* (Tom Snyder) and *Ice Cream Truck* (Sunburst). *PrimeTime Math* teaches math through dramatic stories, whereas *Ice Cream Truck* lets grade 2–5 students become ice cream truck drivers. Students begin with $500 and try to earn as much money as possible by stocking up on the products they think will be in the greatest demand.

Problem-Solving Programs

Problem-solving software promotes critical thinking skills. Most problem-solving software is similar to simulation software in that users are placed in situations in which they manipulate variables and receive information on the results.

For example, *Carmen Sandiego Math Detective* (The Learning Company) teaches pre-algebra, geometry, division, fractions, and percents. The students, ages 8 to 14, embark on 12 missions to Carmen's hideouts. During each mission, they encounter five different math activities. As the students solve the problems, they obtain a secret password. In this particular math activity (Fig. 11.11) the students have to solve six different word problems in order to get a password. The teacher can see a progress report on each student.

**FIGURE 11.11
Carmen Sandiego
Math Detective**
The Learning Company. All
rights reserved.

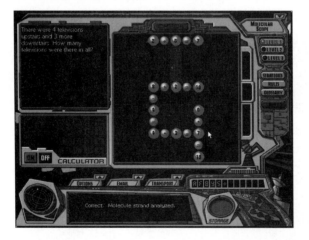

Building Perspective Deluxe (Sunburst) can be enjoyed by students from grade 4 to adult. The program can be played with two or three students working cooperatively at a computer, or one student working independently. *Building Perspective Deluxe* contains three activities that promote geometric and 3-D problem solving. In the *Map Activity,* students complete a path from a flashing arrow on the grid to one of the buildings on the grid. The last geometric puzzle piece they place in the path must be the one with the arrow on it (Fig. 11.12).

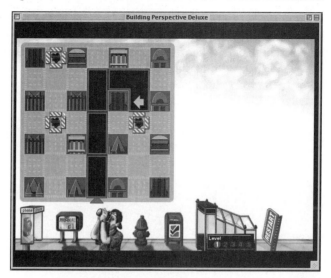

**FIGURE 11.12
Building
Perspective
Deluxe**

Reprinted by permission of
Sunburst Technology.

Critical Thinking Press & Software produces many logic programs, including *What's My Logic?* and *Mind Benders*. *What's My Logic?* is a program for older students and adults. It contains a series of mind-stretching games. Students have to discover the fundamental rule of logic that will let them travel through a maze to the end. *Mind Benders* is a series of logic puzzles for grade 2 to adult. Students improve their deductive reasoning by determining the relationships between people, places, and things. In Figure 11.13, the student is in the process of figuring out the position of each house in the row.

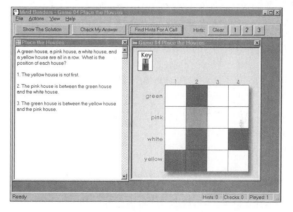

**FIGURE 11.13
Mind Bender**

Reprinted by permission of
Critical Thinking Books and
Software.

Tutorial Programs

A tutorial program gives students instruction in a particular subject and serves as a well-organized private teacher for the learner. A good tutorial usually starts with an overview of the subject matter and then checks the student for mastery of learning concepts. The student can move through the material, answering questions posed by the software. The program provides feedback for correct and incorrect responses, positive reinforcement, and a record of the student's performance. Math is a logical curriculum area for a tutorial because it lends itself to small-step sequencing of material.

High School Advantage 2001 (Encore Software) is a collection of comprehensive tutorials. Eight high school core subjects are presented to the student in an exciting manner. The programs are interactive, using the latest multimedia technology. An example from the *Trigonometry Tutorial* is presented in Figure 11.14.

**FIGURE 11.14
High School
Advantage 2001**

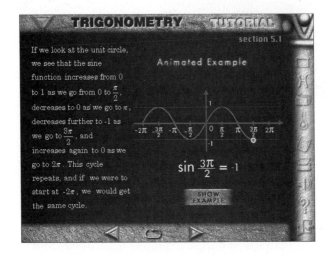

Geometer's Sketchpad (Key Curriculum Press) is not a true tutorial, but it is an exploratory program that teaches geometry in an unusual way. Using *Sketchpad 3* (Fig. 11.15), students manipulate and create geometric figures. They are able to explore freely or use the program as a tool to do assigned problems. The program comes with a user manual and sample activities.

**FIGURE 11.15
Geometer's
Sketchpad**

The Geometer's Sketchpad®, Key Curriculum Press, P.O. Box 2304, Berkeley, CA 94702, 1-800-995-MATH. Used with permission.

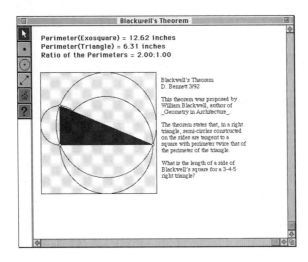

Science Programs

In many elementary schools, science programs have been limited to memorization of textbook facts; teachers have not had the time or money to collect the necessary materials for an exciting hands-on science lesson. Furthermore, the breadth of the science class has depended on the teacher's interests and specific areas of expertise. Because of their general lack of knowledge in science, some teachers have ignored many science topics and most elementary students have received very little science education. Experimentation has occurred primarily in the high school science lab, an experience usually reserved for college-bound students.

The computer has begun to change this unfortunate situation. The science investigation skills of classifying, synthesizing, analyzing, and summarizing data are skills that the computer is designed to reinforce. The computer cannot replace the actual science laboratory, but it can simulate complex, expensive, and dangerous experiments, saving time and money. Because there is a renewed interest in science education, more schools are incorporating the computer into the science curriculum and science software is flourishing. Publishers such as Edmark provide exciting interactive programs such as *Thinkin' Science ZAP!,* and *Virtual Lab: Electricity* and *Light.* Knowledge Adventures produces animated interactive science programs that include *Science Blaster Jr., Solar System Explorer,* and *RedShift 3.*

The Learning Company has *Body Works 6.0,* which provides a complete reference to human anatomy, and *Schoolhouse Rock: Science,* where students complete physical, life, and earth science activities to learn about topics such as sound, light, electricity, genetics, and the solar system.

Finally, Sunburst Communications has a rich and vast assortment of science programs including *Learn About Plants, Learn About Dinosaurs, Learn About Weather, Learn About Simple Machines, A Field Trip to the Sea Deluxe, Science,* and *Gateways: First-Year Biology & Chemistry.* These programs range from elementary to adult levels. The series of early learning programs teaches students about dinosaurs, plants, fossils, animals; the programs for older students or adults instruct them in chemistry, biology, and genetics.

Drill and Practice Programs

Today, quite a few superior science software programs offer drill and practice components. *GeoSafari Animals* (Educational Insights Interactive) uses a game show format with questions based on animal trivia, while *GeoSafari Plants* contains 15 activities on topics such as the human skeleton, rocks, and minerals, space travel, and trees. Other examples of good programs are the *Brain Quest* series (Edmark) and *Senses* (Ventura Education Systems).

Simulation Programs

Science simulation programs such as *Body Works 6.0* (The Learning Company) are designed for repeated use. *BodyWorks 6.0* (Fig. 11.16) makes students feel as if they are actually traveling in the human body and not just exploring a

**FIGURE 11.16
BodyWorks**

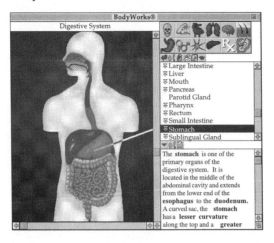

database. The program inspires students to learn the different functions of the systems of the human body. It contains a complete health section that includes information on such topics as first aid, fitness, common illness, and nutrition. *BodyWorks* has colorful graphics on more than 100 glossary entries, detailed movie clips, and sound. Additionally, lesson plans and quizzes improve students' knowledge of human anatomy.

Holt, Rinehart and Winston produces *Interactive Explorations in Physics.* This simulation program has students use tools and techniques to solve problems that make physics relevant to real-life situations. Students conduct experiments, record observations and results, and apply the knowledge gained to problem solving.

Finally, *Physics Lab Simulator* (Visual Touch of America) is a tool designed to help physics teachers demonstrate experiments that ordinarily would need expensive equipment such as a cyclotron or mass spectrometer. Students can examine Einstein's theory of relativity, Rutherford's gold foil experiment, elastic collision, and other phenomena (Fig. 11.17).

**FIGURE 11.17
Physics Lab
Simulator**

Used by permission of Visual
Systems.

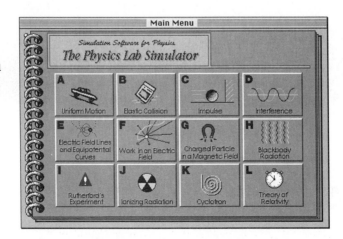

Problem-Solving Programs

The rapidly increasing collection of problem-solving and critical thinking programs serves as evidence of the emphasis on problem solving in science. An excellent example of a science problem-solving program and simulation combination is the classic *Botanical Gardens* (Sunburst), which challenges students to grow a variety of plants in a controlled environment. Through trial and error, students discover the effect of each variable on the plants. During the experiment, students adjust variables such as light, temperature, water, and music and monitor the resulting height of each plant.

The *Return of the Incredible Machine* (Sierra) has 250 unusual mind-melting puzzles. Students build trip-lever contraptions by placing parts such as ropes, pulleys, bowling balls, and cheese-driven mouse motors. When these parts are combined correctly, the machine is able to complete its task. In the example in Figure 11.18, Tutorial 1 lets the user knock the 8-ball off the screen. This program is addictive and meant for the bright middle school student or for any adult brave enough to try it!

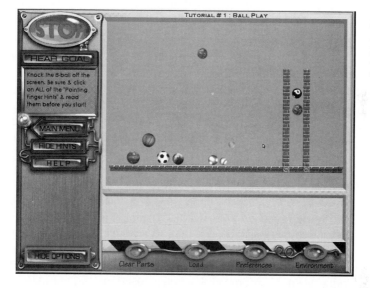

**FIGURE 11.18
The Return of the Incredible Machine**

© Sierra On-Line, Inc.

Another example of a problem-solving program is *Thinkin' Science ZAP!* (Edmark, now Riverdeep). The students in grades 3 to 6 explore sound, light, and electricity working with laser beams, electrical circuits, and sound waves. There are hundreds of simple and complex activities where the student is called upon to seek a solution. In the activity in Figure 11.19, students analyze circuits while solving problems using everyday objects like flashlights, wheels, and fans.

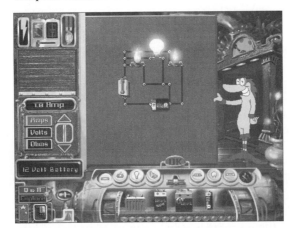

Edmark also created the classic *Sammy's Science House* for primary grades. With its appealing characters and animation, captivating voice, and charming music, this program makes a child curious about science.

Tutorial Programs

Good science tutorials are readily available, especially at the upper elementary, high school, and college levels.

At the high school or college level, *BioTutor, ChemTutor,* and *Physics Tutor* (Interactive Learning, Inc.) help students learn biology, chemistry, and physics. These programs cover the full curriculum for a first or second course in these subjects. While working on these tutorials, the students are given immediate feedback at each step. *SuperTutor Chemistry* (Stanford Multimedia) is a self-paced chemistry tutorial that covers hundreds of topics step by step with animation, voice lectures, exercises, and examples. This software covers one year of high school chemistry. Tutorial software on subjects of current health interest such as drugs and AIDS is also available. *Cocaine and Crack* (SAE Software) is a tutorial that reviews the physical and psychological effects of cocaine and crack, reasons for using and not using these drugs, and forms of cocaine. The program provides a list of objectives, tutorial lessons, and a self-test with multiple-choice questions. *AIDS* (SAE Software) is an interactive tutorial that provides up-to-date factual information about AIDS. It discusses the history of AIDS, how AIDS spreads, risk factors, current treatments, effects on the body, and resources.

Finally, *High School Advantage 2001* covers 10 core subjects. Using *Eyewitness Encyclopedia of Science,* the science components cover chemistry, life sciences, and physics. The tutorials are multimedia and interactive and help the students easily learn the subject matter. Figure 11.20 is a screen shot from the *Chemistry Tutor* where the student is attempting to learn about solutions.

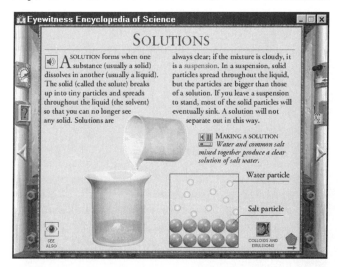

In the past, science tutorial software has been limited to high school and college levels. However, software publishers are beginning to see the potential for science software development in the lower grades. Tutorial programs for the elementary level include the *Science for Kids* series (Science for Kids), the *Learn About* series (Sunburst), and the *Eyewitness* series (DK Multimedia).

Science for Kids is interactive English/Spanish courseware with guided lessons and hands-on activities. The programs in the series are *"Cell"ebration*, for grades K–3; *Forces & Motions*, grades 3–6; and *Simple Machines*, grades 4–9.

The Learn About series provides a simple tutorial that teaches about plants, dinosaurs, weather, and simple machines.

Social Studies Programs

Social studies software excels at presenting current and historical events that foster class discussion and decision making. Students make decisions and then examine the consequences of those decisions. For instance, students can experience indirectly the results of a poorly planned presidential campaign, gaining perspective on political and social realities. Social studies programs are divided into two main categories: application software and computer-assisted instruction.

Application Programs

With **application software**, a teacher can integrate other information into the social studies program. Students can use word processors to write about any subject, spreadsheet and graphics programs to analyze statistical data and to display pertinent information, and database programs to retrieve data and analyze the information. For example, students using the social studies program *New Millenium World Atlas* (Rand McNally) gain access to detailed maps and comprehensive statistics and information (Fig. 11.21). Students can use the software to form patterns and see relationships.

**FIGURE 11.21
New Millennium
World Atlas
Deluxe**

© Rand McNally. Printed with permission.

Teachers can use programs like *TimeLiner 5.0* (Tom Snyder Productions) to create time lines for any subject (see Chapter 13). There are ready-made time lines available for different subject areas.

Computer-Assisted Instruction

A teacher can integrate **computer-assisted instruction (CAI)** programs into the social studies curriculum. To do so, the teacher should examine the purpose of instruction before selecting the software. Teacher A may need only a drill and practice program to reinforce the simple recall of the states and their capitals. Teacher B may need a simulation program to help students study the causes of the Civil War. In social studies, there are many excellent drill and practice and simulation programs that could meet the needs of both teachers.

Drill and Practice Programs Drill and practice social studies programs are easy to use, help in the retention of factual material, are fun because they use a game format, and require minimal teacher supervision.

For example, *GeoSafari* (Educational Insights Interactive) is a drill and practice program that contains multiple-choice quizzes that help with all sorts of geography subject matter such as memorizing the state capitals or learning where states are. In the example (Fig. 11.22), the state highlighted is Washington and the student clicked on the correct answer. In this entertaining quiz game, a player has the choice of selecting from 15 categories; for example, United States attractions and landmarks. Educational Insights Interactive also produces *GeoSafari History*, where students learn about world and U.S. history.

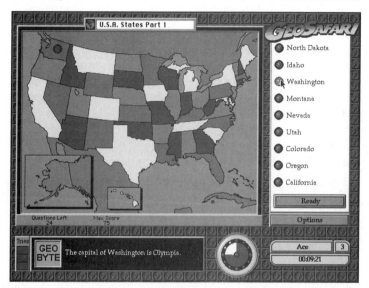

**FIGURE 11.22
GeoSafari
Geography**
Used by permission of
Educational Insights.

Simulation Programs   A well-designed social studies simulation challenges
students to make difficult decisions concerning money, politics, or some
other important factors. The *Carmen Sandiego* series, *The Oregon Trail,* and *The
Amazon Trail* (The Learning Company); the *Crosscountry* series (Ingenuity
Works); and the *Decisions, Decisions* series (Tom Snyder Productions) all help
students gain a better understanding of different people, places, and ideas in
the present or past. Students learn to use the study of history as a basis for decision making and to distinguish between fact and opinion.

A unique program called *Talking Walls* (Edmark) lets students in grades
4–8 explore the stories behind the world's most spectacular walls and see
how this has influenced history. Based on a book by Margy Burns Knight, this
software links cultural and historical facts when it presents a collection of stories of 14 famous walls. In the example, the student is learning about the
Great Wall of China (Fig. 11.23). Students can view pictures, time lines, and

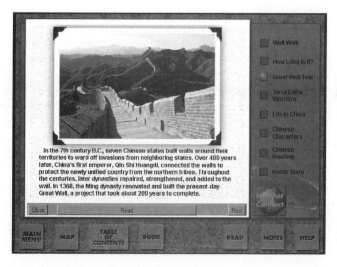

**FIGURE 11.23
Talking Walls**
© Riverdeep Interactive
Learning Limited.

videos to learn about the culture that created the particular wall they are studying. If the classroom has an Internet connection, there are links to the material that is associated with the content of the program. *Talking Walls* has a research component which lets the students take notes, save, and print them. The second program in the series is called *Talking Walls: The Stories Continue.* (See Chapter 12 for an explanation of how this program can be used with special education students.)

Language Arts Programs

Language arts programs are subdivided into the categories of writing, spelling, grammar, and reading (including reference tools). Because of the multitude of good language arts programs, it is often easier to integrate language arts programs into the curriculum than it is other types of programs.

Writing Programs

The computer is an effective tool for motivating and reinforcing the necessary skills to improve a student's writing by linking the various processes involved in writing. We'll discuss both word processing and story writing programs.

We learned in Chapter 4 how word processors can help students save time and reduce effort by moving paragraphs, deleting sentences, and checking spelling. The word processor not only increases students' productivity but also gives students extra time to think about content. We discussed word processors such as *Microsoft Word, WordPerfect* (Corel Corp.), *Write:OutLoud* (Don Johnston), and *AppleWorks.*

Other programs go beyond word processing, such as *Dr. Peet's Talk/Writer* (Dr. Peet's Software), which has a voice synthesizer pronouncing words as they are typed. This program is useful for students with special needs, ESL students, and young students. *MicroWorlds Pro* combines word processing with Logo and lets you create Web pages, while *MicroWorlds 2.0* (Logo Computer Systems Incorporated [LCSI]) is a creative learning tool for exploring language and image. *Write:OutLoud* is an easy-to-use talking word processor with an integrated Franklin spell checker. *Write:OutLoud,* a writing tool for children and adults, can be used by readers and nonreaders. It has been designed for the students who struggle with writing, offering features such as speech, background color, and text color.

In addition to these word processors are story writing programs such as *Storybook Weaver Deluxe* (The Learning Company), *Easybook Deluxe* (Sunburst), and *The Ultimate Writing & Creativity Center* (The Learning Company) and *Kreative Komix* (Visions Technology in Education). These programs let students have the thrill of creating their own printed and illustrated stories. *Kreative Komix,* a recent addition, lets students create animated stories that talk or print out the comic books. The students then can act out the stories using stick puppets. This multimedia program uses hundreds of props, and students record their own sounds or use built-in text to speech with a variety of voices (Fig. 11.24).

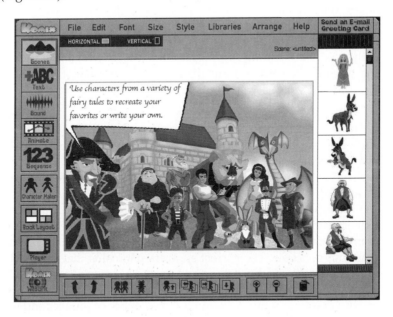

FIGURE 11.24
Kreative Komix
Visions Technology in
Education.

Foreign Language Programs

Using state-of-the-art technology, the *Learn to Speak* series (The Learning Company) provides tutorial programs in Spanish (Fig. 11.25), English, French, and German. These programs let the students record their own speech and compare it with one of the 20 native speakers. The lessons have high-quality sound, pictures, and video.

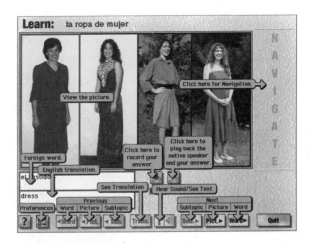

FIGURE 11.25
Learn to Speak
Spanish

Spelling Programs

The many spelling programs involve everyone and everything from sea animals, magic castles, and gulping frogs to jungle adventures and penny arcade activities. *JumpStart Learning Games Spelling,* for ages 5–8, has a student lead a frog through 10 prehistoric mazes, searching for a missing friend. To cross rivers, the student must solve spelling puzzles, using words that are presented in spelling bee style.

Middle School Advantage 2001 (Encore), for age 11 and up, is bundled with *Super Tutor Spelling,* a program that improves spelling through quizzes and games. The student visits different locations, like a museum, library, or music store, and each place offers six different spelling games.

Grammar Programs

Early grammar programs covered a range of skills from subject–verb agreement to recognition of the parts of speech through drill and practice activities. Today, grammar programs are not only drill and practice but are tutorials and simulations.

School House Rock: Grammar Rock (The Learning Company), a drill and practice program, contains videos on grammar from the ABC television program. Students from age 6 to 10 complete 19 multilevel activities and practice grammar concepts. The correct answers win coins that are used to play arcade games. An example of a good grammar tutorial for grade 7 to adult is *Phrase Maze: Grammar through Phrases* (My Word Associates). This program teaches grammar while covering different types of phrases and their application in sentences. The tutorial component explains every answer that a student chooses.

Grammar for the Real World (Knowledge Adventure), a simulation, teaches grammar, sentence structure, punctuation, and spelling. The program is for age 10 and up. As beginners in Hollywood, students must prove themselves at World Studios. They have to proofread letters from TV stars for incorrect punctuation and grammar, fix news anchors' statements before they are broadcast, identify parts of speech, and tailor material to certain audiences. In Figure 11.26, the student is correcting the letter's spelling errors.

**FIGURE 11.26
Grammar for the
Real World**
Used by permission of
Knowledge Adventure/Havas
Interactive.

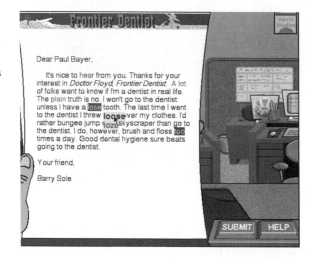

Reading Programs

Many simulations, drill and practice programs, and tutorial programs provide reading instruction. For the elementary schools there is a rich assortment of programs; for example, the *JumpStart* series (Knowledge Adventure) of interactive award-winning programs range from toddlers to fifth grade. The students learn to navigate through a schoolhouse full of interactive educational songs, puzzles, and games with a friendly host.

A delightful beginning phonics program is *3D Froggy Phonics* (Ingenuity Works). This program helps students master basic phonics concepts. *Froggy Phonics* helps the students learn the sounds for each letter and learn early spelling and reading skills. The program consists of 10 animated movies that explore short and long vowel sounds and games that reinforce concepts. In Figure 11.27, the student is learning about the long **A** sound.

**FIGURE 11.27
3D Froggy Phonics**
Used by permission of Ingenuity Works.

Island Reading Journey (Sunburst) is a multimedia program for grades 4 and 5 that contains reading comprehension activities to help the student read for meaning. This program has exercises for 100 intermediate-level books commonly found in your typical classroom or library (Fig. 11.28).

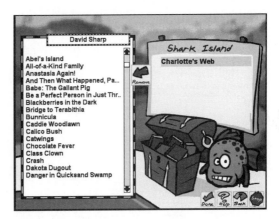

**FIGURE 11.28
Island Reading Journey**
Reprinted by permission of Sunburst Technology.

Spanning grades 3 to 10, *That's a Fact, Jack! Read* is an interactive game show that helps the student review literature. The teacher can choose from 45 CD-ROM discs that cover 450 children's and young adult books that are found in the classroom. This software program is a wonderful method to review literature with individual students or a whole class.

For the high school level there are titles that range from Shakespeare to Steinbeck. The *Literature: The Time, Life, and Works* series (Clearvue/eav) has such titles as *Chaucer, Thomas Hardy, Wordsworth, Dickens,* and *Shakespeare.*

Optimum Resources has an excellent high school comprehension series for grades 9–12. The topics for the high school series are high-interest in curriculum areas such as history, cars, fashion, and famous people. In the program *Famous People* (Fig. 11.29) the students read about Lincoln and have to answer questions about slavery. There are multiple-choice as well as essay questions for each section, and a student's progress reports can be printed.

FIGURE 11.29
Famous People

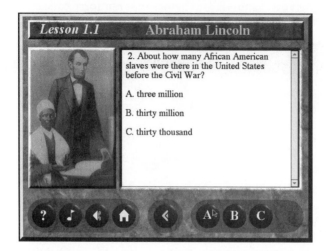

Finally, *Kaplan's SAT & PSAT ACT 2001 Edition* (Encore Software) is tutorial program that uses a step-by-step approach to help secondary students master the strategies for dealing with material found on the SAT, PSAT, and ACT tests. This program covers all pertinent subject areas (Fig. 11.30). The program's instructor reviews basic skills using multimedia lesson topics. Students are able to see their scores improve and track their progress against last year's freshman class.

FIGURE 11.30
Kaplan's SAT &
PSAT ACT 2001
Edition

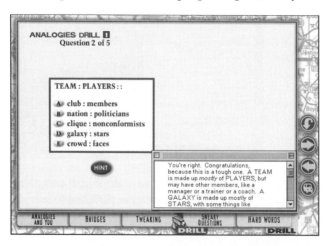

Reference Tools

Microsoft Bookshelf 2001 provides integrated access to nine top reference resources. These reference resources include such high-powered products as the *Encarta Desk World Atlas;* the *American Heritage Dictionary of the English Language,* 4th edition; and the *New World Almanac.*

Grolier Multimedia Encyclopedia Deluxe, Year 2001 (Grolier Interactive) contains thousands of articles (Fig. 11.31), navigational aids, multimedia features, and a dictionary containing hundreds of thousands of words. There is an easy to use *Online Knowledge Exporter,* which gives the students from grade 5 to adult the latest information every month with hundreds of free article updates and special features such as time lines, research helpers, and activities that explore subject areas.

FIGURE 11.31 Grolier Multimedia Encyclopedia Deluxe, Year 2001
© Grolier Incorporated. All rights reserved.

There are also encyclopedias for the younger child such as *Eyewitness Children's Encyclopedia* and *My First Incredible Amazing Dictionary* (DK Interactive Learning).

Classroom Lesson Plans

There are many activities a teacher can use to motivate students in all curriculum areas. What follows are five such activities.

▼   I. Math   ▼

Objective

Students will improve their math skills by using a math simulation program like *Math for the Real World* (Knowledge Adventure) or *Ice Cream Truck* (Sunburst).

Procedure

1. Using a math simulation program like *Ice Cream Truck,* the teacher works through a problem with the whole class.
2. Next, the teacher divides the class into four or five small groups.
3. She or he has each group vote on a leader, keyboarder, and recorder.
4. Each group takes a turn on the computer and sees how much money it can earn.
5. At the end of the day, each group spends time discussing how well the group did using the program. Also, group members establish a goal for the next day or session.
6. The students keep a written record of their activities and progress.
7. They rotate the roles of each member of the group.
8. The teacher should move among the groups asking questions and helping when appropriate.

▼ II. Science ▼

Objective

Use a product like *EasyBook Deluxe* to have younger students create an electronic portfolio.

Procedure

1. Explain how to use a program like *EasyBook Deluxe.*
2. Have the students study a unit on a subject like plants or dinosaurs.
3. While the students are studying this unit, have them create books about what they have learned.
4. When the students have completed the assignment, have them share their electronic portfolio with the class.

▼ III. Social Studies ▼

Objective

Using an electronic encyclopedia like *Grolier* or *Encarta,* have the students create articles for a newspaper.

Procedure

1. Divide the class into small groups.
2. Have each member of the group determine what famous person he or she wants to research. For example, the student might choose Abraham Lincoln or Harry Truman.

3. Using an electronic encyclopedia, have each student research the chosen person and write an article about the times in which this person lived.
4. Have the group then create a newspaper using an electronic program like *Microsoft Publisher.*
5. At the end of the assignment, have the groups come together and share newspapers.

▼   IV. Language Arts   ▼

Objective

Using a multimedia story writing program like *Kreative Komix*, create a book report.

Procedure

1. Students read a book, then talk about the elements that shape the story.
2. Next, have them write down a summary of the events.
3. The teacher then shows the students how to use the software to insert text and graphics.
4. The student prints a hard copy of the report and presents it in class.
5. The class discusses the report and offers suggestions for change.

There is an abundance of language arts software. Appendix A offers a comprehensive and annotated list of award-winning language arts programs.

Summary

In this chapter, we explored how to integrate the computer into the curriculum, select software according to the needs of pupils, collect the appropriate equipment, organize the classroom, and utilize the team approach. Next, we reviewed a variety of programs that are available for math, science, social studies, and language arts.

⊘   General Curriculum and Math Sites

What follows is an annotated list of top-rated Internet sites you can use in all curriculum areas. These curriculum sites range from math lesson plans to science resources.

The Electric Teacher
http://www.electricteacher.com/

The Electric Teacher, created by teacher Cathy Chamberlain, provides a rich assortment of ideas for integrating technology into the curriculum. Categories for resources include Community Resources, Thematic Resources, Literacy and Technology, K–12 Teacher Resources, and Education Listservs and Collaboration Sites. Tutorials help teachers incorporate *Word, Excel, PowerPoint,* and *FrontPage* into the regular classroom. The site also includes a tutorial on the basic use of the Internet, sample lessons, tips for taking quality photos, and help for working with graphics.

Academy Curriculum Exchange
http://ofcn.org/cyber.serv/academy/ace/
Academy Curriculum Exchange offers lesson plans for grades K–12 in a variety of subject areas. To find more than 50 plans for math, click these links: Elementary School, Intermediate School, or High School.

AskERIC Lesson Plans: Math
http://askeric.org/cgi-bin/lessons.cgi/ Mathematics
AskERIC Lesson Plans: Math provides a collection of math lesson plans contributed by teachers for grades K–12. Topics include algebra, applied math, arithmetic, functions, geometry, measurement, and probability. Each lesson plan features an overview, purpose, objectives, activities, and resource materials.

Science Sites

Activity Search
http://www.eduplace.com/search/ activity2.html
Activity Search, from Houghton Mifflin, features a curriculum database where K–8 teachers can search for science lesson plans/activities and other subject areas by grade level. Activities can also be browsed by theme.

Double Helix Science Experiments
http://www.csiro.au/helix/dhexperiments.html
CSIRO provides a collection of over 60 science experiments for grades 3–8.

Amazing Science at the Roxy
http://www.hood-consulting.com/amazing/qt_amazing/asr.html
Amazing Science at the Roxy, provided by Hood Consulting Group, features a collection of physical science lesson plans and experiments for grades 5–12.

Social Studies Sites

Academy Curricular Exchange
http://ofcn.org/cyber.serv/academy/ace/
Academy Curricular Exchange includes over 200 social studies lesson plans for elementary, intermediate, and high school students.

Mr. Donn's Ancient History Page
http://members.aol.com/donnandlee/
Mr. Donn's ancient civilization lesson plan stop and information resource covers ancient Mesopotamia, Egypt, Greece, Rome, China, and others.

Awesome Library Social Studies Lesson Plans
http://www.neat-schoolhouse.org/Library/ Materials_Search/Lesson_Plans/Social_ Studies.html
This site presents a large number of links to a variety of lesson plans representing all areas of the K–12 social studies curriculum.

Education World: Lessons to Celebrate Black History Month!
http://www.educationworld.com/a_lesson/ lesson221.shtml
This site contains 10 classroom activities, other online resources, and award-winning sites for celebrating Black History Month.

Language Arts Sites

AskERIC Lesson Plans: Language Arts
http://askeric.org/cgi-bin/lessons.cgi/ Language_Arts
AskERIC Lesson Plans: Language Arts provides a collection of nearly 100 language arts lesson plans contributed by teachers for grades K–12. Topics include literature, writing composition, reading, and spelling. Each lesson plan features an overview, purpose, objectives, activities, and resource materials.

A to Z Teacher Stuff
http://www.atozteacherstuff.com/
A to Z Teacher Stuff provides hundreds of lesson plans and thematic activities for teaching children's literature in the elementary school. The site also includes *LessonPlanz.com*, a search engine with over 4,000 lesson plans.

Cool Teaching Lessons and Units
http://www.coollessons.org/coolunits.htm
Richard Levine provides an extensive collection of WebQuests and lesson plan sites.

Chapter Mastery Test

To the Instructor: Refer to the Instructor's Manual for the answers to the Mastery Questions. This manual has additional questions and resource materials.

Let's check for chapter comprehension with a short mastery test. Projects and suggested readings and references follow.

1. Give three suggestions for using one computer with 30 students and explain each suggestion thoroughly.
2. Name two advantages of using drill and practice software to learn mathematics.
3. Suggest two ways social studies software can be used to teach U.S. history.
4. Should the teacher use language arts software to improve writing skills? Give reasons to support your position.
5. Using one computer, how can the teacher increase group involvement in the learning process?
6. How can the teacher teach keyboarding skills effectively to young children?
7. What methods can a teacher use to improve problem-solving skills on the computer?
8. How can the computer enhance the development of reading skills?
9. Explain how students might use the computer in gathering, organizing, and displaying social studies information. Include two titles of exemplary software.
10. How can the teacher utilize the computer to report scientific information?
11. What procedures can a teacher use to incorporate a variety of math software into the classroom?
12. What are the advantages of using computer math manipulatives over traditional math manipulative?

Basic Terms

application program (p. 293)
computer-assisted instruction (CAI) (p. 294)
drill and practice (p. 284)
liquid crystal display projection panel (LCD) (p. 278)

problem-solving software (p. 277)
simulation (p. 281)
tutorial (p. 284)
video scan converter (p. 278)

Classroom Projects

1. Visit a school that uses computers and a variety of computer programs. Write a brief report on the criteria used by the school in selecting its software.
2. Devise an organizational schedule for a classroom with only one computer.
3. Discuss the problems inherent in language arts software given the existing curriculum. Research the topic to support your discussion.
4. Using the form in Chapter 10, review five software programs on the annotated list in Appendix A.
5. How does the school work with the media librarian to store, disseminate, and evaluate computer courseware?

Suggested Readings and References

Allen, Denise. "On-Screen Writing: Teaching with Technology." *Teaching PreK–8* 27, no. 5 (February 1997): 18, 23–24.

Anderson, Kimberley, and Cay Evans. "The Development of the Canonical Story Grammar Model and Its Use in the Analysis of Beginning Reading Computer Stories." *Reading Improvement* 33, no. 1 (Spring 1996): 2–15.

Blanchard, Jay S., and George E. Mason. "Using Computers in Content Area Reading Instruction." *Journal of Reading,* November 1985, pp. 112–17.

Brandt, D. Scott. "Tutorial, or Not Tutorial, That Is the Question . . ." *Computers in Libraries* 17, no. 5 (May 1997): 44–46.

Branzburg, Jeffrey. "Six Math Adventures." *Technology and Learning* 19, no. 9 (May 1999): 10.

Buckleitner, Warren, ed. *The Elementary Teacher's Sourcebook of Children's Software* 8, no. 4. Flemington, N.J.: Active Learning Associates, July/August 2000.

Buckleitner, Warren, ed. *The Complete Sourcebook on Children's Software.* Vol. 8 New Jersey: Active Learning Associates 2000.

Buckleitner, Warren, ed. *Children's Software Revue* 8, nos. 2–3 (2000).

Cassidy, Jacquelyn A. "Computer-Assisted Language Arts Instruction for the ESL Learner." *English Journal* 85, no. 8 (December 1996): 55–57.

Cherry, Joan M., et al. "Evaluating the Effectiveness of a Concept-Based Computer Tutorial for OPAC Users." *College and Research Libraries* 55, no. 4 (July 1994): 355–64.

Clements, Douglas H. *Computers in Elementary Mathematics Education.* Englewood Cliffs, N.J.: Prentice Hall, 1989.

Coffee, Peter. "Everyone Can Learn from Sixth-Grade Math." *PC Week* 16, no. 39 (November 27, 1999): 50.

Collis, S., and M. Newman. *Computer Technology in Curriculum: An Instructional Handbook: Courseware Evaluation.* Olympia, Wash.: Washington Office of the State Superintendent of Public Instruction, 1982.

Dvorak, John C. "One Child, One Laptop." *PC Magazine* 18, no. 20 (November 16, 1999): 83.

Educational Software Institute Resource Guide. Omaha, Nebr.: 2001.

Eiser, L. "Problem-Solving Software: What It Really Teaches." *Classroom Computer Learning,* March 1986, pp. 42–45.

Ellis, James D. "Preparing Science Teachers for the Information Age." *Journal of Computers in Mathematics and Science* 9, no. 4 (Summer 1990): 55.

Gonce-Winder, C., and H. H. Walbesser. "Toward Quality Software." *Contemporary Educational Psychology* 12, no. 10 (July 1987): 19–25.

Harrison, Nancy, and Evelyn M. Van Devender. "The Effects of Drill-and-Practice Computer Instruction on Learning Basic Mathematics Facts." *Journal of Computing in Childhood Education* 3, nos. 3–4 (1992): 349–56.

Hodges, Bob. "Task Computing." *Learning and Leading with Technology* 25, no. 2 (October 1997): 6–8.

Hough, Bradley W., and Margaret W. Smithey. "Creating Technology Advocates: Connecting Preservice Teachers with Technology." *T.H.E. Journal* 26, no. 8 (March 1999): 78.

Howie, Sherry Hill. *Reading, Writing, and Computers: Planning for Integration.* Boston: Allyn and Bacon, 1989.

Ignatz, M. E. "Suggestions for Selecting Science Education Software." *Journal of Computers in Mathematics and Science Teaching,* Fall 1985, pp. 27–29.

Ivers, Karen S. "Desktop Adventures: Building Problem-Solving and Computer Skills." *Learning and Leading with Technology* 24, no. 4 (December–January 1996–97): 6–11.

Johnson, Judi Mathis, ed. *Educational Software Preview Guide 2000.* Eugene, Ore.: International Society for Technology in Education (ISTE), 2000.

Kassner, Kirk. "One Computer Can Deliver Whole-Class Instruction." *Music Educators Journal* 86, no. 6 (May 2000): 34.

Lindroth, Linda. "Blue Ribbon Software." *Teaching PreK–8* 5, no. 30 (February 2000): 16.

Mann, William P. *Edutainment Comes Alive!* Indianapolis, Ind.: Sams Publishing, 1994.

Margalit, Malka. *Effective Technology Integration for Disabled Children: The Family.* New York: Springer, 1990.

McGinnis, J. Randy, et al. "Beliefs and Perceived Needs of Rural K–12 Teachers of Science toward the Uses of Computing Technologies." *Journal of Science Education and Technology* 5, no. 2 (June 1996): 111–20.

McMillen, Linda, et al. "Integrating Technology in the Classroom." *Language Arts* 74, no. 2 (February 1997): 137–49.

Reed, W. Michael. "Assessing the Impact of Computer-Based Writing Instruction." *Journal of Research on Computing in Education* 28, no. 4 (Summer 1996): 418–37.

Rittner-Heir, Robbin M. "One Student One Computer." *School Planning and Management* 39, no. 5 (May 2000): 10.

Salpeter, Judy. "Industry Snapshot. Where Are We Headed?" *Technology and Learning* 17, no. 6 (March 1997): 21–30.

Schlenker, Richard M., and Sara J. Yoshida. "Integrating Computers into Elementary School Science Using Toothpicks to Generate Data." *Science Activities* 27, no. 4 (Winter 1990): 13.

Solomon, G. "Writing with Computers." *Electronic Learning*, November/December 1985, pp. 39–43.

Stone, M. David. "One Computer, Many Users." *PC Magazine* 19, no. 2 (January 18, 2000): 135.

Tan, Soo Boo. "Making One-Computer Teaching Fun!" *Learning and Leading with Technology* 25, no. 5 (February 1998): 6–10.

Vockell, Edward, and Robert M. Deusen. *The Computer and Higher-Order Thinking Skills.* Watsonville, Calif.: Mitchell Publishing, 1989.

Wilson, Timothy L.Y., and Kathy Fite. "Integrating the Language Arts Curriculum with Computer Applications in Mathematics." *Reading Improvement* 34, no. 2 (Summer 1997): 66–70.

CHAPTER 12

Computers in Special Education

Integrating the Computer into the Special Education Classroom

Did you know that by using technology with students with disabilities, you can help them realize their potential? Did you know that by using the computer you can help these students achieve equal access to a general education? This chapter will provide answers to how the teacher can help students accomplish these educational goals. You will see examples of hardware devices that will make it easier for students with special needs to function successfully in regular classroom settings. The devices covered range from the discovery switch to the touch screen panel. You will also see some ways in which the classroom teacher can use computer software to help students with disabilities learn. For example, you will examine programs that read to students with low vision and programs that coach students who struggle with the writing process due to language delay. Furthermore, the chapter will give examples of lesson plans that can be used in a variety of situations. You will become familiar with Internet sites containing a rich assortment of content. The sites contain lesson plans, resources, activities, information on professional organizations, and legal issues. There is even an American Sign Language Online animated tutorial, as well as information about general disabilities, physical and health disorders, and learning disabilities.

Objectives

Upon completing this chapter, you will be able to:
1. Describe some special education hardware devices and explain how each works;
2. Discuss some of the software that is available for special education;
3. Discuss some of the important laws passed for special education;
4. Understand some of the problems and issues involved in special education;
5. Utilize special education activities for classroom integration; and
6. Explore some excellent Internet sites on special education that range from lesson plans to organizations.

The Computer and the Special Education Student

The computer has become a natural tool to help the special education student have access to a general education curriculum. The computer can help the student by acting as a tutor. The student may be able to more easily express his or her ideas to the outside world. Using the computer, the student with special needs is often motivated to spend more time working on an instructional assignment and doing well in school. The computer is very patient and private, so the student is not embarrassed to try or to fail. Students with disabilities like to control the rate at which they learn as opposed to having no control over their learning environment. They often receive recognition from the outside world when they achieve something on the computer. Furthermore, the computer increases students' chances of expressing themselves musically or in words. Some students with disabilities can shine when using a computer because they received instruction on computers when they were young. They can model skills for typical students, which is a self-esteem booster.

The computer can speak for those who cannot speak and generate text for those who cannot move their arms. It can help those with low vision by magnifying text. It can read to the blind and help them more easily communicate. The hearing impaired can easily communicate using e-mail and can participate in chat rooms.

For the student with disabilities to get the full benefits of this technology, certain modification may be needed for the hardware or software. After all, more than 50 million Americans have some type of disability, necessitating adaptation of hardware or software for them to use computer technology (Kamp, 1999). **Adaptive** or **assistive technology** devices are defined as "any item, piece of equipment, or product system, whether acquired commercially or off the shelf, modified or customized, that increases, maintains, or improves functional capabilities of individuals with disabilities" (The Technology-Related Assistance for Individuals with Disabilities Act). For a list of adaptive or assistive technologies, see the University of Toronto's Adaptive Technology Resource Centre (ATRC) at http://www.utoronto.ca/atrc/reference/tech/techgloss.html.

The distinction between assistive or adaptive technologies and conventional technologies is blurring as more products are being designed universally for a greater number of individuals. A touch screen can be used as an alternative to the mouse for people with disabilities as well as for those without disabilities. For example, a touch screen can be used in information booths at airports, for voting machines, and in amusement parks. Eventually voice recognition may become the most common form of input for everyone and the keyboard may disappear (Alliance for Technology Access, 2000; Bryant, Bryant, and Raskind, 1998). What follows are ways that hardware can be modified to help the student with special needs.

Hardware

You can rearrange the computer setup, redesigning hardware or designing special software, for students with special needs. The physical layout of the equipment can be changed to make it easy to use. There can be flexibility for monitors and keyboards. The keyboard, monitor, and work material can be repositioned for easier access for a disabled person. Using a power strip, the equipment can be turned on with a single key as opposed to three or four keys.

The keyboard can be redesigned to meet the user's needs. There are many possibilities such as (1) an alternative keyboard with greater space between the keys, (2) a simplified arrangement, (3) a keyboard with larger keys, (4) a left and right keyboard, or (5) an on-screen keyboard. The repeat key disabled would help students with less fine muscle control. The student would get one keystroke per character no matter how long the key is held down. For a user with difficulty pressing two keys simultaneously, the keyboard can be designed so that it has **sticky keys**—that is, certain keys that lock in place—allowing the student with a disability to press a combination keystrokes without pressing keys simultaneously.

If modifying the keyboard doesn't work for the student, **keyboard emulators** could be used. An emulator presents a choice to the student in the form of a whole sentence, phrase, or character; the student then makes a selection in one movement. Sometimes the student moves a mouse pointer by moving his or her hand. If a mouse is too difficult to use, a joystick can be used to control speed and direction. Emulators can be used to generate a sequence of keystrokes that can be recalled as sentences or words.

Many students who have disabilities cannot use a traditional input device such as a standard mouse, trackball, or keyboard. For these students, the computer industry has developed alternative devices such as a foot-controlled mouse, touch screens, onscreen keyboards, alternative keyboards, switches, touch tablets, voice-controlled devices, and word prediction software systems. What follows is a small sample of the many products that are available.

Touch-Free Switch

The **touch-free switch** is an input device that lets students trigger a mouse click without applying any pressure. Edmark's Touch-Free Switch is used in conjunction with a digital video camera and special software that lets the physically challenged student interact with the camera. The digital camera recognizes almost any movement as a mouse click. It is placed on a monitor to see a head movement, on a student desk to recognize a hand movement, or on the floor to see a toe movement.

Discover Switch

The **discover switch** is a talking computer switch for the classroom that attaches to the keyboard. With this switch, the computer user does everything that a standard keyboard and mouse can do. The discover switch shows a keyboard on the computer screen that provides choices for writing, using the mouse, or clicking the graphics in multimedia programs such as *Dr. Seuss* (The Learning Company). The choices are highlighted automatically, and students then press a switch to make their choice (Fig. 12.1). In addition, the discover switch has an on-screen keyboard that can speak words, phrases, and even sentences, which offers nonspeaking students a way to communicate.

FIGURE 12.1
Discover Switch
© Don Johnston Incorporated.
Used with permission.

IntelliKey

IntelliKey (IntelliTools) is for people with a wide range of disabilities who require a keyboard (Fig. 12.2) with a changing face. It can be used for Macintoshes or PC-compatibles. Each standard overlay has a bar code that IntelliKey recognizes. Students who use switches can choose from two built-in programmable switch jacks.

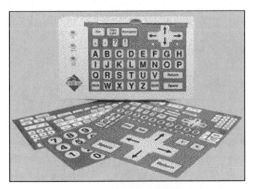

FIGURE 12.2
IntelliKey
From IntelliTools, Inc.
IntelliTools.

Also available are talking keyboards for the classroom, like Discover:Board. The student presses Discover:Board keys for sounds and speech while doing work. Using this keyboard, the student can receive speech feedback with programs such as *AppleWorks, Co:Writer,* or *Kid Pix* as well as with the Internet and online services. It can be used with pictures, text, or just letters.

Touch Screen

The **touch screen** (Fig. 12.3) is a pointing device on which users place their fingers to enter data or make selections. You may have seen the touch screens used in airports, supermarkets, and museums. There are two types of touch screens: those designed with a pressure-sensitive panel mounted in front of the screen such as Edmark's Touch Window and those that require the use of

FIGURE 12.3
*Touch Screen
Panel*
Used by permission of Art
Today.com, Inc.

special, touch-sensitive monitors such as the IBM Info Window System. The software program for the touch screen displays different options on the screen in a graphic button format. For example, in a multiple-choice exam, the student would touch the answer button on the screen, and the screen would change in response to this action.

The touch screen offers a real advantage to disabled students because it is a fast and natural way to enter data, to make selections, and to issue commands. Despite these wonderful benefits, a touch screen is not useful for inputting large amounts of data or for pointing to a single character. Moreover, it is fatiguing to use for a long period of time, and the screen quickly gets finger-marked. Lessons created on one variety of touch screen may not work on another because of software incompatibility. However, touch screen technology is still evolving, and the touch screen currently plays a key role in the educational use of the computer.

Scanner

Wizcom's **Quicktionary Reading Pen** (Fig. 12.4) scans printed words, displays them in large characters, pronounces them aloud, splits words into syl-

FIGURE 12.4
Quicktionary Reading Pen
Reprinted by permission of Wizcom Technologies.

lables, spells them, and defines them when you touch a button. The built-in loudspeaker and earphone jack enable external and private listening. The pen is a perfect device for individuals with dyslexia, a disability where a reader processes words in a reverse order, since phoneme recognition is accomplished without any trouble. In addition, the student who is learning English as a second language finds this educational tool very helpful.

Students with Disabilities

All students display some differences in terms of physical characteristics: some are tall, others short; some are thin, others heavy; some wear glasses, others do not. Students also differ in learning ability. Some students differ from the average either below or above to such an extent that specialized education or an adapted program is necessary to meet their needs. Therefore, the term **exceptional children** refers to students who have physical disabilities or sensory impairment, students who have behavior and/or learning problems, or students who are gifted or have special talents (Heward, 2000). There are many ways that the computer can help students with low vision, blindness, hearing and speech impairment, learning disabilities, and health problems.

Low-Vision and Blind Students

Monitors and Printers

For the impaired-vision student, a standard monitor can display large type and the student can then read three large lines at a time. In addition, there are large monitors which display much larger than normal type. The enlargement program makes the letters appear bigger on the screen and easier to read. If the person is sensitive to light, there is software that reverses the print color. Instead of black on white, it makes the monitor display white on black, which is easier for the visually impaired student to read. Usually a standard keyboard works, but in this case it may be better to have large keytop labels for the students to see. Standard printers can print out any size print so that a person who has impaired vision can see it. A computer allows a blind individual to write and edit papers without the help of a sighted person. Optical character recognition software can convert printed documents into electronic format. The electronic document then can be read using a speech synthesizer.

Speech Synthesis

The **speech synthesizer** is a computer chip that generates sound. This chip gives the computer the ability to search for words and their pronunciations in a database. The computer takes this data, converts it into codes, and delivers it audibly in a voice with a slight accent. The sound is clear enough for most people to understand. The speech quality is better if the computer has to speak only stock phrases rather than read items experimentally. Speech synthesis is very helpful for visually impaired computer users, because they can have the computer read a textbook or encyclopedia or a typed paper. Many products today use computer-generated speech. For example, automobile computers audibly remind drivers to shut the door or fill the tank.

In addition to speech synthesizers, screen reader software or **voice recognition software** is important for students with disabilities.

Voice recognition software lets users communicate with the computer through a microphone. The computer then follows their instructions by pulling down a menu or typing text.

Voice Recognition

Everyone's computer fantasy is to be able to dictate a command to the computer through a microphone and have the computer execute the command on the screen. We have watched starship captains talking to their computers for years. Still in its infancy stage—but evolving rapidly—the voice recognition system shows the most potential for growth in the computer industry. This system converts the spoken word into binary patterns that are computer-recognizable; essentially, it understands human speech. You can enter data or issue simple commands through the system simply by speaking. The speech recognition systems require you to train the system to recognize your pronunciation of words by saying each of the words that will be used. The system develops a pattern for these words and then stores them. After training, the voice recognition system recognizes what you are saying and performs your commands. Some voice recognition systems let you enter and store unlimited words. With this type of system, you can communicate with the computer without using a keyboard or any other input device. In the past, the prevailing type of computer speech recognition was *discrete speech recognition:* The user spoke each word separately and clearly, pausing in between so the system could transcribe the spoken language. This type of recognition was very cumbersome, and there was a need for programs that recognized normal speech.

Continuous speech recognition programs that transcribed normal speech have always been available for highly specialized applications in medicine and other fields, but only recently have products appeared that make this system available to the ordinary person. Dragon Systems' *NaturallySpeaking* and IBM's *VoiceType* are continuous speech recognition products offered at a reasonable price. You no longer have to pause between words; you can dictate directly to your computer as if it were your own personal secretary. You can talk at a natural pace and your words appear on the screen spelled correctly. Individuals who cannot type and disabled persons who cannot use handheld devices are able to easily operate such systems. Screen reader software, like *outSPOKEN* (Berkeley Systems), can describe menus and screen windows. IBM has developed a product that lets the blind student read material that is on the monitor. The student scans the screen using a special computer mouse which emits vibrations that the person can understand. Eventually, voice recognition could relegate the mouse and keyboard to the storage bin. As voice recognition systems improve, the blind will attain complete accuracy when they dictate to their computer.

Adaptive Devices for the Blind

Blind students can use Braille printers, a standard keyboard with Braille key labels, or a **refreshable Braille display.** A refreshable Braille display can be added to a computer system to translate text on the screen into Braille. The display is flat and is designed to be placed underneath the keyboard. There are mechanical pins that raise and lower for each eight-dot Braille cell. The text that is typed is on a single-line display, which follows the movements of the cursor (Fig. 12.5).

FIGURE 12.5
Refreshable
Braille Display:
PowerBraille 40 Cell
Display with
TouchSensor Option
Courtesy of Freedom
Scientific.

The Internet is more accessible to blind students because of the special software that is available. For example, IBM has a *Home Page Reader* (HPR) for computer users who are blind or have low vision. The HPR lets the student access the Web quickly and easily by speaking Web page information. Using this simple interface, the student has no trouble navigating and manipulating Web page elements. The program utilizes IBM *ViaVoice Outloud* text-to-speech synthesizer for speaking. Also, blind students can find talking books and Braille services online.

Hearing and Speech Impairment

For the student who is deaf or hard of hearing, visual output on the screen replaces sound. For example, instead of emitting audible beeps, the monitor blinks. Software programs for the hard of hearing should have captions for spoken elements of the program. Hearing-impaired people can learn to speak by matching words displayed on a screen with the sound waves for each word. As the Internet has grown, more hearing-impaired individuals use online mail programs instead of specially designed telephones for the deaf (TTY). Currently, Web caption editors, like *MAGpie* (National Center for Accessible Media [NCAM]), are being developed. This editor can write video captions in different formats.

Learning Disabilities

More than half of the students who receive special education services have learning disabilities (Fuchs and Fuchs, 1998). As defined by the U.S. Department of Education, a learning disability is "a disorder in one or more of the basic psychological processes involved in understanding or using spoken or written language, which may appear as an impaired ability to listen, think, speak, read, write, spell, or do mathematical calculations." For the student with learning disabilities, the computer can read on-screen print. (Of course, not all students with learning disabilities need this help.) Using a word processing program, these students can easily create several drafts of the same work and spell-check it. Furthermore, the computer can help them read by having large print, graphics, and speech output.

Health Problems

Students who are hospitalized have easy access to their teachers through the Internet. They can communicate in many ways that range from a videocamera to e-mail. They do not have to leave the house or hospital to have access to the huge unlimited library that is online. These are but a few of the ways that the computer can help the student with disabilities communicate.

Software for the Special Education Classroom

Today, many software programs help students with disabilities learn in the classroom. The software ranges from tutorials to drill and practice. In recent years, there has been an emphasis on software that aids students who are diagnosed with reading problems to improve their proficiency. Because of this emphasis, many software programs build vocabulary and help with phonetics skills and decoding. Let us now look at a selection of programs that are especially useful to the special education teacher.

Reading

Don Johnston offered a series of Start-to-Finish books that motivate students who are struggling with reading. They are high-interest, low-vocabulary books that include classic literature, sports biographies, history biographies, original mysteries, and retellings of Sherlock Holmes mysteries. These books range from *The Red Badge of Courage* to *Romeo and Juliet.* Start-to-Finish books help students who are two or more grades behind in reading or unsuccessful readers. They aid students with language disorders, dyslexia, students learning English as a second language, and those with spelling and writing difficulties. The program comes with a computer book, audiocassette, and a paperback book. In Figure 12.6 a page from *Romeo and Juliet* is shown, and the student has the option of listening to the book or reading silently.

FIGURE 12.6
Start-to-Finish Books

© Copyright Don Johnston, Incorporated. Used with permission.

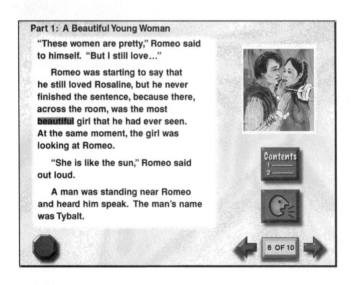

Part 1: A Beautiful Young Woman

"These women are pretty," Romeo said to himself. "But I still love..."

Romeo was starting to say that he still loved Rosaline, but he never finished the sentence, because there, across the room, was the most beautiful girl that he had ever seen. At the same moment, the girl was looking at Romeo.

"She is like the sun," Romeo said out loud.

A man was standing near Romeo and heard him speak. The man's name was Tybalt.

Contents
1 _____
2 _____

6 OF 10

My Reading Coach (Mindplay), for grade 1 to adult, is a reading tutor for students who want instruction in reading proficiency. This program assesses the students' needs, fills in specific learning gaps, and makes sure that each lesson is learned. The program begins with an assessment of the student's encoding and decoding skills, followed by lessons based on the program's evaluation. Each lesson has a video introduction taught by Jim Larrabee, a reading pathologist.

The classic *Living Books* series (Brøderbund/The Learning Company) is perfect for the younger student with disabilities (grades K–4). These storybooks are loaded with "hotspots," where the student clicks on an object to learn about it. The series offers such titles as *Arthur's Birthday Deluxe,* a story about Arthur's big birthday party; *New Kid on the Block,* a humorous introduction to poetry; *Arthur's Camping Adventure,* a tale about a class camping trip and the emergency situation that evolves; and *Green Eggs & Ham,* which presents the classic Dr. Seuss story with word and letter games.

Blue's ABC Time Activities (Humongous Entertainment) for grades preschool–6, grades 7–9, and grades 10–12 lets students explore the world of letters, sounds, and words with the help of a dog named Blue and her pals. This software presents games and leads students through a range of activities such as identifying of letters, vocabulary building, practicing phonics, and creating rhymes. The students collect words and put together their own funny stories. This software is designed for many age levels and it automatically adjusts to the student's reading level.

Simon Sounds It Out (Don Johnston), for pre-K to grade 2, is an interactive phonics tool designed for students to practice letter sounds. This program has a helpful on-screen tutor, which is available for 31 levels of sounds and words. There are colorful graphics, digitized sound, and animation to motivate and entertain the students during the learning process. *Simon Sounds It Out* has a management component that lets the teacher track the progress of multiple students and customize sound and word lessons. This product can be used with ESL students. Furthermore, Don Johnston produces *Simon Spells,* which guides students through individualized spelling instruction at their own pace.

Tiger's Tale (Laureate Learning Systems), for pre-K to grade 2, is software for students with fluency, articulation, and/or language disorders. This program lets students go on adventures with an animated tiger who has lost his voice. Using a microphone, the students talk for the tiger with the help of various animated characters who ask questions to get suggestions. At the end, children can play back the movie they've created, hearing their own voice accompanying the animated tale.

Words Around Me (Edmark), for pre-K to grade 12, can be used for ESL and students with disabilities in the early grades. The program helps students learn over 275 common vocabulary words and 186 important plurals. This program teaches vocabulary words in English or Spanish. The step-by-step design lets users engage in five activities that range from practice in word identification to hide and seek.

Word Processing Applications

Word processing is one of the most commonly used applications for learning-disabled students (Holzberg, 1994). These programs have helped students with a variety of problems, such as improving writing skills: Students who in the past did not write very much become motivated to write. Talking word processors such as *Write:OutLoud 3.0* (Fig. 12.7) can prove very beneficial for the student with learning disabilities. *Write:OutLoud* speaks letters, words,

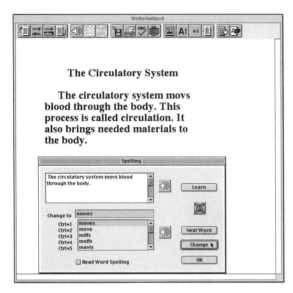

and sentences as they are typed. Students can then self-correct their writing. The word processor highlights as it reads and lets the student include graphics or import graphics from other sources. There are on-screen tools with speech that let students work without menus. The word processor also has large font sizes to make the letters easier to read along with a talking spell checker.

Another program that is helpful for writing is *Co:Writer 4000*, a writing assistant with word prediction capabilities that will work with any word processor. A student just types in a letter and *Co:Writer* suggests word choices that fit the sentences (Fig. 12.8). Using this program, students learn to make word choices. *Co:Writer* reads the words to help them make a choice. In addition, *Co:Writer* has built-in grammar prediction, which helps with such items as capitalization, spelling, and verb tense.

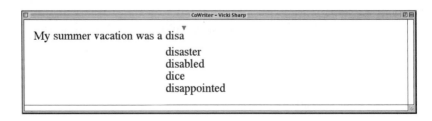

Finally, the Rolls-Royce of the writing assistant programs is *Aurora 3.0* (Aurora Systems, Inc.), located at http://www.djtech.com/Aurora/.

This expensive program (around $495) has everything from word prediction to a talking spell checker.

Math

There are programs that use arcade game formats to aid students in math skills like adding and subtracting. These drill and practice programs are great ways of providing practice for learning-disabled students. There are math tutorials that give visual feedback for the student, as well as simulation programs that let students solve problems without personal risk. Some very fine programs are *Access to Math* (Don Johnston) and *Number Concepts 1 With Oshi the Otter* (IntelliTools, Inc.).

Access to Math is a talking math worksheet that aids students in learning addition and subtraction and multiplication and division. This program gives students feedback on which problems are answered correctly, which need more work, and what part of the work is incorrect.

Number Concepts 1 With Oshi the Otter is a basic addition and subtraction program for very young students or those with disabilities, grades K–2. This program tutors the student on basic addition and subtraction. Oshi the Otter serves as a guide for students doing beginning addition and subtraction problems at the tide pool, practicing counting with sea creatures, and helping an eel decide which school of fish is greater in number.

Drill and practice programs such as *Quarter Mile* (Barnum Software), and the *Math Blaster* series (Knowledge Adventure) are very useful for students with disabilities. These programs let the students work at their own pace and receive immediate feedback on math skills.

Science, Social Studies, and Miscellaneous Programs

There are many interesting programs in social studies and science. *Talking Walls* (Edmark), which was discussed in Chapter 11, helps students discover the stories behind some of the world's most interesting walls. Edmark's *Travel the World with Timmy! Deluxe* lets students learn about people, places, and cultures. They visit five different countries, Argentina, France, Japan (Fig. 12.9), Kenya, and Russia. They learn stories, songs, crafts, and games and practice foreign

**FIGURE 12.9
Travel the World
with Timmy!
Deluxe**
© Riverdeep Interactive
Learning Limited.

language skills. Edmark's *Travel the World with Timmy! Deluxe* has a special talking picture dictionary, and the program has single-switch compatibility. When the program's scanning is turned on, a highlight goes from choice to choice, letting the student use a single-switch device to make a choice. Also, Edmark's *Virtual Lab Series* helps students build practical knowledge about light and electricity. These programs have a built-in tutor and single-switch technology.

DK Interactive's series of social studies and science programs, such as *Earth Quest, Nature 2.0, Human Body, My First Amazing History Explorer, Amazing Animals,* and *My First Amazing World Explorer 2.0,* provide support to the special-needs classroom. In its teacher guides, the publisher shows how this multimedia software can be used in the special education environment.

In addition, *Inspiration* (Inspiration), *Blocks in Motion* (Don Johnston), and *Visual Voice Tools* (Edmark) are three special programs that can help students in visual learning, problem solving, manual dexterity, and voice control.

Inspiration is a powerful visual learning tool that helps students organize their thoughts. (See Chapter 14, "Multimedia for the Classroom"). The students can visually map a story such as *Are You My Mother?* (Fig. 12.10), and in doing so they gain a greater understanding of the story's contents.

FIGURE 12.10
Inspiration
Used by permission of
Inspiration Software, Inc.

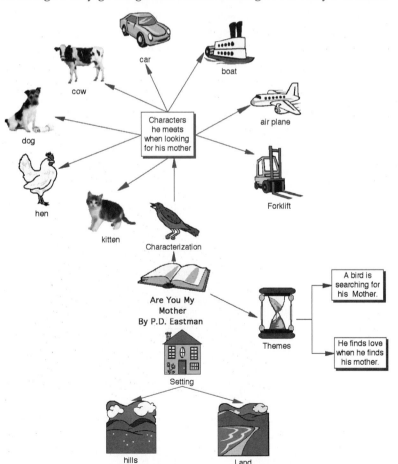

Blocks in Motion (Don Johnston) gives students a sense of confidence (Fig. 12.11) and helps them handle problem-solving tasks and practice their manual

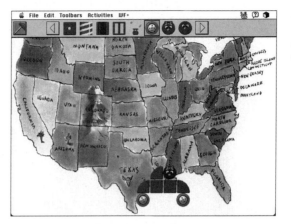

FIGURE 12.11
Blocks in Motion
Screen shot courtesy of Don Johnston, Incorporated.

dexterity. Users create, manipulate, and animate their blocks. This paint and motion program has multiple tools, sound effects, and many programmable options to bring forth the student's creativity. Students can create or import backgrounds, paint pictures, and create scenes with different types of blocks. Motion controllers can assign movement and animation to the created object so the user can explore concepts such as gravity, cause and effect, and much more.

Finally, *Visual Voice Tools* is an assortment of tools that help students develop fine control over their voices. The program begins with simple sound awareness and progresses through multiple aspects of voice. The suggested users are students with a variety of speech disorders, hearing disorders, and physical problems that limit voice output.

New Technologies

The future promises technological breakthroughs to help the student with disabilities function better in the classroom. **Virtual reality (VR)** and **robotics** will play a more prominent role in this future. Virtual reality is "an artificial reality that projects the user into a 3-D space generated by the computer" (Freedman, 2001). VR technology lets the physically disabled student interact with information being presented in all subject areas. The student can immerse himself physically in different environments and experience life on a different intellectual plane. Robotics is "the art and science of the creation and use of robots" (Freedman, 2001). These emerging technologies will be more closely examined in Chapters 16 and 17. Many laws have been passed to try to ensure that students with disabilities receive appropriate educational opportunities.

Laws Affecting Special Education

A little background might help explain why special education laws were necessary. In 1949, no laws existed requiring a school district to educate a student with special needs. If a student was diagnosed as having mental retardation, he or she usually was placed in a separate school or institution for children with disabilities. If there was no school or institution that could accommodate this student, the school district was not required by law to provide an education and it was up to the parent or guardian to find a solution to the problem. The student with disabilities was separated from the rest of the population and discriminated against. Parent groups organized because their children were not being allowed access to a general education, and a movement evolved to educate the student with disabilities. At the same time, other factors contributed to the rise in the need for special education; these included changes in economics, demographic shifts, discrimination, changes in the family structure, substance abuse, and child abuse. As a result of this situation, laws were enacted to make sure that all students received optimal educational opportunities regardless of their disabilities.

Table 12.1 highlights a number of key pieces of legislation that were important in ensuring that all students receive the same educational opportunities

TABLE 12.1

Equal Educational Opportunity Laws

Law	Accomplished
Section 504 of the Rehabilitation Act of 1973 (PL 93-112)	This was the first piece of federal legislation addressing the civil rights of people with disabilities. This act ensures that individuals with disabilities have equal opportunities in programs that receive federal funds.
Education for All Handicapped Children Act (PL 94-142) (1975)	Signed by President Gerald Ford, this key piece of legislation mandated that there be appropriate and free education for students with disabilities.
The Education for All Handicapped Children Act Amendments of 1986 (PL 99-457)	This amendment expanded services for infants and young children who have disabilities or are at risk, and for their families.
The Individuals with Disabilities Education Act (IDEA) (PL 101-476) (1990)	Known as the "Person First" law, this act changed the title of the special education law to Individuals with Disabilities Education Act so that people would recognize the child first and then the disability.
The Americans with Disabilities Act (ADA) (PL 101-336)(1990)	Signed by President George H. W. Bush, this law provided major civil rights protection for people with disabilities by breaking down the barriers in areas of transportation, telecommunication, employment, and public accommodation.
Individuals with Disabilities Education Act Amendments of 1997 (PL 105-17)	President Clinton signed this into law on June 4, 1997. These amendments placed more emphasis on family and parents, general education personnel, and students in the individualized education program (IEP). Another focal point is to ensure access to general education curriculum for students with disabilities.

regardless of their disabilities. Because of the enactment of these laws students with disabilities could no longer be separated from other students and treated unequally. The legislation made schools provide equal access to activities and resources for the disabled students. The federal law requires that students with disabilities be placed in the regular classroom whenever viable. The schools have tried to provide equal access by collaboration, mainstreaming, and inclusion.

Collaboration

Collaboration is a group endeavor that involves students, families, educators, and community agencies. The people work together sharing resources, decisions, and skills for the student's good. The school district provides the resources and support so that these agencies can work cooperatively and focus on the student's needs. In some instances, the special education teacher collaborates with the regular classroom teacher. Their job is to help students with disabilities adjust to the regular classroom. In this case, the special education teacher would team-teach with the classroom teacher and modify the core curriculum to make it accessible to children with needs.

Mainstreaming

After the passage of the 1975 Education for All Handicapped Children Act (PL 94-142), the term **mainstreaming** was adopted to refer to partial and full-time programs that educated students with disabilities with their nondisabled peers. Mainstreaming meant placing students who are diagnosed with disabilities in regular classrooms all or part of the day. A mainstreamed student could attend separate classes within the regular school or could participate in the regular art program only. Students in mainstreaming programs might leave the general-education classroom for the resource room or speech and language services. Special education was in charge of these students and the responsibility for their progress rested with them. Special education services may not be provided in the regular classroom. Often the decision to place a student in a mainstreamed class was based on the educator's assessment of the student's readiness. This implied that the students had to earn the right to be educated in a full-time general-education classroom. Mainstreaming was broadly interpreted, which led to many different implementations. In mainstreamed programs, students are often expected to fit in the regular class where they want to participate, whereas in an inclusive program the classes are designed to fit all students.

Inclusion

Inclusion grew out of mainstreaming and shares many of its goals. Inclusion is based on the concept of least-restrictive environment (LRE). LRE requires that schools make every reasonable attempt to educate students with disabilities with their peers who do not have disabilities. *Inclusion* has all students attending regular classes unless the school can show a reason why this is not feasible. *Full inclusion* requires that all students be educated in a regular classroom regardless of the severity of a disability. A successful inclusion program has a planned system of training and supports. Such a program usually includes the collaboration of a multidisciplinary team comprised of peers, classroom teachers, special educators, and family members. For inclusion, a student is a full member of the classroom and has special education provided in this regular classroom. To have effective inclusion, teachers must be flexible and responsive to the students' needs. Educators should individualize education for all students using assessment techniques. The advocates of inclusion do not want to segregate the students in a separate school or institution.

Reasons for Inclusive Education

Many educational experts feel that **inclusive education**—regular classroom attendance regardless of disabilities—is very important to the well-being of the student with disabilities. They point to the research that seems to support the effectiveness of including these students in regular classroom situations. The students in an inclusive classroom make academic progress comparable to and sometimes better than students who are segregated (Ryndak, Downing, Morrison, and Williams, 1996; Waldron and McLeskey, 1998). They learn from watching the other students in the regular classroom, whereas in a special education classroom, they only have other students with disabilities to observe and copy. In an inclusive classroom students who do not have disabilities learn how to be more sensitive to disabled students and aware of their needs. All students work cooperatively with each other. The students with disabilities become better acquainted with people in the community, thus enabling these students to handle themselves better in the real world.

Problems and Issues

Schools have often disagreed with parents on the interpretation of laws affecting special education, which has led to much controversy. In many instances, when the students with special needs are placed in the classrooms, the regular teacher is overwhelmed and feels he or she cannot meet the needs of the students. The parents of the other students object, because they feel that the special-needs students require too much attention. Also, attendance in a regular classroom does not guarantee that the student with disabilities will acquire the skills she or he needs to function in society. In addition, these laws put extra financial demands on school systems to ensure that all technologies are available to all students in the classroom. For instance, when a school makes purchases of software or hardware, according to law, it must purchase adaptive equipment, such as discovery switches and voice recognition software, to make sure that the special education student can use the equipment. This equipment is far more costly than other technology resources. Schools with budget problems have difficulty deciding to purchase equipment that would benefit only a small population of students. The speed with which technology changes hampers a school district trying to keep abreast of the latest developments. There are software and hardware compatibility issues and huge memory requirements, which are even greater for special needs.

There is also disagreement on how gifted students should be taught. Some programs in the high school are designed for high-achieving students and want to accelerate the curriculum for all students. Some educators believe in a different approach, designed to accommodate the needs of all gifted students. Recently, there has been a trend to eliminate separate programs for the gifted student in favor of setting higher academic standards for all students. However, in 1998, a new legislative initiative called "The Gifted and Talented Students Education Act" provided grants to states to strengthen services for the gifted student (National Association for Gifted Children communiqué, 1998; http://www.nagc.org).

In addition to these school issues, there could be parental problems. Parents may have unrealistic expectations for their children. Assistive technology is terrific and has helped many students, but it cannot suddenly "cure" students with severe physical and mental abilities; it can only help them overcome and succeed in spite of their disability. Software or hardware that requires extensive training is very aggravating for the student with disabilities. Assisted technology should be easy to set up and use so that students can concentrate on learning. Technology does help, but it is not a panacea for all situations. As technology advances, there is hope that this situation will change and frustrations will be eliminated.

Adapting Classroom Lesson Plans for Students with Disabilities

By adapting classroom lessons, the teacher can meet the needs of the student with disabilities. The teacher should divide the class into small groups so that the students can help each other. They then can work in pairs where each complements the other's strengths. Teachers can use a buddy system where a student mentors another student. If appropriate, the teachers can use peer tutoring or cross-age tutoring. For any lesson, they can choose software that is auditory to help the students who have trouble reading. The teacher can have someone read a written script to help with directions. If a student needs auditory feedback, an appropriate software program provides it. Before writing a book report or composition, students could use a graphic organizer like *Inspiration*, which visually represents the material and breaks it down into small steps. If the students need writing help, they can use a talking word processor or word prediction program to aid in the writing process. What follows are six ready-to-use lesson plans that can readily be adapted for the student with disabilities.

▼   I. English   ▼

Objective

Students will read a book and retell the story by creating masks.

Procedure

1. The teacher divides the students into groups of two.
2. She then assigns a short story for each pair to read and discuss with each other.
3. Using a mask-making program like *MaskWorld* (Visions Technology in Education), students print out a mask to help illustrate their story.
4. Next, have the students attach the faces to paper plates, sticks (Fig. 12.12), or paper bags.

FIGURE 12.12 MaskWorld

Used by permission of Visions Technology in Education™.

5. The students then share their story with the class by retelling it.

▼   II. History   ▼

Objective

Using Internet sites such as *The American Civil War Homepage* (http://sunsite.utk.edu/civil-war/), students will learn about the Civil War.

Procedure

1. Divide the students into small groups and have each group research some aspect of the Civil War. For example, the students could find out the causes of the Civil War or contrast and compare the North and South.
2. During this time frame, the students search the Internet looking for information. They have to carefully document the authenticity of their particular sites.
3. Using a word processor, students create a paper explaining their findings.
4. Have the students discuss their papers in class.
5. Continue this project by having the students create a home page on the Civil War.

▼   III. Math   ▼

Objective

Using an art program such as *Kid Pix Deluxe,* the students learn about the different shapes.

Procedure

1. Divide the students into groups of two.
2. Have the students draw a picture using as many shapes as they can.
3. Have the students show their pictures and point out their shapes to the class.

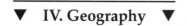

▼   IV. Geography   ▼

Objective

Using the Internet, students will learn about a city, state, or region, and from this information create travel brochures.

Procedure

1. Divide the class into small groups.
2. Have the students choose a city, state, or region.
3. Have the students pretend they are in charge of a tourist bureau for this area.
4. Students will research the region's geographic features, economy, restaurants, state capital, major attractions, hotel accommodations, camping facilities, and any other pertinent information.
5. The students can use the following Internet sites:
   a. State Report Information from Multnomah County Library in Portland, Oregon

   http://www.multnomah.lib.or.us/lib/homework/statesch.html

b. Sites with State Facts Information

http://www.multnomah.lib.or.us/lib/homework/state2hc.html#general

c. Yahoo! Get Local

http://local.yahoo.com/

d. Hometown USA

http://www.hometownusa.com

e. Uscity.net

http://www.uscity.net/

f. 411 Cities

http://www.411-cities.com/

g. About.com's Cities/Towns

http://home.about.com/citiestowns/

h. 2AccessAmerica.com

http://www.accessamer.com/

i. Travel.excite.com

http://travel.excite.com/

j. Travelfacts.com

http://www.travelfacts.com/

6. Students will create a tourist brochure that is not longer than four pages.
7. If the students do not want to limit themselves to these sites, they can use search engines to find other sites.

▼ V. English ▼

Objective

Students will develop their language skills by creating a book that contains the alphabet.

Procedure

1. The teacher divides the students into groups of two.
2. Using a talking word processor program like *Write:OutLoud 3.0,* have each group type the letter A in a large font size. This word processor will speak the letter as it is typed.
3. Tell each group to find a word to illustrate this letter. They can look in the books that are around the room.
4. Using the word processing program, have the students type the word in the book.
5. When the students finish their alphabet books, they can hole punch them and yarn bind them.
6. The students should share their books with the class.

▼   VI. Math—Comparison Shopping   ▼

Objective

Students will learn how to shop by using a program such as *Ice Cream Truck* or *Hot Dog Stand* (Sunburst).

Procedure

1. Divide the class into small groups.
2. Using *Ice Cream Truck,* each group assumes the role of the owner and driver of an ice cream truck. They begin with $500 (Fig. 12.13) and try to make as much money as possible.

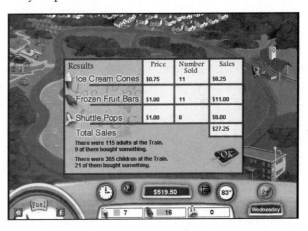

**FIGURE 12.13
Ice Cream Truck**
Reprinted by permission of
Sunburst Technology.

3. As a small group, they have to decide where they want to sell the ice cream, and how much they want to charge. These decisions are based on such factors as day of the week and temperature.
4. The class discusses strategies.

5. The students work on the project during the week.
6. At the end of the week, they discuss results.

Variation

Students conduct experiments to determine what types of ice cream adults and children prefer.

Summary

The computer has been invaluable in helping individuals in special education to realize their potential. In this chapter, you were exposed to some of the key legislation affecting special education. You were also shown different ways of integrating technology into the classroom. In addition, you were given six ready-to-use lesson plans for students with disabilities. After reading the chapter, you should understand some of the software and hardware that is available for these "exceptional" students. Terms such as mainstreaming, inclusion, and collaboration were briefly explained along with the problems and issues facing special education teachers, parents, and students. **Be sure to review the annotated list of award-winning special education programs in Appendix A.**

🖉 SPECIAL EDUCATION SITES

What follows is an annotated list of Internet sites for special education. These sites include information about hardware, tutorials, software, lesson plans, activities, and tips.

The National Information Center for Children and Youth with Disabilities
http://www.nichcy.org

Developed by the National Information and Referral Center, this site provides information on issues and concerns related to disabilities for families and professionals. The focus of the information is on children and young adults.

Teaching Ideas for Early Childhood Special Educators
http://www.mcps.k12.md.us/curriculum/pep/teach.htm

"Linda's teaching ideas" is a collection of teaching ideas for early childhood special education which range from making butter to a great recipe for play dough. There are numerous creative and fun ideas as well as a collection of worthwhile links.

Special Needs Education Network (SNE)
http://www.schoolnet.ca/sne/

This site offers projects to aid parents and teachers of children with special needs as disparate as attention deficit disorder (ADD), autism, blindness, deafness, fetal alcohol syndrome, and many others. It is an invaluable "List of Lists" for links to services to aid these children, and it includes an SNEparentalk-L mailing list for you to discuss topics in the area of special needs education.

National Center to Improve Practice (NCIP)
http://www2.edc.org/NCIP/

This site contains resources for students with disabilities. It includes video clips illustrating how students with disabilities use a range of assistive and instructional technologies to improve their learning and more than 100 links to other sites dealing with technology and/or students with disabilities.

Arc Home Page
http://thearc.org/

Arc Home Page describes the nation's largest voluntary organization committed to the welfare of children and adults with mental retardation and to their families. The site offers many articles, especially with regard to advocacy, and related links.

Disability Resources, Inc.
http://disabilityresources.org/
Disability Resources is a nonprofit organization that publishes the online *Disability Resources Monthly (DRM)*. The site includes the DRM WebWatcher, an easy-to-use guide to WWW resources, and Librarians' Connections, providing information about listservs, professional associations, and assistive technology to librarians who serve people with disabilities.

Special Education at the University of Kansas
http://www.sped.ukans.edu/
The Department of Special Education at the University of Kansas provides a variety of Internet resources on disabilities and special education research projects, including 37 thematic units developed by elementary teachers.

Special Education Resources on the Internet (SERI)
http://www.hood.edu/seri/serihome.htm
SERI is a collection of special education resources including information about general disabilities, legal and law issues, physical and health disorders, and learning disabilities.

Council of Exceptional Children
http://www.cec.sped.org/
The Council of Exceptional Children's site contains publications, products, discussions and forums, a legislative action center, and links. There is a link to Eric Clearinghouse on Disabilities and Gifted Education (http://ericec.org/). *Eric* has a searchable database and is rich in resources and links.

Center for Improvement of Early Reading Achievement
http://www.ciera.org
This site contains information about early literacy acquisition and effective strategies for teaching reading. CIERA publications offer solutions to persistent problems in learning and teaching beginning reading.

HandSpeak: A Sign Language Dictionary Online
http://www.handspeak.com/
HandSpeak is an animated dictionary of sign language. The signs are grouped alphabetically and by categories. A new sign is added daily. It is a great introduction to sign language, a review of vocabulary for the deaf, quick tutorial for parents or teachers of deaf children, or just fun for anyone interested in the topic.

The Parent–Educator Connection
http://www.aea2.k12.ia.us/parenteducator/parented.html
This site provides information to families and educators of students and young adults with disabilities. The site has a wide variety of resources. Click on **Disability Resources** (http://www.aea2.k12.ia.us/curriculum/speced.html) and you will find numerous links.

SCR*Tech www 4 teachers
http://www.4teachers.org/profd/index.shtml
*SCR*Tech* is rich with content that includes online journals, Internet technology lessons, special education links, a technology glossary, technology lessons, tutorials, assistive technology links, and portfolio assessment information. Click on **Assistive Technology,** where you will learn more about assistive technology and how to locate assistive devices, find funding, and do much more.

Houghton Mifflin Special Education WorkPlace
http://college.hmco.com/education/sped_workplace/
This site contains professional resources that include electronic resources, assistive technology resources, links to professional organizations, school reform and standards, information on current legislation, and teaching tools and supports.

About.com's Special Education Resources
http://specialed.about.com/
This site is an encyclopedia of resources that covers topics such as adaptive P.E., autism,

deafness, inclusion, interventions, gifted education, and special schools.

The Adaptive Technology Resource Centre from the University of Toronto
http://www.utoronto.ca/atrc/reference/tech/techgloss.html
The Adaptive Technology Resource Centre provides descriptions of adaptive technologies with links to various products and their vendors.

Texas School for the Blind and Visually Impaired
http://www.tsbvi.edu/
This site includes an assortment of resources and instructional materials such as assessment resources for vision and hearing, instructional resources, adaptive technology resources, downloadable Braille materials, and information about eye diseases.

Children with Disabilities
http://www.childrenwithdisabilities.ncjrs.org/
This site offers information about advocacy, education, employment, health, housing, recreation, technical assistance, and transportation covering a wide array of developmental, physical, and emotional disabilities.

K8's Web Resources for Educators
http://www2.gvsu.edu/~baleikok/teaching.html
Web Resources for Educators is categorized by general and special education links, including ADHD, assistive technology, autism, ESL, general disability, hearing impairments, learning disabilities, lesson plans, visual impairments, and many other educational links.

The Adaptive Technology Resource Centre (ATRC)
http://www.utoronto.ca/atrc/
The Adaptive Technology Resource Centre supports access to information technology by people with disabilities.

LD Online
http://www.ldonline.org/
LD Online, a service of WETS PBS station, is an interactive guide to learning disabilities for parents, teachers, and kids.

disAbility.gov
http://disability.gov/
This comprehensive U.S. site provides a one-stop online access to disability resources, services, and information available throughout the federal government. Topics range from children and youth to tax credits and deductions.

Chapter Mastery Test

To the Instructor: Refer to the Instructor's Manual for the Answers to the Mastery Questions. This manual has additional questions and resource materials.

Let's check for chapter comprehension with a short mastery test. What follows are basic terms, classroom projects, and suggested readings and references.

1. How can the Internet be used to help students with special needs?
2. How does technology benefit students with special needs?
3. What is a speech synthesizer? What is the relationship between a speech synthesizer and voice input?
4. Distinguish among mainstreaming, inclusion, and collaboration.
5. Give two examples of output devices that help students with low vision or blindness overcome their disability.
6. What is word prediction software and why is it helpful for learning-disabled students?
7. Define *virtual reality* and speculate on ways that it can be used with the disabled student.

8. Why are the Individuals with Disabilities Education Act Amendments of 1997 (PL 105-17) important to students with disabilities?
9. What are some ways you can rearrange the computer equipment to make it easier for the student with special needs?
10. What is a touch screen and how can it be used to provide help to students with

disabilities? List some advantages as well as disadvantages for using this technology.
11. How can the computer enhance the development of reading skills for the child with learning disabilities?
12. Give two examples of input devices that help students with physical disabilities use the computer.

Basic Terms

adaptive or assistive technology (p. 309)
collaboration (p. 323)
discover switch (p. 310)
exceptional children (p. 312)
inclusion (p. 323)
inclusive education (p. 324)
keyboard emulators (p. 310)
mainstreaming (p. 323)
Quicktionary Reading Pen (p. 312)

refreshable Braille display (p. 314)
robotics (p. 321)
speech synthesizers (p. 313)
sticky keys (p. 310)
touch screen (p. 311)
touch-free switch (p. 310)
voice recognition software (p. 313)
virtual reality (VR) (p. 321)

Classroom Projects

By adapting the following projects, the teacher can meet the needs of the special education student.

1. Use a multimedia program to develop a presentation for the class.
2. Using the computer, visit the White House site (http://www.whitehouse.gov).

What are some of the advantages and disadvantages of this trip over a real-life visit to the White House?

3. Using word processing software, write a story for the whole class using your classmates' names. Illustrate this story with pictures and sounds. Print the story and read it to the class.

Suggested Readings and References

Abbott, Chris. "Technology that Opens Doors." *Times Educational Supplement* 4206, no. 2 (February 7, 1997): 18.

Alliance for Technology Access. *Computer and Web Resources for People with Disabilities: A Guide to Exploring Today's Assistive Technology.* 3rd ed. Alameda, Calif.: Hunter House, 2000.

Ashton, Tamarah M. "Spell CHECKing." *Teaching Exceptional Children* 32, no. 2 (November/December 1999): 24.

Beigel, Andrew R. "Assistive Technology Assessment: More than the Device."

Intervention in School and Clinic 35, no. 4 (March 2000): 237.

Bender, Renet L., and William N. Bender. "Computer-Assisted Instruction for Students at Risk for ADHD, Mild Disabilities, or Academic Problems." Clearinghouse No. EC304880, February 20, 1996.

Brett, A. "Assistive and Adaptive Technology: Supporting Competence and Independence in Young Children with Disabilities." *Dimensions of Early Childhood* 24, no. 3 (1997): 14–15.

Bryant, B. R., and P. C. Seay. "The Technology-Related Assistance to Individuals with Disabilities Act: Relevance to Individuals with Learning Disabilities and Their Advocates." *Journal of Learning Disabilities* 31, no. 1 (1998): 4–15.

Bryant, D. P., B. R. Bryant, and Marshall U. Raskind. "Using Assistive Technology to Enhance the Skills of Students with Learning Disabilities." *Intervention in School and Clinic* 34, no. 1 (1998): 53–58.

Castells, Manuel . *The Information Age: Economy, Society and Culture.* Boston: Blackwell, 1999.

Cavallero, Clara, and M. Haney. *Preschool Inclusion.* Baltimore: Paul H. Brookes, 1999.

Downing, J. E. *Including Students with Severe and Multiple Disabilities in Typical Classrooms: Practical Strategies for the Teacher.* Baltimore: Paul H. Brookes, 1996.

Fuchs, L. S., and D. Fuchs. "Treatment Validity: A Unifying Concept for Reconceptualizing the Identification of Learning Disabilities." *Learning Disability Research and Practice* 13, no. 4 (1998): 204–19.

Freedman, Allen. *Computer Desktop Encyclopedia.* Point Pleasant, Pa.: The Computer Language Company, 2001.

Hardman, Michael L., et al. *Human Exceptionality and Internet Guide.* 6th ed. Boston: Allyn and Bacon, 1999.

Heim, Judy. "Locking Out the Disabled." *PC World* 18, no. 9 (September 2000): 181.

Heward, William L. *Exceptional Children: An Introduction to Special Education.* 6th ed. Upper Saddle River, N.J.: Merrill, 2000.

Holzberg, Carol S. "Technology in Special Education." *Technology and Learning* 14, no. 7 (April 1994): 18–21.

Howell, Richard. "Technological Aids for Inclusive Classrooms." *Theory into Practice* 35, no. 1 (Winter 1996): 58.

Kamp, Sue. "How Does 'Fair Use' Apply to Software Being Used in the Schools?" *Technology Connection* 5, no. 1, (1999): 19.

King, Thomas W. *Assistive Technology: Essential Human Factors.* Boston: Allyn and Bacon, 1999.

Koseinski, Susan, et al. "Computer-Assisted Instruction with Constant Time Delay to Teach Multiplication Facts to Students with Learning Disabilities." *Learning Disabilities Research Practices* 8, no. 3 (Summer 1993): 157–68.

Kusisto, Stephen. "Planet of the Blind Delta." *Journal of Developmental Disabilities,* December 29, 1998.

Lahm, Elizabeth A., and Beverly L. Nickels. "Assistive Technology Competencies for Special Educators." *Teaching Exceptional Children* 32, no. 1 (September/October 1999): 56.

Lally, M. "Computer-Assisted Development of Number Conservation in Mentally Retarded Children. *Journal of Developmental Disablilities,* September 1980, pp. 131–36.

Lauffer, Kimberly A. "Accommodating Students with Specific Writing Disabilities." *Journalism and Mass Communication Educator* 54, no. 4 (Winter 2000): 29.

Lewis, Rena B. "Changes in Technology Use in California's Special Education Programs." *Remedial and Special Education* 18, no. 4 (July/August 1997): 233.

Lewis, R. *Special Education Technologies: Classroom Applications.* Pacific Grove, Calif.: Brooks/Cole, 1993.

Lewis, Rena B., Tamarah M. Ashton, et al. "Improving the Writing Skills of Students with Learning Disabilities: Are Word Processors with Spelling and Grammar Checkers Useful?" *Learning Disabilities* 9, no. 3 (1999): 87–98.

Lewis, Rena B., Anne W. Graves, Tamarah M. Ashton, and Candace L. Kieley. "Word Processing Tools for Students with Learning Disabilities: A Comparison of Strategies to Increase Text Entry Speed." *Learning Disabilities Research and Practice* 13, no. 2 (1998): 95–108.

Lyman, Michael, and Mary Anne Mather. "Software for Special Needs." *Technology and Learning* 19, no. 4 (November/December 1998): 60.

Male, Mary, and Doug Gotthoffer. *Quick Guide to the Internet for Special Education.* Boston: Allyn and Bacon, 2000.

Mates, Barbara T., Doug Wakefield, and Judith M. Dixon. *Adaptive Technology for the Internet: Making Electronic Resources Accessible to All.* Chicago: American Library Association Editions, 2000.

McNaughton, David, et al. "Proofreading for Students with Learning Disabilities." *Learning Disabilities Research and Practice* 12, no. 1 (1997): 16–28.

Merbler, John B., Azar Hadadian, and Jean Ulman. "Using Assistive Technology in the Inclusive Classroom." *Preventing School Failure* 43, no. 3 (Spring 1999): 113.

Robertson, Gladene, and Leonard P. Haines. "Positive Change Through Computer Networking." *Teaching Exceptional Children* 29, no. 6 (July/August 1997): 22.

Roblyer, M. D., and M. Cass. "Virtual Reality in Special Education: Still More Promise than Potential." *Learning and Leading with Technology* 36, no. 8 (1999): 51–53.

Ryndak, D. L., J. E. Downing, A. P. Morrison, and L. J. Williams, "Parents: Perceptions of Educational Settings and Serves Children with Moderate or Severe Disabilities." *Remedial and Special Education* 17 (1996): 92–105.

Ryba, Ken, and Linda Selby. "Computers Empower Students with Special Needs." *Educational Leadership* 53, no. 2 (October 1995): 82.

Shiah, Rwey-Lin, et al. "The Effects of Computer-Assisted Instruction on Mathematical Problem Solving of Students with Learning Disabilities." *Exceptionality* 5 (1994–1995): 131–61.

Sitko, Merrill C., ed. "Exceptional Solutions: Computers and Students with Special Needs" (February 1997).

Smith, Tom E. C. *Teaching Students with Special Needs in Inclusive Settings.* 3rd ed. Boston: Allyn and Bacon, 2001.

Strong, William S. *The Copyright Book: A Practical Guide.* 5th ed. Cambridge, Mass.: MIT Press, 1999.

Trollinger, Gayle, and Rachel Slavkin. "Purposeful E-Mail as Stage 3 Technology." *Teaching Exceptional Children* 32, no. 1 (September/October 1999): 10.

United States Department of Education. *Twentieth Annual Report to Congress on the Implementation of the Individuals with Disabilities Education Act.* Washington, D.C.: U.S. Government Printing Office, 1998.

Waldron, N. L., and J. McLeskey. "The Effects of an Inclusive School Program on Students with Mild and Severe Learning Disabilities." *Exceptional Children* 64 (1998): 395–405.

Webb, Barbara J. "Planning and Organizing—Assistive Technology Resources in Your School." *Teaching Exceptional Children* 32, no. 4 (March/April 2000): 50.

Wilson, Elizabeth K., and Margaret L. Rice. "Virtual Field Trips and Newsrooms: Integrating Technology into the Classroom." *Social Education* 64, no. 3 (April 2000): 152.

Woodward, L., and R. Gersten. "Innovative Technology for Secondary Students with Learning Disabilities." *Exceptional Children* 58, no. 5 (March–April 1992): 407–21.

Zhang, Yuehua. "Technology and the Writing Skills of Students with Learning Disabilities." *Journal of Research on Computing in Education* 32, no. 4 (Summer 2000): 467.

Zorfass, J., P. Corley, and A. Remzl. "Helping Students with Disabilities Become Writers." *Educational Leadership* 51, no. 7 (1994): 62–66.

CHAPTER 13

Teacher Tool Software, Graphics, Art, and Music

Integrating Teacher Tool Software into the Classroom

Did you know that there are computer software programs especially designed for teachers? These programs can make a teacher's school year easier. They help the teacher plan everyday activities; design notes, letters, labels, and newsletters; and track information. The teacher can utilize a variety of programs including gradebook programs, test makers, worksheet generators, crossword puzzle creators, portfolio builders, certificate makers, and word searches. This chapter will show you how the teacher can use these software programs to help students better accomplish educational objectives. In addition, you will learn how the teacher can use music, graphics, and art software to improve students' performance in a variety of classroom situations. You will also become familiar with Internet sites containing a rich assortment of lesson plans, resources, and teacher utilities.

Objectives

Upon completing this chapter, you will be able to:

1. Discuss the features of a variety of teacher utility software packages;
2. Describe four types of graphics software programs;
3. Discuss the features of an assortment of art and music programs; and
4. Integrate art and music programs into the classroom.

Teacher Tool Software

Teacher support tools increase the classroom teacher's effectiveness. (Moore, Orey, and Hardy, 2000). These programs are meant not for the student but for the teacher—to help in such tasks as recording grades, generating tests, making flashcards, generating puzzles and worksheets, and statistical analysis. Using these software tools reduces time and improves accuracy by assisting the teacher in chores that cannot easily be done in a traditional manner. For example, a gradebook program can quickly weight the students' grades, calculate the means and standard deviations, assign grades, and alphabetize the student list. When shopping for a utility program, you should determine whether the program fits your needs, saves time, and results in a more effective output. In this section, we examine a variety of teacher support tools.

Gradebooks

An obvious advantage of an electronic gradebook is its potential for helping teachers quickly inform students, parents, and administrators about pupil performance in the classroom. An old-fashioned gradebook is useful, but an electronic one is still more advantageous. Why spend hours recording and averaging grades when numerous gradebook programs on the market today can do this burdensome task for you? However, because computers are not always accessible, many teachers feel that they still need to maintain a pencil-and-paper gradebook in addition to an electronic one, which requires double entry. Also, some teachers feel that learning an electronic gradebook program is more difficult than using the old-fashioned gradebook.

A good gradebook should let you enter students' names easily and correct any errors. Once you have typed in the students' names, there should be an option for sorting the names alphabetically, numerically, or by class standing. The gradebook should let you enter a large number of students for each class, record a sufficient number of grades, record absences, and flag students with problems. For each score you enter, there should be a scaling factor to ensure that appropriate scores are figured in student or class averages. Furthermore, you should be able to assign weights according to the value of the class assignments. The program should calculate pertinent statistics—such as the range, mean, and median scores—and should be able to save test information and produce a hard copy. Additionally, you should be able to easily print out copies of graphs and tables depicting the performance of the students and showing comparisons with other class averages. You should also be able to include information on individual student reports, which have value in parent communication, and keep parents apprised of their child's progress. Some programs that are effective for the classroom teacher are *Grade Busters: Making the Grade* (Jay Klein Productions), *Gradebook Plus* (Clearvue/eav), *Grade Machine* (Misty City), and *Grade Quick* (Jackson Software). **Appendix A gives an annotated list of these gradebook programs.**

GradeQuick is a program created to look like a paper gradebook (Fig. 13.1), and the program is very intuitive. *GradeQuick* lets you enter data directly into the gradebook spreadsheet and display the information on one main screen. You can customize this main screen and view any item by just clicking the mouse. For example, you may want to display statistics or show personal student data fields

Name	ID	Fiction	Poetry	Speech	Grammar			Total	Max	Avg	Grade
Long Name		Study of	Using Me	Shakespe	Subject						
Term		1	1	1	1						
Category		Test	Test	Quiz	Homework						
Date		3/5/00	3/12/00	4/1/00	5/15/00						
Possible		100	100	50	50						
1. Adler, Leslie	1	100	**	50.0	√			192.50	200	96.25	A
2. Boyd, Jerry	18	**	75.0	32.0	ok			144.50	200	72.25	C
3. Chang, Julia	5	94.0	97.0	49.0	Good			280.00	300	93.33	A
4. Cohen, Josh	6	100	100	X	√			242.50	250	97.00	A
5. Denton, Bill	14	90.0	81.0	48.0	A			266.50	300	88.83	B
6. Flaherty, Sarah	7	88.0	84.0	45.0	Fail			229.50	300	76.50	C
7. Gardner, Alex	4	92.0	76.0	50.0	NC			218.00	300	72.67	C
8. Guth, Michael	8	66.0	77.0	**	Good			183.00	250	73.20	C
9. Jackson, Martin	9	90.0	88.0	44.0	Pass			259.50	300	86.50	B
10. Johnson, Dave	2	NC	90.0	46.0	Fail			148.50	300	49.50	F
11. Lansing, Eva	10	70.0	88.0	30.0	A-			233.75	300	77.92	C
12. Lee, Thomas	13	97.0	55.0	38.0	Pass			227.50	300	75.83	C
13. Momac, Jennifer	17	72.0	60.0	25.0	√			199.50	300	66.50	D
14. Moran, Jim	19	77.0	50.0	29.0	Pass			193.50	300	64.50	D
15. Nelson, Chris	16	50.0	44.0	24.0	ok			155.50	300	51.83	F
16. Reisner, Nancy	15	86.0	78.0	38.0	A			249.50	300	83.17	B
17. Romero, Maria	3	82.0	89.0	49.0	B			262.50	300	87.50	B
18. Ryan, Patsy	20	83.0	88.0	49.0	X			220.00	250	88.00	B
19. Scott, Elizabeth	11	90.0	87.0	44.0	ok			258.50	300	86.17	B
20. Wilson, Lynn	12	93.0	88.0	42.0	√-			260.50	300	86.83	B

FIGURE 13.1   GradeQuick 5.0

in addition to student averages and test scores. A teacher therefore has control over the content, style, and layout of this program. There is a wide selection of ready-to-print reports. The program displays more than 30 statistics and will print them in any report. *GradeQuick* even has a seating chart feature that allows the teacher to display and print student pictures on the chart.

The more elaborate gradebooks display data as histograms or line graphs, report a wider range of statistics, and have a variety of templates in English and Spanish for parent correspondence.

Grade Busters: Making the Grade (Macintosh and Windows) records 80 students per class, 320 assignments, 25 assignment categories, and 5 grading scales per class and displays the results graphically. Furthermore, it allows you to generate reports in English and Spanish.

Teachers are also using the Web to manage their grades, assignments, calendars, lessons, and attendance. For example, *ThinkWave Web Educator,* found at http://thinkwave.com/, handles these tasks easily. Using *ThinkWave*'s software, the teacher creates a gradebook and selects the information to publish on the Internet. *ThinkWave* then creates student and parent accounts for each student in the teacher's class. Next, the teacher gives students and parents a start key and password so they can access the account. Students can log on to their accounts to see their individual class information. The parents can also log on to see their own child's progress and communicate with the teacher.

Test Generators

A test-generating program resembles a word processor in that it has standard editing capabilities such as deletion and insertion. Many of these programs have font libraries from which you can select different typefaces. There are various test formats, including true/false, multiple choice, fill in the blank, short answer, essay, and matching. Some programs have graphics editors to help you integrate diagrams and pictures into your document. After entering your test questions, you can save them as a database file that can be retrieved on demand. Many programs let you randomize the order of the test questions and the arrangement of the possible responses to multiple-choice questions for makeup tests or alternate tests. The majority of programs let you print final copies of the tests along with answer sheets. Suitable test-making programs are *Test Designer Supreme II* (Super School Software), *Teacher's Tool Kit* (Hi Tech), *Teacher's Resource Companion Deluxe* (Visions Technology in Education), and *Test Creator* (Centron Software).

Test Designer Supreme II combines test creation, test taking, sound, graphics, and foreign languages. This program lets you insert questions from a database and use an overhead projector to give students a timed test on the computer. In addition, you can choose the test format you want and integrate graphics into it. An earlier version of this program, *Test Designer Plus,* was one of the first programs to integrate graphics into a test. Programs such as *Teacher's Resource Companion Deluxe* also integrate graphics and offer a wide selection of options.

Teacher's Resource Companion Deluxe (grades K–12) has an easy-to-use interface that many developers are following. This program lets you create activity sheets, tests, and complete curricular packages. The formats include short essay, multiple choice, true/false, matching, fill-ins, and a word search (Fig. 13.2). You can create a database using your questions for review quizzes or share your questions with other teachers. There are even 500 questions covering all curricular areas. You can use this program in all subject areas, including special education, ESL, foreign language, and geography.

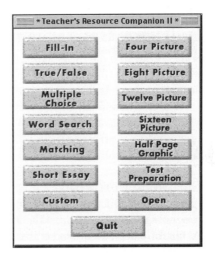

FIGURE 13.2
Teacher's Resource Companion Deluxe
Used by permission of Visions Technology in Education.™

Puzzle Makers

Puzzle makers motivate pupils studying potentially unexciting topics such as state capitals and parts of the body. You can use such programs to develop a crossword puzzle for reviewing Spanish, generate a geographical crossword for studying Europe, or create a math quiz in which equations are clues to a mystery. There are many noteworthy puzzle generators for the classroom, including *Crossword Companion Deluxe* (Visions Technology in Education), *Crossword Studio* (Nordic), *Word Bingo* and *Word Cross* (Hi Tech), *Crossword Creator* and *Puzzle Power* (Centron), and *Crossword Deluxe* (Forest Technologies).

Figure 13.3 is a sample crossword puzzle generated from *Crossword Companion Deluxe.* This crossword puzzle maker is simple to use. The pro-

FIGURE 13.3 Crossword Companion Deluxe

Used by permission of Visions Technology in Education.™

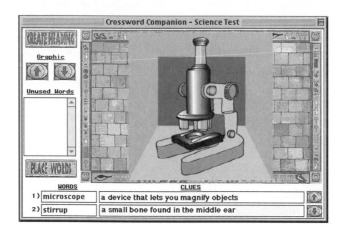

gram lets you create your own crossword puzzles, and it automatically generates a variety of puzzles from the same word list. The product automatically creates clues and inserts a definition, synonym, or sentence selected from a 17,000-word dictionary. You can create picture clues using a variety of picture formats. You can even put your crossword puzzles on your website.

Drill Sheet Generators and Organizers

Some programs, such as *Worksheet Magic* (Teacher Support Software) and *Math Companion* (Visions Technology in Education), produce worksheets in a variety of formats. Other programs, such as *Make-A-Flash* (Teacher Support Software), make flash cards with vocabulary generated by the word processor. Profile tools such as the *Portfolio Builder for PowerPoint* (Visions Technology in Education) and *Scholastic's Electronic Portfolio* assist teachers in the design and management of performance-based portfolios.

Electronic Portfolios

Lately, many educators realize one of the best ways for students to show their progress, knowledge, and skills in school is by creating an electronic portfolio. A **portfolio** is an organized collection of documents that is used by a student to reflect the student's knowledge, skills, and learning accomplishments. There are representational portfolios and developmental portfolios. The **representational portfolio** contains only the student's best work and can be used for employment purposes. A **developmental portfolio** shows a student's growth during a particular time frame and is used as an alternative means of assessment.

A portfolio can be used through a student's years (Fig. 13.4) in school, covering all curriculum areas, and it can include book report lists, computer-

FIGURE 13.4 The Portfolio Builder for PowerPoint

Used by permission of Visions Technology in Education™.

generated examples of student work or projects, paintings, collages, photos, timed writings, letters, poems, short stories, and more. To create a portfolio, students import work created with other software applications. They can import graphics, text, scanned images, full-motion video, and sound clips into a portfolio builder or authoring program like *HyperStudio* or *PowerPoint* (see Chapter 14 for additional information on this topic).

Other Useful Utility Programs

Some programs produce labels, time lines (Fig. 13.5), attendance charts, flowcharts, and lesson plans. The latest version of *TimeLiner, 5.0* (Tom Snyder

FIGURE 13.5 TimeLiner 5.0

Used by permission of Tom Snyder Productions.

Productions), lets you design, illustrate, and print out time lines of any length in Spanish or English. By using *TimeLiner 5.0*, students can sequence events into chronological order. Teachers can print these time lines in any size to display student work in the classroom. This new version of *TimeLiner 5.0* has 400 historical photographs, as well as clip art. You can add movies and sounds to make it a true multimedia time line. You import images from the Web to illustrate the time line and you can also link to the Internet from any event in the time line. This utility lets you convert time lines to slideshows. *TimeLiner 5.0* can be used in all curricular areas. There are even CD-ROMs with ready-made time lines for history, science, and social studies topics.

Lesson Plan Helper (FTC Publishing), written by former teacher Marsha Lifter, generates 350 "tried-and-true" lesson plans for all elementary subject areas. In addition, this program lets you enter your own lessons and has a search feature to find the lesson plan you need.

Teacher TimeSavers and *Research Assistant* (Visions Technology in Education) are two more utilities that lessen the teacher's workload. *Teacher Time-Savers* has assessment and TimeSaver templates. Using the assessment templates the teacher keeps records and calculates the student percentages for different grade levels. The TimeSaver templates let the teacher print name tags, place cards, mailing labels, bookmarks, flash cards (Fig. 13.6), and much more.

FIGURE 13.6
Teacher
TimeSavers *Flash*
Card
Used by permission of
Visions Technology in
Education™.

Research Assistant is perfect for the student or teacher who wants to gather information from any print or nonprint source and place it in a searchable computer database. Students and teachers use the information they gather to write term papers, multimedia presentations, and reports. With only one mouse click, students or teachers can reference their source in the correct bibliography format.

Inspiration (Inspiration Software), a powerful visual thinking tool, helps organize students' ideas and information. For this example (Fig. 13.7), the

FIGURE 13.7
Inspiration
Reprinted with permission of
Inspiration Software, Inc.

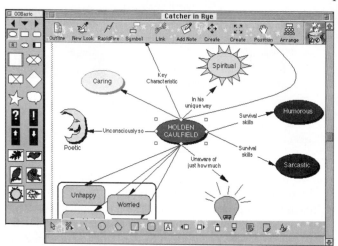

student has created a "character web" to analyze Holden Caulfield, the main character from *Catcher in the Rye*. This program assists students in developing visual diagrams, flowcharts, and knowledge maps. It has an integrated outline view that helps create concise written proposals and reports.

Statistical Programs

In the past, if you wanted to do statistical analysis, you had to do the work by hand or on a mainframe at a university. Today, many microcomputer programs help the classroom teacher make calculations and analyze statistics. Most of these programs handle the simplest statistics, such as mean and standard deviation, while the more complex programs handle multi-linear regression and factor/time series analysis. In a matter of seconds, you can compute a regression, an analysis of variance, or an unpaired *t* test.

Figure 13.8, from *StatView 5.0* (SAS Institute), shows the calculation of an unpaired *t* test, performed simply by double clicking. *StatView 5.0* offers all the tools needed to analyze and present data in one application. Years ago, you had to enter data in a spreadsheet, perform manipulations, and then import the data into a statistical package for analysis. Next, you had to use another program to create graphs. Finally, you had to use a draw program to prepare tables and graphs for presentation. Today, there are many other statistical packages, including *GB Stat* (Dynamic Micro Systems), *NCSS 2000 Statistical Analysis* (Windows [NCSS]), and *Systat* and *SPSS* (SPSS).

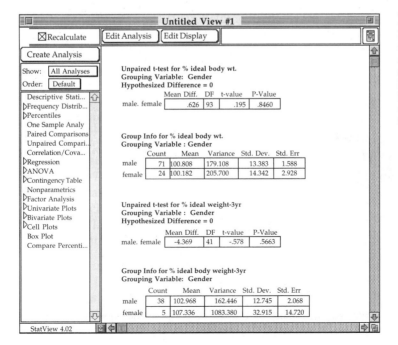

FIGURE 13.8
StatView 5.0

In most cases, you won't need an expensive statistical package because many spreadsheets or gradebook programs have sufficient statistics capabilities. However, if you are doing research or if your grade management program does not provide statistics, then you'll need this type of program.

Graphics Software

Just as utility programs are beneficial for the teacher, graphics are beneficial for the classroom. Pictures shape our perceptions and help us to communicate. When children first begin to read, they are always fascinated by illustrations. When a biology instructor discusses the anatomy of the body, he or she finds it beneficial to show a labeled drawing. The businessperson uses graphics to make important presentational points. The artist draws beautiful landscapes to make a statement. The engineer creates a scale drawing to construct a bridge, and the architect uses graphics to design a building. The statistician creates charts from tables. In our society, people use pictures to educate, to communicate, to express emotions, to build, and to persuade. A picture is indeed worth a thousand words.

The term **computer graphics** refers to "the creation and manipulation of picture images in the computer" (Freedman, 2001). Graphics can be as simple as a pie graph or as elaborate as a detailed anatomical painting of the human body. When discussing computer graphics, we are referring to computer-generated pictures on a screen, paper, or film. Let's divide our discussion of graphics into four categories: design, presentation, productivity, and art software (drawing and painting).

Computer-Aided Design

Computer-aided design (CAD) assists in the design of objects such as machine parts, homes, or anatomical drawings. You must have the proper CAD program to accomplish such tasks. With CAD software, you can easily change or modify designs without having to create actual models, saving time, money, and effort. *AutoCAD 2000* (Autodesk) is a 2-D and 3-D drafting environment that lets the student create, view, manage, plot and output, share, and use drawings. This program can be used by the professional architect, engineer, or drafter. *Quick-CAD Millennium Edition* (Autodesk) is an inexpensive CAD program that turns the computer into a design and drafting tool. Beginning users can produce drawings, plans, and layouts to scale. This user can add to or renovate homes and schools, create school projects, or design furniture.

Many of the programs in this field are simulations that let users create models and show their use. For instance, CAD software allows an engineer to design a car, test it, and even rotate it to gain perspectives. *Car Builder* and *Truck Builder* (Optimum Resource Software) are simulations for education that let students construct, modify, and test cars or trucks. In the process of constructing the car or truck, students design the inside and select the chassis length, the fuel tank, and the tires. When the mechanical selection is complete, students modify the body with data generated through a testing procedure that includes a wind tunnel and a test track. At the end of this testing session, students can save the specifications of the designed truck or car on a disk (Fig. 13.9).

**FIGURE 13.9
Truck Builder**
Used by permission of
Optimum Resource, Inc.

    SIMS and *SimCity 3000* (Maxis/Division Electronic Arts) are popular design programs using principles of CAD. *Sims* is for younger students and *SimCity 3000* is for older students. Both programs are building games in which students create cities or neighborhoods. For *Sims*, students design homes, furnish them, then build neighborhoods and take control of them. In *SimCity 3000*, students become planners, designers, and mayors of an unlimited number of cities. When using any type of simulation, students engage in problem solving. For example, in *SimCity 3000* the students have to consider the consequences of placing police and fire protection in the wrong locations.

    Finally, *3D Railroad Concept & Design, Master 3D Railroad,* and *Train Engineer Deluxe* (Abracadata) provide students with model railroad programs. With *3D Railroad Concept & Design* the student creates model railroad layouts, draws these layouts to any scale, then views them. *3D Railroad Master* lets users have complete control over trains. They select from a variety of rolling stock to build trains up to 100 cars long. In *Train Engineer Deluxe* students run trains as fast as they can through a background of realistic scenery.

Presentation Graphics in Business and Education

In Chapters 6 and 7, we discussed databases and spreadsheets and saw how useful these application programs are. It is not difficult to create graphs from such databases and spreadsheets to illustrate presentations. These types of illustrations are called **presentation graphics,** and businesspeople use them all the time to illustrate salary distribution, inventory fluctuation, and monthly profitability. The images can take many forms, such as the exploded pie chart in Figure 13.10. The section that represents 1973 is separated from the pie for emphasis.

FIGURE 13.10
Exploded Pie Chart

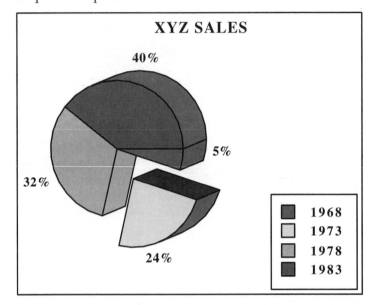

Graphs show a relationship among categories of data. The exploded pie chart compares the results in four different years, with each slice representing a year. Other types of graphs could have illustrated the same data in different ways. Figure 13.11 shows a sample bar graph.

FIGURE 13.11
Bar Graph

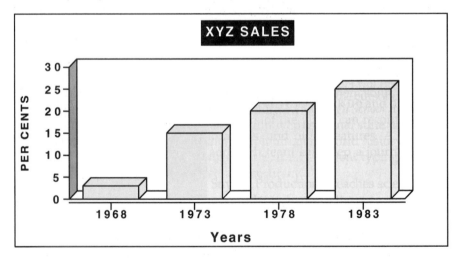

You can use graphics to better understand a student's performance on a series of exams. In Figure 13.12, the teacher charts Jane Smith's scores on six math tests to quickly grasp the effect of an extreme score (10) on this student's performance.

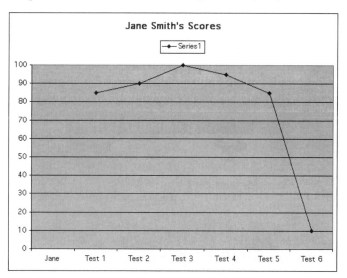

FIGURE 13.12
Excel *Line Graph*
Screen shot reprinted by
permission of Microsoft
Corporation.

Graphing is a means of getting a clearer picture of what the data represent. In education, graphing possibilities are unlimited. In science, students can graph the results of a series of plant experiments in which they alter variables such as temperature and water. In economics or social studies, the teacher might want the class to chart a stock's progress for a year or to graph voting trends. In English, the teacher can chart the incidences of certain words used in student writing to make a point about vocabulary.

Graphic programs such as *GraphPower* (Ventura Educational Systems) and *The Graph Club* (Tom Snyder Productions) are suitable for classroom use. Additionally, if teachers do not want to buy a separate graphing program, they can use an integrated program like *AppleWorks* (Apple) or *Microsoft Office,* which have a graphing component. With *GraphPower* (Fig. 13.13), you can create a bar graph of the area of the continents, one

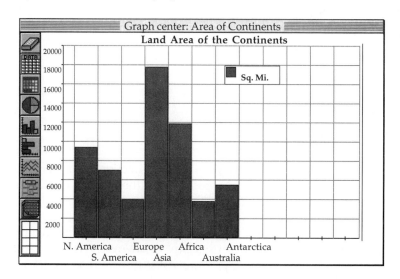

FIGURE 13.13
GraphPower
Used with permission of
Ventura Educational Systems.

example of the use of graphs to develop skills for analyzing and interpreting data. In addition to bar graphs, the program can create pictographs, line graphs, circle graphs, and box graphs. To use this program, you simply enter data in the Data Center and click on a graph icon to instantaneously create a graph. After creating a graph, you can export it to word processing or desktop publishing programs. Furthermore, an online tutorial called the *Graph Tutor* helps you overcome problems. *GraphPower* not only shows how to read graphs but also teaches the different functions of various graphs.

Another suitable graphing program is *The Graph Club*, which is appropriate for grades K through 4. Using this program to analyze data, students can create picture graphs, circle graphs, and bar graphs. *The Graph Club* has a library of over 150 fun pictures and includes an easy-to-use bilingual feature.

Productivity Graphics

To create an award, a poster, a banner, a greeting card, or a certificate, you use productivity graphics software. The best known is *The Print Shop* (The Learning Company), which lets you create a wide assortment of multicolored graphics. This classic program has won countless awards because it is easy to use and it saves hours of time and effort. Figure 13.14 shows a ready-made sign

**FIGURE 13.14
The Print Shop
Deluxe**

Broderbund/Learning
Company/Gores Technology
Group.

from *The Print Shop Deluxe.* Since the introduction of the original *Print Shop*, several versions have been produced. Although the concept remains the same, these programs vary in their capacity to produce color and graphics and use a laser printer.

There are dozens of programs that can be used for productivity graphics. Some of the more popular are *Print Explosion* (Nova), *Print Shop*, and *Kid Pix Studio* (The Learning Company), *Print Artist* (Sierra), and *PrintMaster Platinum*

(Mindscape). These programs produce attractive flyers, banners, and awards. *Culture World Diorama Creators* (Visions Technology in Education) lets children explore other cultures on-screen, then build and print dioramas out of paper. The students can join the Sioux as they hunt buffalo, build a small Ethiopian village, learn about the Alamo, join the isolated culture of medieval Japan, and find out about the Lewis and Clark expedition. For *Cultural World: Lewis and Clark,* the students assemble a diorama, print out figures to populate the diorama, and read an overview of the journey of Lewis and Clark (Fig. 13.15).

**FIGURE 13.15
Culture World:
Lewis and Clark**
Used by permission of Visions Technology in Education™.

Productivity programs offer different templates, fonts, border designs, and clip art. These enhancement programs, designed for users with limited artistic talent, have far-reaching educational benefits. The teacher can produce attractive and interesting bulletin boards, announcements, awards, worksheets, and even transparency masters. The students can design their own letterhead stationery to use in communicating with each other by classroom mailbox.

Art Software

Drawing Versus Painting Programs

When using a **drawing program,** you create illustrations that consist of mathematically defined curves and line segments called vectors. **Vector graphics** "is a technique for showing a picture as points, lines, and other geometric entities" (Freedman, 2001). What this means is that all elements of the picture can be isolated, moved independently, and scaled separately from one another (Fig. 13.16).

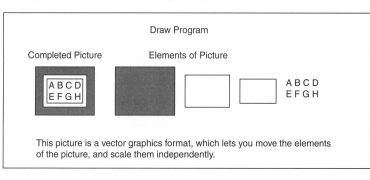

**FIGURE 13.16
*Vector-Based
Drawing***

Vector graphics can be displayed or printed at any resolution or degree of sharpness or detail that a monitor or printer is capable of producing. Drawing programs are similar to CAD programs, without special effects for illustrations. Two popular drawing programs are *Adobe Illustrator* and *CorelDraw*. With draw programs, students can draw geometric shapes, create designs, and construct miniature cities.

Paint programs let the student do painting on the screen with the use of a graphics tablet or a mouse. Paint programs are art-oriented rather than design-oriented, giving the user tools to paint computerized pictures. The pictures that are drawn are made up of dots or pixels. Each pixel consists of data describing whether the pixel is white, black, or a level of color. Unlike draw programs, the picture objects cannot be scaled and separated from one another (Fig. 13.17). The

FIGURE 13.17
Paint Program

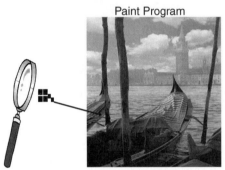

Paint Program

This picture's brush strokes are really made up of dots. The dots are called raster graphics or bitmaps.

pictures created with this format are altered by editing groups of pixels. The bitmap images are resolution-dependent. This means these images will appear jagged and lose detail if you enlarge them.

The majority of paint programs mentioned in this book offer coloring and texturing capabilities. Most paint programs also have brushes of different widths and shapes, drawing tools, a mirror-image function, different fonts, and an undo function.

There are significant advantages to using the computers for painting. If the artist makes a mistake, she or he can easily correct it because there are no real paints or watercolors to spill, drip, or smear. The painter simply clicks the mouse and instantaneously changes the picture or color, enlarges an image, or moves an object. However, there are also disadvantages, including a possible failure to connect with traditional art media and a loss of the opportunity to have hands-on experience with paint, clay, or other more tactile media.

To create images, students can use an input device, such as the keyboard, a mouse, a light pen with a graphics tablet, or a digitizer. The light pen

(Fig. 13.18), which handles exactly like a pencil, translates the students' drawings from the tablet into the computer program so that the drawings instantly

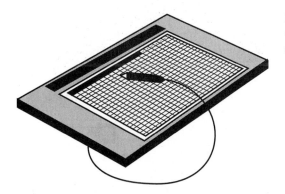

FIGURE 13.18
*Graphics Tablet
and Light Pen*

appear on-screen. The digitizer converts the shades of an image into a digital representation for the computer. A digitizer can be in the form of a scanner or camera; this equipment was discussed in Chapter 3.

    There are many good paint programs available today, including *Canvas* (Deneba Software), *Painter* (Fractal Design), *Painter 6* (Corel), and *Kid Pix Deluxe 3* (The Learning Company). An example of a paint program that is especially appropriate for elementary school children is *Kid Pix Deluxe 3* (Fig. 13.19). This program has 2,500 stamps, over 1,200 graphics, funny paint-

FIGURE 13.19
Kid Pix *Deluxe 3*

brushes, and a collection of wacky tools, each with its own sound. *Kid Pix Deluxe 3* includes a talking alphabet and six unique painting, drawing, and animation projects. Students learn shapes and practice motor skills by working with this program.

    Older students can use the painting component of *AppleWorks* or *Canvas* to create a picture. If they want more advanced programs, they can buy *Paint 6* (Corel), which has a variety of brushes, textures, canvas choices, and art materials.

Art Appreciation

An example of a first-rate program that teaches students about artistic masterpieces is *The World's Greatest Museum* (Voyager/Grolier). This program showcases 150 masterpieces of painting, sculpture, and frescoes, from prehistoric drawings to contemporary art. The art is chosen from 70 of the most famous museums in the world. In addition, *MasterStroke* (Clearvue) introduces students to some of the works and drawing techniques of Old Masters, ranging from Rembrandt to Van Gogh, with six tutorials that cover topics such as color, composition, and animation.

Music Software

After years of silence, the Internet is coming alive with sound and music. Students are getting their music from a variety of sources, allowing small bands opportunities they never had before. Teachers can easily make collections of music, adding richness to their history and cultural discussions. Among the many programs available for creating classroom collections of music are *WinAmp* (Nullsoft) and *SoundJam* (Casady & Green). These media players let you play MP3, CD, and other audio formats; build custom playlists; and track your music by artist, track, song, music style, or whatever is important to you. **MP3** (MPEG Audio Layer 3) has been responsible for revolutionizing music distribution.

Listening to Music

MP3 is an audio compression technology that produces CD-quality sound while providing almost the same fidelity. This technology enables people to download quality audio from the Web quickly. In about five minutes, an hour of near-CD-quality audio can be downloaded from the Internet. This has resulted in an auditioning system for musicians all over the world. Well-known bands post sample tracks from their new albums to encourage sales, and new bands post their music on MP3 sites to develop an audience. If the music is copyrighted, it is offered for a fee or sometimes free, creating a major legal issue. Major publishers are trying to cope with this phenomenon by introducing copyright protection. A premier MP3 site is MP3.com, found at http://www.mp3.com.

Making Music

Recently there has been a resurgence in music programs. Current programs give instruction in playing music, in music appreciation, and in composition and music theory. Some programs provide specific practice in music skills. *Piano Discovery System* (Jump! Music) and *Guitar Method 1* (eMedia) offer comprehensive, self-guided piano and guitar instruction.

Piano Discovery System has arcade-style games and tutorials. *Guitar Method 1*, for ages 8 to adult, takes students step-by-step from basics to playing complete songs.

Numerous software programs teach music appreciation. For example, Clearvue offers comprehensive music CD-ROMs on different musical periods, composers, and instruments. Students learn to understand music while studying musical elements.

Still other music programs are sing-along adventures; they let students experiment with music, teach musical elements, and teach about musical instruments. Using *Making More Music* (Grolier Interactive), students experiment with the elements of music. They become student composers and create their own compositions using familiar tunes and songs, and they save these new musical works. *Juilliard Music Adventure* (Grolier Interactive), for grade 4 to adult, helps students master the tools for composing melodies and creating rhythms. Students produce their own musical performance. This program introduces the student to rhythm, melody, orchestration, and musical styles.

Finally, the award-winning *Music Ace* and *Music Ace 2* (Harmonic Vision) are programs that introduce students to music fundamentals. *Music Ace* has comprehensive lessons, motivating games, and a Music Doodle Pad that lets students become composers. *Music Ace 2* is the second title in the series and it continues where *Music Ace* ended. *Music Ace 2* introduces new concepts such as standard notation, rhythm, melody, and harmony in an engaging format. There are 24 lessons, 2,000 musical examples, 24 games, and a composition tool. The interactive lessons come before each set of games. In Figure 13.20 the student is hearing an excerpt from Beethoven's Sonata Num-

FIGURE 13.20
Music Ace 2
Used by permission of McGraw-Hill School Division.

ber 8 "Pathetique." After listening, she chooses the correct tempo of the piece, in this case slow tempo. In addition, *Auralia* (Rising Software), a top-selling music instructional program, teaches topics like intervals, scales rhythm, pitch, and melody through a drill-based approach.

Classroom Lesson Plans

What follows are seven classroom lesson plans that cover music, art, and graphics.

▼   I. Presidential Election Survey   ▼

Materials

You will need a program that does graphics like *GraphPower, The Graph Club,* or *AppleWorks* and one or more computers.

Objectives

Students will learn how to do a survey and how to graph their survey using a bar graph and a pie graph.

Procedure

1. Working in teams, have the students conduct a survey on the next presidential election.
2. They should record information on socioeconomic level, education, voting preferences, and the like.
3. Using the computer, each team will create a bar graph of the results of their survey. They will graph the relevant factors.
4. Finally, the teacher will lead a discussion of their graphing results.

▼   II. State Data Sheet   ▼

Materials

You will need a program like *GraphPower* or *Excel* and one or more computers.

Objectives

Students will read an almanac for information and learn how to graph their information using a bar graph and a line graph.

Procedure

1. Have each student select three states and research the annual rainfall of those states.
2. Ask the students to create bar graphs on the computer comparing the statistics.

3. Have the students track down state rainfall statistics for three specific dates in the past.
4. Instruct students to construct line graphs showing the changes in the data for each state over a period of time.
5. The teacher and students discuss what the bar graphs mean.

▼   III. Educational Sign—About Drugs   ▼

Materials

You will need *Print Shop Deluxe* or *Print Shop Explosion* and one or more computers.

Objectives

Students will use a productivity graphics program to design a sign, learn about design and placement of objects, and discuss the reasons for not taking drugs.

Procedure

1. Discuss the reasons students should not take drugs.
2. Talk about placement and design with the students.
3. Instruct pupils to use the productivity graphics program to design a sign warning people not to take drugs.
4. After all students have designed signs, discuss what makes certain signs more appealing than others.

▼   IV. Math Riddle Card   ▼

Materials

You will need *Print Shop Deluxe* or *Print Shop Explosion* and one or more computers.

Objectives

Students will use a productivity graphics program to design a greeting card and practice solving math riddles.

Procedure

1. Give each child a riddle or have children find riddles in books.

2. Tell the pupils to design a greeting card, putting the riddle on the cover and the answer on the inside of the card. An example is shown in Figure 13.21.

A train left Chicago at 1:00 P.M. A second train left New York at 3:00 P.M. The train from Chicago traveled toward New York at 40 miles per hour. The train from New York traveled toward Chicago at 50 miles per hour. If the distance from Chicago to New York is 1,000 miles, which train was farthest from Chicago when they met?

They are the same distance from Chicago.

FIGURE 13.21   Print Shop Deluxe *Greeting Card Cover*
Used with permission of Broderbund, Inc.

3. Now distribute the greeting cards and have the students solve the riddles.

▼   V. Math   ▼

Materials

You will need a paint program like *Kid Pix Deluxe* and one or more computers.

Objectives

Students will use the paint program to make various geometric shapes, and they will learn about shapes.

Procedure

1. Teach the students about different geometric shapes as they learn to recognize each shape.

2. Show the students how to use the paint program to create these shapes. Figure 13.22 shows an example.

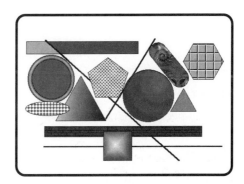

FIGURE 13.22
Shapes in a Draw Program

3. Explain how to fill the shapes with color and how to copy and paste shapes.
4. Have the students use the paint program to make abstract drawings without a fill pattern.
5. When they are finished, have them print out their shapes and color them, making sure all shapes of the same type have the same color.
6. Display these drawings on the bulletin board.
7. As a follow-up activity, have the students make collages with shapes, or create faces.

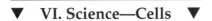

▼ VI. Science—Cells ▼

Materials

You will need a program like *Adobe Illustrator* or *AppleWorks* and one or more computers.

Objectives

Students will use a productivity graphics program to illustrate the parts of an animal or plant cell and paste it in their report.

Procedure

1. Students should draw the cell on paper, labeling its parts.
2. Students then take turns using the computer to create their plant or animal cell.
3. Have the student use a text tool to label each part of the cell: the cell membrane, nucleus, and so on.
4. Save this picture to disk.
5. Tell the students to prepare a report about animal cells or plant cells on the computer.

6. Have the students insert their picture in their report.
7. As a related activity, have the students draw the human body and label its parts.

▼ VII. Music ▼

Materials

You will need a program like *Making Music* and one or more computers.

Objective

Students will identify musical notes.

Procedure

1. Draw eight bars on the board to represent a scale.
2. Turn the computer monitor away from the students and have a student play six random notes.
3. Ask the students to listen carefully to the sounds and draw the bars and notes that represent the sound patterns.
4. Do this two more times so that the students can check their work.
5. Now turn the monitor toward the class and play the pattern. Have them compare their patterns to the ones that are being played.

Summary

Teacher support tools can make a teacher more effective. One of the most popular tools is the gradebook, which lessens the time a teacher spends entering grades, computing averages, and informing parents about students' progress. Other tools that save time and reduce effort are test and worksheet generators, puzzle makers, and statistical packages.

A good paint program or art program lets the user draw without the fear of making a mistake, and a productivity program enables those who are not artistically inclined to create any graphic from an award to a poster. CAD programs are useful in designing room layouts, machine parts, and cars; presentation graphics produce charts and graphs that show relationships within categories of data; and music programs are an effective aid in practicing music skills and theory. We examined seven activities for integrating graphics, art, and music programs into the classroom.

Appendix A offers an annotated list of award-winning teacher utility, graphics, art, and music programs.

What follows is an annotated list of Internet sites for art, music, and teacher utilities. These sites include a wide range of materials—lesson plans and pictures that can be printed, online multimedia presentations for students, interactive games, searchable databases for teachers, and many other resources that can enrich the K–12 curriculum.

 **ART AND MUSIC SITES**

AskERIC Lesson Plans: Arts
http://askeric.org/cgi-bin/lessons.cgi/Arts
AskERIC Lesson Plans provides more than 40 lesson plans for students in grades K–12. Areas include art history and visual arts.

The Art Room
http://www.arts.ufl.edu/art/rt_room/
index.html
The Art Room features a variety of classroom projects for grades 3–12 in the Doorway section. This section also presents other useful art activities, including the Artifacts Center.

Emmett Scott's Arts & Activities
http://www.cartooncorner.com/artspage.html
This site, for grades K–5, provides step-by-step instructions for drawing cartoons, as well as special tricks for creating them.

Joseph Wu's Origami Page
http://www.origami.vancouver.bc.ca/
This is the ultimate origami site, with extensive resources and information for K–12 teachers.

Kennedy Center's ArtsEdge
http://artsedge.kennedy-center.org/
The Kennedy Center's *ArtsEdge* provides a forum where teachers and students can share information and ideas that support the arts in the K–12 curriculum.

Museo del Prado
http://www.mcu.es/prado/index_eng.html
Museo del Prado offers information about the museum itself, a quick tour of 49 of its best-known works of art, its current featured exhibit, and links to other museums on the Web. A Spanish-language version is available.

Collections
http://www.ibiblio.org/wm/paint/
http://dir.yahoo.com/Arts/Artists/Masters/
These two sites offer famous paintings by acknowledged masters.

K–12 Resources for Music Educators
http://www.isd77.k12.mn.us/resources/
staffpages/shirk/k12.music.html
This site contains important resources for music educators and students in all areas of the music curriculum.

GEM: Subject Arts—Music Pre-K to 12
http://www.thegateway.org/index2/
artsmusic.html

The *Gateway to Educational Materials (GEM)*, sponsored by the U.S. Department of Education, provides a collection of art and music lesson plans and instructional resources for grades pre-K–12.

Yahoo! Classical Composers
http://www.yahoo.com/Entertainment/
Music/Genres/Classical/Composers/
This site introduces students in grades 5–12 to hundreds of composers from baroque to 20th century periods. Select a musical period and click on a composer's name to find biographical information, pictures, and descriptions of the composer's work.

Children's Music Web Guide
http://cmw.cowboy.net/WebG/
The *Children's Music Web Guide*, created by Monty Harper, contains a searchable and browsable database of hundreds of children's music sites for grades K–12. Categories include elementary education, fun, live music, media, music education, musicians/bands, resources, and songs.

Internet Music Resource Guide
http://www.specialweb.com/music/
Internet Music Resource Guide features links to a variety of music resources, including bands and artists, magazines, and search sites. For an extensive list of everything musical on the Web, click **General Sites.**

MP3.com
http://www.mp3.com
MP3.com offers thousands of free downloadable songs. The songs consist of different musical styles from all over the world. The site also features comprehensive hardware and software reviews, musical greeting cards, breaking digital music news, and more!

Yahoo! Music
http://music.yahoo.com/
Yahoo's directory contains everything you could want about music. It has information about MP3s, music you can listen to online, and other music topics.

ArtToday
http://arttoday.com

ArtToday is a subscription-based service with 1.2 million downloadable images that range from pen-and-ink, to woodcut, to nouveau retro, to sketch work.

TEACHER UTILITY SITES

School Express Free Worhsheets
http://freeworksheets.com/fws/

School Express provides over 2,00 free worksheets for suitable for grades pre-K–8. Each printable worksheet has a separate answer sheet.

Barry's Clip Art Server
http://barrysclipart.com/

This sites offers thousands of animal pictures to other clip art images. If you can't find it here, try the gallery at **http://gallery.yahoo.com/**.

iFigure
http://ifigure.com/

iFigure provides an extensive collection of on-line calculators and worksheets offering information to help in planning, solving, and making decisions in daily life.

University of Colorado at Denver GPA Calculator
http://carbon.cudenver.edu/register/calc.html

This simple spreadsheet program calculates your GPA by simply entering grade and the number of credits for each class. Another good calculator is the University of California–Berkeley's at http://www.aad.berkeley.edu/Meta-GPACalc.html.

Calculate Your GPA
http://pellam.ucr.edu/~njohnson/gpa.html

This site offers a simple spreadsheet template for calculating your GPA.

Convert It
http://convertit.com/

Convert It features a wide range of calculators for currency rates, temperatures, time zones, measures, and weights.

calculator.com
http://calculator.com/

This site offers online calculators to help solve financial, science, cooking, health, and other everyday problems.

Discover School's WebMath
http://school.discovery.com/homeworkhelp/webmath/

This site provides an array of math calculators featuring instant step-by-step solutions to your math problems from pre-algebra topics to calculus problems.

Discovery School's Puzzle Maker
http://puzzlemaker.com/

Discovery School provides an easy-to-use puzzle generator for teachers and students, grades 3–12. You can create and print customized word search, crossword, and other puzzles using your word lists. You can also build a maze or print specially hand-drawn mazes created around holidays and classroom topics.

FunBrain's Quiz Lab
http://funbrain.com/quiz/

FunBrain's Quiz Lab provides thousands of quizzes designed by teachers around the world. Teachers can create their own quizzes with its easy-to-use authoring tool and allow their students to take quizzes over the Internet at school or at home. You'll get quiz results automatically via e-mail. The registration is free and it is a snap!

Quintessential Instructional Archive
http://www.quia.com/

This *Quintessential Instructional Archive* is another excellent test-maker site to support your curriculum.

Chapter Mastery Test

To the Instructor: Refer to the Instructor's Manual for the Answers to the Mastery Questions. This manual has additional questions and resource materials.

Let's check for chapter comprehension with a short mastery test. What follows are basic terms, classroom projects, and suggested readings and references.

1. Discuss two examples of music software and how each one can help the student in a different phase of the music curriculum.
2. What is the difference between a presentation graphics program and a paint program? Describe the major features of each.
3. How has the availability of paint programs on the computer affected the traditional way of drawing and painting?
4. Define CAD and discuss its primary use.
5. What is a teacher tool program? Explain how it can provide individualized instruction for a class.
6. What is a productivity graphics program? Discuss two uses for this program in the school curriculum.
7. Define computer graphics and explain its importance in today's world.
8. What are the advantages and disadvantages of using a gradebook program?
9. What is an exploded pie chart? How can a teacher use it in the classroom?
10. Explain how graphics programs can be beneficial for the classroom.
11. What is a portfolio and why is it useful for measuring student performance?

Basic Terms

computer-aided design (CAD) (p. 344)	paint programs (p. 350)
computer graphics (p. 344)	portfolio (p. 340)
developmental portfolio (p. 340)	presentation graphics (p. 345)
drawing program (p. 349)	representational portfolio (p. 340)
graphing (p. 347)	vector graphics (p. 349)
MP3 (p. 352)	

Classroom Projects

1. Prepare a report showing why it is important that your school use productivity graphics.
2. Use a presentation graphics program to graphically represent Jane Smith's grades of 50, 60, 70, 88, 97, and 100.
3. Use a productivity graphics program to produce (a) a riddle card, (b) a poster, (c) a calendar, and (d) letterhead stationery. Explain the educational value of each product.
4. Your school will let you purchase only one graphics program. Will you choose a productivity graphics, presentation graphics, paint, drawing, or computer-aided design (CAD) package? Explain and justify your selection.
5. Create a test for the class using a test-making program.
6. Evaluate three test-making programs, discussing their strengths and weaknesses.
7. Use one of the many puzzle utilities to create a product for class consumption.
8. Review three gradebook programs and talk about their differences and similarities. Explain why you would choose one over the others.

Suggested Readings and References

Beltrame, Julian. "Making Music Together on Web Becomes Reality." *Wall Street Journal,* July 6, 2000, p. B1.

Clover, Faith, and Mary Erickson. "Interacting on the Internet." *School Arts* 98, no. 6 (February 1999): 46.

Eiser, L. "Print It! 101 Things to Print with Your Computer." *Classroom Computer Learning,* April 1988, pp. 76, 77.

Freedman, Allan. *The Computer Desktop Encyclopedia.* Point Pleasant, Pa.: Computer Language Company, 2001.

Friefeld, Susan. "Starry Night on Computer." *Arts and Activities* 122, no. 5 (January 1998): 25.

Harris, Judith B. "What Do Freehand and Computer-Facilitated Drawings Tell Teachers about the Children Who Drew Them?" *Journal of Research on Computing in Education* 29, no. 4 (Summer 1997): 351–69.

Holzberg, Carol. "Print Creativity Packages." *Technology and Learning* 17, no. 7 (April 1997): 8–12.

Hostetter, Bryan. "CAD Essentials for the Classroom." *Tech Directions* 56, no. 6 (January 1997): 36.

Kassner, Kirk "One Computer Can Deliver Whole-Class Instruction." *Music Educators Journal* 86, no. 6 (May 2000): 34.

Klinger, Mike. "The One-Computer Music Classroom." *Teaching Music* 3, no. 3 (December 1995): 34–35.

Kultgen, Sherri. "Computer Portfolios." *Arts and Activities* 125, no. 4 (May 1999): 20.

Lifter, Marsha, and Marian E. Adams. *Make and Take Technology.* Gresham, Ore.: Visions Technology in Education, 1997.

Lindroth, Linda. "Blue Ribbon Software." *Teaching PreK–8* 30, no. 6 (March 2000): 16.

Mack, Warren E. "Computer-Aided Design Training and Spatial Visualization Ability in Gifted Adolescents." *Journal of Technology Studies* 21, no. 2 (Summer–Fall 1995): 57–63.

Martin, Joan, Mei-Hung Chiu, and Anne Dailey. "Science: Graphing in the Second Grade." *Computing Teacher,* November 1990, pp. 28–32.

Mendrinos, R. "Computers as Curriculum Tools: Exceeding Expectations." *Media and Methods,* January/February 1988.

Moore, J. L., M. Orey, and J. V. Hardy. "The Development of an Electronic Performance Support Tool for Teachers." *Journal of Technology and Teacher Education* 8, no. 1 (2000): 29–52.

Netochka, Nezvanova. "A Musical Instrument in Perpetual Flux." *Computer Music Journal* 24, no. 3 (Fall 2000): 38.

Rogers, Laurence T. "Computer as an Aid for Exploring Graphs." *School Science Review* 76, no. 276 (March 1995): 31–39.

Schackner, Bill. "Colleges Byte Back when Music Software Jams Networks." *Black Issues in Higher Education* 17, no. 6 (May 11, 2000): 28.

Schrock, Kathleen, and Sharron L. McElmeel. "Newsletter Design to Make Them Take Notice." *Library Talk* 13, no. 1 (January/February 2000): 36.

Sharp, Richard, Vicki Sharp, and Martin Levine. *Best Web Sites for Teachers.* 4th ed. Eugene, Ore.: ISTE, 2001.

Ursyn, Anna. "Computer Art Graphics Integration of Art and Science." *Learning and Instruction* 7, no. 1 (March 1997): 65–86.

CHAPTER 14

Multimedia for the Classroom

Using Multimedia to Integrate the Computer into the Classroom

Did you know that students learn better when they are involved in the learning process? Did you know that this involvement increases as more of the senses are used in acquiring information? Multimedia provides an interactive, multisensory learning experience which motivates the learner and improves the quality of learning. Using this technology, students can have a more exciting and interesting school experience. Students can create electronic portfolios, *HyperStudio* educational stacks, *PowerPoint* or *MovieWorks* presentations, *Kid Pix* and *AppleWorks* slide shows. In addition, they can use programs like *StageCast* to create their own multimedia learning games. This chapter will provide suggestions on how the teacher can use multimedia in the classroom to help students better accomplish their educational objectives. You will be exposed to Internet sites that include software tips, multimedia resources, tutorials, design basics and lesson plans.

Objectives

Upon completing this chapter, you will be able to:

1. Define *multimedia;*
2. Explain the terms *hypermedia* and *hypertext;*
3. Discuss the origins of hypermedia;
4. Identify several major contributors to the field of hypermedia;
5. Explain the basic features of programs such as *HyperStudio, MovieWorks,* and *PowerPoint;*
6. Describe some ways that hypermedia can be incorporated into teaching;
7. Discuss some of the issues surrounding hypermedia; and
8. Describe *QuickTime,* morphing, warping, and virtual reality.

What Is Multimedia?

We are bombarded with the term **multimedia** everywhere we travel: on television, at the shopping mall, in newspapers, and in educational circles. What does this ubiquitous and elusive term really imply? Is it just a catchword tossed about, or does it have a specific meaning? In general and in this text-book, *multimedia* refers to communication of more than one media type, such as text, audio, graphics, animated graphics, and full-motion video.

Multimedia is not a new concept. For years, teachers have made presentations using different kinds of media. Traditionally, they have used slides, movies, cassette players, and overhead projectors to enrich lessons. Now, however, teachers may employ a personal computer and hard disk storage to combine these different media sources in their teaching. A computer-based method of presenting information, multimedia emphasizes interactivity (Pfaffenberger, 2000). Computers offer input and output devices such as laser discs, CD-ROM, DVD-ROM, and stereo sound.

Historical Perspective

In the professional literature, the words closely related to multimedia are **hypertext** and **hypermedia.** Hypertext originated more than 50 years ago. Vannevar Bush, an electrical engineer and Franklin Delano Roosevelt's first director of the Office of Scientific Research and Development, is given credit for first proposing the idea of a hypothetical machine, predating computers, that would mimic the mind's associative process. In 1945, Bush described a work station called a *memex,* which imitated the linking and retrieval of the human mind. Influenced by Bush's associative linking and browsing concepts, Douglas Engelbard conducted research at the Stanford Research Institute in 1960 that led to several significant inventions, including the mouse, an online work environment now named Augment, and the concept of a "viewing filter." With a viewing filter, users could quickly view an abstract of a document or file, thus being able to scan a database for important information (Fiderio, 1988).

These developments were important, but it was Ted Nelson who took the critical step in the development of multimedia. Around 1965, he coined the term *hypertext,* meaning nonsequential writing, and he developed the writing environment called *Xanadu* that lets a user create electronic documents and interconnect them with other text information. Through this endeavor, Nelson was attempting to make literary works available electronically. (Each time a user accessed text on this system, Nelson was paid a royalty.)

In hypertext, text, images, sound, and actions are linked together in nonsequential associations that let the user browse through related topics in any order. At the center of this system is linking. No document or bit of information exists alone; each document contains links to other related documents. Figure 14.1 illustrates the nonlinearity of hypertext.

FIGURE 14.1
The Nonlinearity of Hypertext

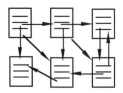

An example of hypertext is a computer glossary from which a user can select a word and retrieve its definition. This definition is linked to other words, and the user can move from it on to other, related terms.

Hypermedia is nearly synonymous with *hypertext*; however, it emphasizes the nontextual components of hypertext. Hypermedia uses the computer to input, manipulate, and output graphics, sound, text, and video as part of a hypertext system. The different forms of information are linked together so that the user can move from one to another. When a teacher uses hypermedia, the computer directs the action of devices such as a video camera, videodisc player, CD-ROM, or DVD-ROM player, tape recorder, VCR tape deck, scanner, video digitizer, audio digitizer, or musical keyboard. Figure 14.2 shows an example of a hypermedia workstation.

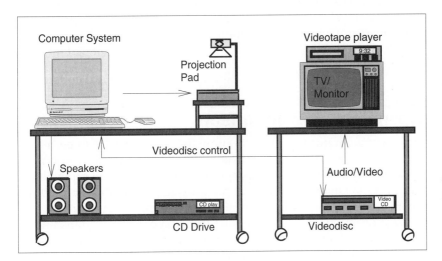

FIGURE 14.2
Using Technology in the Classroom—Hypermedia Workstation
ClickArt Images ©1995 T/Maker Company.

A computer and a monitor are the basic equipment necessary for a hypermedia presentation, with the computer acting as a controller and the monitor displaying images. Depending on the sophistication of their equipment, teachers can add a variety of devices and software programs to enhance the hypermedia creation (Fig. 14.3). For example, they can use the digital camera to take pictures, and the video camera to film a scene while the videocassette player records a television program. The audio digitizer transfers sounds, the scanner adds graphics or text, and the video digitizer transfers noncomputer media such as photos or videotape. The video digitizers let the user convert an analog signal generated by a video camera, television

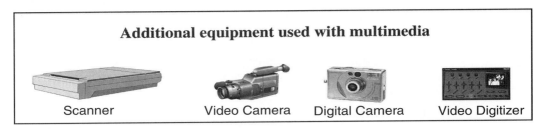

FIGURE 14.3 *Equipment Used with Presentations*

Copyright 2001 www.arttoday.com (scanner and video camera); digital camera courtesy of CUSA; video digitizer courtesy of Freedman, Desktop Encyclopedia, 2000.

tuner, videocassette player, or videodisc player into a digital signal. When this happens, the student or teacher can manipulate these images on the computer and put them into a presentation. A quick way to get slides into your presentation is to use Photo-CD technology. This technology was developed by Eastman Kodak Company to make it easier on individuals who wanted to scan color slides or negatives into a photo-CD. The user simply takes slides or negatives to a service that handles this process and the images are put on a photo-CD at a reasonable cost.

Teachers can use art programs such as *CorelDraw* or *Kid Pix Deluxe 3* (The Learning Company) to enhance artwork, a musical keyboard to provide customized musical accompaniment, and a laser printer to produce high-quality images. Hypermedia components range from sound-enhanced documents that will play on any computer to *HyperStudio* stacks that offer sound, animation, and color.

Hypermedia Authoring Tools

One objective of this chapter is to provide an overview of hypermedia authoring tools and programs and how they operate. While you cannot expect to become a hypermedia-programming expert based on the information in this chapter, you will be introduced to the possibilities of hypermedia. Hypermedia authoring tools are preparing students for the information-intensive society of the future. Hypermedia publishing someday could eliminate publishing as we know it today. Students and teachers will transfer information using sound effects, graphics, music, animation, and video.

HyperCard

One of the first implementations of hypermedia and the best-known one was **HyperCard**, developed by Bill Atkinson at Apple Computer. Atkinson created *HyperCard* in 1987 to run on the Macintosh computer. At that time, *HyperCard* became almost synonymous with hypermedia, although it is important to remember that not all hypermedia used *HyperCard*.

HyperCard was an authoring tool that let users organize information, browse through it, and retrieve it. Information was stored in the form of on-screen *cards* (rectangular boxes on the screen) that contained text, graphics, sound, and animation. You could browse through the cards with the help of buttons, or "hot spots," that you clicked (Fig. 14.4). The cards were displayed one at a time and organized in **stacks**, much in the same way you would organize a Rolodex™ or flipchart. *HyperCard* came with ready-made stacks, but the program also enabled teachers and students to create their own. One of the program's unique features was its simplicity, enabling nonprogrammers to create their own applications without having

What are cards?

Each screenful of information in a HyperCard stack is ◄ ——— **Text**
a "card." A card can be any size, but it's always a
rectangle. Cards contain text, pictures, and buttons.

graphic ———

Universal Wildlife
Preservation Society

300 Animal Blvd.
Chicago, Ill. 10008

——— **buttons**

FIGURE 14.4
Elements of a
Card

to master a complicated programming language. By using a program like *HyperCard*, a teacher could for the first time create innovating multimedia stacks.

　　HyperCard clearly was a user-friendly program, although it required considerable work to construct a stack. Many other authoring tools were developed for hypermedia and performed the same functions as *HyperCard*, for example, *LinkWay* for MS-DOS machines and *TutorTech* for Apple II. Although these programs were a major step forward, they had limited use. Even though they were not as difficult to learn as a programming language, they still required considerable time to program. Everything changed when Roger Wagner produced *HyperStudio* for the Apple IIGS.

HyperStudio

HyperStudio had many of the *HyperCard* features and functions, but *HyperStudio*'s simplicity made it more suitable for most teachers and students. *HyperStudio* did not require scripting (programming) because all its major functions were already built into the software program itself. Nevertheless, programming was available for the advanced user in the form of a scripting language called HyperLogo. *HyperStudio* had many built-in features and functions, including color, videodisc, and CD-ROM support, animation, and scrolling. By examining the present-day version of *HyperStudio* (Knowledge Adventure) closely, you'll gain an understanding of what is involved in working with an authoring tool. *HyperStudio*, like *HyperCard*, displays its information in the form of **cards** (Fig. 14.5) that contain text, graphics, sound, and animation. The cards have **buttons** that let the user navigate through the cards and perform actions such as

**FIGURE 14.5
HyperStudio 4**
Card

Used by permission of
Knowledge Adventure/Havas
Interactive.

playing video and accessing websites (Fig. 14.6). The cards are organized in

**FIGURE 14.6
HyperStudio 4**
Buttons

Used by permission of
Knowledge Adventure.

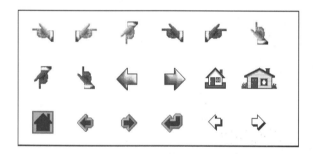

stacks (Fig. 14.7), much in the same way you would organize index cards. *HyperStudio* comes with ready-made stacks, but the program also enables teachers and students to create their own.

**FIGURE 14.7
HyperStudio 4**
Stack

Used by permission of
Knowledge Adventure.

After you open *HyperStudio 4.0* and close its "Tip of the Day," you see the "Home Stack" (Fig. 14.8). The "Home Stack" is the guide to *HyperStudio*.

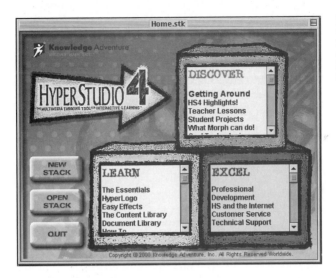

FIGURE 14.8
HyperStudio 4
Home Stack
Used by permission of Knowledge Adventure.

It serves as a visual directory of the different elements in the program. For example, if you click on **Student Projects** in the *Discover* list, you will be asked to choose from a variety of project stacks ranging from poetry to chemistry. To create a stack, you click on the **New Stack** button. A blank card will appear. On that blank card, you can begin to design your new stack.

Let's say you decide to create an African stack. On your first card (Fig. 14.9), you introduce users to Africa. You add the text "African Safari," a map

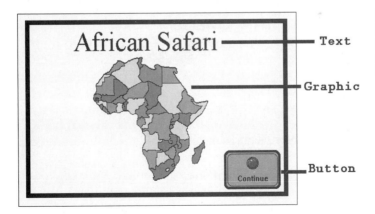

FIGURE 14.9
HyperStudio 4
Stack Card 1
Used by permission of Knowledge Adventure.

graphic, and two buttons—one visible and one invisible. The invisible button is superimposed over the map graphic and its outline is visible only when special keys are pressed. When users press the appropriate key, it makes a roaring sound. The visible button, **Continue,** plays music and provides a nice transition to Card 2 (Fig. 14.10). Card 2, your Facts about Africa card, contains a box with text, an invisible button, and two arrow buttons. When users show this card, a voice reads the text enclosed in the box. The left arrow button takes

**FIGURE 14.10
HyperStudio 4**
Stack Card 2

Used by permission of
Knowledge Adventure.

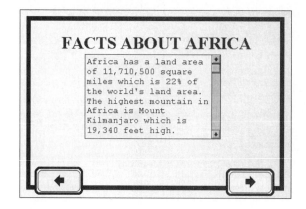

users back to Card 1, while the right arrow button plays a sound clip and then takes users to Card 3. When users open Card 3 (Fig. 14.11), a self-activating in-

**FIGURE 14.11
HyperStudio 4**
Stack Card 3

Used by permission of
Knowledge Adventure.

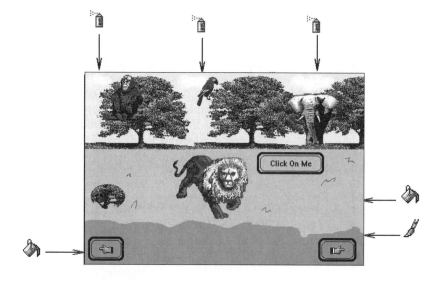

visible button uses animation to send the elephant down a hill. The **Click On Me** button lets the lion run to the bottom of the card. You would have drawn this card with the *HyperStudio* paint tools shown on the outside of the card in Figure 14.11. The left arrow sends users back to Card 2, and the right arrow takes users forward to Card 4 with accompanying sound effects. Finally, Card 4 (Fig. 14.12) has a self-activated scrolling text button. The information enclosed in the rectangular box scrolls the way credits on a movie screen do. The home button returns users to Card 1 to start the stack again.

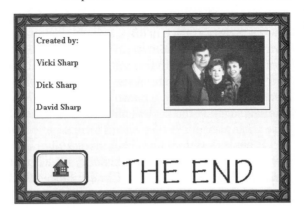

FIGURE 14.12
HyperStudio 4
Stack Card 4
Used by permission of
Knowledge Adventure.

From this example, you can envision the amount of time, effort, and creativity involved in only a four-card stack. *HyperStudio* is a versatile product, and the kinds of stacks a teacher and student can create are endless. A teacher could create a stack to enable students to browse through the permanent collection of the National Gallery of Art in Washington, D.C. She could import color images of the different works of art from the gallery onto the cards in the stack. Students in her class could move through the gallery at their leisure, clicking buttons to move on to new paintings or to return to ones they have already seen. They also can click on buttons to take a tour through the French countryside that inspired Monet's work or to listen to a concert of the music of composers such as Debussy, who were contemporaries of some of the artists represented in the gallery. If students run out of class time, by clicking on the home button they can return to the opening screen and embark again on a new tour of the gallery the next day.

Teachers or students might create a stack that teaches a foreign language, takes the user on a tour of a foreign city, tells an interactive story, discusses endangered animals, or describes a historical event.

Because of *HyperStudio*'s popularity, a large collection of software materials has sprung up to accommodate it. For example, *Sound Companion* (FTC Publishing) lets students place sounds in *HyperStudio* stacks by recording directly through their computer microphone (Fig. 14.13). Students can change

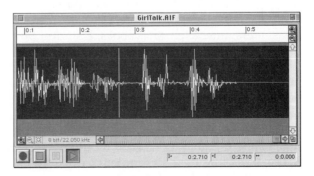

FIGURE 14.13
Sound
Companion
Developer: Jeff Patterson;
Publisher: FTC Publishing.
Reprinted by permission.

the sound tempo and pitch, add echo, and play backward. *HyperStudio Project Resource Kits* (FTP), for grade 2 and up, contains a library of sounds, graphics, and movie files which can easily be moved into a *HyperStudio* stack. Dave Cochran's *HyperStudio Network* at http://www.hsnetwork.com/ has interesting articles about *HyperStudio* along with products like Ann Brundige's collection of creative stacks. There are books like *HyperStudio 3.2 in an Hour* (Sharp, 1999), a tutorial that takes the student through the program step by step, and *Help! I Have HyperStudio. Now What Do I Do?* (McBride and Luntz, 2001), a book that helps the students design multimedia projects with *HyperStudio.* In addition, the *AnswerBox for HyperStudio* (Tech4Learning) is a box that includes step-by-step instructional cards for all the basic *HyperStudio* functions.

Other Hypermedia Authoring Tools

The various hypermedia programs have different skill levels and traits. Advanced programs, like Macromedia's *MacroMind Director,* can run on both Apple and Intel-based platforms and are more appropriate for business applications. Besides *HyperStudio,* there are other programs of this type found in educational circles. For example, there are programs like *Leonardo's Multimedia Toolbox* (NEC), where a "button wizard" can be used to create interactive or navigational buttons. Students or teachers can use a multimedia tool to import pictures, sound, and videos into their presentations. Teachers can use the project management tools to manage student files, menu options, and settings. They can use the geometry tools,—for example, the compass,—to draw geometric figures. The program's combination table/spreadsheet tool lets users enter data in tables and spreadsheets. After the data are calculated, the results can be graphically displayed. *Leonardo's* also has paint tools that let the user draw, paint, and edit lines, rectangles, circles, and free-form objects. Finally, *Leondardo's* animation tools lets users animate images with different effects and movements.

Classroom Suggestions for Using Hypermedia

Teachers and students have a rich selection of software and hardware to choose from in order to develop first-class hypermedia presentations. Students can use a desktop publishing package such as *The Writing Center* (The Learning Company/Gores) to write and illustrate stories that combine text with graphics. They can create their own book reports, research presentations, tours, interactive storybooks, historical portraits, travelogues, animal reports, chronologies of world events, portfolios, and even school yearbooks. They can also create their own motion pictures with sight and sound by using a videodisc player. Teachers can generate slide shows that explain a range of topics from Beethoven to cell mitosis and are accompanied by canned music, sound effects, and digitized human voices. Students can use tape recorders to record interviews on the overcrowding of schools and then turn the interviews into presentations by adding background sounds, such as the noise of children in an overcrowded classroom and sound effects synchronized with words from their scripts.

Numerous other possibilities exist for hypermedia use in classrooms. Using camcorders, teachers can prepare interesting film clips of field trips or school events. A presentation can be combined with computer graphics, photographs, animation, sound, and music. Teachers or students can then add computer titles and credits to their videotapes.

A teacher could also prepare a presentation on the different types of clouds. To make this report more interesting, the teacher could record video shots of actual clouds. A program such as *AppleWorks* would allow graphic screen illustrations to be added. In the finished hypermedia presentation, each type of cloud would have a text explanation, sound effects, and music.

Guidelines for Creating a Multimedia Presentation

To plan a good presentation or multimedia stack, students and teachers should do the following:

1. Consider your teaching objectives. What should users learn? What will they do?
2. Plan ahead. Do a sketch or rough layout of the slides or cards in your stack. Review what is to be communicated. Who is the audience? What approach will best express your message? You should be willing to experiment and be flexible. Look for consistency on each card or slide and check for balance of design. Add interest when it is feasible and organize a card or slide around a dominant visual drawing. Be sure not to clutter a card or slide with too many elements.
3. Look at the format of your cards or slides. Pay close attention to borders and margins. Provide a dramatic graphic for the title card.
4. Add emphasis to the work. For example, use a large font size to call attention to important ideas. When needed, vary the type style by using boldface or italics. Use blank spaces to make designs stand out. Highlight the objects on the page with artwork, but do not overdo it. Let the reader's eyes focus on a particular part of a card or slide.
5. Do not use too many fonts because that detracts from the general feeling of what a card is communicating.
6. Use color wisely. Avoid clashing colors; work with complementary ones instead.
7. If you are only working in black and white, try to avoid too much white space. If this is unavoidable, surround the area with gray or black space.
8. Check your work thoroughly before showing or printing out copies of your work.[1]
9. Have students or other intended audience members preview your work. Watch their reactions. Do they learn what you intended? Are they able to successfully navigate your stack?

---

[1] Vicki Sharp, *HyperStudio 3.2 in an Hour* (Eugene, Ore.: ISTE, 1999), pp. 253–54.

The criteria in the checklist on p. 000 will help you in evaluating multimedia projects.

COMPUTER MULTIMEDIA PROJECT EVALUATION FORM

Title _____ Date _____ Subject Area _____

Grade Level _____ Length _____ Minutes _____

Audience _____ Objectives _____ Prior Knowledge _____

Brief Description

Directions: Examine the following items and determine which ones you feel are important for your class situation. Evaluate your multimedia project and place an X on each line where it meets the criteria.

A. Content

_____ 1. Current

_____ 2. Accurate

_____ 3. Clear and concise

_____ 4. Matches curriculum

_____ 5. No bias or objectionable language

_____ 6. Clear directions

_____ 7. Contents include graphics, text sound, and visuals

B. Graphics and Sound and Visuals

_____ 1. Each slide has text and graphics appropriate to the content

_____ 2. Buttons on each card work appropriately

_____ 3. Graphics or sounds are not distracting

_____ 4. Screens are neither cluttered nor barren

_____ 5. Special effects are used appropriately

_____ 6. Buttons and sounds associated with buttons are appropriate

C. Fonts

_____ 1. There are not too many fonts or type sizes

_____ 2. Shadowing and outlining are not overdone

_____ 3. Type is large enough for reading when projected

_____ 4. There are not too many text ideas on a card

Rating Scale

Rate the multimedia presentation by placing a check on the appropriate line.

Excellent _____ Very Good _____ Good _____ Fair _____ Poor _____

Comments

Pros and Cons of Hypermedia

Before concluding our exploration of hypermedia authoring tools, let's consider some of the benefits and drawbacks of this technology.

Hypermedia as entertainment may effectively mesmerize its audience with spectacular presentations. A student viewing a hypermedia presentation—replete with text, graphics, film clips, still photographs, sound effects, and moving maps—is very likely to be an involved student! One of the teacher's first responsibilities is to motivate students to learn, and the hypermedia presentation addresses this concern. Using hypermedia products, students are not passive receptacles of knowledge; rather, they are actively engaged in their learning, making decisions about how to proceed. The technology facilitates the development of research skills and encourages cooperative learning and problem solving. Reluctant readers are motivated to read, and inquisitive students have the freedom to explore topics independently. All students are able to acquire depth of knowledge on whatever stack, folder, or assortment of screens they are using. Dede (1994) and Lu, Wan, and Liu (1999) see this tool as beyond simple presentations, offering new methods of structured discovery, addressing varied learning styles, motivating students, and in the future applying pattern recognition techniques to help students master higher-order thinking skills. Swan and Meskill (1996) show how hypermedia tools support the teaching and acquisition of critical thinking skills in language and reading. Richard Mayer (1999) reviewed evidence from more than 40 studies that multimedia learning environments can promote constructivist learning that enables problem-solving transfer. Turner and Dipinto (1992) discuss how the hypermedia environment encourages students to be introspective and imaginative. According to Bill Gates (1995), hypermedia authoring may play a major role in preparing students for the intensive information world of the future.

Researchers such as Marchionini (1988) feel there are important contributions that hypermedia systems offer for educators. First, students have quick and easy access to large amounts of information in a variety of formats. Learners can easily use this diverse material stored in a compact form to follow paths that point out relationships between items, or they may create their own interpretations. Second, the environment offers a high level of learner control because users may choose predetermined paths through the lesson or paths that suit individual interests and abilities. Third, hypermedia gives teachers and students an opportunity to change roles, in that students can use the technology to make presentations and teach one another and teachers can learn from the technology's offerings about students' interests and abilities.

While it is obvious that hypermedia has great potential, there are also problems that must be addressed. One key question concerns the overburdened teacher's responsibility in this process: How is a teacher going to find the time to master hypermedia and devise hypermedia presentations? The average time required to put together a quality hypermedia presentation is between 20 and 50 hours. Who is going to train these teachers to use hypermedia programs? Training requires funds and a commitment from the school districts. While there is general agreement that this medium stimulates in-depth knowledge, whether it fosters breadth of knowledge is yet to be determined. Also unclear are the implications of random learning, possible when students determine their own programs. Another problem according to Roblyer, Edward, and Havriluk (1997) is that students need sufficient online time, and their computers must be configured for hypermedia authoring, that is, have the capacity for digitized sound or input video. Finally, some critics question the value of hypermedia, claiming that it is all form and little substance. Teachers who prepare these presentations do spend inordinate amounts of time and energy so that their presentations will look professional on the screen, but perhaps this time is being diverted from substantive learning. A presentation ending with a barrage of images that have a limited connection with a topic may be a way of ensuring emotional involvement, but the cost may be a loss of real learning.

Fiderio (1988); Stanton and Baber (1992); Roblyer, Edward, and Havriluk (1997); Dillon and Gabbard (1998); and Shapiro (1998) describe some of the negatives of hypermedia as a technology: (1) users need guidance because they can become lost in obscure links when they explore various databases; (2) students may be attracted to tangential topics and be diverted away from subject matter that is relevant; (3) teachers also may have difficulty breaking the information into smaller, more organized components; and (4) the cost of hardware and the large memory requirements of hypermedia may make hypermedia prohibitively expensive for many schools. (Recently, this has been alleviated by the relatively low cost of modern equipment.) Other critics caution us not to substitute hypermedia for books and the library.

In conclusion, hypermedia is so embryonic a technology that research on its roles in classrooms is inconclusive and not yet extensive (Toomey and Ketterer, 1995). Do the benefits outweigh the problems? In the end, each individual educator must decide whether to embrace this technology, adopt selected hypermedia software, or cautiously await further developments.

Additional Hypermedia Authoring Software Programs

In response to the time-consuming nature of hypermedia presentations, software was developed that would alleviate this problem. *Modern Learning Aids* (MPG), one of the first programs of its kind, had a multimedia presentation generator that helped produce hypermedia presentations on the computer as easily as operating a VCR remote control. A typical MPG presentation was a lesson on environmental problems caused by clearing the rain forests in Brazil. A VCR was used to present a newscast on these issues; a videodisc of an expedition down the Amazon River depicted forests, inhabitants, and sounds; digitized satellite images and text were added; and, finally, the additional sound of jungle music came from a CD-ROM player. Such a system allowed users to play segments of the presentation in a user-paced mode or in an automatically sequenced video presentation. Today, teachers can choose simpler programs such as *MP Express, Create Together, mPower, Kid Pix, AppleWorks, PowerPoint,* and *MovieWorks.*

MP Express

MP Express (Bytes of Learning) is an easy multimedia presentation tool for Macintosh and Windows. Its streamlined design and simplified user interface let beginners and advanced users produce high-quality presentations in minutes. All the tools and page control information needed to produce effective, professional-looking multimedia are provided on two simple, intuitive floating palettes. Beginners need use nothing more. Advanced users can find customizing options in pull-down menus. The interface and software appear and perform identically on both Macintosh and Windows platforms.

The publisher also provides collections of award-winning multimedia resources, bundled and integrated with *MP Express,* in so-called Multimedia Production Kits. The first of these bundled production kits, released in 1997, was the multiple-award-winning product, *MP Express on the Brink,* which combined *MP Express* with more than 700 pictures, movies, sounds, and music tracks focusing on 56 endangered mammal and bird species of North America, including their habitats. This production kit developed awareness of endangered species and environmental issues. A recent production kit called *MP Express: The Pacific Rim* (Fig. 14.14) features hundreds of multime-

FIGURE 14.14   MP Express: The Pacific Rim
Used with permission of Bytes of Learning Inc.

dia resources, including live-action movies, pictures, backgrounds, music scores, and sounds. This kit also contains teaching ideas and information on Pacific Rim culture, language, religion, and population. With each *MP Express* production kit, students can readily research, write, create, and present multimedia presentations, electronic projects for the next millennium.

Create Together

Create Together (Bytes of Learning) is a multimedia authoring system (Fig. 14.15) which uses wizards to help users through different types of "fill in the blank" templates, including encyclopedias, interactive games, and hyperlinked or

FIGURE 14.15
Create Together
Used with permission of
Bytes of Learning Inc.

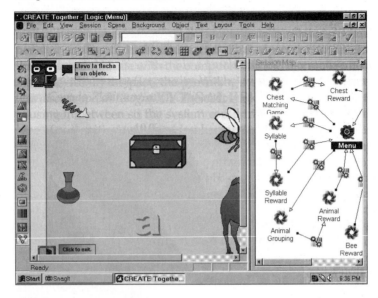

linear presentations. If you want to create these presentations from scratch, you can use the scalable tool sets to make a powerful multimedia presentations. *Create Together* lets you work with other individuals on any network, including the Internet. The user then exports the finished interactive projects to the Web with a click of the button. There is a large collection of clip resources included, and this program works with *MP Express* resource CDs and other multimedia resource sets.

MovieWorks

MovieWorks (Visions Technology in Education) has all the tools that you need to create *QuickTime* movies, videos, and multimedia presentations. This program (Fig. 14.16) has an easy-to-use drag-and-drop interface. The user sim-

FIGURE 14.16
MovieWorks
Used by permission of
Visions Technology in
Education.

ply drags the object on the slide. You can easily combine text, graphics, animation, sound, and video. There is a full palette of tools for adding text and customizing background and original art. You can capture, edit, and create 16-bit, 44 kHz CD-audio-quality soundtracks. You can add movement to your multimedia productions. The linear projects that are created in *MovieWorks* can play from start to finish without buttons. A project can include any combination and any number of objects, that is, text, video, picture, graphic, animation, sound (music or narration), virtual reality, and 3-D. A rendering engine reduces file sizes for delivery over the Internet. There is also powerful video editing feature, which includes analog and digital video capture, transitions, effects, and autosequencing.

Video Editing

Video editing occurs when a user integrates multimedia elements such as text, video, and audio into a presentation and then changes these elements to improve their appearance. Video editing lets the user edit the existing media and get rid of unnecessary parts of the audio or video, record dialog, add video and audio transitions such as fades, and create a more finished product. *Adobe Premiere* is a video editing package that is full-featured but daunting for the beginner. However, several companies have been creating easy-to-use video editing applications for the classroom. Apple's *iMovie2* (Fig. 14.17)

FIGURE 14.17 iMovie2

is a relatively simple to use digital video editing software application that works on the new Macintosh computers. This program has convenient pull-down menus and icons that represent familiar tools and objects. It gives the student the ability to cut and paste video clips. In addition to these programs, there are programs like Ulead's *Video Studio* and Digital Origin's *IntroDV*, a less complicated version of its more professional package, *EditDV*. The video edit program uses a time-line or storyboard interface. For the time-line interface the student lays out the video clips over time. A longer clip is shown across a longer section of the time line either by a rectangular labeled strip or a string of pictures. The storyboard interface lets the user order and reorder video clips by dragging and dropping.

When working on video, it is important to have good storage and also a fast way to transfer data. FireWire, a high-speed serial bus or pathway, lets the user connect up to 63 devices at speeds ranging from 100 to 400 Mbits/sec. Shortly, FireWire will be widely used for attaching digital cameras and other devices to the computer (Freedman, 2001).

Kid Pix Deluxe 3

Kid Pix Deluxe 3, for grades K–8, lets the students produce slide shows and presentations. The new edition of this program has a simplified interface. Students can express themselves with voice painting, photo editing with special effects, and art tools like chalk or magic markers that have realistic sound effects. Also included in this package are digital storybooks, comic books, e-mail drawings and projects, and multimedia movies. Figure 14.18 shows a slide

FIGURE 14.18
Kid Pix Deluxe 3

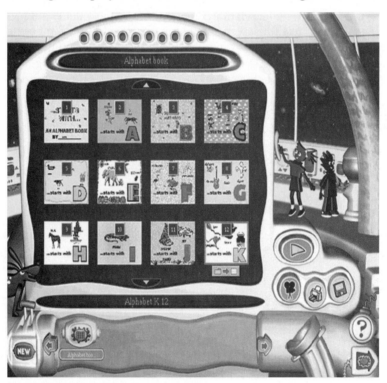

presentation in *Kid Pix*. Notice there are picture buttons underneath which the student presses to print, hear, or save the slide show. To run this show, the student presses the lever located at the bottom of left of the screen. The younger student can easily express himself or herself using this product.

PowerPoint

Finally, *PowerPoint* (Microsoft), a more advanced presentation tool for high school to adult levels, lets users turn ideas into powerful presentations. The program has instant layouts, on-screen directions, and tool tips that let users make compelling multimedia presentations. With *PowerPoint*, users can create overheads for class presentations (Fig. 14.19), slides for a meeting, or daz-

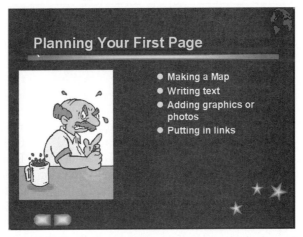

**FIGURE 14.19
PowerPoint 2001**
Box shot reprinted with permission from Microsoft Corporation.

zling effects for an on-screen presentation. Furthermore, a complete set of easy-to-use tools help with the creations. To help users learn it quickly, the product offers prompts, tips, and cue cards along with wizards, templates, and autolayouts. An alternative to buying a separate program like *PowerPoint* is to purchase an integrated package like *AppleWorks*.

AppleWorks

AppleWorks 6 not only has word processor, database, spreadsheet, and drawing and painting modules, but it also has a presentation module. Using the presentation component, users can display the slides on a computer or print them on transparencies. After the transparences are created, they can be displayed on an overhead projector. *AppleWorks* can include *QuickTime* movies and sounds, use visual transitions between slides, and set playing options for the slide. In Figure 14.20 the students have created a slide show on "Web Sites

**FIGURE 14.20
*AppleWorks 6.0***
Copyright © Apple Computer, Inc. All rights reserved.

and Resources for Teachers." Economically, *AppleWorks* is a real find, because of its other components.

Multimedia Formats

All the popular computer magazines mention **QuickTime** or **QuickTime Virtual Reality (VR)** as important formats of multimedia. Other recent and key features include **morphing** and **warping**.

QuickTime

Apple was the first to integrate motion video into its operating system when *QuickTime* was incorporated into Mac OS's System 7. The Windows options are presently called *Audio–Video Interleaved* (AVI) and *QuickTime for Windows* (Freedman, 2001). *QuickTime* is an extension of the Macintosh system software that lets an application display miniature motion picture sequences in a screen window. A *QuickTime* file can contain all kinds of digital media. You can stuff large digital audio and video files into *QuickTime* and use that data in various applications. Any application that is compatible with *QuickTime* can play video, sound, and animation within its program. *QuickTime* is also used on the Web to provide Web pages with animation and video. *QuickTime* lets the user create, edit, publish, and view multimedia content.

The major advantage of these digital files is that no special hardware is required to play the videos for any of these formats. However, there are problems with this software solution. The video quality is low resolution and the viewing window is small. Additionally, the quickness of video playback is dependent on the computer used. Generally, the playback occurs at only about one-half of the normal speed of the computer. Another drawback is the large video file size required to transport and store these files. Presently, a huge amount of hard disk storage space is required to accommodate these large file sizes, although the software developers are working to improve compression ratios to produce a file size more reasonable for typical hard disk capacities. Many users are purchasing Zip, CD-RW, and Jaz drives to hold their work in order to have enough space. Many of these criticisms are answered by *QuickTime 5* (Apple), which improves the compression rate of these multimedia files, has better quality video and audio, and has quick playback.

QuickTime VR

QuickTime VR, an extension of *QuickTime*, lets the user view on-screen in 3-D space. The scenes are created from renderings or multiple still shots taken at all sides. *QuickTime VR* has pushed technology to new heights. Using this extension, the developer can create photorealistic 3-D shots based not on video clips, but on images that are fastened together into one continuous file. Thus, computer users are able to see 360 degrees around an object, with seamless pan and zoom abilities. Users are able to designate an item or items in a scene as buttons that invite interactivity. The first product that used this technology was *Star Trek: The Next Generation Interactive Technical Manual*. Some current programs that use *QuickTime VR* are *Oregon Trail IV* (The Learning Company), *HyperStudio 4.0*

(Knowledge Adventure), and *MovieWorks* (Visions Technology in Education). Students may be able to use VR to create walkthrough presentations of their school or sites of interest.

Morphing

Morphing programs animate a picture sequence by gradually blending one image into another. An example of morphing is the shape-shifting security guard in *Star Trek: Deep Space Nine* or the evil terminator in *Terminator 2: Judgment Day.* I used *Morph Version 2.5,* a program by Gryphon, to morph a picture of my son, David, at 5 years old into a picture of him at 10 years old. This five-second video clip shows his transformation over the five-year period. Figure 14.21 shows four still pictures from this transition.

FIGURE 14.21
Morph Version 2.5
Used by permission of Knowledge Adventure/Havas Interactive.

The morphing software accomplishes the smooth transformation by matching a series of central points set in the beginning image to the ending image. In my short film, I selected the nose in the first image as a central point to be matched to the location of the nose in the last image. I kept adding these central points until the important features such as the mouth, eyes, ears, and head shape were charted. When the points are established, the morphing software sends the dots that are charted in the beginning image to their final location in the ending image, blending their shapes and colors.

The more points you add in morphing, the smoother the transition from one figure to the other. The traditional animation techniques that were perfected in the 1940s required 30 to 35 hand-drawn images to animate a figure for a single second on the screen. Today, a morphing program relieves artists from performing this type of tedious detailed work and also generates a remarkable effect.

Warping

Warping is a completely different type of special effect from morphing. In warping, the key points of one image are used to create an effect that does not involve the blending of two images. By adjusting these main points, you push the selected points of the original image into a different shape. The final production stretches the shape into an image that is completely different from the original one. For example, a rounded human face could be stretched into a narrow face, pointed jaw, and bulging eyes. In the movie *The Mask,* warping was used to stretch Jim Carrey's face whenever he put on the mask.

The *Mona Lisa*'s face in Figure 14.22 is warped using *Kai's Power Goo* (Corel). This program lets the user create liquid images and manipulate them by

FIGURE 14.22 Kai's Power Goo

Used with permission from MetaCreations Corporation formerly MetaTools.

smearing, smudging, stretching, and fusing them. You can superimpose these images and blend parts of one image with another to create a third image.

As motivational devices, morphing and warping have some practical classroom applications. Students can experiment with different images and then copy and paste them to illustrate a story or report. They can create a morphed movie or warped picture for a hypermedia presentation. For example, students might show cell division or plant growth by morphing different pictures together. They might morph pictures of their parents to create new offspring or pictures of themselves and their grandparents to see how they might age.

Virtual Reality

The supreme achievement in multimedia is **virtual reality (VR).** Many authorities in the field consider William Gibson's depiction of cyberspace in his book *Neuromancer* to be the ultimate example of VR. In this book, cyberspace is described as the sum of all interconnected telecommunication networks in this future world (Gibson, 1984). People used this network by plugging their minds into it. A more down-to-earth explanation of VR is a three-dimensional, interactive simulation. Participants in a computer-generated VR environment can manipulate what they see around them.

Historical Perspective

The predecessor of virtual reality was Edward Link's flight simulator. In 1929, he built a carnival ride that enabled passengers to feel as if they were flying a real airplane. This particular ride developed into the flight simulators that are currently used for training aviators. In the 1960s, Morton Heilig created the Sensorama arcade simulator, another predecessor of VR. The Sensorama arcade simulator used sound, motion, images, and even smell to give spectators in this motorcycle ride the feeling that they were experiencing a ride through Brooklyn, New York. In 1965, Ivan Sutherland created a head-mounted computer graphics display that tracked the head movements of the user. The person wearing this device could view simulations shown in graphic frames. Two years later, Frederick Brooks explored force feedback, which "directs physical pressure or force through a user interface to the user so that he or she can feel computer-simulated forces" (Eddings, 1994). In the early 1970s, Nolan Bushnell introduced the popular electronic arcade game Pong, in which players played Ping-Pong against each other or against the game. Although the game seems incredibly simple today, its interactivity was an important development in the field of virtual reality. Finally, Ames Research Center at NASA developed low-cost VR equipment. Because of this development, VR companies such as VPL Research began the ongoing commercial production of virtual reality hardware and software.

How Virtual Reality Works

In VR, users are electronically immersed in a simulated environment, in which they use their sight, hearing, and touch in all three dimensions. The purpose is not only to enter this world but to manipulate it. Participants wear headgear in which computer-generated images are sent to small screens placed before their eyes and to headphones in their ears. The headgear permits users to block out all actual stimuli to concentrate solely on the simulated stimuli. Participants also wear gloves or bodysuits equipped with sensors that communicate changes in body position to the computer, which then communicates the changes to the headgear (Fig. 14.23).

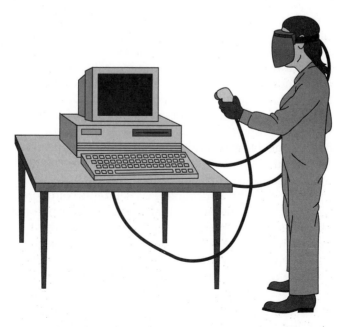

FIGURE 14.23
Virtual Reality Equipment

Let's consider an example. Imagine that you are entering a simulation of the Tate Gallery. You look into one of the exhibit rooms. All around you are paintings and sculptures. As you turn your head, the screens in your headgear adjust to show you what you would be seeing in the actual gallery. If you walk forward, the screens will change again to simulate your movement. As you approach the security guard to ask her a question, her voice becomes louder and louder in your headphones. When you raise your hand to point at one of the paintings, you see a simulated hand on your headgear screen. When you pick up one of the sculptures to examine it from different angles, the screen shows your hands and the different views of the sculpture, and your headphones transmit the angry voice of the security guard.

Virtual reality has found its way into research labs, business, the dentist's office, the military, and video arcade games. In some video games, you direct the action of the game with the movements of your own body, wearing headgear, gloves, and a bodysuit. In 1994, the first virtual reality wedding took place in a computer simulation of the lost city of Atlantis. The couple, Monika Liston and Hugh Jo, was married at the CyberMind Virtual Reality Center in San Francisco, where Liston works. The bridegroom, bride, and minister wore helmets with small built-in eye-level monitors; handheld controllers allowed them to move their virtual reality parts. Guests could view the ceremony on three large TV screens (Snider, 1994). Fakerspace Systems' CAVE products are now used to simulate a virtual reality environment in order to test the design of a new building or learn how to operate a Caterpillar bulldozer. This virtual reality system uses projectors to display images on three or four walls and the floor. Special glasses make everything appear as 3-D images and also track the path of the user's vision (Freedman, 2001).

In education, virtual reality's potential has yet to be explored. What is certain is that this potential is tremendously exciting; virtual reality technology will let students more fully interact with information being presented in all subject areas. Physically disabled students would benefit from VR by being able to immerse themselves physically in different environments. Students and teachers would be able to conduct experiments and experience situations that otherwise might be too costly or dangerous. Imagine networking an educational virtual reality system worldwide in real time. It would be a wonderful way to foster positive interaction among people of different cultures. Consider the usefulness of a virtual reality tour of London. Or your students could don helmets and fly the first spaceship to the moon or enter the human bloodstream to look at the heart.

In a physical education class, students could use a simulation to practice baseball against an all-star baseball player. In a science class, they could explore the laws of physics in a virtual world by testing how changes in gravitational forces affect virtual objects. In a language arts class, students could be visited by a virtual Mark Twain who could talk to them about his books and even answer the students' questions. A student violinist might even practice with the world's finest virtual orchestra and receive individualized tutoring. These are but a few of the options that will be available to educators in the near future. The biggest impediment to this advancement in technology is cost. A smaller concern is the problematic weight of the necessary equipment. Still, a future with virtual reality holds much promise for educators.

Multimedia Software

Floppy disk programs are the technology of the past; software now is packaged in the form of CD-ROMs that hold 650 MB or more of data. The CD-ROM will disappear shortly and be replaced by the DVD (see Chapter 3), a CD-ROM cousin. This disc is capable of storing 17 GB of data, the equivalent of 25 CD-ROM discs.

As evidenced by the software catalogs, almost every software program incorporates some form of multimedia. In fact, just about every program mentioned in this book has some multimedia elements. Let us examine three of these programs and discover what makes them particularly useful in a classroom setting.

Multimedia visual mapping programs like *Inspiration* for students in grade 4 to adult (see Chapter 12) and *Kidspiration* (Inspiration Software) for students in grades K–3 are perfect for planning a multimedia presentation. Students use these visual learning tools to create stories, organize information, understand concepts, and express and share their ideas. Figure 14.24 shows a

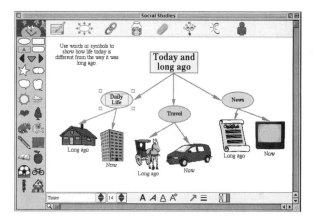

FIGURE 14.24
Kidspiration
Used by permission of
Inspiration Software, Inc.

student representing ideas through symbols. The student can then turn these symbols into outline form.

The Scholastic series programs *What's the Big Idea Ben Franklin?*, *Where Do You Think You're Going, Christopher Columbus?*, and *Shh! We're Writing the Constitution!* are based on books by popular award-winning authors. The CD-ROMs are a wonderful way to explore social studies themes as required for the National Social Studies Curriculum Standards. Each program has a "Learning Cube" for the main menu. From this cube, you go to any of the chapters in the book. Students can see and hear lessons on entertaining videos or take audiovisual side trips with the "Video Explorer." Each lesson has three games that help check and reinforce what the student has learned.

General reference tools such as *2001 Grolier Multimedia Encyclopedia* can address any area of the curriculum. Using this tool students have access to such items as multimedia maps, pictures, videos, animation, sound, and time lines. Users are able to access audiovisual essays that combine photos, music, and narration to give a comprehensive overview of subjects such as the human body or space exploration. The motion videos feature sequences of memorable events such as Dr. Martin Luther King Jr.'s "I Have a Dream" speech. A time line lets students travel along a continuum from prehistoric times to the present.

You can see from this discussion that current computer programs have come a very long way from the static drill and practice programs of the 1970s. These new programs push technology to new heights with their multimedia features and their lifelike animations. In fact, maybe we have traveled too far in the direction of emphasizing multimedia over content. **Appendix A is an annotated listing of award-winning software programs.**

Classroom Lesson Plans

The following five ready-to-use lessons show some of the creative ways you can use multimedia software in the classroom.

▼   I. English   ▼

Objective

Students will learn how to visually map their life using a software program like *Kidspiration* or *Inspiration* (Fig. 14.25).

FIGURE 14.25
Inspiration 6.0
Used by permission of
Inspiration Software, Inc.

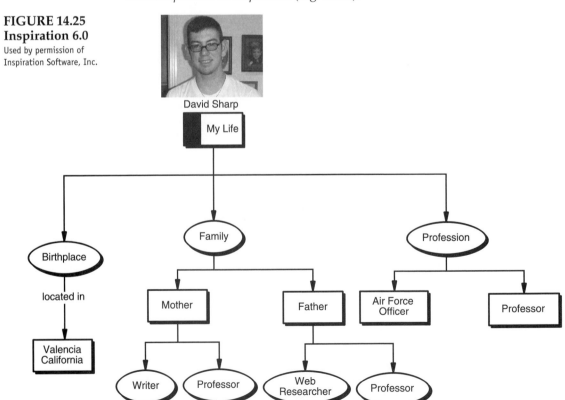

Procedure

1. Have the students write about themselves, their friends, their families, and their future goals.
2. Let the students take digital pictures of themselves, use the scanner to scan pictures they already have, and bring in clip art for their autobiography.
3. Have the students work in teams to experiment with *Kidspiration* or *Inspiration.*
4. Next, let each student use *Kidspiration* or *Inspiration* to create a visual map about her or his life.

Variation

As a variation, you could have the students write about what they will be doing 10 years from now. They can take digital pictures of themselves and change them to make themselves appear older.

▼ II. Science ▼

Objective

Students will learn how to work with a software program like *HyperStudio, PowerPoint, MovieWorks,* or *MP Express* and create a stack in some subject area.

Procedure

1. Divide the students into small groups.
2. Have each group choose an animal to read about and research.
3. Let the students go on the Internet to find information about this animal. They can copy pictures of their animal and download sounds.
4. The students should then plan their stack together.
5. Have the students in each group write a description of the animal, where it lives, enemies, reproduction, eating habits, and prospect for survival in the future.
6. Finally, tell the students to create their stacks and then have them share these stacks with the class.

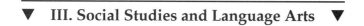

▼ III. Social Studies and Language Arts ▼

Objective

Students will use a software program like *HyperStudio, PowerPoint, MovieWorks, MP Express,* or *Kid Pix Deluxe 3* to create a presentation about a country they would like to visit.

Procedure

1. Divide the students into small groups.
2. Have each group choose a country they would like to visit.
3. Have the students work in groups to research this country, finding about the country's climate, people, money, language, and famous sites. They can go on the Internet or use books from the library.
4. After this task is completed, the students should create an itinerary for their country.
5. Using the Internet, the students should find out the cost of hotels and airline tickets.
6. Next, the students should plan their stack together, collecting pictures of their country, and downloading sounds and movies.
7. Using a multimedia software program like *MovieWorks*, the students should now create their stacks.
8. When the stacks are finished, the students should showcase these stacks with the class.

▼   IV. Math   ▼

Objective

Students will use a software program like *HyperStudio*, *PowerPoint*, *MovieWorks*, *MP Express*, or *Kid Pix Deluxe 3* to create a stack that illustrates mathematical terms such as *fractions* and *percent* (Fig. 14.26).

**FIGURE 14.26
HyperStudio 4.0**
Used by permission of
Knowledge Adventure/Havas
Interactive.

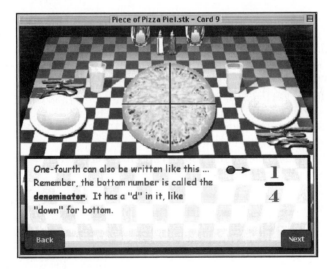

Procedure

1. Divide the students into small groups.
2. Have each group devise a definition for each mathematical term.

3. Next, the students should plan their stack together, collecting pictures and downloading sounds.
4. Using a multimedia software program like *HyperStudio,* the students should now create their stacks.
5. When the stacks are finished, the students should share these stacks with the class.

▼   V. Social Studies   ▼

Objective

Students will use a software program like *HyperStudio, PowerPoint, MovieWorks, MP Express,* or *Kid Pix Deluxe 3* to create a stack about famous generals of the Civil War.

Procedure

1. Divide the students into small groups.
2. Have each group choose a general.
3. Have the students work in groups to research this general, finding out about his life. They can go on the Internet or use books from the library or a multimedia encyclopedia.
4. After this task is completed, the students should create an outline.
5. Next, the students should plan their presentation together, collecting pictures, and downloading sounds and movies.
6. Using a multimedia software program like *MovieWorks,* the students should now create their presentations.
7. When the presentations are finished, the students should present their work to the class.

Summary

We discussed the origins of hypermedia and defined *hypermedia* as use of a computer to input, manipulate, and output graphics, sound, text, and audio in the presentation of information. We learned how hypermedia authoring tools such as *HyperStudio, MovieWorks,* and *MP Express* operate and how they may be used as tools for instruction. We examined some of the unique multimedia software, the special effects that are available for the classroom, and some suggested activities for multimedia software. In the process, you were given five practical lessons for activities that you could use in the classroom. We presented a checklist for evaluating a multimedia presentation and some guidelines for creating a presentation.

Appendix A features an annotated list of multimedia software.

MULTIMEDIA SITES

What follows is an annotated list of Internet sites on multimedia. These sites include a wide range of materials—lesson plans and pictures that can be printed, online multimedia presentations for students, and many other resources that can enrich the K–12 curriculum.

McGraw-Hill School Division
http://www.mmhschool.com/

This K–8 educational publisher of textbooks

and multimedia software provides Web-linked lesson plans for all major subject areas.

Math Forum's Internet Mathematics Library
http://forum.swarthmore.edu/library/
resource_types/software/
The Math Forum provides a comprehensive collection of sites offering downloadable material and software to enhance the teaching of K–12 math.

Compton's Encyclopedia Online
http://www.comptons.com/encyclopedia/
The Learning Company, an educational software publisher, provides an electronic version of latest edition of *Compton's Encyclopedia*. It contains full text of over 37,000 articles, multimedia entries, cross-reference links, over 1,000 pictures, and MIDI and other sound files.

SafeKids.Com
http://safekids.com/
Larry Magid's site provides a safe-surfing haven for software, videos, links, and other multimedia resources. To find these resources, scroll to the safety quiz and click on links and safe searching below the online quiz.

Searchopolis
http://www.searchopolis.com/
N2H2's *Searchopolis* lets you search for thousands of filtered educational websites including multimedia resources. By entering "multimedia resources," you'll find Sun site's fine art site, Professor Brian Smith's guide to multimedia educational materials, and many other multimedia references for grades K–12.

Multimedia Physics Studios
http://www.glenbrook.k12.il.us/gbssci/
phys/mmedia/
Tom Henderson of Glenbrook South High School in Illinois provides a collection of GIF animations with accompanying explanations of major physics concepts. The animations cover common physics principles discussed in a first-year high school physics course.

ExploreMath.com
http://exploremath.com/

This site offers free course pages for teachers and multimedia mathematical activities for students studying algebra, geometry, and other high school math subjects.

SimScience
http://simscience.org/
SimScience provides multimedia learning modules using computer simulations for grades K–12. It covers the science topics membranes, fluid flow, cracking dams, and crackling noise.

SRA
http://sra-4kids.com/
SRA, a division of the McGraw-Hill, provides teachers with hundreds of curriculum-aligned websites and multimedia demonstrations and students with websites, interactive math games, and science animations.

African Studies Center
http://www.africa.upenn.edu/
The African Studies Center at the University of Pennsylvania provides a wide variety of K–12 multimedia resources for exploring the historic and cultural diversity of sub-Saharan African people.

BBC Schools Online
http://www.bbc.co.uk/education/schools/
BBC offers a wealth of online multimedia resources in reading, math, history, and other subject areas for primary, middle, and high school students. To find other interactive activities, be sure to visit the Education and the Learning Zone links.

The Library of Congress
http://www.loc.gov/help/about.html
The U.S. government's Library of Congress provides a wealth of multimedia materials from America's Story to American Memory sites to enrich the K–12 social studies curriculum.

Harcourt Brace School Publishers Learning Site
http://www.harcourtschool.com/
Click on the site map to find a wealth of interactive activities for grades 1–8, including an animated math glossary as well as a multiplication mystery.

Inspiration Software
http://inspiration.com/
Inspiration Software is a visual idea development tool that creates and updates diagrams, flow charts, and other concept maps for educational purposes.

Garth's KidStuff
http://garthskidstuff.com/
Garth Upshaw is the developer of *MaskWorld*, a CD-ROM with creative multimedia activities about myths and masks from the world and people around them.

Children's Educational Software
http://smartkidssoftware.com/
Children's Educational Software sells a great number of K–12 multimedia products online.

Kid Pix
http://www.kidpix.com/html_net/kid_index.html
The Learning Company provides information about its multimedia *Kid Pix* software. The site includes an online painting program.

HyperStudio
http://hyperstudio.com/
Knowledge Adventure provides information about *HyperStudio* software, multimedia-authoring tools enabling students to create interactive reports by mixing digital sources such as clip art, text, photos, video, sounds, animation, and narration. The site includes a showcase section where you can share and view other projects, discussion forums where you can learn more about this hypermedia program, and free training materials.

Jac-Cen-Del Elementary
http://laughery.buddy.k12.in.us/
The Jac-Cen-Del Elementary school in Osgood, Indiana, showcases student-created projects (classroom activities) that use different multimedia software. To learn about other schools integrating software in the classroom, visit Buddy Picks.

Interactive Solutions' MovieWorks
http://www.movieworks.com/
MovieWorks software, developed by Interactive Solutions, is a tool for making a *QuickTime* movie, video, or multimedia presentation.

Leonardo Software
http://leonardosoft.com/
Leonardo Software offers over 100,000 sound effects from aardvarks to zeppelins on compact disc.

Microsoft PowerPoint
http://microsoft.com/office/powerpoint/
Microsoft PowerPoint is a software tool for creating presentations, organizing and formatting your materials, illustrating your points with images or clip art, and showcasing your presentations over the Web. The site includes how-to articles, tips and tricks, as well as support services.

Yahoo! Music
http://musicfinder.yahoo.com/downloads/listen_genres/
Yahoo! Music offers hundreds of streaming audio and video downloads.

Listen.com
http://listen.com/
Listen.com is your guide to online music, offering reviews and links to music by more than 160,000 artists in 500 genres. The site helps you find the music of your favorite artist and every type of music on the Internet, including legal downloadable files such as MP3s and streaming audio and video.

Apple's iMovie
http://apple.com/imovie/
Apple provides information about its *iMovie* software for making desktop movies.

Chapter Mastery Test

To the Instructor: Refer to the Instructor's Manual for the Answers to the Mastery Questions. This manual has additional questions and resource materials.

Let's check for chapter comprehension with a short mastery test. Following are basic terms, classroom projects, and suggested readings and references.

1. What is hypermedia?
2. What are two advantages of using your own authoring tool for a hypermedia presentation?
3. Who invented *HyperCard* and why was it so revolutionary?
4. Define the following hypermedia terms: cards, stacks, and buttons. Give an example of each.
5. What is the major disadvantage of using programs such as *HyperStudio* or *Leonardo's Multimedia Toolbox*?
6. Discuss how you would use the button function in a *HyperStudio* or *PowerPoint* program.
7. In preparing your multimedia presentation for class, name two mistakes that you want to avoid when you produce the final product.
8. If you were to evaluate a multimedia presentation, what criteria would you use and why?
9. Describe a multimedia program for each of the following subject areas: social studies, language arts, science, music, and mathematics. Use Appendix A to help you with your selection.
10. If you were to buy two multimedia programs, which two would you choose? What are the reasons for your choices?
11. Discuss the advantages and disadvantages of multimedia productions in the school setting.
12. Define virtual reality and discuss some of its implications.
13. Explain how morphing and warping work.
14. What is a video digitizer?

Basic Terms

buttons (p. 367)	*QuickTime* (p. 382)
cards (p. 367)	*QuickTime VR* (p. 382)
HyperCard (p. 366)	stacks (p. 366)
hypermedia (p. 364)	video editing (p. 379)
hypertext (p. 364)	virtual reality (VR) (p. 384)
morphing (p. 382)	warping (p. 382)
multimedia (p. 363)	

Classroom Projects

1. Learn a hypermedia application (such as *HyperStudio, HyperCard,* or *MP Express*) and write a short report describing its strengths and weaknesses.
2. Explain a mathematical concept by generating your own slide show, using software such as *Kid Pix Deluxe 3*.
3. Tape record an interview on some important topic. Write a script using the

speaker's words and add your own synchronized sound effects. Using one of the hypermedia authoring tools, create a presentation from this interview.

4. Record an interesting event or trip with a camcorder and combine this with animation, speech, and music, using one or more of the software programs discussed in this chapter.

Suggested Readings and References

Adams, P. E. "Hypermedia in the Classroom Using Earth and Space Science CD-ROMs." *Journal of Computers in Mathematics and Science Teaching* 15, no. 1–2 (1996): 19–34.

Bagui, S. "Reasons for Increased Learning Using Multimedia." *Journal of Educational Multimedia and Hypermedia* 7, no. 1 (1998): 3–18.

Baker, Richard L., and Michael C. Blue. "The Cost-Effective Multimedia Classroom." *T.H.E. Journal* 27, no. 1 (August 1999): 46.

Bornman, H., and S. H. von Solms. "Hypermedia, Multimedia, and Hypertext—Definitions and Overview." *Electronic Library* 11, no. 4–5 (1993): 259–68.

Boyle, T. *Design for Multimedia Learning.* London: Prentice Hall, 1997.

Brewer, Stephen. "Software." *Family PC* 7, no. 7 (July 2000): 72.

Brownstein, Mark. "Batter Up for Broadband." *Byte Special Report,* October 1997, pp. 71–74.

Bruder, Isabelle. "Multimedia—How It Changes the Way We Teach and Learn." *Electronic Learning* 11, no. 1 (September 1991): 22–26.

Brunner, C. "Judging Student Multimedia." *Electronic Learning* 15, no. 6 (1996): 14–15.

Buckleitner, Warren. "Classrooms without Walls." *Instructor (1999)* 110, no. 2 (September 2000): 91.

Bull, Glen, Gina Bull, and Aileen Nonis. "Intent Scripting with HyperStudio." *Learning and Leading with Technology* 24, no. 8 (May 1997) 40–43.

Carr, Tracy, and Asha K. Jitendra. "Using Hypermedia and Multimedia to Promote Project-Based Learning of At-Risk High School Students." *Intervention in School and Clinic* 36, no. 1 (September 2000): 40.

Cates, Ward Mitchell, and Susan C. Goodling. "The Relative Effectiveness of Learning Options in Multimedia Computer-Based Fifth-Grade Spelling Instruction." *Educational Technology Research and Development* 45, no. 2 (1997): 27–46.

Cochran, David, and Robb Staats. *HyperStudio Express 3.1.* New York: Glencoe/McGraw-Hill, 1999.

Dede, Christopher J. "The Future of Multimedia: Bridging to Virtual World." *Educational Technology* 32, no. 5 (May 1992): 54–60.

Dede, Christopher. "Making the Most of Multimedia." *Multimedia and Learning: A School Leaders Guide.* Alexandria, Va.: NSBA, 1994.

D'Ignazio, Fred. "A New Curriculum Paradigm: The Fusion of Technology, the Arts, and Classroom Instruction." *Computing Teacher,* April 1991, pp. 45–48.

D'Ignazio, Fred, and Joanne Davis. "What I Did Last Summer 21st Century Style." *Learning and Leading with Technology* 24, no. 8 (May 1997): 44–47.

Dillon, A., and R. Gabbard. "Hypermedia as an Educational Technology: A Review of the Quantitative Research Literature on Learner Comprehension, Control, and Style." *Review of Educational Research* 68, no. 3 (1998): 322–49.

Eddings, Joshua. *How Virtual Reality Works.* Emeryville, Calif.: Ziff-Davis Press, 1994.

Fiderio, Janet. "Grand Vision." *Byte* 13, no. 10 (October 1, 1988): 237–42.

Finkel, LeRoy. *Technology Tools in the Information Age Classroom.* Wilsonville, Ore.: Franklin Beedle and Associates, 1991.

Fleck, Tim, et al. *HyperStudio for Terrified Teachers.* Huntington Beach, Calif.: Teacher Created Materials, 1997.

Florio, Chris, and Michael Murie. "Authoritative Authoring: Software That Makes Multimedia Happen." *NewMedia* 6, no. 12 (September 9, 1996): 67–70, 72–75.

Freedman, Alan. *Computer Desktop Encyclopedia.* Point Pleasant, Pa.: The Computer Language Company, 2001.

Gates, Bill. "Multimedia Revolution Is Here. Life On-Line." *Gainesville* (Florida) *Sun,* May 15, 1995, p. 7.

Gibson, William. *Neuromancer.* New York: Ace Books, 1984.

Gratton, Marilyn. *Microsoft Powerpoint 2000: One Step at a Time.* New York: IDG Books Worldwide, 2000.

Guglielmo, Connie. "Multimedia Makers Get Point, Click." *Macweek* 5, no. 18 (May 1991): 22.

Hoffman, Joseph L., and David J. Lyons. "Evaluating Instructional Software." *Learning and Leading with Technology* 25, no. 2 (October 1997): 52–53.

Holsinger, Erik. *How Multimedia Works.* Emeryville, Calif.: Ziff-Davis Press, 1994.

HyperStudio Multimedia Journal. Simtech, Inc. (HyperStudio Network).

Johnson, Stuart J. "Multimedia: Myth vs. Reality." *InfoWorld* 12, no. 8 (February 19, 1990): 47–52.

Lifter, M., S. I. Kessler, M. Adams, and J. Patterson. *Multimedia Projects for Kid Pix.* Bloomington, Ill.: Family Time Computing, 1998.

Lu, Gang, Hongwen Wan, and Shouying Liu. "Hypermedia and Its Application in Education." *Educational Media International* 36, no. 1 (March 1999): 41–45.

Marchionini, G. "Hypermedia and Learning: Freedom and Chaos." *Educational Technology* 28, no. 11 (1988): 8–12.

Mayer, Richard E. "Multimedia Aids to Problem-Solving Transfer." *International Journal of Educational Research* 31, no. 7 (1999): 611–23.

McBride, Karen, and Elizabeth DeBoer Luntz. *Help! I Have HyperStudio. Now What Do I Do?* Eugene, Ore.: Visions Technology in Education, 2001.

Milheim, William D. "Virtual Reality and Its Potential Application in Education and Training." *Machine-Mediated Learning* 5, no. 1 (1995): 43–55.

Milligan, Patrick, and Chris Okon. "Mastering Multimedia." *MacUser,* October 1994, pp. 82–88.

Milton, Karen, and Pattie Spradley. "A Renaissance of the Renaissance—Using HyperStudio for Research Projects." *Learning and Leading with Technology* 23, no. 6 (March 1996): 20–22.

Monahan, Susan, and Dee Susong. "Author Slide Shows and Texas Wildlife: Thematic Multimedia Projects." *Learning and Leading with Technology* 24, no. 2 (October 1996): 6–11.

Moran, Tom. "QuickTime VR: A New Spin." *MacWorld,* October 1994, pp. 34–35.

Needleman, Raphael. " 'Action' Takes the Pain Out of Creating Presentations." *InfoWorld* 13, no. 32 (August 12, 1991): 1, 91.

Nelson, Theodore H. *Dream Machines: New Freedoms through Computer Screens—A Minority Report.* Chicago: Hugo Books Service, 1974.

Olsen, Gary. *Getting Started in Multimedia Design.* Cincinnati: North Light Books, 1997.

Pfaffenberger, Bryan. *Webster's New World Dictionary of Computer Terms.* 8th ed. New York: IDG Books Worldwide, 2000.

Pfiffner, Pamela. "Welcome to QuickTime's Virtual Reality." *MacUser,* September 1994, p. 31.

Porter, Anne E. "Scavenged Idea and Virtual Hypermedia." *Computing Teacher,* May 1991, pp. 38–40.

Roblyer, M. D., J. Edward, and Mary Anne Havriluk. *Integrating Educational Technology into Teaching.* Upper Saddle River, N.J.: Prentice Hall, 1997.

Shapiro, Amy M. "Promoting Active Learning: The Role of System Structure in Learning from Hypertext." *Human–Computer Interaction* 13, no. 1 (1998): 1–35.

Sharp, Vicki. *HyperStudio 3.2 in an Hour (Windows and Macintosh Version).* Eugene, Ore.: ISTE, 1999.

Sharp, Vicki. *Make It with Inspiration.* Eugene, Ore.: Visions Technology in Education, 2000.

Sharp, Vicki. *Make It with Office (Macintosh and Windows Version).* Eugene, Ore.: Visions Technology in Education, 1999.

Sharp, Vicki. *PowerPoint 97 in an Hour (Windows Version).* Eugene, Ore.: ISTE, 1999.

Sharp, Vicki. *PowerPoint 98 in an Hour (Macintosh Version).* Eugene, Ore.: ISTE, 1999.

Smith, Irene, and Sharon Yoder. *Inside HyperStudio: Scripting with HyperLogo.* Eugene, Ore.: ISTE, 1997.

Snider, Mike. "In the Heart of Cyberspace." *USA Today,* August 19, 1994, p. 1.

Stamp, Dave, Bernie Roehl, and John Eagan. *Virtual Reality Creations.* Corte Madera, Calif.: Waite Group Press, 1994.

Stanford, Alan. "It's Time for Quicktime." *MacHome,* May 1998, pp. 18–20.

Stanton, Neville, and Chris Baber. "An Investigation of Styles and Strategies in Self-Directed Learning." *Journal of Educational Multimedia and Hypermedia* 1, no. 2 (1992): 147–67.

Stefananc, S., and L. Weiman. "Macworld Multimedia: Is It Real?" *MacWorld,* April 1990, pp. 116–23.

Swan, Karen; Meskill, Carla. "Using Hypermedia in Response-Based Literature Classrooms: A Critical Review of Commercial Applications." *Journal of Research on Computing in Education* 29, no. 2 (Winter 1996): 167–95.

Swartz, James D., and Tim Hatcher. "Virtual Experience: The Impact of Mediated Communication in a Democratic Society." *Educational Technology* 36, no. 6 (November–December 1996): 40–44.

Toomey, R., and K. Ketterer. "Using Multimedia as a Cognitive Tool." *Journal of Research on Computing in Education* 27, no. 4 (Summer 1995): 472–83.

Turner, S. V., and V. H. Dipinto. "Students as Hypermedia Author: Themes Emerging from a Qualitative Study." *Journal of Research on Computing Education* 25, no. 2 (1992): 187–99.

Vaughan, Tay. *Multimedia: Making It Work.* 4th ed. New York: Osborne McGraw-Hill, 1998.

Wagner, Nancy. "Get-Acquainted Slide Show." *Instructor (1999)* 110, no. 2 (September 2000): 28.

CHAPTER 15

Programming Languages

Using a Programming Language to Integrate the Computer into the Classroom

Did you know that learning programming can help students develop better organizational skills? Did you know that when students write a program they have to analyze a problem and show the solution by using a flowchart or algorithm? Programming can be used as another means of motivating students intellectually and developing computer literacy. By learning to program, students better understand the operation of computers and computer software. In addition, some students may develop an interest in programming and become professional programmers. Teachers or students can use a programming language such as Logo to create electronic portfolios, a program like *StageCast* to create multimedia learning games, and a program like *MicroWorlds* to create projects that incorporate movies, photos, sound, graphics, text, and animations. This chapter will provide suggestions on how the teacher can use programming in the classroom to help the students better accomplish their educational goals. You will be exposed to Internet sites that include information on computer programming, and lesson plans on how to use Logo in the classroom.

Objectives

Upon completing this chapter, you will be able to:

1. Trace some of the major developments in the history of programming languages;
2. Differentiate a low-level language from a high-level one;
3. Differentiate between a compiler and an interpreter;
4. Discuss Logo and use it to draw simple geometric shapes and patterns; and
5. Integrate programming into the classroom.

Programming

A controversy exists over whether teachers should be exposed to computer programming. Some authorities feel that programming teaches higher-order thinking and is the key to computer literacy (Jonassen, 1996, p. 228; Miller, 1999; Sarama, Clements, and Seidel, 1998). Students should have the opportunity to learn about the computer by controlling it. If teachers do not have the proper software, they can then write their own. Research has shown mixed results (Pea and Kurland, 1984; Vasu and Tyler, 1997; Woronov, 1994). Other experts feel that teachers are afraid enough of the computer, and programming is not necessary. Instead, the teachers should be shown how to integrate the computer into the classroom by using it as a tutor in subject areas such as language arts, math, and science. Furthermore, teachers should use the computer as a tool for word processing, databases, spreadsheets, drawing, and so on. Whatever position you take, it is important to learn what programming is and its origins. (See Chapter 16 for the research results on Logo programming.)

Flowcharts

The initial step in programming is the creation of a flowchart. A **flowchart** is a graphical representation of the sequence of operations in a program (Freedman, 2001). It uses symbols such as ovals, diamonds, and squares to represent different operation. These symbols are connected with lines and arrows (Fig. 15.1).

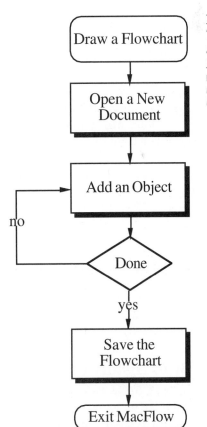

FIGURE 15.1
Top-Down Structure of a Flowchart
Reprinted by permission of Mainstay, publisher of Macflow.

After drawing a flowchart, you are ready to write a program following the flowchart's blueprint. To write any program, you use programming languages that range from BASIC to C++.

Programming Languages

A **program** is a sequence of instructions that informs the computer what tasks are to be performed. You must determine the order in which the computer is to perform these instructions. Programming languages are sequences of words, letters, numerals, and mnemonics that let you operate the computer. Each computer language has its own precise set of rules, syntax, and grammar that differ from those of ordinary language. Also, these rules and structures are rigid; in everyday language, a single word may have many meanings, but no ambiguity exists in a computer language. Each command can have only a single meaning.

Today, there are more than 400 computer languages, including their many dialects. These languages perform a variety of tasks; no one language fits all situations. You determine the language needed by asking: Can I easily use the language? Is the language available on the computer that I am using? Is the language appropriate for the situation?

In some situations, more than one language is appropriate. As different as the languages are, they all have a common base of high and low voltages represented by the 0s and 1s of the binary code. One combination of 0s and 1s, in which the 0 acts as an off switch and the 1 as an on switch, tells the computer to process the data immediately, while another combination tells the central processing unit (CPU) to add. The computer circuitry responds to a group of these commands and performs a variety of assignments.

A **machine language** program, composed of a pattern of 0s and 1s, is far removed from the language understood by human beings. Figure 15.2 shows

FIGURE 15.2
Machine Language

```
10100001 00000000 00000010
00000011 00000110 00000010 00000010
10100011 00000000 00000010
```

a small program written in machine language. This program instructs the computer to read the number stored in the memory address, to add it to the number already in the CPU, and to store the sum in a memory location. Since this abstract language involves a notational system for 0s and 1s, the programmer easily can err, preventing execution of the program.

Brief History of Computer Languages

In 1943, when Howard Aiken built the Mark I, machine language was the only language in existence. The Mark I received its instructions from punched-paper tape that technicians fed into the computer. Mauchly and

Eckert's famous Univac was more difficult to program because a group of technicians had to set thousands of switches and insert cables into the machine. Whenever a user wanted to change a program, he or she had to rewire the entire machine.

Because of the difficulty in using machine language, John Mauchly directed his programmers to develop a language that would let the computer user enter problems in a derived algebraic form. This symbolic language was an improvement over machine language because the programmer could now write a problem in mathematical terms and then use a table to convert it into a two-character code. For example, a plus was coded as *07*. Another computer program would then convert this code into the machine language of *0*s and *1*s. This conversion program was a rudimentary interpreter that translated the program into machine code.

This intermediate code became outdated; nevertheless, it was the first step in a long series of advances that gave the computer user the tools to write programs in a language other than machine language. In the early 1950s, Maurice Wilkes, an English mathematician, designed a computer called the EDSAC, which did not use a machine code but rather a system of mnemonics. Each time the programmer issued an instruction, it was given in the form of a capital letter. For instance, the letter *I* meant *read*. When the user typed this mnemonic on a special keyboard, the computer received the appropriate binary instruction.

Besides designing the symbols, the programmers devised a useful library of generalized subroutines for the EDSAC.[1] The programmers entered a short mnemonic command and the computer would automatically place the subroutine in the program. Wilkes called the subroutines and mnemonics an assembly system. The name *assembly system* still exists today: any language in which a mnemonic represents one machine instruction is called an **assembly language.**

Figure 15.3 shows an example of an assembly program. The top line instructs the CPU to move the contents from main memory into a memory lo-

```
MOV AX, TOTAL
ADD AX, VALUE
MOV TOTAL, AX
```

FIGURE 15.3
*Assembly
Program Sample*

cation named TOTAL and register AX. The next line tells the CPU to add the contents in memory to the contents of AX, and the bottom line instructs the CPU to move the contents to the main memory named TOTAL. This assembly language program produces the same output as the comparable machine language program in Figure 15.2.

---

[1]A subroutine is an independent program that the main program calls upon repeatedly.

Assembly language is cumbersome because of its mnemonic structure. Besides, assembly language is machine-specific, and a program written for one machine does not make sense on a different machine. Because of these drawbacks, prominent mathematicians such as Alan Turing and scientific researchers such as Alick Glennie helped develop high-level languages. A high-level language is more removed from the machine's operation and approximates human language, whereas low-level language is nearer the machine's operation.

In 1951, Grace Hopper and a team of programmers leaped a step by establishing a system capable of translating a program written in a high-level language. The compiler, or translating program, was faster than the line-by-line interpreters, because it could convert an entire program in one step. Hopper's compiler, named Autocode (A-O), was the first to be recognized throughout the world. In 1956, Hopper and her colleagues devised another compiler called the FLOW-MATIC, which permitted businesspeople to program in a language close to English. The market was now ready for high-level language development because compilers could translate entire high-level programs into machine code. Table 15.1 gives a thumbnail sketch of the major computer languages developed in the 1960s, 1970s, and 1980s.

FORTRAN

Shortly after Hopper's compiler, IBM researchers created the first high-level language, **FORTRAN,** an acronym for **for**mula **tran**slation, a language known for its ability to "crunch numbers." The FORTRAN team, headed by John Backus, a mathematician, created their new language with basic notations, for example, assignment statements like M=100. In addition, they added subscripted variables, which told the computer which item in a list of variables was needed. For example, X(5) told the computer "the fifth item in X's list." FORTRAN was easy to use and learn compared to previous languages. The essence of the language has remained about the same over the years. FORTRAN is found on minicomputers and mainframes, but it is not as common on a microcomputer.

Today, FORTRAN, with its capacity for number manipulation and formulas, is still a popular language among scientists, engineers, and mathematicians. Because the education community deals mostly in nonnumeric data, schools see no reason to teach FORTRAN.

Most subsequent languages were direct or indirect descendants of FORTRAN. After FORTRAN's introduction in 1954, COBOL (common business-oriented language), and ALGOL (algorithmetic language) were developed. FORTRAN, COBOL, and ALGOL are considered classic high-level languages, and modern computer languages are variations of these three.

COBOL

As FORTRAN gained in popularity for engineering and science, the business world wanted a language to meet their needs. COBOL, released in 1959, was

TABLE 15.1
Summary Chart of Major Programming Languages

FORTRAN (1954) FORmula TRANslation. John Backus, with a team at IBM, developed FORTRAN, the first high-level language. This language, known for its number crunching, is widely used for science, engineering, and mathematical problems.

ALGOL 58 (1958) ALGOrithmetic Language. Designed by the members of the Association for Computing Machinery and European computer industry representatives, ALGOL 58 is used for mathematical problem solving.

COBOL (1959) COmmon Business-Oriented Language. The Defense Department developed this language, and Captain Grace Hopper of the U.S. Navy perfected it. COBOL is primarily used for business applications.

LISP (1960) LISt Processing. John McCarthy created this language, which is used for special applications such as artificial intelligence.

RPG (1962) Report Program Generator. IBM created and used it to generate business reports.

APL (1962) Kenneth Iverson developed APL; it is used for scientific applications.

SNOBOL 4 (1963) StriNg-Oriented symBOLic Language. David Farber, Ralph Griswold, and Ivan Polonsky of Bell Labs devised the current version of SNOBOL, and it is still in use for text applications.

BASIC (1964) Beginner's All-purpose Symbolic Instruction Code. T. E. Kurtz and J. G. Kemeny developed BASIC at Dartmouth College in order to teach students programming for educational and business applications.

PL/1 (1964) Programming Language 1. IBM created this language to replace COBOL and FORTRAN, which has not happened.

PROLOG (1970) PROgramming LOGic. Alain Colmerauer wrote this language at the University of Marseilles, France. It is used largely for artificial intelligence applications.

Pascal (1971) Niklaus Wirth invented Pascal, a structured programming language, to teach students how to program.

FORTH (1974) Charles Moore, an astronomer, developed this object-oriented language to control telescopes.

C (1975) Dennis Richie created C for the Unix operating system, and it is used for systems and general applications.

Ada (1979) Ada was named after Ada Augusta, the Countess of Lovelace, the first woman programmer. Jean Ichbiah headed a team of programmers that produced Ada, a language based on Pascal, used by the federal government for weapons system tracking.

Modula-2 (1979) MODUlar LAnguage 2. Niklaus Wirth, the author of Pascal, wrote Modula-2, a multipurpose scientific language.

Smalltalk 80 (1980) Alan Kay developed Smalltalk 80 at Xerox's research center. It is an object-oriented language, used for Xerox's original graphical windows system.

C++ (1983) Bjarn Stroustrup designed and implemented this object-oriented extension of C.

Source: Modified from Pamela Milland, "Current Major Programming Languages," in *PC Magazine*, September 13, 1988, Ziff-Davis Publishing.

a high-level language designed for business applications. COBOL uses ordinary English words and syntax, which makes it easier to understand a typical program, find bugs, add or change features, and perform other functions. The beauty of the language became clear to Grace Hopper when she remained behind after touring a computer center in Japan. She and her hosts could not understand each other until she used two COBOL commands. "MOVE," she said, pointing to herself, "GOTO Osaka Hotel." The hosts understood her immediately and took her to her destination (Embrey, 1983). Currently, COBOL is found in the corporate mainframe world. COBOL is rarely used in education.

ALGOL

ALGOL is an algebraic language similar to FORTRAN, which was used primarily for writing programs that solved numerical problems. This language was elegant, but it could not overcome FORTRAN's head start as a language. ALGOL is little used today; however, a number of languages were based in part on this language.

BASIC

In the 1960s, programmers designed languages such as LISP, RPG, APL, SNOBOL, and BASIC because academicians were looking for a way to make computers accessible to students. At this time, there was a scarcity of educational software, so teachers focused on computer programming. John Kemeny and Thomas Kurtz at Dartmouth College wanted a language that would require minimal instruction and that would be easy to learn in an academic setting. FORTRAN and ALGOL did not satisfy these requirements, so Kemeny and Kurtz designed BASIC, which was a blend of the best of these two languages. In 1964, students at Dartmouth College sat down at computer terminals and were greeted by the famous READY> prompt; thus began an era in which the novice computer user could write and quickly execute simple programs.

After BASIC's introduction, word spread about the new language designed for Dartmouth's time-sharing system. Time-sharing permitted several students to interact with the machine at the same time. Students now had access to the computer. They no longer had to use punched-card machines and enlist the help of programmers who would process their programs only when convenient.

Robert L. Albrecht, a senior analyst for Control Data in Minneapolis, heard about the BASIC and lobbied successfully to make it the recommended language for secondary schools. He also started a company called Dymax, which produced instructional books and published a bimonthly magazine called the *People's Computer Company*. Albrecht wanted someone to write a simpler version of this new language that he called Tiny BASIC. He commissioned Dennis Allison, a skilled programmer, to write a series of articles with guidelines for the modified version. Dick Whipple and John Arnold responded with a 2,000-octal code of instructions. The Altair computer, the first affordable microcomputer, responded to commands entered in Tiny BASIC.

Albrecht's magazine continued publishing new versions of BASIC submitted by its readers, and some authors released these versions through public domain. In the mid-1970s, the authors of these programs began selling their versions of BASIC commercially. Many variations appeared. For example, Bill Gates and Paul Allen wrote a version of BASIC using only 4K of memory. For their own versions of BASIC, manufacturers wired interpreters into their computers' ROM. By the mid-1980s, millions of people in the United States and abroad knew BASIC and had learned it on their own computers. The language that was most often taught in the schools was BASIC because it was simple to use and had keywords that resemble English.

Let's compare BASIC with two popular high-level languages, COBOL and FORTRAN. In Figure 15.4, all three languages compute the average of five values.

BASIC	FORTRAN	COBOL
10 INPUT A,B,C,D,E	READ(5,100) V1,V2,V3,V4,V5	ACCEPT Vs
20 LET S=A+B+C+D+E	100 FORMAT(5F3.0)	ADD V-1,V-2,V-3,V-4,V-5 GIVING T
30 LET AV=S/5	S=V1+V2+V3+V4+V5	DIVIDE T BY 5 GIVING AV-OF-ALL-Vs
40 PRINT"AVERAGE=";AV	AV=S/5	DISPLAY"AV="AV-OF-ALL-Vs
50 END	WRITE(6,200) AV	STOP RUN.
	200 FORMAT('AV=',F8.2)	
	STOP	
	END	

FIGURE 15.4
Comparison of Three Languages

Many high school teachers thought BASIC needed structure, so they abandoned it in favor of Pascal.

Pascal

Pascal was named after Blaise Pascal, the 17th-century French mathematician. Niklaus Wirth, author of Pascal, began writing the language in 1968. Because Wirth, a professor of computer science, was dissatisfied with the major languages, he wrote a language that was more precise. At the beginning of a program the writer must define all variables and state each data type, that is, whether the variable contents will be treated as integers or string characters. Pascal has a logical structure that divides a program into simple tasks. Pascal is great for teaching programming techniques and theory. However, it is not good for writing practical applications. Pascal became very popular, and colleges on both sides of the Atlantic adopted it as a classroom aid for teaching programming. Pascal became the leader of a movement to teach structured programming. This movement wanted to change the way software was put together. Teaching Pascal in high school is helpful for later college study of computer science. On the negative side, the majority of teachers are prepared to teach BASIC or Logo because these languages are easier to learn. Pascal has no self-teaching materials and is a more difficult language. A major concern is that most teachers have to take college or university courses to learn Pascal. Finally, Wirth designed Pascal to teach college students, so it is not suitable for the younger child.

Pascal has acceptance as a teaching language, but most professional programmers prefer to use C.

C Language

C was developed because programmers needed a way to let the Unix operating system run on a variety of computers. C is a high-level language that was created at Bell Labs in 1970. This language is able to handle the computer at a low level, just like assembly language. C became the language of choice for commercial program development during the mid-1980s. C became widespread, and a newer variation, C++, appeared. Apple has adopted C++ as its standard house programming language (Pfaffenberger, 2000).

Logo's Development

When artificial intelligence (AI) began to be developed in the 1950s, researchers were looking for a language to express concepts in human words. John McCarthy, a distinguished member of the artificial intelligence community, established an AI lab at Massachusetts Institute of Technology and in 1958 started working on a language that combined the use of lists with a set of symbols. He borrowed concepts from a branch of mathematics named lambda calculus and called his high-level language **LISP,** an abbreviation for **list p**rocessing.

LISP is simply a language of lists of symbols held within parentheses. Presently, LISP is the principal programming language for AI research in the United States, and it's the second oldest general-purpose language in use. LISP has ease, speed, and the ability to write, run, and modify programs. Because of LISP's unique properties, it has many spinoff languages, with **Logo,** a high-level language designed for children, being the most popular. In this book Logo is emphasized, because it is the most widely known of the programming languages used for instruction. It is used throughout the world as a beginning programming language and learning environment for elementary and secondary students.

Historical Background

Seymour Papert, and his MIT colleagues created Logo. Papert, a mathematics professor, had studied with Jean Piaget and worked in artificial intelligence. He felt that school-age children could learn to program, and he was convinced that BASIC was too abstract for the young child. This belief motivated him to create Logo. It was originally used on mainframe computers, but because of advances in computer technology, programs were eventually devised for the microcomputer.

In 1979, the first version of Logo was written for the Apple and the Texas Instruments 99/4 computers. Since then, there has been a proliferation of Logo versions, including *Apple Logo, Logo II,* and *LogoWriter* (Logo Computer Systems) and *Logo Plus, Terrapin,* and *Krell* (MIT versions). Along with these programs came simplified versions such as *Turtle Math* (Logo Computer Systems). Papert's clever innovation, the turtle, was first introduced in the form of a mechanical turtle that crawled on the floor and later as a graphic on the screen. Using simple commands, children were able to write programs that moved the turtle across the screen. For example, if a child gives the commands Forward 50, Right 90, and Forward 50, the turtle will move as follows:

Philosophy and Psychology of Logo

In 1980, Seymour Papert discussed in *Mindstorms* his theories on how a computer should be used in the classroom. He felt a computer is best utilized to aid in the thinking process and not as a piece of hardware that dispenses information. He observed that computer-assisted instruction (CAI) usually meant that the computer was being used to program the child and the child was the passive receiver of information:

> In my vision, the child programs the computer and, in doing so, both acquires a sense of mastery over a piece of the most modern and powerful technology and establishes an intimate contact with some of the deepest ideas from science, from mathematics, and from the art of intellectual model building. (Papert, 1980, p. 5)

According to Papert, Logo creates an environment in which children are free to explore and discover. They can learn geometric concepts, actively test and retest their theories, and develop their intellect. Papert argued that the majority of schools' mathematics programs have nothing to do with reality because the students are taught in a rote, meaningless way. According to Papert, this rote instruction is the reason most children grow up hating and fearing mathematics. Logo combats this problem by letting the child experience a meaningful mathematics environment. Furthermore, Papert saw other ways that Logo could aid learning across all curriculum areas. For example, in his book he presented the case study of a student named Jenny who had difficulty with English grammar. When she used Logo to generate poetry, she discovered the necessity of knowing the difference between a noun and a verb in order to teach the computer how to write poetry. Jenny did a meaningful activity and learned the material.

Papert used the term **Microworld** to describe the Logo environment in which the child freely experiments, tests, and revises his or her own theories in order to create a product. Using the Microworld, the child better understands concepts in analytical geometry, physics, grammar, and composition. It is a playground of the mind in which the learner explores a concept from an intuitive to a formal level. The product can be one the child wants to create to fulfill his or her needs, so the creation of this product is meaningful.

Logo has been used in all areas of the curriculum, even though the majority of programs in schools have focused on it as a tool to teach mathematics. Using Logo, students can explore mathematical topics such as simple geometry concepts, estimation skills, and topology. Students can use Logo for problem solving, breaking down problems into smaller parts, and debugging programs. According to research (see Chapter 16), evidence that Logo can improve problem solving and skill development is inconclusive. In language arts, students can utilize *MicroWorlds Pro* (Logo Computer Systems), which combines word processing with graphics, to create text for describing their Logo graphics work. Using Logo's simple list-processing capabilities, students can teach the computer the parts of speech, subject–verb agreement, or poetry. In science, students can use Legos with a Lego RCX Robotic controller along with *Terrapin Logo* (Terrapin Software) to build objects and control their movements. In the process students learn about physics and develop problem-solving skills. Furthermore, with commercial kits, students can use the computer as a measuring tool. They can write their own simple Logo programs and have the computer generate charts or graphs. For example, students might use a thermistor, a device whose resistance varies with temperature, and use Logo to write a chart-graphic procedure that produces a graph of temperature changes. In social studies, students can use *MicroWorlds Pro* to write about geographical concepts or use Logo to create interesting maps.

Working with Logo

This Logo introduction should familiarize you with the basic concepts of Logo programming. Use the following examples to understand the full potential of this language. Type the sample programs, run them, and save them on a disk. The programs and illustrations are created in *Terrapin Logo*. In general, all Logo programs, including the Windows versions, are similar, so you should be able to make the transition from the chapter examples to your own version.

Open the Logo application, and when the Welcome message appears, type **ST** for **SHOWTURTLE**.

Primitives

Logo **primitives** are commands built into the language itself. More than 100 of these commands exist, but you need to use just a few to program. Table 15.2 lists the primitives that we discuss in this chapter.

TABLE 15.2
Logo Primitives

Primitive	Abbreviation	Explanation
SHOWTURTLE	ST	Shows the turtle.
HIDETURTLE	HT	Hides the turtle.
FORWARD	FD	Moves forward.
BACK	BK	Moves backward.
RIGHT	RT	Turns right.
LEFT	LT	Turns left.
CLEARSCREEN or CLEARGRAPHICS	CS or CG depending on version*	Clears the screen.
PENUP	PU	Does not leave trail.
PENDOWN	PD	Leaves trail.
HOME	HOME	Returns home.

*Use the stop command that is appropriate for your version of Logo. *Terrapin Logo* uses Command G.

Source: Used with permission of Terrapin Software, Inc., Portland, ME.

When you type in one of these commands, you give it a numerical value and the turtle responds. For example, if you assign the command Forward a value of 50, the turtle will move forward 50 steps. Using an abbreviation for the primitive, type in the following instructions. Be sure to put a space between the primitive and the number, and then press Return or Enter after the number.

1. Forward Example

FD 40

Output

Explanation   The turtle moves forward 40 steps.

2. Right Example

RT 90

Output

Explanation   The turtle turns 90 degrees, based on a 360-degree turning ratio.

3. Backward Example

BK 40

Output

Explanation.   The turtle moves 40 steps backward.

4. Left Example

LT 270

Output

Explanation   The turtle turns 270 degrees to the left, based on a 360-degree circle.

5. Combination Example

FD 40 LT 90 FD 40

Output

Explanation   The directions tell the turtle to move forward 40 steps, turn left 90 degrees, and move forward 40 more steps. These instructions allow the turtle to complete a square.

The Total Turtle Trip Theorem states that the turtle must turn a total of 360 degrees to go around a closed figure in order to return to its original direction.

6. HIDETURTLE Example

HT

Output

Explanation   The drawing remains, but the turtle has disappeared from the screen.

7. CLEARSCREEN or CLEARGRAPHICS Example
CS or CG (CS clears the screen for *Terrapin Logo*).

Explanation   The drawings are cleared from the screen.

8. PENUP Example

                            ST
                            PU
                            FD 40

Output

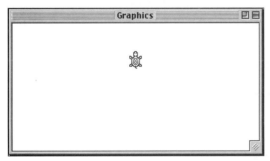

Explanation   The ST command shows the turtle, and the PENUP command tells the computer to move the turtle without leaving a trail. FD 40 moves the turtle forward 40 steps with no trail.

9. PENDOWN Example

                            PD
                            FD 20

Output

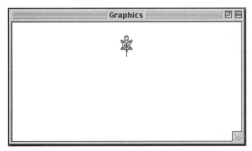

Explanation   The PENDOWN command instructs the computer to reinstate the trail. After you type PENDOWN, every command that follows will leave a trail. FD 20 leaves a trail with 20 steps.

10. HOME Example

HOME

Output

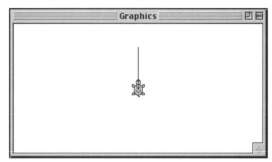

Explanation   The HOME command returns the turtle to its original position.

11. REPEAT Example

After working a while with Logo, you'll notice that you are reusing the same commands; the repeat command shortens this procedure.

Instructions   Clear the screen by typing CS or CG.

REPEAT 4[FD 40 RT 90]

Output

Explanation   This primitive tells the turtle to repeat the directions in the square brackets. In this example, the turtle repeats 40 steps forward and a 90-degree right turn four times. When it stops, it has drawn a square. Using this repeat command, you can create interesting geometric patterns.

Procedures

So far, all the turtle can do is move forward or backward, turn right and left, and follow the REPEAT command to create a square. You have not taught it how to draw a square. Nevertheless, with the primitives you've learned, you can write a **procedure,** or set of instructions, to store in the computer's memory, essentially teaching the computer a new action. Let's teach the turtle how to draw a square.

12. Square Procedure Example

Instructions   Clear the screen and type the following procedure for creating a square. Be sure to leave a space between TO and SQUARE.

```
TO SQUARE
REPEAT 4[FD 40 RT 90]
HT
END
```

Output

Explanation   SQUARE is a new primitive that you are adding to Logo's vocabulary. TO tells the computer that you are about to define a procedure, and SQUARE is the name you've given to the procedure. (You just as easily could have called the procedure SQ or Box.) REPEAT 4 tells the computer to repeat four times what is in the brackets. FD 40 RT 90 creates a square. The HT hides the turtle, and END ends the program. Now you can use this procedure whenever you want by simply typing the word. Let's create a design with the SQUARE procedure.

13. Design Subprocedure Example

Instructions   Clear the screen and type the following procedure:

```
TO DESIGN
REPEAT 8 [SQUARE RT 45]
END
```

After the design has been defined, type **DESIGN** and press Return or Enter.

Output

Explanation   The TO tells the computer that you are about to define a procedure, and DESIGN is the name you've given to the procedure. The REPEAT command instructs the turtle to repeat eight times the procedure SQUARE and turn it 45 degrees each time. For practice, create a procedure for a star or a triangle.

Logo is a powerful language because you can use new words or procedures to define other words and can use a simple procedure to create a more complicated one. As you work with Logo, you should experiment with more complicated projects such as designing a house. This task is not difficult if you break it into smaller components, or subprocedures.

As you become experienced with Logo, you will create procedures for squares or circles of different sizes. These procedures are applicable only to the specified square or circle size. To avoid writing different procedures for each new circle or square, you can use variables.

Variables

Variables let you write only one procedure to cover all cases. A variable is a part of a procedure that changes when you tell it to change. Instead of typing FD 40 in the SQUARE procedure, type in **:SIZE.** In the following example, you can enter any size for the square.

14. Square Variable Example

```
TO SQUARE :SIZE
REPEAT 4[FD :SIZE RT 90]
HT
END
```

Instructions   After redefining the procedure for square, type SQUARE followed by a number, for example, SQUARE 10.

Output

Explanation   TO starts the procedure and SQUARE is the name of the new procedure. The colon is important because it tells the program you are naming a variable location. SIZE (:SIZE) is the name of the variable location for this procedure. There is no space between the colon and the word *size*. (You can use any name for the procedure as long as it is a letter or a word. For example, you can call it :L or :INPUT. Every time you run this procedure, you type the chosen name with a value.) The REPEAT command tells the turtle to repeat four times the set of actions inside the brackets. The HT command conceals the turtle and leaves the small square.

Recursion

Another powerful feature of Logo is **recursion,** which is the ability of a procedure to call itself as a subprocedure, using itself as part of its own definition. The program loops back and starts the procedure again, and this continues until you stop the program.

15. Drawing Recursion Example

Instructions   Clear the screen. Next, create a new square procedure such as the one enclosed in the following rectangle. Finally, type the Drawing Recursion Example.

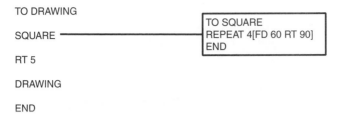

```
TO DRAWING

SQUARE ——————————  TO SQUARE
                    REPEAT 4[FD 60 RT 90]
RT 5                END

DRAWING

END
```

Instructions   After you have defined the superprocedure design, type DRAWING.

Output

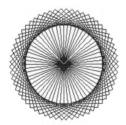

Explanation   TO starts the procedure, and DRAWING is the name of the new procedure. The SQUARE procedure produces a square using FD 60 RT 90. The instructions for this subprocedure are enclosed in the box. The command RT 5 turns this square to the right 5 degrees. When the turtle reaches DRAWING, it repeats the same procedure, drawing a square and turning it 5 degrees to the right. The procedure reaches DRAWING again and repeats itself, continuing forever, if you want it to. Eventually the turtle will retrace its steps. If you hide the turtle, you can see its trail going around and around. To stop this program in the Macintosh version of *Terrapin Logo*, use Command-Period (⌘ .).

Let's work through another example defining superprocedure Effect. After defining this superprocedure, we will use the same stop or halt command.

16. EFFECT Example

```
TO EFFECT :SIZE
FD :SIZE RT 90
EFFECT :SIZE+3
END
```

Instructions   After defining EFFECT, type the name of the procedure with a value, such as EFFECT 3. Once the turtle has retraced many of its lines, quickly use the Command and period key to stop.[2]

---

[2]Use the stop command that is appropriate for your version of Logo.

Output

Explanation   TO starts the procedure and EFFECT is its name. The colon tells the program you are naming a variable location, and the word SIZE (:SIZE) is the name of the variable location for this procedure. FD :SIZE RT 90 tells the computer to go forward the number you enter (3) and turn right 90 degrees. EFFECT :SIZE +3 tells the computer to run EFFECT with its present size (3) and increase it by three. The size will be increased by three every time this procedure is executed.

Because of recursion, the END command is never reached. If you had not used the stop command, the program would have continued running forever.

You can halt a procedure within a program with a conditional statement such as IF S>203[STOP]. If the statement is true, the program ends; if the statement is false, the procedure continues until the statement becomes true. The following procedure shows the previous example with a conditional statement. Type the following procedure.

17. STOP Example

```
TO EFFECT :SIZE
IF :SIZE > 203 [STOP]
FD :SIZE RT 90
EFFECT :SIZE+3
HT
END
```

Instructions   After EFFECT is defined, type EFFECT 3.

Output

Explanation   TO starts the procedure and EFFECT is the name of the new procedure. The colon tells the program you are naming a variable location, and the word SIZE (:SIZE) is the name of the variable location for this procedure. IF :SIZE>203[STOP] tells the turtle to stop when the value is greater than 203. The next line tells the turtle to go forward the number you enter (3) and turn 90 degrees. EFFECT :SIZE+3 tells the turtle to run EFFECT and increase the size by three. HT hides the turtle, and END ends the program once the value for SIZE exceeds 203. It stops and returns control to the user.

Logo's Other Features

By now, you should be familiar with primitives, procedures, variables, and recursion. These powerful ideas apply to other parts of Logo, not just turtle graphics. Besides drawing pictures, Logo has many other capabilities; you can use it to work with numbers, words, and lists.

Logo knows how to add, subtract, multiply, and divide, using the symbols 1, 2, *, and /. You can instruct Logo to add three numbers by typing PRINT.

18. Add Example

PRINT 50+40+66

Output

156

Logo interprets a word as a series of characters with no blanks to separate them, so you can have Logo print out words by typing them.

19. Print Example

Print" Computer

Output

Computer

By working with lists, you can handle complex sets of information. A list is a set of words separated by blanks and enclosed in brackets: [computer monitor printer scanner]. Whenever you work with Logo in this capacity, you must use special commands that operate with lists of words. These commands can randomly pick out a name, a phrase, or a closing message.

Originally, Logo lacked turtle graphics, ran only on mainframes, and used slow printers; however, there has been dramatic improvement in Logo.

Logo now has sound, graphics, excellent color, and telecommunication and database capabilities. For a more in-depth discussion of Logo, refer to the Logo books listed at the end of the chapter.

Other Logo Programming Programs

Let us examine some other programs that students can use to program their computer.

MicroWorlds Pro

MicroWorlds Pro (Logo Computer Systems) introduces students to problem solving and creative thinking. A powerful multimedia authoring tool designed for students in grades 4 and higher to create dynamic, interactive school and Internet projects (Fig. 15.5). Students use this Logo-based toolkit

**FIGURE 15.5
MicroWorlds Pro**

MicroWorlds Pro is a registered trademark of Logo Computer Systems, Inc. The LCSI logo is a registered trademark of Logo Computer Systems, Inc. Used by permission.

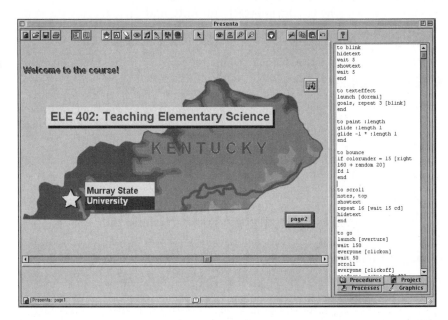

to create projects for any subject in the curriculum. *MicroWorlds Pro* lets students become active Web designers, not just passive Web viewers. Using the Web authoring tools, students can create HTML templates for their *interactive* projects to be displayed on the World Wide Web; add hyperlink connections; make animations; and integrate videos, sounds, shapes, and pictures into their projects.

Students can make animations with just one mouse click and use hundreds of multicolored shapes. Students can drag and drop music, pictures, videos, Web pages, sounds, and shapes into their *MicroWorlds Pro* projects. There are 140 drawing tools and 24 brushes. *MicroWorlds Pro* includes interactive samples within the online help system so that learning *MicroWorlds Pro* is so much easier. In addition, teachers and students can obtain further project ideas by visiting the Project Library at http://www.lcsi.ca.

Crystal Rain Forest

Terrapin Software produces *Crystal Rain Forest* and *Mission Control.* These programs teach Logo programming for students ages 8 to 13. *Crystal Rain Forest* has the students help save a planet by navigating through different screens. For this particular program, the planet Oglo is in trouble and only the student can save its rain forests and its king by finding the magic crystals that are hidden in the forest. The story is exciting, the activities fun, with humor and animation. In this plot, there is a poisoned dart, a snake with a sweet tooth, and a friendly monster. In Figure 15.6 the student must open the door by typing in a simple procedure.

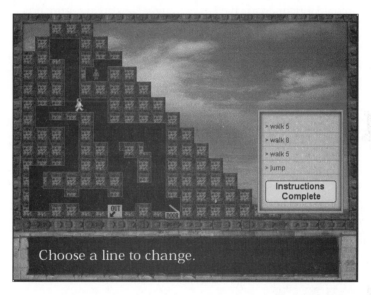

**FIGURE 15.6
Crystal Rain
Forest**
Reprinted with permission
Terrapin Software.

Mission Control, a newer program, has students save the planet from a wacky scientist using programming concepts through a series of sequenced adventures. The students are challenged to activities that include connecting wires to fix a soda machine, controlling motors to move heavy boxes, directing trucks filled with poison to recycling tanks, and using heat sensors to find an escape route. In the process of using this program, they solve problems and learn to build simple procedures. *Mission Control* is self-paced, so students can proceed at their own speed.

Roamer

Roamer (Terrapin Software; Fig. 15.7) is an easy-to-use robot that introduces kindergarten and first-grade students to Logo commands. *Roamer* has Logo on-board in the form of a computer that is dedicated to Logo. Students can see, touch, and follow the Logo turtle as it moves around the room. *Roamer* is a very sturdy design with very few moving parts. Students can easily use the

FIGURE 15.7
Roamer
Reprinted with permission of
Terrapin Software.

colored touchpad to give *Roamer* single-keystroke commands. *Roamer* is battery-powered and lightweight, offering students hours of fun in discovering Logo. *Roamer* can play music, and it has accessories that let you customize it. For example, you can add a nose, ears, or tail, and change its color. If you place a marker pen into the pen pack attachment, you can even watch *Roamer* draw designs. You can also connect *Roamer* to the computer and upload computer programs, as well as merge them with other programs. In addition, you can write programs on the computer and download them to the *Roamer* turtle. There are 16 story-based activities to help students learn problem solving, programming, spatial concepts, and mapping. The activities integrate the *Roamer* floor turtle with the onscreen *Roamer* (http://www.terrapinlogo.com).

Logo-Driven Robots

Using Lego kits, students can build machines in the form of a car, a camera robot (Fig. 15.8), a tower, and a truck that includes motors, sensors, and gears.

FIGURE 15.8
Robotics Kit
Reprinted with permission of
Terrapin Software.

After these machines are built, students connect them with an interface to a computer that speaks the proper dialect of Logo. Using a few simple commands, students write computer programs to control the machines. These commands turn the motors off and on and send them in various directions.

These robotics construction kits are really a relic of the early days of Logo programming when the experimenters with Logo used a "floor turtle," a mechanical robot connected to the computer by a cord. When video display terminals came along, the focus shifted to a "screen turtle" that was faster and more accurate than the floor turtle. *Terrapin Logo* in conjunction with the Lego RCX Robotics controller, which is included in *Mindstorm* and other Lego products, brings back the floor turtle with a few differences. Students are not restricted to turtles but can build all sorts of machines.

A Lego package usually includes an assortment of gears, wheels, motors, lights, and sensors. Students can send commands to Lego motors and lights and receive information from Lego sensors. *Terrapin Logo* can make a robot turn to the right or reverse direction when it touches a wall. Students can engage in all kinds of experimentation, and they can learn the importance of changing only one variable at a time. They can use the scientific method as they invent their machines, and when they have problems with their inventions, they can develop hypotheses and test them. When students use this computer-based system, they engage in data gathering, record keeping, and brainstorming.

Finally, *Stagecast Creator* (Stagecast Software, Inc.) is a tool that lets you create interactive stories (Fig. 15.9), games, and simulations. When the Flower

FIGURE 15.9
Stagecast: *Flower Garden*
© Stagecast Software, Inc. Used with permission. All rights reserved.

Garden is played, the observer sees how flowers are pollinated. This multi-media authoring tool can be used by young students as well as adults. This authoring tool lets you create characters, the rules by which they will interact, and the worlds in which they will exist. Using this program, you can play simulations and games that you have created, see how they work, and then change the rules if you want. When you make these interactive worlds, the computer does the programming. *Stagecast* is a great tool for higher-order thinking skills, and it can be used at any grade level. Using *Stagecast,* you can create complex projects, rather than writing dull reports. The program motivates students and tries to meet the needs of students whose learning styles and intelligence vary. In *Stagecast* the following elements exist: stage or background divided into equal parts, characters or objects, and rules that define the actions of the objects. All the different elements can be seen in Figure 15.10. The background is divided into squares, the object consists of one ball, and the rule that defines the action was created by dragging the ball one square to the right. After you close the rule box, you click **Play** to see the ball move across the screen.

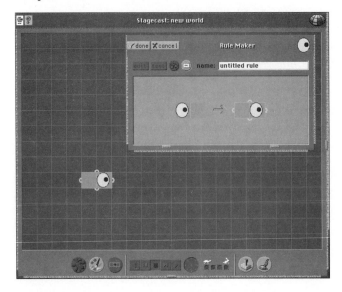

Logo Lesson Plans

The following five ready-to-use lessons show some of the creative ways you can use programming software in the classroom.

▼ I. Develop Logo Programming Skills ▼

Objective

Students will solve problems using algorithms.

Procedure

1. Explain simple Logo commands—Forward, Back, Right, Left, and so on.
2. Hide a reward in the classroom such as a free homework pass or extra reading time.
3. Divide the class into two teams, and choose a representative or human Logo turtle from each team.
4. Have the teams alternate giving the representative a Logo command such as Forward 40. The human turtle then follows these directions by walking Forward 40 steps.
5. The first team to find the reward wins. The teacher can give hints.
6. After the class is sufficiently versed in simple Logo commands, copy a maze onto a transparency and then tape it to the computer monitor screen.
7. Next, have the students drive a computer Logo turtle through the maze.

▼   II. Science or Math Inquiry   ▼

Objective

Using *MicroWorlds Pro, HyperStudio,* or *Stagecast Creator,* create animated presentations.

Procedure

1. Have the class do research on a topic in science or math such as plants, fractals, electricity, or the water cycle.
2. Have each student write a paper that summarizes the research.
3. Divide the class into small groups.
4. Working with a program like *MicroWorlds Pro,* have each group create a simulation that explains the chosen topic. In Figure 15.11 the students designed a project concerning fractals.

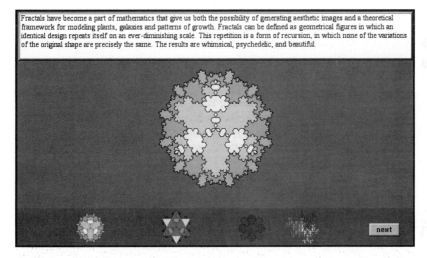

Fractals have become a part of mathematics that give us both the possibility of generating aesthetic images and a theoretical framework for modeling plants, galaxies and patterns of growth. Fractals can be defined as geometrical figures in which an identical design repeats itself on an ever-diminishing scale. This repetition is a form of recursion, in which none of the variations of the original shape are precisely the same. The results are whimsical, psychedelic, and beautiful.

FIGURE 15.11
MicroWorlds Pro

MicroWorlds Pro is a registered trademark of Logo Computer Systems, Inc. The LCSI logo is a registered trademark of Logo Computer Systems, Inc. Used by permission.

5. Finally, let the students use a word processing application to write a summary and explanation of their projects.

The sample animation project shown was developed using *MicroWorlds Pro,* but other programs could be used such as *Stagecast Creator,* or *HyperStudio.*

▼   III. Math   ▼

Objective

Using *Terrapin Logo* or some other programming language, the students will create circles, triangles, squares, and rectangles and design houses.

Procedure

1. Introduce the students to the Logo commands necessary to draw simple shapes.
2. Distribute activity sheets to all students and ask them to physically draw these shapes on paper.
3. Have the students use Logo programming to duplicate these shapes on the computer screen.
4. Finally, divide the class into small groups and have the students design a simple house.
5. Students can experiment and design all sorts of geometric figures using Logo.

▼   IV. Math   ▼

Objective

Using the *Roamer* turtle or some other robotic device, introduce Logo commands to younger students.

Procedure

1. Introduce beginning Logo commands to the class.
2. Divide the class into small groups and give each group a *Roamer* turtle.
3. Construct a small race track with a finish line.
4. Have the groups program their turtle to race on the track using the Logo commands they just learned.
5. The first turtle to reach the finish line wins.

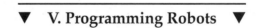

▼   V. Programming Robots   ▼

Objective

Students write simple Logo programs to move robotic machines around the classroom.

Procedure

1. Using the *Terrapin Logo* robot construction kit, build a turtle.
2. Attach the interface to the turtle, connecting it to the computer.
3. Load the Logo files. Now, the students are ready to control the turtle by typing in commands on the computer.
4. Introduce sequences by discussing the steps one takes to boil an egg.
5. Demonstrate the turtle or robot by writing basic commands on the blackboard or overhead.

6. Next, write a small program and have students pretend they are robots by moving forward and backward.
7. Divide the class into small groups and place a world map on the floor.
8. Have the students write a Logo program that makes the turtle travel to a city such as London.
9. Students compare programs to see which one uses the fewest steps.

Additional Projects and Activities

Using a program like *MicroWorlds Pro*, *Stagecast Creator*, or *HyperStudio*, show the following:

1. How peas grow into healthy plants.
2. A food chain in action.
3. A model of the rain cycle.
4. Main bones in a skeleton.
5. Patterns in numbers.

Summary

We discussed the historical development of programming languages, which provided a background on languages ranging from BASIC to C. We showed Logo's four powerful components: primitives, procedures, variables, and recursion. We saw that Logo was derived from LISP by Seymour Papert and colleagues. Papert's theory, based on Piaget's theories, holds that children learn best by constructing their own knowledge, building their own programs, and developing their own designs in meaningful interactions. Children control the computer instead of being controlled by the computer. Logo's intent is to make students analyze what has happened and what will happen in the future. Although Logo was designed with the child in mind, this programming language can be very sophisticated. There are cogent reasons for studying Logo: (1) it is a structured language that encourages good programming techniques; (2) it is a unique tool for exploration; and (3) it is a suitable introductory language. We discussed other software programs and how they could be used in the classroom. We presented five lesson plans to show how programming can be integrated into the school curriculum. **Appendix A is an annotated listing of award winning software programs.**

PROGRAMMING SITES

What follows is an annotated list of Internet sites that contain information on computer programming, lesson plans, on how to use Logo in the classroom.

Terrapin Logo
http://www.terrapinlogo.com/
Harvard Associates in Cambridge, Massachusetts, offers a wide variety of Terrapin Software Logo-related products it makes for schools and home. The site includes an educator's section with a sample lesson and information on using Logo in the classroom.

Logo Foundation
http://el.www.media.mit.edu/logo-foundation/
The Logo Foundation, a nonprofit educational organization, provides information and resources for learning and teaching Logo.

Seymour Papert
http://www.papert.org/
This site includes information on Seymour Papert's written works and the MaMaMedia site he helped to develop as well as links to MIT's Artificial Intelligence Lab and Media Lab, where Papert continues his research.

Math? Logo!
http://www.erzwiss.uni-hamburg.de/
Sonstiges/Logo/logomath.htm#english
The University of Hamburg maintains an extensive list of Logo resources including FAQs and information about Piaget, Papert, Abelsen, and other Logo contributors and teachers.

LCSI's MicroWorlds
http://microworlds.com/
Logo Computer Systems, the creator of *MicroWorlds* Logo software, provides information about its products and an extensive list of Logo links with classroom activities and lesson ideas. The site also offers more than 50 interactive multimedia projects in different subject areas.

Logo
http://www.atlantic.net/~caggiano/logo/
Frank Caggiano's website includes a number of *MicroWorlds* projects that require the free Web Player plug-in available from LCSI site.

A Turtle for the Teacher
http://www.ecu.edu.au/pa/ecawa/sig/logo/
paul_dench/turtle/
Paul Dench's site provides Logo tutorials for the beginner.

Other Logo Tutorials
http://mckoss.com/logo/
http://www.the-hunters.org/logo/
http://library.thinkquest.org/18446/eindex.
shtml
These three sites offer tutorials for the beginner.

Logo Activity Centre
http://atschool.eduweb.co.uk/allsouls/maths/
logo.html
MicroWorlds Logo Activities
http://curry.edschool.virginia.edu/teacherlink/
math/activities/mwactivities.html
These two sites offer activities, tutorials, and lessons in Logo programming.

Lego Mindstorms
http://mindstorms.lego.com/
Lego Mindstorms contains extensive information on special robotics software using Lego products.

BASIC Archives
http://www.fys.ruu.nl/~bergmann/basic.html
This site offers a history of the development of the BASIC and everything a novice needs to know about this programming language.

Computer Science & Business Education Site
http://www.crews.org/media_tech/compsci/
Rod Hames provides handouts, notes, and links to over 200 student-created Web projects done at Alton C. Crews Middle School in Lawrenceville, Georgia.

Chapter Mastery Test

To the Instructor: Refer to the Instructor's Manual for the Answers to the Mastery Questions. This manual has additional questions and resource materials.

Let's check for chapter comprehension with a short mastery test. What follows are basic terms, classroom projects, and suggested readings and references.

1. Trace the development of programming languages.
2. Explain what a programming language is.
3. Give two cogent reasons why programming should and two reasons why it should not be taught in the schools.
4. Explain the main purpose of the following three languages: COBOL, FORTRAN, and Pascal.

5. Describe briefly two characteristics of Logo.
6. Briefly define primitives, procedures, and recursion.
7. Write a program that will draw a square, a rectangle, or a circle.
8. Write a simple procedure using a REPEAT command.

9. Explain what makes the *Roamer* a good teaching tool.
10. What distinguishes *MicroWorlds Pro* from *Terrapin Logo*?
11. What were Seymour Papert's major contributions?
12. Explain what makes Terrapin's robotics kit a good teaching tool.

Basic Terms

assembly language (p. 401)
flowchart (p. 399)
FORTRAN (p. 402)
LISP (p. 406)
Logo (p. 406)
machine language (p. 400)

Microworld (p. 408)
primitives (p. 408)
procedure (p. 412)
program (p. 400)
recursion (p. 414)

Classroom Projects

1. Research the history of a programming language. Prepare a two-page report that answers the following questions:
   a. How did the language originate?
   b. What are its features?
   c. How is the language being used today?
2. Copy a maze onto a transparency and then tape it to the monitor screen. Next, drive a Logo turtle through the maze.

3. Debug the following two programs. The first program produces a square; the second procedure draws a curved line.
   a. Program 1 TO SQUARE
      REPEAT 4[FD 20 RT 60]
      END
   b. Program 2 TO CURVE
      REPEAT[FD 10 RT 10]
      END
4. Experiment and create a design; then print it out for the class.

Suggested Readings and References

Agular, Hugh. "Basic Recursive Techniques." *Computer Language,* May 1985, p. 45.

Anderson R., H. Bennett, and D. Walling. "Structured Programming Constructs in BASIC: Tried and Tested." *Computers in the Schools,* Summer 1987, pp. 135–39.

Athey, Thomas H. *Computers and End-User Software with Basic.* Glenview, Ill.: Scott, Foresman, 1987.

Backus, John. "The History of Fortran I, Ii, and Iii." *Annals of the History of Computing,* July 1979.

Barker, P. *Author Languages for CAI.* London: Macmillan Education Ltd., 1987.

Clements, Douglas H., et al. "Students' Development of Length Concepts in a Logo-Based Unit on Geometric Paths." *Journal for Research in Mathematics Education* 28, no. 1 (January 1997): 70–95.

Clements, Douglas H., and Bonnie K. Nastasi. "Metacognition, Learning, and Educational Computer Environments." *Information*

Technology in Childhood Education Annual, 1999, pp. 5–38.

Clements, Douglas H., and Julie Sarama. "Using Computers for Algebraic Thinking." *Teaching Children Mathematics* 5, no. 3 (November 1998): 186–90.

Coburn, Edward J. *Visual BASIC Made Easy.* Boston: PWS Publishing, 1995.

Cohen, Laura. *Logo Activity Cards: Problem Solving with a Turtle.* Compton, Calif.: Educational Insights, 1985.

Cohen, Rina S. "Computerized Learner Supports in Pre-Logo Programming Environments." *Journal of Research on Computing in Education* 22, no. 3 (Spring 1990): 310.

Davis, William S. *True BASIC Primer.* Reading, Mass.: Addison-Wesley, 1986.

Dodd, Kenneth Nelson. *Computer Programming and Languages.* London: Butterworths, 1969.

Donaldson, Margaret F., and Robert L. Davidson. "PC Logo: A Valuable Tool for Teaching Graphing." *Illinois Mathematics Teacher* 50, no.1 (Winter 1999): 14–19

Dunn, S., and V. Morgan. *The Impact of Computers on Education: A Course for Teachers.* Englewood Cliffs, N.J.: Prentice Hall, 1987.

Embrey, Glenn. "COBOL." *Popular Computing,* September 1983.

Freedman, Alan. *The Computer Desktop Encyclopedia.* Point Pleasant, Pa.: Computer Language Company, 2001.

Gates, Bill. "The 25th Birthday of Basic." *Byte,* October 1989, pp. 268–72.

Goldenberg, Paul E. *Exploring Language with Logo.* Cambridge, Mass.: MIT Press, 1987.

Goldenson, Dennis. "Why Teach Computer Programming? Some Evidence and Transfer." ERIC Document No. ED398886, 1996.

Heimler, Charles, Jim Cunningham, and Michael Nevard. *Basic for Teachers.* Santa Cruz, Calif.: Mitchell Publishing, 1987.

Horowitz, Ellis. *Fundamentals of Programming Languages.* Rockville Md.: Computer Science Press, 1984.

Jarvinen, Esa-Matti. "The Lego/Logo Learning Environment in Technology Education: An Experiment in a Finnish Context." *Journal of Technology Education* Vol. no. 2 (Spring 1998): 47–93.

Jonassen, D. H. *Computers in the Classroom: Mind-Tools for Critical Thinking.* Englewood Cliffs, N.J.: Merrill, 1996.

Kemeny, John G., and Thomas E. Kurtz. *True Basic Macintosh User's Guide.* West Lebanon, N.H.: True Basic, 1989.

Levy, Steven. *Hackers: Heroes of the Computer Revolution.* Garden City, N.Y.: Doubleday Anchor Press, 1984.

List, Peter. *Beginning Visual Basic 5.* Indianapolis, Ind.: Wrox Press, 1997.

Mathinos, Debra A. "Logo Programming and the Refinement of Problem Solving Skills in Disabled and Nondisabled Children." *Journal of Educational Computing Research* 6, no. 4 (1990): 429.

Miller, Douglas S. "Improving Secondary Practical Computer Skills: Logo Test Scores through Graphically Designed Computer Programs and Utilization of Multimedia and Technology." *Information Technology in Childhood Education Annual,* 1999, pp. 5–38.

Muir, Michael. "Talk & Draw: Logo and Artificial Intelligence." *Computing Teacher* 18, no. 7 (April 1991): 31–33.

Muller, Jim. *The Great Logo Adventure: Discovering Logo On and Off the Computer.* Madison, Ala.: Doone Publishing, 1998.

Nastasi, Bonnie, K., Douglas H. Clements, and M. T. Battista. "Social-Cognitive Interactions, Motivation and Cognitive Growth in Logo Programming and CAI Problem-Solving Environments." *Journal of Educational Psychology* 82, no. 1 (March 1, 1990): 150.

Olive, John. "Logo Programming and Geometric Understanding: An In-Depth Study." *Journal for Research in Mathematics Education* 22, no. 2 (March 1, 1991): 90.

Ortiz, Enrique, and S. MacGregor. "Effects of Logo Programming on Understanding Variables." *Journal of Educational Computing Research* 7, no. 1 (1991): 37.

Papert, Seymour. *The Children's Machine.* New York: Basic Books, 1993.

Papert, Seymour. "Different Visions of Logo." *Computers in the School,* Summer/Fall 1985, pp. 3–8.

Papert, Seymour. "Educational Computing: How Are We Doing?" *T.H.E. Journal* 24, no. 11 (June 1997): 78–80.

Papert, Seymour. "An Exploration in the Space of Mathematics Education." *International Journal of Computers for Mathematical Learning* 1, no. 1 (1996): 95–123.

Papert, Seymour. *Mindstorms: Children, Computers and Powerful Ideas.* New York: Basic Books, 1980.

Papert, Seymour, and Nicholas Negroponte. *The Connected Family: Bridging the Digital Generation Gap.* Atlanta: Longstreet Press, 1996.

Pea, Roy D., and D. Midian Kurland. "On the Cognitive Effects of Learning Computer Programming: A Critical Look." Technical Report No. 9. ERIC Document No. FD249919, 1984.

Perminov, Oleg. *The Beginner's Guide to Turbo Pascal.* Chicago: Wrox, 1994.

Pfaffenberger, Bryan. *Webster's New World Dictionary of Computer Terms.* 6th ed. New York: Que, 2000.

Piaget, J. *The Construction of Reality in the Child.* New York: Basic Books, 1954.

Reinhold, F. "An Interview with Seymour Papert." *Electronic Learning,* April 1986, pp. 35–36.

Ross, S. M. *Basic Programming for Educators.* Englewood Cliffs, N.J.: Prentice Hall, 1986.

Ruane, Pat. *Logo Activities for the Computer: A Beginner's Guide.* New York: Julian Messner, 1984.

Sarama, Julie, Douglas H. Clements, and Judith Day Seidel. "Using Computers for Algebraic Thinking." *Teaching Children: Mathematics* 5, no. 3 (November 1998): 186.

Strawn, Candace A. "Logo and Negative Numbers." *Learning and Leading with Technology* 25, no. 4 (December–January 1997–1998): 32–34.

Swan, Karen. "Programming Objects to Think With: Logo and the Teaching and Learning of Problem Solving." *Journal of Educational Computing Research* 7, no. 1 (1991): 89.

Vasu, Ellen Storey, and Doris Kennedy Tyler. "A Comparison of the Critical Thinking Skills and Spatial Ability of Fifth Grade Children: Using Simulation Software or Logo." *Journal of Computing in Childhood Education* 8, no. 4 (1997): 345–63.

Woronov, T. "Six Myths (and Five Promising Truths) about the Uses of Educational Technology." *Harvard Education Letter* 10, no. 5 (1994): 1–3.

Yoder, Sharon. "Logo for Teachers." *Computing Teacher* 18, no. 8 (May 1991): 33–34.

Yoder, Sharon. "Mousing Around with Your Turtle or Turtling Around with Your Mouse?" *Computing Teacher* 19, no. 12 (August/September 1991): 41–43.

CHAPTER 16

Standards, Issues, and Research

The Computer and the School

Did you know there are all kinds of ethical issues regarding the computer and its use in the school? Teachers, administrators, and parents are concerned about educational technology standards, privacy, crime, software piracy, computer viruses, health risks, and computer research. This chapter will discuss some of the research, problems, and issues related to the computer in our society. In addition, the reader will become familiar with Internet sites that contain lesson plans, information on standards, ethics, piracy, and related topics.

Objectives

Upon completing this chapter, you will be able to:

1. Identify and discuss major ethical issues regarding computers;
2. Describe three factors related to computer privacy;
3. Define the term *virus* and explain some precautions for preventing a virus from infecting a computer system;
4. Discuss the National Standards;
5. Summarize the research findings on CAI and (a) gender differences, (b) science simulations, (c) word processing, (d) learning by disabled students, (e) motivation and attitude, (f) Logo and problem solving, and (g) programming; and
6. Discuss three ways to lessen the chance of computer-related injuries.

Ethical Issues

Computers have benefited us in many ways. Computers have improved education, medical care, and business operations. Computers have also helped artists be more creative and allowed factories and businesses to operate more efficiently and effectively.

Unfortunately, no advance comes without disadvantages. In this section, we will examine some of the problems associated with computer technology, including invasion of privacy, computer crime, software piracy, computer viruses, and health risks.

Privacy

The concern for privacy is an issue that is not unique to computerized systems, but such systems increase the likelihood that an individual's privacy will be invaded. Computerized systems have proliferated in recent years, and these systems contain many different types of information. If a person lives in the United States, his or her name appears in federal, state, and local government data banks and in many private-sector files.[1] The Internal Revenue Service keeps records on everyone who files tax returns. State and local governments maintain files concerning taxes and law enforcement, public and private institutions keep records on students' educational performance, and medical data banks store medical records. It is hard to determine exactly who has what information and how this information will be used. The Society for Human Resource Management (SHRM) conducted a research survey of more than 500 members of primarily human resource professional organizations. One startling finding was that 36 percent of the organizations providing e-mail to customers look at their employees' e-mail records for business purposes or security, and 75 percent of those polled felt that employers should have the right to read company-provided e-mail. Personal information such as addresses, telephone numbers, and maps to homes is accessible through the Internet. A technology called a **cookie** keeps records of the online activities on your hard drive. "Cookies are data entries sent from a Web server to a special file on your machine" (Dyrli, 1997). A cookie gives the server the name of the site you visited and information about your choices, and when you return to the site, it requests information from your cookie file and gets even more data on your habits.

With so many different types of computerized systems, financial or academic indiscretions of 10 years ago may return to haunt you. Information that you provided for one purpose may be used for another. The computer poses a threat to our privacy, and we should be concerned about the possibility of unauthorized persons or groups gaining access to personal information simply by entering a system. By looking at statements of charges from the Cigar Warehouse, Ticketron, Toys 'R' Us, Apple Computers, and Foreign Automotive, a "computer detective" can deduce that you like cigars, go to the theater, have children, and own a computer and a foreign automobile. If bills are examined over an extended period, a personal, psychological, and economic profile can be developed, and this information could be used to swindle you out of huge sums of money—or even to blackmail you.

Another concern regarding invasion of privacy is computer record matching, the comparison of files stored in different governmental agencies on the same individual. Law enforcement agencies use computer matching to find a criminal by comparing the Medicare files and Social Security benefits files to identify individuals who are believed deceased but are still receiving Social Security checks. Supporters of this use of the computer argue

---

[1] A data bank is an electronic storehouse for data.

that people who break the law should be punished, and this procedure saves the taxpayers money. Opponents argue that it uses information for a purpose different from what was originally intended. If the people who supplied the information thought that it would be used against them, they might falsify data or not supply the needed information, impeding the operation of the asking agencies and costing the taxpayers money.

In the 1970s and 1980s, a series of laws was enacted to protect privacy by controlling the collection and dissemination of information. The Freedom of Information Act (1970) gave individuals access to information about themselves collected by federal agencies. The Privacy Act of 1974 stated that data collected for one purpose could not be used for another. The Family Education Rights and Privacy Act (1974) regulated access to public and private school grades and anecdotal records stored on computer. Finally, the Comprehensive Crime Control Act (1984) made it illegal for private individuals to modify, destroy, disclose, or use information stored in a government computer.

Crime

Today, there are many examples of computer crime or abuse. The cost to the nation amounts to billions of dollars in lost time and services (Levy and Stone, 2000). Criminals steal computers from people's homes and department stores, manipulate financial accounts, break into secret governmental computer files, and even use computer online services to lure young people to their homes.

Individuals who research fraud estimate that 80 percent of U.S. businesses have been victimized by at least one incident that cost up to $9 billion dollars (http://www.digitalcentury.com/encyclo/update/comfraud.html). According to a survey published by *Information Security Magazine,* the number of companies spending more than $1 million annually on computer security nearly doubled in 1999.

In the early 1980s, there were no clear laws to prevent individuals from accessing military computers or the White House computers. Ian Murphy, a 24-year-old hacker called "Captain Zap," changed this situation when he and three companions used a home computer and telephone lines to hack into electronics companies, merchandise order records, and government documents. (A **hacker** is a computer programming expert or someone who illegally accesses and tampers with computer files.) The group was caught and indicted for receiving stolen property. Murphy was fined $1,000 and sentenced to a 2 1/2-year jail term. After this case, legislators spent several years in research and discussion. The culmination was the Computer Fraud and Abuse Act of 1986, "a U.S. federal law that criminalizes the abuse of U.S. government computers or networks that cross state boundaries" (Pfaffenberger, 1997). Fines and prison sentences are given for illegal access, theft of credit data, and spying. Herbert Zinn, a high school dropout, was the first case to test this law. He was convicted on January 23, 1989, under the Computer Fraud and Abuse Act, of breaking into AT&T and the Department of Defense systems. He destroyed $174,000 worth of files, copied programs worth millions of dollars, and published passwords and ways to circumvent computer security systems. Because Zinn was not yet 18, he was sentenced to only nine months in prison and fined $10,000. However, if Zinn had been 18, he would have received a 13-year prison sentence and a fine of $80,000. The same year, Kevin Mitnick (Fig. 16.1) broke into Digital Equipment Corporation's computer network, and was caught and sentenced to a year in jail.

FIGURE 16.1
Kevin Mitnick
http://www.discovery.com/
area/technology/hackers/
zero.html

In 1994, a gang of Russian hackers, masterminded by Vladimir Levin (Fig. 16.2) broke into Citibank's computers and made unauthorized transfers totaling more than $10 million from customers' accounts. Citibank recovered all but $400,000, and the hackers were arrested in 1995.

FIGURE 16.2
Vladimir Levin
http://www.discovery.com/
area/technology/hackers/
levin.html

Some criminal violations are perpetrated by hackers for simple amusement. The members of the 414 Club, a well-known hackers' organization,[2] made a game out of accessing private computer files. By the time

---

[2]These hackers were called the 414 Club by the FBI because their area code was 414.

the FBI apprehended them in 1983, they had broken into many different business and government computers. And more recently, a group successfully hacked into Microsoft's Network to steal a source code (Berinato, 2000).

Unfortunately, hacking is now associated with theft and fraud, but this was not always the case. In the beginning, the majority of computer hackers were not considered crooks or pranksters but computer geeks who had a curiosity about how things operated. Some of these programmers created "hacks"—programming shortcuts to complete computing tasks faster. The best-known hack was created in 1969 when Dennis Ritchie and Ken Thompson, two employees at Bell Labs' think tank, came up with a standard operating system called UNIX. Today, hacking is more prevalent than ever, but the hackers have gone underground because of fear of prosecution.

As you have probably surmised, only estimated statistics on computer crime are available. Many people are unaware that their rights have been violated, because the data are transferred electronically. In addition, individuals who are aware hesitate to take claims to court because of the inevitable exposure of their private lives. Furthermore, companies prefer to handle computer crime internally to avoid embarrassment and unfavorable publicity.

Software Piracy

Thomas Jefferson (1743–1826) once said, "Some are born good, some make good, some are caught with the goods." **Piracy**—the illegal copying of software—occurs by the thousands of incidents each year. The Software Publishers Association (SPA) and the Business Software Alliance (BSA) had an independent research organization conduct a survey on pirating in 1999. The survey found the following: (1) in the United States $3.19 billion per year in revenue is lost to software piracy; (2) software companies are suffering tremendous losses from software pirates—$12.2 billion globally; (3) between 1994 and 1999, there was a $59 billion loss. Software copies work as well as the originals and sell for less money. Unfortunately, piracy is easy and only the large piracy rings are caught. Even the U.S. government's Department of Justice was involved in stealing copyrighted software. The SPA, a division of the Software and Information Industry Association (SIIA), reports finding many forms of software piracy on the Internet (SPA, 1996). Internet sites have pirated software for free downloading, and bulletin boards give you these links. For example, a college student at the University of Puget Sound, Washington, was caught illegally copying and distributing software via the Internet ("Software Publishers Association Announces Settlement," 1997).

In the 1980s, one of the most popular computer programs was a copy program that was able to duplicate protected software. It is speculated that 30 percent to 50 percent of a typical school's software has been illegally copied. Some teachers have sent illegally copied software to the software manufacturer for repair when they had problems with it. People who would never think of stealing from a department store freely make illegal copies of software, justifying their dishonesty with the following rationalizations:

(1) software developers receive free publicity for their products through illegal copies; (2) software is grossly overpriced and therefore fair game for piracy; (3) teachers believe copying software is for the greater good of their students; and (4) the cost of copying software is borne by the developer and not the customer, and developers have money to spare. The truth is that software developers never condone illegal copying; they expect buyers to use their original copy of their products and make backups as legally stipulated. Software is very expensive to produce and market. The cost of copying software is borne initially by the developers, but it is ultimately paid for by the legitimate buyer (Guglielmo, 1992).

The unauthorized duplication of software violates the federal copyright law and deprives developers of the revenue they richly deserve. The law clearly states that "anyone who violates any of the rights of the copyright owner is an infringement of the copyright" (Federal Copyright Law, Section 501). Reproducing computer software without the proper authorization is a federal offense. The money paid for a piece of software represents a fee for one copy and does not give the user the right to copy freely. Civil damages for unauthorized copying can amount to as much as $150,000. Criminal penalties include jail and fines (Federal Copyright Law, Title 18, Section 2319[b]). Many bills have been introduced in Congress to strengthen the copyright laws and increase the penalties for illegal copying. The software piracy issue is certain to receive continued legal attention. The SPA has tried to help the software industry by having a hotline for reporting software violations (1-800-388-7478). If the SPA finds a violation, it either works with the offending institution or petitions the federal court for a seizure order. This organization represents the leading software publishers in education, business, and home use.

Software developers have produced elaborate copy protection schemes to combat the piracy problem. One method is to build instructions into the program that will override any command to copy the software. The problem with this method is that hackers can easily create a program that gets around the copy protection. Another method uses software fingerprints, an emerging protection method. Fingerprinting is a technique that examines a computer system's individual configuration to collect information that can be used as the system's unique identification. The data are selectively encrypted together to build a unique identifier that sets off a "time bomb" in the software program if the user does not pay. The program will erase itself along with any files that it created. Another method used is to program the software so it is linked to serial numbers inside the chips or logic board of the computer unit. Presently networks have serial numbers and there is electronic registration by almost every software house. Microsoft has added the Registration Wizard to *Office 2000* so that you are forced to register your product. If you do not register the software, it will stop working after the 50th use (Wood, 2000). Yet for every scheme that is devised, a copy buster program is developed to override it.

Unfortunately, schools are a major culprit in educational software piracy. Why do schools copy illegally? Many schools and districts are eager to integrate the computer into the classroom. They have limited funds, and one copy for 32 students is not enough for group participation. Teachers want many copies so that they can have a group of students using the same software simultaneously. They view copying software as equivalent to photocopying teacher-made tests for their classrooms. In the end, the educator is the loser. Companies cannot make a profit selling educational software, so they divert their money to manufacturing products that are more economically lucrative. Software pirates ultimately drive smaller companies out of business.

What can school districts do to dissuade teachers or students from illegally copying software? They can warn teachers about illegally duplicating software and institute some disciplinary action when violations occur. Furthermore, schools can keep software locked away in restricted areas and limit student and teacher access. They can appoint a person or committee to be responsible for keeping records on the software purchased and how it is being used. This group would maintain a log of the software purchased and the machine on which the software resides. In addition, districts can require that teachers supervise students when they use software.

In the classroom, teachers can discuss recent criminal cases or a movie such as *War Games* to make students aware of the problems involved. Teachers can explain the federal and state laws and the differences between a felony, a crime punishable by a year in prison, and a misdemeanor, a crime punishable by a fine or a prison term. After the students have an understanding of the seriousness of computer crimes, they can devise a computer break-in policy for the school. The teacher can give each student a copy of this policy to read and study. Using this break-in policy, the teacher can present hypothetical cases concerning computer ethics breaches and ask the students what punishment they would recommend for the offender.

Teachers should find better ways to combat their budget constraints. Buying lab packs or multiple copies of software is one answer. The district could be encouraged to buy on-site licenses for selected programs, allowing the schools to make legal multiple copies and do multiple loadings of a program.[3]

Schools should also move toward networking their machines, which would enable schools to run a networkable piece of software over multiple machines. Finally, teachers should involve students, parents, and the community in raising money for software. In the long term, it is better to purchase the software than to steal it because the buyer receives technical support and upgrades from the publisher. Most important, it is the honorable and ethical way to operate.

Viruses

Another harmful force in computing today is the **virus,** a set of instructions that infects computer files by duplicating itself. A malicious individual writes

---

[3]*Multiple loadings* is the practice of loading a program from one disk onto several computers.

a code and buries it in an existing program. When the program is loaded into the computer, the virus attaches itself to other programs that are residing in the system. When a person inserts a disk thus infected into a computer's memory, the computer's files become infected. The reverse is also true; that is, a disk used in an infected computer becomes infected. Computers can be infected electronically when a hacker creates a virus and sends it over the phone lines to a local network. Since the network is connected to thousands of computers, the infection is carried to all the connected computers. When the virus arrives at each of these computers, it performs the assignment it was created to do.

A virus program can be nearly harmless, simply producing an obscene or silly message unexpectedly on the computer screen. But it can be a very destructive force, wiping out huge amounts of data. For example, a recent version of a popular utility program contained a virus that destroyed all the data on the user's hard disk. Of course, the company rectified the situation by shipping a new version without the virus. A virus can also find bank accounts with certain names and give the owners large sums of money.

Viruses are very hard to detect because they can be programmed to wreak havoc immediately or to lie dormant until a given future date. Viruses that are programmed to go off at a certain time are called *time bombs*. They start doing the damage at a certain time on a certain date. For example, the famous Michelangelo virus, named after the artist, activated itself on Michelangelo's birthday. Another enemy of the computer user is the *worm*, which is sometimes confused with a virus. The virus is a piece of code that adds itself to other programs and cannot run independently. A worm is "a destructive program that replicates itself throughout disk and memory, using up the computer's resources and eventually putting the system down" (Freedman, 2001). After the worm is finished with its work, the data usually are corrupted and irretrievable. A famous example, called the Internet Worm, occurred on November 2, 1988. This program, authored by Robert T. Morris, a graduate student in computer science at Cornell, was responsible for disrupting the operations of more than 6,000 computers nationwide. Recently, federal agencies experienced attacks by malicious e-mails spreading the "ILOVEYOU" and the "NewLove" worm viruses. At least 14 agencies were affected, including the CIA and the Department of Energy. Strange as it may seem, an industry group warned about the "ILOVEYOU" e-mail worm virus but there was an eight-hour delay before this information was given to federal agencies. This virus was so destructive that it cost an estimated $15 billion worldwide.

A large industry of virus protection software such as Symantec's *Norton AntiVirus* (Fig. 16.3) and *McAfee Anti-Virus Scan* (McAfee) has come into existence to combat the different types of viruses. The software scans for viruses, repairs damaged files, and prints status reports. Unfortunately, these antivirus programs are imperfect at best, because new, undetectable viruses pop up all the time. In 1986 there was only one unknown virus. Presently, between 10 and 15 new viruses are discovered every day Symantec's AntiVirus Research Center, http://www.sarc.com/. Now, according to *Norton AntiVirus* software,

**FIGURE 16.3
Norton AntiVirus**

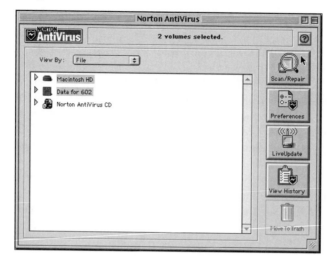

it protects you from over 57,000 viruses, and the number is growing at an unprecedented rate. Thank goodness most are low-level threats.

The best protection against virus infection involves certain precautions, including the following: (1) frequently back up your hard disk; (2) download into a single computer as opposed to a networked system; (3) use virus protection programs to check every piece of software for a virus before loading it into the computer's memory; (4) always write-protect program disks so that they cannot be destroyed; and (5) do not open attachments unless you know the sender, because there are viruses which can be attached to what is now considered "regular" e-mail.

Viruses certainly pose a threat to our computer systems, and this threat is increasing daily as we depend more and more on these technology wizards. However, some warnings about computer viruses are computer hoaxes. In 1997, a famous example, called Good Times, appeared. Many of us received a warning that said, "Beware of e-mail bearing the title Good Times." It went on to say, "Don't open this message; delete it immediately. If you read the message it will unleash a virus that will damage your computer hard drive and destroy your computer." The warning then tells you to e-mail your friends and tell them about this threat. Even some of the experts were scared, and big corporations fell for this hoax. In reality, this e-mail did not contain a computer virus but a self-replicating e-mail virus. This hoax tricked individuals into replicating the e-mail message.

Security

Clearly, there is an urgent need for computer security. Computer owners must take steps to prevent theft and inappropriate use of their equipment. According to an insurance agency, Safeware, an estimated 1.2 million computers were stolen, damaged, or otherwise destroyed during 1999. An estimated $1.9 billion in computer equipment was lost, stolen, or damaged by accidents, power surges, natural disasters, and other mishaps during 1999 (http://www.safeware.com/). Computer theft is a growing global problem costing billions annually.

Today, most computer facilities have some sort of security system. These facilities have means of confirming the identities of persons who want to use the system so that unauthorized users do not gain access. Usually, authorized users are issued special cards, keys, passwords, or account numbers. In elementary schools and high schools, this identification system may consist of a simple list of names. Each person on this list has a key that provides access to a computer room with bolted-down machines. Unfortunately, some users lend their keys and share their passwords. Often when computer users are allowed to choose their passwords, they choose easy-to-remember and easy-to-guess passwords.

One way to avert these problems is to assign access codes that are read by the computer from pass cards. The user does not have to remember this number, so the number can be complex. Even if the card is stolen, the code can be changed when the theft is reported. Recently, U.S. computer makers began offering **smart cards** as a security feature for laptop computers. A smart card can be used as an identification badge consolidating different systems into one card. For example, an enabled smart card can be used for building access, network login, credit card, remote and Web access. The card can also support several different applications such as user identification and Mastercard. Figure 16.4 shows (A) the cardholder's picture, (B) the barcode scan, (C) a seal, and (D) the microchip.

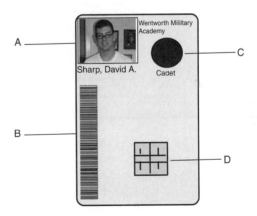

FIGURE 16.4
Smart Card
Courtesy of Vicki Sharp.

Another way businesses and schools are increasing security is by requiring every individual to enter a special code with his or her card. Experts advise going a step further by checking any available personal files for problems and restricting the number of people with access and the type of access they have to the computer. For instance, at most universities, students and professors use the same computer center, but they are not given the same access. Typically, the students have fewer privileges than the professors do. Last, fingerprint recognition is a technology that can be used to control access to a computer or network.

Before access is granted, the individual's fingers are scanned by a fingerprint reader and matched with the stored images of his or her fingerprints.

Another security problem concerns the protection of the operating system and data on the computer. It is essential that security measures protect all operating systems. Unscrupulous individuals have found ways to circumvent the system to print out a list of users' passwords, to give themselves access rights they are not officially assigned, and to spread viruses. For these reasons, all sensitive data should be stored and locked up when not in use. Some large companies use data encryption to store data in a scrambled form, meaningless to anyone without a special data item called a key.

Computer labs are prone to abuse by students who may unintentionally or deliberately alter computer files, trash programs, and create all sorts of havoc. Teachers can safeguard their computers from tampering by purchasing desktop security programs such as *Fortres 101* (Fortres Grand Corporation), *Kid Desk* (Edmark), and *FoolProof* created by SmartStuff Software (Fig. 16.5). Developed for and by teachers, *FoolProof* ensures that students are getting the most beneficial use of their computer learning experience.

**FIGURE 16.5
FoolProof**

FoolProof prevents users from deleting critical files and applications, making unauthorized changes to the desktop, saving unwanted programs, running disallowed programs, or corrupting the operating system, whether accidentally or maliciously.

Computers should also be safeguarded against natural disasters such as power surges, fires, and earthquakes. At the fundamental level, a good surge protector will rule out most power surges. However, disks do wear out and fire destroys, so it is important to make backup disks and store them in a different location. Cartridge backup drives, such as the Zip or Jaz drive, are very popular as a storage medium because of their transportable cartridges.

From this discussion, it should be evident how important security is. How far one goes in implementing a system for security is related to its cost. Usually, the more complicated the system, the more costly it is to carry out. Security will continue to be a problem because the number of computers and users continues to grow. For example, in the period between 1983 and 1984, there were only 92 students per computer in a school; whereas in the period between 1996 and 1997 there were 7 students per computer (Fulton, 1997). Eventually, there will be a computer on each student's desk. The teacher's main job will be to determine how to use this technology as a powerful tool for education. The teacher will also have to provide appropriate security.

Health Risks Using Computers

There has been increased interest in ways to reduce the risks of injury caused by computers. Every computer store has a variety of injury-reducing equipment in the form of wrist pads, antiglare screens, and ergonomic keyboards and track-balls. Unfortunately, it is very easy to improperly use computer equipment to the point of damaging your body. Repetitive strain injuries are a serious medical problem. According to the Bureau of Labor Statistics (http://www.bls.gov/), computer monitors, like other electrical devices, generate electric and magnetic fields in a very low frequency. There is scientific debate over whether low-level electromagnetic emissions cause health problems such as cancer. Regardless, the computer industry has moved to reduce these emissions. Most manufacturers support the guidelines known as MPR-II, established in 1990 by the Swedish Board for Measurement and Testing, or the stricter TCO guidelines, named after the Swedish officeworkers' union that developed them.

You can lessen the chances of computer-related injury by following these 10 suggestions:

1. Position yourself in front of the screen like a concert pianist, relax your shoulders, and keep your forearms and hands in a straight line. Make sure your lower back is supported and your thighs are horizontal. The top of the computer monitor should be slightly below eye level, and it should be positioned to avoid any type of glare. Finally, your feet should rest flat on the floor, and there should be clearance under the work area, between your legs and the desk (Fig. 16.6).

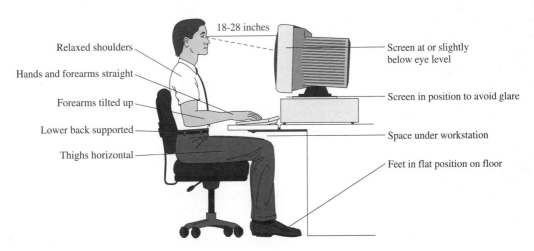

FIGURE 16.6 *Correct Posture for Computer Use*

2. Always work 18 to 28 inches from the monitor. Electromagnetic emissions from the front of any display should be negligible at 28 inches. Furthermore, the left side of the computer and the back usually generate the strongest emissions, so try to stay clear of these areas.

3. Avoid unnecessarily turning up the brightness on the monitor because you may be exposing yourself to higher emissions than the MPR-II guidelines allow.

4. Do not overwork. Take frequent breaks from the computer, at least once an hour. Move around and exercise your legs, arms, and neck. Don't stare at the monitor continually, but look around every 5 or 10 minutes. Remain relaxed.

5. Spend time finding a proper chair for your computer. Try it out and make sure you have ways of adjusting it to suit your individual needs.

6. The equipment you use most often should be close enough that you don't have to stretch to reach it.

7. Check to make sure the keys on your keyboard are not too difficult to press. The keys should give some tactile feedback; do not press too hard on the keyboard. Use function keys to help cut down on keystrokes.

8. Do not grip the mouse too tightly because it will increase the risk of injury. Additionally, choose a mouse that is comfortable for your hands.

9. Never brace your wrists against mouse pads when you are typing because this will eventually cause injury.

10. Finally, if you continually work with graphics, buy an appropriate input device such as a drawing tablet.

National Standards

Educational Technology Standards for teachers, students, programs, and schools have been developed by leading professional groups. These standards discuss what students should know and be able to accomplish with technology. Furthermore, accreditation standards for teacher education institutions discuss expectations for teacher competency in preparation programs.

The International Society for Technology in Education (ISTE), through a National Educational Technology Standards (NETS) project, published a document describing what prospective teachers should know and be able to do with technology. You will find this document at ISTE's website, http://cnets.iste.org/index.html.

The standards define what prospective teachers should learn and what the teachers should teach. The performance indicators show how the prospective teachers will demonstrate that the standard has been achieved. Prospective teachers seeking certification in teacher preparation should meet these educational technology standards. Table 16.1 lists the standards with their performance indicators and the chapters of this book in which they are covered.

Furthermore, the International Society for Technology in Education (ISTE), through a National Educational Technology Standards (NETS) project,

TABLE 16.1

ISTE National Educational Technology Standards (NETS) and Performance Indicators for Teachers

All classroom teachers should be prepared to meet the following standards and performance indicators.

Standards and Performance Indicators for Teachers	Chapter
I. Technology Operations and Concepts	
Teachers demonstrate a sound understanding of technology operations and concepts. Teachers:	2
A. Demonstrate introductory knowledge, skills, and understanding of concepts related to technology (as described in the *ISTE National Educational Technology Standards for Students*).	1, 2
B. Demonstrate continual growth in technology knowledge and skills to stay abreast of current and emerging technologies	16
II. Planning and Designing Learning Environments and Experiences	
Teachers plan and design effective learning environments and experiences supported by technology. Teachers:	1–16
A. Design developmentally appropriate learning opportunities that apply technology-enhanced instructional strategies to support the diverse needs of learners	10–14
B. Apply current research on teaching and learning with technology when planning learning environments and experiences	16
C. Identify and locate technology resources and evaluate them for accuracy and suitability	10
D. Plan for the management of technology resources within the context of learning activities	10–11
E. Plan strategies to manage student learning in a technology-enhanced environment	10–11
III. Teaching, Learning, and the Curriculum	
Teachers implement curriculum plans that include methods and strategies for applying technology to maximize student learning. Teachers:	1–16
A. Facilitate technology-enhanced experiences that address content standards and student technology standards	1–16
B. Use technology to support learner-centered strategies that address the diverse needs of students	12
C. Apply technology to develop students' higher-order skills and creativity	8–11, 13–15
IV. Productivity and Professional Practice	
Teachers use technology to enhance their productivity and professional practice. Teachers:	1–16
A. Use technology resources to engage in ongoing professional development and lifelong learning	14
B. Continually evaluate and reflect on professional practice to make informed decisions regarding the use of technology in support of student learning	10, 16
C. Apply technology to increase productivity	4–9
D. Use technology to communicate and collaborate with peers, parents, and the larger community in order to nurture student learning	4–5, 8–9 *(continues)*

(continued)

Standards and Performance Indicators for Teachers	Chapter
V. Social, Ethical, Legal, and Human Issues	
Teachers understand the social, ethical, legal, and human issues surrounding the use of technology in PK–12 schools and apply that understanding in practice. Teachers:	16
A. Model and teach legal and ethical practice related to technology use	16
B. Apply technology resources to enable and empower learners with diverse backgrounds, characteristics, and abilities	9–10, 12
C. Identify and use technology resources that affirm diversity	9–11, 12
D. Promote safe and healthy use of technology resources	9–11, 16
E. Facilitate equitable access to technology resources for all students	9–12, 16

published a document describing what students should know and be able to do with technology. You will find the standards that apply to K–12 students at ISTE's website, http://cnets.iste.org/index.html.

Computer-Assisted Instruction Research Findings

Computer-assisted instruction (CAI) has been used for over 25 years. CAI refers to applications specifically designed to teach a variety of subject areas to children and adults (Freedman, 2001). In CAI, students receive feedback from the computer, which controls the sequencing of the subject matter. Because of increased access to computers, teachers are concerned about the effects the computer has on instruction. The research literature contains many studies related to computer-assisted instruction, and this section will highlight some of these research findings.

Achievement

Numerous studies have compared the achievement scores of students using computer-assisted instruction with the achievement scores of students receiving regular instruction. Generally, the results indicates that CAI produces equal or greater achievement (Tsai and Pohl, 1977; Goode, 1988; Swan et al., 1990; Harrison and Van Devender, 1993; Kromhout and Butzin, 1993; Chambless and Chambless, 1994; Wenglinsky, 1998; Kuehner, 1999; Mann et al., 1999).

Gene Glass (1976, 1977) introduced a technique called *meta-analysis*[4] in order to generate a clearer picture of the effects of computer-based treatments. Other researchers followed and compiled meta-analysis studies in the area of instructional computing. Kuliks' series of meta-analysis studies were the most

---

[4]Meta-analysis is a statistical technique that allows researchers to summarize the results of a large group of research studies and identify general effects.

comprehensive (C.C. Kulik, J.A. Kulik, and Cohen, 1980; J.A. Kulik, Bangert, and Williams, 1983; C.C. Kulik, J.A. Kulik, and Shwath, 1986; J.A. Kulik and Chen-Lin, 1987; C.C. Kulik, J.A. Kulik, and Chen-Lin, 1991). The results of these studies showed that students who were taught using the computer scored higher on achievement tests than did those students who were taught using other methods. The Kuliks also showed that this analysis produced different results, depending on the grade, ability level, and type of instruction.

Roblyer, Castine, and King (1988) summarized previous literature reviews on the educational effectiveness of instructional computing before they presented their meta-analysis of recent studies. Here is a brief rundown of their findings: (1) there are higher achievement results for college-age and adult students than for elementary and secondary students; (2) the computer produced the greatest achievement gains in science, with math, reading, and cognitive skills yielding about half the effect; (3) computer-assisted instruction software programs were all of approximately equal effectiveness; and (4) lower achieving students showed more gains with CAI than did students who were achieving at grade level, but these gains were not statistically significant.

Using a meta-analysis approach, Khalili and Shashaani (1994) reviewed 36 published studies to see how effective CAI was in improving students' academic achievement. They concluded that computers were very effective in improving academic performance and that duration of computer usage was an important factor.

Using a meta-analytic technique over a 12-year span, Mann and Shakeshaft (1997) did a study that was commissioned by participating New York school districts to see if computer technology made a difference for the region's students, teachers, and schools. The study involved 1,722 elementary and secondary school students and 4,041 teachers. The researchers found that student achievement was higher in schools in which teachers believed that technology had a positive impact on learning. Moreover, overall gain from increased use of computer-related technology for students and teachers was statistically significant.

In a 1997, Christmann, Badgett, and Lucking compared the academic achievement of secondary students across academic areas. These students were instructed by CAI alone, by traditional methodology supplemented with CAI, or by traditional methodology alone. In addition, the study compared the recent results with earlier research findings. The meta-analysis study results showed that the average student receiving traditional instruction supplemented with CAI achieved higher academic achievement than did 57.2 percent of the students receiving traditional instruction alone. However, the effect of CAI on academic achievement showed a decline during the 12-year period; there was a very high correlation between the size of the effect and the number of years.

Sivin-Kachala (1998) did find an increase in achievement from preschool through higher education for regular and children with special needs. Schacter (1999) examined 700 studies on current research on achievement and technology. He found that students who use CAI and other technologies show achievement gains on standardized tests, national tests, and constructed tests.

On the other hand, Richard E. Clark reviewed CAI in meta-analytical studies in 1985. He was critical of the research and suggested that studies by the Kuliks and others overestimated CAI's benefits because uncontrolled instructional methods were embedded in the instructional treatments. Clark (1991, 1994) felt that the existing evidence does not indicate that computers yield learning benefits. In an eastern Canada high school study, Liu, Macmillan, and Timmons (1998) found computer integration produced no significant effect on achievement and there was no change in student attitude toward computers. Also, Baker, Gearhart, and Herman (1994) showed no gains on standardized tests in the Apple Classrooms of Tomorrow.

As you can see from this discussion, recent research findings on CAI suggest that CAI produces achievement equal to or greater than traditional teaching (Wenglinsky, 1998; Sivin-Kachala, 1998; Kuehner, 1999; Mann et al., 1999; Schacter, 1999; Mann and Shakeshaft, 1997), even though there is still lack of consensus among some researchers on the value of CAI.

Gender Differences

Most gender studies try to get at the reasons for males using the computer more than females. Collis and Ollila (1986) examined the gender differences in secondary school students' attitudes toward writing on the computer. Females were significantly less positive than their male counterparts on every item that related to computers.

Swadener and Hannafin (1987) studied the gender similarities and differences in sixth graders' attitudes toward the computer. They found that boys with higher achievement levels in mathematics also had high interest in computers. The boys with low scores had low interest in computers. This finding is completely opposite for females, with the low-achieving female students having the most interest in the computer.

Siann et al. (1988) studied gender stereotyping and computer involvement. They suggested there are some encouraging trends, but males still use computers more than females do.

Williams et al. (1994) examined the effects of factors such as past experience and sex typing on computer-interaction tasks completed by 154 male and 223 female college students. The results of the study did support the pattern of male advantage, but they also highlighted the complex factors involved in computer interactions.

Makrakis and Sawada (1996) surveyed 773 ninth-grade students from Tokyo, Japan, to Stockholm, Sweden. They found that regardless of the country surveyed, males reported higher scores on computer aptitude and enjoyment than females did. Whitley (1997) did a meta-analysis of studies of gender differences in computer attitude and found that males showed greater sex-role stereotyping of computer use, higher computer self-efficacy, and more positive attitudes toward computers than did females. The largest differences were found in high school students; most other differences were small. Liao (1999) did a meta-analysis on the effect of gender differences on attitudes toward computers. These results too suggest that male subjects have a slightly more positive attitude toward computers than female subjects.

Finally, Young (2000) used a student computer attitude survey with 462 middle and high school students. The results of the study showed greater confidence among male students in regard to the computer and the perception of computers as a male domain supported by males.

The majority of studies on gender differences seem to point to males having a more positive attitude toward computers than females. The question that seems to be unanswered is why this is occurring.

Science Simulations

Generally, students learn very well with science simulation software. Moore, Smith, and Avner (1980) found higher student achievement with computer simulations when students had to interpret the results of the experiments to make decisions. If the students only had to follow directions and calculate the results, there was no difference between the experimental and control groups. Summerville (1984) and Fortner, Schar, and Mayer (1986) noted similar findings. Linn (1986) conducted an experiment in which 8 eighth-grade science classes used computers as lab partners for a semester. The students learned to use the computer to collect and display data and save and print out their reports. They used tools such as temperature and light probes that were attached to the computer, and the results were displayed on their computer screens. Linn found that the students instructed in the microcomputer-based labs outperformed 17-year-olds who took a standardized test on scientific knowledge. In addition, these computer-taught students demonstrated a very positive attitude toward experimentation. Farynaiarz and Lockwood (1992) examined the impact of microcomputer simulations on environmental problem solving using community college students. The students showed a highly significant improvement in problem-solving skills after being exposed to three simulation models on lake pollution.

Kumar and Helgeson (1995) reviewed seven computer applications including simulation and found that simulation improved the quality and efficiency of record keeping and data analysis. Finally, Rueter and Perrin (1999) tested the effect of using a computer simulation to teach the concept of a food web to nonbiology majors in an introductory course. They concluded that the use of the simulation resulted in significantly better performance on an open-ended essay question for students using the software and the average student generally scored higher.

The results of the science simulation studies continue to be promising. Even a study that shows no significant difference between students who use the traditional method and students who use the computer is encouraging. Such a finding means that simulations can substitute for laboratory experiments, which is advantageous because science simulations are less dangerous, less time-consuming, and less expensive than actual lab work. They encourage student involvement in the learning process and let teachers give students access to situations that ordinarily would be impossible.

Word Processing

Many studies deal with word processing and its effect on the quantity and quality of student writing, but the evidence is contradictory (Bangert-Drowns, 1993). O'Brien (1984), Feldman (1984), Morehouse, Hoaglund, and Schmidt (1987), Jones (1994), and Owston and Wideman (1997) found evidence in favor of word processing. Owston and Wideman in 1997 did a three-year study (grades 3–5) of two groups of elementary school students and determined that writing quality improved in schools with high computer access, and word processors contributed to the improvement. Gupta (1998) compared Singapore students' composing behaviors using a spelling checker. He found that the spelling checker benefits those students whose writing ability is poor and who have trouble with the mechanical aspects of writing. However, Daiute (1985) found that students wrote less with a word processor. Kurth (1987) found no differences in quality of writing or revisions between a secondary school group that used word processing for their writing and a secondary group that used pencil and paper. Seawel et al. (1994) compared the effects of computer-based word processing and writing by hand on third and fourth graders' attitudes and performance in writing. The third graders made more revisions and edits when using word processors, whereas the fourth graders made more changes in their hand-written drafts.

Roblyer, Castine, and King (1988) summarized the research and said that word processing did not appear to improve the quality of writing. Hawisher (1986) and Bangert-Drowns (1993) reviewed the research on word processing and noted that implementation differences among the various studies could affect their outcomes. Reed (1996) found that the type of word processor that is used affects the students. For example, younger students need more prompts while older ones find this inhibiting. These criticisms highlight the problem, not only for word processing studies, but also for other research concerning computer applications. The inconclusive nature of these studies may be due to the difficulty of quantifying the assessment of writing.

The Learning Disabled

Most research indicates that the learning disabled (LD) benefit from involvement with CAI. Zhang (2000) conducted a year-long research study involving 5 fifth-grade students with learning disabilities. He used a specially designed computer program as a writing tool to assist these students with weekly writing curriculum. The study showed that students had positive gains in their writing behaviors and their written products. Xin and Jitendra (1999), in a meta-analysis study on the effectiveness of instruction in word-problem solving for students with learning problems, found that computer-assisted instruction was most effective for group-design studies and long-term intervention effects. McNaughton et al. (1997) investigated the impact of integrated proofreading strategy training on LD secondary students. This training consisted of using a computer spelling checker and student strategies on proofreading. Students showed an increase in strategy use and percentage of spelling errors corrected on student compositions and proofreading material. Every method improved writing accuracy. Shiah et al. (1994–1995) studied 30 elementary LD students and found that these students performed significantly better on mathematics tests by using a computer rather than using paper and pencil. The researchers found no differences among variations in computer-assisted instruction. Koseinski et al. (1993) conducted a study with six male LD elementary school students. They were taught multiplication facts using computer software programs with a five-second constant time delay procedure. The results of the study indicated that this computer-assisted program was very effective and that the learning generalized with varying degrees of success. Carman and Kosberg (1982) showed a significant positive influence on attention-to-task behavior for emotionally disabled children.

Other studies also support positive effects of CAI with learning disabled (Lally, 1980; Watkins and Webb, 1981; Hasselbring, 1982).

Motivation and Attitude

Teachers face the challenge of motivating students and fostering in them a positive attitude to improve their chances for success in school. For example, an essential element for improving students' spelling is keeping interest high (Ruel, 1977). Many studies report students' positive attitudes toward the computer and how computers motivate students and help them maintain high interest (Kosakowski, 2000; S. Hatfield, 1996; M.M. Hatfield, 1991; S. Clement, 1981).

Yildirim (2000) examined the changes in attitude of 114 preservice and inservice teachers toward computers after they participated in an educational computing class. The results indicated that the teachers' attitudes (anxiety, confidence, and liking) significantly improved after this computer literacy course. S. Hatfield (1996) examined the effective use of computer stations across the curriculum and found overall increased computer use and increased student motivation and interest. Terrell and Rendulic (1996) did a comparative study of elementary school students and found evidence that the use of computer-managed instructional feedback can have a positive effect on student motivation and achievement. Richman's (1994) study showed how innovations in educational technology contributed to motivation and achievement of at-risk students in the New York's Berkshire Union Free School District. Robertson (1978) found that children who had experienced failure in the past responded positively to computer-assisted programs. She concluded that the children involved in the study did not experience a sense of failure over an incorrect response.

In a departure from the other studies, McKinnon, Nolan, and Sinclair (2000) found that an increase in access to computers resulted in a decrease in favorable attitude toward the computer. The findings seem paradoxical because the decrease in positive attitudes toward computers was accompanied by an increasingly positive attitude toward school and the integrated curriculum program in which computers were a major element. Mitra and Steffensmeir (2000) found that if students did not have ready access to computers, their attitudes toward teaching and learning did not change. However, if these students had easy access through a networked institution, this fostered a positive attitude toward computers in teaching and learning. In a 1998 study, Liu, Macmillan, and Timmons found that there was no significant effect of computer integration on achievement, and there was no significant change in student attitude toward computers after the computer integration. Generally, students perceived that using computers had a positive effect on their learning.

Some researchers have tried to find out if students prefer computer-based methods simply because a computer is involved. Other research has focused on the computer's influence on student attitudes toward school and curriculum. Bracey (1982) found that students reacted favorably to computer use for instructional tasks. He reported that students who worked on the computer had a more positive attitude toward the machine than did those students who had not used the computer.

Generally, the CAI studies that focused on students' attitudes toward themselves and school learning were positive. However, the results are inconclusive on the effects on computer instruction as it relates to motivation and school achievement. One reason for this finding might be that achievement in school is not based on a simple set of variables but is the result of a complex set of factors.

Programming

In the 1980s and midway through the 1990s, there were studies that discussed programming languages, such as BASIC. These studies examine the impact that programming could have on different types of intellectual activities. There were proponents who wanted programming taught in the schools (Luehrmann, 1984). Many individuals argue that computer programming improved students' problem-solving ability (Soloway, Lockhead, and Clement, 1982; Casey, 1997; Clements, 1999). Still other supporters proclaim that programming should not be taught for the sake of programming, but instead to help children learn other subjects such as math (Papert, 1980, 1996).

A review of the research on such topics as the effects of programming on achievement, problem-solving, and transferability is inconclusive (Collis, 1990; Bernardo and Morris, 1994; Ennis, 1994; Shih and Alessi, 1993–94). Mayer, Dyck, and Vilberg (1986) concluded that there was no consistent evidence that learning to program had any positive impact on anything else: "There is no convincing evidence that learning to program enhances students' general intellectual ability, or that programming is any more successful than Latin for teaching 'proper habits of mind.' " The general conclusions from these studies were inconclusive and disappointing. Moreover, lately, the only research on programming has been on Logo.

Logo and Problem Solving

In the late 1980s, there was widespread interest among educators on the effects of Logo computer programming language on students. This interest waned for a few years, but recently there has been renewed interest in this topic. The most frequent claim about Logo is that it promotes problem-solving skills or reasoning ability. Some of these studies have found positive results, some have found negative results, and others found no statistically significant differences.

Roblyer et al. (1988) did a meta-analysis on the effects of CAI on problem-solving and general thinking. Their findings indicated that Logo showed promise as a method for developing problem-solving skills, but this finding was not a statistical conclusion. Lu (1991) compared the problem-solving abilities of adolescents enrolled in a gifted program with experienced adolescent programmers. The students were given puzzles and problems to solve. The results demonstrated that the students with programming skill did solve the problems more efficiently, developed more highly structured plans, and systematically monitored their thinking processes better than the nonprogrammers did. Lu concluded that metacognitive skills gained through programming are transferable and do increase with programming experience.

Clements et al. (1993) reviewed the research to discover the benefits of open-ended computer programs such as Logo. They discussed ways that the programs appear to develop problem-solving skill, socioemotional competencies, and subject-matter knowledge. Reeder and Leming (1994) studied the effect of Logo on the nonverbal reasoning ability of rural, disadvantaged third graders. The students were taught Logo for eight weeks and were then compared to a control group that remained in a traditional classroom setting to do homework. The investigators used the Matrix Analogies Test (MAT) to measure these groups. The results of the study showed that the Logo group scored significantly higher than the traditional group and that Logo did enhance the nonverbal reasoning ability of these children. Suomala (1996) studied 38 Finnish eight-year-olds using Logo. The results suggest that Logo promotes the development of problem-solving skills if each student receives sufficient support.

Vasu and Tyler (1997) investigated the effects of using Logo or problem-solving–oriented simulation software on the spatial and critical thinking skills of fifth-grade students. They found that the Logo group had a change in spatial scores, and the simulation group had a significant change in critical thinking scores. There was no significant change found for the comparison group. In "Using Computers for Algebraic Thinking," Sarama, Clements, and Seidel (1998) discussed how three different kinds of software—*Teasers* by Tobbs, spreadsheets, and Logo programming—help students develop algebraic reasoning. Wagner (1998) examined whether use of robotics had a greater effect on elementary school children's achievement in science concepts and problem-solving abilities than use of battery-powered motorized manipulatives or no manipulatives. She found no significant difference in achievement from use of robotics except in programming language problem solving. Both robotics and battery-powered manipulatives made significant achievement differences compared to a traditionally taught class. Douglas Miller's (1999) project in a Florida high school was intended to improve test and programming scores of 9th-through 12th-grade students enrolled in a Logo course. The course's overall objective was to expose students to a higher order of logical thinking skills such as critical thinking, problem-solving strategies, evaluation and analysis, and creativity. The target group improved dramatically in all areas.

Keller (1990) completed a research review on the possible impact of Logo on cognitive development. She found that the teacher plays a critical role in the Logo environment. Some studies showed the difficulties that young children have in learning Logo (Horner and Maddux, 1985; Mayer and Fay, 1987). Grovier (1988) summarized a variety of American and British research related to Logo. She found one key factor: The studies with significant effects were the ones in which the teacher structured the learning.

Pea and Kurland's (1984) research results, however, did not support the connection between Logo and problem-solving skills. Dalton (1986) compared Logo to a curriculum created to improve problem solving and reported that the problem-solving group achieved significantly more than the Logo group or the control group at every level of student ability. David Miller's 1993 article discusses Logo, noting that it is based on long periods of instruction, knowledgeable teachers, and numerous computers. He felt that recent research shows that Logo may confuse children's understanding of angles, not help it. The researcher found that the target group improved dramatically in all areas. In conclusion, numerous studies support the thesis that Logo improves problem-solving abilities; however, the research is still not conclusive.

Problems with the Research

Although a considerable amount of research has been done since the early 1980s, the research is problematic. CAI studies were conducted before microcomputers were readily available. In addition, many studies are not thoroughly reported in the literature, so it is impossible to determine whether the conclusions drawn by the investigators are supported by the data. The meta-analysis that Roblyer et al. (1988) performed included 38 studies and 44 dissertations from a possible 200. The rest of the studies were eliminated because of reasons such as methodological flaws or insufficient data. A good portion of CAI research is anecdotal, based on experiences and not on experimental design. Educators are now beginning to understand what role the computer could play in educating students. However, we still don't know if computers are the answer. Studies have shown that students in most technologically advanced classrooms perform no better on standardized tests than their peers do (Trotler, 1997). There definitely is a need for higher quality computer research to get substantive answers to our many questions.

Research Generalizations

Even with these problems, some relevant generalizations can be made from the research:

1. In science, the computer is a useful tool for simulations. For example, the army and navy use war game simulations. Chemistry instructors can use computer-based simulations as substitutes for lab work. Flight instructors can use flight simulation software instead of putting novices at the controls of actual planes. A simulation program is generally less dangerous, less expensive, and less time-consuming than the real experience.

2. The computer is helpful for individualization. Students working with computers can progress at their own pace. If they need help with math facts, they can turn to the computer for individualized tutoring, freeing the teacher to work with the same child in other academic areas. This type of individualization spreads the range of abilities in a class and allows some students to move ahead.

3. The computer changes attitudes toward the computer, school, and school subjects. The computer does motivate children, and there is speculation that it might improve the dropout rate.

4. The relationship between attitude and achievement is low. There is no strong body of evidence supporting the notion that a positive attitude toward the computer will result in improved achievement.

5. No substantial evidence supports the claim that studying programming improves problem-solving ability or enhances general intellectual development.

6. Research suggests that the computer is best used as a tool or resource rather than as a programming device.

7. Word processing motivates children to write. However, there is no difference between the quality of writing produced using a word processor and that generated with pencil and paper.

8. Gender studies have found that boys work more frequently with the computer than do girls. This finding appears to be a socially developed difference.

Summary

Computers are involved in new types of crime as well as some variations on the traditional crimes. Computer embezzlement and unauthorized access to computer systems are two examples. Software piracy is a problem that computer companies are still trying to resolve. Software houses offer many alternatives to schools tempted to illegally duplicate software: on-site licensing, lab packs, and networkable disks.

Computer security is a topic that is often in the news. A computer user must be concerned with protecting data from loss or unauthorized access. What is needed are proper identification of the user, authorizing passwords, equipment and disk protection, and proper backup of computer files. Backup copies should be kept at different sites to guard against data loss due to fire, theft, or failure of storage media.

There are many research studies on computer-assisted instruction (CAI). The synopsis of research findings presented in this chapter gives an overview of the exciting successes and failures of this field. In Chapter 17 we will consider the future of this technology.

🖉 INTERNET SITES

What follows is an annotated list of top-rated Internet sites. These sites contain articles about viruses, the National Standards, ethics, computer law, software piracy, online quizzes, and other resources.

Arthur Levine: Creating an Education System for an Information Age
http://www.convergemag.com/Publications/CNVGOct00/aurthur.shtm
Meet an education leader whose revolutionary ideas are making a difference in the way we teach. This site offers insight into the mind of Arthur Levine, education leader. Levine believes that change is the biggest challenge that today's educators must face.

Teaching in a Digital Age
http://www.infotoday.com/MMSchools/oct00/sargent&armstrong.htm
Teaching in a Digital Age requires a widespread shift in mindset. So far, this shift has only taken place, if at all, at the classroom level. The George Lucas Educational Foundation has launched a new project called "Teaching in the Digital Age" that is designed to provide the impetus required to bring about change at the school, district, and system levels. Learn how one school benefited from this initiative.

Electronic School
http://electronic-school.com/
The *Electronic School* is an award-winning technology magazine for K–12 school leaders. This online edition of *Electronic School* provides articles from the print edition as well reviews, forms, and links.

Internet Do's and Don'ts
http://www.usdoj.gov/kidspage/do-dont/kidinternet.htm
Internet Do's and Don'ts explains to youths that vandalism in cyberspace is the same as old-fashioned wrongdoing. Ethics and cyber-crime topics covered are computer law, software piracy, and online cheating. This page is part of *Department of Justice Web Page for Kids!*

Safe & Smart: Research and Guidelines for Children's Use of the Internet
http://www.nsbf.org/safe-smart/
The National School Boards Foundation released findings and guidelines from its major national survey on online safety; the report includes data, implications, resources, and guidelines for school leaders and parents.

StateStandards.com
http://www.statestandards.com/
StateStandards.com, a free service from *EdVISION.com,* is a single site for accessing lesson plans based on state curriculum standards. This site offers educational standards for all 50 states and the District of Columbia.

State and National Government Resources
http://www.edvision.com/statenational.htm
EdVISION.com provides a link to the departments of education of each state and the District of Columbia, with extensive information on content standards and other educational topics.

FamilyEducation.com
http://familyeducation.com/home/
This site provides useful information and interactive communication tools to help busy parents help their children succeed. It includes school resources, quizzes, polls, discussion groups, and articles on parenting and education subjects. It also contains a network of local school websites, with school calendars and community-level information enabling parent–school connection.

Education Week—on the Web
http://edweek.org/
This site is for people interested in education reform, schools, and the policies that guide them. *Education Week,* published by Editorial Projects in Education, also includes extensive education information on every state and the District of Columbia.

Internet Fraud Watch
http://www.fraud.org/
This site offers news, updates, and advice from the National Fraud Information Center.

Internet ScamBusters
http://scambusters.com/
This site provides information to help you avoid getting ripped off by Internet scams, fraud, misinformation, and hyperbole.

Consumer.net
http://consumer.net/
Consumer.net provides extensive information on Internet privacy, cookies, junk mail, and other privacy and security issues.

CyberCriminals Most Wanted
http://www.ccmostwanted.com/
CyberCriminals Most Wanted covers hundreds of issues on computer fraud and security from e-mail to shopping.

Computers and Society Social Issues Pages
http://www.ccs.neu.edu/home/perrolle/issues.html
Professor Judith A. Perrolle of Northeastern University in Boston addresses social issues in computing from equity and access to ethics.

Yahoo! Security and Encryption
http://dir.yahoo.com/computers_and_internet/security_and_encryption/
Yahoo's directory offers information on a variety of computer security and encryption issues.

CDT's Resource Library
http://www.cdt.org/resourcelibrary/
The Center for Democracy and Technology provides information on a number of civil liberties issues from Internet filtering to privacy and security.

AT&T Learning Network
http://www.att.com/learningnetwork/
AT&T Learning Network offers the newest models and latest trends in education and professional development and support. The site provides information on cable in education, virtual academy, and other online services and resources.

21st Century Teachers Network
http://www.21ct.org/
The *21st Century Teachers Network* is a place where teachers can learn more about educational technology. Among the highlights are a library of lesson plans and activities that incorporate educational technology, a wide array of discussion groups, and a national event calendar.

Educational World's National and State Standards
http://www.educationworld.com/standards/
Education World presents the objectives of the voluntary National Education Standards for the major subject areas and links to individual departments of education.

Developing Educational Standards
http://PutnamValleySchools.org/Standards.html
Developing Educational Standards is an annotated list of Internet sites with K–12 educational standards and curriculum framework documents, maintained by Charles Hill and the Putnam Valley Schools in New York.

ISTE's National Educational Technology Standards
http://cnets.iste.org/
The National Educational Technology Standards (NETS) Project is an initiative of the International Society for Technology in Education (ISTE) and a consortium of distinguished partners and cosponsors. The site provides online NETS for teachers and students as well as a searchable database of lessons matched to the technology standards.

About.com's Computer Crime
http://lawenforcement.about.com/careers/lawenforcement/cs/computercrime/
Law Enforcement with Cliff Brinson has over 700 sites on computer crime that range from fighting Internet crimes to computer crime research resources.

SPA Software Publishers Association
http://www.spa.org/piracy/policy/
The Software and Information Industry Association (SIIA) has brought together the

leading companies of the software and information industry, expanding market opportunities and forging the way toward a stronger industry. SIIA is the only trade association with a global reach that provides a credible, unifying voice for all businesses that provide the software and information that underpin the digital economy.

California Instructional Technology Clearinghouse
http://clearinghouse.k12.ca.us/
California Instructional Technology Clearinghouse provides over 3,700 selected electronic learning resources that match the California content standards.

Safeguarding the Wired Schoolhouse
http://www.safewiredschools.org/
Safeguarding the Wired Schoolhouse is a must-see for educators and other decision makers. Keeping students safe on the Internet is a concern in every wired school. This site offers excellent information on how to best manage the content that students are able to access. The site presents a checklist of questions that teachers should ask when making content management decisions. The other resources section includes links to some of the best sites on the Internet about child safety, acceptable use policies, filtering, and content management.

Cybercitizen Partnership
http://www.cybercitizenship.org/
The *Cybercitizen Partnership* for parents and teachers provides information on responsible computer use.

Symantec
www.symantec.com/avcenter/
Symantec's site is a very informative site which lists known viruses and gives a list of hoaxes. At this site, you can learn how to remove viruses from your computer and where you can send a suspected threat to be evaluated.

F-Secure Computer Virus Info Center
http://www.f-secure.com/virus-info/
This center lets you search a database to find a particular virus. In addition, it lists viruses alphabetically, with examples. You can also check for news and updates on virus protection.

IBM's Anti Virus Online
http://www.research.ibm.com/antivirus/
IBM's Anti Virus Online site contains a database of viruses and a glossary to help you with the jargon. You can even search for viruses by alternative names There is a test to see how well your virus protection is working.

MacAfee Virus Information Center
http://www.mcafeeb2b.com/naicommon/avert
This site lists more than 50,000 viruses. Here you can learn about major threats and new ones. The site lists virus removal procedures.

Virus.com
http://virus.com/
Virus.com is a global resource for virus protection. This site has up-to-date news, discussion forums, a listing of recent viruses, hoaxes, a virus search engine, informative articles, and much more.

Chapter Mastery Test
To the Instructor: Refer to the Instructor's Manual for the Answers to the Mastery Questions. This manual has additional questions and resource materials.

Let's check for chapter comprehension with a short mastery test. What follows are basic terms, classroom projects, and suggested readings and references.

1. Discuss two issues related to computer privacy.
2. Discuss the AT&T case and explain why it was important.
3. Explain the conflict between the computer user and the software publisher.
4. Why are computer viruses destructive? List some precautions you can take to

prevent one from infecting your computer system.

5. What can ordinary persons do to protect their data from fire, theft, and storage media failure?

6. Discuss the findings of three research studies on CAI.

7. Does CAI research show that science simulations are more effective than laboratory experiences? Explain your answer.

8. Discuss three ways to reduce the risks of computer-related injuries.

9. What is the NETS project for prospective teachers?

Basic Terms

cookie (p. 431)
hacker (p. 432)
meta-analysis (p. 444)

piracy (p. 434)
smart cards (p. 439)
virus (p. 436)

Classroom Projects

1. Research an example of a recent computer crime and prepare a short report. In this report, describe (a) what happened, (b) how the crime was discovered, and (c) how the crime could have been prevented.

2. Prepare a report on two types of computer viruses. Explain how they

affect your computer and how they were discovered.

3. Find three current examples of how computers were used to invade a person's privacy. How could these violations have been prevented?

4. Use research to argue that Logo improves problem solving.

Suggested Readings and References

Ashton, Tamarah M. "Spell Checking: Making Writing Meaningful in the Inclusive Classroom." *Teaching Exceptional Children* 32, no. 2 (November–December 1999): 24–27.

Badgett, Christmann E. J., and R. Lucking. "Progressive Comparison of the Effects of Computer-Assisted Instruction on the Academic Achievement of Secondary Students." *Journal of Research on Computing Education* 29, no. 4 (1997): 325–37.

Baker, E. L., M. Gearhart, and J. L. Herman, "Evaluating the Apple Classroom of

Tomorrow." In *Technology Assessment in Education and Training*, ed. E.L. Baker and H.F. O'Neil. Hillsdale, N.J.: Lawrence Erlbaum, 1994.

Bangert-Drowns, R. "The Word Processor as an Instructional Tool: A Meta-analysis of Word Processing in Writing Instruction." *Review of Educational Research* 63, no. 1 (1993): 69–93.

Bass, George M., Jr. "Assessing the Impact of Computer Based Instruction: A Review of Recent Research." *Educational Technology*, May 1990.

Batchelder, John Stuart, and John R. Rachal. "Efficacy of a Computer-Assisted Instruction Program in a Prison Setting: An Experimental Study." *Adult Education Quarterly* 50, no. 2 (February 2000): 120–33.

Becker, H. J. *The Impact of Computer Use on Children's Learning: What Research Has Shown and What It Has Not.* Baltimore, Md.: Johns Hopkins University Press, 1987.

Berinato, Scott. "After Hack, Microsoft Mistakes Linger." *eWeek* 17, no. 45 (November 6, 2000): 1.

Bernardo, M. A., and Morris J. D. "Transfer Effects of a High School Computer Programming Course on Mathematical Modeling, Procedural Comprehension, and Verbal Problem Solving." *Journal of Research on Computing in Education* 26, no. 4 (1994): 523–36.

Boone, R., and K. Higgins. "Hypermedia Applications for Content Area Study Guides." *Reading and Writing Quarterly: Overcoming Learning Difficulties* 8 (1992): 379–93.

Bracey, G. W. "Computers in Education: What the Research Shows." *Electronic Learning* 2, no. 3 (1982): 51–54.

Brown, Joan Marie. "Technology and Ethics." *Learning and Leading with Technology* 24, no. 6 (March 1997): 38–41.

Bunderson, Eileen D., and Mary Elizabeth Christensen. "An Analysis of Retention Problems for Female Students in University Computer Programs." *Journal of Research on Computing in Education* 28, no. 1 (Fall 1995): 1–18.

Burger, Ralf. *Computer Viruses: A High-Tech Disease.* Grand Rapids, Mich.: Abacus, 1988.

Burns, Patricia Knight, and William C. Bozeman. "Computer-Assisted Instruction and Mathematics Achievement: Is There a Relationship?" *Educational Technology* 21 (October 1981): 32–39.

Campbell, D. L., D. L. Peck, C. J. Horn, and R. K. Leigh. "CAI and Third Grade Mathematics." *Educational Communication and Technology Journal* 35, no. 2 (1987): 95–103.

Carman, Gary O., and Bernard Kosberg. "Research: Computer Technology and the Education of Emotionally Handicapped Children." *Educational Technology,* February 1982, pp. 32–36.

Casey, P. J. "Computer Programming: A Medium for Teaching Problem Solving." *Computers in the Schools* 12, no. 1/2 (1997): 41–51.

Chambless, Jim R., and Martha S. Chambless. "The Impact of Instructional Technology on Reading/Writing Skills of 2nd Grade Students." *Reading Improvement* 31, no. 3 (Fall 1994): 151–55.

Christmann, Edwin, John Badgett, and Robert Lucking. "Progressive Comparisons of the Effects of Computer-Assisted Instruction on the Academic Achievement of Secondary Students." *Journal of Research on Computing in Education* 29, no. 4 (Summer 1997).

Clark, Richard E. "Evidence for Confounding in Computer-Based Instruction Studies: Analyzing the Meta-Analysis." *Educational Communication and Technology Journal* 33, no. 4 (Winter 1985): 249–62.

Clark, Richard E. "Media Will Never Influence Learning." *Educational Technology, Research and Development* 42, no. 2 (1994): 21–29.

Clark, Richard E. "When Researchers Swim Upstream: Reflections on an Unpopular Argument about Learning from Media." *Educational Technology* 31, no. 31 (February 1991): 34–40.

Clement, Frank J. "Affective Considerations in Computer-Based Education." *Educational Technology,* April 1981, pp. 228–32.

Clements, Douglas H. "The Future of Educational Computing Research: The Case of Computer Programming" *Information Technology in Childhood Education Annual,* 1999, pp. 147–79.

Clements, Douglas H., and Julie Sarama. "Computers Support Algebraic Thinking." *Teaching Children Mathematics* 3, no. 6 (February 1997): 320.

Clements, Douglas H., et al. "Students' Development of Length Concepts in a Logo-Based Unit on Geometric Paths." *Journal for Research in Mathematics Education* 28, no. 1 (January 1997): 70–95.

Clements, Douglas H., et al. "Young Children and Computers: Crossroads and Directions from Research. Research in Review." *Young Children* 48, no. 2 (June 1993): 56–64.

Collis, B. *The Best of Research Windows: Trends and Issues in Educational Computing.* Eugene, Ore.: International Society of Technology in Education, 1990.

Collis, B., and L. Ollila. "An Examination of Sex Difference in Secondary School Students' Attitudes toward Writing and the Computer." *Alberta Journal of Educational Research* 34, no. 4 (1986): 297–306.

Colvin, L. B. "An Overview of U.S. Trends in Educational Software Design." *Computing Teacher* 16, no. 5 (February 1989): 24–28.

Cook, Albert M., and Albert R. Cavalier. "Young Children Using Assistive Robotics for Discovery and Control." *TEACHING Exceptional Children* 31, no. 5 (May–June 1999): 72–78.

Daiute, C. *Writing and Computers.* Reading, Mass.: Addison-Wesley, 1985.

Dalton, D. W. "A Comparison of the Effects of Logo and Problem-Solving Strategy Instruction on Learning Achievement, Attitude, and Problem-Solving Skills." *Dissertation Abstracts International* 47, no. 2 (1986): 511a (University Microfilms No. 86–08596).

Davidson, Johan, et al. "A Preliminary Study of the Effect of Computer-Assisted Practice on Reading Attainment." *Journal of Research in Reading* 19, no. 2 (September 1996): 20.

Dence, M. "Toward Defining the Role of CAI: A Review." *Educational Technology,* November 1980, pp. 50–54.

Dye, Lee. "Robots . . . Robots Who Need People." *Los Angeles Times,* September 29, 1997, p. D 8.

Dyrli, Odvard Egil. "Online Privacy and the Cookies Controversy." *Technology and Learning,* March 1997, p. 20.

Ennis, D. L. "Combining Problem Solving Instruction and Programming Instruction to Increase the Problem Solving Ability of High School Students." *Journal of Research on Computing in Education* 26, no. 4 (1994): 486–96.

Farynaiarz, Joseph V., and Linda G. Lockwood. "Effectiveness of Microcomputer Simulations in Stimulating Environmental Problem Solving by Community College Students." *Journal of Research in Science Teaching* 29, no. 5 (May 1992): 453–70.

Feigenbaum, E. A., and P. McCorduck. *The Fifth Generation: Artificial Intelligence and Japan's Computer Challenge to the World.* Reading, Mass.: Addison-Wesley, 1983.

Feldman, P. R. "Personal Computers in a Writing Course." *Perspectives in Computing,* Spring 1984, pp. 4–9.

Fisher, G. "Where CAI Is Effective: A Summary of the Research." *Electronic Learning* 82 (November/December 1983): 84.

Fites, Philip E. *The Computer Virus Crisis.* New York: Van Nostrand Reinhold, 1989.

Flanagan, Patrick. "The 10 Hottest Technologies in Telecom." *Telecommunications* 31, no. 5 (May 1997): 25–28, 30, 32.

Fortner, R., W. Schar, and J. Mayer. *Effect of Microcomputer Simulations on Computer Awareness and Perception of Environmental Relationships among College Students.* Columbus: Ohio State University, Office of Learning Resources (ERIC Document Reproduction Service No. Ed. 270-311), 1986.

Freedman, Warren. *The Right of Privacy in the Computer Age.* New York: Quorum Books, 1987.

Fulton, Mary. "The Data May Not Be Perfect. But If We Don't Start Somewhere and Have Something to Build On, We're Never Going Anywhere." *Education Week* 17, no. 11 (November 1997): 10–11.

Garzella, M. F. "Using an Expert System to Diagnose Weaknesses and Prescribe Remedial Reading Strategies among Elementary Learning Disabled Students." *Dissertation Abstracts International* 52/09-A (Order No. AAD92-07011), 1991.

"Gender Bias: Recent Research and Interventions." *New Jersey Research Bulletin,* no. 22 (Spring 1996).

Glass, G. V. "Integrated Findings: The Meta-Analysis of Research." In *Review of Research in Education,* ed. L. Schulman. Itasca, Ill.: Peacock, 1977.

Glass, G. V. "Primary, Secondary, and Meta-Analysis of Research." *Educational Researchers* 5 (1976): 3–8.

Gleason, Gerald T. "Microcomputers in Education: The State of the Art." *Educational Technology,* March 1981, pp. 7–18.

Goode, M. "Testing CAI Courseware in Fifth and Sixth Grade Math." *T.H.E. Journal,* October 1988, pp. 97–100.

Groner, Jonathan. "Swatting Back at Software Pirates." *Legal Times,* June 1992.

Grovier, H. *Microcomputers in Primary Education: A Survey of Recent Research* (Occasional Paper ITE/28a/88). Lancaster, U.K.: Economics and Social Research Council, 1988.

Guglielmo, Connie. "Managers Clamp Down on Software Piracy." *MacWeek* 6, no. 2 (January 13, 1992): 60–63.

Gupta, Renu. "Can Spelling Checkers Help the Novice Writer?" *British Journal of Educational Technology* 29, no. 3 (July 1998): 255–66.

Harrison, Nancy, and Evelyn M. Van Devender. "The Effects of Drill-and-Practice Computer Instruction on Learning Basic Mathematics Facts." *Journal of Computing in Childhood Education* 3, no. 304 (May 1993): 349–56.

Hasselbring, Ted S. "Remediating Spelling Problems of Learning-Handicapped Students through the Use of Microcomputers." *Educational Technology*, April 1982, pp. 31–32.

Hatfield, M. M. "The Effect of Problem-Solving Software on Student's Beliefs about Mathematics: A Qualitative Study." *Computers in the Schools* 8, no. 4 (1991): 21–40.

Hatfield, Susan. *Effective Use of Classroom Computer Stations across the Curriculum.* ERIC Document No. ED396704 RIENOV96, Dissertations/Theses, Research Technical, June 30, 1996.

Hawisher, G. E. "The Effects of Word Processing on the Revision Strategies of College Students." Paper presented at the annual meeting of the American Educational Research Association, San Francisco (ERIC Document No. ED. 268–546), April 1986.

Haynes, Colin. *The Computer Virus Protection Handbook.* San Francisco: SYBEX, 1990.

Hess, Frederick M., and David L. Leal. "Computer-Assisted Learning in Urban Classrooms: The Impact of Politics, Race, and Class." *Urban Education* 34, no. 3 (September 1999): 370–88.

Hodges, Andrew. *Alan Turing: The Enigma.* London: Vintage Paper Back, Ranlon Century, 1992.

Hoffman, Patricia. VSUM Database, December 30, 1997. VSUM, 3333 Bowers Avenue, Suite 130, Santa Clara, CA 95054. Telephone (408) 988-3773, BBS (408) 244-0813.

Horner, C. M., and C. D. Maddux. "The Effect of Logo on Attributions toward Success." *Computers in the Schools* 2, no. 2/3 (1985): 45–54.

Jones, I. "The Effects of a Word Processor on the Written Composition of Second-Grade Pupils." *Computers in the Schools* 11, no. 2 (1994): 43–54.

Jessop, Deborah. "A Survey of Recent Advances in Optical and Multimedia Information Technologies." *Computers in Libraries* 17, no. 2 (February 1997): 53–59.

Katt, Spencer F. "Hackers Pitch Strikes to Sites' Security." *eWeek* 17, no. 45 (November 6, 2000): 114.

Keller, Janet K. "Characteristics of Logo Instruction Promoting Transfer of Learning: A Research Review." *Journal of Research on Computers in Education* 23, no. 1 (Fall 1990): 3.

Khalili, A., and L. Shashaani. "The Effectiveness of Computer Applications: A Meta-analysis." *Journal of Research on Computing in Education* 27, no. 1 (Fall 1994): 48–61.

Kosakowski, John. "The Benefits of Information Technology." *Educational Media and Technology Yearbook* 25 (2000): 53–56.

Koseinski, Susan, et al. "Computer-Assisted Instruction with Constant Time Delay to Teach Multiplication Facts to Students with Learning Disabilities." *Learning Disabilities Research Practices* 8, no. 3 (Summer 1993): 157–68.

Krein, T. J., and T. R. Mahollm. "CDT Has the Edge in a Comparative Study." *Performance and Instruction*, August 1990, pp. 22–24.

Kromhout, Ora M., and Sarah M. Butzin. "Integrating Computers into the Elementary School Curriculum: An Evaluation of Nine Project CHILD Model Schools." *Journal of Research on Computing in Education* 26, no. 1 (Fall 1993): 5.

Kuehner, Alison V. "The Effects of Computer Instruction on College Students' Reading Skills." *Journal of College Reading and Learning* 29, no. 2 (Spring 1999): 149–65.

Kulik, C. C., C. Chen-Lin, and J.A. Kulik. "Effectiveness of Computer-Based Instruction: An Updated Analysis." *Computers in Human Behavior* 7 (1991): 75–94.

Kulik, C. C., J. A. Kulik, and P. Cohen. "Instructional Technology and College Teaching." *Teaching of Psychology* 7 (1980): 199–205.

Kulik, C. C., J. A. Kulik, and B. J. Shwath. "Effectiveness of Computer-Based Adult Learning: A Meta-Analysis." *Journal of Educational Computing Research* 2 (1986): 235–52.

Kulik, J. A., R. Bangert, and G. Williams. "Effects of Computer-Based Teaching on Secondary School Students." *Journal of Educational Psychology* 75 (1983): 19–26.

Kulik, J. A., and C. Chen-Lin. "Review of Recent Literature on Computer-Based Instruction." *Contemporary Education Psychology* 12, no. 3 (July 1987): 222–30.

Kulik, J. A., and C. C. Kulik. "Timing of Feedback and Verbal Learning." *Review of Educational Research* 58, no. 1 (1988): 79–97.

Kumar, David D., and Stanley L. Helgeson. "Trends in Computer Applications in Science Assessment." *Journal of Science Education and Technology* 41, no. 1 (March 1995): 29–36.

Kurth, R. J. "Using Word Processing to Enhance Revision Strategies during Student Writing Activities." *Educational Technology* 27 (1987): 13–19.

Lally, M. "Computer-Assisted Development of Number Conservation in Mentally Retarded Children." *Journal of Developmental Disabilities*, September 1980, pp. 131–36.

Leeds, Matthew. "Desktop Videoconferencing." *MacWorld*, November 1994, pp. 87–92.

Levy, Steven, and Brad Stone. "Hunting the Hackers." *Time Magazine*, February 21, 2000, pp. 39–44.

Liao, Cliff Yuen-kuang. *Gender Differences on Attitudes toward Computers: A Meta-Analysis.* ERIC No: ED432287, Clearinghouse Number IRO19657, 1999.

Linn, C. "Learning More—with Computers as Lab Partners." Paper presented at the annual meeting of the American Educational Research Association, San Francisco, April 1986.

Liu, Xiufeng, Robert Macmillan, and Vianne Timmons. "Assessing the Impact of Computer Integration on Students." *Journal of Research on Computing in Education* 31, no. 2 (Winter 1998): 189–201.

Lu, G. C. *Expert Adolescent Programmers: The Cognitive Consequences of Programming.* Doctoral Dissertation, Columbia University Teachers College (Dissertation Abstracts Order Number DA9136407), 1991.

Luehrmann, A. "The Best Way to Teach Computer Literacy." *Electronic Learning* 3, no. 3 (April 1984): 37–42, 44.

Lundell, Allan. *Virus! The Secret World of Computer Invaders That Breed and Destroy.* Chicago: Contemporary Books, 1989.

MacArthur, C. A., J. A. Haynes, D. B. Melouf, and K. Harris. "Computer Assisted Instruction with Learning Disabled Students: Achievement, Engagement, and Other Factors Related to Achievement." Paper presented at the annual meeting of the American Educational Research Association, Washington, D.C., April 1987.

Makrakis, Vasilios, and Toshio Sawada. "Gender, Computers and Other School Subjects among Japanese and Swedish Students." *Computers and Education* 26, no. 4 (May 1996): 225–31.

Mann, D., and C. Shakeshaft. *The Impact of Technology in the Schools of the Mohawk Regional Information Center Area.* Technical Report, 1997. ERIC Document NO.-ED 405893 (800) 443-ERIC

Mann, D., C. Shakeshaft, J. Becker, and R. Kottkamp. *West Virginia's Basic Skills/Computer Education Program: An Analysis of Student Achievement.* Santa Monica, Calif.: Milken Family Foundation, 1999.

Mayer, R. E., J. L. Dyck, and W. Vilberg. "Learning to Program and Learning to Think: What's the Connection?" *Communication of the ACM* 29, no. 7 (1986): 605–10.

Mayer, R. E., and A. L. Fay. "A Chain of Cognitive Changes with Learning to Program in Logo." *Journal of Educational Psychology* 79, no. 3 (1987): 21.

McAfee, John. *Computer Viruses, Worms, Data Diddlers, Killer Programs, and Others.* New York: St. Martin's Press, 1989.

McGrath, Diane, et al. "Multimedia Science Projects: Seven Case Studies." *Journal of Research on Computing in Education* 30, no. 1 (Fall 1997).

McKinnon, David H., C. J. Patrick Nolan, and Kenneth E. Sinclair. "A Longitudinal Student Attitude toward Computers: Resolving an Attitude Decay Paradox." *Journal of Research on Computing in Education* 32, no. 3 (Spring 2000): 325–35.

McNaughton, David, et al. "Proofreading for Students with Learning Disabilities." *Learning Disabilities Research and Practice* 12, no. 1 (1997): 16–28.

McNeil, Barbara J., and Karyn R. Nelson. "Meta-Analysis of Interactive Video Instruction: A 10 Year Review of Achievement Effects." *Journal of Computer-Based Instruction* 18, no. 1 (1991): 1–6.

Milbrandt, George. "Using Problem Solving to Teach a Programming Language." *Learning and Leading with Technology* 23, no. 2 (October 1995): 27–31.

Miller, David. "Research into LOGO—What Are the Lessons for Primary Schools?" *Scottish Educational Review* 25, no. 2 (November 1993): 104–8.

Miller, Douglas S. "Improving Secondary Practical Computer Skills: Logo Test Scores through Graphically Designed Computer Programs and Utilization of Multimedia and Technology." *1998 Information Technology in Childhood Education Annual*, 1999, pp. 5–38.

Miller, Mark D., and William D. McInerney. "Effects on Achievement of a Home/School Computer Project." *Journal of Research on Computing in Education* 27, no. 2 (Winter 1994–1995): 198–210.

Mitra, Ananda, and Timothy Steffensmeier. "Changes in Student Attitudes and Student Computer Use in a Computer-Enriched Environment." *Journal of Research on Computing in Education* 32, no. 3 (Spring 2000): 417–33.

Moore, C., S. Smith, and R. A. Avner. "Facilitation of Laboratory Performance through CAI." *Journal of Chemical Education* 57, no. 3 (1980): 196–98.

Morehouse, D. L., M. L. Hoaglund, and R. H. Schmidt. *Technology Demonstration Program Final Evaluation Report*. Menononie, Wis.: Quality Evaluation and Development, February 1987.

Nadeau, Michael, and Bram Vermeer. "Coming 'Soon': 3-GB CD-ROMs." *Byte,* October 1994, p. 4.

Novice Editorial Staff. "Working at Home." *PC Novice,* September 1994, p. 61.

O'Brien, P. "Using Microcomputers in the Writing Class." *Computing Teacher,* May 1984, pp. 20–21.

Olsen, Florence. "Internet2 Effort Aims to Build Digital-Video Network for Higher Education." *Chronicle of Higher Education* 46, no. 33 (April 21, 2000): A49.

Owston, Ronald D., and Herbert H. Wideman. "Word Processors and Children's Writing in a High-Computer-Access Setting." *Journal of Research on Computing in Education* 30, no. 2 (1997): 202–20.

Palumbo, David B., and Michael W. Reed. "The Effect of BASIC Programming Language Instruction on High School Students's Problem Solving Ability and Computer Anxiety." *Journal of Research on Computing in Education* 23, no. 3 (Spring 1991): 342–69.

Papert, Seymour. "Educational Computing: How Are We Doing?" *T.H.E. Journal* 24, no. 11 (June 1997): 78–80.

Papert, Seymour. "An Exploration in the Space of Mathematics Education." *International Journal of Computers for Mathematics Learning* 1 (1996): 95–173.

Papert, Seymour. *Mindstorms: Children, Computers and Powerful Ideas*. New York: Basic Books, 1980.

Parker, Donn B. *Ethical Conflicts in Information and Computer Science Technology*. Wellesley, Mass.: QED Information Sciences, 1990.

Paul, Lawrence. "Keying Injuries Proliferate, Defying Clear Cut Remedies." *PC Magazine,* August 8, 1994, p. 81.

Pea, R. D. "The Aims of Software Criticism: Reply to Professor Papert." *Educational Researcher* 16, no. 5 (June/July 1987): 4–8.

Pea, R. D., and D. M. Kurland. *Logo Programming and the Development of Planning Skills*. Technical Report No. 11. New York: Bank Street College of Education, 1984.

Phelps, David. "SPA Reaches Settlement with Internet Software Pirates, Credits Teamwork with Internet Access Provider," http://www.spa.org, 1997.

Potter, Dianne. "Virus? Or Just a Hoax?" *Presentations Magazine,* November 2000, p. 24.

Reed, W. M. "Assessing the Importance of Computer-Based Writing." *Journal of Research on Computing in Education* 28, no. 4 (1996): 418–37.

Reeder, Lillian Kay, and James S. Leming. "The Effect of Logo on the Nonverbal Reasoning Ability of Rural and Disadvantaged Third Graders." *Journal of Research on Computing in Education* 26, no. 4 (1994): 558.

Richman, John A. "At-Risk Students: Innovative Technologies." *Media and Methods* 30, no. 5 (May–June 1994): 26–27.

Rizzo, J. "Erasable Optical Drives." *MacUser,* November 1990, pp. 102–30.

Robertson G. *A Comparison of Meaningful and Nonmeaningful Content in Computer-Assisted Spelling Programs.* Saskatchewan, Canada: Saskatchewan School Trustees Association Research Center, 1978.

Roblyer, M. D. "Technology and the Oops! Effect: Finding a Bias against Word Processing." *Learning and Leading with Technology* 25, no. 7 (1997): 14–16.

Roblyer, M. D., W. H. Castine, and F. J. King. *Assessing the Impact of Computer-Based Instruction: A Review of Recent Research.* New York: Haworth Press, 1988.

Ruel, Alfred A. *The Application of Research Findings.* Washington, D.C.: National Education Association, 1977.

Rueter, John G., and Nancy A. Perrin. "Using a Simulation to Teach Food Web Dynamics." *American Biology Teacher* 61, no. 2 (February 1999): 116–23.

Ryan, Bob. "Alpha Ride High." *Byte,* October 1994, pp. 197–98.

Salerno, Christopher A. "The Effect of Time on Computer-Assisted Instruction for At-Risk Students." *Journal of Research on Computing in Education* 28, no. 1 (Fall 1995): 85–97.

Sarama, Julie, Douglas H. Clements, and Judith Day Seidel. "Using Computers for Algebraic Thinking." *Teaching Children Mathematics* 5, no. 3 (November 1998): 186.

Schacter, J. *The Impact of Education Technology on Student Achievement: What the Most Current Research Has to Say.* Santa Monica, Calif.: Milken Family Foundation, 1999.

Schroeder, Erica. "Voice Recognition Making Some Noise." *PC Week* 12, no. 20 (May 23, 1994): 7.

Seawel, Lori, et al. *A Descriptive Study Comparing Computer-Based Word Processing and Handwriting on Attitudes and Performance of Third and Fourth Grade Students Involved in a Program Based on a Process Approach to Writing.* ERIC Document EJ482040, 1994.

Shashaani, Lily. "Gender-Based Differences in Attitudes toward Computers." *Computers and Education* 20, no. 2 (March 1993): 169–81.

Shashaani, Lily. "Gender-Differences in Computer Experience and Its Influence on Computer Attitudes." *Journal of Educational Computing Research* 11, no. 4 (1994): 347–67.

Shashaani, Lily. "Gender Differences in Mathematics Experience and Attitude and Their Relation to Computer Attitude." *Educational Technology* 35, no. 3 (May–June 1995): 32–38.

Shashaani, Lily. "Socioeconomic Status, Parents' Sex-Role Stereotypes, and the Gender Gap in Computing." *Journal of Research on Computing in Education* 26, no. 4 (Summer 1994): 433–51.

Shiah, Rwey-Lin, et al. "The Effects of Computer-Assisted Instruction on Mathematical Problem Solving of Students with Learning Disabilities." *Exceptionality* 5 (1994–1995): 131–61.

Shih, Y., and S. M. Allesi. "Mental Models and Transfer in Learning in Computer Programming." *Journal of Research on Computing in Education* 26, no. 2 (Winter 1993–94): 154–75.

Siann, G., A. Durndell, H. Macleod, and P. Glissov. "Stereotyping in Relation to the Gender Gap in Participation in Computing." *Educational Research* 30, no. 2 (1988): 98–103.

Sivin-Kachala, J. *Report on the Effectiveness of Technology in Schools, 1990–1997.* Washington, D.C: Software Publishers Association, 1998.

Software Piracy. Software Publishers Association, White Paper, 1992.

"Software Publishers Association Announces Settlement with College Student." http://www.spa.org/piracy/releases/puget.htm, 1997.

Software Publishers Association. News Release. http://www.spa.org/, October 1995.

Software Publishers Association. Reports published on the World Wide Web, http://www.spa/.org/, Fall 1996.

Soloway, E., J. Lockhead, and J. Clement. "Does Computer Programming Enhance Problem Solving Ability? Some Positive Evidence on Algebra Word Problems." In *Computer Literacy: Issues and Directions for 1985,* ed. R. J. Seidel, R. Anderson, and B. Hunter. New York: Academic Press, 1982.

Stuart, Rory. *The Design of Virtual Environments.* New York: McGraw-Hill, 1996.

Summerville, L. J. "The Relationship between Computer-Assisted Instruction and Achievement Levels and Learning Rates of

Secondary School Students in First Year Chemistry." *Dissertation Abstracts International* 46, no. 3 (1984): 603a (University Microfilms No. 85–10891).

Suomala, Jyrki. "Eight-Year-Old Pupils' Problem-Solving Process within a Logo Learning Environment." *Scandinavian Journal of Educational Research* 40, no. 4 (December 1996): 291–309.

Swadener, M., and M. Hannafin. "Gender Similarities and Differences in Sixth Graders' Attitudes toward Computers: An Exploratory Study." *Educational Technology* 27, no. 1 (1987): 37–42.

Swan, K., Gueerero, F., Mitrani, N. M., and Schoener, J. "Honing in on the Target: Who among the Educationally Disadvantaged Benefits Most from What CBI?" *Journal of Research on Computing in Education* 22, no. 4 (1990): 38–403.

Takahashi, Dean. "Which Disk Will Slip?" *Los Angeles Times*, March 14, 1995, p. 1D.

"Technology and Achievement Have Positive Correlation, Study Says." *Electronic Education Report* 6, no. 8 (April 28, 1999): 7.

Teh, George P. L., and Barry Fraser. "Gender Differences in Achievement and Attitudes among Students Using Computer-Assisted Instruction." *International Journal of Instructional Media* 22, no. 2 (1995): 111.

Terrell, Steve, and Paul Rendulic. "Using Computer-Managed Instructional Software to Increase Motivation and Achievement in Elementary School Children." *Journal of Research on Computing in Education* 26, no. 3, (Spring 1996): 403–14.

Tessler, Franklin N. "Safer Computing." *MacWorld*, December 1994, p. 96.

"The Tech Isn't Perfect, but Video Conferencing's Day Is Near."*Fortune: Winter 2001 Technology Guide* 142, no. 12 (2000): p. 242.

Thomas, Rex, and Elizabeth Hooper. "Simulations: An Opportunity We Are Missing." *Journal of Research on Computing in Education* 23, no. 4 (Summer 1991): 497–513.

Thomas, Rex, and Sylvester C. Upah Jr. "Give Programming Instruction a Chance." *Journal of Research on Computing in Education* 29, no. 1 (Fall 1996): 96–108.

Tien, James M. *Electronic Fund Transfer Systems Fraud: Computer Crimes*. Washington, D.C.:

U.S. Department of Justice, Bureau of Justice Statistics, 1985.

Trosko, Nancy. "Making Technology Work for Your Students." *Technology Connection* 4, no. 2 (April 1997): 20–22.

Trotler, Andrew. "Taking Technology's Measure." *Education Week* 17, no. 11 (November 10, 1997): 6–13.

Tsai, San-Yun W., and Norval F. Pohl. "Student Achievement in Computer Programming: Lecture vs. Computer-Aided Instruction." *Journal of Experimental Education*, Winter 1977, pp. 66–70.

Vasu, Ellen Storey, and Doris Kennedy Tyler. "A Comparison of the Critical Thinking Skills and Spatial Ability of Fifth Grade Children Using Simulation Software or Logo." *Journal of Computing in Childhood Education* 8, no. 4 (1997): 345–63.

Viadero, Debra. "A Tool for Learning." *Education Week* 17, no. 11 (November 1997): 12–14.

Waddell, Steve, and Keith L. Doty. "Robotics." *Tech Directions* 58, no. 7 (February 1999): 34–40.

Wagner, Susan Preston. "Robotics and Children: Science Achievement and Problem Solving." *Journal of Computing in Childhood Education* 9, no. 2 (1998): 149–92.

Wanat, Thomas. "Internet-Savvy Students Help Track Down the Hacker of an NCAA Web Site." *Chronicle of Higher Education* 43, no. 29 (March 28, 1997): A30.

Watkins, Marley W., and C. Webb. "Computer-Assisted Instruction with Learning-Disabled Students." *Educational Computer*, September/October 1981, pp. 24–27.

Wenglinsky, H. *Does It Compute? The Relationship between Educational Technology and Student Achievement in Mathematics*. Princeton, N.J.: Educational Testing Service Policy Information Center, 1998.

Whitley, Bernard E., Jr. "Gender Differences in Computer-Related Attitudes and Behavior: A Meta-Analysis." *Computers in Human Behavior* 13, no. 1 (January 1997): 1–22.

Wiegner, Kathleen. "Software Predicts Radio Wave Action." *Los Angeles Times*, October 12, 1994, p. D4.

Williams, Sue Winkle, et al. "Gender Roles, Computer Attitudes, and Dyadic Computer Interaction Performance in College Students."

Sex Roles: A Journal of Research 29, no. 7–8 (June 1994): 515–25.

Wood, Christina. "Register Your Software—or Else!" *PC World* 18, no. 10 (October 2000): 35.

Woodward, L., and R. Gersten. "Innovative Technology for Secondary Students with Learning Disabilities." *Exceptional Children* 58, no. 5 (March–April 1992): 407–21.

Wright, R. "Multimedia: What Is It?" *MacValley Voice*, October 1990, p. 2.

Xin, Yan Ping, and Asha K. Jitendra. "The Effects of Instruction in Solving Mathematical Word Problems for Students with Learning Problems: A Meta-Analysis." *Journal of Special Education* 32, no. 4 (1999): 207–25.

Yildirim, Soner. "Effects of an Educational Computing Course on Preservice and Inservice Teachers: A Discussion and Analysis of Attitudes and Use." *Journal of Research on Computing in Education* 32, no. 4 (2000): 479–95.

Young, Betty. "Gender Differences in Student Attitudes Toward Computers." *Journal of Research on Computing in Education* 33, no. 2 (Winter 2000): 204–13.

Zellermayer, M., G. Salomon, T. Globerson, and H. Givon. "Enhancing Writing-Related Metacognitions through a Computerized Writing Partner." *American Educational Research Journal* 28, no. 2 (1991): 373–91.

Zhang, Yuehua. "Technology and the Writing Skills of Students with Learning Disabilities." *Journal of Research on Computing in Education* 32, no. 4 (Summer 2000): 467–78.

CHAPTER 17

Epilogue: The Future

Schools of the Future

Future technology breakthroughs will make it easier to integrate the computer into the classroom. Students will be heavily involved in distance learning, have robots aiding them in the instructional process, be downloading their books, and be wearing computers. Using virtual reality, students will visit museums, see different countries, see chamber groups in concert, learn how to fly airplanes, work in science labs, and engage in all sorts of exciting educational experiences. Shortly, many of the predictions made in this epilogue will become a reality.

Future Trends

Examining the research leads to some natural questions: What will the future bring? What are the trends for microcomputer development? Will we have more artificial intelligence applications? Will there be more networking in the schools? Will there be an emphasis on distance learning? Will there be further developments in multimedia technologies? How will this affect teaching? Let's try to answer some of these questions.

Computer Hardware

Recent developments such as the wireless computer and wireless computer network, distance learning, flash memory chips, and liquid crystal displays will play a more prominent role in the computer's future. The cathode ray tube (CRT) monitor will be replaced by a large active color matrix flat screen display or a plasma display. The displays could have poster-size screens as well as screens we can hang on the wall or unfold from our pocket. The displays could evolve from two-dimensional displays into large three-dimensional displays. If we want to access the Internet, we can use the pocket Net computer, a computer that fits in a pocket, to log on anytime from anywhere. Mainframes will be replaced by desktop computers resembling large laptops. By 2005, EInk Immediate Technology will be producing paper-thin displays consisting of liquid ink embedded in paper-thin plastic sheets. EInk is also creating electronic books with flexible plastic pages that can display downloaded text, erase, and reprint themselves. Each book will consist of hundreds of pages that a student can thumb through, with text that can be changed. Students then could easily attach the book to the PC and download whatever they wanted to read.

Another major computer trend is the development of equipment that is smaller, faster, and easier to use. These computers will have thinner and lighter screens with advanced voice recognition. Nanotechnology and quantum computing are two areas in which researchers are trying to supplant the silicon chip. These concepts involve using molecular or subatomic particles as logic components. A powerful microscopic computer that used the position of individual atoms or spinning electrons to calculate numbers would leave today's machine in the scrap bin. Microscopic computing would require very little power, and it would be perfect for wearable computers such as wristwatches. Researchers predict that in a few years advances in technologies could produce a powerful watch-size computer that would require minimum battery power. Resembling a Dick Tracy two-way wrist radio, this device would work with voice commands, have wireless Internet access, and have holographic projection displays. We could then eliminate monitors, keyboards, mice, and other peripherals. Every child in the classroom could then have a personal computerized watch.

Xybernaut has produced wearable PCs which let people perform a wide range of mobile tasks easily and safely. This wearable PC is small and lightweight, but it is powerful (Fig. 17.1). These computers can be touch or voice

FIGURE 17.1
Wearable Computer
Used by permission of Xybernaut Corporation.

activated. IBM has a belt computer, weighing a few pounds, that lets users surf, edit documents, and dictate while they are moving around. There are wearable computer prototypes that are in the form of undetectable glasses and belt clips. Every time we turn around, someone has introduced a new computer that is quicker and can run more complex programs. The standard has quickly transformed 750-megahertz machines to gigahertz machines. Look for even faster machines in the near future.

Computers will all have sophisticated **voice recognition systems** and be capable of running many applications simultaneously. We will be talking to our computer like Dave did in the classic movie *2001: A Space Odyssey.* The question is, Will the computer listen to us or will it be like HAL 9000, a murderous machine? Every computer will have built-in speech, and instead of typing commands, we will just tell our computer to launch an application or print that document. Improved color inkjet printers will continue to figure prominently in the printing device market. Furthermore, color laser printers will become increasingly popular because of drastic price reductions and superior printing capabilities.

Apple Computer has changed the design of new computers with its revolutionary cube. This computer is not bulky and it houses the components of most desktop computers inside an eight-inch cube (Fig. 17.2).

FIGURE 17.2
Apple LCD Display, Cube, Mouse, and Speakers
Copyright© Apple Computer, Inc. All rights reserved.

The memory needed to run different applications has increased. In the early 1980s, most microcomputers needed only 16K of random access memory (RAM) to run the available educational software programs. Today, there are machines with over 1 GB of RAM, and Mitsubishi is on the verge of introducing one chip with 4 GB of RAM.

Because of their large memory, the new microcomputers are much more powerful and can perform a myriad of tasks. The price of the memory chip has decreased and will continue to do so in the next few years. In 1994, DEC's Alpha 21164 chip was the fastest microprocessor in the world. It could perform 600 transactions per second and there was a 300 MHz version of this chip (Ryan, 1994). While these figures still seem high, analysts say desktop PCs will hit speeds higher than 3 GHz (Howard, 2001).

Not only has memory size increased, but storage devices have increased their capacity to store data. The 5 1/4-inch floppy disk faded into oblivion and the 3 1/2-inch disk will be disappearing forever. The hard drive capacity has increased and by 2005 could hold over 100 GB per platter. There are online storage depots such as Idrive.com and FreeDrive.com which give up to 25 MB of free storage. This enables the user to store material quickly at one location and travel to another to retrieve it. Furthermore, the 250 MB Iomega removable Zip disk has become a popular option for storage. In addition, the Iomega's Jaz drive holds 2 GB of information and has 2 GB removable cartridges. In 2001, Samsung Electronics, the South Korean electronics giant, unveiled a combination CD-RW and DVD-ROM optical disc drive for notebooks, which offers rewritable media through the CD-RW disc drive while also providing DVD-ROM support. The trend is toward smaller disks that hold more information, such as the 1.8-inch disks already available for some portables. CD-ROM discs and laser discs are being replaced by DVD. The DVD is the same size as the CD-ROM, but it is capable of holding 17 GB of data with digital images equal to laser discs (see Chapter 3). With a reduction in price and faster access time, it is evident the erasable optical discs have emerged as a viable alternative to magnetic disks. These discs have the capacity to store gigabytes of information, and they do not wear out as floppy disks do. In addition to these features, optical discs offer the ability to reproduce high-quality color graphics, images, and animation. Furthermore, storage could occur in another dimension such as holographic storage. Holographic storage disks could hold millions and millions of holograms, and the transfer rates could reach 1 GB per second. This technology holds promise for interactive video. These advances are just the tip of the iceberg—in the near future this huge amount of storage capacity will seem minuscule.

Along with the changes in storage devices are changes in input devices. The movement is away from the keyboard as the primary input device. There are now more touch screens, pens, and variations on the mouse.

Wireless Networks in the Schools

Anthony Nguyen, a network administrator at California State University, Northridge, feels that in the near future, we will see **wireless networks** gaining ground in the schools. The wireless networks will eliminate expensive cabling and add flexibility, permitting users to move the machines freely around a room. This will reduce the cost of running cables throughout the building. Having wireless-network access could eliminate the cost of upgrading computer equipment. Some colleges provide wireless-network access and require students to purchase laptop computers with wireless-network cards; thus, these colleges feel they can avoid the cost of upgrading computer hardware.

Major producers in the wireless field are Apple, Lucent, Intel, IBM, and Symbol Technologies. Computers equipped with compliant network devices, with necessary software, can interact on the same network at speeds up to 11 Mbs within a distance of 400 feet, whether they are Macintosh or PC. (The wireless network was discussed in Chapter 8.) Besides wireless networks, every school will be engaged in **distance learning.**

Distance Learning

Online learning is becoming increasingly popular. Mr. Nguyen feels that this is related to the explosion of network bandwidth via high-speed connection at home, such as DSL or cable. Today, online instructional materials are loaded with multimedia, such as sound and movie clips, which can make learning more interesting.

Moreover, the influx of students in higher education institutions is outpacing the growth of the infrastructures of many colleges. This leaves colleges no choice but to open up a virtual campus, teaching through telecommunications and other methods, such as the Internet, print-based instruction, and satellites. Private higher education institutions are particularly eager to implement online education because they can recruit more students and offer instruction at lower cost. Public institutions, in turn, are forced to jump in to stay competitive and to retain their students. The same trend is now happening in high schools and even at middle schools in some rural areas.

The two major players providing software to facilitate the distance learning setup are WebCT (http://www.webct.com) and Blackboard (http://www.blackboard.com). WebCT allows a free download and trial of its software. Once you have your courses online, you will pay a license fee based on your projected enrollments. Blackboard offers free course setup on its server with a limited storage space. Going beyond that limit, you will have to pay a fee. You can also buy its software to install on your server. Blackboard's long customer list is available at http://company.blackboard.com/customers.cgi. Many of those customers are K–12 schools. A newcomer in the field is Metacollege (http://www.metacollege.com/), which offers marketing schemes similar to Blackboard's. (Distance learning was discussed in Chapter 8.)

Of all the new developments, the **voice recognition system** seems to hold the greatest promise. (See Chapter 12 for a more detailed discussion.)

Voice Recognition Systems

In the future, we will no longer need a keyboard to communicate; we will use speech instead. Voice recognition has come a long way from the system introduced by Convox in 1991. The *Voice Master Key System II,* as it was called, could recognize only 64 words. Users typed in the words they wanted the system to listen for, repeated each twice, and then typed in the desired keyboard responses. After this programming, users only needed to say a command to direct the computer to execute it. This type of voice recognition was *discrete voice recognition* because it required a pause between each word.

From this type of voice recognition system we moved to *continuous-speech systems,* or systems that understand natural speech without pauses. The new voice recognition systems are speaker-independent; that is, they do not require user training. These products are still not 100 percent accurate, but shortly we will see breakthroughs in speech recognition technologies. Many of these advances will be linked closely to artificial intelligence, the principles of which are being used to improve the voice recognition system.

Artificial Intelligence

Artificial intelligence (AI) is a range of computer applications that are designed to simulate human intelligence and behavior. For instance, with AI, a machine or robot can recognize pictures and sounds. In the future, we may be able to walk up to any computer or robot, ask it for problem-solving help, and receive information useful in solving the problem.

In a short amount of time, the differences between the machine and an intelligent person will be reduced drastically. At UCLA and other universities, scientists are working on computer programs and, in some instances, on robots that will emulate conditions of life such as evolution. The computer ants program at UCLA is a product of an infant science called artificial life. David Jefferson, a computer scientist at UCLA, feels that the artificial ant colonies are a small step toward the creation of life itself. If these scientists are successful, electronic creatures capable of independent thought and action may emerge—a prospect both exciting and frightening. At Los Alamos National Laboratory, there exists a whole repertoire of self-reproducing computer codes. These are just variations of the computer viruses that have disrupted computer networks over the last few years.

AI systems are designed for particular fields to make evaluations, draw conclusions, and provide recommendations. They help doctors make diagnoses on diseases and treatments, they help drill oil wells, and they aid stockbrokers in making analyses.

This type of software will have a similar impact on education. Teachers are already demanding and using programs that have been made more interactive through artificial intelligence. The AI language will definitely increase the number of programs that respond in human ways. The software we will be using in the near future will tackle concepts and ideas. This software will accept a range of English-language commands and be easier to use. In the future, you will be able to converse with your average computer and ask for help. The computer will automatically bring up the appropriate application to aid you in solving your problem. We will see real AI as Alan Turning, the famous mathematician, defined it: "A machine has artificial intelligence when there is no discernible difference between the conversation generated by the machine and that of an intelligent person" (Hodges, 1992).

Robots

A **robot** is a computer system that performs physical and computational activities. The robot can be created in a human form; however, industrial robots are not designed this way. The advantage of a robot is that it can perform many different human jobs often better than a person might perform them, or at least more efficiently or quickly. Robots are being designed with artificial intelligence features so they may respond more effectively to unusual situations. In the future, robots may be in the classroom serving as teachers' aides. Robots will spend time with the students, individually drilling them on math skills. In the chemistry lab, robots will handle dangerous chemicals. Robots will also help the disabled student with homework.

As the average age of the population increases, the need and cost of assisted care will also increase. Under development are automated "smart apartments" that will help the old and disabled live more independently and comfortably. These apartments would have different types of machines to assist incapacitated individuals. The robots in such an apartment would differ from the industrial robots found on the factory floors; these service robots extend human abilities and help people rather than replace them. Horner Robotics (http://www.HORNERrobotics.com) has robots that can carry food, drinks, and other personal items for people who need home care. Some other possibilities are robots that dust, clean floors, reach items on top shelves, respond to voice commands, push wheelchairs, and walk dogs. Jean-Claude Latombe, chairman of the computer science department at Stanford University, says, "One of the fastest-growing areas for robotics today is robot-assisted surgery." Stanford is doing brain surgery with robots. During radiation surgery for a brain tumor, the surgeon is not even in the same room with a patient. Instead, the doctor sits at a computer console in a nearby room and monitors what is happening during the operation (Kaplan, 1994). Robots are also being used as targets in weapons training. Dan Fetterly's remote-controlled robot can move like a human, run up to 9 miles per hour, carry 100 pounds, and spot any target (Dunn, 1998). K. G. Engelhardt, formerly Manager of Robotics for the NASA Regional Technology Transfer Center and director for the Center for Human Service Robotics at Carnegie Mellon University, has been developing robots for 17 years. She has written a program that introduces teachers to robots. The *Teachers Corps* program utilizes robots and robotics-related technologies to learn exciting ways to teach scientific, biological, and engineering concepts (http://www.robotics.usc.edu/~behar/robot.html).

In summation, people are using robots for jobs that range from working in an automobile plant or gathering things at the bottom of the ocean to mowing the lawn to brain surgery and teaching. Now if we could only manufacture a robot to write up our reports or do our homework. (Look at "Peering into the Future" at http://www.infoworld.com/printlinks.)

Computer Use by Persons with Disabilities

Many devices are currently available to aid the disabled pupil, including Braille keyboards and computer-operated telephone devices for the deaf and screen reading programs for the blind. (Many of these devices were mentioned in Chapter 12.) Screen reader programs like *Job Access* (Henter-Hoyce, Inc., a division of Freedom Scientific) for Windows computers or *OutSPOKEN* (ALVA Access Group) for Macintosh computers let the blind surf the Web. Using speech synthesizers, the software reads text in a computerized voice and names the icons as the individual encounters them. The blind person then uses the keyboard to navigate and the software interprets whether a user has tabbed to a button or graphic or other element. There are products for the speech-impaired like *Speech Enhancer Spectrum VP* (Electronic Speech Enhancement Inc.), which uses the latest voice processing technology to turn unclear speech into sound that can be understood by any person. Until this development, the only help for the speech-impaired was the amplifier, which did not improve voice clarity.

IBM's *Blue Eyes* research program is now working on a face-recognition system. Using this technology, the computer can recognize faces, track gazes, and even sense moods. For gaze tracking a computer camera is mounted on the person's computer display and this camera follows the person's iris. Depending on where the person focuses his eye, the monitor then senses what information he wants and calls it up. What a boon this is for the disabled person, who would not be required to make a mouse click. In addition, face recognition systems could be used for security. This means the keyboard would lock out any unauthorized person who tried to use your computer.

Desktop Videoconferencing

Videoconferencing lets you be in two places at the same time. Instead of moving large sums in an armored car, a bank can relay video messages on how much money it wants to transfer. A teacher can confer with an ill student at home without leaving the classroom. A businessperson can attend a long-distance conference without leaving the office. Around 1992, videoconferencing equipment cost $100,000, filled a room, and required satellite hookups and expensive data lines (Leeds, 1994). Today the industry is expanding because of better compression of data, miniaturization, lower costs, wider availability of digital telephone lines, and faster processors. Nevertheless, videoconferencing is still difficult to configure, provides marginal video and audio quality, and lacks compatibility between systems; thus videoconferencing can be done only with people who use the same system.

Desktop videoconferencing is becoming common in schools and classrooms across the United States. (See the discussion on desktop videoconferencing in Chapter 8.) A typical desktop video system has a multimedia-equipped computer with the proper audio/video cards, a modem, a microphone, and a small video camera, like Logitech QuickCam. Using this equipment, a person can transmit an image, along with sound, through the phone lines to a recipient's monitor instantly, so that two people can see and hear each other. This process lets individuals on opposite ends of the globe have two-way video conversations. Presently, there are drawbacks to using videoconferencing because the sound is sometimes garbled and the visual image slow and jerky. The reason for these drawbacks is that the quality of the image is dependent on the bandwidth or connection speed. This situation will change when bandwidth and hardware are improved. Regardless, this technology offers unique possibilities in the classroom.

Technology Classrooms

Smart Classrooms

The Hueneme School District, located in Ventura County, California, was one of the first to receive international recognition for its leadership in developing technology. According to superintendent Dr. Ron Rescigno, students have made marked improvement in their achievement.

The district offers technologically designed classrooms, called Smart Classrooms, organized by curriculum area. Each Smart Classroom is a state-of-the-art, completely furnished facility that follows unique design principles. The computer configuration of these classrooms allows for seamless exchange of data, voice, and video; total integration of equipment; computer instruction; and in-service training. Electronic connections are concealed under desks but are easily accessed with a simple command. Color monitors are recessed underneath desktops, and keyboards are housed in drawers that pull out for each student.

The Smart Classroom design emphasizes student interaction and academic success. Students learn to use different applications such as desktop publishing programs, word processing programs, and databases while gaining knowledge in all areas of the curricula. Students engage in observations, explore different scientific phenomena, perform manipulation activities, and assume responsibility for their own learning with self-administered quizzes and answer checks.

Each student has an individual workstation with access to a CD-ROM disc drive, printer, and laser disc player. Each teacher has a workstation with a color printer and color scanner. The teacher's workstation controls an overhead projection system mounted on the ceiling that projects to a motorized screen that could be used with a large group. Infrared electronic blackboards and conventional white boards are attached to the wall behind the teacher's desk. Furthermore, the lighting system is designed to eliminate glare.

Twenty-First-Century Learning Environments

Creative Learning Systems, Inc., of San Diego, California, has pioneered the whole-laboratory approach to technology education, introducing the Technology Lab 2000 in 1987 as the first such system ever sold. This company currently provides custom and semicustom learning environments to North American schools under the trade names of SmartLab, SmartStudio, and Creative Learning Plaza.

Creative Learning Systems emphasizes the following core principles in its learning environments:

- A learning facilitation model, not stand-and-deliver teaching.
- Learner-focused instruction, which engages young people and helps instill the love of learning that is so necessary to creating communities of lifelong learners.
- Constructivist approaches, which allow learners to make meaning out of their experiences.
- Portfolio-based assessment, not prescriptive "single-answer" testing.
- Project work that requires collaboration.
- Learning that is self-directed.
- Cross-curricular project work to better reflect the real world, rather than arbitrary separate subject matter.
- A brain-based system of learning.

The educational program incorporated into SmartStudio uses a series of integrated curricular resources that challenge the student to discover the underlying principles of technology and apply them, through critical thinking, problem solving, and decision making. The scenario helps students acquire the skills and confidence needed to live and work in the technological environment of tomorrow.

Although the SmartStudio incorporates an extensive collection of cross-platform computer equipment and peripherals, it is anything but another version of the computer classroom. Rather than dominate the instructional program, computers serve as the tools by which learners access the language and the images of a broader technological arena. The environment is a total integrated system of furnishings, equipment, computer-mediated instruction, software, and hands-on computer-based learning. The instructional resources are self-paced, interactive tutorials. The materials launch learners into a variety of technological experiences and support self-designed projects that expand students' understanding of technological phenomena. The SmartStudio gives learners access to information in areas such as robotics, audio engineering, Web design, entertainment engineering, multimedia production, satellite technology, and lasers, to name just a few.

Figure 17.3 shows a floor plan of a SmartStudio for Pre-Engineering Studies planned for purchase by a Colorado school district in 2001. Islandlike

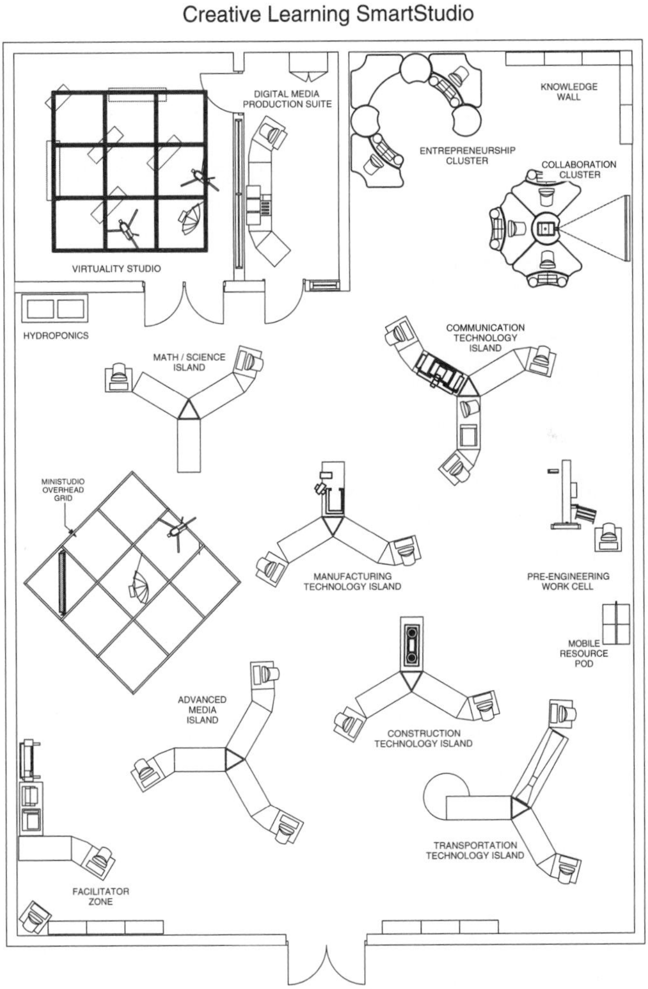

Creative Learning SmartStudio

FIGURE 17.3
SmartStudio

Used by permission of Creative Learning Systems, Inc.; for more information contact Bret Vedder at bvedder@clsinc.com

arrangements of versatile, leading-edge laboratory furnishings form a series of activity zones within which students work and learn collaboratively. Each station is also reconfigurable to accommodate new activities or advanced explorations. Learner teams participate in computer-integrated enterprises in which all phases in the creation of a product are linked and interdependent.

Math, science, and technology-related areas of study are presented in an integrated curriculum. The power of the SmartStudio is realized when the vast array of activities are seen not as finite exercises, but rather as open-ended investigations, each leading to the next, linked by the common thread of curiosity.

One of the greatest changes in this new mode of learning is the teacher's role. The teacher is no longer the all-knowing instructor, but rather a facilitator of learning. The teacher-facilitator is freed to circulate, to facilitate creative contributions, and to help learners make connections and develop higher-order critical thinking skills.

Electronic Books

The electronic book, or **e-book,** is gaining in popularity and may someday replace the traditional paper book. The e-book displays electronic versions of books, letting you set bookmarks, do keyword searches, and make notes in margins. An example of an e-book is the *Rocket eBook* (Fig. 17.4) designed by

FIGURE 17.4
Rocket eBook
Courtesy of Gemstar, Inc.
(http://eBook-Gemstar.com/).

Gemstar, Inc. This handheld book has scroll buttons on the side. You can connect to any phone line to get books, magazines, or newspapers. When this device is perfected, students may dispense with their backpacks loaded with books, and instead have a lightweight electronic book.

Software

Software manufacturers are producing high-quality multimedia programs that follow sound educational principles. For example, the *JumpStart Series* (Knowledge Adventure), designed especially for children from kindergarten through grade 6, Scholastic's, *Why Mosquitoes Buzz in People's Ears* (pre-K to grade 2), Edmark's *Talking Walls Series* (grades 4–8), and *Body Voyage* (Time

Warner Electronic Publishing, designed for junior high school students to adults) are innovative multimedia programs. Prices for educational software and computers are now reduced, and parents are taking advantage of these lower prices by buying more computers and software.

Today, students interact with the computer programs in a more realistic fashion because of developments in artificial intelligence. Programs such as *Crosscountry Canada* (Ingenuity) and *Math Mind Benders* (Critical Thinking Books & Software) have elements of artificial intelligence. Publishing houses are moving in the direction of integrating software with the state-adopted texts and the National Standards. Lab packs and networkable products are now available as well. In the future, every textbook will come with a supplemental disk. Programs such as *Grolier's Multimedia Encyclopedia*—which combines sound, still sequences, animations, and full-motion video, photographs, and simulations—are the norm. Virtual reality is being integrated into every software package along with *QuickTime VR* (see Chapter 14 for a full discussion).

Thoughts on the Future of Computers in Education

The following paragraph is from an interview with Dr. George Friedman, adjunct professor at the University of Southern California. Dr. Friedman was formerly research director at the SpaceStudies Institute, Princeton, and vice president of publications at the Institute of Electrical and Electronic Engineers. He retired in 1993 as Vice President Engineering and Technology at Northrop.

> Presently, American children are scoring quite poorly on worldwide tests in science and mathematics. Paradoxically, they are enormously computer literate; often shamefully outdistancing even their well educated parents. The opportunity here is to devote this computer literacy—and great desire to play and compete on the computer—to an effective educational tool which can increase their test scores not only in science and math but in ALL subjects, academic or not. This will not be easy but reasonable extrapolations of computerized instruction, expert systems, other domains of artificial intelligence and virtual reality can motivate, interest, and teach our children the necessary life and work skills in a far more effective environment than the present classroom. An important part of this plan is to employ the communication technologies necessary for distance education, so that rather than the students and professors being trapped in an inflexible classroom, the students, instructors, educational institutions, and coursework are distributed throughout a dynamic cyberspace where learning is conducted at any time and any place.

Author's Concluding Thoughts

We would all like to see technologically advanced computer labs such as SmartStudio 2001. Furthermore, we would want every student in our classrooms to have a computer that is connected to a wireless network. If a robot aide could decrease our workload, few of us would not order one tomorrow. Many of the items on our wonderful wish lists may never materialize. Unfortunately, schools do not have the money to buy the equipment to implement a technology-based program. The more sophisticated computer equipment will be found primarily at the college and university level. Elementary and secondary schools will not be able to afford this costly hardware. But there's another problem: the lack of teachers trained to manage this new technology. Still, most states now require that teachers complete a computer course for certification. Because of this requirement, there will be more trained teachers who can integrate the computer in the classroom.

What does the future hold? Computer use will increase, and the computers will be smaller, faster, more efficient, and less expensive. More emphasis will be placed on computer ethics, and the Internet will be available to all schools and children. Multimedia software will be even more sophisticated, offer speech recognition, be less expensive and more transparent, and will be menu- and icon-based. Computer storage capacity will be improved, and optical drives will allow teachers and students to access software more easily. More networkable machines will be available; advances in networking will lead to better communication between classrooms, schools, and school districts. One classroom will be networked with another classroom on a national or state database. Eventually, classrooms will be networking with classrooms in other countries. Students and teachers will commonly use desktop videoconferencing and publishing programs as well as scanners, digital cameras, and fax machines to import pictures and graphic images into their documents. The computer will be used with a DVD-RAM disc and database.

Teachers will be "teaching" less because the computer will have a more prominent role in the classroom. Computers will allow teachers to assume the role of facilitators, designing learning experiences and individualizing instruction. There will be less drill and practice and more problem solving and real, meaningful learning activities. Many more of our universities will have virtual degree programs, offering classes via the Internet. Books are still going to exist, but maybe as a supplement to technologies like the Internet. There may be only electronic books in our future, with the traditional book disappearing forever. Ahead of his time, one Illinois state superintendent of schools wanted laptop computers instead of books. The computer is a remarkable invention. Its possible impact on the curriculum is staggering, but it needs to be given a chance to show what it can do for children in the schools. It is up to educators to inspire, motivate, and excite students and colleagues about this remarkable instrument for learning.

Lessons We Have Learned

We have learned quite a few things from our experiences with the computer. History has taught us that technology will not solve all our educational problems. Programming or networked computers do not offer quick answers to how to educate students. The computer is an especially useful tool when working with the learning disabled (see Chapter 12). We are living in a society where technology is constantly changing and the skills that students need to compete are ever changing. These skills are different depending on the person's needs and competencies.

Educators generally want technology integrated into the classroom, but there are no firm guidelines for accomplishing this task. Stand-alone computers and networked computers each have their advantages and disadvantages. Networked computers let teachers standardize material across schools, districts, and classrooms. Stand-alone systems let teachers individualize the curriculum and control scheduling. We have learned that teachers usually do not have the time to develop computer materials or curricula. Distance learning has allowed people to attend class and conferences online, rather than traveling to other locations. However, there is still something wonderful about face-to-face instruction.

From the history of educational computing we can see that technology is developing faster than teachers can keep abreast of these changes. Teachers can no longer use the same handouts, homework, worksheets, or lecture notes. Educators must continually change to take advantage of technological advances. Finally, even in this new technology world, teachers will always be essential, and their understanding of how to use this technology in the classroom is indispensable.

Summary

Computers are not just a passing fancy; they will be with us for a long time. They have made life both easier and more complicated. We can accomplish a great deal more by using a computer, but we have to work harder to keep up with the technology. In the end, we must consider the future of this exciting technology. We will definitely have smaller, faster, easier-to-use, and more powerful computers. Future software and hardware will be multimedia, be networkable, include voice recognition, be based on artificial intelligence, and involve robots. Education will integrate computers into the curriculum as much as possible, but problems with funding and lack of adequately trained teachers may limit what is accomplished in classrooms. We can only speculate on what will happen in the future. What we do know is that the coming years will be exciting!

Chapter Mastery Test

Following the mastery test are basic terms and suggested readings and references.

1. What are some lessons we have learned from our experiences with educational technology?
2. Why is the voice recognition system the wave of the future?
3. Define artificial intelligence and speculate on how it could be used in the classroom.
4. How can the computer help disabled children?
5. What has slowed the use of computers in the schools? How can these obstacles be overcome?
6. Explain how computers in the classroom will change the traditional roles of teachers, students, and parents.
7. What are some future directions for computer use in the classroom? Defend your choices.
8. Why will wireless technology play an important role in the schools?

Basic Terms

artificial intelligence (AI) (p. 470)

desktop videoconferencing (p. 473)

distance learning (p. 469)

e-book (p. 476)

robot (p. 471)

voice recognition system (p. 468)

wireless networks (p. 469)

Suggested Readings and References

Apicella, Mario. "Robots Are Marching Toward a More Intelligent and More Mobile Future." *InfoWorld* 22, no. 47 (November 20, 2000): p. 72.

"The Best of What's New." *Popular Science,* December 1997, pp. 44–81.

Bork, Alfred. "The Future of Computers and Learning." *T.H.E. Journal* 24, no. 11 (June 1997): 69–77.

Bramscum, Deborah. "Monitors and Health." *MacWorld,* December 1994, pp. 175–76.

Crawford, Walt. "Faster, Better, Cheaper: A Decade of PC Progress." *Online* 21, no. 1 (January–February 1997): 22–26, 28–29.

Crawford, Walt. "Jargon that Computes: Today's PC Terminology." *Online* 21, no. 2 (March–April 1997): 36–41.

DuBois, Grant. "Membership Swells for the E-Book Club." *EWeek* 17, no. 41 (October 9, 2000).

Dunn, Kate. "Inventor's Robot Is a Big Hit on the Shooting Range." *Los Angeles Times,* April 27, 1998, p. D7.

Dvorak, John C. *Dvorak Predicts: An Insider Look at the Computer Industry.* New York: Osborne McGraw-Hill, 1994.

Ediger, M. "Computers at the Crossroads." *Educational Technology* 28, no. 5 (May 1988): 7–10.

Feigenbaum, E. A., and P. McCorduck. *The Fifth Generation: Artificial Intelligence and Japan's Computer Challenge to the World.* Reading, Mass.: Addison-Wesley, 1983.

Flanagan, Patrick. "The 10 Hottest Technologies in Telecom." *Telecommunications* 31, no. 5 (May 1997): 25–28, 30, 32.

Freedman, Alan. *Computer Desktop Encyclopedia.* Point Pleasant, Pa.: Computer Language Company, 2001.

Galloway, Jerry P. "The Effects of QuickTime Multimedia Tools on Writing Style and Content." In *Technology and Teacher Education Annual,* ed. J. Willis, B. Robin, and D. A. Willis. Charlottesville, Va.: Association for the Advancement of Computing in Education (AACE), 1994.

Hodges, Andrew. Alan Turning: The Enigma. Vintage Paper Back, Ranlon Century, London, 1992.

Hogan, Mike. "PC of Tomorrow." *IDG,* January 1998, pp. 132–42.

Howard, Bill. "2001: The Future Is Now." *PC Magazine,* January 2, 2001, p. 99.

Jerome, Marty. "The Fastest PCs in the World." *PC Computing,* August 1997, pp. 183–88.

Kahney, Leander. "White Pine Brings CU-See Me to Version 3.1." *MacWeek* 11, no. 48 (December 9, 1997).

Kaplan, Karen. "Robots Roll Up Their Sleeves." *Los Angeles Times,* March 10, 1994, p. 1D.

Leeds, Matthew. "Desktop Videoconferencing." *MacWorld,* November 1994, pp. 87–92.

McDonald, Glenn, and Cameron Crotty. "The Digital Future." *PC World,* January 2000, pp. 116–34.

Neel, Dan. "Wearable PC Goes to Work." *InfoWorld* 22, no. 47 (November 20, 2000): 10.

Pfaffenberger, Bryan. *Webster's New World Dictionary.* New York: Que, 1997.

Robertson, S., et al. "The Use and Effectiveness of Palmtop Computers in Education." *British Journal of Educational Technology* 28, no. 3 (July 1997): 177–89.

"The Tech Isn't Perfect, but Video Conferencing's Day Is Near." *Fortune Winter2001 Technology Guide* 142, no. 12 (2001): 242.

Viscusi, Vance. "21st Century Classroom." In *Computers in Education,* 8th ed. New York: Dushkin/McGraw-Hill, pp. 31–33.

Willis, William. "Speech Recognition: Instead of Typing and Clicking, Talk and Command." *T.H.E. Journal* 25, no. 6 (January 1998): 18–22.

Withrow, Frank B. "Technology in Education and the Next Twenty-Five Years." *T.H.E. Journal* 24, no. 11 (June 1997): 59–62.

Appendix A
Recommended Software

The majority of the programs that follow are award winning and have been cited in numerous magazines.

Art and Web Design Programs

Adobe GoLive, Adobe (Macintosh, Windows). Grades 7–Adult

GoLive lets students create professional dynamic websites. The program is integrated with other Adobe products such as *Illustrator* and *PhotoShop.*

Adobe PhotoDeluxe, Adobe (Macintosh, Windows). Grades 7–Adult

PhotoDeluxe lets you personalize your photographs with special effects. This program has step-by-step directions that explain how to combine photos, add special effects, and remove redeye. Templates let you add your photos to calendars, greeting cards, and so on.

Adobe PhotoShop, Adobe (Macintosh, Windows). Grades 10–Adult

This program is the standard for photo design and is a production tool for images that you can print and use on the Internet.

CorelDraw, Corel 10 (Windows). Grades 6–Adult

CorelDraw is an excellent illustration and image-editing software package with powerful tools. This program lets you create exciting designs that add spice to your school reports and projects.

DeBabelizer, Equilibrium (Macintosh, Windows). Grades 10–Adult

DeBabelizer is a high-powered automated application for students working with graphics, animations, and digital video, the Web, and desktop products. This program can automatically perform an unlimited number of graphic processes on an unlimited number of images for any specification for an entire batch and output everything to more than 90 bit-mapped file formats.

Disney's Magic Artist, Disney Interactive (Windows, Power Mac OS). Grades 3–Adult

Disney's Magic Artist is a drawing program that has realistic-looking tools such as whipped cream and bubbles, paints that smear, musical selections, and much more. The program includes a tutorial on how to draw Disney characters.

Dreamweaver, Macromedia (Macintosh, Windows). Grades 9–Adult

Dreamweaver is a professional Web design program for the advanced student. *Dreamweaver* can be customized using HTML, JavaScript, and XML.

Hallmark Card Studio Deluxe, Sierra On-Line/Havas (Windows). Grades K–Adult

Hallmark Card Studio lets students customize more than 3,000 Hallmark cards. There is a photo editor to incorporate classroom pictures.

ImageBlender, Tech4Learning (Macintosh, Windows). Grades 3–12

ImageBlender helps students find images for their Web pages and projects. This program is an editing gem that lets students effortlessly crop these images, add a bevel, text, and much more. *ImageBlender* has a wonderful assortment of paint tools and graphic effects.

iMovie 2, Apple (Macintosh). Grades 1–Adult

This video editing program can be downloaded from Apple's site. Beginning students or teachers can edit their own video footage by using drag-and-drop procedures.

JumpStart Artist, Knowledge Adventure (Macintosh, Windows). Grades K–4

JumpStart Artist is a creative drawing program that lets students explore the art world. They are introduced to fine art examples, where they use spray paint and colored chalk.

Kid Pix Deluxe 3, The Learning Company (Macintosh, Windows). Grades K–8

Kid Pix Deluxe 3 (the latest version) lets the student create a digital storybook, multimedia movie, or comic book by adding original art, sounds, music, or animations. The program has a set of art tools, and it has slide show capabilities. It has been a favorite for years.

Kid Pix Studio Deluxe, Brøderbund/ The Learning Company (Macintosh, Windows). Grades K–8

Kid Pix Studio Deluxe lets students do photo editing with special effects, voice painting, sound effects, and real art tools like chalk and magic markers.

Print Artist 4.0 Gold, Sierra/Knowledge Adventure (Macintosh, Windows). Grades 2–6

An easy-to-use program, *Print Artist* lets students design posters, signs, greeting cards, and more, in a matter of minutes. The program features more than 10,000 full-color graphics, 1,500 professionally designed layouts, and 600 spectacular photos.

Print Explosion, Nova (Macintosh). Grades K–Adult

The student can produce greeting cards, signs, banners, and more. This program gives you rich graphics, layout features, and text effects.

Print Master Platinum 10, The Learning Company (Windows); *Print Master Gold 10* (Macintosh). Grades 3–Adult

With this useful program, you can create cards, posters, newsletters, Web pages, labels, slide shows, and calendars.

Print Shop 11 Deluxe Brøderbund/The Learning Company (Windows). Grades K–Adult

This classic program comes in different flavors, such as *Print Shop Pro,* and *Print Shop 11 Deluxe.* With the *Print Shop*'s clip art, borders, and fonts, you can create calendars, posters, signs, banners, greeting cards, personal stationery, and advertising material. In addition, *Print Shop* offers easier-than-ever Web publishing.

SiteCentral, Knowledge Adventure (Macintosh/Windows). Grades 4–Adult

This Web-authoring tool has ready-made templates that help students make a Web page. *SiteCentral* is very easy to use because of its drag-and-drop interface. The program includes an extensive animation library and clip art, along with special art effects.

Web Workshop 2.0, Sunburst (Macintosh/Windows). Grades 2–8

Students can easily create Web pages with the standard drawing tools, dozens of backgrounds, and clip art library. The program has one-step publishing that lets students send their projects to their Internet server or publish free on Sunburst's site.

Web Workshop Pro, Sunburst (Macintosh, Windows). Grades 6–12

Web Workshop Pro is a sophisticated Web publishing program with advanced editing and assembly tools. The program has one-step publishing that lets students send their projects to their Internet server or publish free on Sunburst's site.

Authoring Tools/Presentation Software

Create Together, Bytes of Learning (Windows). Grades 3–Adult

Create Together is a multimedia authoring tool which uses wizard guides for hyperlinked or linear presentations. If you want to create these presentations from scratch, you can use its scalable tool sets. You can also collaborate with other students on any network.

HyperStudio 4.0, Knowledge Adventure (Macintosh, Windows). Grades 7–12

HyperStudio is an extremely popular authoring program that is used worldwide. It offers many built-in features and functions, including color, laser disc, and CD-ROM support, animation, scrolling, and exporting to the Web.

Leonardo's Multimedia Toolbox, NEC (Macintosh, Windows). Grades 7–12

Students or teachers can use *Leonardo's* to create multimedia presentations. This program has paint tools that let students draw, paint, and edit lines, circles, rectangles, and freeform objects. *Leonardo's* also has animation tools that let users animate images with different effects and movements.

MicroWorlds Pro, Logo Computer Systems (Macintosh, Windows). Grades 4–8

MicroWorlds Pro is a multimedia authoring tool that introduces students to problem solving and creative thinking. Students use this Logo-based toolkit to create and combine graphics, text, animation, music, and sound in interactive books, newsletters, maps, and other products.

MovieWorks, Visions Technology in Education (Macintosh, Windows). Grades 4–Adult

MovieWorks has all the tools that you need to create *QuickTime* movies, videos, and multimedia presentations. This program has an easy-to-use drag-and-drop interface.

MP Express, Bytes of Learning (Macintosh, Windows). Grades 2–Adult

This program is an easy-to-use multimedia presentation tool for children as well as adults. Its streamlined design and simplified user interface let beginners and advanced users produce high-quality presentations in minutes.

PowerPoint, Microsoft (Macintosh, Windows). Grades 9–Adult

PowerPoint is a presentation tool that lets high school students turn ideas into powerful presentations. The program has instant layouts, on-screen directions, and tool tips that make compelling multimedia presentations. *PowerPoint* lets you create overheads for class presentations, slides for a meeting, or dazzling effects on-screen.

Database Programs (See Spreadsheets and Integrated Programs)

FileMaker Pro, Filemaker Incorporated (Macintosh, Windows). Grades 7–Adult

An easy-to-use but still powerful and sophisticated piece of software, *FileMaker Pro* offers many layout possibilities to meet the varied needs of student and teacher without compromising output or performance.

TableTop Jr. (younger students) and *TableTop Sr.* (older students), Brøderbund/TERC (Macintosh, Windows). Grades 1–12

Using these tools, students can sort, manipulate, and create data sets. Both programs provide databases for students to explore.

Desktop Publishing and Writing

Amazing Writing Machine, The Learning Company (Macintosh). Grades K–6

This program inspires children to write and illustrate their own stories, journals, essays, letters, and poems. They can design pages from scratch or use predesigned templates. The program has a built-in spelling checker and a rebus tool that transforms words into pictures.

Easy Book Deluxe, Sunburst (Macintosh). Grades 3–8

With *Easy Book Deluxe,* children create real books with a minimum of effort. They simply write their stories and illustrate them with simple paint tools. The program determines the page layout and is even able to print on both sides of the paper.

Imagination! Express, Edmark (Macintosh, Windows). Grades 1–6

Edmark has reached a new plateau in education with this sensational multi-media desktop publishing program. Students create interactive books and print out beautifully illustrated stories. The program features a multitude of illustrated backgrounds, hundreds of character and prop "stickers,"a text placement feature, a sound record option, and music capabilities.

Kid Works Deluxe, Knowledge Adventure (Macintosh, DOS/Windows). Grades K–4

Kid Works Deluxe, is a combination word processor, text-to-speech program, and paint program in a simple-to-use package. Students learn to express themselves in Spanish or English and listen to the computer read their own stories.

Microsoft Publisher, Microsoft (Windows). Grades 5–Adult

Microsoft Publisher performs a variety of choices from creating a business card or flyer to producing a newspaper. The program requires less learning time than a program such as *QuarkXPress* or *PageMaker,* but it is more complicated than *Imagination! Express.* You can work from scratch or work through a series of questions posed by the program to determine how to build your publication.

PageMaker, Adobe (Macintosh, Windows). Grades 11–Adult

The publishing package that launched the desktop publishing revolution, *PageMaker* gives advanced users the ability to produce professional documents quickly. The program uses an intuitive electronic pasteboard that enables you to lay out and view text and graphics easily on a page. Several templates and predesigned publications come with it.

QuarkXPress, XTensions (Macintosh, Windows). Grades 10–Adult

This program is becoming the standard for desktop publishing, possessing a full range of features for the sophisticated user.

Stanley Sticker Stories, Edmark (Macintosh, Windows). Grades Pre-K–2

Students create their own animated storybooks featuring the Edmark characters Sammy, Trudy, Millie, and Bailey.

Storybook Weaver Deluxe, The Learning Company (Macintosh, Windows). Grades 1–4

Storybook Weaver Deluxe gives young students a simple interface with which to create elaborate storybooks that combine graphics, sounds, and text. The easy-to-use word processor has a spelling checker, a thesaurus, and text-to-speech capabilities. This program operates in both English and Spanish and has drawing tools and an excellent collection of graphics.

Student Writing Center, The Learning Company (Macintosh, Windows). Grades 4–10

Student Writing Center is a quality word processor and desktop publishing program. This program comes packed with features, including a spelling checker, a bibliography maker, a thesaurus, process writing capabilities, and grammar tips. Included in this package are 30 predesigned letterheads and borders and more than 150 clip art pictures.

Ultimate Writing & Creativity Center, The Learning Company (Macintosh, Windows). Grades 2–6

Students create reports, signs, journals, storybooks, and newsletters. This program has the ability to have documents read aloud and to add animation.

Writing Trek, Sunburst (Macintosh, Windows). Grades 4–6, 6–8, and 8–10

Students participate in 12 structured real-world learning projects. They develop an understanding of writing, experience literary examples, answer questions, and complete their own writing projects.

Early Childhood

Arthur's Camping Adventure, The Learning Company (Macintosh, Windows). Grades Pre-K–2

In *Arthur's Camping Adventure,* Mr. Rathburn takes Arthur and the class on a camping trip. In the process of trying to solve an emergency, students engage in six delightful activities that involve challenging puzzles, problem solving, and critical thinking skills.

Chato's Kitchen, Scholastic (Macintosh, Windows). Grades Pre-K–2

Chato's Kitchen is about a mambo-loving cat called Chato. This multicultural story is about friendship and learning to get along with each other. There are interactive games and writing exercises that reinforce the lessons.

Clifford Reading, Scholastic (Macintosh, Windows). Grades Pre-K–1

Clifford Reading takes place at a carnival, where students engage in a collection of six early reading activities. For example, *Monique's Word Painting* activity has students drag letters onto a blank canvas to form words and see them illustrated.

Disney's Mickey Kindergarten, Disney Interactive (Windows). Grades Pre-K–1

This program teaches math, counting, logic, addition, creativity, and telling time. The setting is downtown Disney, where Mickey Mouse, a star reporter, is trying to find something to write about. He discovers writing material as the students play seven different games with quality music and graphics.

Dr. Seuss Pre-School and Kindergarten, The Learning Company (Macintosh, Windows). Grades Pre-K–1

Dr. Seuss contains readiness activities in reading that teach alphabetical order, letter recognition, phonics, word recognition, and spelling. The Dr. Seuss characters introduce the students to these multilevel activities.

JumpStart Series, Knowledge Adventure (Macintosh, Windows). Grades K–2

Knowledge Adventure has a series of early learning programs in reading and math. Students learn to navigate through a schoolhouse full of interactive educational songs, puzzles, and games with a friendly host.

Math Blaster for 1st Grade, Knowledge Adventure (Macintosh, Windows). Grades Pre-K–8

By playing five activities, students practice counting, addition, and subtraction facts, sorting sets, measuring, telling time, and counting money. This program not only has math drill and practice activities, but also has activities that involve higher-level thinking skills.

My Amazing Human Body, DK Multimedia (Macintosh, DOS/Windows). Grades K–4

A 3-D skeleton teaches the students about topics that range from human anatomy to health. They engage in activities such as building a body and playing a "taking me apart" game.

My First Amazing Diary, DK Multimedia (Macintosh, Windows). Grades K–3

Using this program, students engage in written expression. *My First Amazing Diary* lets you create pictures of yourself, family members, or friend by combining different facial features.

Oz—The Magical Adventure, DK Multimedia (Macintosh, Windows). Grades Pre-K–3

Oz—The Magical Adventure has nine fascinating puzzles that take place in the Land of Oz. The program promotes problem-solving skills and is great with special education students because of its auditory directions and picture signs.

Putt-Putt Joins the Circus, Humongous Entertainment (Macintosh, Windows). Grades Pre-K–3

Putt-Putt Joins the Circus teaches logic and problem solving in a very entertaining fashion. Students steer a car through the different screens, meeting people and collecting useful objects. The *Putt-Putt* series consists of a whole collection of programs that include titles such as *Putt-Putt Enters the Race, Putt-Putt Travels through Time,* and *Putt-Putt One-Stop Funshop.*

Reader Rabbit's Math, with ADAPT, The Learning Company (Macintosh, Windows). Grades 1–4

The setting is a Pirate Island where the students engage in nine exciting activities. There is a customized feature that uses a pretest and the teacher can keep track of each student's progress.

Reader Rabbit Personalized First Grade, The Learning Company (Macintosh, Windows). Grades K–2

Students are taught spelling, word recognition, math, and music in this delightful *Reader Rabbit* program. Students must help Reader Rabbit save Wordville's annual musical performance by completing a series of activities, including collecting props, costumes, and musical instruments. There is a pretest to diagnose student strengths and weaknesses.

Reader Rabbit's Ready for Letters, The Learning Company (Macintosh, Windows). Grades Pre-K–1

This fun-filled program uses six activities with wonderful cartoon characters and lifelike speech and animation. Children learn letters, find shapes and colors, match words and letters, and spell.

Richard Scarry's Busytown, Paramount Communications (Macintosh, Windows). Grades Pre-K–2

The adorable characters from Richard Scarry's books come alive in 12 original playgrounds. *Richard Scarry's Busytown* will keep young children busy for hours with activities that let them experiment with objects, manipulate real machines, and practice working behind a counter. Furthermore, they can build a house, become a doctor, or fight a fire. Another new title produced by Paramount is *How Things Work in Busytown.* In this program, the Busytown characters teach cause-and-effect relationships.

Stickybear ABC Deluxe, Optimum Resource, Inc. (Macintosh, Windows). Grades Pre-K–1

Stickybear ABC Deluxe teaches the alphabet using four different activities. The students learn phonics, how to pronounce, select, write, and identify letters. The program is easy to use with terrific graphics and a management component.

3D Froggy Phonics, Ingenuity Works Inc. (Macintosh, Windows). Grades Pre-K–1

3D Froggy Phonics helps students master basic phonics concepts. This engaging phonics program helps the students learn the sounds for each letter and learn early spelling and reading skills. Students can also see videos that illustrate letter sounds.

Graphics Programs

Graph Club, Tom Snyder Productions (Macintosh, Windows). Grades K–4

This graphics tool can be used for self-directed exploration, presentations, lessons, or class projects. Students learn to sort, classify information, construct graphs, and analyze data.

Graphing & Managing Data, Gamco (Macintosh, Windows). Grades 3–6

The students collect and organize data, read and interpret data that is displayed in tables, charts, and graphs. In addition, they can conduct surveys, record and evaluate data, and draw conclusions.

GraphPower, Ventura Educational Systems (Macintosh). Grades K–8, Special Education

GraphPower develops students' ability to analyze and interpret data by teaching students how to create an array of graphics including pictographs, bar graphs, and circle graphs. An online tutorial helps users overcome graphing problems.

Graph Workshop, Cognitive Technology Group (Macintosh, Windows). Grades 4–12

Students quickly produce pictographs, line graphs, circle graphs, and bar graphs. There are tutorials, integrated draw tools, and built-in statistics. This program is easy to use and has a comprehensive teacher's guide with line masters.

Probability Toolkit, Ventura Educational Systems (Macintosh, DOS). Grades K–8

Probability Toolkit is an engaging program that helps students develop a basic understanding of probability and statistics. This educational tool has a variety of interesting simulated experiments involving marbles in a jar, colored spinners, colored chips, dice, and cards. The results of each experiment can be graphed in many different formats such as bar graphs, circle graphs, or line graphs. Furthermore, a detailed instructor's guide and activity sheets accompany the program.

Language Arts/Reading Programs

Bailey's Book House, Edmark (Macintosh, Windows). Grades Pre-K–1

When children enter the enchanting environment of *Bailey's Book House,* they learn the alphabet, make rhymes, and develop visual memory and discrimination. They create adventure stories filled with spaceships, flying carpets, and monsters.

Corporate Climber, JayKlein Productions (Macintosh, Windows). Grades 7–Adult

Corporate Climber helps you learn and master the English language. The user enters the corporation as a probationary employee and embarks on an entertaining and educational journey through the company's 10 divisions. In the process, students learn about subject–verb disharmony, spelling, apostrophes, pronouns, and much more.

English Express Deluxe, Knowledge Adventure (Macintosh, Windows). Grades 5–Adult

This program is designed to teach English as a Second Language (ESL) students. Students hear standard pronunciations and make connections among spoken and written words and sentences and images representing the words' meanings to help them acquire language skills naturally.

Grammar for the Real World, Knowledge Adventure (Macintosh, Windows). Grades 5–12

Grammar for the Real World, a simulation, teaches grammar, sentence structure, punctuation, and spelling. Students have to proofread letters from TV stars for incorrect punctuation and grammar, fix news anchors' reports, identify parts of speech, and tailor material to certain audiences.

High School Advantage 2001, Encore Software (Macintosh, Windows). Grades 9–12

This six-set of CD-ROMs teaches 10 core subjects with a multitude of lessons, animations, and activities. The students work at their own pace with exercises in such subjects as vocabulary, reading, writing, and science.

High School Reading Comprehension, Optimum Resources (Macintosh, Windows). Grades 9–12

Optimum Resources has an excellent, high-interest comprehension series for high school students. The curriculum areas covered include history, cars, fashion, and famous people. There are multiple-choice as well as essay questions for each section, and a student's progress reports can be printed.

Hollywood High, Grolier Interactive (Macintosh, Windows). Grades 7–12

Hollywood High encourages creative writing and provides an opportunity for students to listen to their own written work and make revisions. When students use *Hollywood High,* they choose characters, expressions, and scenery for their play. They write scripts, add actions, edit the scripts, and then listen to and watch the characters perform.

I Love Spelling, DK Interactive Learning (Macintosh, Windows). Grades 2–6

I Love Spelling, for ages 7 to 11, is a collection of classic spelling games, such as spelling bee and hangman, and anagrams that are packaged in a cartoon format.

Island Reading Journey, Sunburst (Macintosh, Windows). Grades 4–5

Island Reading Journey is a multimedia program that contains reading comprehension activities to help the student read for meaning. This program has exercises for 100 intermediate-level books commonly found in classrooms or libraries.

John Steinbeck Library, Mindscape/Penguin Books (Macintosh, Windows). Grades 9–Adult

John Steinbeck Library: Of Mice and Men tells the classic tale of two men trying to find their niche in the world. The students learn about the history of the early 1900s in California. The CD-ROM contains film footage, archival photos, maps, and period music.

JumpStart Series, Knowledge Adventure (Macintosh, Windows). Grades Pre-K–6

The *JumpStart* series presents award-winning programs where students learn to navigate through a schoolhouse full of interactive educational songs, puzzles, and games with a friendly host.

Kaplan SAT & PSAT ACT 2001 Edition, Encore Software (Macintosh, Windows). Grades 9–12

Kaplan SAT & PSAT ACT 2001 Edition is a tutorial program that uses a step-by-step approach to help secondary students master the strategies for dealing with material found on the SAT, PSAT, and ACT tests. This program covers all pertinent subject areas.

Kreative Komix, Visions Technology in Education (Macintosh, Windows). Grades 2–Adult

Presently there are two programs in this series, *Super Hero Comic Book Maker* and *Fairy Tale Comic Book Maker.* These multimedia programs have all the necessary background and props to bring students' favorite comic book or fairy tale characters to life. Students can click on text and record their own voices and animate characters in a sequence. Furthermore, students can create characters, print stick puppets, and make puppet show backdrops.

Lawrence D. Duck: Language Arts Private Eye, Lawrence Productions (Macintosh, Windows). Grades 3–8

Lawrence D. Duck investigates unsolved mysteries. Students help this able detective by clicking on footprints and answering language arts questions such as identifying a part of speech or putting in capital letters.

Leap into Phonetics, Leap into Learning (Macintosh, Windows). Pre-K–1 (ESL)

Leap into Phonics teaches pre-K through first graders the eight beginning phonemic awareness phonic skills, rhyming, auditory memory, sound segmentation, alphabet, sound substitution, blending sounds, identifying environmental sounds, and nursery rhymes.

Literature Classic Companions Series, Clearvue/eav (Macintosh, Windows). Grades 5–8

Literature Classic Companions are CDs designed to increase students' skills in writing, interpreting, and enjoying literary classics. The CDs range from *American Literature,* with stories like *The Red Badge of Courage* and *The Grapes of Wrath,* to *The Nature of Evil* CD with stories like *The Turn of the Screw* and *Jane Eyre.* Each CD offers a word processor on-screen, activities, and a database of quotations.

Living Book Series, Living Books (Macintosh, Windows). Grades K–5

This excellent series of delightful interactive books comes in English and Spanish. The titles continue to grow in number. Four of the more popular books are *Arthur's Teacher Trouble, Just Grandma and Me Deluxe, Little Monster at School,* and *Green Eggs and Ham. Arthur's Teacher Trouble* tells of the grade-school adventures of a shy aardvark. *Just Grandma and Me* is a story about a grandma and grandson's adventures at the beach. *Little Monster at School* is a funny story about the trials and tribulations of a new kid at school. *Green Eggs and Ham* has clickable games and is based on the classic Dr. Seuss tale.

Macbeth, Hoffman + Associates (Macintosh, Windows). Grades 9–Adult

Students using this program are taken on a guided tour of the play *Macbeth.* They learn about the life and times of the characters, Shakespeare, and Scottish history.

Reader Rabbit Learn to Read System, The Learning Company (Macintosh, Windows). Grades Pre-K–3

Reader Rabbit Learn to Read is a delightful reading program for the beginning reader. This is an easy-to-understand set of reading activities that teaches letters and sounds, as well as the most frequently seen sight words.

Reading Blaster 5th Grade, Knowledge Adventure (Macintosh, Windows). Grades 4–7

Reading Blaster is an exciting adventure game that reinforces reading, spelling, and vocabulary. As with *Carmen Sandiego,* students earn clues to find the identity of a crook.

Reading SEARCH: In Search of Lost Folk Tales, Great Wave Software (Macintosh, Windows). Grades 1–6

Students are sent to one of four ancient sites to collect clues so that they can unscramble one of the 70 folktales. This program is good for comprehension practice. It has animated characters and keeps track of progress.

Romeo and Juliet, Cambrix Publishing (Macintosh, Windows). Grades 8–Adult

Students read and listen to the play, which is enhanced by synchronized on-screen text presented with hypertext study notes. This CD-ROM disc is helpful for the special-needs student.

School House Rock: Grammar Rock, The Learning Company (Macintosh, Windows). Grades 1–5

School House Rock: Grammar Rock is a drill and practice program, containing videos on grammar from the ABC television program. Students complete 19 multilevel activities and practice grammar concepts. The correct answers win coins that are used to play arcade games.

Stories & More: Time and Place, Edmark/Riverdeep (Macintosh, Windows). Grades 2, 3

This high-quality program teaches reading comprehension with a multicultural flavor. Students choose one of three delightful stories that emphasize different cultures, places, and times. The stories are beautifully illustrated, and they can be read silently or read by the narrator. There are pre and post activities. A similar program by Edmark is *Stories & More: Animal Friends,* which teaches reading comprehension through the following stories: *The Trek* (by Ann Jonas), *The Gunnywolf* (retold by A. Delany), and *Owl and the Moon* (by Arnold Lobel).

That's a Fact, Jack! Read: Mystery and Adventure, Tom Snyder Productions (Macintosh, Windows). Grades 2–8

That's a Fact, Jack! Read is an interactive game show that helps students review literature. The teacher can choose from 45 CD-ROM discs that cover 450 children's and young adult books that are found in the classroom. This software program is a wonderful method to review literature with individual students or a whole class.

Why Do Mosquitoes Buzz in People's Ears? Scholastic (Macintosh, Windows). Grades Pre-K–2

Why Do Mosquitoes Buzz in People's Ears? is a traditional African story that has specially composed music, animated video segments, and narration by James Earl Jones. This program contains games that reinforce reading skills and a record-keeping feature that records a student's progress.

Math Programs

Applied Math, Plato (Macintosh, Windows). Grades 3–8

Students master measurement, conversion, and estimating, as they relate to a work setting. They move through three types of activities which include tutorials and mastery tests.

Carmen Sandiego Math Detective, The Learning Company (Macintosh, Windows). Grades 4–8

Carmen Sandiego Math Detective teaches pre-algebra, geometry, division, fractions, and percents. The students embark on 12 missions to Carmen's hideouts. During each mission, they encounter five different math activities.

Fraction Fireworks, Edmark (Macintosh, Windows). Grades 3–6

This program is a basic introduction to fractions. Students experiment with numerator and denominator to see how a fireworks display will look.

Geometer's Sketchpad, Curriculum Press (Macintosh, Windows). Grades 9–Adult

Using *Sketchpad 3,* students manipulate and create geometric figures. They are able to explore freely or use the program as a tool to do assigned problems. The program comes with a user manual and sample activities.

Geometry World—Interactive Explorer, Cognitive Technologies Corporation (Macintosh, Windows). Grades 5–Adult

Geometry World teaches and reinforces geometry concepts in a unique 3-D environment. The areas covered include the Pythagorean theorem, angles, lines, polygons, circles, perimeter, area, and solids. There are activities on tessellation, tangrams, Venn diagrams, and geoboard.

Ice Cream Truck, Sunburst (Macintosh, Windows). Grades 2–6

Ice Cream Truck, an exciting simulation, lets lower grade students become ice cream truck drivers. Students begin with $500 and try to earn as much money as possible by stocking up on the products they think will be in the greatest demand.

Interactive Math Journey, The Learning Company (Macintosh, Windows). Grades 1–4

This program has 25 math games that include interactive books, challenge games, and songs. Some of the games are multiple level, and the record-keeping function tracks the student's progress.

KidsMath, Great Wave Software (Macintosh, Windows). Grades K–3

In *KidsMath,* eight entertaining activities teach a range of basic math skills, from counting and fractions to developing positive attitudes toward math. Great Wave Software has produced two other very useful programs: *NumberMaze* and *Decimal and Fraction Maze.*

Math Advantage 2001, Encore Software (Macintosh, Windows). Grades 9–12

Math Advantage 2001 covers eight core math subjects, pre-algebra, algebra I, algebra II, geometry, trigonometry, precalculus, calculus, and statistics. There are animated examples, narrated text, quizzes, games, and over 3,000 problems. The in-depth tutorial has a hint system, with step-by-step problems solutions, and real-life examples of math applications.

Math Arena, Sunburst (Windows, Macintosh). Grades 4–6

Sunburst's *Math Arena* is a unique program that lets students practice the essential math skills, including money, probability, and geometry. The students play in a training or a competition mode, by themselves, with two or three other people. Then 20 puzzles range from Venn diagram sorting puzzles to probability exercises.

Math Blaster: Algebra, Knowledge Adventure (Macintosh, Windows). Grades 7–Adult

This tutorial program reviews and gives practice in algebra basics. More than 670 problems cover different areas of algebra. New problems can be added with the editor feature.

Math Blaster 9–12, The Learning Company (Macintosh, Windows). Grades 4–6

This version covers multi-operand equations, adding fractions, logic, and more. It has more than 50,000 problems and 10 levels of difficulty. It includes an easy-to-use spreadsheet and graph program. The *Math Blaster* series covers the ages of 6 and up with programs such as *Math Blaster 6–9, Math Blaster 9–12, Math Blaster Pre-Algebra, Math Blaster Algebra,* and *Math Blaster Geometry.*

Math for the Real World, Knowledge Adventure (Macintosh, Windows). Grades 5–8

Math for the Real World teaches fractions, decimals, time, money, charts, and measurement. The program lets students use their math skills in a real-world context by joining a band and traveling to 10 cities across the United States.

Math Heads, Grolier Interactive (Macintosh, Windows). Grades 3–7

Students use TV channels to practice their pre-algebra skills. They learn about such topics as multiple representations, proportions, and estimation.

Math Munchers Deluxe, The Learning Company (Macintosh, Windows). Grades 2–12

The students race through a grid to capture a solution to a math challenge while avoiding evil troggles. The program offers 20 topics that range from prime numbers to factors.

Math Shop Deluxe, Scholastic (Macintosh, Windows). Grades 2–12

This program, which supports the NCTM standard, covers thousands of math problems at five levels of difficulty. Students solve problems at the Arcade Alley shops. For every correct problem, they earn money they can use to play games at the Math Shop Arcade.

Mathville, Ingenuity Works (Macintosh, Windows). Grades K–9

Mathville is a series of CD-ROMs that support the NCTM standard. These programs are based on everyday math and supplement the typical teacher's math program. The problems and activities in each program cover a variety of topics and difficulty levels. The series handles grades K–9 and can be used for remedial practice for high school students. It is a good basic program for the reluctant learner.

Mighty Math Calculating Crew, Edmark (Macintosh, Windows). Grades 3–6

Mighty Math Calculating Crew helps students improve their math problem-solving skills. This program invites students into an animated world of math adventure. They are given practice in handling topics such as multiplication, division, number lines, money, and 3-D geometry.

Millie's Math House, Edmark (Macintosh, Windows). Grades Pre-K–1

Millie's Math House is an award-winning multimedia program that teaches beginning math skills. Children learn about numbers, patterns, sizes, and shapes in six interactive activities with animated characters, colorful graphics, and lively music.

MindTwisters, Edmark (Macintosh, Windows). Grades 3–4

MindTwisters focus on math facts, rounding, measuring, telling time, counting money, and much more. In this action-packed game show format, students race against the clock and other players to enter their answers. The teacher can set the program's challenge level to match individual student skill level.

PrimeTime Math, Tom Snyder Productions (Macintosh, Windows). Grades 4–9

The *PrimeTime Math* series for students teaches math through dramatic stories about professional people. Students engage in real-world stories of wilderness, medical emergencies, search and rescues, fires, and crimes. By using this program, they see the application of math in the real world.

Princeton Review Algebra Edge, The Learning Company (Macintosh, Windows). Grades 7–Adult

This package contains two algebra programs, *Algebra Smart* and *Grade Builder Algebra I.* Using 60 interactive lessons, *Grade Builder Algebra I* covers an entire year of algebra I. The students have fun mastering the topics with games and unlimited practice problems. *Algebra Smart* is an interactive tutorial that covers a full year of algebra I. It has more than 500 practice problems with step-by-step solutions, algebra games, and 130 videos that take you through 12 key lessons.

Puzzle Logic, Ventura Educational Systems (Macintosh, Windows). Grades 6–Adult

Puzzle Logic consists of 17 challenging puzzles which build thinking skills. The puzzles are very different, ranging from Magic Squares to the Tower of Stars. Students choose challenging puzzles and then find themselves in an interactive environment where they use a variety of math and logic skills to find a solution.

Stickybear's Math Splash, Optimum Resource (Macintosh, Windows). Grades K–5

Stickybear's Math Splash guides students ages 5 to 10 on a water-filled wacky adventure. The software contains four inventive drill and practice activities.

TesselMania Deluxe, The Learning Company (Macintosh, Windows). Grades 4–12

TesselMania! inspired by the work of M. C. Escher, helps students explore transformational geometry while stretching their imaginations and developing spatial and visualization skills. Students create their own interlocking puzzlelike designs, connecting art and geometry.

The Quarter Mile 6.0, Barnum Software (Macintosh, DOS/Windows). Grades K–9

The Quarter Mile is an addictive drill and practice program. It covers whole numbers, fractions, decimals, percents, integers, equations, estimation, and math tricks. Students are in a competitive drag race with themselves. (Students can opt to race "wild running horses" instead of cars.) The program offers an excellent teacher management component and many additional features.

Trigonometry Explorer, Cognitive Technologies Corporation (Macintosh, Windows). Grades 7–Adult

This program is a comprehensive overview of trigonometry. The students manipulate angles and objects, hear explanations, and receive feedback.

Music Programs

Auralia, Rising Software (Macintosh, Windows). Grades 4–12

Auralia is a top-selling music instructional program, teaching topics like intervals, scales, rhythm, pitch, and melody. It uses a drill-based approach, and students progress through various levels in 26 categories.

Backstage Pass: The Ultimate Rock & Roll Trivia Game, Sierra On-Line (Windows). Grades 7–Adult

This clever trivia game tests student knowledge on a variety of musical topics that range from disco to folk music. The time period covered is from the 1950s to the present.

Guitar Method 1 version 1.2, eMedia (Windows). Grades 3–Adult

Guitar Method 1 takes students step-by-step from basics to playing complete songs. The program has an enhanced audio soundtrack and an animated Fretboard.

Juilliard Music Adventure, Grolier Interactive (Macintosh, Windows). Grades 4–Adult

Juilliard Music Adventure helps students master the tools for composing melodies and creating rhymes with Juilliard. The students produce their own musical performance. This program introduces the student to rhythm, melody, orchestration, and musical styles.

Making Music and *Making More Music,* Grolier Interactive (Macintosh, Windows). Pre-K–12, Adult

Making Music lets children experiment with the elements of music. It contains games and open-ended creativity activities. *Making More Music,* the sequel, brings the students to the next knowledge level. Using this program students experiment with the elements of music. They become student-composers and create their own compositions using familiar tunes and songs, and they save these new musical works.

Music Ace and *Music Ace 2*, Harmonic Vision (Macintosh, Windows). Grades 3–Adult

Music Ace and *Music Ace 2* are programs that introduce students to music fundamentals. *Music Ace* has 24 comprehensive lessons, motivating games, and a Music Doodle pad that lets students become composers. *Music Ace 2,* the second title in the series, continues where *Music Ace* ended. It introduces new concepts such as standard notation, rhythm, melody, and harmony in an engaging format.

Music Appreciation, Clearvue (Macintosh, Windows). Grades 4–Adult

Clearvue offers comprehensive music CD-ROMs on different musical periods, composers, and instruments. Students learn to understand music while studying musical elements. There are CDs such as *Dynamics and Tone,* and *Rhythm and Melody.*

Musition, Rising Software (Windows). Grades 3–Adult

Musition is a complete music theory program that covers topics ranging from note reading to transposition. This program uses a drill-based approach where students progress through different levels of difficulty and receive immediate feedback.

Pianomouse Meets the Great Composers, Pianomouse.com (Macintosh, Windows). Grades 3–12

This program provides an excellent introduction to eight famous composers' lives and their musical work. Students choose a musician to study, for example, Beethoven; listen to his biography; and then play games to test their knowledge.

The Piano Discovery System, Jump! Music (Windows, Macintosh). Grades 1–12, Adult

Based on the classic *Miracle Piano,* this program turns your computer into a piano and teaching machine. *Piano Discovery* comes with a MIDI keyboard and has arcade-style games and tutorials.

Problem Solving and Logic

Brain Buster, DK Interactive Learning (Macintosh, Windows). Grades 3–Adult

This amusing program helps students develop critical thinking skills by teaching word recognition, spatial relationships, estimation, creative thinking, and logic. *Brain Buster* is fast and exciting, with questions on everything from math to science.

Building Perspective Deluxe, Sunburst (Windows, Macintosh). Grades 4–Adult

Building Perspective Deluxe has three challenging activities that help geometric and three-dimensional thinking skills. Students contrast and compare different pictures of a city block with different heights to predict configurations of views that are not visible.

I Spy School Days, Scholastic (Macintosh, Windows). Grades K–4

Students work in nine unique play areas, tackling clever riddles and racing against the clock trying to break codes. Students even have the option of making their own Spy picture riddle.

Kids MENSA, Grolier Interactive (Macintosh, Windows). Grades 5–8

Kids MENSA offers 100 number puzzles with 10 levels of difficulty. There are many secret codes to break and "Fun Facts." Students will find a terrific hint system with a variety of puzzles which keeps this program interesting.

MENSA, Grolier Interactive (Macintosh, Windows). Grades 7–Adult

MENSA's Mind Teasers has over 500 math, word, logic, and spatial relations problems. This CD has six difficulty levels and a helpful hint system with explanations. There is also a *MENSA Ultimate Challenge,* created for grade 9 and up, which has brand-new puzzles, games, and riddles with in-depth self-analysis to improve thinking.

Myst and *Riven,* The Learning Company (Macintosh, Windows). Grades 7–Adult

The classic *Myst* is an advanced problem-solving program that involves students in reading for information. The program's *QuickTime* movies are quite unusual and the music has an eerie quality that draws users into a surrealistic setting. *Riven,* the sequel to *Myst,* has greater graphic detail, full-motion video, and puzzles that are integrated into the story line.

Nancy Drew: Stay Tuned for Danger, Compu-Teach (Windows). Grades 5–9

Our heroine Nancy Drew visits a soap opera star and becomes involved in a mystery. This case has 3-D characters and codes and puzzles to solve. The students learn to interpret nonverbal clues, gather and synthesize information, use critical thinking skills, and much more.

Oz—The Magical Adventure, DK Multimedia (Macintosh, Windows). Grades K–3

Students solve intriguing puzzles in the magical Land of Oz. They reorder switches to guide water to a tank, plant flowers, and discover how to move frogs across toadstools.

PhysiciaElementa Collection, Intellectum Plus (Windows). Grades 12–Adult

Intellectum Plus produces a series of interactive problem-solving programs that address elementary physics concepts such as force, motion, and friction. These programs are appropriate for grade 12 to adult. The software is based on advanced problem-solving methodologies incorporating artificial intelligence features.

The Return of the Incredible Machine, Sierra On-Line (Macintosh, Windows). Grades 5–9

The Return of the Incredible Machine has 250 unusual, mind-melting puzzles. Students build trip-lever contraptions by placing parts such as ropes, pulleys, bowling balls, and cheese-driven mouse motors. When these parts are combined correctly, the machine is able to complete its task.

Thinkin' Science ZAP! Edmark/Riverdeep (Macintosh, Windows). Grades 3–6

The students explore sound, light, and electricity working with laser beams, electrical circuits, and sound waves. There are hundreds of simple and complex activities calling on the student to seek a solution.

Thinkin' Things FrippleTown, Edmark/Riverdeep (Macintosh, Windows). Grades K–3

The students join the Fripples in activities that test thinking strategies. There are four parts: Navigation, Rule Determination, Creativity, and Deductive Reasoning.

Thinkin' Things Galactic Brain Benders, Edmark/Riverdeep (Macintosh, Windows). Grades 3–8

Thinkin' Things Galactic Brain Benders consists of five activities that build problem-solving, evaluation, and reasoning skills. Students test hypotheses, analyze information, and improve inductive and deductive reasoning.

The Time Warp of Dr. Brain, Sierra On-Line (Macintosh, Windows). Grades 7–Adult

The Time Warp of Dr. Brain is just one in a series of programs developed by Sierra On-Line that includes *The Island of Dr. Brain* and *The Lost Mind of Dr. Brain.* These programs have strong math and logical thinking elements. Students employ different strategies to solve puzzles that employ language, spatial reasoning memory, music, and so on.

What's My Logic? and *Mind Benders,* Critical Thinking Press and Software (Macintosh, DOS/Windows). Grades 2–Adult

What's My Logic? is a series of mind-stretching games for older students and adults. Program users have to discover what the fundamental rule of logic is that will let them travel through a maze to the end. There are 30 different fascinating, very challenging mazes. *Mind Benders* is a series of logic puzzles for grades 2 to adult. Students improve their deductive reasoning by determining the relationships between people, places, and things.

Programming

Crystal Rain Forest and *Mission Control,* Terrapin Software (Macintosh, Windows). Grades 8–13

Terrapin Software produces *Crystal Rain Forest* and *Mission Control.* These programs teach Logo programming for students from age 8 to 13. *Crystal Rain Forest* has the students help save a planet by navigating through different screens. The story is exciting, the activities fun, the humor and animation engaging. *Mission Control* has students save the planet from a wacky scientist using programming concepts through a series of sequenced adventures. The students are challenged to activities that include connecting wires to fix a soda machine, controlling motors to move heavy boxes, directing trucks filled with poison to recycling tanks, and using heat sensors to find an escape route.

MicroWorlds Project Builder, Logo Computer Systems (LCSI) (Macintosh, Windows). Grades 4–8

MicroWorlds Pro introduces students to problem solving and creative thinking. Students use this Logo-based toolkit to create projects for any subject in the curriculum. *MicroWorlds Pro* lets students become active Web designers, not just passive Web viewers.

Roamer, Terrapin Software (Macintosh, Windows), Grades K–1

Roamer is an easy-to-use robot that introduces students to Logo commands. *Roamer* has Logo on board in the form of a computer that is dedicated to Logo. Students can also connect *Roamer* to the computer and upload computer programs, as well as merge them with other programs.

Stagecast Creator, Stagecast Software (Macintosh, Windows). Grades 2–Adult

Stagecast Creator is a tool that lets you create interactive stories, games, and simulations. The student can create interactive animated worlds for science, reading, social studies, and more. This authoring tool lets you create characters, the rules by which they will interact, and the worlds in which they will exist.

Terrapin Logo, Terrapin Software (Macintosh, Windows). Grades K–Adult

Terrapin Logo is a full-featured computer language that can be used by the beginner and the experienced programmer alike. This program is a version of the language developed at MIT. The examples used throughout the Logo chapter in this book were generated with *Terrapin Logo.*

True BASIC Version 5.1, True Basic Inc. (Macintosh, Windows). Grades 8–Adult

True BASIC is an easy-to-use and fully structured programming language. Students write less code to solve harder problems. This elegant program can be used to generate professional-looking graphs. The examples used in the BASIC section of this book were generated using *True BASIC.*

Visual Basic 6.0, Microsoft (Windows). Grades 9–12, Adult

The standard learning edition of this program is designed for the beginning programmer. It comes with *Visual Basic* as well as an interactive CD-ROM tutorial.

Puzzle Utilities

Crossword Companion Deluxe, Visions Technology in Education (Macintosh, Windows). Grades K–12

A very easy-to-use crossword puzzle maker. You can write long clues, add graphics, mix numbers and letters, and much more. This program automatically creates clues, has 17,0000 words to use in the puzzles, creates picture clues, and incorporate custom crossword puzzles into your website.

Crossword Creator, Centron (Macintosh, Windows). Grades 4–Adult

Using *Crossword Creator,* students can create crossword puzzles for the Web. In a matter of minutes, students can make puzzles and choose colors, sounds, and font sizes. The program creates the HTML code automatically.

Phonics Companion, Visions Technology in Education (Macintosh, Windows). Grades K–12

Using *Phonics Companion,* you can create phonics-based activity sheets, games, classroom posters, and much more. The easy-to-use program features crossword puzzles, bingo, story starters, and flash cards.

Puzzle Power 3.2, Centron (Macintosh, Windows). Grades 2–Adult

This software program gives you a collection of puzzle-making software that includes *Crossword Creator, Wordsearch Creator, Cryptos, Anagrams, Cross Sums,* and more. You can have three types of multimedia themes, pictures, sounds, and movies.

Word Bingo, Hi Tech (Macintosh, Windows). Grades 4–Adult

With this program, you can create a set of bingo cards on the vocabulary words that the students are currently learning. This easy-to-use program comes with Spanish capabilities, some very useful clip art, and excellent documentation.

Word Cross, Hi Tech (Macintosh, Windows). Grades 3–Adult

This crossword puzzle maker is simple to use. It lets you create your own crossword puzzles and automatically generates a variety of puzzles from the same word list. You can customize *Word Cross* to help students learn new vocabulary words.

Wordsearch Studio, Nordic Software (Macintosh, Windows). Grades K–Adult

Wordsearch Studio creates word puzzles that help vocabulary and spelling skills. The student simply types in the words or imports a list and the program creates the puzzle. There are 100 premade puzzles.

Reference

Compton's Encyclopedia, Compton's/Learning Company (Macintosh, Windows). Grades 2–Adult

This comprehensive encyclopedia lets students have easy access to over 40,000 articles. In addition, it contains a thesaurus, dictionary, atlas, and time-lines as well as an Internet directory with links to websites.

Eyewitness Children's Encyclopedia, DK Interactive (Macintosh, Windows). Grades 2–6

Eyewitness Children's Encyclopedia relates the content to information that students learn in school, at home, and in everyday life. A variety of 3-D landscapes transport children to virtual worlds such as the rainforest, inside the earth, and deep space.

Eyewitness World Atlas, DK Interactive (Macintosh, Windows). Grades 2–6

This atlas has detailed maps, videos, photographs, charts, and graphs. Students travel the world with help of expert research, accurate satellite imagery, and wonderful 3-D graphics.

Grolier Multimedia Encyclopedia Deluxe, Year 2001, Grolier Interactive (Macintosh, Windows). Grades 5–Adult

Grolier Multimedia Encyclopedia Deluxe, Year 2001 contains thousands of articles, navigational aids, multimedia features, and a dictionary containing hundreds of thousands of words. There is an easy-to-use Online Knowledge Exporter, which gives the students grades 5 to adult the latest information every month with hundreds of free article updates, and special features such as timelines, research helpers, and activities that explore subject areas.

Microsoft Encarta Reference Suite 2001, Microsoft (Windows). Grades 6–Adult

Microsoft Encarta Reference Suite 2001 is a reference library and research tool that lets students find information they need. The award-winning software programs included are *Encarta Africana 3rd Edition, Encarta Encyclopedia Deluxe 2001, Encarta Interactive World Atlas 2001, Encarta World English Dictionary 2001, Free* Encarta Online Deluxe!* This reference suite contains 277,400 articles, 25,300 illustrations and photos, 81,100 sounds and pronunciations, and 31,500 Web links.

Microsoft Encarta Encyclopedia Deluxe 2001, Microsoft (Windows). Grades 6–12

Microsoft Encarta contains more than 36,000 articles and thousands of multimedia pictures, videos, audio, and animation clips. There is a powerful search engine that lets students quickly find information. The program has a new interface.

My First Amazing Dictionary, DK Multimedia (Windows). Grades Pre-K–2

My First Amazing Dictionary is an excellent reference tool for beginning readers. This program has four games that improve word recognition. The dictionary explains the meanings of 1,200 child-oriented words with clever animations, illustrations, and narrations.

20th Century Day by Day—Millennium, DK Multimedia (Windows). Grades 6–Adult

20th Century Day by Day—Millennium chronicles the history of an entire century. The topics range from the Wright Brothers' first flight to the Apollo 11 moon landing. There are thousands of photographs, biographies, sound clips, and videos.

Science Programs

A.D.A.M. Essentials High School Suite, adam.com (Macintosh, Windows). Grades 9–Adult

A.D.A.M. Essentials High School Suite is a multimedia exploration of human anatomy, physiology, and biology. This suite includes the award-winning *A.D.A.M. The Inside Story, Nine Month Miracle, Life's Greatest Mysteries, Interactive Physiology—Cardiovascular Module.* The program merges an extensive database of information with stunning imagery, sparkling animation, and brilliant sound.

BioTutor, ChemTutor, and Physics Tutor, Interactive Learning Inc. (Macintosh, Windows). Grades 9–12

BioTutor, ChemTutor, and *Physics Tutor* help students learn biology, chemistry and physics. These programs cover the full curriculum for a first or second course in these subjects. While working on these tutorials, the students are given immediate feedback at each step.

BodyWorks 6.0, The Learning Company (Macintosh, DOS/Windows). Grades 6–Adult

With this program, students feel as if they are actually traveling in the human body and not just exploring a database. The program inspires students to learn the different functions of the systems of the human body. *BodyWorks* features a health section, colorful photographic graphics, more than 100 glossary entries, detailed movie clips, and sound. Additionally, lesson plans and quizzes improve students' knowledge of human anatomy.

Brain Quest Series, Edmark (Macintosh, Windows). Grades 1–6

The *Brain Quest* series is an entertaining drill and practice program. Students answer questions regarding math, reading, science, and social studies. Games can be saved, but there is no record-keeping function.

Bumptz Science Carnival, Grolier Interactive (Macintosh, Windows). Grades 3–6

This program has 200 different puzzles and 12 short animated movies. Students apply the principles of gravity, light, and buoyancy as they explore an amusement park.

ChemRacer 2713: The Legend of Kid Chem, Ohio Distinctive Software Inc. (Macintosh, Windows). Grades 4–Adult

ChemRacer teaches students the elements of the periodic table and associated facts in an amusing way. The game alternates between an arcade racing challenge and an identify-the-elements game. Points are awarded for correct answers; games and high scores can be saved.

ClueFinders 6th Grade Adventures, The Learning Company (Macintosh, Windows). Grade 6

The sixth-grade version of the motivating *ClueFinders* series gives students 24 hours to stop plants that are destroying their town. Students engage in nine activities to solve the mystery. These activities teach sixth-grade science, math, geography, history, reading, and problem solving. The program tracks students' progress and prints customized workbooks.

Eyewitness Encyclopedia of Science, DK Multimedia (Macintosh, Windows). Grades 5–Adult

Students explore chemistry, math, physics, life sciences, and a who's who of science. This program contains 1,700 entries, 20 videos, and 66 animations.

Farmer Greenfield's Virtual Harvest, Ohio Distinctive Software, Inc. (Macintosh, Windows). Grades 3–12

This software package is reminiscent of the classic *Botanical Gardens* created by Sunburst. Using this simulation program, students plant, grow, and harvest their own gardens. In the process, they check for bugs and blight, and they control water. If they do what is correct, they are rewarded with points. There are 10 difficulty levels and a narrated glossary.

A Field Trip to the Sea Deluxe, Sunburst (Macintosh, Windows). Grades 4–8

A Field Trip to the Sea Deluxe explores sea life, geography, and related issues. Students click on illustrations of plant and animal life and see enlarged pictures with text. There are research tools, a notebook, field guide, and camera.

GeoSafari Animals and *GeoSafari Plants,* Educational Insights Interactive (Macintosh, Windows). Grades 3–12

GeoSafari Animals uses a game show format with questions based on animal trivia. The question categories include Dog Show, Animal Tracks, Bird Call, and Name That. *GeoSafari Plants* contains 15 activities on topics such as the human skeleton, rocks and minerals, space travel, and trees. The student can play individually or in teams. There are hundreds of questions on topics ranging from space to dinosaurs.

High School Advantage 2001, Encore Software (Macintosh, Windows). Grades 9–12

High School Advantage 2001 covers 10 core subjects. Using the *Eyewitness Encyclopedia of Science,* the science component covers chemistry, life sciences, and physics. The tutorials are multimedia and interactive, and help the students easily learn the subject matter.

Interactive Explorations in Physics, Holt, Rinehart and Winston (Macintosh, Windows). Grades 9–Adult

In *Interactive Explorations in Physics,* students use tools and techniques to solve problems that make physics relevant to real-life situations. They conduct experiments, record observations and results, and apply the knowledge gained to problem solving.

Learn About Series, Sunburst (Macintosh, Windows). Grades K–2

Sunburst Communications has a rich and vast assortment of science programs, including *Learn about Life Sciences, Plants, Learn about Life Science: The Senses, Learn about Earth Science: Weather, Learn about Earth Science: Astronomy, Learn about Physical Science: Simple Machines,* and *Learn about Physical Science: Matter, Measurement, and Mixtures.* These programs have extension activities that include matching and sorting games and an expressive writing section.

Magic School Bus Explores the World of Bugs, Microsoft (Windows). Grades K–5

Ms. Frizzle and her students are looking for four lost bugs. They visit the meadow, rainforest, jungle, and pond in search of these missing bugs. During their search, they learn how bugs survive and why they live where they do.

RedShift 3, Maris/Knowledge Adventure (Macintosh, Windows). Grades 7–12

RedShift is loaded with astronomy information. This program lets students journey through space and time, predicting and simulating events like eclipses.

Sammy's Science House, Edmark (Macintosh, DOS/Windows). Grades Pre-K–2

Sammy's Science House has five fun-filled activities that help children with sorting, sequencing, observing, predicting, and constructing. Students learn simple scientific classification and develop logical thinking skills painlessly by building toys and machines, classifying plants, and sequencing movies.

Scholastic's Magic School Bus Explores the Solar System, Microsoft (Macintosh, Windows). Grades 1–5

Children ride a school bus on an interplanetary adventure to investigate planets and moons. This program features realistic NASA and JPL videos and nine science experiments in which students make craters on the moon, put rings around Saturn, and see how big Jupiter is by filling it up with other planets. Another program in the same format explores the human body.

Schoolhouse Rock: Science Rock, The Learning Company (Macintosh, Windows). Grades 2–6

In *Schoolhouse Rock: Science Rock* students complete physical, life, and earth science activities to learn about topics such as sound, light, electricity, genetics, and the solar system.

Science Court Series, Tom Snyder Productions (Macintosh, Windows). Grades 2–6

The *Science Court* series teaches science concepts to elementary and middle school students. Some of the programs in the series are sound, statistics, gravity, particles in motion, machines, water cycle, fossils, and inertia. The program unfolds as a courtroom drama, and there are demonstrations and explanations as the lawyers battle over a case. Programs contain animated video clips with hands-on activities.

Science Seekers—Hidden in Rocks, Tom Snyder Productions (Macintosh, Windows). Grades 5–8

Science Seekers can collectively improve critical thinking skills as students take notes, manipulate variables, analyze the results, draw conclusions, and offer solutions to problems.

SuperTutor Chemistry Plus, Stanford Multimedia (Windows). Grades 9–12

SuperTutor Chemistry is a self-paced chemistry tutorial that covers hundreds of topics step by step with animation, voice lectures, exercises, and examples. This software covers one year of high school chemistry.

Thinkin' Science ZAP! Edmark/Riverdeep (Macintosh, Windows). Grades 3–6

The students explore sound, light, and electricity working with laser beams, electrical circuits, and sound waves. There are hundreds of simple and complex activities where the student is called upon to seek a solution.

Tommorow's Promise Science, CompassLearning (Windows). Grades 9–Adult

These programs offer core reading science explorations with scored online activities. Students work at their own pace, and assessment tools help the teacher evaluate, track, and report student achievement.

Virtual Labs: Light and *Virtual Labs: Electricity,* Edmark/Riverdeep (Macintosh, Windows). Grades 6–12

There are two programs in this series. *Virtual Labs: Light* lets students safely run virtual laser experiments that would be dangerous and impractical to run in the real world. In the same vein, *Virtual Labs: Electricity* is a simulation program where students do experiments in a lab or create their own electricity experiments without the hazards of playing with electricity.

Social Studies Programs

Amazon Trail IV: Rain Forest, The Learning Company (Macintosh, Windows). Grades 4–10

Students travel through the jungles of South America, encountering five rain forest habitats. They experience hardships, risk possible death, meet different creatures, and learn navigational skills and history.

Brain Quest Series, Edmark (Macintosh, Windows). Grades 1–6

The *Brain Quest* series comprises entertaining drill and practice software programs. Students answer questions regarding math, reading, science, and social studies. Games can be saved, but there is no record-keeping function.

Crosscountry Canada Platinum, Ingenuity Works (Macintosh, Windows). Grades 4–Adult

Students play the role of truck drivers on a mission to pick up and deliver certain commodities. Students practice map reading, logical thinking, and record keeping as they deliver the products all over Canada. Other programs in the series are *Crosscountry California, Crosscountry USA,* and *Crosscountry Texas.*

Decisions, Decisions 5.0 Series, Tom Snyder Productions (Macintosh, Windows). Grades 5–12

The *Decisions, Decisions 5.0* series help students gain a better understanding of different people, places, and ideas. Students learn to use history as a basis for decision making and to distinguish between fact and opinion. Some of the titles in the series are *The Cold War, Immigration, On the Campaign Trail, Prejudice, Violence in the Media, Building a Nation,* and *The Environment.*

GeoSafari Geography, Educational Insights Interactive (Macintosh, Windows). Grades 3–12

GeoSafari Geography contains multiple-choice quizzes that help with all sorts of geography subject matter such as memorizing the state capitals or learning where states are. Educational Insights Interactive also produces *GeoSafari History,* where students learn about world and U.S. history.

History of the American Legal System, ABC-Clio (Macintosh, Windows). Grades 6–12

This encyclopedia presents articles and images concerning issues regarding the U.S. legal system. The material covered is from the 17th century to the Clinton presidency. There are photographs, videos, audio clips, and even primary source documents.

Land of the Inuit—An Exploration of the Arctic, Ingenuity Works (Macintosh, Windows). Grades 4–Adult

Using this wonderful program, students learn about the Arctic. An Inuit shaman acts as guide while students read, watch, and listen to tales of early Arctic explorations. Students then test their knowledge of the content with 12 interactive challenges.

MaskWorld, Visions Technology in Education (Macintosh, Windows. Grades 2–Adult

Using this delightful program, students can print outline masks; experiment; and create scenes, stories, and myths on their own. There are 24 myths from around the world. Each story comes complete with characters, props, and a script.

Microsoft Encarta Africana 2001, Microsoft Learning Group (Macintosh, Windows). Grades 5–Adult

This encyclopedia discusses African history and culture using text, pictures, audio clips, and videos. *Microsoft Encarta Africana* offers closed captioning and text to speech, so text can be read if desired.

Neighborhood MapMachine, Tom Snyder Productions (Macintosh, Windows). Grades 1–6

Students can create maps with buildings, lakes, trees, roads, and other elements. They learn geography skills that include compass directions, distance scale, and grid coordinates. These maps can be printed out in a variety of sizes.

The Oregon Trail IV, The Learning Company (Macintosh, DOS). Grades 5–12

The Oregon Trail IV transports students to the 1850s, where as pioneers they must outfit their wagons for the journey west from Independence, Missouri. If students make the right decisions, they reach their destination. During the journey, students learn about the time period.

SimCity 3000 and *Sims,* Electronic Arts/The Learning Company (Macintosh, Windows). Grades 5–Adult

Sims and *SimCity 3000* are popular design programs using principles of CAD. *Sims* is for younger students, while *SimCity 3000* is for older students. Both programs are building games in which students create cities or neighborhoods. In *SimCity 3000,* students measure their ability to plan by how much their population grows and how healthy their tax base is. For *Sims,* students designs homes, furnish them, then build neighborhoods and take control of them.

Talking Walls, Edmark (Macintosh, Windows). Grades 4–8

A unique program called *Talking Walls* lets students explore the stories behind the world's most spectacular walls and see their influence on history.

TimeLiner 5.0, Tom Snyder Productions (Macintosh, Windows) Grades 3–12

TimeLiner 5.0 lets you quickly design and print out time lines of any length in Spanish or English. This award-winning program has an excellent graphics library with more than 400 historical photographs and clip art. Tom Snyder has included in this package 150 ready-made time lines in history, social studies, and science.

Where in the USA Is Carmen Sandiego? Deluxe Version, The Learning Company (Macintosh, Windows). Grades 6–12

Students search for criminals across the United States, using geography facts. There are enhanced graphics and more cases to solve. The *Where in the World Is Carmen Sandiego? Deluxe Edition* has students searching for criminals across the globe. Using these programs, students learn geography in an entertaining manner.

World Discovery Deluxe, Great Wave (Macintosh, Windows). Grades 3–12

World Discovery is an inventive drill and practice program that features 19 highly detailed maps from around the globe and 12 games that teach political and historical places, people, and events.

Special Needs

Access to Math, Don Johnston (Macintosh). Grades K–7

Access to Math is a talking math worksheet that aids students in learning addition, subtraction, multiplication, and division. This program gives students feedback on which problems are correct, which need more work, and what part of the work is incorrect.

Blocks in Motion, Don Johnston (Macintosh, Windows). Grades 1–Adult

Blocks in Motion allows students to create, manipulate, and animate blocks. This paint and motion program has multiple tools, sound effects, and many programmable options to bring forth the student's creativity.

Blue's ABC Time Activities, Humongous Entertainment (Macintosh, Windows). Grades P-K-6, 7-9, 10-12

Students explore the world of letters, sounds, and words with the help of a dog named Blue and her pals. This software is designed for many age levels and it automatically adjusts to the student's reading level.

Co:Writer 4000, Don Johnston (Macintosh, Windows). Grades 6-Adult

Co:Writer 4000 is a writing assistant with word prediction capabilities that will work with any word processor. A student just types in a letter and *Co:Writer* will suggest word choices that fit the sentences. Using this program, students learn to make word choices. *Co:Writer* has built-in grammar prediction which helps with such items as capitalization, spelling, and verb tense.

Kidspiration, Inspiration (Macintosh, Windows). Grades K-4

Kidspiration encourages students to organize their ideas. This fun program makes it easy for them to represent their ideas using user-friendly symbols. Students can hear their work and record their own words. In the classroom, teachers can immediately use the program's 45 built-in student activities.

My First Amazing World Explorer, DK Multimedia (Macintosh, Windows). Grades K-5

Students travel the world trying to find a person named Joe. In this interactive journey, they use scrolling map scenes, pop-up screens, videos, and games. DK Multimedia has a series of social studies and science programs.

My Reading Coach, Mindplay (Macintosh, Windows). Grades 1-Adult

My Reading Coach is a reading tutor for students who want instruction in reading proficiency. This program assesses the students' needs and fills in specific learning gaps, making sure that each lesson is learned.

Number Concepts 1 with Oshi the Otter, IntelliTools, Inc. (Macintosh, Windows). Grades K-2

Number Concepts 1 with Oshi the Otter is a program designed for students with disabilities that tutors students on basic addition and subtraction.

Simon Sounds It Out, Don Johnston (Macintosh, Windows). Grades Pre-K-2

This program is a phonics tool that lets students practice letter sounds. It has a helpful online tutor that leads students through 31 sequenced sounds and words.

Start-to Finish Books, Don Johnston (Macintosh, Windows). Grades 4–12

These books motivate students who are struggling with reading. The books range from *Red Badge of Courage* to *Romeo and Juliet*. They aid students with language disorders or dyslexia, students learning English as a second language, and those with spelling and writing difficulties. The program comes with a computer book, audiocassette, and a paperback book.

Smart Driver, BrainTrain (Windows). Grades K–12

Smart Driver helps students with learning disabilities develop cognitive skills. Students drive a car around a track while obeying the signals and signs and avoiding obstacles.

Tiger's Tale, Laureate Learning Systems (Macintosh, Windows). Grades Pre-K–7

Tiger's Tale is software for students with fluency, articulation, and/or language disorders. This program lets students go on adventures with an animated tiger who has lost his voice. Using a microphone, the students talk for the tiger with the help of various animated characters who ask questions to get suggestions. At the end, children can play back the movie they've created, hearing their own voice accompanying the animated tale.

Travel the World with Timmy! Deluxe, Edmark (Macintosh, Windows), Grades Pre-K–1

Edmark's *Travel the World with Timmy! Deluxe* lets students learn about people, places, and cultures. They learn stories, songs, crafts, and games and practice foreign language skills. Edmark's *Travel the World with Timmy! Deluxe* has a special talking picture dictionary, and the program has single-switch compatibility.

Virtual Labs: Light and *Virtual Labs: Electricity*, Edmark (Macintosh, Windows). Grades 6–12

The *Virtual Lab* series helps students build practical knowledge about light and electricity (see Science Programs). These programs have a built-in tutor and single-switch technology.

Visual Voice Tools, Edmark (Windows), Pre-K–Adult

Visual Voice Tools is an assortment of tools that help students develop fine control over their voices. The program begins with simple sound awareness and progresses through multiple aspects of voice. The suggested users are students with a variety of speech disorders, hearing disorders, and physical problems that limit voice output.

Words Around Me, Edmark (Macintosh, Windows). Grades K–12

This program is useful for ESL and special education students. Using *Words Around Me,* students learn more than 275 common vocabulary words and 186 plurals. This is a step-by-step approach that lets users engage in five activities for practice.

Write: OutLoud, Don Johntson (Macintosh, Windows). Grades 2–8

Write: OutLoud is an easy-to-use word processor that talks. Students can listen to their work as they type it. The spelling checker lets students hear and see suggested replacement words. The program features a handy on-screen ribbon that lets students quickly access the program's options.

Spreadsheets and Integrated Programs (See also Database Programs)

AppleWorks 6.0, Apple (Macintosh, Windows). Grades 7–Adult

AppleWorks combines a word processor, spreadsheet, database, drawing, painting, and presentation module smoothly and flawlessly. The program lets the student quickly build graphs, slide shows, and pictures. It is packaged with clip art images, sounds, movies, and templates that duplicate what students are learning in school.

The Cruncher, Davidson (Macintosh, Windows). Grades 5–Adult

The Cruncher is an enjoyable and easy-to-use spreadsheet tool that teaches how a spreadsheet works, when to use one, and how to create one. The spreadsheet comes with ready-to-use templates and projects and an easy-to-use step-by-step tutorial.

Lotus SmartSuite, Lotus (Windows). Grades 7–Adult

This program includes a spreadsheet, word processor, time and contact manager, presentation graphics software, database, and PC multimedia recorder. *SmartSuite* brings you an easier way to publish documents to your website. You can access Internet news and weather with a click of the mouse and also analyze Web data in *Lotus 1-2-3.*

Microsoft Excel, Microsoft (Macintosh, Windows). Grades 7–Adult

Microsoft Excel is an award-winning spreadsheet. It combines its spreadsheet with graphics and a database. The program has more than 16,000 rows and 250 columns. *Excel's* features include multiple fonts, auditing tools, a dialog editor, drag-drop cell operation, and 3-D chart types. The latest versions of this program are *Excel 2000* for Windows and *Excel 2001* for Macintosh.

Microsoft Office 2001, Microsoft (Macintosh). Grades 9–Adult

This program includes five applications—*Microsoft Word, Microsoft Excel,* the *Microsoft PowerPoint Presentation* graphics program, the *Entourage* e-mail and personal information manager, and *Microsoft Internet Explorer.* There are additional clip art, templates, and wizards to give users extra value for their money.

Microsoft Office 2000 Standard Edition, Microsoft (Windows). Grades 9–Adult

This program includes five applications—*Microsoft Word, Microsoft Excel,* the *Microsoft PowerPoint Presentation* graphics program, the *Microsoft Outlook Express* e-mail, and *Microsoft Internet Explorer.*

Spreadsheet 2000, Casady and Green (Macintosh, Windows). Grades 7–Adult

Spreadsheet 2000 lets you use drag and drop for almost every part of your spreadsheet, including cell tiles, formulas, and charts from floating palettes into your new document. Using your mouse, you connect these elements to create your calculation chain. The program contains 49 templates for school and home.

WordPerfect Office 2000, Corel (Windows). Grades 9–Adult

WordPerfect Office 2000 includes the following software programs: *WordPerfect, Quattro Pro, Corel Presentations, Trellix 2, Corel Print Office, Corel Central,* as well as hundreds of templates, hundreds of fonts, and thousands of clip art images. You can install the entire suite or only specific programs that you use.

Works 6.0, Microsoft (Windows). Grades 9–Adult

Works 6.0 is a versatile and simple integrated software that includes a word processor, data management program, spreadsheet, and calendar. The calendar lets you manage your schedule, keep track of events, and set up reminders.

Teacher Utilities

Calendar Machine Plus, Visions Technology in Education (Macintosh, Windows). Grades 3–8

Calendar Machine Plus is a classroom utility designed for students and teachers. This program not only prints calendars, but it includes lesson plans, has a searchable 900-event and holiday database, and has much more.

Easy Grade Pro, Orbis Software (Macintosh). All Grades

Easy Grade Pro has a wide range of tools including grading, attendance, seating, analysis, and reporting. Unlike other grading programs, *Easy Grade Pro* integrates all classes into a single file and at the same time lets each class be managed individually. The program has many options that range from multiple subjects in reports to adding and rotating furniture.

Gradebook Plus V6.1, Clearvue/eav (Macintosh). All Grades

Gradebook Plus V6.1 is an intuitive program that any novice can use. The program helps you with oral reminders such as "Don't forget to back up." With this program, you can create form letters, add any of 15 user-definable comments to reports, and annotate sound to student reports. On-screen editing and a mini–word processor allow you to create reports and letters.

Grade Busters: Making the Grade, Jay Klein Productions (Macintosh, Windows). All Grades

Grade Busters: Making the Grade records 80 students per class, 320 assignments, 25 assignment categories, and five grading scales per class and displays the results graphically. Furthermore, it allows you to generate reports in English and Spanish.

Grade Machine, Misty City (Macintosh, Windows). All Grades

Grade Machine is loaded with features such as e-mail capability for student progress reports, student pictures in seating charts, on-screen color for grades, unlimited length for student notes, and much more. This program has a comprehensive Help system that enables the teacher to get answer to frequently asked questions.

GradeQuick, Jackson Software (Macintosh, Windows). All Grades

GradeQuick is a gradebook gem that is as simple to use as a paper gradebook. There are no confusing windows to set up or long, involved procedures. You simply start this program and it immediately lets you calculate grades and statistics. *GradeQuick* easily displays or prints student pictures on seating charts, enters attendance with a click, and posts reports on the Web.

Inspiration, Inspiration Software (Macintosh, Windows). Grades K–12

This program is a visual learning tool that helps students develop ideas and organize their thinking. Students or teachers can create concept maps, story webs, semantic maps, storyboards, bubble diagrams, and outlines.

Learner Profile, Sunburst (Macintosh, Windows). All Grades

Learner Profile records and organizes data for student assessment portfolios. You can instantly record your observations of pupil learning; the observational information can be uploaded to the computer, where it becomes part of the database. This program is very fast and easy to use, and it eliminates burdensome paperwork.

Lesson Plan Helper, FTC Group (Macintosh, Windows). All Grades

This helper provides the user with a database of more than 300 lesson plans in all elementary curriculum areas. All the lessons can be changed to meet the teacher's objectives.

Make-A-Flash, Teacher Support Software (Macintosh, Windows). All Grades

This utility makes flash cards for vocabulary words, math, or any subject area. There are multiple templates available, and you can also create your own.

Math Companion 1 and *2,* Visions Technology in Education (Macintosh, Windows). Grades K–8

Math Companion 1 is a wonderful utility that lets teachers create math activity sheets in four different formats with graphic capabilities. For example, you can create color-in activity sheets and math anagrams. You choose from 110 NCTM math objectives. *Math Companion 2* covers money, time, counting, place value, sets, fractions, and elementary geometry. You can create flashcards, bingo cards, illustrated money problem, math color-ins, and more.

The Portfolio Builder for PowerPoint, Visions Technology in Education (Macintosh, Windows). Grades K–8

The Portfolio Builder for PowerPoint lets students easily combine sound, videos, text, and graphics to create a representation of their work. In a matter of minutes, a student can import work created with other software applications, graphics, text, scanned images, full-motion video, and sound clips into this portfolio builder.

Scholastic's Electronic Portfolio, Scholastic (Macintosh). Grades 3–8

This program is a multimedia tool in which teachers can create, manage, and present multimedia student portfolios using scanned images, sounds, full-motion video, graphics, and textual data.

SPSS/PC, SPSS (Windows). Junior high and above

SPSS/PC is a popular statistical package for IBM and compatibles. It is menu driven and has interactive data analysis and an online glossary of statistical terms.

StatView 5.0, SAS Institute (Macintosh). Junior high and above

StatView is a state-of-the-art graphics and statistics program that includes some very advanced features, including outstanding documentation. You can use the program to import data from spreadsheets, databases, word processors, telecommunications programs, and text files.

Teacher's Resource Companion Deluxe, Visions Technology in Education (Macintosh, Windows). Grades K–12

Teacher's Resource Companion Deluxe has an easy-to-use interface that many developers are following. This delightful program lets you create activity sheets, tests, and complete curricular packages. The formats include short essay/free write; multiple choice; true/false; matching; two-, four-, and eight-picture fill-ins, and a word search.

Teacher Tool Kit, Hi Tech (Macintosh, Windows).

Teacher Tool Kit is simple to use and offers excellent online help. It does word searches, word scrambles, word matches, multiple choice, true/false, and short-answer tests. The program lets you randomize questions and print out clean page layouts with answers.

Test Designer Supreme II, SuperSchool (Macintosh, Windows).

Test Designer Supreme II combines test creation, test taking, sound, graphics, and foreign languages. This program lets you insert questions from a database and use an overhead projector to give students a timed test on the computer. In addition, you can choose the test format you want and integrate graphics into it.

TextBridge, ScanSoft-Xerox Imaging Systems (Macintosh, Windows).

You can save time and effort and avoid typing errors with *TextBridge.* Using a scanner and this excellent OCR software, you can convert less-than-perfect documents into professional, electronic text.

Timeliner 5.0, Tom Snyder Productions (Macintosh, Windows). Grades 3–12

See Social Studies Programs for a write-up of this award-winning package.

TimeLiner Machine Plus, Visions Technology in Education (Macintosh, Windows). Grades 3–8

Using this program, you can create your own custom time lines for lesson plans, research projects, and events. There are ready-made time line activities and 350 lesson plans with a searchable database of more than 900 historical events.

Vocabulary Companion, Visions Technology in Education (Macintosh, Windows). Grades K–12

With this nifty utility, you can create instructional material covering phonics, word analysis, and vocabulary development. The program has 200 language arts objectives and a database of over 12,000 words. You can print out scrambled words, concentration, anagrams, color-ins, flash cards, and much more.

Typing Programs

All the Right Type, Ingenuity Works (Macintosh, Windows). Grades 2–Adult

All the Right Type is a simple-to-use typing program that links word processing to keyboarding. It includes a record-keeping feature and the lessons are customized for the student's use in a classroom setting. The program is very exciting with its futuristic graphics and a spaceship pacer game.

JumpStart Typing, Knowledge Adventure (Macintosh, Windows). Grades 2–5

Using this program, the student builds typing proficiency in five different sporting events, ranging from skateboarding to rock climbing. *JumpStart* even has a diagnostic test to determine the student's typing ability and the program adjusts the product to match the abilities of the user.

Mario Teaches Typing, The Learning Company (Macintosh, Windows). Grades K–5

Mario Teaches Typing is a fun-filled program with all the Mario characters and scenes. Students progress at their own pace through each adventure-filled level.

Mavis Beacon Teaches Typing, The Learning Company (Macintosh, Windows). Grades 5–Adult

Mavis Beacon Teaches Typing uses animated graphics, facts from the *New Grolier's Multimedia Encyclopedia* and *Newsweek* magazine, riddles, rhymes, and jokes to teach typing. Lessons range from 10 to 120 minutes. This new edition features a 3-D classroom, Internet access, audio spoken feedback, and six arcade games. The children's version is called *Mavis Beacon Teaches Typing! for Kids.*

Stickybear Typing, Optimum Resources (Macintosh, DOS/Windows). Grades 1–6

Three activities, including an arcade game, sharpen students' typing and keyboarding skills. The program can help the more advanced typists who need to review and brush up. Pupils choose the level of difficulty and track their progress as they improve.

Type to Learn, Sunburst (Macintosh, Windows). Grades 2–Adult

This popular typing program teaches students to type while reinforcing spelling, composition, grammar, and punctuation. There are 22 lessons that cover all letter and number keys. To practice your typing, there are four games and a speed-building exercise. In addition, Sunburst has record keeping, numerous teacher options, and a congratulatory certificate when the course is completed.

Typing Tutor, Knowledge Adventure (Macintosh, Windows). Grades 5–Adult

The new edition of *Typing Tutor* is loaded with video clips, games, animation, color, and graphics. The samples are from 100 well-known books.

UltraKey, Bytes of Learning (Macintosh, Windows). Primary–Adult

UltraKey has many features including realistic 3-D graphics, voice-supported instruction, live classroom video demonstrations, teacher classroom management capabilities, and Internet support.

Web Tools

CyberSnoop, Pearl Software (Windows). All Grade Levels

CyberSnoop lets the teacher customize lists of sites for individual students. It also has an extensive array of fully researched websites that are updated on a daily basis.

FoolProof Security, Smartstuff Software (Macintosh, Windows). All Grade Levels

FoolProof prevents users from deleting critical files and applications, making unauthorized changes to the desktop, saving unwanted programs, running disallowed programs, and corrupting the operating system, whether accidentally or maliciously.

FrontPage 2000, Microsoft (Macintosh, Windows). All Grades

Using *FrontPage 2000,* students can create and manage good-looking websites. They can quickly create Web pages with WYSIWYG tables, hyperlinks, thumbnail images, counters, graphics, and so on. This program even has management features to keep the site at a top performance level.

SiteCentral, Knowledge Adventure (Macintosh, Windows). Grades 4–Adult

SiteCentral is an easy-to-use drag and drop Web page authoring tool. This program has ready-made templates that help students make websites. *Site-Central* includes an extensive animation library and clip art, along with special artist effects.

WebPrinter, Blue Squirrel (Macintosh, Windows). Grades 7–Adult

Using *WebPrinter,* you can turn your printer into a printing press. *WebPrinter* takes Web pages that you want to print out and automatically reduces, rotates, and realigns the type into booklet form. *WebPrinter* works with any printer.

Web Wacker, Blue Squirrel (Macintosh, Windows). Grades 7–Adult

This program lets you save to your computer hard drive Internet sites that include text, graphics, and HTML links. This capability is ideal for presentations and working with students off-line.

Web Workshop Pro, Sunburst (Macintosh, Windows). Grades 6–12

Web Workshop Pro provides an easy-to-use Web design program for older students. This program lets students maintain complex websites with editing tools, easy-start templates, and all sorts of text options. There is free one-step publishing on Sunburst's website, and Sunburst provides the teacher with a Teacher Guide that has 10 very useful classroom activities.

Web Workshop 2.0, Sunburst (Macintosh, Windows). Grades 2–8

Web Workshop is a gem for the beginning student. It contains clip art, familiar paint tools, and a simple interface that makes it easy for the student to create a Web page.

Web Zinger, ImageOn (Macintosh, Windows). Grades 7–Adult

Web Zinger is a fully automated research engine. Students type in what they need and this Web research assistant locates websites by topic, visits, analyzes the sites, and downloads graphics and text.

Word Processing Programs

AppleWorks 6.0, Apple (Macintosh, Windows). Grades 7–Adult

See the Spreadsheets and Integrated Programs section.

Microsoft Word 2000 (Windows) and *Microsoft Word 2001* (Macintosh). Grades 12–Adult

Word is a feature-laden word processor that first became popular in its Macintosh version. It lets students generate tables, design forms, and create newsletters, indexes, résumés, and outlines. There is additional clip art, templates, and wizards to give the user extra value. You can even create graphically rich Web pages using *Word.*

WordPerfect, Corel (Macintosh, Windows). Grades 12–Adult

WordPerfect is a sophisticated, full-functioning word processor program. This best-selling word processor includes Grammatik, a grammar checker; advanced drawing features; and an equation editor. *WordPerfect* is well known for its fast technical support.

Appendix B
Directory of Selected Software Publishers

A.D.A.M. Software Inc.

1600 RiverEdge Parkway, Ste. 800
Atlanta, GA 30328
800/755-2326
404/980-0888
404/955-3088 (fax)
www.adam.com/

Addison-Wesley Publishing Co.

Pearson Education Order Department
PO Box 11073
Des Moines, IA 50336-1073
800/282-0693
515/284-2607 (fax)
www.aw.com/

Adobe Systems Inc.

345 Park Avenue
San Jose, CA 95110-2704
800/833-6687
408/536-6000
www.adobe.com/products/main.html

AIMS Multimedia

9170 DeSoto Avenue
Chatsworth, CA 91311
800/367-2467
818/773-4300
818/341-6700 (fax)
www.aims-multimedia.com/

AlphaSmart

20400 Stevens Creek Boulevard, Ste. 300
Cupertino, CA 95014

888/274-0680
408/252-9400
408/252-9409 (fax)
www.alphasmart.com/

Apple Computer Inc.

1 Infinite Loop
Cupertino, CA 95014
800/767-2775
408/996-1010
www.info.apple.com/education/aesmenu.html

AppleWorks

1 Infinite Loop
Cupertino, CA 95014
800/MY-APPLE
408/996-1010
www.apple.com/appleworks/

Aurbach & Associates, Inc.

9378 Olive Street Road, Ste. 102
St. Louis, MO 63132
800/774-7239
314/432-7577
314/432-7072 (fax)
www.aurbach.com/

Barnum Software

3450 Lake Shore Avenue, Ste. 200
Oakland, CA 94610
800/553-9155
510/465-5070
510/465-5071 (fax)
www.thequartermile.com/

Baudville

5380 52nd Street S.E.
Grand Rapids, MI 49512
800/728-0888
616/698-0888
616/698-0554 (fax)
www.baudville.com/

Bytes of Learning

60 Renfrew Drive, Ste. 210
Markham, Ontario, Canada
L3R 0E1
800/465-6428
905/475-8650 (fax)
www.bytesoflearning.com/main.html

Classroom Connect

8000 Marina Boulevard, 4th Floor
Brisbane, CA 94005
800/638-1639
888/801-8299 (fax)
650/351-5100
650/351-5300 (fax)
www.classroom.net/

Cognitive Learning Media

235 Montgomery Street, 27th Floor
San Francisco, CA 94104
800/938-94104
415/765-1900
415/765-1902 (fax)
www.cogitomedia.com/

CompassLearning

9920 Pacific Heights Boulevard
San Diego, CA 92121
800/244-0575
www.compasslearning.com/

Compu-Teach, Inc.

PMB 137
16541 Redmond Way, Ste. C
Redmond, WA 98052
800/448-3224
425/885-0517
425/883-9169 (fax)
www.compu-teach.com/

Computer Associates International, Inc.

1 Computer Associates Plaza
Islandia, NY 11749

800/225-5224
631/342-5224
631/342-5329 (fax)
www.cai.com/

Corel Corporation

1600 Carling Avenue
Ottawa, Ontario, Canada K1Z 8R7
800/772-6735
716-447-7366 (fax)
www3.corel.com/

Critical Thinking Books & Software

PO Box 448
Pacific Grove, CA 93950
800/458-4849
831/393-3288
831/393-3277(fax)
www.criticalthinking.com/

Discovery Channel Multimedia

800/889-9950
www.multimedia.discovery.com/

Disney Interactive

800/228-0988
818/846-0454 (fax)
disney.go.com/DisneyInteractive/

DK Publishing, Inc.

95 Madison Avenue
New York, NY 10016
800/356-6575
212/213-4800 x220
212/213-5240 (fax)
usstore.dk.com/shop/

Don Johnston Inc.

26799 West Commerce Drive
Volo, IL 60073
800/999-4660
847/740-0749

847/740-7326 (fax)
www.donjohnston.co

Edmark Corporation

PO Box 97021
Redmond, WA 98073-9721
800/691-2986
425/556-8430 (fax)
www.edmark.com/prod/

Electronic Arts

Direct Sales
PO Box 7530
San Mateo, CA 94403
800/245-4525
415/572-2787
www.ea.com/

FileMaker, Inc.

5201 Patrick Henry Drive
PO Box 58168
Santa Clara, CA 95052-8168
800/ 325-2747
www.filemaker.com/

Forest Technologies

765 Industrial Drive
Cary, IL 60013
800/544-3356
847/516-8280
847/516-8210 (fax)

Fractal Design Corp.

335 Spreckels Drive
Aptos, CA 95003
408/688-8800
408/688-8836 (fax)
www.fractal.com/

FTC Publishing Group

PO Box 1361
Bloomington, IL 61702
888/237-6740
www.ftcpublishing.com/

Grolier Interactive

90 Sherman Turnpike
PO Box 1703
Danbury, CT 06816
800/353-3140
203/797-3130 (fax)
Attn: Customer Service
www.gi.grolier.com/

Hi Tech of Santa Cruz

202 Pelton Avenue
Santa Cruz, CA 95060
800/336-2558
831/425-5654
831/425-8041 (fax)
www.teachertools.com/

Humongous Entertainment

3855 Monte Villa Parkway
Bothell, WA 98021
800/499-8386
425/486-9258
www.humongous.com/

IBM Software

New Orchard Road
Armonk, NY 10504
888/SHOP-IBM
877/411-1FAX (fax)
www-4.ibm.com/software/

Ingenuity Works Inc.

1123 Fir Avenue
Blaine, WA 98230-9702
800/665-0667
604/431-7996 (fax)
www.ingenuityworks.com/

Inspiration Software, Inc.

7412 S.W. Beaverton Hillside Highway, Ste. 102
Portland, OR 97225-2167
800/877-4292
503/297-3004

503/297-4676 (fax)
www.inspiration.com/

Jackson Software

361 Park Avenue
Glencoe, IL 60022
800/850-1777
847/835-1992
www.jacksoncorp.com/

Jay Klein Productions Inc.

2930 Austin Bluffs Parkway, Ste. 104
Colorado Springs, CO 80918
719/599-8786
719/599-8312 (fax)
www.gradebusters.com/

Knowledge Adventure

1311 Grand Central Avenue
Glendale, CA 91201
800/545-7677
310/793-4307 (fax)
www.knowledgeadventure.com/

Lawrence Productions

1800 S. 35th Street
Galesburg, MI 49053
800/421-4157
616/665-7075
616/665-7060 (fax)
www.lpi.com/

The Learning Company

6493 Kaiser Drive
Fremont, CA 94555
800/358-9144
800/395-0277
800/821-5895
www.learningco.com/
www.mecc.com/school/products.htm

Logo Computer Systems Inc. (LCSI)

PO Box 162
Highgate Springs, VT 05460

800/321-5646
514/331-1380 (fax)
www.lcsi.ca/

Mainstay

591-A Constitution Avenue
Camarillo, CA 93012
805/484-9400
805/484-9428 (fax)
www.mstay.com/

McGraw-Hill Children's Publishing

PO Box 1650
Grand Rapids, MI 49501-1650
800/443-2976
800/453-2253 (fax)
www.instructionalfair.com/

Microsoft Corp.

1 Microsoft Way
Redmond, WA 98052-6399
800/426-9400
206/882-8080
www.microsoft.com/

Milliken Software

1100 Research Boulevard
St. Louis, MO 63132
800/325-4136
800/538-1319 (fax)

MindPlay

160 W. Fort Lowell
Tucson, AZ 85705
800/221-7911
520/888-1800
520/888-7904 (fax)
www.mindplay.com/

Neufeld Learning Systems

7 Conifer Crescent
London, Ontario, Canada N6K 2V3
800/624-2926

519 /657-3220
www.neufeldmath.com/

Nordic Software Inc.

800/306-6502
www.nordicsoftware.com/

Opcode Systems, Inc.

1818 Elm Hill Pike
Nashville, TN 37210
800/444-2766 ext. 2367
877/999-4199
www.opcode.com/

Optimum Resource Inc.

18 Hunter Road
Hilton Head Island, SC 29926
888/784-2592
843/689-8008 (fax)
www.stickybear.com/

The Princeton Review

2315 Broadway, 3d Floor
New York, NY 10024
800/955-3700
212/874-8282
212/874-0775 (fax)
www.review.com/

Queue Inc.

338 Commerce Drive
Fairfield, CT 06430
800/232-2224
203/336-2481 (fax)
www.queueinc.com/

SAS Institute's StatView

SAS Campus Drive
Cary, NC 27513
919 /677-8000
919 /677-4444 (fax)
www.statview.com/

ScanSoft, Inc.

9 Centennial Drive
Peabody, MA 01960
978/977-2000
408/395-7000
www.scansoft.com/

Scholastic Inc.

555 Broadway
New York, NY 10012
800/541-5513
800/392-2179
800/724-6527
www.scholastic.com/

Schoolmusic.com's Software Catalog

5 Overlook Drive, Ste. 4
Amherst, NH 03031
888/622-2299
603/673-8825 (fax)
www.schoolmusic.com/software/

Sierra, Inc.

3060 139th Avenue SE, Ste. 500
Bellevue, WA 98005
425/649-9800
www.sierra.com/

Simon & Schuster Interactive

1230 Avenue of the Americas
New York, NY 10020
800/545-7677
212/698-7000
212/698-7555 (fax)
www.simonsays.com/subs/index.cfm?areaid=58

SmartStuff's Foolproof Solutions

PO Box 82284
2100 SE 10 Avenue
Portland OR 97282
800/671-3999
503/231-4334 (fax)
www.smartstuff.com/

Sunburst Technology

101 Castleton Street
Pleasantville, NY 10570
800/321-7511
914/747-4109
www.sunburst.com/

Super School Software

1857 Josie Avenue
Long Beach, CA 90815-3432
800/248-7099
562/594-8580
562/594-4942
www.superschoolsoftware.com/

Symantec Corp.

175 W. Broadway
Eugene, OR 97401
800/441-7234
541/984-8020 (fax)
www.symantec.com/

Tech4Learning Inc.

PO Box 16538
San Diego, CA 92176
877/834-5453
www.tech4learning.com/

Terrapin Logo Software

10 Holworthy Street
Cambridge, MA 02138
800/972-8200
617/547-5646
800/776-4610 (fax)
www.terrapinlogo.com/

Tom Snyder Productions

80 Coolidge Hill Road
Watertown, MA 02172-0236
800/342-0236
617/926-6000 ext. 276
800/304-1254 (fax)
www.teachtsp.com/

True Basic Inc.

12 Commerce Avenue
West Lebanon, NH 03784
800/436-2111
802/296-2715 (fax)
www.truebasic.com/

Ventura Educational Systems

910 Ramona Avenue-E
Grover Beach, CA 93433
800/336-1022
800/493-7380 (fax)
www.venturaes.com/

Videodiscovery

1700 Westlake Avenue N., Ste. 600
Seattle, WA 98109-3012
800/548-3472
206/285-9245 (fax)
www.videodiscovery.com/

Visions Technology in Education

PO Box 70479
Eugene, OR 97401
800/816-0695 (fax)
www.visteched.com/

Voyager Company

888/292-5584
802/864-9846 (fax)
voyager.learntech.com/cdrom/

Appendix C
Recommended Mail-Order and Online Software Sources

Amazon.com, Inc.

www.amazon.com/

Attainment Company (special education)

PO Box 930160
Verona, WI 53593-0160
800/327-4269
www.attainmentcompany.com/

Beyond.com

3200 Patrick Henry Drive
Santa Clara, CA 95054
800/977-6171
408/855-3000
408/327-6400 (fax)
www.beyond.com/edutainment.htm

CCV Software

PO Box 6724
Charleston, WV 25362-0724
800/843-5576 (east)
800/541-6078 (west)
800/321-4297 (fax-east)
800/457-6953 (fax-west)
www.ccvsoftware.com

ClassroomDirect.com's SQC.COM

PO Box 830677
Birmingham, AL 35283-0677
800/599-3040
800/628-6250 (fax)
www.classroomdirect.com/SQC_index.htm

Educational Resources

1550 Executive Drive
Elgin, IL 60123
800/860-7004
www.edresources.com/

Educational Software Institute (ESI Online)

4213 South 94th Street
Omaha, NE 68127
800/955-5570
402/592-2017 (fax)
www.edsoft.com/

Education Technology, Inc. (ETI)

2102 NE 30th Street, Ste. A
Tacoma, WA 98403
800/677-6221
253/474-5200
253/474-3550 (fax)
www.edtech.com/

Egghead Software

22705 East Mission
Liberty Lake, WA 9019-8553
800/EGG-HEAD
www.egghead.com/

eToys.com

www.etoys.com/

Forest Technologies

765 Industrial Drive
Cary, IL 60013
847/516-8280
847/516-8210 (fax)
www.foresttech.com/

Interact CD-ROM Store

www.interactcd.com/

KBkids.com

1099 18th Street, Ste. 1000
Denver, CO 80202

877/452-5437
303/ 228-9000
www.kbkids.com/soft/

Kids Domain

kidsdomain.com/

Learning Services

PO Box 1036
Eugene, OR 97440
800/877-9378 (west)
800/877-3278 (east)
541/744-2056 (fax-west)
508/251-7631 (fax-east)
www.learnserv.com/

MacConnection

730 Milford Road
Merrimack, NH 03054
800/800-2222
www.macconnection.com

MacMall

2555 W. 190th Street
Torrance, CA 90504
800/328-2790
310/354-5600
www.cc-inc.com/macmall/

MacWarehouse

1720 Oak Street
Lakewood, NJ 08701
800/397-8508
www2.warehouse.com/default.asp?home=mac

MacZone

707 South Grady Way
Renton, WA 98055-3233
800/248-0800
www.maczone.com

MicroWarehouse (PCs)

1690 Oak Street
Lakewood, NJ 08701

800/397-8508
www2.warehouse.com/

PC Connection

730 Milford Road
Merrimack, NH 03054
800/800-5555
www.pcconnection.com

PCMall

2555 W. 190th Street
Torrance, CA 90504
800/863-3282
310/354-5600
www.cc-inc.com/pcmall/

PcZone

707 South Grady Way
Renton, WA 98055-3233
800/419-9663
www.zones.com

Smart Kids Software

888/881-6001
www.smartkidssoftware.com/

Software Express, Inc.

4128-A South Boulevard
Charlotte, NC 28209
800/527-7638
704/522-7638
704/529-1010 (fax)
www.swexpress.com

TigerDirect.com

7795 W. Flagler Street, Ste. 35
Miami, FL 33144
800/879-1597
305/415-2200
305/415-2202 (fax)
www.tigerdirect.com/

Tucows

800/371-6992
416/531-5584 (fax)
www.tucows.com/

Tukids

800/371-6992
416/531-5584 (fax)
download.tucows.com/perl/TUKIDS.html
cyberlynk.tukids.tucows.com/

Yahoo! Shopping: Internet Marketing Associates

877/275-9955
813/571-7631
http://shop.store.yahoo.com/meter/
http://search.yahoo.com/bin/search?p=educational+software

ZanyBrainy.com

877/969-5437
www.zanybrainy.com/

ZDNET Reviews

(Ziff Davis Software Library)
www.zdnet.com/products/stories/reviews/0,4161,2611159,00.html

Glossary

Abacus   An ancient calculating device consisting of beads strung on wires or rods that are set in a frame.

ABC   An abbreviation for the Atanasoff-Berry Computer, the first electronic digital computer.

Access time   The time a computer needs from the instant it asks for information until it receives it.

Acoustic coupler   A type of modem that lets the user insert the telephone handset into a built-in cradle that sends and receives computer signals through telephone lines.

Active matrix   A screen, generally used in portable computers, in which each pixel is controlled by its own transistor.

Ada   A high-level programming language developed in the late 1970s and named after Augusta Ada Byron, Countess of Lovelace and daughter of Lord Byron.

Algorithm   Generally a set of instructions for a person to follow in order to solve a problem. A computer program is an algorithm that tells the computer what to do in a step-by-step manner—in a language that it comprehends.

Analog device   A mechanism that handles values in continuous variable quantities such as voltage fluctuations.

Analytical Engine   A sophisticated mechanical calculating machine designed by Charles Babbage in 1833. Conceived before the technology was available, it was to have been capable of storing instructions, performing mathematical operations, and using punched cards for storage.

Applet   In Java, a small program that is embedded in a Web page and when downloaded is started by the browser.

Application program   A program written for a certain purpose, such as word processing.

Arithmetic Logic Unit (ALU)   The central processing unit component responsible for the execution of fundamental arithmetic and logical operations on data.

Artificial intelligence (AI)   Use of the computer to simulate the thinking of human beings.

ASCII   The American Standard Code for Information Interchange, a standard computer character set that allows for efficient data communication and achieves compatibility among computer devices.

Assembler   A computer program that converts assembly language programs into executable machine language programs.

Assembly language   A low-level programming language that uses mnemonic words and in which each statement corresponds directly to a single machine instruction.

Assistive technologies   Equipment that increases, maintains, or improves the capabilities of individuals with disabilities.

Authoring language   A computer language used to create educational software, such as drill and practice lessons.

Authoring system   A program requiring little knowledge, used to create computer-based lessons and tests.

Backup disk   A second copy of a program or document.

Bandwidth   The amount of data that can be transmitted through a communication network.

Bar code reader   An input device that scans bar codes and converts the bar codes into numbers that are displayed on the screen.

BASIC   Beginner's All-purpose Symbolic Instruction Code, one of the most commonly used high-level programming languages.

Baud rate   The speed at which a modem can transmit data.

Binary   The number system a computer uses. It has only two digits, 1 and 0.

Bit   An abbreviation for binary digit, either 1 or 0 in the binary number system.

Block   In word processing, a unit of text that is transferred from one location to another.

Bookmark manager   A software program that lets you organize and collect Uniform Resource Locators (URL's) in a hierarchical manner.

Boolean logic   Devised by George Boole, a system of algebra that used the operations of informal logic.

Boot   The process of starting the computer.

BPS   An abbreviation for bits per second, the measurement of data transmission speed. Presently the fastest modem transfer over phone lines is 56 kilobits per second (kbps).

Broadband   Refers to high bandwidth that transmits 1.5 Mps over fiber optic cables.

Browser   Software that lets users surf the World Wide Web. *Netscape Communicator* and *Internet Explorer* are the two most popular browsers.

Bug   A mistake or error in a computer program.

Bulletin board system (BBS)   A computer that serves as a center for exchange of information for various interest groups.

Bus network   Network with a single bidirectional cable or bus line that carries messages to and from devices. Each workstation can access the network independently.

Buttons   "Hot spots" that are clicked to initiate an action.

Byte   A unit of computer storage that consists of eight binary digits (bits). A byte holds the equivalent of one character, such as the letter C.

C   A computer language developed by Bell Labs for the Unix operating system.

Cable modem   A device that lets the individual access the Internet via television cable connection.

Cathode ray tube (CRT)   The basis of the television screen and the typical microcomputer display screen.

CD-ROM (compact disc read only memory)   A means of high-capacity storage (more than 600 megabytes) that uses laser optics for reading data.

Chat room   A real-time Internet discussion on some topic.

Cell   In an electronic spreadsheet, the intersection of a row and column.

Central processing unit (CPU)   The "brains of the computer," where the computing takes place. The CPU is also called the *processor*. It is made up of a control unit and the arithmetic logic unit.

Chip   A piece of semiconducting material, such as silicon, with transistors and resistors etched on its surface.

Circuit board   A board onto which the electrical components are mounted and interconnected to form a circuit.

Clipboard   A temporary memory storage area where text or graphics can be copied from a document and stored until pasted in elsewhere in the document.

COBOL   Common Business-Oriented Language, a high-level programming language used for business applications.

Compiler   A program that translates the source code of a program written in a higher-level language such as BASIC into a machine-readable, executable program.

Composite color monitor   A monitor that accepts an analog video signal and combines red, green, and blue signals to produce a color image.

Computer   A machine that accepts information, processes it according to a set of instructions, and produces the results as output.

Computer-aided design (CAD)   Use of the computer for industrial design and technical drawing.

Computer-assisted instruction (CAI)   Use of the computer as an instructional tool.

Computer conferencing   Communication between two or more computers in real time.

Computer graphics   Using the computer to create and manipulate pictures.

Computer-managed instruction (CMI)   A computerized record-keeping system that diagnoses a student's progress, provides instruction, and analyzes progress.

Connect time   The time spent online from logging on to logging off.

Constructivism   A learning theory emphasizing experience-based activities.

Control unit   The component of the central processing unit that receives programmed instructions and carries them out.

Cookie   A text file that a server writes to a person's hard drive without his or her knowledge. The purpose is to track the individual's computer usage.

CPS   An abbreviation for characters per second, a term used to describe the number of characters printed per second by the printer.

Cursor   The blinking light that shows the user where he or she is working on the computer screen.

Cyberspace   The use of computer technology to create virtual space.

Daisy-wheel printer   An impact printer that produces a typewriter-quality print. This printer has its type characters set around a daisy wheel, similar to a wagon wheel minus an outer ring.

Database   A collection of information organized according to some structure or purpose.

Database management system   Application software that controls the organization, storage, and retrieval of data in the database.

Debug   Find the errors in the computer's hardware or software.

Delete   To remove information from a file or disk.

Demodulation   Used in telecommunication, the process of receiving and transforming an analog signal into its digital equivalent, which can be used by the computer.

Desktop   A computerized representation of a person's work as if he or she were looking at a desk cluttered with folders.

Desktop publishing (DTP)   The use of the personal computer in conjunction with specialized software to combine text and graphics to produce high-quality output on a laser printer or typesetting machine.

Desktop publishing software   Programs like Microsoft Publisher, Adobe PageMaker and QuarkXpress. These applications let the computer be a desktop publishing workstation.

Developmental portfolio   A collection of student work that shows a student's growth during a particular time frame and that is used as an alternative means of assessment.

Digital camera   A portable camera that records images in a digital format.

Digital Subscriber Line (DSL)   A digital technology that offers high-speed transmission over standard copper telephone wiring.

Digital computer   A computer that operates by accepting and processing data that has been converted into binary numbers.

Digitizer   A device that translates analog information into digital information for computer processing. Examples include scanners and digital cameras.

Direct-connect modem   A modem that lets the user connect directly to the computer and plug into the phone jack, bypassing the telephone handset.

Discover switch   An "intelligent" switch that lets people with physical disabilities use a variety of software programs that feature single-switch scanning.

Display   The representation of data on a screen in the form of a printed report, graph, or drawing.

Distance learning   The receipt of an education from a remote teaching site by computer or television.

Documentation   The set of instructions, tutorial, or reference material that is required for the computer program to run effectively. Documentation can be online help or printed material.

DOS (disk operating system)   A program that lets the computer control its own operation. This program's major task is to handle the transfer of data and programs to and from the computer's disks.

Dot-matrix printer   An impact printer that produces characters and graphic images by striking an inked ribbon with tiny metal rods called pins.

Dot pitch   The smallest dot that a computer monitor can display. The smaller the dots, the higher the resolution.

Download   The process of sending information from a larger computer to a smaller one by means of a modem or network.

Drag and drop   A technique that uses the mouse to drag objects on the computer screen.

Drawing programs   Programs that use vector graphics to produce line art.

drill and practice   A type of computer instruction that lets students practice information with which they are familiar in order to become proficient.

DVD-RAM (digital video disc–random access memory)   The read/write version of DVD-ROM.

DVD-ROM (digital video disc–read only memory)   Similar to CD-ROM in appearance, this disc format has the capacity to hold 4.7 gigabytes. The capacity will shortly change to 17 gigabytes.

E-book   A handheld computer, similar in size to an organizer, that displays electronic versions of books, letting you set bookmarks, do keyword searches, and make notes in margins.

Electronic mail, e-mail   A system of transmitting messages over a communication network via the computer. Pine is an e-mail service most commonly used at universities, and Eudora Lite is a mail application used most often by the general public.

E-mail address   A name and a computer location (often referred to as a host), for example, vicki.sharp@csun.edu, where vicki.sharp is the name and csun the location.

Encryption   The process of coding information so that it cannot be understood unless decoded.

Ergonomics The science of designing computers and furniture so that they are easy and healthful to use.

Ethernet One of the most popular types of local area network connections.

Execute Carry out the instructions given in machine language code.

Expansion slot A slot inside the computer that accepts boards which add to the computer's capabilities and features.

FAQs (Frequently Asked Questions) Files found at Internet sites that answer frequently asked questions. It is a good idea to check for FAQs and read them.

Fax machine An input/output device that lets the user transmit text and images between distant locations.

Fiber optics A medium consisting of glass fibers that transmit data using light.

Field A record location in which a certain type of data is stored.

File A collection of related records.

Filtering software A program that tries to prevent the user from accessing adult material on the Internet.

FireWall A security system that protects a network against threats from hackers from other networks.

FireWire A 400 Mbps port that connects peripheral devices such as digital cameras.

Flame An argumentative posting of an e-mail message or newsgroup message in response to another posting.

Floppy disk Covered with magnetic coating, such as iron oxide, the mass storage device used primarily with microcomputers.

Flowchart A graphical representation of the flow of operations that is needed to finish a job. It uses rectangles, diamonds, ovals, parallelograms, arrows, circles, and words.

Font A group of letters, numbers, punctuation marks, and special characters with the same typeface, style, and weight.

Footer In word processing, repeated text such as a title that appears at the bottom of the page.

Format Prepare a disk so the user can store information on it. During the formatting process, the computer's disk drive encodes a magnetic pattern consisting of tracks and sectors.

FORTRAN FORmula TRANslator, one of the oldest high-level programming languages, suited for scientific and mathematical applications.

Frame In desktop publishing, a moveable and resizable box that holds graphics and text.

Free-form database A database that allows the user to enter text without regard to its length or order.

FTP (File Transfer Protocol) The basic Internet function that lets files be transferred between computers. You can use it to download files from a remote host computer as well as upload files from your computer to a remote host computer.

Full-duplex A protocol that lets the user send data in both directions simultaneously.

Function key A key located on the keyboard that the user programs to perform a specific task.

Gigabyte A unit of measure that equals approximately 1 billion (1,073,741,824) bytes.

Gopher A program that lets the user browse the Internet using menus.

Graphical user interface (GUI) A graphical interface, as opposed to a character-based computer interface such as MS-DOS. An example of a popular graphical interface is the Macintosh operating system.

Graphics tablet   A plotting tablet that the user draws on to communicate with the computer.

Gutenberg, Johann   Revolutionized communication with the invention of moveable type.

Hacker   A computer expert; sometimes one who illegally accesses and tampers with computer programs and data.

Half-duplex   Synonymous with local echo, a protocol that lets data be sent in both directions but only one direction at a time.

Handheld computer   A small mobile computer that lets the user write on-screen with a stylus. This device provides tools for everyday use such as a notepad, word processor, appointment calendar, address book, and fax modem.

Handshake   A method of controlling the flow of data between two devices.

Hard copy   Computer output that is on paper, film, or other permanent medium.

Hard disk   One or more disk platters coated with a metal oxide substance that allows information to be magnetically stored.

Hard drive   The computer's main storage device.

Hardware   The physical components of the computer system, which include the computer, monitor, printer, and disk drives.

Header   In word processing, repeated text such as page numbers that appear at the top of the page.

Hierarchical database   A database that stores things in a top to bottom organizational structure.

High-level language   Language that is further away from the machine's operation and approximates human language. Low-level language (like machine and assembly) is nearer the machine's operation.

Home page   The main page in a website, at which you find hyperlinks to other pages.

Host   The computer that serves as the beginning point and ending point for data transfer when accessing the Internet.

HyperCard   An authoring tool that lets the user organize information and retrieve on-screen cards that contain text, graphics, sound, and animation.

Hyperlink   A graphic, an icon, or a word in a file that when clicked automatically opens another file for viewing.

Hypermedia   A system nearly synonymous with hypertext (however, it emphasizes the nontextual components of hypertext) that uses the computer to input, manipulate, and output graphics, sound, text, and video in the presentation of ideas and information.

HyperTalk   The programming language that is used with HyperCard.

Hypertext   Nonsequential associations of images, sound, text, and actions through which the user can browse, regardless of the order. An example of hypertext is a computer glossary from which a user can select a word and retrieve its definition.

Hypertext Markup Language (HTML)   The basic language that people use to build hypertext electronic documents on the Web.

Inclusion   Education of students with disabilities with their peers who do not have disabilities.

Initialize   *See* Format.

Inkjet printer   A nonimpact printer that uses a nozzle to spray a jet of ink onto a page of paper. These small, spherical bodies of ink are released through a matrix of holes to form characters.

Integrated circuit chip (IC chip)   *See* Chip.

Integrated learning system (ILS)   A central computer with software consisting of planned lessons in various curriculum areas.

Integrated program   An application program that combines several tasks such as word processing and database management in one package and allows for the free interchange of information among applications. These applications do not offer as much capability as a single application.

Integrated software packages   Sofware packages like *Microsoft Works* that contain more than one application in one single package (e.g., word processor, database, spreadsheet).

Interactive video   A system consisting of a computer, videodisc player, videotape, and software that provides the student with immediate feedback. It includes management features so lessons can be customized to specific student needs.

Interface   The place at which a connection is made between two elements so they can work harmoniously together. In computing, different interfaces occur, ranging from user interfaces, in which people communicate with programs, to hardware interfaces, which connect devices and components in the computer.

Internet   A system of worldwide networks that enable the user to send electronic mail, conduct research, chat, and participate in newsgroups.

Internet appliances   Low-cost devices that handle e-mail and Web browsing and do this job faster than an ordinary modem connection.

Internet relay chat (IRC)   A real-time Internet service that allows you to do conferencing all over the world.

Internet service provider (ISP)   An organization that charges a fee for users to dial into its computer for an Internet connection.

Interpreter   A high-level program translator that translates and then executes each statement in a computer program. It translates a statement into machine language, runs it, then proceeds to the next statement, translates it, runs it, and so on.

Java   A programming language designed by Sun Microsystems to write programs that can be downloaded from the Internet with a Java interpreter. Many World Wide Web pages on the Internet use small Java applications, or applets, to display animations.

JavaScript   A scripting language for Web publishing.

Joystick   A small, boxlike object with a moving stick and buttons used primarily for games, educational software, and CAD systems.

Kbps   An abbreviation for kilobits per second, a computer modem's speed rating, measured in units of 1,024 bits. This is the maximum number a device can transfer in one second under the best of conditions.

Kerning   In typography, the adjustment of space between pairs of characters like "B A" so that they print in a pleasing manner.

Keyboard   An input device similar to a standard typewriter but with extra keys, such as the function keys and the numeric pad.

Kilobyte (K)   A unit of measure for computers that is equal to 1,024, or 2^{10}, bytes.

Laser disc   Large-sized optical disc that utilizes laser technology for the purpose of video.

Laser printer   A printer that produces high-quality text and graphic output by tracing images with a laser beam controlled by the computer.

Leading   In typography, the vertical spacing between lines of type that is measured from baseline to baseline.

Light-emitting diode (LED)   When charged with electricity, a semiconductor diode that gives off light.

Light pen An instrument, used in conjunction with a video display, with a light-sensitive, photoelectric cell in its tip that sends an electrical impulse to the computer, which identifies its current location.

Linotype machine The first successful automated typecasting machine.

Liquid crystal display (LCD) A display that uses a liquid compound, positioned between two sheets of polarizing material squeezed between two glass panels.

Liquid crystal display projection panel A projector that receives computer output and displays it on a liquid crystal screen placed on an overhead projector. The projector displays on a large screen the program that the computer generates.

LISP Acronym for list processing, a high-level programming language frequently used in artificial intelligence systems that combines the use of lists with sets of symbols.

Local area network (LAN) A network that provides communication within a local area, usually within 200 or 300 feet, as found in office buildings.

Logo A high-level programming language designed for children that contains many functions found in LISP.

Low-level language A programming language, like assembly language, that is close to the machine's language.

Machine language A programming language composed of a pattern of 0s and 1s that is far removed from the language understood by human beings. This is the only language that computers understand.

Macro A group of routines or commands combined into one or two keystrokes.

Magnetic disk A device that stores data magnetically in circular tracks that are divided into sectors.

Magnetic ink character recognition (MICR) A character recognition system that reads text printed with a special magnetic ink. All the checks issued by banks are coded with this special ink and characters so that an MICR unit can read them.

Magnetic tape A reel of tape that is usually around 1/2 inch wide that can store about 25 megabytes of data magnetically in a linear track.

Mail Merge A word processing feature that prints customized form letters.

Mainframe computer A high-level computer designed for sophisticated computational tasks.

Mainstreaming Partial and full-time programs that educate students with disabilities with their nondisabled peers.

Mark I An electromechanical calculating machine designed by Howard Aiken at Harvard University and built by IBM.

Megabyte (MB) A unit of measure that equals approximately 1,048,576 bytes.

Megahertz (MHz) A measure of frequency equal to 1 million cycles per second.

Memory The circuitry inside the computer that lets it store and retrieve information. Generally, memory refers to the semiconductor storage (RAM) that is directly connected to the microprocessor.

Microcomputer system A computer that uses a single chip microprocessor, one that is less powerful than that of a minicomputer.

Microprocessor A chip that contains the central processing unit of the computer.

Microworld The Logo environment in which a child freely experiments, tests, and revises his or her own theories in order to create a product.

Millisecond (ms) Equivalent to 10^{-3}, or one-thousandth, of a second.

Minicomputer A midlevel computer whose capabilities are between those of a mainframe and a microcomputer.

Modem   Short for MOdulator/DEModulator, a device that lets two computers communicate with each other via telephone lines.

Modulation   Used in telecommunication, the means that a modem uses to convert digital information sent by computer to its analog form, so that the information can be sent over telephone lines.

Monitor   A video display that resembles a television set, designed to handle a wider and higher range of frequencies.

Morphing   A special effect that changes one image into another image.

Mouse   A popular input device that is used instead of the keyboard to make menu selections.

MP3   Moving Pictures Experts Group (MPEG) audio format that produces CD quality audio using a 12:1 compression rate.

Multimedia   A subset of hypermedia that combines graphics, sound, animation, and video.

Nanosecond (ns)   Equivalent to 10^{-9}, or one-billionth, of a second.

Napier's rods   A device used for multiplying large numbers, invented by John Napier, a Scottish mathematician, in 1617.

Netiquette   The etiquette used in cyberspace.

Network   Computers that share storage devices, peripherals, and applications. A network can be connected by telephone lines, satellites, or cables.

Newsgroups   Similar to public bulletin boards where you can read messages that others have written and contribute to the discussion.

Online   When a computer is interacting with an online service or the Internet. For example, a person goes online to read his or her e-mail.

Online help   The capability of a program to display onscreen guidance while an individual uses the computer.

Online service   Any commercial service like America Online (AOL) that gives access to electronic mail, news services, and the Web.

Operating system   *See* DOS.

Optical Character Recognition (OCR)   A device that recognizes printed or typed text.

Optical disc   A round platter that has information recorded on it with laser beam technology. It is capable of storing large amounts of information.

Optical mark reader (OMR)   A device that reads penciled or graphic information on cards or pages. Lamps furnish light reflected from the card or paper; the amount of reflected light is measured by a photocell.

Output   After processing, the information that is sent from the computer to a peripheral device.

Page layout   In desktop publishing, the process of arranging text and graphics on the page.

Paint programs   Graphics programs that let individuals simulate painting on the computer screen with the use of a mouse or graphics tablet. Paint programs create raster graphic images.

Parity   A modem-checking technique for memory or data communication errors.

Pascal   A high-level structured programming language, designed by Niklaus Wirth in the late 1960s.

Peripheral   The devices that are connected to the computer under the microprocessor's control, such as disk drives, printers, and modems.

Personal data assistant (PDA)   A small, handheld computer that accepts input on the screen from a stylus.

Piracy   The act of copying software illegally.

Pixel   Short for picture element, a linear dot on a display screen. When this dot is combined with other dots, it creates an image.

Plasma display   A display produced by a mixture of neon gases between two transparent panels, giving a very sharp, clean image with a wide viewing angle.

PLATO   Programmed Logic for Automatic Teaching Operations, developed by the University of Illinois and Control Data Corporation. This early computer system was designed for instructional use.

Plug-ins   Programs built to extend a browser's capabilities. Plug-ins let you see and hear video, audio, and other kinds of multimedia files.

Portal   A web site that acts as a starting point to the Internet, usually on a specific subject area.

Predetermined functions   Ready-made formulas that allow the user to quickly solve problems.

Presentation graphics   Combining text and images, software that produces and displays graphic screens.

Printer   A device that produces computer output.

Problem-solving software   Computer assisted software that helps students develop critical thinking skills with the intent that these skills will transfer to other areas of the curriculum.

Program   A series of instructions designed to make a computer do a given task.

Protected and hidden cells   A spreadsheet program feature that protects a group of cells from being altered or erased.

Public domain software   Software that is not copyrighted and can be freely copied and distributed without payment or permission.

QuickTime   Apple designed this program so that small movies could be shown on the computer screen.

QuickTime VR   An extension of *QuickTime* that lets the user view on-screen movies in 3-D space.

Quicktionary Reading Pen   A device that scans printed words, displays them in large characters, pronounces them aloud, and defines them when you touch a button.

RAM (random access memory)   Volatile memory. Whenever the computer is turned off, information stored in RAM is lost.

Raster graphics or bit-mapped graphics   Images made up of a pattern of pixels or dots. These images are limited to the maximum resolution of the computer display or printer.

RealAudio   A plug-in that lets you listen to live or prerecorded audio transmission on the World Wide Web.

Real time   The immediate processing of data as it becomes available. In telecommunication, when you are online you can be connected to other people who are online at the same time.

Record   A collection of related fields that are treated as a single unit.

Refreshable Braille display   A device that is added to a computer system to translate text on the screen into Braille.

Relational database   A database that links files together.

Representational portfolio   Contains only the student's best work and can be used for employment purposes.

Resolution   The clarity or degree of sharpness of a displayed character or image, expressed in linear dots per inch.

Ring network   A group of computers that communicate with each other in a ring, without a file server.

Robotics   A branch of engineering that is concerned with training and the creation of robots.

ROM (read only memory)   Memory that retains its contents when the power supply is turned off. Often referred to as hardwired, internal memory, it cannot be altered or changed.

Scanner   A device that digitizes photographs or line art and stores the images as a file that can be transferred into a paint program or directly into a word processor.

Search engine   A program that lets you find information on the Internet.

Shareware   Copyrighted software that is distributed free but must be paid for if the customer is satisfied.

Simplex   Data transmission that works in one direction at a time.

Simulation   Software that approximates the conditions of the real world in an environment in which the user changes the variables.

Site licensing   A software licensing system in which a person or organization pays a set fee to run copies of a program on a large number of computers.

Software   A program that instructs the computer to perform a specific job.

Software suite   A collection of programs that are usually sold individually (e.g., *Microsoft Office 2001*).

Sort   An operation that reorders data in a new sequence, usually alphabetically or numerically.

Spam   Unsolicited messages sent via the Internet.

Speech recognition   A computer program that can decode human speech into text.

Speech synthesizer   An output device that generates sound. This chip gives the computer the ability to search for words and their pronunciations in a database.

Spider programs   Automated electronic software programs that follow the links on a page and put all the text into one huge database.

Spreadsheet   A computerized version of a manual worksheet, with a matrix of numbers arranged in rows and columns, that facilitates calculations.

Star network   A communications network in which all the computers are connected to a file server or host computer.

Sticky keys   Certain keys that lock in place—allowing a student with a disability to press combination key strokes without pressing keys simultaneously.

Streaming audio   Compressed audio that is sent in real time via the Internet

Streaming video   Compressed movies that are sent in real time via the Internet.

Structured programming   Programming that uses a limited number of branching instructions and emphasizes modularity.

Style sheet   A file that contains instructions that apply character, paragraph, and page layout formats to desktop publishing and word processing documents. Style sheets include settings such as tabs, margins, columns, and fonts.

Supercomputers   The largest and fastest of the mainframe computers with the most advanced processing abilities.

Surge suppressor   Also known as a surge protector, a device that protects the computer from damaging electrical surges.

SYSOP   Acronym for SYStem OPerator, the person who runs a bulletin board.

System disk   The disk that contains operating software and can also be used to boot the computer.

Tag   In HTML, a special code, that identifies a part of a document so that the Web browser can ascertain how to display it. Tags are enclosed in angle brackets like the following example <H2>.

Telecommunication   The electronic transmission of information, including data, television pictures, sound, and facsimiles.

Template   A predesigned document that includes text or formulas that are needed to create a standard document.

Terabyte   A unit of measurement equal roughly to 1 trillion bytes (actually 1,099,511,627,776 bytes).

Thermal printer   Using heated wires, a printer that burns dots into a costly special paper.

Time bomb   A computer virus that is programmed to go off on a specific day and time.

Touch-free switch   An input device that lets students trigger a mouse click without applying any pressure.

Touch screen   A display that has a pressure-sensitive panel mounted in the front. The user makes choices by touching the screen in the correct location.

Trackball   A movable ball that moves the cursor on the screen as it is manipulated.

Trackpad   A pressure-sensitive pad that is smaller and more accurate than the trackball.

Transistor   An electronic gate that bridges the gap between two wires and lets the current flow.

Tutorial   Similar to a tutor, a program that explains new material and then tests the student's progress.

UNIX   Originally developed by AT&T Bell laboratories, an operating system used on different types of computers that supports multitasking.

Upload   Transfer of information from one's computer to a remote computer.

URL (Uniform Resource Locator)   A site address on the World Wide Web. For example, the URL for the California State University home page is http://www.csun.edu.

Usenet   A leading network system of bulletin boards that services more than 1,500 newsgroups.

User-friendly   A term that means easy to learn and use.

User group   A group of users of a specific type of computer who share experiences to improve their understanding of the product.

Utility programs   Programs that perform a variety of housekeeping and control functions such as sorting, copying, searching, and file management.

Vector graphics   Images made of independent objects that can be sized, moved and manipulated.

Videoconferencing   A multiuser chat in which the live images of the users are displayed on each participant's computer screen.

Videodisc   A read only optical disc that uses an analog signal to store and retrieve still and moving pictures, sound, or color.

Video scan converter   A device that changes the personal computer or laptop output so it can be displayed on a television monitor.

Virtual reality   A computer-generated world in which a person is able to manipulate the environment. The user generally wears a head-mounted device and special sensor gloves.

Virus   A program that infects computer files by duplicating itself.

Voice recognition   A system that converts the spoken word into binary patterns that are computer recognizable; it understands human speech.

VRAM (video RAM)   Chip used to transfer and hold an image on the computer screen.

Warping   A process similar to morphing, involving the altering and manipulation of a single image.

Wide area network (WAN) A network that uses long-distance communication or satellites to connect computers over greater distances than a local area network does.

Wildcard character A character such as an asterisk that is used to represent one or more characters.

Window An onscreen frame where you can view a document, database, spreadsheet or application program.

Windows A graphical interface developed by Microsoft Corporation for IBM and IBM-compatible computers.

Wireless communication A method of linking computers with radio waves or infrared. There are no interconnecting cables or wires.

Word processor A software program designed to make the computer a useful electronic writing tool that can edit, store, and print documents.

Word wrap In word processing, when words go beyond a margin they are automatically wrapped to the beginning of the next line.

World Wide Web (WWW) An Internet service that lets you navigate the Internet using hypertext documents.

Worm A program that can run by itself and replicate a full working version to other computers. After the worm is finished with its work, the data are usually corrupted and irretrievable.

Index